DEAREST CHUMS AND PARTNERS

DEAREST CHUMS AND PARTNERS

JOEL CHANDLER HARRIS'S LETTERS TO HIS CHILDREN ❧ A DOMESTIC BIOGRAPHY

EDITED BY ❧ HUGH T. KEENAN

THE UNIVERSITY OF GEORGIA PRESS   ATHENS AND LONDON

Designed by Sandra Strother Hudson
Set in Berkeley Old Style by Tseng Information Systems, Inc.
Printed and bound by Thomson Shore
The paper in this book meets the guidelines
for permanence and durability of the Committee on
Production Guidelines for Book Longevity
of the Council on Library Resources.

Printed in the United States of America
97 96 95 94 93 C 5 4 3 2 1

Library of Congress Cataloging in Publication Data
Harris, Joel Chandler, 1848–1908.
Dearest chums and partners : Joel Chandler Harris's
letters to his children : a domestic biography / edited by Hugh T. Keenan.
p.   cm.
Includes bibliographical references and index.
ISBN 0-8203-1480-3 (alk. paper)
1. Harris, Joel Chandler, 1848–1908—Correspondence.   2. Harris,
Joel Chandler, 1848–1908—Family.   3. Authors, American—19th
century—Correspondence.   4. Journalists—United States—
Correspondence.   5. Children—United States—Correspondence.
I. Keenan, Hugh T.   II. Title.
PS1813.A4   1993
818'.409—dc20   92-8235
[B]   CIP

British Library Cataloging in Publication Data available

Frontispiece: Joel Chandler Harris in the library of the Wren's Nest,
his home in Atlanta's West End
(Joel Chandler Harris Collection, Special Collections Department,
Robert W. Woodruff Library, Emory University).

To the memory of my mother, Jewel Owens Keenan

CONTENTS

Foreword by R. Bruce Bickley, Jr.
ix

Acknowledgments
xiii

Introduction
xvii

Abbreviations and Short Titles
xxxiii

Notes on Text and Editorial Practices
xxxv

Chronology
xxxix

Genealogical Chart: Children and Grandchildren
of Joel Chandler and Esther LaRose Harris
xlvii

PART ONE · 1890–1896
Fatherly Admonitions to the Boys
1

PART TWO · 1896–1897
Home News for Lillian
59

PART THREE · 1897–1898
Two Little Dearies Together at Saint Joseph's
135

PART FOUR · 1898–1899
More Stories for the Girls
211

PART FIVE · 1899–1900
Advice for the Absent
303

PART SIX · January–June 1901
A Turning Point
365

PART SEVEN · 1901–1908
Renewed Spirits & New Projects
405

Appendix
Register of Previously Printed Letters
507

Recommended Readings
513

Index
517

FOREWORD

This edition of Joel Chandler Harris's 280 surviving letters to his six children, written across two decades, is a substantial contribution to Harris studies. Given the resurgence of interest in Harris by Julius Lester and other writers and critics, this is also a timely piece of scholarship. *Dearest Chums and Partners* alters and enriches our knowledge of Harris's personality; his expectations for himself and his children; his literary sensibilities, methods for composing, and interactions with his publishers; his involvement with the Catholic church; and his social, political, and moral values, generally. The book is also an engaging collection of turn-of-the-century family correspondence, entertaining and informative in its own right.

The letters in Dr. Keenan's "domestic biography" present a fuller picture of Harris and his relationship to his children than Julia Collier Harris provided in the letters she excerpted in *The Life and Letters of Joel Chandler Harris* (1918). Julia's biography of her father-in-law has been a major source of family information for later biographies and critical studies. Yet it was also an affectionate study, selective in its details about family dynamics and Harris's own personality. Dr. Keenan's collection, which includes as its introduction a helpful distillation of the letters' themes, fleshes out our portrait of Harris—rounding some lines, sharpening or deepening others, and adding new color tones in several places. This volume reveals a more complex and intriguing self-portrait of the artist than we have seen previously.

One of the strongest impressions presented by this collection is that of Harris's powerful empathy with his children, his sustained, morally earnest concern for them, and his disciplining force in their lives. He was heavily involved in their upbringing and in their later lives, as well, and wrote them regular, typically voluminous, letters. He offered his sons pointed advice about education, professional writing style, careers, courtship, and marriage—and generally assumed that they would heed it. While his two daughters, Lillian and Mildred, were away at Saint Joseph's Academy, a Catholic convent school, he wrote them long weekly letters containing family and neighborhood news, social and moral advice, and humorous diversion. In return, Harris expected weekly letters from his daughters—often reproving them when they did not respond. "There is absolutely nothing in this neighborhood worth writing about," Harris regularly lamented tongue-in-cheek—and then he would write a half-dozen pages, hoping for at least a page or two of the girls' news in response. Yet throughout the letters—and despite Harris's often irritating intrusions and moralizing—we see a generous, highly supportive parental response. Somewhat more distant and authoritative with his sons, more the "chum and partner" with his daughters, Harris obviously loved all his children, shared a great deal of his own person with them, and hovered protectively and supportively around them until his death.

A second dominant pattern in the correspondence is Harris's sustained verbal dexterity and his complex literary technique. His letters to Mildred and Lillian comprise, in effect, a literary tour de force. Harris adopts multiple personae, male and female; invents anecdotes and short parables to make instructive points or provoke a laugh; produces riddles, puns, dialect humor, and slapstick; indulges in sheer fantasy; folds in scenes from his own books in progress, to try them out on his daughters; is by turns playful, ironic, sarcastic, somber, and flippant. Harris's literary vision is highly self-conscious and multiplex in many of these letters, because he is often writing simultaneously for at least four audiences: (a) for himself, (b) for his daughters, (c) for the nuns at the academy, who screened everything the convent girls received (and sent), and, it would appear, (d) for the edification of children and parents everywhere. Harris probably contemplated reprinting at least some of the correspondence later; after his death, dozens of excerpts from these letters were, in fact, published by the family in *Uncle Remus's Magazine*. Students of Harris's humor and literary technique will learn a great deal from a close study of his rhetorically complex correspondence.

Finally, *Dearest Chums and Partners* would be a significant volume even had Harris been a less prominent figure. The book is a fascinating anthropological study in the comings and goings of a large, diverse, and extremely active New South household at the turn of the last century. We read with fascination as the family gossips about neighbors and in-laws; prepares and eats meals; cleans house and raises flowers, vegetables, and *scores* of animals and pets; sends children off to school or work and welcomes them home; attends funerals, political gatherings, and spirited college baseball games; nervously takes pictures with an early Kodak box camera; reads and discusses daily news events, from fires and race riots in Atlanta to the Spanish-American War; gives birth to and raises a string of grandchildren; relates to domestic servants; and resists or succumbs to illness and death.

As Harris punned in a letter of 1902, "This is a funny world if you look at it right—and left." In this important collection, a celebrated American local colorist, journalist, and folklorist looks right—and left—at the world his children inhabited, to find in it both childhood fun and adult responsibilities. At the same time, Harris looks right and left at himself, while we stand just a gnat's eyebrow away, watching over his shoulder.

R. Bruce Bickley, Jr.

ACKNOWLEDGMENTS

For more than eight years I have researched the published and unpublished works of Joel Chandler Harris, principally at Emory University, the major depository of his materials. This research resulted in several essays on his work as a children's writer and folklorist and in the editing of a collection of essays by others on Harris's life and works. The past five years have been concentrated on the editing of his letters to his six surviving children during the period of 1890 to 1908. This was also the period of his most prolific literary production and the height of his popular and literary acclaim. These letters seemed to me to present a singular story both of his domestic life and of his literary observations on his own work and that of others. My efforts have been directed toward clarifying this story.

What promised initially to be an easy task of transcribing the letters and arranging them in sequence proved more difficult than imagined. Supplied dates proved to be wrong in many instances; many letters to the girls were addressed only to "Dear Daughter," and if the envelope was missing, one could not readily tell whether the letter was to Lillian or Mildred. Birth and death dates of several members of the family were missing as well. To do this work properly, I have sought information, help, and advice from many sources and individuals. First of all, I am indebted to the staff of the Special Collections Department, Robert W. Woodruff Library, Emory University, for the aid and encouragement they gave me during the extended period spent deciphering the handwritten letters and typing copies from both microfilms and the fragile originals. Particularly am I indebted to Dr. Linda Matthews, head of Special Collections; Virginia Cain, processing archivist; Beverly Allen, reference archivist; and Kathy Knox, archives reference associate, for their help and kindness. My thanks are extended to Norma Watterson, curator of the Uncle Remus Museum, for permission to publish the three Harris letters at the Uncle Remus Museum and for locating the originals and allowing me to collate them with my transcription of the copies in the Emory collection. I appreciate the support of Carole Mumford, executive director, Joel Chandler Harris Association (the Wren's Nest, Atlanta, Georgia), and of Karen Kelly, assistant director, in supplying information about the Harris family genealogy and furnishing photographs.

My gratitude is due to the present descendants of Joel Chandler Harris who not only permitted but encouraged this project. Especially do I wish to express my appreciation to the successive literary executors of the literary rights for the initial permission and its extension: the late J. Robin Harris, Lucien Harris III, and James N. Grant, Jr., present executor. The late Mildred Wright and also Elizabeth Chapman, daughters of Mildred Harris Camp, were especially accommodating to one prying into the history of the family. Dorothy Dean Harris, in a gracious interview, shared her memories of her husband, Joel Chandler Harris, Jr., and his family in Atlanta. LaRose Wagener Grant provided not only useful information about her mother, Lillian Harris Wagener, but also illustrative materials from those she had inherited. Myrtle W. Wagener made copies of and gave permission for the use of two letters to Lillian and Mildred.

The staffs of the following other colleges, universities, and institutions were courteous and helpful in my examination of the Harris materials in their various libraries and collections: The American Academy of Arts and Letters; Atlanta-Fulton County Public Library; Atlanta Historical Society; Clark Library (UCLA); Columbia University; Department of Archives and History, State of Georgia; Duke University; Georgia State University; Huntington Library; New-York Historical Society; New York Public Library; New York University; Princeton University; Scripps College; Stanford University; Tulane University; University of California, Los Angeles; University of Georgia; University of Virginia; and Yale University. To all of them I express my gratitude. Photographs of the Harris rabbit monogram and rabbit leads from *Uncle Remus's Magazine* are courtesy of the Special Collections Department, Pullen Library, Georgia State University.

A number of assistants, far more skilled than I in the mysteries and aberrations of personal computers, took my typed copies and put them into the appropriate electronic guises and the necessary permutations while seeing the manuscript through numerous corrections, reprintings, and recorrections. To David Remy (who began the project), Leah Hughes Barcik (who entered most of the letters), Scott Gissendanner and LeAnne Benfield (who made final corrections), and Sonja Gardner (who performed electronic wizardry without effort), I owe thanks for their hard work, long hours, and cheerful attitudes. Dr. Virginia Spencer Carr, chair of the Department of English, Georgia State University, generously provided professional advice and encouragement, research funds, and the services of student assistants and staff. I am obliged to Georgia State University for a research grant which purchased a word processor for this project and paid for the services of a student assistant. I wish to thank Patricia Bryan, administrative assistant to Dr. Carr, for critiquing the in-house proposal which secured this grant and for reading various drafts of the introduction. To the former chairman of the department, Dr. Paul Blount, I am grateful for a quarter's leave of absence many years ago that allowed me time to read through all the Harris materials at Emory University long before I even contemplated this project.

Finally to two colleagues: to Dr. R. Bruce Bickley, Jr. (Florida State University), who as an established scholar of Harris studies welcomed my beginning investigations, I owe a debt for generous aid and a graceful foreword; and to Dr. Glenn L. Sadler (Bloomsburg University), I owe thanks for his hospitality and practical advice gleaned from his experience editing the letters of George MacDonald. For information on matters genealogical, I am indebted to Kenneth H. Thomas, Jr., who sent me to the *Christian Index* and provided other information, and to Mary Galiano, secretary, the Shrine of the Immaculate Conception, Atlanta, Georgia, who found the baptismal records of Linton and Joel Chandler Harris, Jr. To the staffs of Oakland Cemetery and Westview Cemetery, I am indebted for information about burial records and grave sites of the Harris family members. Franklin M. Garrett, the premier historian of Atlanta history, kindly granted me an interview and supplied information by telephone. All of these persons and institutions have been helpful in making this collection of letters better and more detailed than I ever imagined or thought possible.

The notes have been made more extensive at the suggestion of the two readers of the manuscript for the University of Georgia Press. I owe them thanks for telling me what a broader readership might wish to know. For the faults and errors that doubtless remain, I take full responsibility.

INTRODUCTION

Writing on 13 March 1898, to his older daughter, Lillian, then a boarding student at Saint Joseph's Academy, Washington, Georgia, Joel Chandler Harris defined for her and for himself the essential qualities of personal correspondence. From his recent reading of excerpts of the letters from Miss Dorothy Osborne to Sir William Temple, he had observed that her seventeenth-century letters were just "as fresh and charming now as they were the day they were written" because "She gossipped about herself; her hopes, her expectations, her troubles, real and imaginary, and in doing so made a contribution to our permanent literature. She was serious, but not too much so. Indeed, her vivacity and spirit in the face of real troubles, are something wonderful." In general, these are the subjects and the attitudes found in Harris's own weekly letters to his daughters, Lillian and Mildred, when they were away at boarding school. Their responses to his epistolary guides unfortunately have not survived. But his letters have and are, indeed, "fresh and charming" and contain "something wonderful" in their details and changes of tone.

To capture the informality of such letter writing, he further suggested to Lillian that "it might be good practice for you to write your thoughts— your views, your little day-dreams, your opinions about things. By doing this you will get yourself in the habit of thinking in an orderly way. But in writing letters to me or to a friend, don't try to be too precise[.] Just let your pen move naturally with your thoughts, and don't forget that the rules you learn in rhetoric are not applicable to letters, or that formality in a friendly letter subjects the other person to all the rigors of a snow storm." That kind of free association and warmth characterizes the best of Harris's letters to all six of his surviving children but especially those to his daughters Lillian and Mildred, with whom he indulged in more flights of fantasy or what today is called "free writing."

As a result, the surviving 280 letters, some of which are fragments, written to his two daughters, Lillian and Mildred, and to his four sons, Julian, Lucien, Evelyn, and Joel Chandler Harris, Jr., have both literary and autobiographical importance. Excerpts from letters to the girls were used in *Uncle Remus's Magazine* early in this century for their literary value. And Julia Collier Harris drew generously upon them in writing the biography of her father-in-law and a short magazine piece. Until now, however, the letters have not been published in a complete meaningful sequence.

This book aims to use Joel Chandler Harris's own words to fill in the domestic autobiography for the years 1890–1908. His first book, *Uncle Remus: His Songs and His Sayings: The Folk-Lore of the Old Plantation* (1880), had established his literary and commercial success. By 1890 his reputation was at its height. And as Dr. R. Bruce Bickley, Jr., has pointed out, "The 1890s proved to be Harris's most productive decade."[1] It was marked by thirteen books plus at midpoint (1895) the reissue of his first book, *Uncle Remus: His Songs and His Sayings*, with the superlative new illustrations by Arthur Burdett Frost. The variety of his work included additional books of Uncle Remus tales, novels, five children's books, local-color short stories, an autobiographical narrative, a translation of French folktales, and a public school history text. He was busy also with journalistic assignments for magazines such as *Scribner's*. And the period of 1900–1908 was almost as productive. He wrote essays for such new publications as *World's Work* and fiction for magazines and books in addition to assuming the arduous duties of editorship of a new family magazine called *Uncle Remus's Magazine*.[2] Each year a book or two had appeared by the famed author of Uncle Remus, so that by the year of his death (1908), he was the acknowledged author of some thirty books, as well as of numerous tales, short stories and sketches, essays, and articles in many well-known national magazines and newspapers.[3] As the editor of *Uncle Remus's Magazine*, he with his son Julian had launched in June 1907 a new magazine that had proven a successful hybrid of a chamber of commerce publication and a literary quarterly.

During the period of 1890–1908, the family life of Joel Chandler Harris experienced many changes as well. The boys grew up and began

The Wren's Nest (Joel Chandler Harris Collection, Special Collections
Department, Robert W. Woodruff Library, Emory University).

professional careers. Some of them married and began their own families. The two daughters, Lillian and Mildred, went away to a convent
boarding school, Saint Joseph's Academy. When the daughters returned,
they brought their friends with them for extended visits. The neighborhood boys and girls dropped in. The daughters grew old enough to
have beaux come calling in the parlor or on the front porch. Harris observed wryly that one could imitate "a cat to perfection" and "also talk
like a frog." There were tennis games in the backyard and church fairs
on the front lawn. Out in town there were baseball games of interest
to him and his youngest son between the West End Lobsters and the
Saint Charles/Highland Avenue Club. Joel Jr. went on fishing trips and
to summer camp. Mrs. Joel Chandler Harris customarily spent the summers in Canada with her parents, and often one or more of the children

accompanied her. Thus often the home was overflowing with people and company, and then again it was relatively empty. In his letters to the children, Joel Chandler Harris takes note of all of these changes both in his professional life and in his domestic arrangements.

Though Harris's letters to his children chronicle his relations with the world outside—his negotiations with publishers; books he was writing; and state, national, and international events that concerned him as the associate editor of the Atlanta *Constitution*—they go into greater detail about the domestic affairs within his home, the Wren's Nest in West End, Georgia. The family pets, the friends of his children, their amusements and ambitions, neighborhood gossip, detailed observations about the foibles and faults of the household servants (often three in number), and the rituals of meals and dress are all typical subjects in Harris's letters to his children.

Of course, not all surviving letters are interesting, but even the lesser ones contribute to the domestic autobiography. As Richard Ellmann has observed about the more mundane letters of a far greater literary writer, James Joyce,

> Letter-writing imposes its small ceremonies even upon those who disdain the medium. An audience of one requires confrontation too, and even a perfunctory message discloses a little with what candour, modesty, or self-esteem its writer ranks himself in the world. Some accompanying hint of his appraisal of that world is bound to appear in the way he asserts or beseeches a tie with his correspondent, the degree of familiarity he takes for granted, the extent to which he solicits action or approbation, the alacrity and tenacity with which he joins issue. He may present himself in various guises, as machine, badger, deer, spider, bird. Whatever his mode, if he is a practicing writer his assembling of words can never be totally negligent; once enslaved by language forever enslaved.[4]

Like Joyce, Harris was enslaved by language. Oddly enough, both professed to admire Cardinal Newman's prose style. But unlike Joyce, he did not disdain letters. He cultivated the art of writing personal letters and frequently takes occasion in his letters to his children to coach them in that art, by criticizing their efforts and analyzing his own letters. He wrote voluminous ones as well to business associates, professional colleagues, family friends, and other family members as the collections of Harris materials in college, university, and public libraries attest.

The few letters that Harris wrote during this period to his wife, Esther LaRose Harris, to his daughter-in-law Julia Collier Harris, and to the family as a unit have been excluded from this edition. These total twenty-one letters.[5] But they are outside the scope and interest of the present edition. In the letters to his children, Harris seemed to be more at ease and more freely revealed himself. He was not generally comfortable in sustaining a heavy nineteenth-century paternal role, though he could play a heavy paternal role with the sons, especially Julian. He preferred to treat them all as equals, even calling his daughters, Lillian and Mildred, his "dearest chums and partners" in one memorable letter (26 February 1899).

To the end of his life he remained often closer to children than to adults. He began a very successful "Children's Department" in *Uncle Remus's Magazine*, which led to a lengthy correspondence with one girl, Dorothy Loye.[6] He proposed to the fourteen-year-old sister of a daughter-in-law that they write alternating chapters of a story to be called "King Philpo."[7] He was open with children and versatile in his dealings with them. On the other hand, in his professional correspondence, he was more limited. In seeking from publishers both acceptance of and the best contract for his writings, he alternated between a passive stance (or sometimes even a coquettish feminine style) and that of a straightforward businessman or man of letters.

His letters to his children cover a wider variety of subjects and change more widely in tone, manner, and even persona, depending on the occasion, his feelings, and those of the children with whom he was corresponding. Perhaps it is Harris's natural empathy with children, both his own and those of others, that has ensured his lasting reputation and influence as a writer of children's literature. This empathy is reflected in the black narrator of the Uncle Remus tales when he modulates his tales to the moods of the Little Boy and to the exigencies of the occasion.

The premise of this collection is that these letters are both the truest autobiographical record of the author and his family life during 1890–1908 and also artful in their design. Though the texts of these various groups of letters overlap in time, they differ significantly in content and attitude. Like many parents, Joel Chandler Harris addresses himself differently to each child. Overall those to the boys—Julian, Lucien, Evelyn, and Joel Chandler Harris, Jr.—are the more adult or parental in their tone. The majority are to his eldest son, Julian, and these take the most severe, critical attitude. The letters to the other three sons are less severe.

This collection begins in 1890 with the first letters to a sixteen-year-old Julian, who has been sent for a visit to his mother's parents in Canada before becoming a working man at seventeen. In the same letter chastising Julian for not letting his parents know of his safe arrival, he also encourages him to polish his writing skills. In subsequent letters to him during that visit, which extends into 1891, he advises him to keep a journal and to gather materials that may be published in the Atlanta *Constitution*. He encourages his son's efforts at writing by showing the stories to others and conveying the praise of these readers. He pushes Julian to practice his French with his Canadian grandparents so that he may converse in French with his mother upon his return. He directs him toward a career in the newspaper business. At the same time, Joel Chandler Harris warns him that doing newspaper work alone can ruin his style and damage his ability to do other kinds of writing. Correspondence in that year about the unexpected death of his young brother Linton shows the closeness of father and son.[8]

Joel Chandler Harris writes frankly to Julian about his own negotiations with the *Century Magazine* and *St. Nicholas*, his success at selling his Uncle Remus sketches to a syndicate of newspapers besides the *Constitution*, and the announcement of the publication of *Daddy Jake* and *Balaam and His Master*. When, at the instigation of the *Constitution*, Julian goes to work on the Chicago *Times-Herald* to widen his experience in journalism, his father advises his son about his career and reassures him of a place at the Atlanta newspaper. Later when they are more closely associated as editor-in-chief and editor of *Uncle Remus's Magazine*, Joel Chandler Harris continues to play a heavy mentoring role. In other letters, he can confide his fears of financial difficulties to Julian as well as write him a note of light-hearted birthday greetings.

The letters written to the younger brothers contrast with those to Julian. In two letters written in 1891 to Evelyn, who was on a visit to Harris's hometown of Eatonton, Georgia, his father addresses subjects dear to this teenaged boy's heart—the ducks in the backyard, the peaches for dessert, and the news of the neighbor girls. In another written in 1895, while he is at Warm Springs, Georgia, to finish writing *Mr. Rabbit at Home*, he confides more maturely to Evelyn that the relationship between him and his wife's niece Essie LaRose has become strained. This information is inserted in "confidential" passages of a letter written to Evelyn, who was visiting his LaRose grandparents along with his mother and the niece. As he did for Julian, he gives Evelyn advice on improving his writing when this younger son was taking the waters in 1899 at Poland Springs, Maine. And he gives him much the same advice as he gave to Julian to observe the French customs when he visits his LaRose grandparents and to write them up for the *Constitution*, thus grooming another son for the newspaper business. Though a strict disciplinarian, he writes disapprovingly of the public correction he has just observed being administered to children in his own neighborhood. Later letters to Evelyn give his amused observations on the courtship of Essie and Charles Kelly. And after Evelyn marries, he invites him in 1904 to move into the Wren's Nest temporarily rather than to take a job in Macon, where chances for advancement in the newspaper business are poor.

The single surviving letter to Lucien shows similar efforts to control his sons' lives. In a letter written to Lucien during a visit to the Canadian grandparents in 1892, Joel Chandler Harris advises him as to how to go about courting Aileen Zachry and congratulates himself on the finesse with which he gets her to swap photographs with his son.

With the youngest son, thirteen-year-old Joel Chandler Harris, Jr., his father takes an easier tack in 1901, writing with amusement about the neighborhood and the tennis games being held at the Wren's Nest, when the boy is on summer vacation at Porter Spring, Georgia. When in turn this son, at age fourteen, is visiting the Canadian grandparents in 1902, his father continues to write about the exploits of the family dogs and domestic matters such as the Sunday school class his wife has begun to hold in their home. In 1906, when J.C. or Jake, as Joel Jr. was called, returns to Canada on another extended family visit, his father gives him news about the preparations for starting *Uncle Remus's Magazine*. And in the second letter (28 October 1906) along with more news about the magazine, he encourages J.C. in the art of letter writing in the same way that he had counseled the other children: "Your last letter was quite the thing, and I liked it very much. It was interesting and well-written; in other words, there seemed to be no effort on your part to write well and yet the well-known sign of style was there—the thing that everybody recognizes instantly, though nobody can say precisely what it is. I call it the flavor of individuality. But there is not one person in a million that can put himself on paper. The way I do, I just imagine that I can hear my thoughts, and that gives them a certain vitality that they could not have if I did otherwise." This comment, along with those in other earlier letters about the right way to learn English grammar, syntax, and diction, shows Harris persisting as a teacher of English composition through letters to and from the children.

As the letters to Joel Jr. show, his father was easier with him than with Julian, but he still exercised some control over the youngest boy's life. According to Jake's widow, his father would not permit him to attend the University of Georgia because it did not have the proper moral reputation. Instead he was sent to Georgia Tech, although his interests were not at all mechanical or scientific.[9]

As Harris often said, he appreciated the "bracing" that mature men such as Joseph Addison Turner and Evan P. Howell had given him as a young man. It is clear that he took a similar attitude toward his own sons, pushing them into the responsibilities of manhood. He was also candid both in encouraging their writing abilities and in discussing his own works, while remaining pragmatic about the monetary profits from literature. Though he could be sympathetic and sometimes amusing, on most occasions he remained more a parent than a chum with his sons.

Lesser in number, these letters to the boys provide a foil to the more numerous and generally more affable ones written to Lillian and Mildred. With his daughters, Harris was inclined to be playful, creative, and indulgent. He was generous in sending them money and paying for trips, clothes, and amusements. But unlike his freer tack with the sons, usually he kept his daughters more dependent by such means as sending a check to be cashed by an older woman and dispersed as their chaperon or to be cashed by a male such as their grandfather or, in the case of Lillian, her husband. His personae are more varied in writing to the girls. He does not hesitate to adopt a feminine point of view and to gossip with them about parties, dresses, and hats and about their boy- and girlfriends or about those of their friends.

As the girls grow older, Harris writes with humor about their serious courtships and subsequent marriages, as well as about his continued annoyance at his wife's industrious housecleaning. He chronicles his wife's attendance at parties and flower shows, family matinees at the theater, church bazaars, and vacation trips to Canada and Chattanooga.

His letters to the girls include his humorous and often critical observations about the other children and later about his grandchildren, starting with Stewart Harris, the first grandchild and the son of Lucien. He writes about the domestic lives of the household servants, especially Rufus the butler and Chloe the milker and sometime cook. He includes anecdotes about the family pets, such as the numerous cats, chickens, pigeons, guinea pigs, the canary bird, the dogs, the donkey Nelly, and the pony Lily. A singular feature of the letters to the girls is the free-hand sketches he often drew to illustrate these domestic creatures or the servants or other family members.

His gossip about domestic affairs in the West End neighborhood includes quarrels, divorces, embezzlement, wasted inheritances, loud singing voices (male and female), and fires in West End, besides those in Atlanta and Macon. His accounts of trips to fairs, card parties, and the theater prove he was no recluse. The Atlanta performance of the famed actor James O'Neill in the money-making vehicle *The Three Musketeers* was a marked disappointment for him.

Harris's letters to the girls also contain fragments of stories, riddles, poems, essays, and editorials, some of which were fully developed in books. He indulges in flights of fancy for his and their amusement. He experiments with language not only in brief passages of black dialect but also in baby talk, German-English dialect, and even Afrikaans. In two letters to Lillian, he tells a story using the distinctive style of popular fellow comic journalist George Ade, capitalizing both the high-flown and the ordinary words. He frequently sends the girls copies of his latest work and solicits their opinions. He also discusses his works in progress, books by others, and the newspapers he has forwarded after reading them. Often such information is very detailed. For example, in a series of letters to Lillian in 1896, he enumerates like the journalist he is trained to be the rapid composition of the manuscript of *Aaron in the Wildwoods*. Having begun it on 28 October 1896, he has written sixteen thousand words by 11 November and thirty-five thousand words by 21 November. In his letter of 13 December, he reports that, having finished it a week prior with a total of forty-eight thousand words, he is starting now on a new book. The whole manuscript of *Aaron in the Wildwoods* had taken less than six weeks. Other letters to the children give similar specific details that are valuable in reconstructing Harris's strengths and weaknesses as a writer.

On a more personal note, he often exaggerates the drinking habits of the family members. And he frequently criticizes the alcoholism of Frank Stanton, a poet and a colleague on the Atlanta *Constitution*, and recounts the sprees of others. Unlike the letters to the sons where he frequently warns them against being drinkers, he treats such matters more as a joke with the girls. For example, he is glad that Mildred only wants a pony for Christmas because that is a small glass of beer. He even rhymes at length about the tipsy Christmas fruit cake, but he never mentions his own drinking problems, which allegedly resulted in his death from cirrhosis of the liver.

Harris draws a distinction between Lillian and Mildred in his letters to them, even in those written jointly to them during the period when they were in school together at Saint Joseph's Academy (1897–99). Then it was his custom to write each of his daughters one letter a week and often to send a joint letter as well. The letters to Lillian begin with her entrance into Saint Joseph's in the fall of 1896 and are followed by the announcement of the birth of the first grandchild, Stewart Harris.

At first Harris writes to Lillian about her experiences at school, the activities of the family at home, and those of her friends in West End. He praises her academic successes, coaches her in her writing abilities, and advises her about writing a memorable graduation speech. After she graduates in 1899, his letters focus on her clothes, her boyfriends, and her travels. They conclude with Lillian's marriage to Fritz Wagener in 1908 and his advice to the young married couple in the few months before his death.

The letters to Mildred, the acknowledged tomboy in the family, take up athletic subjects: details about tennis, baseball, and swimming. He writes about significant public events, such as the Atlanta celebrations planned for the Spanish-American War heroes—Adm. George Dewey, local hero Lt. Tom Brumby, and Rear Adm. Winfield Scott Schley—and about the public address of William Jennings Bryan. He writes to her about the lengthy visit of James Whitcomb Riley to the Wren's Nest in 1900 and about the brief one of publisher Walter Hines Page. The letters also include gossip about the personnel at the Atlanta *Constitution* and the operation of the newspaper.

To both girls he writes at length about the extremes of weather through the year, the flowers in bloom, the vegetables in the garden, the meals served, and his illnesses and those of his wife, other family members, and neighbors. Furthermore, his adoption of a female persona in some letters leads him to take an active interest in women's fashions, social rivalry, and gossip. He even fantasizes about how he would look in one of the new dresses being made for them or about how it would be if he hid his face behind a lace fan on the streetcar. In one letter he signs himself "Queen of May."

His feminine interests also include an enjoyment in overhearing the ladies gossip about the neighbors. In an early letter (7 February [1897]) to Lillian, he justifies his obvious interest in gossip "because it gives me a clue to character, and there's nothing richer than human character. To me the most serious person is the most humorous if I can but get him to open his mouth and speak freely, and sometimes the most humorous are the most serious." His easy adoption of a feminine persona is due perhaps in part to being reared solely by his mother and grandmother. In his literary work, he found it easy to use the feminine persona, as witness his Aunt Minervy Ann, a black storyteller who, though not as famous as Uncle Remus, is just as skilled a narrator. He also created Drusilla, the realistic teenaged black girl, who serves as nurse, storyteller, and literary critic in the Little Mr. Thimblefinger stories. And as his book-reviewing persona in *Uncle Remus's Magazine*, he chose Anne Macfarland, a fictitious Georgia aristocrat living in London. To all of these females he gave more biographical details and depth than he ever did to Uncle Remus.

At times, he mocks the roles he imagines that the daughters assign him as they read his letters: "the Parental Bore" or "Popsy the Clown." A famous letter to Lillian and Mildred of 19 March 1899 analyzes at length the difference between his persona as an editorial writer at the *Constitution* and that of the "other fellow" who does creative writing at home. All of these references show that Harris was deeply aware of the significance and advantages of role-playing for his public, professional, and private lives.

In following the letters arranged chronologically in this book, the reader will experience the domestic life of the Harris family during the years 1890–1908, as they reveal their common life more fully than any biography has yet done. The full and varied life of Joel Chandler Harris and his family presented in his own words takes a middle course between that presented in Julia Collier Harris's *Life and Letters* (1918) and that in Paul M. Cousins's *Joel Chandler Harris* (1968). Life in the Harris household was not as universally harmonious as Julia Harris made it appear in her journalistic account by suppressing significant contrary evidence. Nor was Joel Chandler Harris the reclusive, antisocial creature that Cousins's more scholarly biography suggests and that some more recent critics have emphasized, tracing this to a neurotic pattern beginning in childhood and acted out in his literary works.[10]

On the other hand, neither Julia Harris nor Paul Cousins mentions the understandable tension induced when Essie LaRose, a niece of Mrs. Harris and near to the age of Lillian and Mildred, came to live for several years with the Harrises until her marriage to Charles Kelly. Moreover, Julia omits much of the criticism that the famous author consistently directed toward her devoted husband, Julian. Neither biographer quotes the 1905 letter to Julian in which Harris is nearly despondent because his income is diminished after he retired from the *Constitution* and found that the free-spending habits he had encouraged in his family threaten all of them. While writing about this change, though, Harris is able to shift to a more optimistic view, bracing himself as it were.[11]

More importantly, perhaps, none of the biographers has traced Harris's extensive interest in the Roman Catholic Church from the time that Lillian entered Saint Joseph's Academy. Not only does Harris regularly close his letters with best wishes for Sister Mary Bernard and Sister Mary Louis, her teachers, but he also praises their character and teaching in the body of the letters. As all correspondence to and from the girls was read by the nuns, he often addresses them quite familiarly, writing little dramatic skits with roles for the nuns. They sent letters and small gifts to the family and in turn he asks the girls to take their picture. But he always defers to the rules of the school and the authority of its mother superior. He remarks upon the Catholic news at home, such as the institution of a Manning literary society for the ladies in West End, named after Cardinal Manning, and wishes that they had chosen Cardinal Newman instead. He often praises Newman's literary style as being superior to Nathaniel Hawthorne's and admires the theological content of his works and that of Cardinal Wiseman and other Catholic writers. He is reputed to have lent his copy of Newman's *Apologia* frequently to others.[12] He was a subscriber to the *Catholic News* and often remarked upon the Catholic fiction he had been reading.

When Mildred joins Lillian, Sister Sacred Heart is added to the nuns remembered regularly in each letter. Harris frequently had visits from such local priests as Father Bazin, Father O'Brien, and Father Gunn. He sent contributions and presents of barrels of apples to the nuns. He contributed generously to the rebuilding of the boys' orphanage at Saint Joseph's after it burned. He was distressed at the stinginess of the Catholic congregation at West End. When they proposed to build a chapel, he paid for the lot near his home. And each year a bazaar, with Harris in attendance, was held on his front lawn to raise money for Saint Anthony's Church. But always he keeps a light touch, teasing his wife about her thinking of putting a crucifix on the table when Father Jackson was to be their dinner guest and describing with amusement the rush she was in to catch the streetcar after teaching the Sunday School class at home.

At the same time, Harris was friends with many Protestant preachers in the neighborhood and observes with amusement that his children frequently attended parties and dinners at the Episcopalian church and the Baptist ones. And even though all of his children were brought up as Catholics, none of them married a coreligionist.[13] The only time he is critical of any denomination is the occasion of the debate in the Park Street Methodist Church over discontinuing the use of a common cup for communion out of a fear of disease. In his letters concerning the Spanish-American War, he is careful to distinguish between American and European Catholics, especially the Spanish, while supporting the peace plans of the pope. Quite naturally Harris's views about the Catholic faith are expressed more extensively in letters to the girls while they were at Saint Joseph's. Part of his fervor may be a result of his program of entering wholeheartedly into anything that deeply touched the well-being of his children. A greater part may be the influence of his wife, who as a French Canadian Catholic was educated in a convent. But he shows no interest in the tenets of any other Christian faith. And all of his work and life reflect both a deeply rooted moral sense and a great tolerance.

Immediately after the death of Joel Chandler Harris, it was evident that these letters to the children could serve another purpose and appeal to a wider audience. To sustain the vital connection of *Uncle Remus's Home Magazine* with its founder-editor, portions of forty letters to the daughters were published in subsequent issues. Later Julia Collier Harris made use of the letters in writing her biography of Joel Chandler Harris and in a brief article for the *Ladies Home Journal*. The register of letters at the end of this volume identifies all letters so used. Unlike Julia's earlier publication, all of the letters in this volume are presented in their entirety. Most of them are on deposit in the Joel Chandler Harris Collection, Special Collections, Woodruff Library, Emory University. Three letters in the collection are copies of those from the Uncle Remus Museum, Eatonton, Georgia.[14] No other letters to the children are known to exist in the various colleges, universities, or public and private libraries that house Harris materials. Two letters addressed in 1908 to Lillian and Mildred are used through the permission of their owner, Myrtle W. Wagener. It is possible that others are also in private hands, but my efforts have failed to find them.

I hope that readers will become better informed about the personal and literary life of Joel Chandler Harris as they follow the sequence of letters set forth in this volume.[15] I also hope that they enjoy the many playful, surprising, and informative details in this revealing domestic autobiography of the writer and his active role in the lives of his children. As Julia Collier Harris, his daughter-in-law and biographer, summed up his life, "He had the heart of a child, the tenderness of a woman and the fortitude of a brave man."[16] These letters bear full witness to this range of the character and personality of Joel Chandler Harris.

NOTES

1. *Joel Chandler Harris* (Athens: University of Georgia Press, 1987), 49.

2. Bickley, 49–62.

3. Two of these books were published posthumously (1909) after appearing first as serials in magazines: *The Bishop and the Boogerman* and *The Shadow Between His Shoulder-Blades*.

4. *Letters of James Joyce* (New York: Viking Press, 1966) 2:xxxv.

5. The nine letters to his wife and the six letters to family addressed as "Dear Folks" or as "Family and Friends" are in box OP 1, folder 1; the six letters to daughter-in-law Julia are in folder 7; all being in series 1, subseries 1, the Joel Chandler Harris Collection, Special Collections, Robert W. Woodruff Library, Emory University (hereafter SC, EU).

6. See Julia Collier Harris, *The Life and Letters of Joel Chandler Harris* (Boston: Houghton Mifflin, 1918), 543–63 (hereafter cited as *Life and Letters*).

7. See the account of JCH's scheme for them jointly to write a book, each contributing alternate chapters in "King Philpo." *Uncle Remus's Home Magazine* 31, no. 2 (May 1912): 7, 18. The story was never written.

8. Julian's dignified, mature letter of sympathy concerning the death of Linton survives. See letter to "Dear Papa and Mama," 28 September 1890, box 21, folder 4, Julian LaRose Harris Collection, SC, EU.

9. Personal interview with Mrs. Joel Chandler Harris, Jr., Atlanta, Georgia, 27 September 1990.

10. See Paul M. Cousins, *Joel Chandler Harris* (Baton Rouge: Louisiana State University Press, 1968), 119, 171–74, 179, 188–89. For an extreme view of Harris's neuroticism, tracing it from youth and seeing it reflected in abnormal families in his novels, see Michael Flusche, "Underlying Despair in the Fiction of Joel Chandler Harris," *Mississippi Quarterly* 29 (Winter): 91–103. Such shallow psychological speculation is readily denied by the contents of the letters Harris wrote his children.

11. Letter to Julian, 8 August [1905].

12. For some of these details, see Michael Kenny, S.J., "Joel Chandler Harris (Uncle Remus)," *Messenger* 50 (September 1908): 225–42; and Msgr. John B. Ebel, "Wise 'Uncle Remus' is Joel Chandler Harris," *Register*, 20 August 1942, 6.

13. Evelyn Harris, *A Little Story About My Mother* (Atlanta: privately printed, 1949), 55.

14. These three letters are listed in the records at Emory University as copies of those

at the Uncle Remus Museum, Eatonton, Georgia. Only two could be located at the museum when I rechecked the originals there on 9 December 1991: a letter to Lillian and Mildred, "Thanksgiving, 1898" [24 November 1898]; and a letter to Mildred, "Sunday, 27 January [1901]." The one remaining to Mildred, "October 19, 1901," is only a photocopy of the original typed letter.

15. The scholar may wish to consult also the essay by Julian LaRose Harris, "Joel Chandler Harris as His Eldest Son Remembers Him," *Atlanta Journal Magazine*, 19 May 1946, 16. This is the only published portion of his detailed autobiography, contracted with E. P. Dutton & Co. in 1946 and abandoned in 1948 after returning the advance. For the notes and drafts of the six chapters completed, see box 23, Julian LaRose Harris Collection, SC, EU. Evelyn Harris's *A Little Story About My Mother* (Atlanta: privately printed, 1949) is far more general but conveys a good impression of the private domestic life and sociability of the family as expressed through visits of friends and church festivals on the lawn.

16. Draft note on an envelope, box 20, folder 12, Joel Chandler Harris Collection, SC, EU.

ABBREVIATIONS AND SHORT TITLES

Candler	Allen D. Candler and Clement A. Evans. *Cyclopedia of Georgia*. 3 vols. Atlanta: State Historical Association, 1906.
Dictionary of Georgia Biography	Kenneth Coleman and Charles Stephen Gurr, eds. *Dictionary of Georgia Biography*. 2 vols. Athens: University of Georgia Press, 1983.
Cousins	Paul M. Cousins. *Joel Chandler Harris*. Baton Rouge: Louisiana State University Press, 1968.
Garrett	Franklin M. Garrett. *Atlanta and Environs*. 2 vols. New York: Lewis Historical Pub. Co., 1954. Reprint. Athens: University of Georgia Press, 1969.
Life and Letters	Julia Collier Harris. *The Life and Letters of Joel Chandler Harris*. Boston: Houghton Mifflin Co., 1918.
Martin	Thomas H. Martin. *Atlanta and Its Builders*. 2 vols. Century Memorial Publishing Co., 1902.
SC, EU	Special Collections Department, Robert W. Woodruff Library, Emory University, Atlanta, Georgia.
Strickland	William Bradley Strickland. "Joel Chandler Harris: A Bibliographical Study." Ph.D. diss., University of Georgia, 1976.

Contemporary issues of the Atlanta *Constitution* and of the Atlanta city directory have also been invaluable resources. Less frequently cited sources are given in full in the notes to individual letters.

NOTES ON TEXT AND EDITORIAL PRACTICES

The spellings and punctuation are those of the holographs. Harris often played with comic spellings, even resorting to imaginative ways of dating his letters, i.e., "Febiwary" and "Aprile the two-eye." Since these minor details are indicators of his playful manner, they have not been regularized. He played also with proper names, referring to his children and grandchildren by such pet family names as these: Lillian, "Billy"; Mildred, "Tommy"; Lucien, "Tootsie"; Julian, "Buba Juju"; Julian and Julia as a couple, "Lovey and Dovey"; Stewart, "Toodly-bo"; Stewart's brother Chandler, "Chubby." He puns on the names of visitors, such as Father Gunn, asking if he will go off. But strangely for a newspaperman, he often misspells names when there is no apparent reason. Only twice does he get the name of the first daughter-in-law, Aileen, right; the rest of the time she is Alleen or Aleen. He misspells the name of the Swede who comes to the house and works on a bust of the author for several months, often calling him Okaberg in letters to the girls. He does get the name Okerberg right in a letter to Julian.

Such obvious errors are usually not marked by a *sic*. In contrast, Harris's spelling of ordinary words and his grammar and syntax are usually impeccable. He shows a real care for phrasing, often calling attention to his own lapses when he falters. The practice in this edition is to use *sic* only when necessary. Reconstructed syllables and words have been put in square brackets. Usually no notice has been taken of the notes added to letters by later commentators or editors. I have restored the passages marked out when they were edited for the *URM* or the other earlier uses.

The editorial abbreviations at the end of each letter—AL, ALS, TL, and TLS—designate whether letters are autograph copies unsigned, autograph copies signed by hand, typed copies unsigned, or typed copies signed by hand. Since these are family letters, the title "Daddy" or "Dad" has been counted a signature equally with the author's name. If the signature is typed only, the abbreviation used is TL.

Harris's corrections of obvious errors in his letters have not been noted unless the writer calls attention to them in making the corrections. Technical information about the type and size of paper for each letter is omitted, also. Harris used a wide variety of paper stock during the period 1890–1908. Unfortunately most of the family letters written before 1900 are on large newspaper proof sheets that are highly acidic and today very fragile. Fortunately most of those in the Emory collection have recently been deacidified and encapsulated. Films have been made of these originals as well. Five main types of paper may be noted, however:

1. large brown newspaper proof sheets, ranging from 10⅞ by 15 inches to a later size 9¼ by 16 inches.

2. white business notepaper printed with "The Constitution/Atlanta, GA./ Editorial Rooms" and measuring 9¾ by 7¹³⁄₁₆ inches for the flat sheet and 4⅞ by 7¹³⁄₁₆ inches when folded.

3. personal blue or white notepaper with the rabbit monogram designed by Oliver Herford and measuring for the flat sheet 12 by 9⅜ inches and 6 by 9⅜ inches folded; or 9¾ by 7⅞ inches and 4⅞ by 7⅞ inches folded.

4. letters typed on large sheets 8 by 13 inches.

5. white business notepaper printed with "Uncle Remus's Magazine/ Office of the Editor/ Edited by Joel Chandler Harris/ Atlanta, Ga." carrying the rabbit logo and measuring 10¾ by 6¾ inches for the flat sheet and 5⅜ by 6¾ inches folded.

The transcription includes at the beginning of each letter the salutation if there is one and the date as given by Harris with supplemental information in brackets; and at the end of the letter the abbreviations AL, ALS, TL, TLS, the number of pages, the mailing address on the envelope if it survives, and the postmarked date (PM). These details help in reconstructing the lives of the family members. Harris's various abbreviations of Georgia on the envelopes have been normalized to Ga. In the postmarks, names of months have been spelled in full and the year written in full, not 92 but 1892 for example. Otherwise, addresses are true to the envelope information. Where no such information is appended, the envelope is missing or has been detached and cannot be identified.

Harris often marked up his personal letters as if they were newspaper copy to be typeset. He also frequently added up the total number of words in his text. Even while writing personal letters, he often retained some stance of his profession as a journalist. Most of his hand markings are represented here in the typeface he specified: equal marks appear as hyphens; words or passages underlined once are italicized; material underlined twice is set in small capital letters; and material underlined three times is set in capital letters. Words or passages underlined five or more times are set in italics followed by a note in brackets giving the actual number of underlines appearing in Harris's original letters.

CHRONOLOGY

This chronology has drawn upon R. Bruce Bickley, Jr., *Joel Chandler Harris* (Athens: University of Georgia Press, 1987), 13–14; and William R. Bell, "The Relationship of Joel Chandler Harris and Mark Twain," in *Joel Chandler Harris: The Writer in His Time and Ours*, ed. Hugh T. Keenan, *The Atlanta Historical Journal* 30, nos. 3–4 (Fall–Winter 1986–87): 105–10.

No birth record for Harris survives. An earlier date of 1846 has been proposed by W. J. Rorabaugh in "When Was Joel Chandler Harris Born? Some New Evidence," *The Southern Literary Journal* 17 (Fall 1984): 92–95. The "new" evidence consists of six citations in census and other published sources from contemporaries that suggest, if any or all are accurate, that JCH was born somewhere in the period 1845–47. For additional citations supporting this hypothesis, see Kenneth H. Thomas, Jr., "Roots and Environment: The Family Background," in *Joel Chandler Harris: The Writer in His Time and Ours*, 44. See also the letter to Lillian and Mildred, 10 December 1898, where JCH remarks on celebrating his fiftieth birthday. Nowhere in the letters does JCH suggest an earlier birth year.

1848   December 9: Joel Chandler Harris is born to Mary Harris in Eatonton, Putnam County, Georgia, father being unknown.

1856   JCH begins education in private schools in Eatonton at expense of wealthy neighbor Andrew Reid.

1862–66   From March JCH is employed as printer's devil for the *Countryman* published on Joseph Addison Turner's plantation, Turnwold, where he hears plantation fables from old slaves. He also publishes a few essays, reviews, and poems, mostly in the *Countryman*.

1866–67   May–October/November, JCH works as typesetter for Macon *Telegraph*; in fall he becomes a private secretary to William Evelyn, publisher of New Orleans *Crescent Monthly* for a few months.

1867–70   In spring JCH becomes printer and editor for *Monroe Advertiser*, Forsyth, Georgia.

1870–74   In fall JCH becomes associate editor of *Savannah Morning News*. On 21 April 1873, he marries Esther LaRose, daughter of Capt. Pierre LaRose and Esther DuPont LaRose, of Upton, Quebec, Canada. Julian LaRose Harris, their first child, is born 21 June 1874, Savannah, Georgia.

1875   Lucien ("Tootsie"), his second son, is born August 21, Lansingburg, New York.

1876   Having left Savannah because of a yellow fever epidemic, JCH moves to Atlanta and becomes associate editor of Atlanta *Constitution*. JCH and family move to 201 Whitehall Street. He publishes first Uncle Remus sketch in *Constitution*, October 26. Evan Howell, his third son, is born December 8.

1877   JCH's mother comes to live with family in five-room cottage on Whitehall Street.

1878   JCH writes strong editorials for "free silver" during Hayes administration. JCH's first novel, *The Romance of Rockville*, is serialized in *Constitution*, April 16–September 24. Evan Howell dies of measles May 18. In summer Esther takes Julian and Lucien for visit to her parents in Canada. Evelyn, his fourth son, is born September 18 in Upton, Quebec, Canada.

1879   First Uncle Remus fable, "The Story of Mr. Rabbit and Mr. Fox as Told by Uncle Remus," is published in Atlanta *Constitution*, July 20. Mary Esther ("Rosebud"), his first daughter, is born December 29 and named for wife and mother.

1880   JCH's first collection of Uncle Remus materials, *Uncle Remus: His Songs and His Sayings: The Folklore of the Old Plantation*, is published by Appleton.

1881   JCH and family including his mother move to 312 Gordon Street (later numbered 1040 and called the Wren's Nest), West End, a town annexed by Atlanta on 1 January 1894 as its Seventh Ward, with approval of the Georgia legislature on 20 November 1893. International Cotton Exposition is held in fall in Atlanta.

1882   Lillian ("Billy"), a second daughter, is born March 1 at the Wren's Nest. April 30–May 2, JCH meets Mark Twain, George Washington Cable, and publisher James Osgood in New Orleans to discuss possible speaking tour using Uncle Remus sketches. JCH declines. In June he attends Tile Club dinner, New York City. Embarrassed by invitation to read his stories at a second dinner, planned by Richard W. Gilder, editor of *Century Magazine*, he leaves for Atlanta and cancels trip to Boston and to Hartford to see Twain. Harris's first daughter, Mary Esther, dies of diphtheria on October 28.

1883   *Nights with Uncle Remus* is published by Osgood. In spring Harris visits publisher in Boston and Twain in Hartford. Linton Edmund, a fifth son, is born June 18. JCH buys the Wren's Nest, house at 312 Gordon Street, and five or more acres from the *Constitution*.

1884   *Mingo and Other Sketches in Black and White* is published. While house is being extensively remodeled, Esther and four children visit her parents in Canada for summer, first of annual trips. In fall JCH goes to Lithia Springs to recover from illness.

1885   Mildred ("Tommy"), a third daughter, is born July 28 at the Wren's Nest.

1886   JCH is visited by A. B. Frost, his most talented illustrator and also his best known. Frost illustrates JCH's story "Free Joe" for *Century Magazine*. Henry Grady makes his famous "New South" speech on December 22 to New England Society, New York City.

1887   *Free Joe and Other Georgian Sketches* is published.

1888   Joel Chandler Jr., called "J.C." and also "Jake," his sixth son and the last child, is born February 5 at the Wren's Nest. JCH resigns from West End City Council over reassessment of his property.

1889   *Daddy Jake the Runaway and Short Stories Told After Dark* is published; the title novella is the first to feature children as protagonists. Its Gaston protagonists are named Lucien and Lillian after his own children. Henry Grady dies December 23. Clark Howell becomes managing editor of *Constitution*.

1890   In March JCH is on a fishing trip to Florida, part of the time at Saint Augustine. In July Julian goes for extended visit to Canadian grandparents and briefly attends Freres Maristes College. On September 21, Harris's fifth son, Linton, dies of diphtheria at age seven.

1891   *Balaam and His Master and Other Sketches and Stories* is published. Harris's mother dies March 30. Esther LaRose, niece and namesake of Mrs. JCH, comes from Canada to live with family, remaining there until her marriage to Charles J. Kelly. In summer JCH makes business trip to New York City.

1892   *On the Plantation* (JCH's fictionalized autobiography) and *Uncle Remus and His Friends* (illustrated by A. B. Frost) are published. Lucien spends summer with Canadian grandparents.

1893   *Evening Tales*, a translation of French folktales, is published. JCH goes to Savannah, Georgia, in November to cover hurricane destruction for *Scribner's Magazine*.

1894   *Little Mr. Thimblefinger and His Queer Country*, the first of a series of six books planned for children, is published.

1895   In spring and summer JCH writes editorials on side of "free silver" issue of 1896 presidential campaign. New edition of *Uncle Remus: His Songs and His Sayings*, with illustrations by A. B. Frost, is published. Second children's novel, *Mr. Rabbit at Home*, is published. Lucien marries Aileen Zachry on December 11. Couple lives with JCH and family for a few months. JCH deeds them a lot from his property to build a house.

1896   Third children's novel, *The Story of Aaron*, is published. *Stories of Georgia*, a public school history text, is published. A domestic novel, *Sister Jane*, appears. Julian becomes engaged to Julia Collier. He goes to Chicago *Times-Herald* to learn newspaper business. Lillian enters Saint Joseph's Academy, Washington, Georgia. First grandchild, Stewart Harris ("Toodie"), the son of Aileen and Lucien, is born October 27. Lucien begins building a house on nearby lot given to him by JCH.

1897   Fourth children's novel, *Aaron in the Wildwoods*, is published. Wife's niece Essie and his son Evelyn visit grandparents in Canada. In fall, Mildred enters Saint Joseph's Academy. Julian marries Julia Collier, October 26. JCH gives them a lot at the corner of Gordon and Lawton. (Other children—Evelyn, Lillian, and Mildred—are also given lots when they marry.) Evan P. Howell resigns as editor-in-chief of the *Constitution*. Clark Howell, his son, takes his place. Joel Chandler Harris III, called "Chubby" and the second child of Lucien and Aileen Harris, is born December 17.

1898   *Tales of the Home Folks in Peace and War* is published and dedicated to Lillian. JCH receives instruction in the Catholic church. Knut Okerberg does bust of JCH.

1899   *Plantation Pageants*, the fifth children's novel in the series, and *The Chronicles of Aunt Minervy Ann* are published. Niece Essie LaRose marries Charles Kelly in fall. Lucien Jr., the third son of Lucien and Aileen, is born September 9, 1899. Charles Collier Harris, the first son of Julia and Julian, is born November 23.

1900   JCH retires from the *Constitution* on September 5 and accepts yearly contract with McClure's Publishing Co. *On the Wing of Occasions* is published. James Whitcomb Riley is the guest of the family for two weeks at the Wren's Nest.

1901   January–February, JCH is ill with grippe for three weeks. Pierre LaRose Harris, the second son of Julia and Julian, is born September 13. Julian begins building a house on his lot given by JCH.

1902   *The Making of a Statesman and Other Stories* and *Gabriel Tolliver: A Story of Reconstruction* are published. JCH receives an honorary degree from Emory College. In winter/spring JCH has severe tooth infection, resulting in septic fever. In spring Julian and Julia move into new house nearby. JCH spends fortnight at Lithia Springs, Georgia, recovering health. In June he goes to Warm Springs for rest.

1903   JCH gives up yearly contract with McClure Phillips Co. *Wally Wanderoon and His Story-Telling Machine*, the sixth and last of the series of children's novels, is published. Evelyn marries Annie Louise Hawkins, October 27. Charles Collier Harris, son of Julia and Julian, age four, dies December 29.

1904   In January, Mrs. Pierre LaRose, Mrs. JCH's mother, dies. *A Little Union Scout* and *The Tar-Baby and Other Rhymes of Uncle Remus* (poetry) are published. Pierre LaRose Harris, age three, dies April 29. Aileen Harris, the first granddaughter and the fourth child of Lucien and Aileen, is born September 25.

1905   JCH returns to *Constitution*, doing three or four editorials before leaving to resume writing projects and to assist in planning of the *Uncle Remus's Magazine*. *Told by Uncle Remus* is published. On May 15, JCH is notified of his election on April 20 with the recommendation of Mark Twain to the American Academy of Arts and Letters. When Pres. Theodore Roosevelt makes a speech in Atlanta, he insists that JCH join him on the platform and at the luncheon that follows at the Piedmont Driving Club, October 20. Evan P. Howell, former editor-in-chief and major owner of the *Constitution*, dies.

1905–6   The early deaths of both her children cause emotional and physical illnesses for Julia, requiring frequent rest cures. In 1906 Evelyn leaves the *Constitution* to become an advertising manager for Bell Telephone Co. That same year J.C. Jr. visits grandfather and other relatives in Canada.

1907   *Uncle Remus and Brer Rabbit* is published. JCH invited to a private dinner with Pres. Theodore Roosevelt in November at the White House, with son Julian and writer Don Marquis. JCH becomes editor of *Uncle Remus's Magazine*, a family monthly. First issue, June, carries initial installment of Harris's *The Bishop, the Boogerman, and the Right of Way*, published as book in 1909.

1908   Lillian Harris marries Frederick ("Fritz") Wagener, Jr., January 15 "at the Sign of the Wren's Nest." In May, *URM* absorbs *The Home Magazine*, published by Bobbs-Merrill Co. of Indianapolis. It becomes known as *Uncle Remus's Home Magazine*. JCH becomes seriously ill; after being baptized a Catholic, he dies of acute nephritis on July 3 in Atlanta.

GENEALOGICAL CHART
CHILDREN AND GRANDCHILDREN
OF JOEL CHANDLER AND ESTHER LAROSE HARRIS

Joel Chandler Harris
1848 [1846?] [1]–1908
m. 1873
Esther LaRose
1854–1938

Julian LaRose Harris
1874–1963
m. 1897
Julia Collier
1875–1967

- Charles Collier Harris
  1899–1903
- Pierre LaRose Harris
  1901–1904

Lucien Harris, Sr.
1875–1960
m. 1895
Aileen Zachry
1876–1958

- Andrew Stewart Harris
  1896–1986
- Joel Chandler Harris III
  1897–1966
- Lucien Harris, Jr.
  1899–1983
- Aileen Harris Scruggs
  1904–1984
- Mary Harris Rowsey
  1908–1979
- Remus Anthony Harris
  1916–1979

Evan Howell Harris
1876–1878

Evelyn Harris
1878–1961
m. 1903
Annie Louise Hawkins
1880 [2]–1954

Mary Esther "Rosebud" Harris
1879–1882

Lillian Harris
1882–1956
m. 1908
Fritz Wagener, Jr.
1882–1964

- LaRose Wagener Grant
  1908–
- Fritz Wagener, Jr. [III]
  1911–1976

Linton Harris
1883–1890

Mildred Harris
1885–1966
m. 1909
Edwin Camp
1882–1955

- Mildred Camp Wright
  1910–1989
- Elizabeth Camp Chapman
  1912–

Joel Chandler Harris, Jr.
1888–1964
m. 1911
Hazelle Pancoast White
1888–1919
m. 1922
Dorothy Dean
1898–

Notes:
1. Westview monument to JCH gives 1849 as date of birth.
2. Annie Louise Hawkins born 1879 according to Emory University list (Special Collections); Westview monument gives date of birth as 1880.

PART ONE ❧ 1890–1896
FATHERLY ADMONITIONS
TO THE BOYS

I am not a great success as a lecturer, and if I take that attitude occasionally
it is because I have more interest in your future career
than I have ever had in my own.

—*Letter to Julian, 20 July 1890*

[To Julian]

6 July, 1890

My Dear Boy: I wrote you a letter last Sunday, but as it was written while I was still suffering from the strain which my uneasiness and anxiety placed on me, I did not mail it. I will send it to you this week, for there are some things in it that you might [wish] to see; but in reading it you must bear in mind that it was written under the pressure of excitement.—I received your letter, enclosing a piece headed "My Trip." The difficulty is that it is not about your trip at all, but is only an episode of your trip. When you send me a real letter for the paper I will put this episode in it. Can't you take time to write about 1200 words for the paper? But you must certainly improve your handwriting. Get some wider paper—get foolscap and large envelopes. I could hardly read your letter at all. When you write, don't be in a hurry.—Another thing: you must learn how to talk French. You will never have another opportunity. Don't disappoint me in this. It will be a great pleasure to me to hear you talking French to your mother when you return.—You must help your grandfather and grandmother all you can. You can make yourself useful in a thousand ways.

With the $14 you can get your grandmother to take you to St. Hyacinthe, and to Montreal[.] I will send you some money later on, so that you can buy you a suit of winter clothes and an overcoat. Find out how much they will cost in Montreal. Don't go to a Jew store, but to some substantial establishment.[1]—There is no news at home. One day with another, it is the same as when you left. Such points as I think may interest you I will give in another letter. But don't be alarmed when you receive my famous letter of reproval which I will mail to-morrow.[2]

Your affectionate
Dad[3]

ALS
4 pp./1 sheet folded
1. A reference to the quality of clothing, as the context makes clear, and not an anti-Semitic remark. JCH always bought the best quality of clothing for himself and wanted the same for his son. JCH would have been familiar with some nineteenth-century Jewish dry goods stores in the South, especially in Savannah and Atlanta, whose owners often began as peddlers before becoming merchants of inexpensive goods and only later sellers

3

of higher quality, more expensive items. See Steven Hertzberg, *Strangers Within the Gate City: The Jews of Atlanta, 1845–1915* (Philadelphia: The Jewish Publication Society of America, 1978), 16–19, 33–37, 81–92, 101–13, 144–49, 153–54. For a modern parallel of Chinese merchants going from street peddlers to store owners, see also Gwen Kinkead, "A Reporter at Large (Chinatown—Part 1)," *The New Yorker*, 10 June 1991, 50, 63–68, 71.

2. Julian, having gone by train to Grandfather LaRose's farm in Quebec, failed to meet his father's friend Mr. E. W. Barrett in Washington, D.C. He became ill in New York, was delayed for several hours, and failed to telegraph his parents of the delay. See *Life and Letters*, 257–64.

3. Unless otherwise noted, this and the text of all other letters by JCH to his children come from the originals found in the Joel Chandler Harris Collection, SC, EU.

Sunday Box 111

[July 1890]

Dear Julian: I enclose a clipping from the Washington Post,[1] one of many of that kind that have appeared in the newspapers during the past week[.] Please have it inserted in the Upton Bugle or in the St. Hyacinthe Poppy. You can imagine what a charming episode it has been to us all—how pleased your mother was when a telegram from Barrett[2] came, announcing that you were not in Washington, and that you could not possibly have arrived. It was a beautiful scene—one long to be remembered; a scene such as can only be found (with this exception) in books. This mammoth exhibition of thoughtfulness on your part has cost me in one way and another $43.75.

To add to the anxiety of your friends here, J. M. Todd[3] telegraphed from Central, S.C., on his way back, that no such passenger as Julian Harris had been on his train. This telegram I kept from your mother[.] What an easy matter it would have been to sent [sic] a telegram from Washington that you were going through!

Well, I trust you will have a good time. You have arrived at the age when carelessness and indifference to the feelings of others have taken possession of you, as they do of all youngsters, but try to be as respectful to your grandfather and your grandmother as possible. Bear in mind that they have lived long out of the world, so to speak, and try not to trial them with that supercilliousness [sic] so often affected by boys of your age[.] Remember that learning is merely an accomplishment and

Esther LaRose Harris and her son Julian (both seated, right) with some of their French Canadian relatives: (seated) Esther's parents, Pierre LaRose and Esther Dupont LaRose; (standing) a nephew; uncle Wilfred LaRose Dupont; and sister-in-law Petula LaRose (Joel Chandler Harris Collection, Special Collections Department, Robert W. Woodruff Library, Emory University).

not a virtue, and if they seem to you to be ignorant, bear in mind that, in time, you will seem to be ignorant to your descendants.

Remember, too, that we love you, that we and all who know you expect great things of you—remembering this, let every act of yours bear some definite relation to your self-respect. We are all well here, though Lucien is moping. The place is just as you left it, except the hole made in the air by your absence, and it is a pretty large one, too.

I am waiting for those long letters.

Your Dad

[Postscript on back of p. 6]

Dear Julian: This letter was written the Sunday after you left. There are some things in it you ought to read. You will overlook the seeming harshness caused by excitement.

> Your affectionate
>
> Dad

ALS

7 pp.

1. For clipping originally glued to top left of this sheet, see next item.
2. E. W. Barrett.
3. Conductor on the train.

WHERE IS THIS BOY?[1]
Joel Chandler Harris' Son Missing on His
Trip to Washington

Julian Harris, the fifteen-year-old son of Joel Chandler Harris (Uncle Remus), of the Atlanta CONSTITUTION, is badly wanted by his father and friends.

A few days ago Mr. E. W. Barrett, correspondent of the CONSTITUTION here, received a letter from Mr. Harris stating that his son, Julian, would leave Atlanta Sunday morning for Canada, to visit relatives. He would reach Washington Monday morning, and would stop over three or four days before proceeding on his journey. Mr. Barrett was asked to kindly look after the young man, and to show him such favors as might be necessary and convenient. This letter stated that he would stop at the Metropolitan.

Mr. Barrett notified the clerk at this hotel to say to young Mr. Harris to remain at the hotel until he came in from Takoma Park, about noon Monday. When Mr. Barrett went to the hotel at the time named, he was told that no such party had arrived. This appeared strange, and when Mr. Barrett reached the Capitol he found a telegram asking if Julian had arrived safely. An answer was sent, saying that he had failed to reach Washington, or else he had gone to some hotel other than the Metropolitan.

This telegram caused Mr. Harris, Captain Howell, and other members of the CONSTITUTION staff to become alarmed, and since its receipt a larger number of messages have been sent to Mr. Barrett to spare neither time nor money in ascertaining the whereabouts of the young man. He had left Atlanta Sunday morning and his failure to reach Washington could not be explained.

All day yesterday efforts were made to learn something of him, but without avail. Late in the afternoon, Mr. Barrett notified detective headquarters, and left a description.

The young man is of a quiet, retiring disposition, and no one who knows him would for a moment believe that he has concluded to run his trip on his own schedule and to suit himself.

1. Copy of news article glued to letter.

P.O. Box 111,

Atlanta, July 20. [1890]

Dear Julian: Your last letters show a great improvement of the first, not only in writing, but in expression. I suppose you wrote the first in a great hurry, being anxious to get out and around, and make your influence felt on the worthy habitans of the Province of Quebec. I see from your various letters that you are having a good time, and that is what I want you to have. Are you keeping up with your short-hand? And are you perfecting yourself in spoken French? I remind you of these things in order that even during your play you may have an eye to your future[.]

But I am not a great success as a lecturer, and if I take that attitude occasionally it is because I have more interest in your future career than I have ever had in my own. A dog caught one of Tootsie's[1] bantams the other night, and the next night he sat up for him. When the dog appeared, the gun was lying across Tootsie's lap, and he cocked it and pulled the trigger at the same time, so that, with a terrific explosion, the whole load went into the calf-pen.

Tootsie, however, is coming out in great shape. He has been moping about the house and reading ever since you left, until the other day, when he joined a literary society composed principally of Lora Venable and the Burgess Smith girl. Friday evening he was invited to a party given by Ivy and Alice May Lee. He decked himself out in a new hat and a pair of patent leather pumps (having on his clothes, of course) and appeared on the festive scene in great shape. Walter Forbes says that

Tootsie was the life of the party, full of wit and humor. He certainly made a fine impression.

Buck Richardson is the same roaring Bull of Bashan, loose-jointed and light-headed. I don't know how he is getting on with Winnie, but I am looking for developments. He Buck [sic], Lucien, Joe Swartz and Evelyn, slept last night in a little tent under the smoke tree, and they say they had a fine time.[2] Evelyn has learned to swim a few strokes, but he is afraid to take advantage of this fact. Linton still has one or the other of his feet wrapped in a dirty, greasy rag, and he presents a picturesque appearance wherever he goes.[3] Sometimes he hides the rag with a dirty old sock. Mildred has become a great elocutionist. She went to the school exhibition, and can now repeat all the songs and dialogues she heard there, and she does it with surprising accuracy. J.C. is right now in the middle of the whooping-cough.[4] He stands up under it very well, but he is having a tough time. The boys will tell you all the juvenile news when they write—if there is any. The cows are holding up well, but I expect they are eating their heads off. I am afraid to make a calculation. Miss May has the billious [sic] fever, and Bill and the old lady look as lonesome as ever. There are some family visitors at Richardson's, and things look like there has been some sort of a family disturbance over there; but Buck neglects his cow and rocks the cook with a regularity that goes to show his own serenity.

My dear boy, I am neglecting my work to write you this stuff, and I must stop. Write to me when you spare the time from your arduous duties, and give my love to all.

Your affectionate

Daddy

Address letters to me

    Box 111

ALS

6 pp.

1. Tootsie, family nickname for his brother Lucien Harris and the second son.
2. Obvious error "He" marked out by later hand.
3. Linton, a younger brother of Lucien, Evelyn, and Julian Harris.
4. Joel Chandler Harris, Jr.

Four of the Harris children: (seated) Mildred and Joel Chandler, Jr. ("Jake");
(standing) Lillian ("Billy") and Evelyn (Joel Chandler Harris Collection,
Special Collections Department, Robert W. Woodruff Library,
Emory University).

[To Julian]

P.O. Box 111.

Atlanta, July 27. [1890]

My dear Boy: Your last letter was charming. I was so proud of it—of the style and the expression—that I showed it to Mr. Reed.[1] His remark was "That boy is a good writer." Then after a while he said: "He is a splendid descriptive writer." This is very gratifying to me, and I tell you about it in order to encourage you to do better all the time. Do you know what genius is? It is large talents united with the ability to take pains—native ability wedded to persistent industry. If you will only take pains you will make a tremendous success in everything you go at.

I suppose that by this time you are getting somewhat homesick, and we are still missing you. The baby is always asking about Bubber Juju,[2] and your mother and I sit on the porch after supper and wonder what our young man is doing. Still, we know that you are enjoying yourself, and that is enough.

Miss May Grigsby has been very sick, and there has been a good deal of sickness in the street leading from the store to Murphy's, with the whooping cough to fill out the sandwiches. Miss Kate Ware has been sick, but has gone home. Buck went to Savannah last night on what he calls a pleasure trip. My own impression is that his daddy, like yours, needs the money that is thrown away in mere pleasure trips. This, however, is not a "slam" at you, for you will get a great deal more out of your trip than the money's worth, or else I will be disappointed. I dreamed last night. That your mother and I were with you in France, and that in walking across the country—it seems we were tramping—we came to a town called Bordeaux. It appeared that the French spoken at Bordeaux was so much like that spoken in Upton that you could converse fluently. Dreams are queer things.—Mr. Doyle is building a snug cottage on the G. A. Howell corner next to the end of the street carline, and Mark Berry is building next to A. G. Howard.—Evelyn now has the stamp craze, and it has struck in deep. One result of it, I suspect, is that the big calf is seriously sick with the scours.[3] She may die, but she looks better this morning. Your alleged game rooster has his feathers coming out, and is somewhat better looking, but he is still the most disgraceful looking object I have ever seen. He must be disposed of in some way.

Write your ideas about it, and remember that by the time you return, you will have recovered from your chicken fever.—Banks had four kittens recently, but Lucien has drowned two.—I will try and fix up your letters in one for next Sunday's paper. Meantime, write something about Upton and the people you meet up with—the impressions they make on you—and don't forget the folk-lore stories that are to be found in that neighborhood. Get your grandpa to help you on this.

Your affectionate

Dad

ALS

5 pp.

1. "Wallace P. Reed, on the editorial staff of the *Constitution* and one of [JCH's] warmest friends" according to *Life and Letters*, 267.

2. I.e., Julian. The baby is Joel Chandler Harris, Jr. (b. 1888).

3. A water diarrhea or purging among cattle.

[To Julian]

P.O. Box 111.

3 August. [1890]

My dear boy:

I have written you two letters since hearing from you, and this is the third. I suppose you are too busy to write to an old man, whose letters are uninteresting. This is a perfectly natural feeling. I don't like to write letters myself, and I never do unless I feel it to be my duty. You are probably too young to understand what duty means. It gets to be a bigger and a more important word as we grow older.

I haven't had time yet to patch your letters together. Mr. Reed has been on a tremendous drunk, winding up in the calaboose, and this has been supplanted by a "booze" on the part of Mr. Stanton, who has just turned up while I am writing. He looks sad and sorry.[1] Ah, Lord! I trust you will never fall into such a muddy ditch. I don't see how the Almighty can ever forgive an intelligent human being for making a sot of himself. You will see that I have had very little time of my own, except at night, and the weather is too warm then for work. The Century has just accepted the story[2] I was writing in the spring when I had to drive you boys out of the room. It will make fourteen pages in the magazine, and

Editorial staff of the Atlanta *Constitution,* circa 1890: (seated) Clark Howell, Jr.,
managing editor, and Joel Chandler Harris, associate editor; (standing)
Wallace P. Reed, editorial writer, J. K. Ohl, city editor, and Frank L. Stanton,
poet and writer (Joel Chandler Harris Collection, Special Collections
Department, Robert W. Woodruff Library, Emory University).

will appear in the December number. If it wasn't so hot I could make a
great deal of money by this literary work. I think next year I'll stay in
Canada during the three hot months and try to do some literary work.—
I hope you are keeping up your short-hand, as you promised, and I shall
be very much disappointed if you don't learn to speak French fluently. I
haven't time to write a long letter, especially as I haven't heard from you
lately[.] Be good to yourself.

Your affectionate

Dad.

ALS

3 pp.

1. Wallace P. Reed and Frank Stanton, newspaper colleagues on the Atlanta *Constitution*.

2. "A Conscript's Christmas," later published with five other stories as *Balaam and His Master*, according to *Life and Letters*, 270.

Box 111,

18 August. [1890]

Dear Julian:

The elephant business prevented me from writing to you last Sunday—I mean the elephant business in conjunction with your own seeming indifference. I didn't know then that you were carrying on such an extensive correspondence. That is certainly a fair excuse for not writing oftener to your mother and me. If you have to cut anybody on that account, don't cut your mother. She was very much troubled because you neglected her so long, and she was very proud to get a letter at last. Cut me instead of your mother. Your eloquent plea for your dunghill rooster shall save him. He is utterly harmless. The ducks run him, and he never gets within 50 feet of the old buff. He goes off by himself. You were badly swindled in him, as well as in your celebrated Maricopa Chief, which is simply a yellow legged country chicken. I am almost tempted to send to my friend Grice in Fort Valley and get you a sure enough game to look at, so that you will know them when you see them.

I think if your grandpa were to sell out and come here, he would be forty years younger. I may be able to visit Upton next spring, but not this summer. I should like very much to see the folks—and of course your mother would. You seem to be very anxious to stay in Canada. No doubt you are having a good time, but there are other things to think about. I am willing you should stay until about the 1st of December. You will probably want to visit in Lansingburg and Albany three or four days—or you probably will not. You can do as you please about that. But I think you ought to be at home so as to bring us all a Christmas present, including yourself. Don't you think so? What about your clothes? You must find your summer clothes uncomfortable. What shall I do about them? Consult with your grandmother, and find out how much money you will want for 1 common winter suit, 1 nice winter suit, 1 overcoat, and shoes. You ought to have attended to this before, as I suggested sometime ago. Mr. Reed is on another jag, and Mr. Stanton is just off one. I have had no opportunity to go anywhere. Evelyn is in Eatonton, and pretends to be having a good time. Lucien is just so: sometimes very good, and sometimes very hard headed. He sticks at home like a tick on a cow.

Love to all.

Your affectionate
Dad

ALS
4 pp.

P.O. Box 111.
1st September, 1890

Dear Julian:

I enclose you sight exchange on New York for $50. This will leave you some money over, and I want you to take care of it as well as you can. You will have enough to go to the French school[1] if you are still in that mind. I think it is a very good idea. It will be a very poor return for me, and a great disappointment to boot if you come back here with only a smattering of French. I want you to know the principles of it thoroughly, so that you can enjoy its literature. You ought to be able to explain to your grandfather that you will have to begin the business of life next year, and that you cannot afford to remain in Upton any longer unless you propose to settle there. He will understand that. He would have been a great deal better off if he had come to Atlanta when I bought the West End place. No youngster who has any promise of a career can afford to bury himself in Upton, or in any other country place. Not that I object to country places. I think it is quite as important as any other part of his education that a boy should be brought up in touch with the rural regions, and that he should appreciate them to the fullest extent. That is the reason you are in Upton now. When you get as old as I am you may want to go back there and live—having discovered that life has very little to offer outside of the contentment of home. It will be time enough for you to spend a longer season in Upton when you have made this and other discoveries. I am now trying to look at life through your eyes, and I frequently catch myself mapping out a proud career for you. But this will be a vain imagining unless you have that within you which will enable you to resist the various temptations that are spread out before a young man. The real success in life is the will power that enables one to resist these. But I am not much of a preacher, and this is not intended to be much of a sermon—being merely a roundabout way of saying that your fortune is altogether in your own hands. I am not much of a Puritan myself, and I have tried to so conform my views to yours as to enable you to say that I have never denied you anything that would tend to give you real pleasure. All that I ask in return is that you won't drink whiskey or other spirits. I don't want any Bob Adair around me—I see him occasionally and the sight is too pitiful. Your mother and myself have just returned from Eatonton with Evelyn. The new railroad is now about halfway between the factory and the town. Evelyn met us out there on horseback. I was glad to see that he has developed into a good rider. We had a very good time at the barbeque. I drove Mrs. Lawrence out behind Prince. I think Charley was in hopes that in the hurrah of going and coming the buggy would turn over and break her neck. Coming back I passed everything on the road, and the old lady was badly frightened.

There is no news here—and the boys will send you all the gossip.

You can get the draft cashed in St. Hyacinthe.

Your Dad:[2]

~

ALS

5 pp.

1. Frères Maristes College, which Grandfather LaRose proposed he attend to study French (*Life and Letters*, 270).

2. Note JCH's use of journalist's closing mark after signature as a signal for end of copy. JCH frequently uses this symbol to close subsequent personal letters to the children.

15 September.

[1890]

Dear Julian:

I have not written sooner for several reasons. In the first place you owe me a letter; you have never answered the one in which I enclosed a draft on New York. I suppose, however, your school and your work keep you pretty busy. In the second place, Linton has been very sick. He is still very sick, but the doctors—Crow and Hobbs—think he is improving a little.[1] In addition to the tonsilitis which your mother wrote you about, he has had polypii in his nose. In other words, a polypus in each nostril. I have heard of this disease, but never saw it before. A polypus is a sort of growth in the nostril—in the case of a man gristle; in Linton's case a sort of pulpy flesh, not greatly different in appearance from the lights of a chicken, though a little darker. I suppose these polypii have been growing in Linton's nose for some months, and that they were greatly aggravated by the tonsilitis. This afternoon Dr. Hobbs cut them out, and I judge from their size and length that they must have extended throughout the nostril. The operation would have been a very painful one, but for the use of cocaine, but Linton says it didn't hurt him at all, and he seems to be very much better. He is very hoarse, and his throat is still very sore, but he is bright and patient under it all. He gets mad sometimes when we irritate him with our attentions and anxiety, but, altogether, he is the most courageous and patient chap I ever saw. You may judge from all this that he has been very sick. He is still very sick, but has retained his strength and nerve to a remarkable degree.—I have no news to write, the principal item being the fact that Mr. Reed got drunk again Friday, was sent home Saturday, and escaped from the clutches of his wife at noon to-day. He was still at large at last accounts—going about town like a lunatic and making a spectacle of himself on every corner. But this news is stale, and I shall write about it no more.

The calves are both in good condition, and so are your fowls, so far as I know. Your celebrated game has renewed his feathers, but not his courage if he ever had any. He doesn't stay around where old Buff can trample on him. Lucien has a three ounce bantam that tries to train

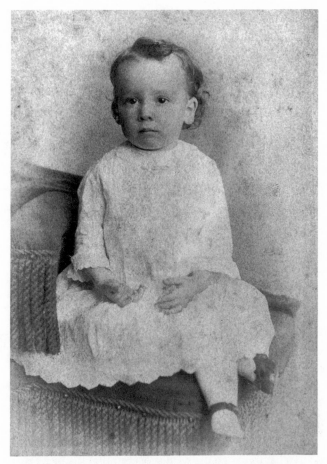

Linton Harris, circa 1885 (Joel Chandler Harris Collection,
Special Collections Department, Robert W. Woodruff
Library, Emory University).

Maricopa in the art of scrapping, but the great chief refuses to come
to time. The Pekin ducks are the only game fowls on the place except
Linton's hen. I think I will write to my friend, Grice, of Fort Valley, in
October, and get a trio of games—the real article.

Lucien started to school to-day, and I hope he will follow the advice
you gave him. I am very sorry you didn't follow it yourself. Linton has

been going a week to Alice McGehee. Evelyn and Lillian are going to the Academy.

I am too sleepy to write you a long letter. I trust you will write to me when you can seize time from your arduous duties.

Your affectionate Dad[2]

～

ALS

6 pp./4 sheets folded

1. Dr. Arthur G. Hobbs, specialist in eye, ear, and throat, had offices at 14½ Whitehall; Dr. Walter A. Crowe, a general physician and neighbor, lived at the corner of Oak and Lee streets in West End and practiced from his home. Dr. Crowe is mentioned frequently in other letters. Information from the Atlanta city directory for 1891.

2. "Dad" added in another hand.

[To Julian]

22 September, [1890]

My Darling Boy:

In the midst of my grief and despair I can scarcely summon courage enough to write you of the death of Linton[1]—your little brother and partner. If there had been time, I would have telegraphed you money to come home on, but the change came so suddenly that there was hardly time to send for Dr. Crow. The trouble was not with his throat—that was getting along very well—but with his heart. Though his throat was improving all the time, he never seemed to rally, and at the last, too late to apply any effective remedy, we discovered that his heart was affected. The change took place late Saturday evening; he was very bright Friday, looking at his cigarette pictures and talking about you; and at 5-o'clock Sunday morning he died, without a struggle and with no pain whatever, like a tired baby going to sleep. From beginning to end, he made no complaint, and was never fretful nor irritable, and the last words he said were: "I feel better." It is a great blow to us as it must be to you. I have always fancied that you cared more for him than for the rest—perhaps it was only a fancy—but I know that you were chiefly in his thoughts, although you were away.

Of such dispensations as this, we have to make the best. So I am told. But I should like somebody to tell me how. While we are thinking about it, let me advise you to take Linton for your pattern so far as his patience was concerned. I cannot write you a long letter, and I hardly know what I have written. Your Mother sends her dearest love and we both bless you, and trust that heaven may guard you safely.

> Your affectionate
>> *Papa*

Our love to all.

ALS
4 pp./2 sheets folded
1. Linton, b. 18 June 1883; d. of diphtheria on 21 September 1890, according to *Life and Letters*, 275.

6 October—[1890]

Dear Julian: If anything could possibly have that effect, your beautiful letter has drawn you closer to your mother's heart and mine.[1] A boy of your age may sometimes have such tender and true sentiments in his mind; but I think it would be difficult to find a man of any age capable of giving them more beautiful expression. All this we are proud to know and we hope that the gift of expression will grow on you.

Dismissing other things, let me suggest to you that you have a very rare opportunity to claim for your own the literary field that is richer and broader in French Canada than in any other portion of the globe. That field has still to be filled. It has been touched on here and there by awkward and adventurous hands. Fiction based on the lives and characters of these quaint and simple people could be made more picturesque than any I know of. Think about this and study the habitan in his native simplicity. You may be able to make a mint of money.

I think your grandfather is right about the law. There is in it the certainty of recompense to a bright mind, and it could easily be made the handmaid of literature. But this is a matter you will have to decide for yourself. It will do you no harm to take a turn at the newspaper business, for you have plenty of time to be a lawyer or anything else.

Your affectionate

Papa

Our love to all.

[Postscript:]

Dear Julian:

I send you a stray Canadian quarter; it will do to buy chewing gum. Tell grandma I received her letter and will write soon.

Mama

ALS

3 pp.

1. For text of this letter to "Papa and Mama," dated 28 September 1890, see box 21, folder 4, Julian LaRose Harris Collection, SC, EU.

P.O. Box 111.

Atlanta, 26 Octo. [1890]

Dear Julian:

No doubt you think I have been neglectful or indifferent because I haven't written, and yet I have been thinking about you every day. But I have been unusually busy. I am trying to earn a respectable living by writing a serial for St. Nicholas, and I now have 138 pages of MS. And the exposition has bothered me.[1] I haven't been out yet, but there has been a good deal of confusion in the office on account of it—Strangers coming in to see me, and old acquaintances. Cephas Leonard and Nona Leverette are here, and they break somewhat into my writing moments.[2] The town has been very gay with the crowds, and yesterday Barnum's circus added to the whirl and tumult. Your mother is writing to you to-night, and she will give you all the local news of any account. I think you are mistaken when you say that I have nominated you as the black sheep of the family. Let us hope that there will be nothing of that kind in this particular family. But I have said that I thought you lacked the plodding and persistent elements that are more valuable in this world than genius. I am not at all sorry about your shorthand, nor am I disappointed. It was your fad and not mine. You took it up of your own accord. It is an affair that calls for a good deal more patience than the average boy can command. I took it up myself and dropped it, and I have never regretted it. I do not think you will regret it. It is useful, of course, and frequently invaluable, but I do not think that it helps the intellect; in fact I am very sure that it hampers originality and destroys the individuality of those who make a business of it. I hope you are still sticking to your French.—Do you know what would be a good thing to do? Keep a journal, and write in it your experience and observation each day, and all the incidents that occur. Make notes of the patois, or dialect that the farmers speak. To do this would seem monotonous to you now, but it would be invaluable to you hereafter, and some of the simplest notes would be of great aid to you, particularly if you propose to get your bread by the sweat of your mind.—I hope all this is not tedious to you. I am not lecturing, nor issuing orders. I am merely making suggestions. Now, as to coming home. If you really want to stay until next June, so as to learn French pretty thoroughly, I don't know that I have any objections, except such as grow out of a desire to see you; and these I can waive. I don't know that you could be in a better place. I am sure that your experience on the farm and in the neighborhood generally will be worth a great deal to you hereafter. The work you have done will insure you a sound and strong body, and that is worth more than all the education you could get. Perhaps I may be able to come in June. I think you are almost too young to jump into the newspaper business, but just the right age to do what you are doing. Write me your views, and give my love to all.

Your affectionate

Dad

ALS

4 pp.

1. The Great Piedmont Exposition, a fair that opened October 15 and closed November 1, 1890, according to the Atlanta *Constitution*, October 5, 1.

2. Probably friends from Eatonton. Cephas may be C. D. Leonard (*Life and Letters* 1, 14–21); Nona is probably related to Frances Lee Leverette who often wrote about JCH.

P.O. Box 111.

Sunday, [November] 16, [1890]

Dear Julian: Your letter in to-day's paper is admirably done. Mr. Reed praises it very highly. The error in the headline is mine. I had it Les Habitans, but our Greek proof reader changed it to habitant, and left the plural. Habitant is the dictionary word, but habitan is the Canuck dialect, and it ought to have been spelt so throughout the letter. Speaking of this, you ought to jot down in your note-book, the words and phrases of patois that you hear—the speech of the common people. They will be of immense importance to you hereafter if you should dabble in literature, and they will be interesting if you should not. You say you don't understand how you you [sic] can put your observation and experience on paper. Maybe I left out a word or two in my letter. You can certainly make notes of what you see and hear—the thousand and one little intimations and suggestions that float in the air—the traditions that are cropping out among the older. I think you would find your Aunt Josephine a perfect mine of these things.[1] Why do I pick her out? Because she is not French and everything she has heard struck her as strange and queer at first, and has stuck in her memory. I am sending you a book about Emerson. It is time you were beginning to take a little interest in thoughtful things, and you will find in this little book some remarks on style that may be profitable to you—By the by, in looking around for the book, I find it is misplaced, but I'll send it to you if I have to buy it. Another thing—when I make a remark or a suggestion, don't take it too seriously. You are old enough to have discovered, or, at least, to have suspected, that, except in the matter of morals, it is impossible to map out a young man's career by means of advice. All that I can do is to give you some of the results of my own experience. I am much more interested in seeing you grow up strong-bodied and clean-minded than I am in your career. A clean-minded man will be everything that he should be. I should like to see you with a will strong enough to resist all forms of temptation. Your career will then take care of itself. And yet I shouldn't like to see you puritanical and narrow-minded. I want you to grow up to be a wholesome, hearty, liberal-minded man. You have indi-

Atlanta *Constitution* Building, circa 1890 (courtesy of the Atlanta
Historical Society).

viduality enough to make your impress on the public in various ways, and when you get a little older you will know which way to choose.

There is no news of any importance. The oldest heifer was sent off the other day. She was nine months old and ought to have a calf when she is eighteen. Mayflower will have a calf the last of December. Nita went off on the 23d October.[2] Buck Richardson has been sick and amused himself (so your Mother says) by spitting on the bed and floor. I'll send you some money by Dec. 15, or as soon as my Daddy Jake check comes to hand.[3] Your grandfather is the best judge of whether you should board with the Brers or not.[4] I told your mother I was afraid they would teach you bad habits and she was very much shocked. I hope to send you enough money to enable you to buy some Christmas presents for the folks. Maybe the $1.44 was for cigarettes or something of that kind. Be good and write soon to

Your Loving
Papa

ALS

6 pp.

1. Josephine LaRose, an aunt of Mrs. JCH, often referred to in letters to Canada.

2. Nita, the other cow.

3. *Daddy Jake the Runaway and Short Stories Told After Dark*, published 1889.

4. Probably a joking reference to the Marist brothers. See note 1 to letter of 1 September 1890.

P.O. Box 111.

---

7 December. [1890]

Dear Julian: I suppose you think I have been very neglectful, but I have been writing every night on the new story, and now it is nearly done. S. S. McClure has offered me $2,500 for the serial and book rights of the story, and I have written to him that he can have them if he'll pay $2,000 cash down, and $500 in July.[1] This is (will be) a right snug sum to make in two months, won't it? I hope to forward you a check on or before the 15th. Meanwhile, I hope you are not really needing the money. Maybe I'll send you some in a day or two. Write the Constitution an account

Julian Harris, age sixteen, in Canada. An inscription on the back of the photograph reads: "'*The Missing Link*'/ *Weight 125* lbs." (Joel Chandler Harris Collection, Special Collections Department, Robert W. Woodruff Library, Emory University.)

of the Christmas and New Year's festivities among the habitan's [sic].
You can couple what you observe yourself with such details as you can
get from your "gramp" and "gram." You wrote about not wearing your
overcoat on a very cold day. Do you know that you have to take care of
yourself in that climate? An attack of pneumonia might undermine your
constitution and destroy your health entirely. Don't let your high spirits
lead you into taking risks. Mark Twain told me that the first winter he
spent in the north he wore no overcoat at all, and he has been paying for
it every since with rheumatism of the loins. But, alas! behold the force
of habit! When you are at home I am hectoring you, and when you are
away, I am "lectoring" you, or words to that effect. I saw Pearl and Ruby
to-day. They are certainly beautiful girls, but as I don't know t'other from
which, I can't say which is the beautifullest. I'll say this, though—they
are the prettiest girls for miles around. I had never seen them before.
Did you know that our friend Nelson is in jail? I have a suspicion that
you found out something about him long ago, for I remember that you
dropped him very suddenly. The fellow seems to be a natural-born thief,
with no principle whatever. It is a pity that a man who could be useful
to himself and to others should allow his depravity to get the better of
him. I hope you won't fall into any bad habits. The boy that can conquer
himself at your age can conquer the world. Everybody that I know is
constantly asking about you—how you are getting on, and sometimes
these questions are asked by people who are strangers to me. It is very
gratifying to me to know that you have made an impression on people.
Lord, Lord! don't disappoint 'em, and don't disappoint your mammy and
daddy. (More "Lectorin'.") Hannie Frazer is the most ridiculous little
spizerinktum you ever saw. Her voice is like a small tin-horn on Christmas Eve. Next Tuesday I'll be 42 years of old, a fact that goes to prove
my great 40-two'd. (Laughter and applause.) Lucien seems to be getting
along better at Gordon than he ever did anywhere else. The discipline
is good for his health. He is growing, too, but not as rapidly as you did.
Your letter was too much for him. We laughed at him so that he got mad,
and has been pouting with you, but he vows that he wants to see you
mighty bad: and it is the truth. I believe he thinks more of you than
he does of anybody in the world. He is a curious compound of affection

and bad temper. Not long ago, a country rooster—Cowlan—who goes to the academy took a notion that he ought to whip Lucien.[2] So one evening, he waited for Tootsie and sent up after him. Whereupon Lucien went out and cuffed him around considerably. Shortly afterwards the Thompson boy—Ed—who is not as large as Lucien, concluded that he could whip him; so he sent up after Tootsie, and challenged him. Lucien told him he didn't want to fight him on account of his size, but Thomson whaled Tootsie over the head with a stick, and Tootsie lit into him and smashed him in the face and swept the road with him. It is the general opinion that the boys will let Tootsie alone after this. They seem to be mad because he wears military clothes and puts on airs. Write soon to your Dad.

Mamma says she won't write to-night, but will write during the week.

ALS

4 pp.

1. Semiautobiographical story published as serial by McClure in newspaper and then by Appleton as a book, *On the Plantation* (1892). See *Life and Letters*, 294.

2. Gordon Military Academy.

[To Julian]

P.O. Box 111,
14 December, 1890

The Constitution
Atlanta, Ga.
Editorial Rooms.

My dear Boy: I enclose a cheque for $25 made payable to your "gramp." I suppose he can have it cashed with greater facility than you can; and I suppose you will accept the cheque in lieu of a long letter. It is much more interesting, I dare say, than anything I could write, for all the news that I know you get in the papers. I send you to-day a copy of the December Century containing my story.—I want you to feel easy about the money. I send you this much now so that you can use as much of it as you see proper in buying Christmas and New Year's presents for "gramp" and "gram" and the rest. The first week in January I'll send you another cheque for $25.—I suppose you are never homesick. Well, we still miss you greatly, but we feel that your visit will be a profitable one for you in more ways than one. You will see in the paper that Carter's house burned yesterday. But for the Atlanta fire department Blacknall's house would have gone.—We are not going to have much of a Christmas, but I'm sorry you are not to be with us. Hereafter, we'll try and have you.— I'll write you a longer letter later in the week. Love to all.

Your loving *Dad*.

ALS
2 pp.

P.O. Box 111,

—————————

22 December, 1890

Dear Julian:

I judge from your last letters that you are having as much snow as you want and something over. Well, that is what you wanted. You must bear in mind that you are not acclimated to the severe weather and you must positively take care of yourself. The fresh air will not hurt you, but I am afraid that the contrast between the warmth of the house and the cold air outside will be a terrible strain on your lungs. I think a little fresh air in your sleeping room wouldn't hurt—but your gramp will know how to regulate that. The portrait of yourself in one of your letters with a pipe in the mouth is very suggestive. I hope you haven't begun that sort of thing at your age, and I shall be very sorry if you have. It is not a crime, and it is not even a vicious habit, but it would grieve me to know that my nice big boy was sucking away at a filthy pipe. If you have begun it, quit it now while you can. Wait until you are through growing before you begin on tobacco. Mind you! I'm not lecturing, but just venturing a piece of advice. I suppose Lucien has written you about Tom Latham and the blue stag. Tom and G. Adair made a raid on the yard when nobody was at home. I always objected to your going into partnership. Lucien, I am told, gave George a regular salting down on the street car yesterday, remarking in a casual way that George and Tom were cowards, thieves and liars. Eveylyn [sic] heard a part of this friendly conversation, and he says that George was very lamblike. I suppose Lucien and Tom will have a row, and if Tom has any grit in him he will get hurt, for Lucien is in a very bad humor about the chicken. It is a very pretty bird. Maricopa is really a beautiful fowl, and I suppose some of your other partners will come and get him. I believe all the boys for miles around were in partnership with you, and I'll be very glad if they don't come in and claim the cows and calves.—About Rudyard Kipling: don't be impressed too much by his style. It is vicious English, and he allows himself to be unnecessarily vulgar. I wanted you to read his stories in order to give you an idea of the "go" that a little enthusiasm will give a thing. The man certainly has a genius for telling a tale in an off-hand way.—McClure, the syndicate man couldn't come to time. I told him he might have the story for $2,000 cash down and $500 in July, but, as I suspected, he was a little weak in the pocket. I have sent it to St. Nicholas, and now have an offer from Miss Gilder, of the Critic, or the suggestion of an offer. I'll have no trouble, I think, in selling it, but it strikes me as a very poor affair. I'll have out a book in March or April, entitled "Balaam and His Master, and other Sketches and Stories"—Houghton, Mifflin & Co., Boston; London: Osgood, McIlvaine & Co.—I suppose somebody has told you that Johnny Caldwell has built another brick store by the side of the first one. I am told we are to have electric cars sometime in the spring. This will enable you to visit Mr. and Mrs. Moseley with impunity, for it will be a "loop" running around by the cemetery. We should like to have you here for Christmas and all of you, but as that cannot be, I can only hope you will have a merry one and a happy New Year—and the same to Gramp and Gram and Josephine.—You might pad out your letter to The Constitution with a description of some of the general aspects of winter there—how the people do and what they do when they are snowbound.

My love to all. Your affectionate

Dad

ALS
6 pp.

[To Julian]

P.O. Box 111.

_____

1 January, 1891.

The Constitution
Atlanta, Ga.
Editorial Rooms

My Darling Boy: We were all very much pleased at getting letters from you to-day. We were not getting uneasy, but just a trifle restless at the failure to hear from you. I suppose the boys and the other children had a very good time Christmas. They say they did. And then, when the keen edge had been taken off of expectation, and there was something of a lull in the hurly-burly, we sat around the fire and talked about you. You see there was something missing, and in its place there was the big hole caused by your absence. I think it was felt by all. I made few remarks about it myself, but your mother and Lucien and Evelyn—in fact all of them had something to say about Julian and Bubber Ju-ju. The big hole is still here—in the daytime, but mostly at night when we are sitting in my room after supper. Lucien is especially loud-spoken in his desire to see you. Just at this present time your mother is rocking J.C. to sleep, and he remarked a few moments ago that he wanted Bubber Ju-ju to come home right now, right to-night. I observe that you have been having some such feeling, and you boldly announce that you are about to be homesick and want to take the necessary medicine at once. I am not at all sorry to see you hoist the signal of distress. I was beginning to fear that there was no place in your mind for homesickness, and that would be very bad—for us who love you. I used to read about a man who loved to travel merely for the pleasure of coming back home again, and I have often thought that he was a man who knew how to enjoy life. I hope you have not forgotten that your visit was protracted at your own suggestion. I thought, and still think, that the suggestion was a good one. Your contact with new scenes and new people, and your struggle with the language of all Gaul will be of as much benefit to you in the long run. The language itself will open up a new literature to you[.] I think the last of April or the first of May would be a good time for you to come home. In fact if I had my heart's desire you would be here now, but I console myself with the idea that you are making your stay there count for your own good. Lucien took a two days' hunt in the country last week—no, this week—going with Ovid, and stopping at the house of Mr. Tom Powell ten miles out on the Sandtown road.[1] He was very successful, killing a good deal of game. He brought home two rabbits and a squirrel. To-day he went calling with Forbes, and to-night he is at Forbes's house. He is improving considerably in his manners and methods. Mrs. Josiah Carter was out to dinner to-day, and Bob and Jack Adair were both drunk, all of which goes to show that very few changes have taken place.[2]

But I am getting tired. This is the first letter I have written since last year, and I am out of practice. Your mother will probably write to you to-night, but just now she has gone to sleep in the bed with J.C. She is snoring, which is a sign that she hasn't had a whole night's rest since last year. Write soon to your Affectionate Dad[.]

My *love to all.*

ALS
4 pp./2 sheets folded
1. Ovid, family dog.
2. Wife of Josiah Carter, journalist on Atlanta *Journal* in 1880s and 1890s (Garrett 2:57).

                                                        20 *January.* [1891]

Dear Julian:

I mailed you yesterday some copies of your letter. Mr. Reed said: "It is a remarkable letter to come from a boy. He seems to know just what will interest outsiders, and his style is good." I have heard a good many comments on it—all favorable. We think your picture is splendid, and we appreciate it very much. Your mother kisses her hand to it occasionally, and I have my copy at the office on my desk, where I can look at you as I work. I can see no change in you, except a maturer, or, rather, a more settled expression on your face.—No, I sent no check in my last letter. In fact, I have been waiting to hear from St. Nicholas about my boy's story. The matter seems to hang fire. I think it will turn out all right. In any event my Frenchman shall have his check in a few days. Consider whether you wouldn't want to stop over in Albany and Troy a few days as you are journeying home. I can send you a letter of introduction to Governor Dave Hill, who threatens to become a very big man before long. You could have an opportunity of doing a piece of newspaper work by interviewing him—I mean a piece of work that would be widely quoted.—Mamma is cooking, and does it so well that we don't sympathize with her as we should. Celia has the grip, and hasn't been around in several days. The result is that we are having chocolate cake and stewed prunes until you can't sleep sound at night. Tell the Captain that it is a great blessing to have an Albanian-Canadienne who can cook. His daughter here can rattle the pots and make as much fuss by yelling at the children as any living person. Notwithstanding all this the children are well. They seem to thrive on the stewed prunes and the fussing. Evelyn has the stamp craze in its most aggravated form. It has broken out all over him, and I think it is about to strike in, for to-night he was complaining of the belly-ache. Or he may have felt that way because Mayflower is about to have a calf.

But I am in a hurry—I'll write again before the week's out, just to show you how industrious an old man can be.

Your affectionate

Dad

My love to all. Mamma will write when the cook comes.

ALS

5 pp.

[To Julian]

P.O. Box 111.

Atlanta, 10 February. [1891]

My dear son:

Of course you are prepared to make allowances for me when I fail to write promptly. I do the best I can. It is true, I might have answered your letter several days ago, but I wanted to be as good as my word and enclose you a check when I did write. I was waiting to get the half yearly reports from my publishers, and to see how my syndicate venture with Uncle Remus sketches would turn out. The sketches which you see in the Sunday Constitution I have been trying to get in a number of other papers simultaneously with their appearance here. My syndicate now consists of The N.Y. Sun, The Boston Daily Globe, The Phila. Times, The Wash'n Evening Star, the Chicago Inter-Ocean, the St. Louis Republic, the San Francisco Examiner, the Courier-Journal, and the N.O. Times-Democrat. The price varies from $4 to $5 each, according to length, making the returns 4 times 9 or 5 times 9, as the case may be, which is a very comfortable weekly addition to my income if I can keep it up.[1]— Very well. The book publishers have been heard from, and the syndicate is in sailing trim, the breezes seeming to be fair. Wherefore and whereupon, I enclose a cheque for $25. Naturally, this is the most interesting part of this letter.—I gather from the tone of your letters that you are getting somewhat homesick. Indeed, I have been afraid that you wouldn't get homesick, a condition of affairs that would have betrayed a hardness of heart and an unregenerate spirit altogether out of keeping with your character. I think you have been very brave in sticking it out so long, and it has given your mother and me great pleasure to know that you have made such progress in French.—This being the case, I am ready, whenever you please, to discuss the precise date of your homeward voyage; and it is a date which I shall leave you to set, merely remarking that we are about as homesick to see you as you are to see us. Your mother thinks I ought to appoint the date myself; but I tell her that is better for you to do so, in order that all your arrangements may be made to fit. I shall expect you to tell me in your next letter when you desire to start from Canada, so that I may send you a cheque in time to meet your views and wishes.—Mayflower has a baby calf, another heifer—and this is about all the local news that occurs to my mind. Lucien wrote you a long letter the other night.—The New York Sun of Sunday had a sketch and portrait of your dad. The sketch said I had maried a Miss La Bosse. I shall write to the editor and say that your mother was not La Bosse before I married her, but that she is certainly La Bosse now. Evelyn is trying to learn to milk, and he is succeeding very well.—I didn't tell you what I thought of your New Year letter because I took it for granted that its appearance in the paper would satisfy you in regard to my opinion of it. I thought it was very good, for it was a very difficult piece of work to do. You certainly have a knack with the pen, and you will have a "fetching" style if the reporting business doesn't destroy it forever. I may be wrong, but I believe that reporting is death to the literary style if it is persisted in, or if it isn't accompanied by some higher work. But what is the use of my running on in this way? You will be what you will be, and your success is in your own hands to make or mar. Your affectionate

Dad

ALS

4 pp.

1. Harris's syndicate was his direct marketing of Uncle Remus sketches to newspapers.

[To Julian]

20 March, 1891

My Dear Son:

While we misunderstood your letter for a few hours, you will find by the letter which you will receive from your Mother before this reaches you, that the misunderstanding was not of long duration. We appreciate to the fullest extent your will-power, and your power of self-denial. For my part I deem it a certain omen of success for you. It means patience, fortitude, and all the other qualities that compel success. Say to your grandfather that I have not the slightest objection to you writing your name in full.[1] I do not remember changing it; but if I did, it was because you had been writing it in a simpler way. I have been sick at home with a cough for several days, and I feel very weak and nervous—so I will not write you a long letter. I enclose you a cheque for $50. Come at once, and try to catch the vestibule train from Washington 10:30 a.m., which puts you here at 6:30 the next morning. Love to all.

Come at once.   Your affectionate Papa

ALS

2 pp.

1. I.e., Julian LaRose Harris.

[To Evelyn]

P.O. Box 111.

_____

1 August [c. 1891][1]

My Dear Boy:

I need not tell you that your letter gave me great pleasure. Of course, it would be a pleasure to hear from you under any circumstances, but your letter was in the nature of a surprise.[2] It was well-written—well thought out, and put up in good shape. In short it was interesting, and that is what a real letter should always be. My letter, however, doesn't count. I'm handicapped. All the rest will be writing to you, and they'll take all the sauce out of the pudding[.] They'll tell you all the news and leave me to send you this dab of dough. Everything is about as you left it except the ducks. They have mysteriously disappeared until only five are left. We had a very fine rain yesterday—the first in—well, you know how long. Lucien and John say they walked out to the "The Farm" and back yesterday. I'm sorry to say I don't believe it. I don't believe either one is such a fool. They got back about 3 p.m. I don't know any "gal" news, and therefore can't expect to entertain you.

It is very funny about the Macon fad in Eatonton[.] Such prominent Macon men as Huff and A. O. Bacon say that Macon is the deadest town in Georgia.[3] Mr. Huff told me the other day—(we were standing on Tyner's corner)—that he could stand in his tracks and see more people—more life and movement—in twenty minutes than he could see in Macon in two days.[4] But there are some mighty clever people in Macon, and there is more vacant land in the city than Atlanta has. But don't pester yourself about taking up for Atlanta. The town doesn't need it. Harry called Sunday night, and I made him and Essie go in the parlor.[5] They seemed to enjoy themselves very much.—Mamie Richardson wants to come up and spend a week with Lillian.—You are right about Charlie Wylie. He is one of the smartest boys in Georgia.

Be good. Have as much fun as you can, and don't bother much about us old folks, except to remember us with love, as we do you. My regards to Mr. C.D. and Mrs L., and to all the rest. Write when you can.

Your affectionate

PAPPY.

ALS

6 pp.

1. Emory University's supplied date [c. 1890] is wrong because Julian was in Canada in August of 1890 and Essie LaRose came to live with the family in 1891 (*Life and Letters*, 372).

2. According to note at top this letter "Sent to Eatonton, Ga."

3. Augustus O. Bacon (20 October 1839–14 February 1914), Macon lawyer and United States senator (1894–1914), according to the *Dictionary of Georgia Biography* 1:44–46.

4. Tyner's drugstore was at 30 Marietta Street, downtown Atlanta.

5. Essie LaRose is Mrs. JCH's niece, who came to live with the family in 1891 (*Life and Letters*, 372).

[To Evelyn]

[Atlanta, Ga. c. 1891][1]

4 August.

My Darling Boy:

You must bear in mind the fact that an old man can't write a letter every day in the week, especially when he has nothing to write about.— Everything is going on here all right. Harry sent Essie some very fine peaches, and I have had three of them.—Winnie went off Tuesday. Julian and a lot of girls went with her to the "*daypo*[.]" When parting time came, everybody thought that Julian would kiss her, but he merely lifted his hat, bowed haughtily, and retired. If he is grieving after her he doesn't show it. He is as serene as a setting duck.—By the by, the old duck has come off—result 000. Her eggs disappeared one by one. Whether she broke them and ate the shells or whether some varmint got them it is impossible to say. There are now five young ducks waddling around.— Everything is quiet and dull—plenty of rain and cool weather[.] I have set about to get Tootsie a place. He is getting ripe for it.—The little gals are right where you left them—flip and flirtatious.—I'll send you a postal order Monday or Tuesday.—What about Cephas? We'd like to have him. He may find it dull, but we'll do the best we can. There is absolutely nothing to write about. Give my regards to all, and remember me with love as I do you. Have a good time and don't worry about writing every day.[2]

Your affectionate,

Pappy

ALS
3 pp.
1. Emory University's supplied date [c. 1890] must be wrong. C. 1891 is probably
correct; see note to the letter to Evelyn, 1 August [c. 1891].
2. Written on letter "This letter sent Eatonton, Ga."

[15 June 1892]
Wednesday.

Dear Julian: Everybody is well here, and there is no news. Winnie went
with Essie and Tootsie to the Culberson shindig. I fancy you got a letter
yesterday saying she would go just because popper wanted to go and
not because she'd enjoy it. For how could she enjoy it with her dear
charmer away? She looked very pretty, and so did Essie. Winnie has that
interesting, far-away look which belongs to a gal in love. She seems to
be most hopelessly gone on you. Tootsie was in one of his "moods" at the
party; and they say he stirred up the animals (as it were) with a long
pole. He came home about 12 o'clock, and I heard him laughing after he
got in his room.

I'll send that cheque Friday. Be good to yourself and remember that
the only genuine pleasure there is in this world is in pleasing those who
love you.

Your affectionate
Papa

ALS
1 p.
Envelope: The Constitution / Atlanta, Ga. / Julian Harris, / The Wigwam, / Indian
Spring, / Ga.
PM: 15 June 1892

[16 June 1892]

Dear Julian:
I send you a cheque for $12.50. Mr. Collier will probably have to pay
25 cents to have it cashed, maybe 50 cents. He can take the cheque and
return you $2.

The winsome one is very well I thank you.

> Your Affectionate
>
> Dad

Just endorse the cheque to George Collier, and tell him howdy.

> JCH

ALS

1 p.

Envelope: The Constitution / Atlanta, Ga. / Julian Harris, / The Wigwam, / Indian Spring, / Ga.

PM: 16 June 1892

[To Lucien]

14 August, 1892

My Dear Boy:

You are not hurting yourself by writing to your Dad. You must bear in mind that your absence leaves a large round hole here which is troublesome to think about. You can't fill it by writing, of course—only your presence could do that—but the more letters I get from you the better I will feel. You must bear in mind, too, that my letters are six or seven times longer than yours. Perhaps I'm asking you to take up too much of your time in writing to an old played-out citizen, and I guess I'll have to take what you give me, but it strikes me that it wouldn't strain you much to write four of your bobtailed pages twice a week—just to keep your poor old dad from getting lonesome.

The matter I wrote you about in my last letter was all O.K. in spite of Harry's letter. He showed me your letter to him, and I straightway made him explain it to me. He said he had already written the explanation to you. I have been trying to engineer the thing so that a settlement could be made without compromising you in the least, and it will surely turn out that way unless you act in a foolish, unreasonable manner. The note of apology would be the correct thing to do if you never expected to speak to her again. In this instance it will lead to a correspondence between you, which, if you are as sensible as I think you are, will be mutually pleasant. In regard to the picture—that was engineered skillfully, I think. Harry was here one night—he comes frequently now—

and I told him to take one of each kind home, examine them by sun-light, and make *his* choice. He took them home, and the inevitable result followed. Aleen went over to see Nell, saw the pictures, and took posses-sion of the full-face one. Harry protested that I would be mad, but she walked off with it anyhow. She said that all she asked was that Julian shouldn't know about it—therefore Julian *doesn't* know about it. Out of that transaction will come a picture from the girl. Perhaps you think it queer that an old chump like me should take such an interest in this matter. Well, in the first place it is your affair, and I'm rather stuck on you; and, in the second place, I want to prove to you that my theory of forcing the female sex to come to terms is the only practical one.[1] Ben has made his disappearance, as the niggers say. Harry says he still likes Ben, but he says it in a tone of voice that convinces me that B. doesn't stand as well as he has stood in Harry's estimation. There has been trouble of some sort. There is one thing you must remember about Harry—he is a perfect echo of Aleen, whomsoever she likes, he likes; whomsoever she despises, he despises.

Mrs. Leonard has been here with her two oldest girls. She came Tues-day and left Friday—making us very glad twice in one week. Uncle Bob Shropshire found a negro in his pantry the other night. The nigger had a light and was squatting down on the floor. Uncle Bob crept up, placed his double-barrel gun between the nigger's legs, banged aloose and tore up the floor. The . . . [p. 6 missing]. I tell her it's the very worst thing I ever heard of in my life. Ah! it is a terrible situation. Ovid brought Essie a basket of flowers yesterday. Tell Zepherine that Essie will probably be married before the year is out, and then Snoosh can ride on the street cars without paying. We are going to buy Essie a new pair of socks, and Ovid will have a plug hat. It will be a lovely couple. I gave Flip to Chloe yesterday. He had become a nuisance.[2]

Heavens! how this letter has spun out! Tell the Captain howdy, and give everybody my love.[3] Write soon to your ever affectionate

Dad.

ALS
7 pp.; p. 6 missing
Envelope: Lucien Harris, / Upton, / Province Quebec, / *Canada East*
PM: 14 August 1892

1. Lucien married Aileen Zachry, 11 December 1895.
2. Ovid and Flip were family dogs. Chloe Henderson was the black milker and sometimes maid and cook (*Life and Letters*, 179).
3. Capt. Pierre LaRose, JCH's father-in-law.

2 July, 1895.
Box 111.

The parts I have marked *Confidential* you will of course keep to yourself.[1]

Dear Evelyn:

We have enjoyed your letters immensely. They are just the thing. You seem to have the knack of putting in "the light touch," and that, after all, is what makes things go.—I have been too busy to write—just pushed to the wall with matters and things. I went to Warm Springs Saturday and got back to-day.[2] I intended to write to you from that famous resort, but didn't find time. All the folks that you and I met there were on hand—except the Macon girl—and I just had to sit up and talk to them when I ought to have been writing to you. You'll know how to excuse me—though I wouldn't know how to excuse you: such is the advantage that youth has over age. You certainly know how to write a good letter, and that is an accomplishment that but few ever acquire. Occasionally I see Charles,—that is to say when he gets on the street car with that air of proprietorship that so well becomes a red-headed boy. As to Brader, he is more of a puzzle than ever.[3] I don't know where he combs his hair now, but certainly not over here.—Pat has a job in the Southern Passenger Association, and seems to be getting along very well. He is now stuck on Helen Jefferson, who seems to be as stickable as the Tar Baby.—At the Springs, Dr. Jordan asked about you very particularly, and so did Callahan—the chief bottle-washer and towel wringer. The bar room is still in a place so public that it may easily be avoided, and the new pool is 150 feet long and 50 feet wide. You remember Gertrude? Well, Gertrude swam entirely around it without stopping, showing that wind is superior to water. Women and men go in together, owing to bathing suits and an abject desire on the part of both sexes to display that which they have the least of, namely: calves.

Confidential

I hope Essie is happy.[4] She certainly seems to be, and happiness is what we all are looking for. She wrote me a letter, which was about the coldest document of the kind I ever received. I'll answer it presently, but not in kind. I think it was dictated by—Mrs. Josephine, who seems to be a regular female Tardler [Tartar?]. I hope Essie will profit by Mrs. Josephine's advice and instruction. If she does she will grow fat in front and rear and become a leading dish-washer. Do you know, my dear boy, I was never as sorry for anybody in my life as I am for Essie? I am sorry because she is so blind to her own interests. I am sorry because she is so utterly—But what's the use? A thousand years from now we will never know the difference, and if we do we'll talk about it in whispers.

not confidential

You'll find your grandfather to be a remarkably good man—a man who has seen the world and knows it, and who will give you a lot of good advice disguised as a joke. You will find, if you study what he says, that he looks clean through people just as if they had glass windows in their bowels. He is as good a man as your mother, and that is saying a great deal.—I hope you miss us a little, but not too much. Too much would be the greatest plenty. We are here thinking and talking about you every day, and it is a big thing when two old people are engaged in that business. Of course, we could think and talk about other people, but we don't, and so there it is. Our big boy is constantly in our minds, and we hope we are in his. Shucks! We know we are—and what a comfort that is!

(Confidential again.)

What about Essie? What is her attitude? What sort of game is Josephine putting up? What sort of a line is she playing up there? Is Essie as snappy and as quarrelsome as ever? Does she heat you agreeably, or has she sprinkled sugar over her temper? It is important that you should keep your eyes open, as you well know how to do, and tell your daddy the inwardness of things. Now, I don't mean that you should spy or turn yourself against anybody, but that you should observe closely and give me the facts in your own way and with a touch of your own good humor.

(not confidential)

We see nothing of Harry, and don't need to, because the cows give down just as much milk as ever, and everything seems to be in a weaving way. Annabelle was bellowing to-day, and that might be owing to Harry's constant absence, but if she continues to-morrow I'll send her where she can be cooled off. I'll just tell Ed to take her—and he can carry her to Wotton's if he wants to.[5]

But the plain truth is, there is nothing to write about, and that is the reason I am writing you such a long letter. Being a notorious writer, I can sit down and write you whole volumes about nothing. The cats and dogs continue to be kind-hearted, and Ovid, the dog, knows your name and whines when we mention it—which is a great tribute to an auburn-haired disposition. Continue thus, my son, and keep your temper auburn-haired. It is a great thing in life, and it goes a long way toward making life worth living. If Mrs. Josephine is not too large in front to bear an additional burden you may give her my regards.[6] My love to your grandfather and grandmother, and to Essie, if she is in the humor to accept so small a favor. I read with delight of your success at fishing, and have an idea that the stories you send us about it are a sort of preparatory work for the writing of real fiction.

Consequently I am your

    Affectionate *Pa*,

    and

    so is your *Ma*

ALS

7 pp.

Envelope: Evelyn Harris, Esq. / Upton Station, / Province of Canada, / *Canada East*

PM: 2 July 1895

1. Harris's note at top.

2. Warm Springs, Georgia, then a modest resort town.

3. Brader Warner, a neighbor and frequent visitor to the home, about whom JCH often gossips, especially in letters to his daughters. Full name is given in letter to Mildred, 15 April 1900.

4. Harris's wife's niece "Essie," or Esther LaRose, came in 1891 to live in JCH's home and remained until she married.

5. Probably James L. Wotton, a neighbor residing at 234 Lawton and identified as an electrician at Southern Bell Telephone and Telegraph Co. in the 1896 Atlanta city directory. The Wottons, whose name JCH sometimes misspelled as "Wotten," are referred

to in subsequent letters, especially their daughter Kathrine, whose name is sometimes misspelled "Catherine."

6. Josephine LaRose; see photograph in box 14, folder 14, Harris Collection, SC, EU. She was an aunt of Mrs. JCH.

Warm Springs, [Ga.]
July 21, 1895

Dear Evelyn:

I am here for a week to finish up the Thimblefinger business.[1] But, in replying, address your letter to Box 111, as there is no telling when I may pull up stakes and go home.—I am writing with a fountain pen that Julian made me a present of, and it moves as easily as a pencil.—I left home yesterday, and nothing had occurred up to that time worth writing about. Everything was running along in the same old groove, and "*hit*" greased. When I left Miss Laura and Miss Alleen were there. Miss Laura kissed me goodby, but Miss A. refused, so I take it for granted that she finds in me some trace of the disagreeable. This is easy enough found in me if a body will look for it closely enough. Miss Laura is not as close an observer as Miss Alleen.—I was much interested in what you wrote about your grandpa. I expect he is inclined to exaggerate my good qualities (if I have any.) I sent him the money because I happened to have it to spare, and he was just as welcome to it as if I had been sending it to myself.—I hope everybody is happy. Those who are young ought to be happy because they are young, and those who are old ought to be happy because they are alive. Essie, I presume, is having a good time. At least I presume so from all the rumors and hints that I hear. She has cut my acquaintance as a correspondent, but I shall continue to write to her occasionally.[2] There is no need whatever for you to feel lonely. People who know how to think ought never to lack for company, or for sources of pleasure and amusement. Pat Leonard has returned home. He got a job in the Passenger Association at $10 a month, but it seems to have been too much for him. I have somewhat changed my views about him[.] A boy who has no patience is not likely to succeed at anything. Everything comes to those who wait, and everything gets away from those who are restless. I have noticed that all my life. It is nothing to seize an opportunity, but another and quite a different thing to wait for the opportunity to develop itself.—I am glad your grandpa thought of the boys the first thing. It shows he has a big heart. Those boys are as near and dear to him as his own children, and they ought to be.— The apples in the front yard are about gone. They were very good this year—so the children say. The trees in the long row are literally covered. The garden is in a better condition than it ever has been. Yesterday, for instance, we had asparagus for dinner. I turned 68 new chickens loose in the lot Friday, and now we shall have fried chicken and chicken pie every Sunday until you get back. Julian is miffed with Adamson and the consequence is he comes home at night sometimes at eleven p.m., and sometimes at 2, 3, and 6 a.m.—The tailor has made Lucien's suit, and is now making mine and Julian's.—If you will count the words on one of these pages, you will see that one of them is a long letter by itself; so don't be alarmed if you find my name at the bottom of this. Dr. Jordan is here and says he is sorry you can't go to ride with him. He has his horses here, and very fine ones they are. There is a good crowd from Atlanta, and the big swimming pool is immense. I went in last night and at half past four this morning. Consequently I'll have to take a nap today. My love to all and to yourself especially. If you get out of money let me know.

Your Dad

ALS
3 pp.
1. Second book, *Mr. Rabbit at Home* (1895).
2. Niece Essie LaRose.

Saturd'y, 31. [c. 1895]

Dear Evelyn:

I feel that I've treated you very badly, but you are a great big boy and can stand it. You are not only a great big boy, but a great big good boy. I enjoy your letters immensely. Your last was especially good, showing that you are developing your critical faculty, which is another name for judg-

Evelyn Harris, February 21, 1896 (Joel Chandler Harris Collection,
Special Collections Department, Robert W. Woodruff Library,
Emory University).

ment. Your ideas are very good—just about what I would say if called on
to give an opinion of these masterly young Constitution men.—Julian
has not yet returned. He went from Tallulah to Porter Springs, which is
not only a long journey, but a very picturesque one—among mountains
all the way, and on top of a mountain after you get there. He writes
that he'll be home to supper Sunday night. He's had a long vacation,

and I hope he'll come back improved in mind and body.—So far as I can see, your old friends, your dear companions, have about deserted the ranche [sic]. Charles never comes, and the only token of friendship and remembrance that I've received from that quarter is a request from Mrs. Kelley [sic] that I will lend her my mowing blade—which I did with feelings of mingled respect and veneration.—Why don't you try to cheer Mama up? I judge from her letters that she is having a terrible case of the blues. It is a great pity. She is not used to old people, and I dare say the sight of her father and mother in their old age, is calculated to wind her feelings up to a very high pitch. It is what we'll all have to come to unless, happily, we die young.—Take for example the case of old man Freeman who lived on the corner of Gordon and Garner (or Evans) Streets. I saw him Friday and had a talk with him. I didn't want to talk, but he talked anyhow, and after he got off the car, I said, "Ding your old hide, I hope that's the last talk I'll have with you for some time." And so it was. That night he took too much morphine, and yesterday there was crape on the door. The old lady looks more shocked than grieved. I saw her at the front gate yesterday afternoon informing passers-by of the suddenness of the event. Such is life, and such also is death. When you get a little older you'll find that death is as much a part of life as life itself.—Mama, gazing on the spectacle of old age, has changed her tune. What is funny is her surprise in gazing on old age. But she's the dearest and bestest mama that you'll ever have, and she always wants to do right. We've been married nearly twenty-three years and I wish we could live it all over again. . . . . These dots mean a lapse of twenty-four hours. When I was right in the midst of my high-flown moralizing, Ida Grigsby put in an appearance and began to chatter and look over my shoulder. I turned the pages down and told her I was writing an Editorial for Sunday on a very solemn subject, which little girls ought not to read in naked handwriting, but ought to wait until I had put on its breeches by appearing in print.—I see, however, I have waited in vain. There is nothing else to write about. There were four eggs in the wren's nest in the mail-box, and the little bird was setting as hard as she could, but some scamp came along and filched one, and now I am afraid the wren is disgusted[.] Nothing consoles me for this but the fact that Jesse and Andrew Cobb got a tremendous whipping the other day for smoking. The affair occurred in the backyard of the Cobb plantation, and invitations were extended to the whole public. At any rate a very large crowd was hanging on the Gordon street fence watching it before the conclusion came. Honestly, I never knew a white woman to whip her Children as Mrs. Cobb whipped hers that day. I think it was beastly cruel and unnecessary. You will live to see those boys go to the dogs unless providence intervenes to save them, and I sincerely hope that Providence will step in to save them. Nothing else will after that beastly whipping.—Everything is all the same. Chloë swallowed the old churn and has at last got rid of it. Tootsie swallowed a peach seed the other day and I don't know how he is going to get rid of it, unless we cut off his appendicitis—the one that hangs on the outside. Miss Aleen complains that none of you write to her—but that kind of talk belongs to the frenzied condition of the family when they let their tongues wag. My dear boy, this is all. Love your Dad and continue to write to him.

With Love,
Your Dad

ALS
4 pp.

[5 April 1896]
Box 111
Easter Sunday [1896]

Dear Julian: We received your letter and though it was comparatively short and sweet we understood that you would have made it longer if you had had time. There is nothing going on here that is worth telling. Garnsey[1] returned the other day. He will leave for Chicago Wednesday and will doubtless hunt you up.

To-day has been a great day—chicken for dinner, and Mamma with a new easter hat; an old one trimmed over, a sort of pancake affair, so that when Mamma came to the house from the street-car she looked like an

Esther LaRose Harris (Joel Chandler Harris Collection, Special Collections
Department, Robert W. Woodruff Library, Emory University).

apple dumpling with a tulip stuck in it, and a broad smile across it. Such is life in the south, if my memory serves me. The weather has been cold, wind blowing like flugens until to-day. By-the-by, when you take beer consult the weather bureau. If there is a northwest wind we can stand in the front porch and smell the beer on your breath. I mailed you a letter the day after you left. It was from "The Family"—that dainty little family that seems to know a good thing when it seize sees it. Heavens! Observe my spelling. This is because I have been correcting some of Evelyn's type-written copy. I have finished my story, all except some inside work—the hand oil finish, etc. It will make 85,000 words, and I don't care whether it succeeds or not, since I had so much pleasure in writing it.[2] Don't overwork yourself. Now is the time to store up strength and energy to be used later. I think Mr. Howell is very fond of you. He has a natural hesitation about telling me how he feels toward you, but he lets fall a hint occasionally. The old man—good old soul!—continues in the weaving way, rolling home almost every afternoon as drunk as a lord. Presently you'll hear about a sudden death—that Clark has been made Editor-in-chief and so on. As to the boys about town, of course I know nothing about 'em. They are no doubt the same as ever. Our own household is unchanged[.] J.C. wrote you before you got to Chicago,[3] and wondered very much why he didn't get an answer the next day. It is this kind of thing that makes us young people tired. For instance why can't I get a reply to this to-morrow morning? I hope you are comfortably situated and that your surroundings are pleasanter than you expected. Write when you can, and holla when you get in a hole.

All send love.   Your affectionate

Dad

ALS

2 pp.

1. John Henderson Garnsey, of Joliet, Illinois, friend of JCH and family. See *Life and Letters*, 343.

2. Probably *Sister Jane* (1896). Garnsey convinced JCH that it was worth publishing. See *Life and Letters*, 343–45.

3. Julian was sent by Clark Howell to gain experience on a Chicago paper. See next letter.

[To Julian]

Monday Evening—not afternoon [1896]

Condensed for information
by
Joel Chandler Harris,
Author of
A number of Books and Things
and
Co-Author of Several Children.

Scene—Clark Howell's Room (repapered.)

Clark (after the usual greetings.)—Did you see that Iowa matter?

Harris–   What Iowa matter? Was it in the paper?

C.–   *Yes!* State going our way.

H.–   I didn't see it.

C.–   (Hunting over paper once, returns to 1st pages, and finds it at bottom of second col.) Here it is.

H.–   Now, Clark! Why in the ding-dong-nation don't they emphasize that kind of stuff?

C.–   Hell! They don't know how.

H.–   Why don't you raise Cain?

C.–   No use; they don't know how.

H.–   WELL!! What are you going to do about it?

C.–   Do? I've already done. That's the reason I wanted Julian to go to Chicago.

H.–   Heavens! Did he have to go there to learn that?

C.–   Heh-heh! Why, no! But I wanted him to learn all about everything.

H.–   Humph!

C.–   When he comes back, there won't be any more trouble.

Your affectionate
Dad.

TL
1 p.

[To Julian]

[29 April 1896]

29 afternoon

My dear Boy:

Stamp received. Thanks! Such thoughtfulness drops out of the cloudless sky of Kidland like a thunderclap. You know how I am—how ingenious I am in avoiding letter-writing. Of course I ought to have written before, but I said to myself. "He is getting about a letter a day from home, and if I push him with mine he'll think he ought to return the whole fusilade."

Everything is the same here. Your suggestion of a freeze-out[1] is out of your own hatchery. No eggs of that sort are laid here. Clark looked over the marked paper you sent him and was very much pleased with it. Don't imagine things and then mistake them for facts. It will be time enough for you to walk on the ice when the freeze-out comes, and I've heard you're a pretty good skater. Reed is at work, and Stanton is making feints and threats in the same direction. By-the-way, don't let that Monroe lecture business worry you. You are no more responsible for the collapse than I am. Just leave me to deal with him—or, better, let him deal with himself. Answer no more of his letters, but just let him rock along.

Of course I'll send Mr. Kohlsaat a book.[2] Would he prefer one of the new edition—or one of the Tumblebug—excuse me! Thimblefinger books?[3] How about the Rosenfeld insurance? I'm ready for him whenever he presents the matter. But I think bills are sent direct from New York. I was thinking the other day (vaguely) of running up to Chicago sometime in May and spending a day or two with you[.] At night we should both have different engagements. If I come I'll drop in at the Saratoga.

Our roses are fine and numerous. We sent you some the other day. Twas Mamma's suggestion, of course. I cut 'em, she pack 'em, and Ebby mailed 'em. No doubt they were a mess when you received them but the scent they bore with them came right out of the yard.

Sewer hits us this summer—90 cents a foot all along the front and the Lord knows how much to make connections in the back yard. Maybe you think I'm worried about it. Shoo! I'm too old for that. I've got the money ready to pay for it right now.

All send love. How is our "family?" Do they still keep the mails warm? Or is there a cooling off? They were sick last week, so I saw in the papers.

Your 'fectionate

Dad

ALS

3 pp.

1. Julian's job at the *Constitution*?

2. H. H. Kohlsaat, of Chicago *Times-Herald* where Julian was working. See *Life and Letters*, 347.

3. Probably the new edition of *Uncle Remus* (1895) with A. B. Frost's illustrations; second reference is to his children's books, *Little Mr. Thimblefinger* (1894) and *Mr. Rabbit at Home* (1895).

[To Julian]

Sunday 3rd May [1896] [1]

My Dear Boy:

That was a good letter you had in to-day's Constitution, timely and full of interesting stuff. Get acquainted with Henricksen, and also with Harvey. The latter can give you some interesting information about the independent silver campaign. He's the author of "Coin," you know.[2]

I'm sorry to see from your letter to Mama that you are mentally troubled. The truth is, at your age, and with your ability—which is a source of constant pride to me, and has been for years—you ought to have no mental troubles that you cannot instantly dispose of. Worry is the thing that weakens and dampens energy and ardor. There's no such thing as over-work. Over worry is the trouble that kills. Get in the habit of contentment. There is absolutely nothing in your way if you can retain your health, and the way to do that is to stop worrying over trifles. Not that I think you are doing that. You have too much of my own disposition, I hope, and too much will power of your own, I know, to worry over trifles.

In the office they are having their usual spring carpentry and carpentry [sic]. The editorial rooms have been repapered, and on the fifth floor a great many changes have been made in the rooms—all for the better, I hope. In the general cleaning-up, John Whittaker and his brother have been discharged. Whittaker had been with the paper twenty-eight years—just long enough to convince him beyond all question that the paper couldn't get along without him. It is coming out as usual, however.

I notice what you say in your letter to your mother about Atlanta and Chicago, salary, etc. It is all just and proper. I think you will have no trouble to contend with here—except in the matter of wages. They never did pay good salaries here, and I suppose they never will. But on The Constitution an ambitious man is more in the public eye than on any other paper in the world. The public all over the country is familiar with the paper, and it is far more widely known in the United States than any paper except the N.Y. Herald. That is curious, but it's true.

Stanton is not sober yet. Wallace spent last night in the station-house. It is all very pitiful. Reed's wages are garnished for months ahead, and I suppose he thinks it is as cheap to get drunk as it is to work. For Stanton, there is not even a trifling excuse to be found. He simply takes pure and unalloyed delight in everything that is low and disreputable.

Everything is the same at home. The donkey is fat and melodious, the roses are in great shape (and we'll send you some more shortly,) the birds are busy, and everything is lovely except that the weather is too dry.

The family are all well, including five new kittens under the barn, Trilby's two in the cellar, and the old cat's two on the back porch.

But my eyes are getting tired. Write when you can.

Your affectionate
Dad.

I have a bill of yours from Muse & Co for $30.[3] They sent it to you through the mail and I opened it. What shall I do with it?

ALS

4 pp.

1. Emory library-supplied date [c. 1897] is wrong, as free silver was campaign issue in 1896, not 1897. Papers were full of it in 1896. See Atlanta *Constitution*, 3 May 1896, 19, for letter to which JCH refers.

2. William H. Harvey's *Coin's Financial School* (1894), a popular amateur treatise in which "Coin," a young but wise financier, delivers six lectures in Chicago for free silver before actual contemporaries whom he defeats by his arguments. It sold approximately one million copies and spurred a number of books in rebuttal. See the introduction by Richard Hofstadter to the reprint of William H. Harvey, *Coin's Financial School* (Cambridge, Mass.:

The Belknap Press of Harvard University Press, 1963). Henrickson, unidentified, perhaps was a newspaperman working for the same Chicago paper as Julian.

   3. Atlanta clothing store.

[May 1896]

Sunday again

Dear Julian:

I am writing a play, and have got as far as the 1st scene of Act I. I am afraid I am getting too many villains in it. As the 1st scene is short I'll describe it:

Scene, Street car—Time Saturday night. (super to be used as passengers) Clark Howell, returning home. Enter Tootsie with bundle and a heavy smile.

C. Howell—airily—Hellow, Tootsie!

Tootsie—grimly—How are you, Mr. Howell?

C. Howell—*What-do you know?* How's everybody? They tell me you are married. How's that? Where's your wife?—*Whadder you know?*—Everything in bloom—did you ever see the like in your life? How's your wife?—*What you know?*—What have you got in that bundle?

Tootsie—wincing—Strawberries, Mr. Howell.

C. Howell—amazed—Straw berries! You don't tell me. All that bundle strawberries? What in the world you going to do with 'em? hey!

Tootsie—irritated—Feed 'em to the chickens!

C. Howell—after a long and painful pause—*Whadder you know any way?* Well, old man Joe must be fond of strawberries!

⁓   ⁓

The fact is everything has been lovely for the past two days. Weather warm—apple trees literally clothed in white and pale pink blooms, and the purple wisteria blossoms trailing like flowers. On our rose bushes the buds are beginning to show; and, contemporaneously, the red spider and the green amphidae [aphids?]—now *is* that their name? Well, any how, I'm squashing 'em as fast as I find 'em, and it don't make any difference how much name you pile on 'em after that. I have had new steps put on the front terraces, and Juliana may ride by and look at 'em if she'll

bow when she passes. And, bless you! The chickens are in the pen—
that is, those that are lazy enough to stay there. Mamma had a little
strawberry patch planted this spring—a pretty little patch about the size
of Evy's right foot—and they are all in bloom. I reckon she'll gather as
much as a tin cup full if the season is a good one. We had strawberry
shortcake for dinner today, but it didn't grow in our garden. The grass
on the terraces is growing as if it didn't want to stay in the ground at all,
and the trees are all putting out, and the violets are still blooming and
the pansies and pretty soon a sewer will be built along the front—and
then a long farewell to a lot of money. The dogs are quarrelling over a
bran sack, one pulling at one end and the other at the other—or may be
it is the other pulling at one end and one at the other—in consequence
of which I don't know whether I'm sitting up or standing down. And—
oh, yes!—the donkey is very lively—so much so that J.C. wants to know
why he is more active at his behindest end than he is at the other. Not
being able to speak Spanish I couldn't tell him—a fact that goes to show
how much I've lost by not going to college and then to Mexico.

Clark showed me your letter last Monday and said it was a fine one.
I'm glad you are catching on. If you make the T.-H. men fond of you, you
will have two strings to your bow.[1] Anyhow, it is well to have as many
friends as possible.

Between ourselves and the bed-post, you'll be an uncle sometime next
fall. I haven't been told so right out, but I can shut my eyes and see
things. If it's twins, watch out! I'll join you in Chicago.

⁓

Lord, I forgot and made an editorial mark because I was through. I'm
tired in the fingers.

Write when you can to
        your affectionate
            Old Dad

ALS
3 pp.
1. *Times-Herald.*

[To Julian]

Wednesday, May 20. [1896]

My Dear Boy:

Have you made arrangements for the enclosed? I wouldn't ask you about it if I didn't have an idea that you had broken it up into small notes. Answer at once.

I have just read the Alkahest, or, rather, your story and squibs in the Alkahest. You tell Evelyn that you are sorry your name was signed to the story—but it is by far the best thing you have done in that line, and shows a development that both pleased and astonished me. I enjoyed it immensely, and yelled at the close. It is very neat, very deft, and yet strong and vigorous. The squibs are perfect—bright, snappy and telling. I don't know when I've been so proud and pleased. In fact I'm prouder than if I had done it myself. It speaks to me of great possibilities for my young man. Your letters to Evelyn are in the right key. Having my shrinking, doubting, self-effacing disposition, he needs bracing, and you are just the chap to do it. That's the way Turner (in Putnam long ago) and Evan Howell (in Atlanta) braced me, and it does a world of good.

I've written you two or three letters recently—short ones. Count 'em in with this, and they'd make a long one; which is the kind I want from you when you have time and are in the humor.
All send love.

Your affectionate
Dad

ALS
2 pp.

[c. 1896]

Friday *afternoon*—late

Dear Evelyn:

Your letter was a most pleasant surprise. I forebore asking you to write, feeling that the request would make it a duty, and that sometimes, when even our inward desires take the shape of duties, they become irksome. Most boys of your age, or, rather, most young men, are so busy with their own plans, conceits, and operations that they forget about the old folks. They say, "Oh, Well! What's the use of doing so and so?" and so forth and so on. I have used the same formula myself—alas, on too many occasions.—I had no trouble whatever in reading your letter. Handwriting should be individual, and yours is very much so. It is uneven, but time will correct that.—I hope the water is having on you all the effect I expected it to have.[1] I feel sure that by the time you are through with your visit, you will find your trouble entirely gone. It came from exhaustion, and not from disease; but it is in the nature of a warning to you to take things easy and not to permit yourself to be destroyed by *conscientiousness*—a quality which, in a sensitive mind, may become intemperate in its operations. Yet it is a fine, a vital, quality when it doesn't become morbid. I have had the same difficulty. I used to be kept on a perpetual strain for fear my work wasn't pleasing the proper persons. But I finally controlled it until now my conscientiousness is concerned with doing my *best* and not my *most*—if the expression is proper. With respect to newspaper work, since it is for the day only, I have no conscientiousness whatever. You will lose yours in good time, for I discover in what you write, especially in this last letter, certain touches and suggestions that belong exclusively to the mind that [is] preparing to do creative work. I have never found this touch in Julian's work since he became a sort of executive, but he had it when he was younger, though not nearly so finely developed as yours. His was conscious—he labored for the effect; whereas, it seems native to your mind, and therefore unconscious. Don't ask me to describe it, or to lay my finger on it. It is elusive; it flees if you but look hard at it; but the impression it makes lingers. I would suggest to you to train your observation. Note closely everything about people's ways, and manners, and gestures; not *critically* but kindly. The Lord made us all and we cannot help our peculiarities, but we can at least enjoy those of other people, and profit by them (in a literary way, at least) it harms no one.—There isn't a mite or a smattering of news anywhere in the neighborhood—except that Rufus has a pair of No. 9 shoes, apparently made from the model of a war vessel. They make a noise when he walks as of a file of men pouring at regular intervals spadefuls of gravel on a tin roof from a great height.—C.K. was on hand last night, bringing an armful of cut roses and pinks and carnations.[2] The bundle was so large I thought at first he had found a baby on the front step and was bringing it in. It made me tremble, for I knew I would be charged with its authorship (even at my age) by thoughtless people.— The two cats came to time with a scuttleful a piece the other night. Out of the abundance we have saved one white one and one somewhat like old Mrs. Kitty Banks.—I hope Lucien is better. He was very much worse off than you were or have been; but in spite of that I knew that, as soon as he got a bellyful of the water, he'd go whickering around among the females.—Julian and Julia were to go up this afternoon. Give them my love; to Lucien also; and likewise the same for yourself. The folks are all out or they'd join me.

Your loving
Daddy

ALS
3 pp.

1. Note on letter: "Sent to Lithia Springs, Ga." Evelyn was there to drink the mineral waters for their medicinal properties. Lithia Springs (formally known as Salt Springs) became a well-known southeastern resort boasting a luxury hotel—Sweet Water Park Hotel—and two smaller inns, the Piedmont Chautauqua (established in 1888) housed in a Moorish style building, private summer cottages, a lake, and other recreational facilities. Lithia Springs, approximately twenty miles west of Atlanta, was only a thirty-five minute train ride on the Georgia Pacific Railroad and branch line. Henry Grady was a promoter of Chautauqua. Other wealthy Atlanta businessmen developed various portions of the resort. *Cf.* scrapbooks at Lithia Springs Public Library; Garrett 2:167–69. For a personal history by the daughter of the owner of Sweet Water Park Hotel, see Inez Watson Croft, "Lithia Springs: Recollections of the Golden Age of Southern Health Resort," *Atlanta Historical Bulletin* 13 (March 1968): 9–16. Members of JCH's family often vacationed there; see references to Lithia Springs in other letters.

2. Rufus, black male house servant; C.K., probably Charles Kelly, a neighbor and beau of Essie LaRose, whom he later married.

PART TWO  1896–1897
HOME NEWS FOR LILLIAN

You mustn't take it for granted that life is a joke because my letters are frivolous. When a good little girl gets a letter from home it ought to be pleasant, and in that way I am trying to please you.

—*Letter to Lillian, 25 October 1896*

Box 111.

Dear Lillian: We had the dirtiest, nastiest ride home you ever saw or heard of. Mamma looked as if he [*sic*] had been beat over the head and ears with a bag full of fine cinders and dust. And there were some girls on the train going to Rome to school. Two of them sat and blubbered a good deal, and rubbed dust and dirt in their eyes until they looked like play-actors in a monkey show. I think you did very well for a little chap that has never been away from home before. You will find everything all right in a few days as soon as you find out how sweet and good the sisters are. I hope you will soon get on friendly terms with these lovely women[.] Naturally, you won't find everything there the same as it is at home; but you are old enough now to know that the reason we are sending you [to] that school is because we want to be proud of you some day. Especially your daddy. And he feels it in his bones (as the saying goes) that you will not only like the teachers and the school, but that you will settle down to work and prepare to make a name for yourself. To work and to play, too. Don't forget to play as much as you can. Be friendly with the girls; and, above all, make confidants of the sisters. Find out what they'll permit you to read, and I'll send it to you.—Mildred says she wants to go to the Sister Joseph Rock-Ademy, too, and J.C., for the first time, is sorry he isn't a girl.—It's a good deal duller here than it is at St. Joseph's. The kittens are getting sore-eyed, and the calf is able to make railroad time to the lot, with his tail over his back. Mrs. Glenn, at the tavern, has a rug and a fan that Mamma forgot to leave at the Academy.—As we came back we saw some houses afire behind the Agnes Scott Institute, and all the girls were standing out looking at it. Your mamma couldn't see much of it, her eyes and ears were so full of dirt. Mildred wants to know if Miss *Josie* came from *Joseph's* Rock-Ademy. She's very funny.— But it's getting dark. I'll write again shortly. Meantime write to me and tell me all about the school. Mamma and the rest send love—and there's no need to tell you that a big chunk is sent by

      Your affectionate

        Dad

ALS
4 pp.

St. Joseph's Academy postcard (courtesy of Gary L. Doster).

[To Lillian]

22 Sept. [1896]

My Dear Daughter: [1]

I was delighted to get your letter, and it was a great relief to Mamma and myself to know that you are reasonably well satisfied with your surroundings. I was sure, after what I saw, that you would be. I went with you, fully intending to bring you back home if the surroundings were not such as I hoped they would be. You may be sure, therefore, that I was fully satisfied. I have never been more agreeably disappointed than I was when I saw the scheme of the school, the contentment of the children, and the enthusiasm of the sisters.

Everything is going on here like a yoke of oxen in the big road, slowly, dully, hot and dusty. Washington is not any hotter than Atlanta has been during the past week. Friday, for instance was the hottest day of the year. The weather man's thermometer marked 97°—ours 98°. And there has been no rain since you left. Saturday night was cool, but to-day it is hot; yet the *cold wave* flag is up. This means, I hope, that we are to have some cool weather. Mamma caught the noble and gifted Edward stealing Julian's belt, and there was quite a scene.[2] Edward betrayed deep emotion. He fell on his knees to Julian (at the dining-table) and vowed that he was innocent. Then he arose, brushed away his manly tears, *and produced the belt!* Such is life in West End. Edward says he will never steal anything again as long as he lives, consequently I have had all the drawers locked, for I have noticed that when one of the colored brethren reforms he is "slicker" than ever. We are sending you the juveniles in a separate envelope to-day. Thursday I'll send 2 Harper's Round Table and St. Nicholas—if it comes. Mamma has never found her trunk, which shows how easy it is to lose anything on the Georgia road. A man travelled on that road some years ago and lost his memory, another lost his mind. As for me, I sent mine by express. They do say that mosquito bites prevent malaria. But ask the sisters to buy you a dime's worth of oil of pennyroyal, and rub a few drops on your hands and face and they'll not bother you. Kerosene is just as good[.] There is nothing here to write about. It is beginning to look like fall, and as soon as we have a rain everything will be lovely. Write soon to

Your loving

Dad

ALS

4 pp.

1. The group of letters with salutation "Dear Daughter" or "My Dear Daughter" and dated Fall 1896—Spring 1897 most likely were all written to Lillian, for she entered Saint Joseph's Academy first in 1896. Mildred joined her in September 1897.

2. Edward, unidentified house servant.

[To Lillian]

26 *September.* [1896]

My Dear Daughter:

At my request, Julian sent you some candy which you ought to get to-day. He received your letter to-day, in which I find a large and growing demand for CANDY. I didn't know you had such a habit. It is as keen as my appetite for raw tobacco. I don't think you'll like the stuff he sent, for it is not candy at all, simply marsh mellows and chocolate—oh, a fearful mixture! I hope you had your paregoric bottle handy. I'll send some papers and magazines Tuesday. I can't think to buy stamps.—I'm just dying to see that book that is going to surprise everybody—the one you mentioned in your Julian letter.—We have Rufus with us now.[1] I observed him carrying some water to the donkey to-day, and here's the way he looked: [stick figures of goat, man, chicken, and donkey labeled "Thompson," "Rufus," "chicken," and "This is the donkey."] About that time the calf got out of the pen: [stick figure sketch of man running, having dropped a bucket, preceded by donkey and goat] So you see we are having lively times in Wes' Een', Ga., occasionally. Banks came back to work this week.[2] His explanation was: "I tell you, suh, I had mo' biles dan I ever have saw on one pusson. I couldn't set down onless I sot on a bile, an' I couldn't lay down onless I laid on 'em. Take 'em all together, de biles was lots bigger dan I was."

Julian said he sweetened the candy with a telegram and in order to make the telegram and the candy more palatable, I write this letter. I don't know when you'll get it, for I forgot to buy some stamps.—(I stopped a moment to send Rufus to West End for 25 2-cent stamps.) There is no news here: just the same old thing over and over—dry weather, dust, climate warming up a little, and, as I write, the clock striking five—the same old five o'clock it struck yesterday. The vestibule clock has been fixed and is now ticking slowly and deliberately, but it gets there at the same time as the other clocks. Mamma cleaned up the parlor Friday and had the whole house turned upside down on that account. The small kitten has sore eyes, but I think it is on account of the dust your Mamma and Chloë raise.

You must take all the out-door exercise you can and so get in the habit of it. That is even more important than your books. And you are not to feel obligated to reply to *every* letter I write. One or two letters a week to me or to some family member will be all you are expected to write.

With my love:

Your affectionate

Daddy

ALS

4 pp.

1. Rufus was the black butler for a number of years and is often mentioned in many of Harris's letters to the daughters; he was a member of Chloe Henderson's family.

2. Banks is the black gardener.

[To Lillian]

Sunday. [October 1896]

My Dear Daughter:

I read your little story with much interest, and thought it very good. You could have made it better by making it longer, but I suppose you had to cut it down to suit the size of the paper. You know I always told you that if you'd give your talents any showing you'd make a writer.— Charles went to New York to-day. They say he looked right pale under the gills when he left. It's the first time he's gone so far away from home, and I think the idea made him seasick. From the way you are squealing for the "relics" from this house, I think you are beginning to be homesick yourself. Well, it doesn't hurt. We may put Thompson in a coop and ship him down. Or the donkey. But we'll send you whatever you want—if your want is reasonable. Mama will send the pictures (and my magnifying glass) when she sends your aprons. Also photographs of Mildred and J.C.—The roses are doing pretty well, but everything else is about the same. We had a new chicken-house built—a cheap affair, but better than the old one. The pen has been made larger. The old one was like this: [author's sketch of outline] The new one is like this: [author's sketch of outline] I sent St. Nicholas some days ago, and yesterday Youth's Comp'n, Round Table and McClure's. Aaron will be out Oct. 10, and I'll send you a copy, which you can present to the library.[1] Is the rent for your school-books for the full term? I'll send the money during the week. There's nothing going on in West End society. Even Mrs. Mattie Coleman has no news that she'd care to tell[.] I sometimes see Mamie Z. with Jeffy Jimmerson's sister. Mrs. Z., Laura and Lula were here last night. The weather here is betwixt and between. It's too hot for fires and too chilly without them. Ovid don't know whether to cry to come in the house or to stay out of doors.—The programme you sent is a very good one. I should be glad to know that you are taking as much out-door exercise as possible.

Things are beginning to look quite fallish. At night I can hear birds flying in the air overhead. A terrible hurricane swept over Florida, Savannah and on up the coast last week, killing and drowning many people, and destroying millions of dollars' worth of property.[2] How would you like to get the weekly Constitution? That has everything the Sunday paper contains, as well as the junior.[3]—This letter is not a satisfactory one to me, for I'm not feeling in fine feather. Ate too much hash last night, slept too hard, and now I'm paying for it. Mildred has a new plaid cloak, very pretty, and a highland cap. J.C., not to be outdone, has a new boil on his leg, and a new splinter in his finger.—John Matthews and John Webster (*half seasoned*) had an altercation with a car conductor the other night. Policeman Duke arrested them and they had to stand trial in Recorder's court next day. Result: $3.75 and costs each, and a notoriety that will last them many a long day.

You don't have to answer every letter you get as soon as you get it. Take your time. A letter to some member of the family once or twice a week is enough.

Mama was writing you awhile ago.

> Your loving
>> *Dad*

ALS
5 pp.
1. *The Story of Aaron* (1896).
2. The storm occurred 29–30 September 1896. See the account in the Atlanta *Constitution*, 1 October 1896.
3. *The Constitution, Jr.*, was designed for children.

[To Lillian]

11 *October* [1896]

My dear Daughter:

I had a headache all the week, else I would have sent you a basket of fruit. The headache is gone now for the time being, and I hope to be able

to ship you the stuff early this week. I'll try to send you with this letter some photographs of members of the Royal Family—a pretty tough
crowd, if you'll let me speak for them.—Mamma's in trouble again. She
drove to town the other day, and the horse she calls Lily walked off with
the buggy. A nigger man had to catch her, and on top of that the police
(think of their immense impertinence!) warned mama that she wouldn't
be allowed to leave the celebrated horse called Lily lying around loose
again. So there we are, and what's to be done? It's a big job to anchor a
small horse, but that's the problem before us. Mama was so mad about
it that she went off and had her last winter's hat fixed over at immense
expense and increased her bill at Keeley's.[1] Oh, I hate to see your Mama
get mad! I have to pay a round sum for it; and the older she gets the
more I have to pay. When you get married I hope you'll do your husband
that way, because these men ought to be taught their place. They are
puffed up with pride and nothing will take it out of them like having
bills to pay—the nasty things!—I hope you liked *Aaron*[.][2] It's a pretty
good-looking book outside, but, oh, the inside! Don't mention it to your
girl friends. I also have *one* copy of a new edition of *Daddy Jake*, which
has been reprinted so as to "size up" with Kipling's Jungle books. That
I'll keep to show you Christmas, unless you get the wrong check on
you, as mama's trunk did, and become one of the lost pieces of luggage
until after we eat the Christmas cake. That is, if we have any. Our main
dessert now is *evaporated apples*. By the way, would those sweet women,
the sisters, mind if I sent you A BARREL of apples? I don't mean all for
yourself, to eat at one sitting, but to be dished out and handed around
from time to time. Now I know mighty well Sister Bernard wouldn't
mind it, nor Sister Alphonso—nor Sister Sacred Heart—but of course
where there are so many nice ones, one must be severe, and I'm going
to wait before sending A WHOLE BARREL OF APPLES [underlined four times
in text] to hear what the severe one says about it. Maybe the severe one
wouldn't like it—and, then, again, maybe she would—but it all depends
on her—so there now!

The little yellow kitty is dead. It just died itself, and mama didn't have
a thing to do with it. All the other cats are alive and well, and would
sent love if they knew how nice you are. The Bunkey is in the lot with

Dunker's horse—Oh, nonsense, I mean the donkey is in the lot with Bunker's horse, and seems to be doing well. The little calfy is also doing well. At any rate it chewed a button off my coat while I was scratching its back.—The chickens are all in the new pen, and they seem to like it. They don't have to walk as far and scratch as hard for something to eat as they used to. They just sit around under the fig bushes[.] [sketch of hen under bushes] The little children in the neighborhood—especially Harold Goodman and Nora Belle Rosser—have been giving birthday parties. They are all six years old this year, but nobody knows how young they will be twenty years from now. Why should they be six this year, instead of some other year? I've puzzled myself over this until I begin to "favor" Ida Grigsby or Mrs. Wooten's Molly.—The Benevolent Society had an Irish wake the other night, and your mama went and sat up with them. She said she had a good time, but the way she looked and the way she said it was enough for me. I hid my face behind my collar-button and wept.

Hooray for Bryan![3]

Your affectionate

Dad

ALS

5 pp.

1. The Keely Co., dry goods store at 64 Whitehall.

2. *The Story of Aaron* (1896).

3. William Jennings Bryan, the "free silver" presidential candidate in 1896; defeated by William McKinley, he was still given an enthusiastic reception in Atlanta that December (Garrett 2:334).

[To Lillian]

20 October. [1896]

My Dear Daughter: Mama would have written to you yesterday, but she had the headache—caught it from me, I presume. Evelyn came home last evening with a headache, and Julian has a very troublesome cold. So you see we are in fine feather in this beautiful fall weather. And it *is* beautiful weather. Some of the maple leaves are so red that you'd think Mildred and J.C. had poured pokeberry juice on them. And still the drought—dust everywhere, and the donkey squalling like all-forty whenever he hears an acorn fall.

Evelyn's trouble comes from his wisdom tooth, which is now working its way through his overworked jaw. Julian has a troublesome cold, and Tootsie is worried with the idea that somebody is going to lift Mr. Andy Stewart out of office.[1] Tootsie is the tragedian of the family. He is always imagining that old man Trouble is waiting for him round the corner with a stuffed club. But what difference does it make about old man Trouble, when you remember that the Lord is closer to you than Trouble ever can get?

And so the Severe Sister is not to have any of the apples? Do you know why? Because there is no severe Sister. All are patient, and gentle because they are good. I wish everybody including myself could be as good. But I'm afraid the gentle sisters will shake their heads and declare that I am terribly frivolous to be writing such rattle-brained letters to my daughter.[2] But this is not exactly a case of frivolity, for you know yourself I am terribly stuck-up and dignified when I get all by myself[.] It's only when I write to the girls that I'm giddy. But what am I doing? writing about myself! This should never be!

What I started out to say was that Charles had had a hard time with his wisdom tooth and that Evelyn is trying hard to follow suit. I'm afraid these dear boys are too young to have wisdom teeth. Which reminds me that Mrs. Kelly comes over a good many times during the week to talk about Charles. She was here yesterday morning. So was her celebrated dog Jack. Jack's hair has grown out, and I think, from the way he looked yesterday, that Mrs. Kelly had used him as a mop to wash the windows with and then brought him over here to dry. *the windows with*[3] (just see how I repeat! It's a sign of old age.) Trilby must have had the same idea, for she tried her best to wipe the floor with Jack. [author's small sketch of dog] We have 10 or twelve chickens, four brown leghorn hens and a leghorn rooster. The old Langshan has been turned out of the pen, and he walks round and round it all day crowing, as much as to say, "Look-look—look-a-here! See how I keep the rest from coming out!"

The apples will be along as soon as Mildred can bring them out of the pantry. Don't you see her coming? [author's sketch of Mildred with basket of apples on her head] Oh, I forgot—these apples we were talking about were to be in a barrel by themselves. Very well—as soon as you get through with your home-made cake and candy you'll have the apples.

Paul Barker died of typhoid fever Friday. We didn't know he had been sick till after he died.

There's no news of any importance.

> Your affectionate
> *Daddy*.

ALS

4 pp.

1. Andrew P. Stewart, tax collector for Fulton County; Lucien ("Tootsie") had just become his clerk.

2. The sisters at Saint Joseph's Academy, Washington, Georgia, read all of the letters to and from the girls attending the school. Therefore, Harris often addresses a wider audience than his daughters.

3. Italic text struck through in original.

[To Lillian]

25 October. [1896]

My Dear Daughter: We are all pretty well, now; except Mama, and her ailment isn't serious. She was fooling with the stove-pipe in the hall yesterday, and it came unjointed in some way, and about 28 pounds of soot, or *sut* (as we say in Georgia) poured down on her devoted head and face. She looked like Dinah in the minstrel show, only worse. She was so black that the whites of her eyes appeared to be as big as the door-knobs in Julian's room. When she first washed her face she looked worse than ever. She had to go in the tub headforemost, and then, as a final effect,—something lah-de-da, you know—nothing would do her but she must put some ammonia in the water for her face. So she poured it in and poured too much, and when she got through with that, her face looked like a boiled lobster. Then on top of that she smeared her matronly countenance with vaseline; and this made a beautiful moonlight effect by gaslight, showing the lights and shadows of home life in West End, ([sic] edited with notes by that well known humanitarian Joel Chandler Harris, author of the beautiful song, "*Don't Make any Noise;*

Mama's Bathing." Now, you think all that's fun—and it is (on paper), but you wouldn't have enjoyed it if you had been here. For I know mighty well I had to crawl under the bed, and the three cats went out at the back door with such velocity that the carpet smoked—or it may have been the soot rising. And you ought to have heard the racket, when I (from under the bed) asked: "Aunt Dinah Harris, why *did* you want to crawl into the stove-pipe?" And even at the supper-table, there was considerable gloom when I remarked, casually, that there are more than seven hundred different ways of getting dirty respectably. I was told to go somewhere and select me a perfectly clean wife. I answered that the Church does not allow divorces. The reply was that I was not a Catholic—to which I answered that having become (as it were) a brother-in-law of the church, with the hope and expectation of a closer relation when I felt good enough, I felt bound to conform to the rules in so far as I could. Well, it was a great time.

As I write Mrs. Fleming and Mrs. Warner are in the sitting-room, and Lucien is entertaining them. The yard is full of children and a donkey, and the fact that they are not making any fuss convinces me that they are up to some desperate prank—such as pulling up the onions to see if they all smell alike from one end of the row to the other, or smoking acorn pipes, or counting their collections of political buttons. That reminds me that Mildred went about everywhere last week wearing a button with this awful warning: "Don't pull my leg." I said to her, "Mildred, you are a girl; you ought not to be wearing such a button as that." She replied: "Yes, papa, I know I'm a girl, and that's the reason I'm wearing the button; I don't want anybody to pull my leg." I need hardly say that she is no longer wearing that or any other kind of political or advertising button.—We are going to house the donkey for the winter in the Richardson cow-house, which has now been without a tenant for some time[.] The house is not too small for the donkey, but I'm afraid the donkey's voice is too large for the house. She must have plenty of room for the echo to roll in when she asks the wall-eyed Rufus why in the name of goodness her breakfast isn't ready.—Mr. Donker—(Oh, nonsense!) I mean Mr. Bunker is making great preparations for getting married this fall. He has had Babe curried, and the backyard swept, and a new plank nailed on the barn. I judge from this that he is really in earnest.—Mrs. Abernethy has a new cow. I don't know what her name is, but her hind legs are shorter than her fore ones, and this gives her the appearance of always travelling up hill. As this must be tiresome, you will see that even cows have their troubles.—That Forest of Terror must be a dangerous place. Nobody knows what may be lurking in a grove about the size of a theatre hat—it isn't much larger, is it?—and I'd advise you never to venture in it unless you are armed with a box of sardines, four store biscuit [sic], and a bottle of pickles.—I'll send the apples during the week. Meantime, I see you are asking for money. Do you want "sound money" or free silver? When Julian comes he'll bring you some.—I think your letters are improving, and I hope you are studying hard enough to get all the advantages the sisters are ready to give you. You mustn't take it for granted that life is a joke because my letters are frivolous. When a good little girl gets a letter from home it ought to be pleasant, and in that way I am trying to please you. And I'm hoping all the time that you are trying to please me by doing your duty in all ways[.] Write when you can to

Your loving *Old Dad*

ALS

4 pp.

1896—27 Oct. (night)
10:30 o'clock

Dear Lillian:

Your nephew is now sleeping soundly in Aileen's room.[1] He weighs seven pounds and was born at 9 a.m. He seems to be about 81 years old, but will get considerably younger in a few days. Everybody is happy, and all send love to you, including

Your affectionate

Dad.

Say to the sisters that the apples were shipped Monday, freight prepaid. I hope you'll all enjoy 'em.

ALS

1 p.

1. Stewart Harris, son of Lucien and Aileen Harris.

[To Lillian]

1 *November.* [1896]

My Dear Daughter:

That report is lovely, as you girls say. I never saw a better. In fact, if it wasn't signed by Sister Mary Bernard, I'd be inclined to believe it is a joke. I am proud of it, for it shows that you are studying hard. I would know that, however, without the report, for your last letters grow better and better, and the last one is the best. You are unconscious of this improvement of course; but it is plain to me. Just keep right on as you are going, and, with it all, *be good,* and *patient,* and learn how to laugh at things that irritate you. And be generous and kind, and you'll soon find that the most beautiful part of life is that which you spent in doing good to others. That is hard to do of course, but it is not harder than your lessons.

Thank Sister Bernard for her kind letter. I'm sure we are perfectly satisfied that you are doing better than you ever have done, and I can see by the tone of your letters that you are satisfied, and that means a great deal. I'll send some apples for Christmas. You'll be at home, but the sisters and the girls who spend their holidays at the academy will enjoy them.

The news here is so scattered about that it is hard to gather it up. In fact there's nothing but the baby. You remember I told you he was very old—well, it's a fact. He is bald-headed, and all his teeth have dropped out, and his head is wobbly, and he is too decrepit to walk. And he's irritable, too, just like an old man. When he yells for his food, he talks just as the donkey does, only not so loud. But he sleeps most of the time and this is another sign of extreme old age; and he can hold nothing in his hands. He may grow younger as he gets older, and I hope he will, because we don't want to have an old man like that in the house.

You said something about my being a grandpa. But the way I look at it, this baby is too small and wrinkled to count. If I'm to be a grandpa I want to be one sure enough; I want to be the grandpa of something you can find without hunting through a bunch of shawls and blankets— something that can open its eyes and comb its hair. If *this* is what you call being a grandpa anybody can be one, for all you've got to do is to get you a *squall* and wrap it up in a shawl, and there you are! Mamma hovers around and looks wise and seems to think that every time the clock strikes, the squall ough [sic] to be smothered with a quart of catnip tea. Tootsie looks considerably subdued. He goes around with an air of "Well, this beats me! What else is going to happen." If Mildred were to pop a paper bag in the hall, he'd think the doctor had come with a twin for the baby. They all say the baby is going to be very pretty. He has a nose like Tootsie, a mouth like Aline, a head like a simlin, and a voice like the donkey. He's getting on pretty well, too.[1] No name has yet been found that is quite good enough, and I suppose the upshot of it will be that he'll be called Bill, or Sam, or some equally romantic name. I think that Mildred has more fun with the baby than anybody. She is hanging around all the time, and if she can't hold it, she'll sit by the hour and watch it.

With the exception of the baby, everything is about the same as when you left. We have had some rain, and some very pleasant weather. Essie went to Stoke's last night to a Hallow-E'en party. If she had a good time I haven't heard about it. Mildred and J.C. have joined the singing-class in the Sunday school, and go to town every Saturday by themselves. And so you're in the choir. Well, you *are* getting along. I shall never get through congratulating myself that we placed you under the care of those devoted Sisters. It will be worth more to you in all ways than any other experience you'll ever have.

You ask me to write you a funny letter. Alas! I never could be funny. I've tried and tried, but somehow I'm always too solemn. My hat sits too heavy on my head.

But enough! I'm weary with much writing, as you will be with much reading.

My regards to Sister Bernard.

Your affectionate:

Granddaddy

oh shucks! I mean

Daddy.

The clipping you sent is pure fiction, invented by Wallace P. Reed.[2] I'll send for the library my "Stories of Georgia."[3] I wish you'd read them and tell me whether they are interesting.

ALS

4 pp.

1. Simlin, a kind of squash. "Tootsie," JCH's nickname for Lucien.

2. Wallace Putnam Reed, editor of *History of Atlanta, Georgia* (1889) and newspaper colleague at the Atlanta *Constitution*.

3. *Stories of Georgia* was published in 1896, so the letter was probably written that year.

[November? 1896]

Dear Lillian:

This is no letter. It doesn't count. I simply wish to remark that you'll find your tooth money inside. The man can write his own name on the cheque. I also enclose some stamps.

All well here. The baby has been named *Stewart* Harris [.] Mr. S. has given it a fine carriage and has raised Lucien's wages.[1]

Your affectionate

Dad.

I'm writing this without my glasses and I don't know whether it's spelled right or not.

ALS

1 p.

1. Probably Andrew P. Stewart, Fulton County tax collector. Lucien was listed as his clerk in the 1896 Atlanta city directory.

[To Lillian]

11 *November.* [1896]

My Dear Daughter: I intended to write Sunday afternoon, but, meanwhile, I expected a short note from you as a sort of encouragement. Besides, I am now deep in another book. "Aaron in the Wildwoods."[1] I have 16,000 words already written.—And so you are homesick! Well, that is funny, at this stage in the game. Don't you remember how dull it was for you at home—nothing to do and nothing *to* do it with, nowhere to go and nobody to go there with you? I thought that by this time you would begin to feel at home at the academy. I suppose the tooth-ache had something to do with it. Why not have your tooth treated or pulled by the Washington dentist. That would put an end to the pain.—Or are you blue because your money is out? Well, to make the blue green I enclose $5. I hope you'll feel better when you get it. I have kissed it *good-bye* and you can kiss it *howdye*.—I see I am celebrated in *Gleanings* as the editor and compiler of a whole barrel of apples. The apples were no doubt sweeter to the taste and more wholesome, too, than *The Story of Aaron*.—Julian said he would telegraph you Monday. The election business, and now Mr. Evan Howell's candidacy for the senate have kept J. pretty close to his work.[2] Moreover, like many other young people, especially boys, he makes many promises that he intends to fulfill and then finds something in the way. Expect him when you see him. He has the best intentions about it in the world, and would have gone long ago if intentions would have carried him.—Having the blues and the time for you to come home so near? That is indeed funny. Where, oh where, are the Carter's Little Liver Pills that cure all ills? Mama is constantly afraid that you are ill, and when she fails to receive a letter from you promptly, she gets uneasy. Please have it arranged so that if you were to get sick we'd know at once by telegraph. Healthy people don't have the blues, and I don't have 'em even when I'm sick.—There's nothing to write about here except Rufus bringing up coal and that is not an interesting subject. In fine, if you were here now, I'm afraid you'd find it intolerably dull. You couldn't play with the baby, and you couldn't hang around in Aleen's room. So what would you do? On the other hand, when you come home for the holidays, the baby'll be ripe for nursing, Aleen will be entirely well—she is sitting up a little now—and you'll have a pretty good time generally. Everybody thought that your present for the baby was exquisite.

Some day when you are feeling better, and have nothing to do, take your pen between your hands and drop me a few lines[.]

Your affectionate

    Dad

ALS

3 pp.

1. Published 1897.

2. Evan P. Howell sought the Democratic nomination for senator in October 1896 and was defeated by Alexander Stephens Clay, state party chairman. This defeat and the subsequent failure of the *Evening Constitution* led to his retirement as editor-in-chief of the Atlanta *Constitution* on 5 April 1897 (*Dictionary of Georgia Biography* 1:485).

[To Lillian]

15 *November.* [1896]

My Dear Daughter: Your nice letter, with its dainty green embellishment, was very welcome, as, indeed, your letters always are, whether long or short, with or without embellishment.—On the editorial page of to-day's Constitution you will see a piece signed "Charles Kelly." That is our Charles, and the article shows that he has a distinct talent as a writer. It is a fine piece of work for a young man who has had no experience. I send you also in the same package a copy of *Life*, containing a very clever review of Aaron. You might cut it out and save it after the girls are through with the paper.—If the dentist treats your tooth, have him send his bill to me. If he pulls it, pay him yourself, and I'll send you more money when that $5 gives out, or disappears.—Mr. Bunker and his bride have returned, but are now living a very secluded life. I saw Mr. B. in his backyard. When I first glanced at him I thought he had his coat off, but it was only the broad and dazzling smile that he wore. The late Mrs. B. will have been dead a year next month. Such is life—with us men, and if that isn't good grammar it's the truth anyhow.—Why couldn't you play with the baby? Ask me a hard one next time. Because his head is too wobbly. *Muddy* (or should it be *Modie?*) won't hardly allow your mama to touch him, and this, of course, makes her feel very happy—so happy that I challenged her yesterday to go to confession to Fr. Kennedy, who knows her voice. She vowed she wouldn't, and she didn't. She went to Fr. Bazin, who doesn't know her—and what a tale she must have poured into the good man's ear! She had been quarreling, fuming, fussing and fretting for two weeks all because she imagined *Muddy* and Aleen *didn't want her to hold her own grandchild*. When she got back from church, she went right in and took the baby, and they were glad enough, for he had a case of colic as big as a street car. He had colic for twenty feet all round him, and his howls described a still wider circle. I don't understand how one small baby can have such a big colic. But he seems to fatten on it. Aleen now goes into the dining-room. Tootsie is still banished upstairs, and it's a good thing for his peace of mind, for the baby made political speeches until long after midnight— made the speeches, and then applauded himself[.] If babies shed tears when they cried, this one would now be as dry as a last year's orange peel. If he had teeth, and eyelashes and hair he would really look very much like a human being. Mildred says he's *cute,* but she said that about the new stove in the dining-room—and I suppose one is about as cute as the other. I have great hopes, however, when I remember how you looked when you were a baby—and when I remember how I must have looked.—There's no news. Mrs. Kelly gave your Mama a quilt made out of the scraps saved by Julian when he was cash-boy at Rich's. This is considered to be a very big thing—not the quilt, but the event, and ———— oh, dear! The baby is squalling as I write at the top of his voice, and his voice is a seven-story one.

So I'll close in the midst of the storm, and go outdoors and grabble for moles.

Your affectionate

Daddy.

ALS

3 pp.

[To Lillian]

Sunday 'fore Thanksgiving

[21 November 1896]

Dear Billy Ann:

I thought I had the headache this afternoon, but it was nothing in the world but a gum-bile behind my right ear. It is a small affair, but it has a very red face, and it speaks in a tone of voice that can be heard all over my head. I wouldn't mind this if it didn't become personal in its remarks. And yet—to quote from the epistles of Miss L. Harris to her pop—such is life. And such, indeed, it is! A pimple to-day, another to-morrow, the next day the tooth-ache, and so on and so forth; first one thing and then another, especially another. It's mighty funny that people can't feel well when they're sick, and be perfectly comfortable when they have pains. I don't know that we'd be any better off, but it would be a wonderful change, wouldn't it? There's another thing I've found out, when Pain comes to our little partys [sic], it always comes back to pay a party call. Just mention that to your talented dentist, and tell him to wall up your tooth so Pain can't get in to pay its party call.

Did I tell you? I've nearly finished another book—*Aaron in the Wild-woods*. Thirty-five thousand words are already written down, with only 10,000 more to write. No doubt I told you something about this in a former letter: I'm always gossiping about my poor little affairs. They pester me almost as much as Ovid's fleas pester him, and I'm always lifting one hind foot and dragging the other, trying to scratch myself on the back, as Ovid does. And it tickles me as much as it does Ovid for somebody else to scratch me on the back. Oh, you don't know what preposterous frauds WE AUTHORS are: I mean we authors!! The books are getting some very nice notices—better than they deserve, for, when all is said, I know how far they fall below what I want them to be.

Essie wrote you a long letter yesterday, and I've no doubt she told you all the female news. John and Harry and Nell are here to-night. John came to see the baby, and the baby is showing his appreciation by howl-ing like a wildcat. I never heard a baby cry as much as he does, and, I never saw one that had a more unmusical voice. I took his photograph awhile ago and here it is: [sketch][1] I hope he will get to liking us better after awhile and so become more contented with his lot, which he now seems to think is a hard one. The portrait above is nearly life-size. You can have it framed at very small expense.

As I said in a former communication, there is no news in this neigh-borhood. Mr. Cobb has been nominated as a supreme court judge, and I'm very glad of it. He is a good *judge* of law, but not a good speaker.[2]

It is likely the baby will be christened the first pretty day. To-day was too cloudy.

Your affectionate *Dad*

Manuscript page from Joel Chandler Harris's 21 November 1896 letter to Lillian, showing the author's sketch of grandson Stewart Harris (Joel Chandler Harris Collection, Special Collections Department, Robert W. Woodruff Library, Emory University).

ALS
3 pp.
Envelope: Return to Box 111, / Atlanta, Ga. / Miss Lillian Harris, / St. Joseph's
Academy, / Washington, / Wilkes county, Ga.
PM: 22 November [1896]
    1. Handwritten note: "Harris print *1896/STEWART HARRIS/taken from* life."
    2. Probably Andrew J. Cobb.

[To Lillian]

[28 November 1896]

Sunday night, 28. [1896]

My Dear Billy-Ann: I hope you received your box and the Yellow Kid
Saturday.[1] The news of market is as dry this week as ever. Something
refuses to happen. You'll probably see the baby's picture in the Eve. Consti. Monday or Tuesday. Mr. Wilkinson tried to make a good cut, but
it is hard to draw the lack of expression in a baby's face.—Mr. Davis,
our neighbor, died last night about 1 o'clock, and was buried to-day.
Mrs. Abernethy says he had some insurance on his life, so his family will
not be left entirely destitute.—We had some open cars several days ago,
but during the last day or two the weather has been cold. There was a big
frost last night, which nipped my rose-bushes and thinned out the apple
crop in the front yard. To-day, however, the wind suddenly changed and
the weather has been bland, though fires are comfortable to-night.—A
hen came off with *three* whole chickens this morning, showing that there
are still some sound eggs to be found here and there in the suburbs.—
We have been having fresh asparagus right along; peas are up; and this
week we'll plant beans and more peas.—Brader has just come in, fresh
from business victories "down the road," a part of the country that seems
to be his fairy land. Down the Road is located wherever you want it, and
seems to be more mythical and insubstantial than the land of Nod, for
our Cousin Cain did go there and marry.—The scare seems to be over in
this part of the burg. All the scarlet fever cases are getting better—there
were but two—and everybody seems to be feeling better except those
who want something to talk about.—Aleen is doing her own cooking—
that is to say, she is doing the heavy standing around, while the stove

does the sizzling and frying.—J.C. has been setting traps for pigeons, but the pigeons seem to know all about that sort of thing, for they walk about the trap with a far-away look that speaks volumes.—The old cat cried at the back door last night, and when it was opened, she walked in with a baby cat, placed it on the rug before the fire, and asked us to admire it as much as we could. This we did to some extent, whereupon she curled around it and rocked it to sleep. Speaking of such things, reminds me to take pleasure in informing you that Essie has a little brother, a brand new one. Her step-pa wrote her a letter giving her the news and when she got to that point, she hurled the missive across the room, and proceeded to shed large gobs of sobs—all of which shows you that girls can be girls and little children too. I suppose Essie feels that her nose has been knocked out of joint by the stranger. She feels better about it now.—I'll attend to your pictures for you. The others being taken with a jerk, could not be profitably printed. The next will be better, I hope.— Tell Father O'Brien that I hope he put in a good word for Atlanta when the Bishop was in Washington. He will understand what I mean. Give him my kindest regards.—Mildred is as wild as ever. Whatever J.C. does she wants to do, and usually does it. I let her run and play with the boys because it is good for her health. She is as hardy as any of them—can run fast, jump as far, and throw as hard as any chap of her age in the town. She'll go back with you next fall.

My regards to Sister Bernard and Sister Mary Louis.

Your affectionate

Daddy

ALS

3 pp.

Envelope: Miss Lillian Harris, / St. Joseph's Academy, / Washington, Ga. / Wilkes County.

PM: 29 November [1896]

1. The Yellow Kid, a popular comic strip created by Richard Felton Outcault in 1895 for Joseph Pulitzer's New York *World* and lured away by William Randolph Hearst for his New York *Journal* in 1896. The ensuing competition for this comic strip gave the name to "Yellow Journalism"—the use of sensational stories, vivid comic strips, and colored pictures to lure the reading public. (David Manning White, "Comics," *Encyclopedia Americana*, 1990 ed.)

[To Lillian]

Sunday evening [November 1896]

My Dear Daughter:

Mamma enjoyed fixing the box as much as you did the eating of the contents; and I think Mattie enjoyed cooking the stuff, for she went about it very cheerfully, and seemed to take a great interest in the matter.[1] And we are all glad that you liked it.—Your report is perfectly splendid as the girls say. The first one was good enough for me, but this beats it out of sight. And now you say you are going to excel even this magnificent record! Well, please, ma'm, permit one little 99 to slip in somewhere, so that I may know that the report comes from a real human being. But, seriously, I am very proud of the report and so is your mother, and we thank our stars that we were fortunate enough to have an opportunity to place you with those devoted sisters, who have the art of developing young minds. More than that we are grateful that providence so arranged it that you might be under the especial supervision of Sister Mary Bernard who seems to have the gift (and it is a heaven-born gift) of imparting something of her own knowledge and exquisite culture to her pupils. I knew from the third letter I received from you that you had fallen under some sweet and yet powerful influence, and that you had begun to learn how to *think* and think *right,* which is the end and aim of all education.—Of course, my famous portrait of the baby was a caricature. He is a very nice-looking baby, but he seems to me to be always in trouble. When he's not crying, the expression of his face shows that he has something on his mind. He works his hands and blinks his eyes, and appears to want to know why he came to this country anyhow—a country where everybody seems to have the colic and live on soothing sirup, and where the whole population has to be jogged on somebody's knee in the most terrific manner if it so much as whimpers. He's crying now, and somebody is jolting him up and down in the most fearful manner. If he holds together awhile longer he will make a famous football player, and will be able to emerge from a railway collision serene and smiling.— Tootsie says he is going to begin building his house before long, and I think that will be a good idea. This will give Aleen an opportunity to do some housekeeping on her own account, and I have no doubt she will be better satisfied.—To-day the weather has been cold and rainy—what the English call "nawsty weather, don't cher know." Thermometer down to 42°, with indications that the ground will be frozen in the morning. But in the northwest they have been having the most severe blizzard since 1888. That was when you were quite a little girl. Snow blockades, frozen cattle, and probably many people killed by the severity of the cold. So, after all, we are better off in Georgia.—In regard to that surprise, you'll have to send a night message to Julian—not a "half-rate" message, but one not to be sent till after six p.m. The lady at the hotel can arrange it for you. I would say the Sisters could arrange it, but they are so kind that it seems a pity to suggest any addition to their kindness. Julian, getting the telegram at night, could whisper the message in my left ear when he comes home in the early morning—and I, not being in a humor to receive secrets in my left ear, will likely throw a shoe at him. This, he will declare, is evidence of my literary ability, and remark, "Pop; you are too modest. You don't know what a great man you are." And then will come your surprise—or, rather, *our* surprise.—Having a baby in the house, we are now thinking about selling the donkey.—Mr. Bunker's new wife has arranged her windows so that the lady members of our family can't see what she is doing. I think it's a shame, don't you? In fact, it's dreadful. Anyhow, she needn't have taken all that trouble— *we* don't care what she has nor what she does. So there, now!

Well—this is the end of the page, and it's late. I've been interrupted right along every five minutes.

Your affectionate

Dad

ALS

4 pp.

1. Mattie Henderson, sister to Chloe. Mattie served as cook and sometimes as nurse for JCH's family (*Life and Letters*, 179).

[To Lillian]

[December 1896] Sunday Evening.

My Dear Pods:[1] Please fetch home a copy of the almanac, or calendar you are using[.] I want to hang it up as a curiosity. Writing to Essie Friday, you say: "It is just two weeks to Christmas"! That means, of course, that it will be just two weeks before you come home. I don't know whether the rest "caught on," but 'twas as plain as day to me. Therefore I enclose with this a cheque for $10 made payable to the Sisters of St. Joseph's. They will get it cashed for you. Find out what the fare to Atlanta is, and if you have a surplus you can buy presents for some of your friends at St. Joseph's and bestow them before you leave. You need not save any money except enough to get you here. I'll have some for you for Christmas—and if you want $5 more to use in Washington, just write a postal card thus:

$5

L.H.,

and I'll send it at once. The reason I'm apparently so liberal is because you've done so well in your studies and seem to have improved so much in every way. Otherwise—oh, wouldn't I have been mean and stingy! (By the by, I think *stingy* ought to be spelt with a *j*, don't you?)—I haven't sold the donkey; the boy never came back. But anyway, you are too large now to ride as Mildred does, without a side-saddle. So you needn't be so anxious for me to keep the donkey. J.C. wants to sell her to get some money to help buy a bicycle.—Jesse Cobb is at Young Harris institute [*sic*],[2] and is anxious to get up a correspondence with the daughter of the Old Harris institution, if I may allow myself to become architectural in design.—We had the snow and sleet. The north front of the house is still full of it, and although the weather is mild, the flower beds are still covered with it. It puts my teeth on edge every time I see it. Rufus and J.C. caught a rabbit near Mattie's house the day after the snow[.] It was nearly five inches deep,—not the rabbit, but the snow.— Now don't read all sorts of meaning into what I write. Most positively, I didn't intend to intimate that you couldn't get 100 in all your studies. What I meant was that even one 98, however lonely it might appear, would throw over the report the glamor of naturalness. This will apply to anybody's report. I think that if it is possible for any one to be perfect in that way, it is possible for you. But remember, please, that I had rather see you with perfect health and digestion than to see you absolutely perfect in your studies. Therefore, please, ma'm, don't study your eyes out just to get 100 in everything. Don't come home looking pale and sad, and complaining of the headache.—That was a very good story in Gleanings.

You are sure to get there after awhile if you have any ambition that way. But to talent must be added experience, and it takes time to make the union perfect.—Give my kindest regards to Sister Bernard, and say to her again how grateful we feel for the tender interest she displays toward you. It is fortunate indeed that you fell under her care as a teacher and as an adviser.

Your affectionate

Daddy

ALS

3 pp.

1. "Pods" was JCH's mother's pet name for Lillian, according to *Life and Letters*, 293.
2. Now Young Harris College, Young Harris, Georgia.

13 December. [1896]

Dear Lillian: Before I forget it—mama wants to know if it wouldn't be well for her to send by express the large valise, so that you may be spared the trouble of bringing your trunk? It is a matter you may decide for yourself. As to the date of return: you have placed it on the day when the train will be crowded with people coming here to Mr. Bryan's lecture.[1] With the permission of the sisters (who will know how to decide better than you or I) wouldn't it be better for you to come on the 22nd? The impression here is that the trains on all the roads will be crowded to suffocation, especially as the fare is to be reduced to half rate. Now, as I say, the Sisters will know better how to decide this matter than I do. I merely throw out a suggestion. Let me know in time. Mama will be out shopping the day you come, and she'll meet you at the depot. You'll take dinner at Durand's, gad about with Mama an hour or two and then come home—in time for supper, I hope; but you know how Mamma is when she gets up town.[2]

The Kid continues to weep copiously, from which I conclude that he is of a melancholy if not a despairing nature. This he must inherit from me.—Oh, did I tell you the Zachrys have bought the Birch place, corner of Queen and Baugh? They have already moved, and seem to be pretty well satisfied with the change. Some of them are over here pretty much every day. We had Lula for dinner yesterday, and also some turnip greens, and to-day we had the same old chicken-pie, with the usual fight over the gizzard. You will find it very much like home when you return, with Mama crying out every quarter of an hour—"I'll call your papa if you don't behave!" or "Joel, can't you come to these children?" and then, if I make no response: "Your papa says I spoil you, but he's the one that does the spoiling. *Mildred!* why *don't* you behave? *I'llsendyoutobediflhavetospeaktoyouagain!*" This last all in one word as it were. And so we go on raising our children, at a loss whether to pet them or bump their heads together. The donkey is still one of our treasures, and still lifts her voice in song whether things go right or wrong.— Lucien is talking about beginning on his house this week; he has already made a contract I believe[.]—Julian is still rushing along at the same old gait, doing the work of two or three men and coming home in the morning utterly fagged out. He threatens to rest this week, but it is probably only a threat. I have been urging him not to put on so much steam but to same [save] some fuel for the years to come, but ambition is gnawing at his vitals—as if ambition could possibly have any connection with a night editor of a daily paper. It is almost equal to being president of a barber shop in Washington, Ga., Wilkes county.—Oh, pshaw! I seem to have something in my mind to tell you—some piece of news—but I can't think what it is. Consequently, it can't be of much importance.— This is Julian's off-night. He went to bed at nine this morning, rose at eight this evening and is now reading in my room.—I began *Aaron in the Wildwoods* the night of the day after the baby was born and finished it one week ago—writing 48,000 words in less than six weeks. To-morrow night I'll make an experimental beginning on another book. A story of village life in the south before the war.[3] I'll try not to forget to send the Sisters a barrel of apples for Christmas. I'll have them shipped the last of the present week, or on the 20th by express.

There's no news here, as usual. The place is the same day in and day out except that you are not here, and we'd miss you more if we didn't know you were in such devoted hands. My regards to Sister Mary Bernard and the rest.

> Your affectionate
> Daddy

ALS
7 pp.

Lillian and Mildred Harris (Joel Chandler Harris Collection, Special Collections Department, Robert W. Woodruff Library, Emory University).

1. Reference to visit of defeated presidential candidate William Jennings Bryan in 1896. According to Garrett (2:334), some 3,000 met Bryan at Atlanta Union Depot on 22 December 1896. He gave a lecture, "The Ancient Landmarks," at the Grand Opera House on December 23.
2. Durand's Restaurant, Union Depot.
3. Probably the manuscript of "One Mile to Shady Dale," published as *Gabriel Tolliver*.

[To Lillian]

4 January. [1897]

Dear Miss Pods: First, about Charles. You know perfectly well that we have no objection to your corresponding with him. Yet, at the convent, it is a different matter. We, as well as you, must be governed by the rules. If the Mother Superior decides that this particular case is an infraction of the rules, and that it would be a bad example for the other girls, or set them wondering why *you* should have a young man correspondent, and thus give them an idea that they are victims of partiality, then it would be better not to correspond with Charles.[1] You see the question has a wider bearing than your own personality, and the Mother Superior must judge of its importance. You must remember that very few girls have been raised as you have—on perfectly familiar and confidential terms with their fathers and mothers. Very few of them have had the course of reading that you have followed, and fewer still have been taught to discriminate between the romance of fiction and the realities of life. You have read pretty much everything that you have desired to read; yet I have been particular that the *most* you have read is sound and sweet at the core, and therefore wholesome. This has been done so quietly, that you have never known that the process was going on. This great plot has been going on and you never even suspected it. You remember that there was something of a fuss made about three or four years ago about you reading the newspapers. As you know, I didn't make any fuss about it, for I knew and still know that even the sensations in the newspapers carry their moral with them. Up and down the columns of the newspapers it is writ large,—"Be good! Men, women and children, be good!"

Whoa! Wait—let me get my foot out of the stirrup. Now!—My goodness! I was on my high horse. Yet, high as he is, he should be mounted sometimes. To conclude the matter, the question is not whether it is wrong for Lillian Harris to correspond with a young man who is almost like one of her own family, but whether the fact of the correspondence will be a good example for your friends and companions. *That* question the Mother Superior must decide, and you may be sure she will decide it correctly from her point-of-view[.]

It's a mighty good thing I had that important correspondence to write about, for there's not much floating around here. I can't tell you any town news for you get the Evening Constitution. I am having it sent to you. It strikes me as being a pretty good paper. The Journal seems to be very much worried about it.—In regard to Evelyn, I meant that C.D. wanted him to report for the Evening Consti., while Mr. Adamson insisted on retaining him on the morning paper.[2] In consequence of which, his salary was doubled and he is no longer regarded as a newpaper "kid." He's old by the side of the Evening paper. Mr. Cramer seems to be the managing editor of the Baby, in fact of two Babies, for he has one at home. He and Albert Howell are going to house-keeping on Peachtree Street. Mr. Stanton, our cherished poet-laureate, is not well. In fact, he has not been well for a couple of weeks. He has a curious disease. He can't keep out of a whisky shop, and when he gets in there, his elbow keeps bending until he gets drunk. It is sad for the Muse and sadder still for the family.

Julian has gone to Nassau on a two-weeks' vacation, as the guest of the Florida press association. Nassau is in the Bahamas, so he will have a taste of salt-water before he gets back. The card club met last at Mrs. "Dr." Smith's. Essie won first prize—a pair of silver manicure scissors. Lula got the "consolation" prize. You'll see about it in Tuesday's Constitution. I never heard how Mrs. W's card party came out. Belle and Bob and Brader called to-day. Chloe has been sick with the grippe, and is still unable to work. Mrs. Bunker has called, and Mama likes her very well. She is very much like Winnie about her upper face. You heard Daisy Doyle was dead.

There is absolutely nothing else to write about except the baby, and he's "des ez tute en ez tweet" dat what drammer tay, en he pullin' Milsie's hair wright now, yas he ar', bess un tweet life! And so forth and so on.

Your loving
Daddy

ALS
4 pp.
1. Charles was a neighborhood boy and friend of the family (*Life and Letters*, 370).
2. C.D. was Charles Daniel, city editor of the evening *Constitution*. See letter to Lillian,
16 January [1897]; Robert L. Adamson, city editor of the Atlanta *Constitution*.

[To Lillian]

9 *January*. [1897]

Dear Daughter: I take my pen between my hands to drop you these few
lines. If you have the grippe you are in good company, for J.C. has it, and
looks as peaked as a chalk doll that has been left out in the rain. Everything is about as you left it, except the baby, which has added another
wrinkle to its forehead.—They had the card-party—oh, yes! they had
it, and Mama was in fear and trembling for fear the Zachry's would club
together and manage it. Lula objected to Mr. Hartman because she didn't
know his pedigree, and when Essie invited him anyhow, Lula got her
revenge by throwing her vote against Bob Goodman for president, elect-
ing a Mr. Harper. Kathrine[1] (that's the way it's pronounced)—Kathrine
Wooten was made secretary and treasurer. I didn't go into the room,
and consequently missed many funny things that would have interested
you. There was one girl whose laugh sounded as if she had her head in
a bucket of warm soapsuds. I don't know who she was.—Julian stayed
at home three days this week, and I suppose he feels better for it. *I hope
your hair is not falling out.* As we used to say on the plantation—"Come
see me Sunday and I'll have your head looked."—If you get sick have a
telegram sent to the house, and Mama'll drop down to see you. She may
come anyway before long.—It's a good thing to be a little bit homesick,
but a little of it goes a long ways. This is not my regular letter. I'll write
again Sunday.

Your affectionate

Dad.

ALS
1 p.
1. The "rine" part of the name is written perpendicularly to "Kath" to indicate falling voice.

10 *January.* [1897]

Dear Lillian: I'm just through writing my editorial stuff, and I have that tired feeling that comes over us when we eat too much fried chicken. We had some to-day—but quite by accident. The hen, or rooster, or whatever it was, was too old and tough to bake or "smother," and so Mattie hid its age and toughness with batter, and fried it. J.C. got hold of a piece—the drum-stick—and tried to tear off a "hunk" of it with his teeth. He pulled harder and harder, and finally the "hunk" came off; but J.C. was pulling so hard that his hand hit against the tin waiter under his plate, upset the salad, and hurled some of the batter in Mama's hair. So there are now other reasons why she will have to comb her hair. This thing of combing hair has grown to be an epidemic in this house. Do they ever do such things at St. Joseph's academy? I hope so.—They had their little card party, as I wrote you, and it was pretty tame—No skirt-dancing, or anything of that kind. A day or two afterwards Rozzy Howell invited Essie to a "Heart" party—you know how they play Hearts with cards—some of the peachtree [sic] crowd were there, and Essie says they were pretty tough. I judged from the way she talked that she was thoroughly disgusted with their manners.—One queer thing happened the other day. A plasterer working on Lucien's house had a black dog. This dog, not quite as large as Thompson, concluded he would refresh himself, and so he went and sucked the young cow. I thought this was queer, and doubted it. But Banks declared he saw him, and Chloe says the cow (Lucille) didn't give much milk that night.—Mattie came back from Athens "tetotally ruint wid de grip," and couldn't go back into the kitchen until Thursday.—Mrs. Bunker's reception day was last Wednesday, and she had one caller—Mrs. Abernethy,—who went over to borry a cup of sugar. I think it is too bad, after we go and fix a reception day, and arrange for it, and dike out, and do up our back hair, and put on our nicest frock, that people won't flock in and pass the time of day— but such is life in West End, Atlanta, Ga., A.D. 1897.—Saturday the baby went to town to have his picture taken. They say he was very good. Doubtless one will be sent to you. Your own pictures are fair, but they do not represent you at your best. I think you were feeling ill—the first symptoms of your bad cold. But they'll do until you can have better ones taken.—At Mrs. Wagner's crystallized wedding, Mrs. Young picked up a bowl in each [hand], intending to have some fun with Mrs. W.[1] The said Mrs. Y. put the bowls behind her suddenly, there was a collision, and the finest, a $12 affair, was broken; whereupon Mrs. Y. proceeded to weep. Tell all the ladies you meet never to try to joke at all, especially at a crystallized wedding. It cost Mrs. Young $12 just to *think* she was going to play a joke. The only news I know is that the pony still objects to the shape of Rufus's legs, so that all the neighbors have to be called in to catch the creature.—By the by, there was great trouble among the deacons and sub-deacons of the Park street Methodist Church the [other] day. It was on the subject of communion. Dr. Longino rose and contended that it was unhealthy and dangerous for all the members of Park street Church to drink wine out of the same cup.[2] So there were various propositions suggested: 1. That each member should bring his own cup; and 2. That there should be a number of cups and a dishwasher [hole in ms.] in the back of the church. This [hole in ms.] like sacrilege, and it would be if our Methodist bretheren had a proper idea of communion; but Mrs. Culberson told me the facts. The propositions were actually made. I thought this was funny at first, but now that I have written it out, it seems more like a disgusting display of ignorance and worldiness on the part of the deacons and sub-deacons.

Well, be good, and sometimes when you are at your orisons slip my name in edgewise. Take care of yourself and don't get sick.

Your affectionate

Daddy

ALS

3 pp.

1. Crystal wedding, i.e., fifteenth anniversary when glass presents are appropriate. Probably Mrs. Frederick Wagner of 270 Gordon.

2. Probably Dr. Thomas D. Longino, veteran of Wheeler's Cavalry, C.S.A., losing candidate for mayor of Atlanta in 1905; died in 1911. (Garrett 2:472, 596.)

[To Lillian]

16 Jan. [1897]

Dear Billy: It has been raining off and on—especially on—all day. Consequently, everybody but the baby and I has been going about looking extremely billious. The rose-bushes are dripping, and the moles have begun their spring plowing.

Meantime society here in West-End is all torn up over the Sawyer-Goodman card club. It seems that, in the shuffle (to speak by the card) Mrs. Wotten's plump darlings Nell and Harry were left out in the cold. Their names were not on the list. Naturally, this made everybody in that house furious. Essie was and is supposed to be responsible for all the damage that has been done to Nell and Harry, and Mrs. Wotten is up in arms.—At first she said she was coming to see Essie and ask her why she ignored two such prominent and powerful members of West End society. Mrs. W. must have reconsidered that movement, for she hasn't called. She has done better than that. She has poured her tale of woe into Miss Laura's ears, and Miss Laura brought it all over here in a two-bushel basket (so to speak) and laid it fresh and hot at the dainty feet of the female members of this family. It is wonderful what memories you ladies have! Miss Laura remembered every word her Aunt "Lal" said, and embellished it, no doubt, to suit her own ideas of society diction. The echoes of it are ringing in my head yet. "And who is Essie LaRose anyhow? And as for Rob Goodman—why I wouldn't let Nell go with him—I honestly would not. Why they must think that somebody wanted to belong to their old card club. Well you can just tell them for me that Nell shouldn't belong to it. Nell is already getting up a card party, and not one of the Harrises shall have an invitation—not one single one. And you may tell them I said so if you want to. What did the Harrises serve for refreshment?—not apples, surely. *Chocolate!* Why *any*body could have *chocolate* and cakes[.] Well, you can just tell them that Nell will not have *chocolate;* she'll have Neopolitan ice-cream, and you can tell them that!"

I judge from this that the cream is to be transported from Naples, else it can't be genuine Neapolitan ice-cream; and if it isn't genuine anybody can have it,—and so there we are right where we started. It would be a thing to weep over if it were not so funny. You mustn't blame Mrs. W. too much in your thoughts, for human nature is but human nature after all.

To-morrow afternoon The Evening Constitution will make its appearance.[1] I'll try to have it sent to you. Charles Daniel is city editor. There was quite a contest between him and Mr. Adamson over Evelyn, but Mr. Adamson won.[2] Evelyn seems to be getting ahead very rapidly[.] I know he works hard, and those who work hard at anything are sure to succeed if they have any ability in that particular direction. I don't know what effect the evening paper will have on the Journal. Some say the Journal will issue a morning paper. They will find it a very costly venture.—Mama's pony has developed a new streak of hoss nature. She don't want the harness put on, and it takes a grown man to do the job. Consequently it sometimes happens that when your poor mama gets ready to drive the pony isn't ready to be driven—truly a sad state of affairs. But there are no other sad affairs to be considered. At this moment (I am writing Sunday night) Brader is in the sitting-room reading with his glasses on, and Essie is in there writing to Charles. The situation is indeed tragic—Brader laughing at the milk-and-water jokes in Puck and Essie making a prolonged and laborious effort to write Charles in English. Little does Brader know what is going on. He says he is now obliged to wear glasses, but they add mightily to his gloomy air of discontent[.] Why is it that Brader and all the women frown and look solemn when they are reading humorous or comic papers? Please tell me that. I have seen you read Puck, Judge and Life from cover to cover without a smile, and yet you say you think they are funny.

Mr. Lumpkin, your old professor of Elocution, was found dead in his bed this morning. The cause was heart disease.

Give my regards to Sister Bernard and Sister Mary Louise.

I'll fix up your papers to-night so you'll get them earlier. I trust the keen edge of your homesickness has worn off by this time. We sent you a package Friday which no doubt reached you in time—a marshmallow waist and some worsted candy.

Your affectionate

Dad

ALS

4 pp.

1. For a few months (Monday, 18 January 1897–Wednesday, 31 March 1897), the Atlanta *Constitution* published an evening paper called the *Evening Constitution* to compete directly with the *Journal*.

2. Robert L. Adamson, city editor, Atlanta *Constitution*.

[To Lillian]

31 Jan. [1897]

Dear Billy-Ann:

You know what I said about writing to Charles. I haven't the slightest objection, and I don't think the Sisters have really. They object to the example only. I see you are still wearing the cross of honor. Well, that is right. Your report, too, is very satisfactory[.] It is *more human,* you know, to find a few 98s among the 100s. And, speaking of chills, have you been cold this winter? Don't say a word to anybody, but out in the back-yard is a piece of ice ten inches thick. It came out of a tub, and is solid. I had to wrap myself in a blanket to look at it. The mercury went downstairs last week and stayed there till yesterday. It rained and the rain froze as it fell until the streets and sidewalks were slicker than glass. One man on the sidewalk who went to bow to a lady in the street car sat down upon himself with a dull sickening thud. He had his hat in his hand when he concluded to fall, and how he got it under him, I never could tell. It was a high hat when he went down. When he rose it wasn't taller than a fried egg. By good luck I kept from falling, but I had some narrow escapes. Friends, acquaintances and strangers fell at my side and all around me as thick as autumn leaves, but a clear conscience and a sober mind preserved me.[1] My water-meter has collapsed, and that means ten dollars for another—and the rooster's comb was friz, (or is it fruz?) and the stoves wouldn't give out any heat, and I changed the name of my new story from "1 MiLE TO SHAdy DALE" [*sic*] to "A Quarter of a Mile from the North Pole."[2] The only characters in it are to be a broken down thermometer and an iceberg. All the news has fruz (or is it friz?) up, and consequently I can't send you any; likewise, consequently, this letter must be dull and short.

Julian has returned from his Bahama voyage with tonsilitis. He seems to have bad luck all around. Miss C. is going to Boston for a three-month's stay, and her pa and Jacob Haas want to sell the animals at the park.[3] Of course The Constitution will have to oppose this, and maybe it will say something to hurt pa's feelings. Such is life in Atlanta, Ga. Mr. Whitcomb, the old man, fell and hurt himself on the ice, but Brader could come over here the darkest night and never fall—and you know how slick our front steps must have been. Everybody is well and sends love. My regards to Sr. Bernard and Sr. Mary Louis, and thank them again for their kindness to you.

Your affectionate *Dad*

ALS

2 pp.

1. *Cf.* Dante's *Divine Comedy* or Milton's *Paradise Lost* for source of image.

2. Published as a serial in *The Era*; then as a novel *Gabriel Tolliver* (1902). Harris's capitalization seems consciously eccentric.

3. Probably Julia Collier, who later married Julian; her father, Charles A. Collier, vice-president of the Capital City Bank and Atlanta businessman; Jacob Haas, cashier of Capital City Bank and prominent Atlanta businessman. Probably the Atlanta zoo in Grant Park.

7 February [1897]

Dear Lillian: I'll get you a Kodak with pleasure.[1] To that end, I have instructed both Julian and Evelyn to scour the town and find one that is nice enough. But, listen, Miss Pods: don't study too hard. Take care of your health. I'd rather see your report chokefull of 98s than to pay a doctor's bill. Study is a good thing, but "too much of a good thing is a plenty," as we say in Georgia.—Will the Sisters send their bill, or shall I just "up and send" a cheque on my own motion? I think your tuition was due on the 1st. Is it the same as last term—$82?—There is the same dreadful dearth of news here. You get all the city news in the Evening Consti., and as to neighborhood news, why, you must know that Dame Gossip has been compelled to keep in doors with her head wrapped in flannel and a hot rock to her feet. To-day is the first day she could come out, and —ting! goes the door bell, and I hear the joyful voice of Miss

Laura in the hall, mingled with the strident tones of "Muddies'" abler foghorn. I suppose we shall get all the news mixed with some scandal, but as I have to write this letter in the dining-room I'll not get the benefit of it. You can guess, however. "Did you see Miss Nora's new dress?" "Did I? Well I should say! Anybody could see it a mile off." "*Why* does she chose such colors and have such queer contrasts?" "Heighho (sigh) don't ask me, child. It's too ridiculous." "And did you notice Nell's hat?" "Heh-eh-eh-eh-(giggle) Oh, wasn't it a fright?" "Fright: don't mention it. *Why* don't we get somebody to go with her when she buys her things?" And so on and so forth.—Tootsie is about getting ready to move in. His house will be finished this week. Julian gave him a fine mantel, and I think Mamma is "doing about" for him in the way of stove, carpets and dining-room furniture. Everything comes to those who have the nerve to wait and wear an expectant look. The back fence is up, and it makes things look queer.—Oh! Mama has just come in (the visitors have "gone to see the house") and *she* says that Lula invited some young lady to the card-party to be held at her house after awhile (it is her turn, you know) and Nell heard of it, and advised Lula to countermand the invitation, the reason being that the young lady in question and Kathrine Wooten don't speak when they meet. It seems that the young lady in question had remarked that Miss Wooten needn't hold her head so high, because her pa "was nothing but a circus-rider." Now wasn't that awful? Of course Kathrine's father wasn't a circus-rider, but just think of the horrible slam Nell was enabled to give Lula, because Lula hadn't invited Nell. My dear, I hope you'll look at the world around you as I do as you grow older. If you do it will be a mixture of plum-pudding and mincepie all the year round. I enjoy gossip because it gives me a clue to character, and there's nothing richer than human character. To me the most serious person is the most humorous if I can but get him to open his mouth and speak freely, and sometimes the most humorous are the most serious. You remember Jincy in *Sister Jane*.—When Tootsie moves, a new set of furniture—*birch-wood:* think of that!—is to be placed in your room, and it is to be a *pink* room, and it is to be yours all by yourself: everything spick and span, everything new; all the cobwebs knocked down, all the dust blown out, all the fleas killed, and all the flies friz.[2] And if the blankets are too hairy, we'll have 'em shaved.—Mama isn't joking about coming to see you. When the weather breaks up a little and settles down into something that can be depended on, she'll come.—The donkey got to playing with the calf the other day and, in the midst of their various and assorted gambols, the calf fell down. Whereupon the donkey jumped on him and proceed [sic] to dance the highland fling. The calf was supposed to be dead, but it wasn't hurt.—Essie and Rob have gone over to Jenny Smith's (I'm writing Sunday afternoon)—I don't know whether they are going to have a card-party, a base-ball game, or a plain converzationy.—Mrs. Grigsby's tenants have moved. Essie got a letter from Ida, who announces that she has two beaux—a perfect riot of gallantry it would seem.—*Aaron in the Wildwoods* begins in to-day's Constitution.[3] I hope you'll like it. It is somewhat and somehow in a new vein.

Well, my little budget of talk is exhausted. I'll try to mail this so you'll get it Monday night, but maybe I won't have the opportunity. It was my fault that you didn't get your paper in time. I neglected to bundle them up. I'll do better next time.

From your loving

Daddy

ALS

4 pp.

1. The introduction of the Kodak camera to the American market in June 1888 led to a popular rage for snapshots. Subsequent letters by JCH give Lillian advice on how to take good pictures. Some of her snapshots remain in the Emory collection. On the popularity of the Kodak camera and snapshots, see Richard Conniff, "When 'fiends' pressed the button, there was no place to hide," *Smithsonian*, June 1988, 106–10, 112, 114–17.

2. Tootsie is Lucien Harris. Lucien and Aileen Harris lived with the JCH family after their marriage (11 December 1895) and the birth of their first child, Stewart. JCH gave them a lot next door; they built a house and moved into it by 14 February 1897.

3. Atlanta *Constitution*, 7 February 1897. Published as a book in 1897.

[To Lillian]

14 Feb. [1897]

My Dear Daughter:

In regard to the Kodak, I'm going to write to Mr. Garnsey about it, so as to find out where to get a good one. So if there is some delay about it, you mustn't fret or be worried. I don't know that there will be delay; I hope not; but if there is you mustn't think your daddy has forgotten it.—As usual there is a great supply of no news[.] The beef seems to be a little tougher than usual, and we still have chicken for dinner Sunday. That's the reason I cackle so when I write to you. It is so loud I'm afraid the Lovetts will hear me.—J.C. was teaching Rufus how to spell the other day. He could spell sat and cat, and I asked him to spell hen.

"Dem out dar in the pen?" "Yes." He paused and scratched his head. "Dey so Many out dar I dunner which'n ter spell. Ef I try ter spell 'em all, it'll be too hard." "Well, spell the one under the fig-bush." "Dat'n yonder?" "Yes." "She's a black hen. I never did like ter spell dat kinder hen." Of course I could say no more. He never did admit that he couldn't spell the word.—Please say to Sister Bernard that I didn't expect my account to be credited with the apples I sent. I see the bill is for $70.84 only. Still, if she insists on it, I'll not complain.—Essie and Charles are now trying to correspond. It is easy for Charles, of course. But Essie works as hard over one letter as if she were splitting rails. It is in the nature of physical culture. All her muscles will be well developed if she keeps it up. She started to go to ride with Mama awhile ago, having just finished a letter to you, but Rob Goodman came just as she got in the buggy, and she jumped out to explain. She is still explaining and Mama and Mildred are gone.—The children tried hard to have some fun with valentines, but I don't think they succeeded to any great extent. Mamma had her picture taken the other day. She will have a half dozen of each negative. They are entirely different[.] In fact, they don't look like the same person. One of each will be sent to you.—Did you get any valentines? I was in hopes some young lady would send me one, something like—"Sure as the vine grows round the stump, so sure you are my sugar lump."—Speaking of long letters, I notice that you don't think about length when you write to me. I'm not complaining, because I know you would write me great long ones if you had anything you thought would interest me. And that's the way with me. Everything is quiet except the cats at night, and they only have time to give one squall before Thompson shows them the way over the fence. I've been trying to trim my rose-bushes, but the ground is so wet I can't get at them very well.—The weather is very pleasant

now, but pretty soon we'll have high winds and more cold weather.—
Mama fixed you up a box of trumpery stuff, (candy and things) which
I hope you'll find to your taste.—Lucien seems to be very serious over
his new adventure, (housekeeping), and it is just as well he should, for
he and Aleen will find it more serious than they suspect.[1] And it should
be, for it is the serious things of life that give substance to character. As
I'm not very serious myself, you can well imagine that my individuality
lacks substance. You are already serious enough for the whole family.—
You have fewer correspondents now than formerly. That is the reason
you don't get as many letters. Julian hardly has time to write, and Lucien
and his wife—well, they have their own affairs to look after: So that
after all you have to fall back on Dad, the old reliable. Essie went down
to the Manning society the other day. I don't think she would enjoy it
if she joined.[2] I imagine it is composed of [a] lot of ladies who imagine
they take an interest in really serious subjects. Mrs. Shehan Moody is
president. They want Mama to join, but imagine Mama writing an essay
on the works of Eusebius,[3] and reading it at the request of Mrs. Shehan
Moody! If the Society will take up the works of Cardinal Manning and
read and digest them, the members will get more information than by
writing essays on subjects in which they have no interest.[4]

But all this is not news and I'm at the end of my row. Write when you
can, and whether your letters are long or short they will be welcome to
your affectionate

Dad

My regards to Sister Bernard and Sister Mary St. Louis.

J. C. H.[5]

ALS

4 pp.

1. Lucien and Aileen had just moved next door into their new house.

2. Essie LaRose, niece of Mrs. JCH.

3. Probably Eusebius Pamphili (266?–340?), Bishop of Caesarea, called the Father of
Church History.

4. Henry Edward Manning (1808–92), English cardinal and Archbishop of Westmin-
ster, writer, and reformer.

5. "Joel Chandler Harris" also at the bottom of the page in author's hand.

21 Feb. [1897]

Dear Lillian: Everything here is dull as Rufus's complexion. Mr. and Mrs. L. Harris and Master S. Harris have moved to their new possessions on Walton avenue, and appear to be enjoying themselves as well as two old married people could be expected to do.[1] Your new furniture has been moved in and it is very beautiful.—Some new people have moved in the Grigsby place, Lucien's back fence has been white washed, the donkey is very well, Mrs. Frazier is fatter than ever, and B. Goodman is in the sitting-room. So there you are—all the startling events in a lump.—Mrs. Ed Matthews died the other day, and we hear that Miss Carrie (Mrs. Moore) had a hemorhage (now that's spelled wrong)—hemorrahge—no, hemorrhage (My goodness! I can't make it look right!). Well, anyhow, you know what I mean.—I believe things are getting duller here. Even the Lovett children have been keeping out of sight.—Oh, yes! last night Mrs. Wotton's setter-dogs killed eight hens for Mrs. Abernethy—and they were fine hens, too.—Charles sends his regards. He understands the situation thoroughly. He certainly writes a beautiful letter, and it is in writing, rather than in drawing, that I think his talent lies.—You see what a nice man I am: I didn't send your papers last week; but that was only partly my fault, for in the moving, cleaning and general uproar, the papers were misplaced, and couldn't be found when I wanted them. Oh, I hope I'll grow up to be good and thoughtful, and learn how to keep everything in its place. If I can be as good as I want to be, I'll be a nice man when I grow up.—I'm coming along with "1 Mile to Shady Dale"—about 150 pages completed. I hardly know whether it is worth the trouble; but I always feel that way. How is "Aaron in the Wildwoods" striking you? What does Sr. Bernard say about it? She is a good judge. Give her my regards and say to her that I pay my bills promptly because that is the best way to deceive people. Next time, I'll defer payment a couple of months, and so on and so on, until your last year won't cost me anything. Isn't that cute? It's either that, or she'll have to educate that poor Orphan Tomboy Mildred for nothing. Somebody—maybe Essie—was asking the other day what "philanthropist" meant. Mildred who didn't hear the words, said: "Oh, I know—a philopœna is twins." Some one explained that "philanthropist" was the word. "I know," says Mildred. "A philanterper is a man what takes up his bed and walks, and gives all his dry goods to the poor." So you see what we are all coming to in West End. Even the children lack education; and this being so, what's to be done with the old folks?—I don't wonder that Sister Bernard smiles about that Manning society. It would be fine if they'd read Cardinal Manning's works, and then form themselves into a Wiseman society to read Cardinal Wiseman's books, and finer still if they'd devote themselves to the entrancing volumes written by Cardinal Newman, the poet of the Church. But instead of that, here they go attitudinizing, and pretending to do something that only the learned doctors of the Church have done. It is, indeed, really too funny. It is like a parcel of hens scratching for acorns under the most beautiful tree in the world. With people who think, the main thing about the acorn is the tree that grows from it. If an acorn is safe in the ground, let it stay there, for there is where it belongs. You and I, my dear, will enjoy the tree. You may be sure that if our hens find any acorns they'll not know their right uses.—But how easy it is for a young man to grow serious and begin to lecture. I'm afraid I'm too smart to be healthy. That's the reason I'm thin[.]

Now, I've written all I know and some more besides, and you'll have to excuse your friend and dear Daddy till next time. And give his regards to those you love, and beg those gentle sisters (especially Sister Bernard and Sister Mary Louis) to put his name in their saintly petitions, to the end that whatever is wrong about him may be made right.

With the love and devotion of

Your *Dad*

I'm sending you a little picture of Mamma.

~

ALS

4 pp.

1. Mr. and Mrs. Lucien Harris and son, Stewart. The Atlanta city directory (1898) gives their address as 224 Lawton; the number is 252 Lawton in 1902. JCH seems to have interchanged w and l in spelling street. Walton Street was a familiar downtown Atlanta street.

[To Lillian]

[28 February 1897] [1]

Sunday before Lent. [1897]

My dear Daughter:

You have had cake, candy, Kodak, Mama and Mildred and now you ought to be happy and contented for two or three days at least. I hope your Kodak will turn out to be a good one. It is larger than Mr. Garnsey's and takes a tolerable picture—in fact a fine picture, as some of the specimens I saw showed—which is a detestable English sentence to be written by an author to his daughter. Untangle it and make it musical, so as to practice in that line; thus "in fact a fine picture if some of the specimens shown me are what they were represented to be." That's better but not good.—There is a diptheria [sic] sign hung up at the Grigsby place. Aleen's baby seems to be somewhat unwell, and I think she is worrying for fear he has the disease or may have it. I hope her fears may prove groundless. The family at Grigsby's appear to be German's or Swedes, and they must have brought disease with them. Yet if the nurse has been careful with the baby there's no danger; but a negro nurse is about as untrustworthy a piece of furniture as can be found.—Belle Sawyer is staying with Essie, and to-night Bob and Brader are both on hand. Brader is especially on hand, having a high old revel with himself, adjusting collar, cuffs, and brushing imaginary specks from his panties. Bob, I think, is fond of Belle, and Brader is fond of himself, so that we have to [sic] love matches on hand. Of the two, Brader's affection for himself is the most genuine and far-reaching.—Your mama never goes away but there's trouble. Last night I was childish enough to allow J.C. to sleep with me. He went to bed at the usual hour, fell asleep at once, and lay like a log. I congratulated myself. I thought, "The poor child has been misrepresented." I watched him closely, and he never stirred hand nor foot. I finished my writing and went to bed, being careful to make no stir. J.C. still lay like a log. I fixed myself comfortably amd was just dozing off, when I heard a snort in my ear, and there was J.C. walking about on top of me with elbows and knees. How he managed to do it I don't know, but he never once used hands or feet. He ran about over me like a cow in plowed ground. I finally rescued myself and placed him on his back, where he lay quietly; but sleep was gone from me for an hour. Finally she came near again, and I was just beginning to dream a story about bubbles that are inhabited,[2] when—bang!—I heard something go, and—biff—I felt something strike me. "Be still, sad heart," said I, "and let's see what it is." J.C. had butted the headboard with his head, and had trampled in my face with his knees, which are as hard as the hoofs of a Texas pony. It was then that I began to long for the presence of my dear, dear wife, who has to put up with this sort of thing every night, and I envied you—oh, so much! I said to myself, "Here am I the victim of this new fangled method of somnambulism—this dismal scheme of teaching parents their place—while my dear daughter is candying, and marsh mallowing and kodaking! Little does she know of the miseries of her poor afflicted daddy, who never knew before what it is to be both ma and pa!" But, with the exception of many bruises and blue places, I am feeling better to-night. J.C. is in Essie's room on the sofa. I may have to buy a sofa or have the wall re-papered, but what do I care for expense [. . .] long as I am able to get a good night's rest?[3] I understand now why Mama is so hale and hearty. It's the exercise that J.C. gives her while they are both asleep. Why, I'd rather practice with dumb bells— I'd rather have a scrap with Corbett—[4] I'd rather be run over by a run-away horse—than to sleep in the same room with J.C., much less in the same bed. But such is life in Wes 'Een—and I never shall forget it.—I see the *Sunny South*[5] is offering prizes to those who can make the most words from the letters in Holiday. Suppose you try for it? The words must be English words found in any standard dictionary. I enclose the offer. Get as many words as you can, send me a list of them, and I'll send you a list that I have made. Then you can copy the whole, send it to me, and I'll put in fifty cents for you, and you'll be sure to get some kind of a prize.—My regards to Sister Bernard. Say to her that I highly appreciate all she has done and is doing for you, and also her remembrances of me.

Your loving

Dad.

ALS

4 pp.

1. Ash Wednesday was on March 3 in 1897.

2. *Cf.* Bubble-land in *Plantation Pageants* (1899), chapter 6.
3. Missing text is indicated by [. . .] in transcription.
4. "Gentleman Jim" was James John Corbett (1866–1933), the boxer who defeated John L. Sullivan for the world's heavyweight title in 1892.
5. *Sunny South*, Atlanta home weekly, founded by John H. Seals in 1875, became the weekly edition of the *Constitution* in 1903. Discontinued in 1907, it became the nucleus of the new *Uncle Remus's Magazine*, edited by JCH and Julian Harris and supported by stockholders of the *Constitution*. See Frank Luther Mott, *A History of American Magazines* (Cambridge, Mass.: Harvard University Press, 1957) 4:92. For more recent and more complete information on both the *Sunny South* and *Uncle Remus's Magazine*, see the entries in Sam G. Riley's *Magazines of the American South* (New York: Greenwood Press, 1986). The *URM* continued the literary home magazine format of the *SS*.

[To Lillian]

[February/March? 1897]

Sunday evening

Dear Miss Billy-Ann: "I take this present opportunity of dropping you these few lines, trusting you are well and doing well." That's the way people began letters when I was a boy, and I don't know but it's a very good way. It showed that the writer didn't know what to say—Brader has just knocked, and I have turned him in as Essie skipped across the hall to hide herself. Brader, by the way, is now supposed to be seriously engaged in business. He started out last Monday to establish local agencies in various Georgia towns for some sort of an insurance company. He returned yesterday and is now here describing his various experiences, and giving all to understand that he is a person of considerable importance any way you fix him. He is so unlucky, however, that I'm afraid his insurance company will fall to pieces in his able hands. It's a pity, too. I can't say that Brader deserves success, but it's not his fault. The trouble is with his bringing up. He has had no one to stimulate his ambition and to show him that, next to religion, the highest achievement of our natures is self-respect—not the self-respect that leads to pride, but that which leads us to be honest and virtuous for our own sakes. Religion is better than that of course—being the best of all. If Brader had the right kind of self-respect he would have gone at any kind of work that presented itself, and by this time he would have been well on

his way to success.—But what have you done that I should be delivering a lecture on Brader? Indeed, you don't deserve to be treated so, and
I'm a very inconsiderate daddy; but you know [how] we old people are:
we put on airs and pretend to be very wise—however, I'll not let you
see everything that is behind the scenes.—Besides Bob has just come
in, and brings word that Mattie Byington is married to Mallory Dixon. I
suppose it must have been a runaway match. If so, it shows a sad lack of
confidence between Mattie and her Mother and Father. I hope when my
dear daughter concludes to elope (should she ever come to such a trifling
conclusion) that she'll whisper the fact to her Mother and Me, so that
we can creep out of the house on tiptoe, and hand her bundles over the
back fence. Seriously I'm sorry for Mattie, if it is an elopement[.] She is
sure to regret it. Marriage is too sacred an event to be made a plaything
of, or to be entered into in a secret way.—Mr. Stanton, our esteemed
poet, is still wobbling. I don't know what is to become of him.—Our
violets have been a surprise to me. The more we pick 'em, the more they
are. I have had the two flower beds on each side the front steps planted
in pansies—lev'm dozen even. Some of them are already in bloom. The
violets are very beautiful.—We had a thunderstorm from the northeast
at 4:30 this morning. The rain it rained, the wind it howled, and the leak
it leaked. I had to set slop-tubs and water cans in my room, and these
articles being made of tin, I was soothed by a fuss that made me dream
that Mildred had at last decided to practice on the piano.—Lucien is at
his house now, and Aleen is doing the cooking. Julian took tea there
this evening, and is still there. The baby is fat and saucy, and cries very
little.—We have another hen on.—Mattie has served notice that she and
Jesse are going to Nashville in a few weeks. Consequently we must get
another cook. Meanwhile, we have Chloë to fall back on.—We have had
lettuce out of the garden and by Tuesday we'll have asparagus. It's a sign
that winter is about over. The grass is green and the wild cherry tree
in the back yard is putting forth its leaves—and at night you can hear
the willis-whistlers. You can hear them in Washington if you'll stand in
the back piazza of the convent and listen when everything is still—soft
whistles sounding far away. They used to tell me it was the frogs; but
I exploded that notion when a boy. I pursued the sound one night for

more than two miles and it was as far away at last as at first. Besides, frogs don't whistle.

But, good-night. You must be tired of all of this by this time. I have written a long letter with nothing in it but my love, which is a good deal though it may not show to great advantage. My kindest regards to Sisters Bernard and Mary Louis.

Your affectionate Daddy.

ALS

4 pp.

[To Lillian]

[February/March? 1897]

Sunday night.

My Dear Daughter: Your welcome little note was received, and by this time I suppose there's a letter in the P.O. awaiting my coming.—Your mother tells me she informed you of the particulars of the elopement. Compare her letter with mine and behold, once for all, how much more knowing a woman is than a man. A woman knows there's a mouse behind the wall though she's never heard it: a man knows it only after the creature has bounced out and run up his breeches-leg. My lecture about the elopement was apropos of nothing. I had no text, being in that particular somewhat like Sam Jones.[1] The elopement was a family affair, planned to avoid expense. Consequently I hasten to endorse it. It gives me an idea. I shall know how to avoid expense when my girls marry— no "infair,"[2] no trousseau, no railway tickets to buy—everything saved. It is a great scheme.—But how was a dull old man to know that this elopement was different from other elopements? On the other hand, how was your mama *not* to know? She's a woman, and that either explains the mystery or deepens it, I forget which.—Mama says the dress-maker didn't get your dress done in time to send it last week; but you will have it in time for next Sunday.—Clark Frazier has had scarlet fever, but is getting better. Edna Wade has it, and is supposed to have a serious case. Dr. Crow thinks those people at Grigsby's had both scarlet fever and diptheria; at any rate Clark was taken down after playing with one of the little boys. But I think it's the sewer—the man-hole is right in front of Wade's and Frazier's.[3] We have one in front of us, but I had it arranged so that nothing would stop in it.—Aleen took dinner with us to-day. The baby brought his dinner with him.—Everything is beginning to look like spring here, and the weather is warm. We have had some hard rains and a long spell of cloudy weather.—I have planted out 1,000 new straw-berry plants, the finest varieties.—There is nothing new to write about, and, besides, I'm just recovering from an attack of sore throat, hacking cough and headache—nothing serious, but calculated to make one wish that one could feel as well when sick as one feels in good health. It's funny (isn't it?) how bad you feel when you're sick. I suppose it was intended to be that way.—The street car men are stiffening up the soft spots on their line out this way, tearing up the old cross-ties and putting in new ones, and soldering the ends of the rails together. Yesterday for a change we had open cars, and the fresh air was very[.] [4]

We've set another hen, and we've had lettuce out of the garden and oodles of asparagus. And the crab-apple tree is in blossom. So you see we are getting along pretty well. Our poet, too, has about recovered, and promises not to do so any more.[5] I'm hard-hearted, but I feel like crying when I see little Val and think of his poor, weak father[.] Yet we all have our failings.—Julian found me awake the other morning when he came from work, and was talking to me when Rufus came to wake me up. Rufus stuck is [sic] head in at the door: "It 8 o'clock, Mr. Harris," he said. "No, Rufus," I replied, "it lacks 5 minutes of 8." "It 8 o'clock out here 'mongst de cuckoo," he insisted. Later in the day I inquired why he said "mongst" the cuckoo. "Heh! she got so many chains, an' weights an' funny noises."

Well, I've written myself out, and have written nothing. All send love. My regards to Sisters Bernard and Mary Louis.

    Your affectionate

    Daddy

ALS

3 pp.

1. Samuel Porter Jones (1847–1906), Georgia evangelist notable for theatrical reli-gious revivals and financial success, was known as the "Apostle of Prohibition." See entry in the *Dictionary of Georgia Biography*.

2. Scottish and local United States term for a wedding reception.

3. Jeremiah D. Frazier (residence at 324 Gordon); George H. Wade (residence at 341 Gordon); Willis H. Grisby (residence at 241 Lawton).

4. Page 3 is possibly from another letter. There is no physical sign of break between sheets two and three, but the text lacks proper transition. Transcript in URM 28, no. 1 (September 1910), 4, supplies the adjective "fine," so the previous sentence ends: "the fresh air was very fine."

5. Frank Stanton.

[To Lillian]

7 March [1897]

My Dear Daughter: Confidentially, between you and me, entre nous, sub rosa, (and likewise nix cum a sous) I'm the most worthless and forgetful daddy you ever had. I get absorbed in my work, and forget to send your papers when they should be sent. And then when you fail to get them you sit and bite your fingers and say to yourself that you are forgotten; whereas, you are well remembered, but the papers are forgotten. And then along comes one of the dear sisters—or two of them—and they see you looking doleful. Then this dialogue occurs:

Sr. M. L.—That child is not feeling well. I think she ought to have a pill.

Sr. B.—*A* pill, did you say? Two pills at the very least. See how she droops? It's her liver. Two pills, *of course.*

Sr. Sacred Heart (at foot of stairway)—Did I hear you say 'liver?' *Three pills* for the liver. Don't forget—*three.*

Chorus behind the scenes.

Oh, a *doctor* must be a *cheerful* giver—(treble)

One pill for a *shake* and *two* for a *shiver* (alto)

And *three* for that *awful* thing the *liver* (bass)

Consequently you must be feeling very much better.—All your commissions shall be atten[ded][1] to—the new films, the development of th[e] old ones, et cettry, and so forth. Right [. . .] I intend to do these academic chores th[e] first thing in the morning. If I'm the sa[me] man I was, I shall probably forget [. . .] and then abuse myself for being such a heartless, cruel monster as to forget my errand that a young lady desires me to undertake—especially when the aforesaid young lady is so well and favorably known to me.—I declare, your Mama is a perfect martyr—such adventures—such experiences—such waiting for trains—such awful spectacles of engines laying [sic] sprawling, their eyes knocked out and their boilers cold—such going without dinners and things! It would take a whole letter to relate them. But there were some streaks of sunshine amid the general gloom. She had seen you and she had seen the sisters, and she enjoyed every moment of her stay there. It was only when she started away that gloom began to gather. It was quite four o'clock when she arrived, and there was an expression on her face—well, I'm glad I wasn't a railway schedule! She says she had an elegant time at the convent, and she talks about it even when I want to go to sleep. Mama is enthusiastic, and I'm glad of it. When we lose enthusiasm appreciation goes with it, and then two-thirds of the joy of living are taken away.—Why, of course I received your report and appreciated the wonderful record you are making. But don't study so hard as to give you a distaste for your text-books. Health, my dear—health—that is the main thing at your age. Still, I like your reports; they are a great satisfaction to me, and if you can get such records and not overtax your mind, all right.—Some one at the office had taken your name from the subscription list of the Evening Consti. I have had it put back, but if you have not received it when you get this, write two words to say so, and I'll settle the matter for good and all.—I started you a bundle of papers to-day. You'll get it with this. I'll send the funny papers to-morrow and you'll get them Wednesday—that is to say, if my memory—but we'll not talk about the shaky old thing, until we get it a pair of crutches.—The diptheria [sic] across the way drove Aleen and Lucien home again[.] They were afraid the baby would catch it. They are still here, and will remain until the health department announces that the yellow placard may be taken down. It is now hinted that the disease wasn't diptheria at all, but simply sore throat. At any rate, the children are all getting well and are just as dirty as ever.—Mama made a mistake and sent you only 10 yards of cheese (it) cloth. She says you can get the other 2 yards in Washington, Wilkes County.

My regards to Sisters Bernard and Mary Louis.

Your affectionate

Daddy

ALS
3 pp.
1. Lower right margin of page 1 is torn away. Missing text is indicated by [. . .] in
transcription. Where possible, letters have been supplied.

[To Lillian]

4 April 1897.

Dear Billy-Ann:

I sincerely regret that there is no news here of an exciting nature.
The most thrilling incident I can think of occurred yesterday afternoon.
Mama was planting—or, rather, setting out—some California violets.
The ground was not dry, in fact, it was mud. After scratching around in
the mud awhile, Mama inadvertently scratched her head. This was not
on the programme, for the mud was more necessary to the violets than
it was to mama's hair. We have two dozen Parma violets and three dozen
California's. These will make a brave show next fall.—We will divide up
the common violets and set them out as soon as the rain stops. We'll
have enough to go around all the rose beds. And next fall we'll have
violets without number. Speaking of rain, we've had a right smart of it,
I can tell you. The sun shone out this afternoon for about half an hour,
but the rain kept falling, and I suppose we shall have more to-morrow;
but it is all right. It is in the course of nature, and therefore Providential.

You have seen about the baby Constitution. The King of France, and
twice ten thousand men, marched up the hill and then marched down
again. Some changes will have to be made among the men on the morning paper—just what I don't know. The Evening Consti. was started to
give a job to Brother-in-law Cramer. Ida wanted to come home to live,
and so Mr. Cramer had to be provided for. The Evening Consti. is gone,
but Mr. C. is here and will have to be fixed.[1] This is natural, and perhaps
it is just. I hope it will turn out to be so—that is to say, I hope no deserving man will be thrown out of a job on that account.—If I think of it
(you know what a tremendous memory I have) I'll have the Journal sent
to you in place of the defunct Evening Consti. The Journal is a pretty
good paper, and has held its own very well.

I just turned your films over to Mr. Wilkinson, our artist, who has had some experience in getting Kodak pictures developed and printed. He will see that they are properly attended to. I presume he will have the job done at once. If so, I'll send the pictures during the week.

Aleen and Lucien had dinner with us to-day, and we had fresh beans for dinner—not out of our garden, however. Our vegetables are growing finely, considering the lack of sunshine during the past month.—Your report was very fine. I am proud of the many 100s but I am also a trifle proud of the 98 and 99 in French. It shows that, like your pappy, you are a true Georgia cracker. You will be able to get over this after a while; for the present Sister Bernard will have to excuse your 98s and 99s in French.

As I said, there's nothing here to interest you, and my invention fails me—By-the-by, I forgot to mention that Chloë brought us some *souse* yesterday, and those who ate it—your mama, Essie and I—have bitterly repented of it. Moral: don't eat *souse* out of season.

Your affectionate

Daddy

ALS

3 pp.

1. Probably Robert B. Cramer, listed as special correspondent of the Atlanta *Constitution* in the 1898 Atlanta city directory.

[To Lillian]

[April 1897]

Dear Billy Ann:

I enclose your "developed" films.

They have but one trouble—

All, all are double.

Consequently, take notice:

1. Don't get nervous.

2. Hold your "gun" steady when you go to take a shot.

3. Press the button steadily, and not with a jerk.

4. The slightest movement of the "gun" ruins the picture.

5. When you "shoot" again take some soothing syrup for your nerves.
A part of these directions came from the photagrapher [sic]. Others
come from me.
   Your loving
      Dad

ALS
1 p.

[To Lillian]

Sunday evening. [Spring 1897]

My Dear Daughter: I know you are feeling better now, for you have mama
with you. We had a vague idea that she would return home to-day, but
we were not disappointed when Evelyn returned from the train without
her. She enjoys being with you, and you enjoy being with her, and so
there you are.—You keep on saying that you have to study very hard,
so hard that you have resumed your glasses. Now, (do you know?) the
information worries me. It is so easy for a well-disposed and an ambitious girl to overdo the matter.—There is another picture still to come.
The trouble is that your camera has the jerks. Why is it? Can't you hold
it steady when you press the button? Practice with it when it's empty,
for it is a somewhat costly business to spoil 7 films out of 12. I'm not
complaining of the cost, but merely saying that a little care and attention would put an end to it. I'll send you some more films Wednesday
or Thursday. If necessary, oil the machinery that does the work, so that
only a slight pressure on the button will cause it to snap.—Ella Pope
and Annie Howell are both at home. They couldn't graduate. Reason:
they were expelled for their April Fool-ishness. You heard about the
Lucy Cobb girls going bareheaded about town on the first of April, didn't
you?[1] Well, Ella and Annie are out, and they don't seem to be proud of
it a little bit. I don't think it was the fault of the girls that they were
able to commit such a breach of discipline, but with the teachers whose
laxity gave the giddy young things so fair an opportunity. For instance:
would it have been the fault of Julian and Lucien if they had been seen
idling around stores at West End day after day when they were growing
up? I rather think not. It would have been wholly my fault. Therefore I

think it is wrong to make a few young girls suffer for the failure of the Lucy Cobb teachers to establish discipline. A good old gentleman (Dr. McDonald) was praising my boys on the car the other day, and bewailing the fact that his own sons had done him no credit. I was within one of telling him that his boys had gone wrong before they came to manhood, simply because his discipline had been wrong.

But I'm getting prosy—a sure sign of a lack of something interesting to write about. The fact is, if news were as plentiful as strawberries, I'd send you a lot of it. Now you'll ask why I don't send the strawberries. The truth is, we are not prepared to send them. Next season, I'll get boxes and crates and send you some of the finest you ever saw. I tried to get some boxes the other day, but didn't know where to go, nor did the commission merchants know where to direct me.—Lula is staying with Essie while the Mama is away, and while I write Miss Laura is singing at the piano—a little of which goes a long way with me. Mr. Jim Holliday called on Lula and Essie this afternoon, and he put in his time teaching them how the game of *faro* is played. How does that strike you?—Bob and Brader have just come in, but the song goes on just the same, and there is a vim about the higher notes calculated to convince an old man that true love (in music at least) is shrill and thin, and in the highest of high keys.

The roses are gorgeous, but there are so many buds that it is no satisfaction to cut those that are in bloom. Still, we get some fine ones.— To-day the weather is chilly again—wind blowing from the northwest— and we had to have a fire in the sitting-room. Alleen and the baby were here to dinner. The youngster is very bright and pleasant. He knows how to patty-cake with his hands, and has a voice that will come in fine should he ever be an auctioneer. But he cried only once to-day, and then in subdued and velvety tones. He remained until Miss Laura was through singing and then had to be taken home. And no wonder. The silence that came after the shrill love song was absolutely appalling. I could feel it.

Write when you can. Regards to Sister Bernard.

Your affectionate

Daddy

ALS
4 pp.
1. Lucy Cobb Institute (1858–1931) at that time was a fashionable finishing school for young women at Athens, Georgia.

18 April. [1897]

Dear Lillian: I wrote as usual, the usual number of pages, the usual amount of uninteresting remarks, mailed the letter as usual, and there is no reason whatever, so far as I can see, why you didn't get it as usual. I have received replies from two letters I sent to Boston, and they were mailed on the same day and in the same way. But, you naughty, naughty gal, the fact that you didn't get a letter from me was no reason why you shouldn't write to your poor old pappy. Consequently, when I failed to hear from you I thought (and still think) you were feeling too badly to write more than the short letter to your mamma. Well, I hope you will soon be better. I don't want your studies to interfere with your health. A perfect report is a very pleasant thing in its way, but it's not one-thousandth part so important in my eyes as perfect health. I am not so anxious for you to get ahead in your books as I am for you to have robust health. I understand how the Sisters feel about it. They think I ought to get the worth of my money in the shape of book-learning for you. They are compelled to take that view because they know that the great majority of parents look only at material results. Well, I am different from the majority of parents. I do not look at material and immediate results. I would be getting the worth of my money if you didn't recite but one lesson (out of a book) each week. It is worth more than I pay to have you brought in daily contact with those gentle sisters so that you may have the example of their refined manners, their forbearance and their gentleness. You can learn book lessons anywhere, but you cannot learn the things I want you to learn any and everywhere. Therefore I am sending you to St. Joseph's Academy, Washington, Wilkes county, Ga., U.S.A. You may fail to receive this letter. If you do, I shall have to make an official examination into the state of the postal service between Atlanta and Washington. One of the inspectors told me yesterday that it was impossible for a letter to be lost between the two points, but I told him he was mistaken, and I think the postal clerk who went out of Atlanta last Tuesday, or the postmaster at W., will shortly have trouble on his hands [.] No doubt it would be a pity for either one to lose his job—but such is life in Uncle Sam's service.

I enclose the pictures in the box. There were only five good ones. The remedy is that you must have a rest for your camera when you take a picture. You can't take a picture with it by holding it unsupported in your hands. Those that you did take, however, seemed to be very good ones. That of yourself was taken in a bad light. The camera should be in shadow and the subject in a fairly strong light.

The plates you sent are simply exquisite [.] I don't know how they can be improved upon. Mama came near having a conniption fit over them. She will attend to your request in regard to Lycett's [.] [1]

To-day has been a beautiful day, but there was an east wind this morning, and so I rose with a headache, which never left me till this afternoon, when the wind began to blow from the south. You'll think this is my imagination; but wait till you get old, and fat, and superstitious, and you'll have a [sic] imagination too.

To return to the beautiful plates—Mama expected to receive a small box with some easter eggs. She never dreamed of receiving such a handsome gift. She has examined the whole dozen a dozen times. I told her she'd wear the paint off, but she declares it is burnt in, and I expect it is, for with all her handling of the plates, the paint seems as fresh as ever. They certainly are lovely pieces.

And now to return again to the day. Everybody was out but me. The church was crowded, the music fine, and the sermon by Father Schadewell most excellent. I intended to go, but my head ached so severely that I was afraid to risk it.

I told you in the letter that was *lost* (but which will be found again) that I would probably take my vacation in June, in which event, I'll come down to your closing exercises, take my stand in the audience and make faces at you when you come out to recite a piece.

I have told you no news, but there is none to tell. Evelyn subscribed to the Journal for you, and if you don't receive it regularly let me know.

My regards to Sister Bernard, Sister Mary Louis, and to Bernardine, the lass you are to fetch home with you.

Your affectionate

Daddy

ALS

4 pp.

1. Name of an Atlanta china company, Lycett Studio.

[To Lillian]

25 April [1897]

My Dear Daughter: [1] There's nothing of importance here to write about. We have had another kitten-killing, at which Mama is an expert. Annabel has a new calf, but she doesn't promise much milk. We have been buying milk recently for the first time in 17 years. Speaking of calves, the baby is teething, and is not so gay as usual. Teething, you know, will sober the gayest baby. He is not falling off, and he is not sick, but he has a sort of reflective air. [2] You know Mattie is gone. Well, Chloë and her family are cooking for us. The greater part of last week, we had in the kitchen Chloë, Lizzie, Ed., Rufus, Johnson, and the mule and wagon. Of course they were not all in the kitchen at once, but off and on—relays and reliefs. I don't know whether Johnson or the mule made up biscuits, but certainly one or the other. Chloë seemed to be hard run even then, so I told Banks that he had better come and bring his wife and family to help Chloë and her family cook for us this week.—The roses have begun to bloom feebly, but they have been very much hurt by the cold north winds that have been blowing for a month until the last two or three days.

The bushes are full of buds, but they are very shy about opening. The winds have hurt the pansies, too. They bloom, but in a sickly way. I noticed some ripe strawberries [in] the garden to-day—some very fine ones, but not enough, so far, to give each of the family one apiece. There are thousands of young ones, and the vines are still blooming, but no doubt something will occur to prevent them all from ripening. The cold winds have hurt all the vegetables except the lettuce (have peas) and the asparagus.[3]

But fie upon the pen that will persist in writing of "sallid" and "greens" to a young lady, when, as a matter of fact Lula Z. is going to give a card party for the benefit (no, for the pleasure of) Miss Louise McIntosh, whom she is to entertain for a few weeks at her suburban home on Bah street. (By the way, Baugh has been changed to Oglethorpe.) I learn, by special messenger that Miss Lula was writing her cards of invitation yesterday, and that not by any means nor on any account will she invite Miss Belle Sawyer. Poor Miss Belle! Not only will Miss Lula not invite Belle, but the affair is to be [. . .] carried out in full dress, which means, I suppose, that the dresses are to be so full the girls will boil over the tops of them to a considerable extent. I don't know what poor little Essie will do, for she can hardly fill the dresses she has.[4] My special messenger say that Miss Louise McIntosh has been visiting Catherine Wooten, and that Miss L says she has been having "*A bum time*" there. This shows that the young lady has a large vocabulary and more refinement than she knows what to [do] with. I hope that my dear daughter will think twice before she uses such language as that. To be candid, however, I think the phrase was manufactured for the occasion by someone who told my special messenger. Well, anyhow, the chief features of this suburban card-party on Bah street are to be the absence of poor Belle Sawyer and the presence of full dresses. (I always heard them called Evening dresses until now.) I think Essie will go even if she has to wear one of your Mama's Mother Hubbard's. And then, after the card party is [. . .] over, Miss McIntosh is to have an engagement *every night* while she remains in the suburban homes just to show Miss Catherine Wooten that *all* the popularity and *all* the society are most distinctly and emphatically *not* on the other side of town.

My regards to Sister Bernard, and say to her that I am glad and grateful that she is praying for a special favor to me. I think I know what it is, and the idea is growing more and more pleasing to me every day. Say to her that if he [sic] had been raised a Protestant she would know how hard it is to root out of the mind the mean prejudices and doubts and fictions that have been educated into it. This is the task I am engaged in now. There are only small and insignificant weeds in my mind at this time, but I want to have them all cleared out and thrown over the fence in the trash pile.[5] My regards also to Sister Mary Louis.

Your affectionate

Daddy

ALS

4 pp.

1. Ascribed to Mildred in *URM* but probably to Lillian.

2. Stewart Harris, son of Lucien and Aileen Harris.

3. Typical Harris puns.

4. Niece Essie LaRose.

5. Allusions to JCH's conversion to the Roman Catholic Church. Though a firm believer for a number of years, he was not confirmed until he lay upon his deathbed. His letters to the daughters which praise the work of the sisters at Saint Joseph's Academy often mention Catholic authors, such as the scholarly Cardinal Newman and popular writers; issues facing the Catholic church; and friendships with various priests.

[To Lillian]

2 of May. [1897]

Dear Miss Billy-Ann: Weather cold; wind blowing a gale from the nor'-west, thrashing out the roses, and making thin-skinned people feel as if they had lost home and friends and country; old Annabel ailing; calf so poor that it falls down when it tries to bleat; hens deserting their nests, and allowing their eggs to get cold; birds pecking at the strawberries; bucket falling in the well; J.C. cutting a hole in the toe of his Sunday-go-to-meeting shoes; donkey trying to climb the wire-fence; pigeons gobbling up the chicken's food; apples rotting; stove smoking; dry goods bill heavy; bonnet bill heavier; street cars behind time; Chloë trying to get in the stove to cook; Rufus dropping plates from the ceiling; milk bill growing; cow-doctor's bill coming in; dust blowing everywhere; kitten getting its tail under the rocking-chair; Brader with his hair soaped smooth on each side; the pony wallowing herself black; planks falling off the fence; Lizzie helping Chloë to harden the biscuit—

Now, how do you suppose I can find any news to write while all this is going on? More than that, how do you suppose I survive the infliction?

Well, I'll tell you, Billy-Ann: I laugh at it. I'm just as happy, almost, when things are going wrong, as I am when they are going right; and for very good reason. It doesn't amount to a row of pins. There's nothing funnier than to see small troubles disappear when you laugh at them. They seem to get ashamed of themselves and run away.

I went to see Mildred confirmed this afternoon and enjoyed it very much. More than a hundred were confirmed I think, and among them three or four colored people. At the close the Bishop delivered a little address, and in the course of it made a remark that caused me to laugh. He said: "If all people were good Christians it would put a stop even to the scandals in Atlanta." I daresay our enterprising town appears to be very lively to outside folks, especially to those who live in Savannah, where everything goes on in a sort of mild dream. I remember running to catch a street car when I first went to Savannah. The people on the car looked at one another and whispered, and one old lady in a corner said to a companion: "If you think he's crazy, let's get off." Savannah folks don't like Atlanta. I got even with some of them the last time I was there. The train arrived about 8 o'clock, a.m., and I went to a restaurant to get my breakfast. The waiter seated me at a table where there were three old gentlemen. I knew one of them but he didn't know me. While waiting to be served I turned to him and said: "What town is this?" He shuffled about with his feet. "I didn't catch your remark, sir," he replied. "I asked the name of the town; it is a very pretty place." He regarded me with amazement, but finally told me it was Savannah. One of the others leaned his elbows on the table, and asked me what part of the country I was from. "Atlanta," I replied. Well, I wish you could have seen their faces! The old gentleman to whom I had first spoken swelled up in the worst comical manner, and ordered the waiter to carry his breakfast to another table; whereupon, I made myself known to him, and I never saw a man enjoy a joke more. In fact, he paid for my breakfast.

Still, this is not news. In fact, I've written it instead of inventing news. I have had marble chips spread over the walk from the gate to the front steps, and around the side of the house. When I have a few more bar-relsful put down it will help matters wonderfully.—Inspector Whiteside is now looking into the loss of your letter. Father O'Brien tells me that the Washington P.O. is not in a very good condition. This investigation will no doubt lead to a reform. No complaint has been made by the Washington people because, as Father O'B. says, the P.M. belongs to a *prominent family*. This is of course confidential. Don't mention it to your classmates, for it might get out, and if the family really is prominent it might make things unpleasant for Fr. O'B.

Yes, you have not many more weeks between now and vacation. Your last report was good; good enough for me. Mamma is coming down this month if she can raise the money. I expect she'll have to borrow it from me.

My regards to Sister Bernard and Sister Mary Louis. And please remember that I'm your affectionate

    Queen of the May

    ⌒

ALS
4 pp.

[To Lillian]

                                     9 May. [1897]
My Dear Daughter: During the past few days we have been fairly feasting on home-made strawberries. To-day, we had three short-cakes for dinner, and two large bowlsfull of berries left over for supper. We'll have almost as many more to-morrow: and all this from the little patch you saw when you were here. I set out 500 new plants in March, and next year (if all goes well), we'll have enough berries to supply the neighborhood. To-day we had green peas for dinner out of our garden, being somewhat ahead of anybody in West End, although we planted later than our neighbors. This must be luck, for I take no special pains with the garden, leaving it pretty much to Banks. The old cow is in a bad way. Her udder has hardened, and the probability is that she'll be of no more service. But I'll not grumble about it. She has been a faithful old cow and will make good West End beef.—I have se [set?] 75 little chickens, but had to buy them. You shall have fried chicken when you come home. Mama was talking about {going/coming} down one day this week—probably

next Friday, and I'll try to have your pictures mounted in time for her to {bring/take} to you. There's just about as much news here as there is under a barn. The weather is warm, and we have a profusion of roses. La France seems to be out-doing herself this year, giving us some buds larger than I have ever seen from a hot-house, and delightfully fragrant. I trimmed the bushes very close in March, and now they are paying me back. I never saw as many buds. But for the cold weather and high winds the flowers would have been more perfect, but they are perfect enough for me. I'm not grumbling.—Which reminds me that J.C. has placed a "grumble-box" on the dinner-table. Whoever grumbles must place a copper in the box. Julian had to put in two cents the other day. He says he grumbled, but I never heard him.—Evelyn is now doing night-work, his hours being from 1 p.m. to 2 a.m. He has a wheel [bicycle] and rides it home in 15 minutes. From 9 p.m. to 2 a.m. he helps Julian with the telegraphic dispatches, editing them and writing heads. The experience will do him good. Lucien also has a wheel. The family took supper with us to-night, but went away immediately after, taking Mama with them. The baby is growing nicely and seems to be a right clever baby, which is surprising when you remember he's some kin to me. I suppose Essie will tell you the girl-news when she writes. If there's any I haven't heard of it—except this, that all the girls, without regard to age or beauty unite in saying that Bob Goodman is a worse bore than Brader. My opinion is that all boys and a great many old men are bores. They are so conceited. Why is it that we have such a marvelous admiration for ourselves and for our most foolish opinions? And why is it that an old man is never more tiresome than when he is trying to convince young people that their own opinions are foolish? When old people find out how foolish they have been they are called wise; when they discover how foolish they are, they have reached the pinnacle of wisdom. They have nothing more to learn.

I have discovered one thing, namely; that one little field sparrow can whip a whole colony of English sparrows. Another one of the Lombardy poplars has blown down. And still I am not grumbling.

I have nothing more to write about, even admitting that I have already written about something. I read your street-car episode. It was very good, but when you write for print, you seem to be afraid you'll say something. You seem to "haul in your horns" just when you have reached the point of expectation. That is timidity. But why be timid in print? Be modest and truthful, but go about it boldly; plunge into the matter even though you have to hold your breath.

Meanwhile, pardon this dull letter, and give my regards to Sisters Bernard and Mary Louis.

Your affectionate

Daddy

ALS

4 pp.

23 May. [1897]

8 p.m., and upwards.

My Dear Lillian: I can give you the news in a nutshell: It is warm and dry; Mama has the headache, and I have the toothache; the children have a new bull-terrier pup named Muldoon; old Annabelle is still in the hospital; and the little white kitten we had is dead.

Thus you will see that things are running along in their native and natural groove, with an occasional jar, as when you ride on a street car that has a wooden leg.

Evelyn saw Julian riding out to Fort McPherson with Miss Julia Collier one afternoon recently. That night, he approached Julian with a very serious face.

"I'm sorry to hear you are sick?"

"What do you mean?"

"You certainly do look pale. You ought to have known that you can have my bicycle whenever you want it."

"Will you tell me what you mean?"

"Why, I hear you are not able to walk."

Julian saw the point, and ceased to press his inquiries.

Well, Lloyd has some young lady for a guest. They went to Lucien's this afternoon, and then all went for a walk, Lucien with the young lady and Nell and Alleen bringing up the rear. J.C. met them on the street, and came running to the house with this inquiry: "Who is Lucien's new wife?"

I tried to put a mixture of oil of cloves and chloroform on my tooth this afternoon, and the result is a blistered mouth. You may imagine the extent of my lacerated feelings. Mama has a summer cold, and is going about the house with the woebegone look of a woman who has buried her husband and said good-bye to all her friends.

The old cat's little kitten is big enough to run about the yard. The donkey was tied to the cherry tree this afternoon by a long rope, and the kitten was playing about nearby. Presently the kitten ran halfway up the tree. The donkey, not being used to such proceedings, went forward to investigate. He was close to the cat when he saw me, and at once he set up one of his eloquent brays. The kitten turned loose of everything and fell to the ground, but, as the Negroes say, "hit lit a runnin'" and disappeared as suddenly as if it had been shot out of a gun. So you will see that we are having gay times in Wes' Een'.

Our verandah has now come into play, and it is pleasant to sit in the big chairs or swing in the hammock. But for the dry weather, the weather would be fine, but the grass is beginning to look the worse for wear and the *sizzle* of the grasshoppers sounds like meat a-frying in a skillet.

My vacation will begin on the 25th of June, and I think I'll come right down to Washington and spend a day or two until your long-drawn out school concludes to fold its tent. If the town gets too dull for me, I'll go out to the big poplar, and see if it is larger around the waist than Mama or *me*—which isn't good grammar. But the tree doesn't care anything about grammar.

Bob and Brader are both on the veranda talking to Mama's headache; Essie having rushed of [sic] to Alleen's. They say the two B's do as other bees do except to make honey. They buzz and drone monotonously until the mind of the listener fairly shrivels. I reckon it's so, too, for men are poor sticks at best, and it's an awful calamity when they fall below the average.

Of course I had to forget about your films. That's ME all over. But I'll

Commencement Day photograph, 23 June 1897, St. Joseph's Academy; Lillian Harris is in the third row, second from left (Joel Chandler Harris Collection, Special Collections Department, Robert W. Woodruff Library, Emory University).

attend to it this week. The pictures that you *do* take are splendid. The others that you *don't* take are not so good.

Aaron will be published in the fall to meet the holiday trade.—Evelyn is talking about going to Canada. Essie says she'll wait until Mrs. Bunker goes. Charles will probably return next week. He always sends his regards to you when he writes to me or to Mama.

Heigh-ho! I've written a long letter and said nothing. But that's because of the state of the news market.

My regards to Sr. Bernard and Sr. Mary Louis. All send love.

> Your affectionate
> > Daddy

Mr. Rob Otis has just come, and so Mildred has gone for Essie.

ALS
4 pp.

[To Lillian]

30 *May.* [1897]

Dear Billy ann [*sic*]: Your report is horribly good. It makes cold chills run over me to think of the amount of vitality you must expend to get a perfect report. And yet I suppose I would be disappointed and disgruntled if you were to send me poor reports. For my part, I took a distaste to text-books very early in life, and I never see one but it sends a shiver of apprehension over me.—Mama intended to write, but she has had a very bad cold. One day, she was too ill to sit up, and even now she talks in a wheezy tone of voice. Under the circumstances, it has been practically impossible for her to do anything except sniffle and try to clear her throat.—Jesse Cobb has returned from his school and called to see us last night, choosing the romantic hour of 9 p.m. for that purpose[.] Time has evidently dealt Jesse a severe biff. He has cooled down considerably[.] He speaks in a very low and subdued tone, and talks much more sensibly than he did. At least Essie says so; I didn't talk with him myself.—Essie had two callers this afternoon—Rob. Otis and a Mr. Bell.—Quite a cat-(no, a dog-)-astrophe happened in our neighborhood last night[.] Roy had a stray dog named Patsy, which he was very fond of. He and Grace and our children were playing on the sidewalk when Patsy made the mistake of getting under a street-car. You have heard Mildred squeal? Well, she and Grace squealed in concert, but Patsy never heard them. Grace and Roy cried, but Patsy never saw them. Mama heard the extraordinary squealing, and she knew—she just knew—that J.C. had been hurt. She knew it because she had been feeling all the afternoon that something had happened. And wouldn't I go and see about it? Because if it was J.C. she just couldn't bear to go and find it out herself. But we soon learned that Patsy was no more, and everything quieted down again, except the still small voice of Miss Laura who was trying to learn to ride a bicycle in the front of the gate.—Charles will be home to-morrow. He has been planning to surprise his mother, but she, woman-like, read one of his letters to Mr. K., and so found the secret out. It is well-nigh impossible to deceive your sex, my dear.—I have a new bull-terrier pup, white with a speck of brindle on the right ear. His forgiven name is Muldoon. He threatens to be a very fine dog of his kind, though he will never be as beautiful as Mingo was.—The old cow is no better. She is a wreck. I'm sending her out to a swamp near Chloë's, where she may drink branch-water and feed on various "errubs" (which is Chloë's word for herbs) and so, perchance, recover.— J.C. went to his first professional game of baseball yesterday, and was absolutely charmed by it. I think I'd enjoy such things myself if I could make up my mind to go and see them.—I "haven't done a thing" (as the boys say) but forget your films again, and now I'm afraid you'll think I'm too stingy to buy them. But it isn't that. It's just pure forgetfulness. I'll try and remember to get them the first thing in the morning.—I remember Archbishop Gross very well. General Toombs once told me that the Archbishop (he was then Bishop of this diocese) was one of the most brilliant men he had ever met.—If there is anything else you need to complete your *tout ensemble* (as we French say) let us know. If you are to read an essay, you will need a piece of blue ribbon to tie it with, and a fan to hide your embarrassment. I'll come down on the 21st, so as to get a front seat where I can make faces at you when you come forth on the scene.—This is all I have to say at this time, except that the baby is blooming, and the strawberries are nearly all gone. Likewise the dry weather continues with some small promise of rain to-night.

My regards "to all inquiring friends," especially to Sister Bernard and Sister Mary Louis.

>Your affectionate
>>Daddy

ALS
4 pp.

[To Lillian]

6 June. [1897]

My dear Daughter: You are gradually finding out what a fraud your father is. No papers went to you last week. Cause why: Tooth! I haven't been feeling well. Cause why: Tooth!! I don't feel like writing now. Cause why: TOOTH!!! Just one small tooth. I went to have it pulled out Friday, after it had tormented me for three or four days. But Dr. Rosser said he'd save

Chloe Henderson, milker, and sometime maid and cook, for the
Harris family (Joel Chandler Harris Collection, Special Collections
Department, Robert W. Woodruff Library, Emory University).

it by killing the nerve.[1] Well, he killed the nerve; and the affair has left me a physical wreck. It seems that after the nerve was killed, its remains generated a sort of gas, which filtered into my old jaw-bone, and even into my empty head, and you can imagine the various fancy forms of misery that have been my portion. This morning the Doctor bored into the nerve cavity, so as to give the gas an opportunity to escape. Another twelve hours of gas manufacture, and my head would have become a balloon, and the community would have witnessed the phenomenon of a fat man floating through the air supported by his gaseous head. That would have been a spectacle for the population to gaze upon and talk about. I neglected likewise, to turn in the list of words, but nothing is lost by that except a third-rate paper-covered novel: and I have something better than that—"Slav Tales," a collection of the most delightful fairy stories I have read in years.

Essie has about made up her mind to go to Tarenton [Taunton?] when Evelyn does, and he says he will leave about the 28th. Charles has returned, and seems to be much improved. He has fallen into his old friendly habits, and drops in upon us once or twice a day. Bob and Brader continue their merry-go-round. Brader is on the porch while I write.—Did I tell you Ovid is to be married on the 22nd? Julian is to be the bridesmaid—no, no—the best man. I go so little into society that I get the technical terms mixed.—Muldoon is growing very fast, and the cats are giving him a wider berth, yet they sometimes give him a swipe which cools him down. Alleen's baby is not well. Dr. Crow says they have been making its food too strong. It is not as fat as it was, and its eyes have a weak expression; still, it is very lively and cunning.—Pat L. borrowed a dollar from me the other day. I was glad to accommodate him, for he will now avoid me rather than pay it back.—The club will have its picnic Wednesday night. The members were to ask outsiders. Essie invited Charles, but he is going to Chattanooga; so your cousin is left unless she goes with Lucien and Alleen, who are to be the chaperones. She seems to think that would be something terrible; nevertheless she will go.—Mamie Z. makes herself very scarce recently. I have seen her but once since—well, "since the woods were burnt."—And so you weigh only 89 when you should be weighing 115? Well, that is one of the results of chewing a larger intellectual cud than you can digest; and the fact worries me as badly as my gaseous toothaches.

We have had some rain, but not enough. The roses are not flourishing. We ate the last of our strawberries to-day. We have been having beans out of the garden for a fortnight.—Well, I know not what else to say, except that all send you their love. Give my regards to Sister Bernard and Sister Mary Louis.—I will leave here on the late train and get to Washington on the evening of the 21st. If the sisters will permit it, you might go home with Miss Blanch—but no; you will be too busy with your preparations. I'll stop by the Academy as I go to the hotel. However, you can arrange that according to your own desires. Maybe you can meet me at the depot; or maybe not; anyhow, I'll come the 21st, and remain in the village until you are ready to come to this town.

    Your affectionate

    Daddy

ALS

4 pp.

Envelope: Return to Box 111. / Atlanta, Ga. / Miss Lillian Harris, / St. Joseph's Academy, / Washington, / Wilkes County, *Ga.* / Ga. R.R. /

PM: 7 June 1897

1. Probably Dr. Clarence V. Rosser, dentist and neighbor at 428 Gordon.

[To Lillian]

15 June—night. [1897]

———

Dear Sis: I should have written Sunday, but the weather was too hot. When I got through with my editorial work I was exhausted. And so Monday and Tuesday. To-night, it is cloudy and cooler, and so I have taken my pen between my hands to drop you these few lines. The most remarkable part about the whole matter—whatever the whole matter may be—is that there is no more news Wednesday than there was Sunday.—Everything seems to be in a stagnant condition[.] The chickens stand in the pen panting, their arms—no, their wings—half extended, and the birds have ceased to fly about as nervously as they used to do. All on account of the heat. Well, I am very fond of hot weather, and I haven't been uncomfortable, but if I had set under my Welsbach lamp Sunday, Monday, or Tuesday nights (as I am going now) I should have had a bad quarter of an hour.[1] Anyhow, you've no time to read my letters. They're too long and dull. By the time you get through your studies you have to take your beef iron and wine, and by the time you get through with your beef firin [iron] and wine, you have to go to bed. I spoke about you meeting me at the depot for only one reason; viz, to-wit, that is to say: Julian had intended to send you some flowers, and I thought it well to get them into somebody's hands so they could be taken care of. I'll let him send them by express Tuesday—or, I may bring them. There's no telling what I'll do, I'm so old and full of notions.—A Mr. Bell has been coming to see Essie. He had an engagement with her last night. Lula and Laura wanted him to go to Lakewood, but he pleaded the engagement. Then they asked him to bring the young lady, and they nagged him so that he promised. But he came out and stayed here instead, and this morning they are furious. At least I judge so, for sweet Alleen came down and said he was no gentleman, so there! Whether he is not a gentleman be-cause he refused to break his engagement, or because he didn't want to go to Lakewood—which is a pretty tough place for ladies, I don't know.[2] Laura and Lula went to town expecting him to come and bring Essie, but they had to return home. I'm sorry for their disappointment, but I'm not sorry that Essie didn't go.—Well, it is useless for me to write a long letter. I'll see you Tuesday some time—if I can get up courage to go to the Academy alone. You must be on the look-out, for if I go in the gate and don't see you, I shall feel strongly tempted to turn back. Anyhow I'll meet you at the daypo [sic] Thursday morning, and we'll come home together.—Yes, I know Mr. Benson very well. He is one of the most de-lightful men I ever met. His brogue is rich as cream, and delicate as a faint whiff of the shamrock bloom. All send love. My regards to those gentle sisters

    Your affectionate

    Daddy

ALS

3 pp.

Envelope: Return to Box 111, / Atlanta, Ga. / Miss Lillian Harris, / St. Joseph's Academy, / Washington, / Wilkes County, *Ga.* / *Ga.* RR.

PM: 16 June 1897

1. Welsbach light, named for its inventor, Baron Carl Auer von Welsbach.

2. Lakewood Park, an amusement park laid out (1894) on the site of the old Atlanta waterworks by Lakewood Park Company. In 1914–15 its 375 acres became the site for the annual Southeastern Fair, first held in 1916. *Cf.* Garrett 2:299, 664–65. Today, four substantial exhibit halls remain and are used for a flea market and a small movie studio. A concert amphitheater has recently been built on the grounds.

[June 28? 1897][1]

Sunday afternoon.

Dear Evelyn:

Your note, short, sweet and reassuring came duly to hand. It is too hot to write a long letter, so I am replying to your note with a notelet just to assure you we are all well. There have been no changes here. I hear it has been decided not to cut salaries but to get rid of one or two men. L. Hanisse was one. Probably he'll be the only one. Everything seems to be running smoothly. Stanton is sober—too sober, I'm afraid. Our friend Mr. Cramer is on hand, jocund and rosy, reaping the benefits of a fortunate matrimonial alliance. I see little of Mr. Adamson, of course, but that little is a plenty. Julian is still going courting. The baby is teething some more, and, as Mrs. Zachary would remark, "it aint so rotten well." Tootsie went to church today, and says he'll have to keep on now that he's begun, else they'd miss him. J.C. is still worrying with his cough, Bob Jones is dead, and the yaller cat has kittens again. I am glad I am not a yaller cat. 'Twould be too great a strain on my constitution. Ed Love has gone to the fire department, and sends you his regards. So does Reynolds, motorman. The new elevator man is the white drayman who hauls the Constitution to the Post Office—a very clever old man. Charles comes over occasionally—also Brader likewise Bob.

All the rest of the news you will find in The Constitution.

Please send me Essie's address. She forgot to leave it here, and the poor girl will be distressed if she doesn't hear from us soon. I thought your Mama had it, but she doesn't remember it. Consequently Essie will fear the worst.

My love to the dear old folks.

Your affectionate

Daddy

ALS

3 pp.

1. Note on Emory typed copy: "Evelyn Harris was in Upton, Canada when this letter was written." *Cf.* the reference to this trip taken by JCH's niece Essie and son Evelyn in letter to Lillian ("My Dear Daughter," 6 June [1897]).

PART THREE  1897–1898
TWO LITTLE DEARIES
TOGETHER
AT SAINT JOSEPH'S

I always told you our family ought to go on the comic stage. We'd make the biggest hit ever heard of just by transferring to the boards the parts we play at home, and acting them as we do every day. By next June I'll have a circus wagon ready, and then we'll hire an Italian band and take to the road.

—*Letter to Lillian and Mildred, 9 January 1898*

[To Mildred]

Box 111.   *16 September.* [1897]

My Dearest Tommy: As I was passing through the backyard yesterday afternoon, I heard considerable noise at the Guinea pig pen. I thought at first the young ones were squealing for something to eat, but when I crept nearer I found that the little white one was talking. At first I couldn't understand what he was saying, but after listening awhile I managed to catch some of the words, and presently I had no difficulty in understanding what was said. The young ones caught sight of me, and one of the brown ones started to run. "What do you want to run for?" said old Whitey. "Why, pa, there's that old man watching us. What is he going to do?" "Just what he does every day. I'm not afraid of him." "Well, I am, pa—he looks so big and rough." "That's because he's a man, my daughter, I'm not so smooth myself." "Oh, look at him, pa! What is he doing now?" cried another of the brown ones. "Taking a chew of tobacco, my son. I'd like to have some myself." Then the little white one began to talk again, as if in answer to a question I didn't hear. "That great big girl that used to come here and kick up such a racket? Well, I heard somebody say she'd gone off to school. Goodness knows! I hope she'll learn how not to tickle my nose with a straw." "She never tickled *my* nose," said one of the little brown ones; "but I remember she flung an apple at our house and it nearly scared me to death." "Why she didn't throw the apple," explained the old white one, "it dropped from the tree." "Pa, what does 'dropped from the tree' mean?" asked the brown one. "Oh, don't ask such foolish questions; go to bed!" exclaimed the old white one. "But that girl could throw," he went on, turning to his wife. "I believe you!" said the old lady; "I saw her fling something they call a ball, and it hit that Rufus in the shin." "You shouldn't say *shin,* my dear; that is naughty. You should say *chin,*" remarked the old man solemnly. "Much *you* know of *shins* and *chins,*" snapped the old lady. "But, ma,["] said the little one, "Why did they call her Tommy?" "Well," replied old Mrs. Guinea Pig, "that was because she could throw rocks and play ball better than the boys could. "I liked her well enough until she said one day that my eyes were red because I drank too much beer," remarked the old white one. "Well[,] I don't know but it's true," said the old lady; "You certainly do

137

act mighty funny sometimes. I hate for our children to see you go on so. For my part, I'll be glad when the Tommy girl comes back. She won't be gone long. I remember that when J.C. forgot to give us something to eat, she used to come out and give us some herself." "That's so," said the old white one; "but I think she thought more of that brat on the other lot than she did of us." "What[,] that brat is her nephew," said the old lady. "Ma, what is a nephew?" asked little Whitey. "Oh, some kind of a blood cousin," said the mother. "Watch out!" cried one of the little ones; "There comes that abominable dog. They call him Muldoon. He'll stick his nose against this pen once too often." "Oh, he's got a new collar," cried little Whitey. "Yes, indeed," exclaimed the mother. "They think a great deal more of him than they do of us." "Well," said old Whitey, "his day will soon be over. There are some young chickens in the pen next door,—three brown ones and a white one." "Oh, ma! look at the big old fat man laugh," cried one of the brown ones. "Make him go away." "Don't bother," said the old lady. "How can I do anything penned up in this place?" About that time, an apple fell in the box and the whole crowd disappeared like a flash.

There is no news here. Everything is just the same. The Journal got out an extra this morning saying that Flannigan had escaped. But he had merely hid in another cell, while the sheriff and his men were hunting all over DeKalb county.—J.C. is going to school. He seems to be having an easy time. His hard time comes when he gets home and there is no Mildred to play with. Tell Lillian that Miss Collier got back all safe, and said the last she saw of Mildred on the cars, "She was smiling and eating a sandwich." I sent her word that Mildred always smiles when there is food before her.

Give my love to Lillian, saving some for yourself, and my regards to Sister Mary Louis, Sister Bernard, and Sister Sacred Heart.

Your affectionate

Daddy

ALS

3 pp.

Envelope: Return to Box 111, / Atlanta, Ga. / Miss Mildred Harris, / St. Joseph's Academy, / Washington, Ga. / *Wilkes County*

PM: 16 September 1897

Joel Chandler Harris with one of the family's two watchdogs, a pit bull named Muldoon, in the backyard of the Wren's Nest, 1902 (Joel Chandler Harris Collection, Special Collections Department, Robert W. Woodruff Library, Emory University).

[To Lillian]

[20 September 1897]

Monday Eve (*or Aft.*) 20

My Dearest Billy: Your letter was short and sweet—and it is a pity, because Mamma is very anxious to hear about her girls. We have not heard a word from Mildred. Will you kindly give Sister Mary Louis a hint to make Tommy write if it is only a line or two. I'd like to know just how she feels about matters and things, and what her views are about eating and sleeping away from home—I hope Sister Mary Louis has been able to explain to your satisfaction. She seems to have been flirting (if I may use the word lightly) with several of you girls at once.—The news here is like the weather, dry. I see very few people except Rufus and Chloë. Rufus has a new bloomer dress which he wore Sunday. It is cut bias behind, with a yoke in front, and a ruffle around the bottom to make room for his feet.—Muldoon has a new collar, and I have four new Leghorn hens. The roses are blooming very nicely, and poke-berries are ripe, which is very good for the mocking-birds.—J.C. is now umble-come-tumble with Luther, and we have a great riding of donkeys, and various processions of howling kids, going up and down seeking whom they mought [*sic*] devour.—Banks stuck a nail in his foot, and now has to haul it in a dray on account of the swelling.—I went out yesterday to the Stewart place to see the famous Jackson cotton[.] I'm glad I did. It is quite a spectacle, being entirely different from our cotton. I can give you a rough outline of the difference—[sketch detailing plants] [1][.] I am writing you this because I don't know what else to write. Get a bottle of Paine's Celery Compound and take according to directions. *Don't fail in this,* and while you are taking it stop your wine. I am sending you some films. Get Sister Bernard and Mary Louis in the light and take a good picture of each. And also of Sister Sacred Heart. And if you can catch Father O'Brien do so. I'll write a longer letter later in the week, and enclose cheques to the Dear Sisters, simply enclosing with this my Kindest regards.

> With Love from your
> Affectionate
> Daddy

ALS
2 pp.
Envelope: Return to Box 111, / *Atlanta, Ga.* / Miss Lillian Harris, / St. Joseph's Academy, / Washington, Ga. / Wilkes County
PM: 21 September 1897
1. Notes by two plants: "3 *ft/6 bolls*/our cotton" and "15 ft/82 *bolls*/Jackson limbless." *Cf.* picture and article on Jackson African Limbless Cotton in Atlanta *Constitution*, Sunday, 2 October 1898, 9.

[To Mildred]

[22 September 1897]

An *Ode on* Weeps.
They say that Mildred cried O, and cut up such a dido
　　The Sisters knew not what to do.
Said Sister Sacred Heart, "I'll try and do my part,
　　"And help her out with my boo-hoo."
But Sister Mary Bernard, who from Northern lands had journeyed,
　　Declared that she would help out too;
Said Sister Mary Louis, (a correspondent cu'ous)*
　　"I'll drop a letter in her shoe."
And there never were such doin's, such weepin's, and boo-hooin's
　　Seen in St. Joseph's house before
And Father O'Brien comes creeping up and pryin',
　　"And," says he, "I'm not denyin' that this is real sighin',
　　But when it comes to cryin'
　　Just watch me rise and walk the floor.["]

———

And, that's the news that comes from here, from a little bird that hums here
　　　　And he said it was a sight to see
　　　Sweet Mildred a-cryin' and all the rest a-sighin'
　　　　With hearts as full as hearts could be.
　　　　(Carefully copied from the New Edition of Poems by
　　　　W. Shakespere. London: Lovingood, publisher)

*She wrote Lillian lev'mteen letters this summer.

AL

1 p.

Envelope: Return to Box 111, / Atlanta, Ga. / Miss Mildred Harris, / St. Joseph's Academy, / Wilkes County, / Washington, *Ga.*

PM: 22 September 1897

[To Lillian]

[27 September 1897]

Sunday afternoon (and still

a-heating)

Dear Daughter: I have just written to Mildred, and write this note to en-close the promised cheques. Don't count this as a letter. I'll write more at length Tuesday. I am having the Journal sent to you, and I think I'll send The Constitution—if I can think to do so. Mamma is fixing up some mysterious package or box for you—or something of that sort. I'll see that she puts in the sweetenin'. I am sending you two bundles of papers—among them St. Nicholas—But this is not a letter. Therefore, I'll close with love to you and regards to the good sisters. When Sister Sacred Heart wants the money for Mildred's music and for your painting and firing [?],[1] tell her to please send bills.

Your 'fectionate

Daddy

ALS

1 p.

Envelope: Return to Box 111, / Atlanta, Ga. / Miss Lillian Harris, / Washington, / Wilkes county, / *Ga.* / *St. Joseph's Academy* / Ga. R.R.

PM: 27 September 1897

1. This word is not clear. Perhaps it is firing, as girls did china painting and products would be fired. It might be finery, but there seem to be two letter is in the word.

[To Lillian]

[28 September 1897]

Dear Bill-Ann: "Tis now the afternoon of the 28th, and I am writing with a new fountain pen. I hope there is something in it worth getting out, for there is not much out of it worth getting in—certainly not much in the way of news.—Essie has gone back to St. Hyacinthe, and is using "is" in the plural and "shall" for "will" with renewed energy and vigor. As she gets farther north, her grammar seems to fall to pieces, which is funny, considering how sensitive she is to criticism. She seems to have found her match in Aunt Josephine—the Lady of the Tumors—and is very glad to get out of reach of that railing and irritating voice.—We had quite a sensation in our neighborhood last night. Mama, who has a fine ear and eye for these things, heard some loud talking, followed by some equally loud wailing. By her desire, I went to the big gate to discover what it was and what it all was about. I soon found that the Voice (it deserves a capital V) emanated from the Lovett Mansion. Something had gone wrong at that Mansion, and Lord Lovett was making a riotous speech at the top of his Voice. Whether this vociferation was occasioned by the Total Deafness (I continue the Capitals) of Lady Lovett, or by the Heartrending Conduct of the Children, I couldn't discover; but I observed not without a Secret Satisfaction, that when Lord Lovett took occasion to rest his Voice, he improved the Opportunity to Pound most severely on his Children, who are no doubt the Idols of his Heart. I returned and made a Faithful Report of My Observations, as becomes A Dutiful Husband. But this was not Satisfactory to Mama, who, with that Insatiable Curiosity characteristic of her Charming Sex, insisted on Investigating the Trouble for Herself. So, taking J.C. by the Hand, she wended her way out upon the Public Thoroughfare, and so to within Hearing Distance of the Lovett Mansion. The Uproar continued, and likewise the Pounding upon the Children, but to what End (except the several and various Ends of the Youngsters) and to What Purpose, even your Inquisitive Mama failed to Discover. Hence we are in the Midst of a great Mystery, with no Clue to carry us out, or to lead us, as it were, to the Light. And the Mystery is this: that a Man so Lazy as Lord Lovett should suddenly break out like a raging Volcano without sending word to his Neighbors and warning them of what was about to occur. It must have been something very Terrible, for the Children of Lord Lovett have [been] Running About, seeing What Mischief they could do for, lo, these many Weary Months.[1] We will now dismiss the Lovett Episode with such Benediction as seems

Suitable to a perverse and hard headed generation.—The baby is said to have a very bad cold, (I have not seen him to-day), brought about, no doubt by too much care.—Julian seems to be preparing for the ordeal. He has ceased to be Gay. Indeed, he is almost solemn. He continues to call the Bride-Elect "Miss Collier," and she, on her part, reciprocates by continuing to call him "Mr. Harris" very Sweetly, I must admit, but still, somewhat Coldly. Mama has just rigged out to call on the Young lady.[2] She has on a Magenta waist with a scarlet front, surmounted by a black lace bretelle, and supplemented by a black silk skirt.[3] The bretelle gives her a fluffy look, but I dare not say so, lest she should weep and refuse to go.—J.C. has four bantams, three hens and a red rooster. They are not entrancing in their appearance, but he seems to think they are what they should be.—I hope Mildred, under the gentle ministrations of the Sisters, is becoming reconciled to the Academy. For your promptness in taking Celery Compound, many thanks. Bumps are a sign of bad blood, and the compound will drive them out, and give you a good complexion. Don't stop at one bottle, but get another when that is out, and take according to directions. And if Mildred looks weary or tired, make her take some too. It is better than pills, for it is a tonic too. You will not need wine while you are taking the compound. Persevere until all the bumps have disappeared.—When next you write me a "long" letter, count the words in this and then in yours, and thus discover what a long letter really is. My love to Mildred, and tell her to write again. Regards to the Sisters.

From your loving

Daddy

ALS

3 pp.

Envelope: Return to Box 111, / Atlanta, Ga. / Miss Lillian Harris, / St. Joseph's Academy, / Washington, / Wilkes county, Ga. / Ga. R.R.

PM: 29 September 1897

1. The R. O. Lovett family lived at 333 Gordon. Mr. Lovett was a lawyer.

2. Capitalization of words and stilted style continues in imitation of George Ade's popular fables in slang.

3. Bretelle, a decorative shoulder-strap like a suspender.

[To Mildred]

[3 October 1897] [1]

3 *September.* [1897]

My Dearest Tommy: Your letters are very cute indeed—cute and short. I notice you say that my letters are "dear." That would be true if they were written for publication—$20, $30, and $50 a thousand words. The publishers sometimes think they are too dear.—Mamma says she can't write to-day. She has a bad cold and is dalki'g through her doze. Says she: "Dell de girls I ca'd wride do-day; by Doze is stobbed ub." Says I: "I hobe you don't wride wid your doze; I don't wride wid bine." She would have said something in reply, but she had to sneeze, and while she was preparing to do so, I made good my escape.—J.C. is now experimenting in top-spinning. I suppose by that, that the top season has arrived. He does pretty well; but I have been telling him that he should have you here to show him how to spin a top.—Toodie is looking peaked and puny. He has been sick again on account of his teeth, and had to have the doctor. But he's better to-day—in fact, well enough to come down here. Still, he is not lively, but fretful, and has lost some flesh. We'll soon have cold weather, and then Toodie will be all right. I showed him your picture to-day and he took it and kissed it, and then looked at me and said *"Ai?"* "You are right, young man," said I, "she's the girl that loves you." *"Ah?"* And so on and so on.—I hope Lillian wasn't scared when the trunk reached her to be paid for. It was Evelyn's fault. He left the matter in the hands of the baggage transfer, and the man just sent it off c.o.d. Evelyn then wrote her a letter and sent her some money. We're a funny crowd. We always get mixed up when there's anything unusual to be done. Still, if Lillian wasn't scared when she had to pay the expressage, or if the good sisters didn't think we were all crazy, why there's no harm done.—One afternoon not long ago, while your mama was up town, Nelly chewed her rope in two, and got loose. Rufus chased her around awhile, but she finally went out at the big gate. Rufus would have gone after, but it was getting late, and I told him to let her alone. Then I shut both gates, intending to get rid of the donkey for good and all. But it was not to be. Just then Mama stepped from the car and asked me what I was doing at the front gate at that time of day. Nelly was then standing under the electric light at Frazier's. I pointed in that direction. Then there was a scene! "Rufus! Why didn't you send Rufus after her? I never did see such a man. That's the way! Something always goes wrong when I'm away." Then Mama rushed to the house, flung her hat on the bed, and rushed out again with J.C. The upshot of it was that they drove the donkey back in triumph. I never will get rid of that donkey. She sticks to us like a redbug. Wouldn't the sisters like to have a donkey warranted to eat a panel of fence a day? I think Nelly would enjoy the picket-fence around the Academy. The pickets are so small she wouldn't have much chewing to do.—When the weather gets cold enough, I'm going to send four boxes of marsh-mallows to you and Lillian so that you can have some fun roasting them.—You'd find it much duller at home if you were here than it is at the Academy. Be as much of a tomboy as the sisters will permit, and continue to write me those pretty little letters. They are so very short. I think you might send two a week, but if it would be tiresome to you no matter. Little girls mustn't be made too tired.— I'll write to Miss Billy Ann Tuesday. My best regards to Sr. Mary Louis, Sr. Bernard, and Sr. Sacred Heart.

    From your devoted
      Daddy

ALS
3 pp.
Envelope: Return to Box 111, / Atlanta, Ga. / Miss Mildred Harris, / St. Joseph's Academy, / Washington, Ga. / Wilkes county. /
PM: 4 October 1897
  1. Dated by detached envelope with note "Amusing acc't of donkey's escape."

[To Lillian]

                          6 October. [1897]
My Dear Billy-Ann: I intended to write to you yesterday afternoon, but we had distinguished company: the baby and he [sic] sick. He is cutting five teeth at once, and his gums were so sore that he wouldn't eat, or drink, or sit still, or move about, or sit up, or lie down, or go, or stay. In short, he was in such a tantrum that Alleen couldn't nurse him while Ida got dinner, and so we had them all down here. The kid is better to-

day. His teeth are about through, and, as a consequence, he is at peace with all the world and the rest of mankind.—We have all our stoves up, and this morning Rufus built a fire in the dining-room, the result being that the weather is hotter than it has been any day this season. To add to the horrors of a terrible situation the stove has been smoking, and is still engaged in that business.—It is funny—or, rather, not at all funny—that you haven't said anything about receiving or not receiving your trunk. I hope the trains are still running. If not, you stand a desperate chance of getting home by Christmas. If you have to walk, you could get here in time by starting now.—Of course you would have written a line if you had received your trunk, or failed to receive it; therefore, I think the worst has happened—you have and you have not received it. I wish something unique would happen to me that way. I'd like so much to receive and not receive something at the same time. The next thing to an experience of that kind would be to learn that Sister Mary Louis has written a letter to someone.—Julian is going ahead fixing up. He has bought 2 overcoats, 2 hats, 2 pairs of shoes, 5 suits of clothes, and ever so many other things of various lengths and thicknesses. He puts me in mind of an old maid up a tree. He wants everything except a ladder— and a ladder is the very thing he wants.—Mamma is also fixing up. She's to have some new duds of some kind, goodness knows what. Yet I'm painfully aware of a yard of real Duchesse lace that is to be grouped under her chin, the group to cost anywhere from $12 to $15. Being old, I do not complain, and I am only telling you these things in order to interest you.[1]—I saw Mrs. Zachry this morning.[2] She looked like she had been flung over the fence and hauled around the backyard, which is the way Mama looks when she's house-cleaning. I have never been able to understand why a lady had to be so dirty in order to clean a house that is already clean. Does Sister Mary Louis, or Sister Sacred Heart have that appearance when there is cleaning to do on Academy Hill?—I hope Mildred is feeling pretty well by this time. Usually it takes her a long time to feel pretty well, but when she does reach the much-desired point, she feels better than anybody in the neighborhood.—Mrs. Bunker has returned, and has begun to give her bell-like voice to the breeze.[3] If the breeze has ears as uncultivated as mine, it will blow hereafter in some other part of the country. It's not the bell-like voice I object to, but the size of the bell.

You'll think, of course, that I haven't written you all the news, but I have, and some more besides. Essie seems to be getting a trifle restless; but I suppose that is a mere symptom which any French young man can cure with the tip of the hat and a "Bon jour, Ma'mselle!" I had the Journal sent to you, but I don't know whether you are receiving it. In short, I know less now than I did when I knew more. My knowledge-box is a refrigerater which condenses, and a good deal of vapor escapes in the process. As to girl news, I know none. I see 'em on the car and hear 'em giggle, and that's all there is to it. Mamie Zachry looks like she needs squills. All the rest of them I'd give Jamaica Ginger.[4]—The baby is better to-day.

Here I must close, after having written a good many things that I can't vouch for.

Regards to Sister Sacred Heart, Sister Bernard, and Sister Mary Louis, that favored letter-writer.

From your loving
Daddy

ALS
3 pp.
Envelope: Return to Box 111 / *Atlanta, Ga.* / Miss Lillian Harris, / St. Joseph's Academy, / Washington, / Wilkes county, Ga. / Ga. R.R.
PM: 7 October 1897.
1. JCH refers comically to the clothes and preparations for Julian's marriage to Julia Collier on 26 October 1897.
2. Probably Mrs. James B. Zachry of 357 Lee Street.
3. Probably Mrs. Frank R. Bunker of 294 Gordon Street.
4. Squills and Jamaica Ginger were patent medicines.

11 October [1897]

Dear Billy-Ann and Tommyldred: You'll have to excuse me this time for bunching your letters, but I'm sick with a cold. My left eye aches, I have a fever blister on my nose, and a gum-boil on my chin. And I'm filled with a desperate determination to "blow my doze," as Mama says, every minute in the day. This is what I get for making fun of Mama in the letter that Lillian says she didn't get. I wrote to her last Wednesday, and it was a real letter, too—a great deal longer than those she used to get from Sister Mary Louis. It rained all night Sunday night, and all day yesterday—which was a welcome relief from the long drouth we had been having.—The baby is very much better—well, in fact, and has an appetite like a hippopotamus. J.C. is ailing again—fever, cough and all the old symptoms of bronchitis.—Towards the close of Mildred's last letter, she seemed to grow somewhat impatient. In fact she seems not to want to write. Well, just say to her that if it worries her to write her old daddy, she can postpone it as long as she pleases. If it is a task for her to write, she needn't write. Of course I am delighted to hear from her, but if it is too much of a task, or is tiresome to her, why, then, she can write only when she wants to.—I hope her cold is better, and that she has found out how to be happy at the convent.—I presume Burdeen's people are afraid of the yellow fever, but there is not a particle of danger. There has been a case in town, but nobody was afraid of it. The child that had it is well, and that is the end of the matter for this season. We have already had a frost here.—I don't know a particle of news that would interest you two girls, and I'm not able, feeling as I do, to write you a letter that is worth reading.—I sent Lillian the first copy of *Aaron in the W. w.* that came from the press; but it was intended for both of you to read, and, after that, it is to go in the Academy library.[1] I forgot to put my name in it, but that will make no difference. It could easily be a better book, but in that case it would have to be written by someone else.—I hope Lillian received my last Wednesday's letter after she wrote. Is her face "as big as the full moon" on account of the bumps, or on account of a gain in flesh? I hope it is the latter,—and, with this hope I shall have to close, for I am to [sic] badly stewed up to write at greater length.

> From your devoted
> Daddy

ALS
2 pp.
Envelope: Return to Box 111, / *Atlanta, Ga.* / Miss Lillian Harris / St. Joseph's Academy, / Washington, / Wilkes county, Ga. / Ga. RR.
PM: 12 October 1897
1. *Aaron in the Wildwoods* (1897).

Monday night. [16 November 1897]

[sketch of guinea pig][1]

Dear Lillian and Mildred:

To begin with I'll write to both of you at once. This is because I have nothing to write about. Nothing happens that the newspapers don't get, and sometimes they get a good many things that don't happen. At home nothing happens, except that the vestibule clock has begun to run again. The weather is warm, and the violets are not doing well, but occasionally we have a very pretty rose. The leaves are falling very rapidly, and Mamma is doing her best to have Rufus clean off the front; but the more Rufus cleans the more leaves fall, and so we are in a considerable of a fix.—Toody doesn't come down as often as he did; I mean he doesn't come in the house as often.[2] Ida had him down this afternoon, and wanted to bring him in the house, but I told her we had drawn the line since Mildred went away. He might come as far as the well, but we didn't want him in the house. So he didn't go in. Brader comes over occasionally to brush his clothes, but Charles has deserted us. J.C. went to the dog and pony show the other day, and has had a good deal to say about it. But that's nothing. He has a good deal to say about everything, especially when we have pig's feet for supper.—Banks came around to-day.[3] He says he has heart-trouble and seems to be very proud of it. He remarked with a sort of triumphant smile that the doctor said his heart had a "murmur." This means that he has an aneurism of the heart, and is therefore not long for this world. I didn't explain the matter to him. I have hired a man named Calvin to do my work.—I hope the girls went to the circus—and yet I suppose the sisters would hesitate about taking them. Well, you know how I am. I like to see young people have all the harmless fun they can.—I do hope that my dear little Mildred is trying to be good. If she gets too hard-headed, I hope somebody will drop me a line about it. Such a letter would make me feel very badly; but I want to know the facts.—Julian was to start home Sunday, so Julia wrote your mama. They were to return with George Adair and his wife. Alleen saw George to-day (Monday), so I suppose the two darling ducky-dories have returned also. Or they may have stopped in the capital of our common country to make sure that Mr. McKinley is doing his whole duty.[4]—We should have been very glad to entertain Burdeene a few days, or, at least, to meet her at the depot, and see her safely on the way. Why didn't Sister Sacred Heart make some arrangement of that kind? I told you to tell her to.—But here I am at the end of my row.[5]

> Your loving
>> Daddy

ALS

2 pp.

Envelope: Return to Box 111, / Atlanta, Ga. / Miss Lillian Harris, / St. Joseph's Academy, / Washington, *Ga.* / Wilkes County

PM: 16 November 1897

1. Signed "By Dad."

2. Toody, pet name for Stewart Harris, the first grandchild and son of Lucien and Aileen Harris.

3. Banks was the Negro gardener.

4. President McKinley, newly elected.

5. Bottom of sheet.

[Letter to Lillian and Mildred, fragment starting page 2.]

[November 1897]

very deep tone of voice if I want Mildred to take private elecution [*sic*] lessons. That depends on whether the Sisters think she has any talent in that line, and likewise on the price. If she has a talent that can be developed, I have no objection.—I'll be sending you a barrel of apples for Thanksgiving, and I expect your Mother will have a box for you.— Essie is in Upton. I judge from her last letter that she finds it somewhat dull as compared with *Sant-ya-san´* [*sic*]. I also think that she'll be after coming home before long. Perhaps your grandmother will come with her.—Alleen is looking better, and so is Toody-Boo, since Ida has been able to devote all her time to him. Alleen has hired a woman to cook, wash and iron, and pays only 50 cents a week more than she paid for the washing alone.—You'll see something in Sunday's paper about the killing of two brothers named Harris in Waco, Texas.[1] They were brothers of Percy Harris who used to board with Mrs. Abernethy.—J.C. remains very much pleased with his guinea pigs. They seem to have an attraction for him.—Chloë has a new son, who is said to be very black and greasy.—Toody-Boo knows Mildred's picture from all the rest, and tries to hug and kiss it every time he get[s] a chance.—To-night, Mama has a very severe headache, the result of the strain of fixing up for Julia 'n Julian—and she fixed up very nicely too—everything according to the latest modes, fashions, styles and authorities, with Rufus on hand to catch the ceiling if it fell, and Ed in the kitchen to taste of the dishes before they came to the table. Evelyn was on hand, too, and he did some very good talking. J.C. was on hand, too, and behaved very prettily. He picked some rose buds for Julia, and he presented them very politely when she went to leave.—

Well, this is all I know, and, after all, it is not worth knowing. Write when you can to your loving

Daddy

ALS

2 pp. of 3

1. See Atlanta *Constitution*, Sunday, 21 November 1897, 4, for this news item which dates the letter.

[To Lillian and Mildred]

Sunday Evening [late November 1897]

Dear Girls: Howdye? I don't know what date this is because my "vaccinate" is beginning to itch. Anyhow, it's Sunday, and my time to write. Just because the negroes on Decatur street have become infected with the small-pox, the city authorities, including Julian's new poppa,[1] have decided that Tom, Dick, Harry and Susan Jane shall be vaccinated. Well, it does no harm, and it is the only way to reach the negroes. When they see the whites yielding to compulsory vaccination, they are readier to yield themselves, if only for the sake of imitation. The disease is confined entirely to the negroes, and there have been no deaths among them.—The letters you write, dear girls, are very modest and shy. You seem to be afraid of shedding ink; but if it is bad to shed ink, think what a black-handed criminal your daddy is. It is bad to shed blood, but even Job wanted his enemy to write a book, though probably in that day, writing a book did not involve the shedding of ink.—Anyhow, I'm not complaining, merely teasing. I'm so glad to get even a short letter from each of you that I have no room to complain.—It is very cold here to-night, and everything will be friz up in the morning—and so I have just this moment been out and shut the water off so as to keep the pipes from freezing[.] This was mama's suggestion, though I don't think it's cold enough for that; but then Mama has been vaccinated. She stood it right well, too, for an old lady. When she bared her arm it was so large, and fat and white it looked for all the world like the wide side of a bolster, only wider. Rufus was also vaccinated. He showed his teeth as if he were trying to laugh, but he rolled his eyes around in a very dismal way— especially when he saw Dr. Crow's knife. Toody-Boo was on hand this afternoon, and spent quite awhile here rushing around from stove to fireplace.[2] Lucien and Alleen didn't come. They thought Julian and his wife would be out. But this last couple are not inclined to visit much— not just yet. I think they are trying to get acquainted with each other. But Julian is at work. They were out to see us last Tuesday, on their way to the woods. They had Ellinor, and came by for J.C. Coming back, they stopped long enough for Julian to indulge in a lot of guying. It's funny that I, who am so fond of guying people, should dislike to hear others engage in it.—I'm glad to hear there is a hope that Burdeene will return with you. She'll be very welcome, as you know, and we'll treat her just as if she were home folks. Evelyn is now doing day work. That is, he gets to work about twelve M.,[3] and returns home on the last car at night, sometimes a little earlier.—I don't think Essie will be home before Christmas. I knew she'd like to come, but grandma can't come before Aunt Josephine returns from Montreal—though it is possible that Josephine may go home earlier than she expected.[4]—Till to-day, we've been having what the British call "nawsty weather, dontcherno." Clouds, rain and gloom. I tried to have the blues, but somehow they wouldn't "take." When I feel like I ought to have the blues, so as to do like other people, something is sure to happen to take my mind off, and set me to laughing [.] A lady once told me she thought it would be dreadful if she couldn't have the blues; and there are a great many people who are never happy unless they are unhappy.—Mildred is getting so she writes very nice letters, and, somehow, by a word, or a turn of expression, she happens to put herself into them. She'd be great if she'd be good—I don't mean prim and solemn, but good enough to mind and to attend to all her duties, which are smaller and easier now than they ever will be again.—Mrs. Fulgin (how do you spell her name?) has gone to Macon to keep her baby from being vaccinated. Toody-Boo will not be vaccinated, as he is teething, and as both Alleen's servants have been vaccinated.— Roy has turned his pigeons out, and now feels better.—J.C.'s bantam hen is laying, and his guinea pigs continue to whistle for food though they get plenty. This is all I know. Regards to the Sisters.

> Your affectionate
> Daddy

ALS
3 pp.

1. Reference to Julian's father-in-law, Charles Collier. Julia and Julian were married 26 October 1897. Smallpox had spread from Griffin, Georgia, to Atlanta. See Atlanta *Constitution*, 23 November 1897, 8, for one of the first notices about smallpox inoculation in Atlanta.

2. Toody-Boo, JCH's pet name for Stewart Harris.

3. *Meridiem meridies* (noon), Latin abbreviation.

4. Mrs. JCH's relatives: niece, Essie LaRose; mother, Mrs. Pierre LaRose; and Aunt Josephine LaRose.

[To Lillian and Mildred]

Sunday evening. [December 1897]

Dear Girls: I'm about to write, with nothing to write about. And this reminds me that it would be better if each of you would write one letter a week, the letters to be to both mama and papa. This will save you the worry of writing two letters each week. Therefore let Lillian write one letter to Mama and papa, and Mildred one letter to Mama and papa each week. Make them as long as you can or as short as you please. I'm glad you liked the apples, and I'm pleased to know you divided with the girls. I know you didn't forget the sisters. We had L. and A, and the baby for Thanksgiving.[1] The baby wrote a letter to Mildred. He used the Portuguese language so as to make it interesting[.] He told everybody what he was writing, but I couldn't hear what he was saying. He held the pencil in both hands and perspired freely[.] It was a big undertaking.— Roy and Fritz brought Mrs. Cobb's old chicken-eating cat over yesterday, and asked if I would let the dogs kill it. I consented, thinking the cat would get away. But I didn't know Muldoon. They carried the cat in a sack to the middle of the pasture, put it down and called the dogs. They were very much surprised to see the sack jumping up and down, and they also jumped up and down. Finally the cat rushed out when the dogs were not looking, and had a good start. Muldoon, however, caught sight of it, and was off like a shot. The cat got as far as Richardson's fence and jumped to the top; but Muldoon was there also, and jumped as high as the fence, pulling the cat down again. You can guess the rest. For about two minutes, Muldoon's whole nature seemed to be changed and he made short work of the cat. I was sorry when it was too late, but the cat didn't suffer any at all. Muldoon broke its neck almost instantly. But I have made up my mind not to have any more such affairs in my back yard.—Brader has just come in to return a book, and he will sit up with Mama's headache for some hours. She had just said she hoped he wouldn't come.—I heard a man on the car say that he heard Santa Claus would fail to come to Atlanta this year for fear of catching the small-pox. How true it is I don't know, but I thought the news would interest Mildred. For my part, I should think that Santa Claus would have experience enough to get vaccinated.—I hope Burdeene will come with Lillian. What is to prevent her coming? We should be delighted to have her—and I wouldn't say so if I didn't mean it. Therefore, I put in this petition to Sister Sacred Heart: Won't you please, dear Sister, permit Burdeene to spend the holidays with Lillian? She will be taken care of as if she were our own daughter, and while she might enjoy herself better somewhere else, I'm sure she'd be as welcome here as if she were one of ours. Now, then, Sister Sacred Heart! won't you listen to reason?—We are not having very gay times here now, owing to. . . [.][2]

ALS

4 pp.

1. Lucien and Aileen Harris, with son Stewart, born 27 October 1896.

2. Letter on short sheets, rest of original text missing. For continuation in printed, edited version, see *URM* 24, no. 4 (December 1908), 28.

[13 December 1897]

Sunday Night.

Dear Girls: Again we have Brader with us, but we are not as bad off as Miss Emma, who burnt her foot, and then went to the store and clerked on it until she is now threatened with dyspep—no, elyslipperus—oh, pshaw! erysipelas.[1] So there she is. But that doesn't prevent mama from trading up there.—We are having more sensations here than a mule can tote. The old Mobley house burned the other night, and not a thing was saved except a wheelbarrow and a door-knob. Mrs. Ellis and hubby, and Miss Hardman were up town. Miss H. lost all her clothes, which she had bought to go to Europe in. I always thought they went in ships, but I heard Mama tell Mrs. Young that Miss Hardman had bought these clothes to go to Europe in.[2]—And that's not all. The boys jumped a big gray rabbit in the yard and the dogs ran it around and und[er] the house, and under the barn, and then under the servants' house, and there they caught it. It is now in Fritz Wagner's pen. And J.C.'s vaccination is taking, and he's so proud of it he wants to show it to everybody[.] He went to bed early to-night, seeming to be proud of the fact that he wasn't feeling well enough to sit up long.—Well, there isn't anything the matter with Goodly-Boo.[3] He's as lively as a cricket. He can say wa'-wa' when he wants his morning dram.—So we are to get you girls in our stockings Christmas Eve? Well, Mama's may be large enough to hold you, but mine are not. Just think it's only twelve more days. Don't let Burdeene back out. She may not have much fun, but it will be a change for her, and maybe she'll enjoy it. I'll send the sisters a barrel of apples in time for Christmas Eve if I can get some good ones. The violets are blooming very prettily, and I hope we'll have some for Christmas. The roses also continue to bloom, so you see we have had no *very* cold weather. Yet it is sometimes chilly, and sometimes drizzly. We can't have everything the way we want it. I think Mildred's Christmas appetite is somewhat too large for Santa Claus's bundle. I'm writing this because I have nothing else to do. I'll try and write a longer letter during the week if I can think of anything to write. It is very dull here. All are well except J.C.'s vaccinate [sic]. My regards to Sister Bernard and the rest, and love to you both.

From your affectionate
Daddy

ALS
2 pp.

Envelope: Miss Lillian Harris, / St. Joseph's Academy, / Washington, Ga. / *Wilkes County*

PM: 13 December 1897

1. Erysipelas, "An inflammatory specific disease, usually confined to the skin, but sometimes extending to the subjacent connective tissue, and accompanied by fever, Saint Anthony's fire." (*Funk and Wagnall's New Standard Dictionary of the English Language*, 1959, s.v. "erysipelas.")

2. *Cf.* this with JCH's familiar humorous paragraphs in the Atlanta *Constitution* and other newspapers earlier.

3. Stewart Harris, son of Lucien and Aileen Harris.

[1897?]

Sunday afternoon—and hot

Dear Mildred: Your letters are short and sweet. I am glad you like hash; we are preparing to have it twice a day when you come home Christmas, and, as for alcoves, why you can sleep in the lumber room upstairs— a glorious place on a stormy night. You can hear the rain pattering up there, and, in the pauses of the wind, the Booger Man will sneeze. I should like to sleep up there myself if I were a little girl.—By this time, no doubt, you have gained twenty more pounds. That's the reason your shoes don't fit. Well, I'll take Rufus to town with me tomorrow, and let him try on girl's shoes till he finds a pair to fit him, and these I'll send to you. If your feet keep on growing you'll need two alcoves to stand in, and two beds to sleep in.—All the children around here are up and about. Roy looks a little paler since you left, and I think he is suffering some. His mouth twitches a little more than usual, and his finger-nails are longer. I think he is grieving after you.—The donkey continues to make remarks at regular intervals, and the rooster to crow. The baby wants to walk so bad he tries to run. Mrs. Fuljon's [sic] baby is looking pale. I think the nurse feeds it on green persimmons. By-the-by, the persimmons are ripe, and J.C. says they are fine. The Goodman boys were over here yesterday, and Harold's pants fit him quicker than ever. The Rosser kids haven't been over since you left, consequently we've been able to hear the donkey when he had anything to say. Tootsie is carrying Alleen and the baby to ride this afternoon, and I suppose they'll have a very pleasant time, owing to the dust, which is as thick as a piece of pine bark.—I'm glad to know that you are to learn how to hold your hands while playing the piano. When you get to be a young lady, I'll show you how not to walk pigeon toed.—J.C. went doodle-hunting yesterday. I don't know what success he had, but I suppose he bagged a good deal of game.—Banks stuck a nail in his foot and it flew to his head. Anyhow, he hasn't been back to work,—and Johnson's got a new wagon.— This is all the news I know at present. If we could have rain maybe I'd have something more to write about.—I hope you won't lose your high spirits. You can be good and nice, and still be as lively as a tomboy. Play all you can, and tell Sister Mary Louis not to make you study too hard.

> Your 'fectionate
> Daddy

ALS
2 pp.

[To Lillian and Mildred]

> 19 December. [1897]

Dear Girls: I enclose two cheques, both payable to the Sisters[,] one for the Sisters, the other for yourselves. You may pay Burdeene's fare if she'll let you, if not you can get some presents for somebody. Tell Mildred to write at once to Mama and tell her what presents she wants bought for her to give to others. Mama will not write this week, as she'll be so busy fixing for Christmas, and I'm not going to write a long letter myself— mainly because there isn't anything of interest to write about. We have the cutest present for both of you that you ever saw. *Fine!* Some of us will meet you at the train. All well here, but the weather is gloomy[.] We don't know yet when Essie will return. But Brader will return to-morrow night. You'll say this letter is short. Well, the week will be short and then you'll be with us. Regards to all.

> Your loving
> Daddy

ALS
1 p.

[To Lillian and Mildred]

9 Janiwary. [1898]

Dear Girls: I missed you so much, including Burdeene, that I went to bed with the sick headache on Wednesday, and did no work until yesterday. I hope Mildred will try to get at least a piece of her mind satisfied. I think she's "putting on" anyway. Her home-sickness is like the kind of love they have on the stage, "for this occasion only." Burdeene was so glad to get away that she has actually written a letter thanking us for setting the clocks up every day while she was here. Thank her for her pretty letter, we appreciate it very much. She added a great deal to our enjoyment not only by her mere presence, but by playing on the piano; in short she made everything that much lovelier.—I saw the man from whom I bought the apples—Mr. Hods—and he showed me the express receipt. The barrel was shipped on the 23d. We are going to stir up the matter and see what has become of the apples. They were addressed "Sisters of St. Joseph, Washington, Ga," and express prepaid. Well, there's no use worrying about them, only I'm sorry the sisters didn't get them.— Chan Harris is getting along fine so far as sleeping is concerned.[1] He eats, sleeps and grows. Stewart Harris is fat and reckless. Alleen Harris is up and about and looking very well. Lucien Harris is about the same. Lily Harris calls for more vittles. Lucille Harris is glad it isn't fly-time. Valentine Harris looks forward to spring. Daisy Harris takes things easy. Nelly Harris continues to talk over the fence.[2] All that news is important.—Mamma had some tickets to the Lyceum yesterday, but she went to the Grand instead.[3] The man at the door took 'em all right, but the gentlemanly usher informed her that she was in the wrong pew— and then what a stew! They unlocked the ticket-box and recovered her bogus tickets, and then she borrowed a dollar from Miss Philadelphia Baltimorie Hoppie, who clerks at the Woman's Exchange. Julian in the meantime was telephoned to, and had to leave his "poor sick wife" (as he said, though she was pretty well, I thank you) and come down to see about. By that time Mamma was sitting in a front seat, looking sporty, and saying "Ha-ha-ha!" to everything, while J.C. was looking at the Liliputians [sic] through the wrong end of the operating glass.[4] So there was nothing for Julian to do but to pay the lady the dollar and smother his

Grandson Joel Chandler Harris III in the front yard of the Wren's Nest, 1899
(Joel Chandler Harris Collection, Special Collections Department, Robert W.
Woodruff Library, Emory University).

injured feelings.—I always told you our family ought to go on the comic
stage. We'd make the biggest hit ever heard of just by transferring to the
boards the parts we play at home, and acting them as we do every day.
By next June I'll have a circus wagon ready, and then we'll hire an Italian
band and take to the road. Maybe Burdeene would like to come along.

Well, this is all I can think of now, and I don't believe I thought of
all of that. I'm afraid for Mama to read this letter, and so I'll just slip it

in an envelope and put it in my pocket.—Essie and grandma will leave Wednesday, with their baggage packed for Troy.[5] They will stay with Sophia a week, and then start home, reaching here about the 20th. Give my regards to the sisters, and my love to Burdeene.

> Your loving
>
> Daddy

ALS

3 pp.

Envelope: Return to Box 111, / Atlanta, Ga. / Miss Lillian Harris, / St. Joseph's Academy, / Washington, Ga. / Wilkes county

PM: 10 January [1898]

1. Joel Chandler Harris III, second son of Lucien and Aileen Harris. He was born 17 December 1897.

2. Daisy, the family cow; Nelly, the donkey; Lily, the horse.

3. Two Atlanta theaters, now demolished.

4. Opera glass.

5. Niece Essie LaRose and Mrs. JCH's mother, Mrs. Pierre LaRose.

[To Lillian and Mildred]

16 January. [1898]

Dearest Girls: We were glad to get your letters. Mildred writes very cutely for a little Tomtit of her age and size. She seems to be improving very much. If there's any news in this neighborhood I haven't heard it. The Journal will go to Lillian until the 1st of June, and no doubt both of you can get all the news out of that able paper.—And so Father O'Brien nabbed Sister Sacred Heart's apples? Well, well, well! Who'd have thought it? I'm going to ask Father Bazin what he thinks about it. And they were the finest apples I could find in town, ring-streakedy and striky, and mellow and sweet. And so he nabbed 'em? Well, well! Language is powerless to describe the description. But wait! Maybe Mr. Benson got 'em. Maybe anything except that which I hear.—I hope Burdeene has recovered from her melancholy. I felt right sorry for the poor child, she pined so much. Brader has not been well at all since she left. He took up her pining mood as soon as she went away, and has lost three or four ounces of flesh, about all he could spare. Sweet little Burdeene! dear little Brader! The dumb-bells are ringing over the tomb of their buried hopes.—Burdeene's Mama wrote us a beautiful letter thanking us for making her daughter happy during Christmas. The thanks were so beautifully expressed that I felt right proud until I happened to remember Burdeene's homesickness, and then I fell on Brader's bosom and shed large sobs. That is, I shed one sob on the bosom and the rest in the air, for Brader doesn't like to have his shirt front rumpled.—Alleen went to town yesterday. She is looking fine and feeling well.[1] Stewart is cutting an eye-tooth and his vittles don't seem to agree with him. Still, he's not sick. Chinny Harris continues to drink and sleep just like any other toper. His appetite is something awful. The weather has been cold and cloudy to-day—wind blowing from the northwest. Yesterday (Saturday) we picked thousands of violets. You should have seen them early in the morning[.] They made a lovely show on the vines—are the plants called vines? We have never had so many.—I enclose you some lucre. Bah! lucre is so filthy that I send it to you gladly. I have to get rid of it some way. Brader has just come in [sketch of Brader's head, labeled "B. on a bust"]

I can't help thinking of poor Burdeene when I look at him in all his youthful beauty. Well, well! Such is life in old Wes' Een'. The cows are all up and about and so is the Donkey. Lily has had her mane trimmed. The Leghorn hens are laying, and J.C.'s bantams are following suit.— I'm reading the proofs of a book of short stories to be published in the spring. One portion of it will be a surprise to Lillian.[2]

But my ammunition has run out. My regards to the sisters, my love to Burdeene and to yourselves.

      Your loving

      Daddy

P.S. *And so Father O'Brien got the apples! Well! Well!*

ALS

2 pp.

1. After birth of second son, Joel Chandler Harris III.
2. *Tales of the Home Folks* (1898), dedicated to Lillian.

[To Lillian and Mildred]

The last Sunday night in Janiwary. [1898]

To two little Dearies:

Sweet dearies: Everything is the same except the weather, and it's hard to say weather [sic] the weather will grow better or no. It snew all the morning, sometimes very heavily, but as luck would have it, the ground was warm, and the snow that had snew'd made haste to melt. The melting was much finer than the snow, and I felt so good over it, I went behind the parlor door—in that dismal room where nobody ever stays—and hugged myself. I suppose I must have looked funny for when I glanced around, my portrait was smiling heartily. Its mouth is still crooked, but I hope it will be straight in the morning.—Oh, no! I forgot; everything is not the same. Grandma and Esther LaRose arrived Wednesday, in fine health and spirits.[1] The railroads don't charge anything for hauling appetites; if they did, neither of the poor creatures would have had a cent left. Indeed, both would have been compelled to walk from Charlotte. Grandma looks a little thinner than she did years ago, but has not changed otherwise, being as lively as ever. Esther LaRose has fattened up some, and I don't wonder. She weighs 105 before dinner and 112 afterwards. This is no joke. I had the man to come out and weigh her. His name is Bell—you have heard of him before. He was here this afternoon, and brought the scales with him. Harry Lloyd was here too, and lifted Esther onto the scales. She squealed some, but not as much as you might have supposed.—We had the whole family to dinner, Julia 'n Julian, Alleen and Lucien—and also Turkey. Think of that! *And* celery! *And* cranberry sass!—Mildred's letter was so long it got lost in the mails. I hope she's not ill. I was sorry not to hear from her. Tell her to write occasionally when she has time. Her letters are very cute when she writes, but letters that are unwritten are not cute at all.—Essie says she'll write to you to-morrow. She says she'd write to-night, but is expecting company. I know one thing—when the company comes he'll find tar, pitch and turkentine dripping from the parlor mantle. I never saw a piece of hard oiled pine sweat and stew as that parlor mantle does. Well, there's one comfort, turkentine will keep off yellow fever it is said. If that is true we'll never have any yellow fever in the parlor.—Stewart was also with us briefly to-day, but quite long enough to set the house in an uproar. He's very rough and boisterous, and wanted to pull down the hallstove, hot as it was and roll it over the floor. It's a wonder he's still alive, but he is, and in very good health, too.—And so Lillian will soon be sweet sixteen! Well, from sixteen to womanhood is not a very long jump, and I hope she will be as lovely a woman as she is a girl.[2] You see, I was already thinking she was a woman. The four years to that point will soon pass away, and if those years are lived wisely and usefully, they will count for a great deal. But I must *not* get to lecturing. I never was good at it.—Clarence Caldwell ran away and married a Newman girl the other day. They say she has money. Well, you watch 'em and see how it turns out. A girl that runs away to get married is always a candidate for misery; and she usually gets elected. I hope I'll never have anything of that kind in my family. In fact I know I won't, for no sensible girl ever runs such a terrible risk.— Grandma sends her love to you both.—I suppose Mama will write to-morrow or next day. She will send Mildred's shoes to-morrow, in spite of the fact that Mildred failed to write.—Chubby Harris is doing very well, and Alleen has a new cook, and the violets continue to bloom.— I'm sorry I didn't know Father Bazin was in Washington. I'd have written to him about the apples that Father O'Brien said were so nice.—Brader has been here only once a day since Essie returned. My regards to the sisters.

> From your loving
>> Daddy

ALS
3 pp.
1. Mrs. Pierre LaRose, Mrs. JCH's mother, and niece Esther LaRose, who lived with the family of JCH.
2. "*Has been*" crossed out and "is" substituted.

[To Lillian and Mildred]

Sunday Evening. [31 January 1898]

Dear Billy and Tommy: You didn't say a word in your letters about the nice candy (2 boxes) that Mamma sent you a week ago to-day. I hope the postal clerks didn't get hold of it and confiscate it. If they did they are a sweet lot. I went up to see the Kidlets this afternoon. They are both well and happy. Chubby has had his picture taken. I saw the proofs, and one of them is very good. Toodlum-Boo is as rough in his ways as a sea captain.[1] If I were his papa I'd give him a spank poultice. One or two of these poultices would cure him sound and well. I have tried the same remedy on all of my boys, and it never fails to cure after a few applications.—Mamma's neuralgia has completely disappeared, and she is now wobbling about with her usual agility.—Essie's Lenten experience has been a serious one thus far. She went to the theatre Saturday, and to-day she has been ill, not ill enough to go to bed, but too ill to feel well.— Grandma knocks along about as usual. If she feels ill she never speaks of it—you know how she is. She has received a good many callers, and she says it's wonderful what fluent talkers we have among the women here. I believe they are to be found in all parts of the world. For my part I like to hear 'em talk occasionally. Mrs. Kelly, for instance, can talk all day without changing her tone. It is as restful as the murmur of a running brook.—Essie sleeps in the back room with Grandma, while Mama has taken your room. Now, the back room is right over that part of the cellar which the John Thomas Henry and the Tabitha Ann cats have selected for rehearsal before starting on their tour around the neighborhood. They have selected this part of the cellar because they can hear the echo of their song, and thus decide how to pitch their voices when they go out to amuse the neighbors. Well, they gathered there Friday night and began their rehearsal. They were not vehement. In fact, they sang in a minor key. But Essie was not feeling well, and was not prepared to enjoy the elaborate programme that had been prepared. Her LaRose temper (of which both of you have a slice) arose, and thus she arose and inquired in a loud voice if there was no remedy on earth for that sort of thing, and then she said words and made statements similar to those you have heard from the lips of angry people. This was at 12 o'clock. For a few moments she made more noise than the cats, and I was afraid she would disturb them, or at least cause them to miss a note; but they paid no attention to the interruption. They had trained themselves to place their minds firmly on the task they had set themselves. When they heard competition overhead, they simply sang the louder. And then Essie, being nervous anyway, sat down on the carpet and cried. But even this did not disturb the cats. They continued to rehearse until 4 a.m.[2] So Essie says. I didn't hear them myself[.] Being a peaceable man, and not given to sitting up in bed to disturb cats, the whole affair went on and off without any assistance from me. Essie says it was a huge success, but she uses different words to describe it. She has become quite accomplished in English, especially in the employment of those words and phrases that we called "idiomatic," which means that they are peculiar to our mother tongue, and can't be translated into any other language. I'm certain that Essie made a dozen remarks which she couldn't turn into French even if her health depended on it.—Charles was here to-day, and Harry and Don Alexander called. Brader is here now. Bob has deserted the ranch, having doubtless received a timely hint from Brader.—J.C. continues to play with the big boys, including Rufus.

⌒

I daresay the good sisters wonder why I don't write you serious letters, containing fatherly maxims, and a lot of advice, such as we sometimes see in the correspondence of parents to their children. Well, the reason I don't do it (I'm fully capable of it; I'm just mean enough to) is because I want you to be glad to get *letters* from me, and not prosy advice which is calculated to make young people tired. I remember my own childhood too well to want to add to the natural anxieties of children. And (between us three) that's the reason your brothers are such clever boys.

Mama will try to get a box off Tuesday, but the time is very short, and she'll have to do a good deal of hustling. My regards to the sisters and love to Burdeene.

> Your loving
> Daddy

ALS

3 pp.

Envelope: Miss Lillian Harris, / St. Joseph's Academy, / Washington, / Wilkes county, *Georgia. / GaRR.*

PM: 31 January 1898

1. Chubby is Chandler Harris; Toodlum-Boo, Stewart.

2. Text has "4 g.m.," perhaps JCH's allusion to G.M.T., "Greenwich meridian time," but more probably a simple slip of the pen.

[To Lillian and Mildred]

[7 February 1898]

Sunday Evening

Dearest Girls: That was a very sad fire you both wrote me about. It is terrible to be aroused in the middle of the night, and see the red reflection of fire through the windows, and it is more terrible still to hear the noise of roaring and crackling of the burning buildings, and to see the red tongues of the flames shoot upward and curl downward, and whirl about the burning centre. And that particular fire was a very sad one. Yet we may hope and believe it was all for the best, for surely the people will open their hearts and purses and come to the aid of the orphans.[1] I see Mrs. Horne has started a subscription list here, heading it with $100. I enclose a cheque for $25. Please hand it to Father O'Brien with my best wishes. The name is left blank. He can write his own name in; or any other that is most convenient. (The truth is I have forgotten his initials.[2] Ask one of the sisters to write it in the cheque.) Mildred's letter had a touch of genuine piety in it. I hope she'll continue to feel the need of praying even when the fire is forgotten.—As usual, the news here is the same it was before, except that Mrs. Ray is very ill, and has been moved to Mrs. Taylor's because three of her children are down with scarlet fever. Dr. Longino is in charge of the sick children, and he didn't know the disease was scarlet fever until after they had been ill two weeks—and all the neighbor children had been in to see them. All that time the rest of the Ray children were going to school, and there's no telling how many youngsters have been exposed.—We've had some very cold weather—mercury down to 12. You may imagine how I felt, but not how Rufus looked when he came into the yard the coldest morning. Here's his photograph from memory: [JCH's profile, full-length sketch of Rufus]

We had to cut off the water and hug the fire, and even then it was cold. Yesterday it rained and friz as it fell, but after dinner the weather cleared, and the ice melted from the trees, and it is now fairly comfortable—by the fire. And er-er-oh, yes! Brader has just come, but Essie has gone to Lucien's. To-morrow night, Brader and Bob will both come, and *then* where will Essie go? It is very sad when you come to think of it. Burdeene should be here by all means. Your grandmother seems to be enjoying herself fairly well. She is very lively for her age, and I think she's improved some since she arrived. The warmer climate—*she* says it is warmer—seems to agree with her.[3] She went to church this morning, and has also been to Lucien's. We don't see much of Julian— though even little Billy Matthews comes out three times aweek to see his folks. Perhaps he is not as completely wedded as Julian is. Mr. Collier seems to stand it without a murmur.—Alleen is flying around "right smart," and looks well. The babies are in good health, and, between eating and drinking, seem to be flourishing.—I think the letters of both of you are improving[.] Well, keep it up, and write as much as you can.— You see how forgetful I am! I have neglected the sister's bill for tuition since you went back. This is pure thoughtlessness. Please send me the figures of the full amount, including Mildred's music and your painting, and I'll remit at once. I think Sister Sacred Heart should give parents a gentle hint when they neglect to send the money promptly.—One thing puzzles me: how could the fire start in the bath-room? From the stove? From a match dropped on the floor? My regards to the sisters, and love to Burdeene.

From your loving

Daddy

ALS
3 pp.
1. Fire at adjacent Saint Joseph's Home for Boys.
2. Rev. James M. O'Brien, chaplain of orphanage and pastor of Saint Joseph's Church.
3. Mrs. Pierre LaRose, mother of Mrs. JCH.

Sunday Evening. [14 February 1898]

Dear Lillian: I enclose cheque for $182.20. I imagined it would cost more than $2 to drench Mildred, but no doubt drenches are cheaper in Washington than in Atlanta. I notice that you and Mildred are putting on airs drinking chocolate. Well, if you like that sort of thing, I suppose chocolate is the sort of thing you'd like. Now, don't think I'm begrudging this little pleasure because I mention it. Goodness knows, I want you to have chocolate and anything else in reason. I'm just remarking on the queer taste some people have. I believe our whole family, except me, is afflicted with chocolate palate. J.C. is constantly begging me for chocolate candy, and I am as constantly forgetting it: but, as I tell J.C., everything comes to those who go to bed and wait.—I sent you last week "The Two Orphans," at Essie's request. It is a little too watery for me, but no doubt you and Essie find a great satisfaction in weeping over the woes that accumulate in books and on the stage. I'm afraid that if you two saw real woe of the kind stories and plays deal in, you wouldn't feel like weeping at all.[1] There's less romance in real life and a great deal more suffering than books give any account of.—Please say to Father O'Brien that your mama and myself do not need any thanks for our small donation to the orphans. We both found a sincere pleasure in sending the money. I trust we'll be able to duplicate the amount a little later when Father O'Brien begins the work of rebuilding.—Louise Goodman returned Essie's call with promptness. She has grown tall, and an Alpine hat makes her seem taller. She said to Essie: "I used to be very timid; I thought I was dull by comparison with other people. But Mama told me I was as bright as *anybody*. She said I was the *brightest* of her children. Since she told me *that* I haven't had a *spark* of timidity. Indeed, I know now that I *am* bright."—Now, I'm not telling you this, my dear, to give you a poor opinion of Louise, but to show you how a very sweet and amiable girl may be spoiled by injudicious praise at home. Don't never [sic] think that you are brighter than other girls, for when you get to that point you'll not *try* to be brighter. That is why conceit is dangerous. Poor Mrs. G., sitting at home, has spoiled both Rob and Louise by instilling such notions into their minds.[2]—The weather has warmed up, and we had ripe jonquills for dinner. The violets are also in bloom, and the canary bird was singing so to-day I had to fling a towel at his cage.— Julian and Julia called to-day, and spent an hour. They seem to be very happy. Charles fell in the gymnasium at Sharon, and cut the skin over his eye. One of the sisters had to sit up with him at night. No doubt he feels that he is quite a hero.—I have saved my small-talk for Mildred's letter, which is enclosed.

> From your loving
> Daddy

ALS

2 pp.

Envelope: The Constitution, / Atlanta, Ga. / Return to Box 111. / Miss Lillian Harris, / St. Joseph's Academy, / Washington, Ga. / *Wilkes county* / *Ga. R.R.*

PM: 14 February 1898

1. Probably one of the nineteenth-century translations of the *Two Orphans*, subtitled "an emotional drama in four acts and several tableaus of powerful interest." This popular play was a translation of *Les deux orphelines* by Adolphe d'Ennery and Eugene Corman.

2. Probably the Charles M. Goodman family at 257 Peeples.

[To Lillian]

[6 March 1898]

Sunday evening, 6th.

Dear Billy-Ann: Your sixteenth birthday had been so long in my mind that it seemed to be an old story.[1] I have been thinking about it for some time, wondering to myself if I really have a daughter who has reached the point where by straining her eyes a little, she may see the fair lights of womanhood gleaming in the distance. And not such a great distance! In two years you will be a young woman in your own right. You will be of age at eighteen, according to the laws of Georgia, while a gawky boy of eighteen must wait four more years before he is legally of age! Aren't you sorry for the poor boys? It is no wonder that a grown young woman of eighteen feels herself so much older and more mature than a calfy boy of eighteen. The surprise I have in store for you I had intended for your birthday, but circumstances were against me, and so you will have to wait until the 19th, possibly a few days later. Oh, you'll be astonished— don't forget that!—And then here's a little bug I want to put in your ear: When I fail to mention anything, or fail to refer to anything you have said or done, you need not think that I have forgotten it, or that I am not pleased with it; as, for instance, your birthday, and your report. Why, the report was every bit as good as it should be. Perfection is a fine thing, no doubt; But I don't think human beings should try to do something superhuman in the hope of attaining perfection. Only those who draw who draw [sic] themselves away from the world can even approach perfection of life and conduct—the sisters, for example. Ask the saintliest among them if she has reached perfection, and she will be shocked; she will imagine you are making fun of her. Ask the greatest painter, poet, musician or writer, and, if he be not eaten up with conceit, he will tell you with a sigh that he has not even approached it. It is an attribute of God alone and we can can [sic] only make it our ideal. You do as well in your studies as you can—a great deal better than I used to think you would.—And then that little essay on Lowell—I thought and think it was finely done; taking your age, experience and opportunities into consideration. I could say more in this line, but you know there is sometimes danger that a sixteen-old Miss will put on airs. You are too diffident for that, but to praise you seems like praising a part of myself: you know how I feel about that sort of thing.—It's funny to read your inquiry: "Am I really coming home on the first of June?" You are, to a certainty, if you are strong enough to bear up under the shock, so to speak. You know I promised myself and you that you were not going through the fearful ordeal of preparing for a public examination. And then you must remember that April 30 is only eleven weeks off.— Those films arrived safely, and Evelyn will get them when they are done; whereupon I will at once proceed to send them to you.—Evelyn wrote the criticism of Anna Held for The Constitution. I'll send you a copy of the paper in the bundle. It is the best piece of writing he has ever done, the diction showing that he will have when he "finds himself" the light touch so hard to attain. Ah, well! I wish everybody's children were as nice as mine and doing as well. I think (see how insane I can be at times!) that the average of the world would be a little higher in a short time. And yet, as we used to say in the country, all my children are not "out of the woods" yet. Some of them may disappoint me—not the girls, of course; but some of the boys.

And now, for gossip and comment I refer you to my letter of this date to Miss Tommie Harris, of Washington, Ga., Wilkes county.

> Your loving
> Daddy

ALS

3 pp.

Envelope: Return to Box 111, / The Constitution, / Atlanta, Ga. / Miss Lillian Harris, / St. Joseph's Academy, / Washington, Ga., / Wilkes county, / Ga. R.R.

PM: 7 March [1898]

1. Lillian was born 1 March 1882.

[To Mildred]

Sunday evening, 6th [6 March 1898]

Sweet little Tom: My mind is made up. I have determined to write you a letter all to yourself, and to send it to you in an envelope all by itself. I can see Billy putting on all sorts of airs because she is so old as to be sixteen; I can see how she holds herself. "I thank you, Mildred," says she, "You must treat me with more politeness hereafter. Remember, child, I am now *sixteen*." Oh, but these sixteen-year-olds are awfully stuck-up. *I've* seen 'em. *I've* watched 'em out of the corner of my eye, (when mama wasn't looking, of course), and I know how they carry on. It is quite aggravating, enough to discombobble the minds of young ladies of eleven and twelve and thirteen. Yes, and I've seen something else, too. I've seen the same sixteen-year-olds very jealous and envious—oh, perfectly green with envy—when the young ladies of eleven and twelve come to be sixteen. It is easy to guess why. It is because those who were once sixteen have grown to be twenty and twenty-one; yes, you may count it up yourself—*twenty-one*. They are almost old maids, and oh, wouldn't they give just anything to be sixteen again! Let us hope that Billy is enjoying herself now, for in three years and five months, dear Tommy, *you* will be sixteen, and then *you* can do some crowing— (ahem! please excuse the slip; I mean you will be enjoying the honors that Billy now wears.)

Now, although it may seem a long time to you at present, three years and a half will fly by very rapidly. By that time you'll be in the graduating class—or may be you'll graduate the month before—and *then* there'll be hot times in the old town where (as Chloë says) "we lives at." You write very cute letters, and your handwriting is improving, and, you say yourself you are getting along finely in music, and so forth; so what is there to grumble about? Oh, pardon me! you think June has gone lame. Well, you are very much mistaken. June will arrive on schedule time, and you'll enjoy your vacation all the more for having exercised a little patience—especially when you are obliged to exercise it.—Mama will of course send a hamper basket of stuff for Easter, and I hope Sister Bernard—no, Sister Doctor Mary Louis—will lay in an extra stock of cholera drops and paregoric and other medicines calculated to soothe and regulate a pair of nightmares imported into Washington from West End.—If there's any more news here I haven't heard it. J.C. threatens to write to you. The dogs got in a fight with another dog one night recently and tried to pull him in two. He didn't like this operation, and uttered his reproaches in a very loud tone of voice. He said they were bad neighbors and very inhospitable. When he did get away he ran through the empty barrels and over the loose shingles, making such a racket that Mama declared the parlor chimney had fallen in. The donkey is sick. She has either had too much to eat or not enough.—Speaking of donkeys Brader continues to call. He will doubtless be over to-night. Julian and Julia were here this afternoon. Julia is looking extremely well. Julian is about the same. Stewart also came. He is beginning to say a few words very plainly. *The strawberries are beginning to bloom.* There'll be some here in June.—Father O'Brien preached to-day. Ask Sister Mary Louis to say to him (he will be home Tuesday) that my contribution sent a few weeks ago was an *emergency donation.*—(I'm getting so I can't write letters).[1]—My regular contribution is still to be paid.—Everybody is well. Chubby Harris is fat and good natured. He is shedding his long hair, and is right bald in front and half way the head. It makes him look like a Brownie.[2]

Heighho! I don't know anything else, except to say that this is from
  Your loving
    Daddy

ALS
3 pp.
1. "Contribution" is struck through and "donation" substituted above.
2. Palmer Cox's Brownies. "Chubby" was the nickname of Joel Chandler Harris III, second son of Lucien and Aileen, born 17 December 1897.

[To Lillian]

                    Sunday evening, [March] 13th, '98
Dear Billy-Ann: There are two things I don't understand. First, I can't imagine what you found in my last letter to please you more than my other letters have pleased you. It was written in a vein more somber and serious than usual. Was this the element that imparted to the affair a

new charm? Why, in that case I can write you the most serious letters you ever read, long essays calculated to make sermon-writers envious. Is it possible that you have been knowing me for sixteen years without discovering that seriousness is my hobby? Or have you come to the conclusion that a good-humored person must necessarily be giddy and light-headed?—Second, I can't understand how you and Mildred got it into your heads that you were not coming home on the first of June. When did I hint that you were not to come? Or did you think I was joking when I said you should come? Well, some of my jokes are serious, and this is one of them.—I see you are pumping yourself up to be greatly surprised sometime this month. But you must bear in mind that I said, or at least intended to say that I had a pleasant surprise for you— not a *great* one. But please don't make too many preparations for it. You may be disappointed. It is a very simple affair, after all—not of sufficient importance to arouse great expectations.[1] I really don't know what day the surprise will be sprung on you, but before long.—Anyhow, it is not good form for a sixteen-year-old young lady to be surprised, and I think it is in shocking bad taste for her indulgent parent to make an effort to do so.—I notice that you are sometimes at a loss what to say in your letters. This is natural, owing to the fact that you have so few things external to yourself to write about. But it might be good practice for you to write your thoughts—your views, your little day-dreams, your opinions about things. By doing this you will get yourself in the habit of thinking in an orderly way. But in writing letters to me or to a friend, don't try to be too precise[.] Just let your pen move naturally with your thoughts, and don't forget that the rules you learn in rhetoric are not applicable to letters, or that formality in a friendly letter subjects the other person to all the rigors of a snow storm. I was reading in a literary periodical the other day some extracts from letters written in Cromwell's time by Miss Dorothy Osborne to Sir William Temple, whom she afterwards married. These letters are as fresh and as charming now as they were the day they were written. This is because Miss Dorothy put *herself* in her letters. She gossipped about herself; her hopes, her expectations, her troubles, real and imaginary, and in doing so made a contribution to our permanent literature. She was serious, but not too much so. Indeed, her vivacity and spirit in the face of real troubles, are something wonderful.—As Mildred seemed to be very proud of her "private letter," as she quaintly calls it, I'll write her another, and you'll find in that such gipsy-gossip as I used to put in yours; but which I'm afraid to indulge in now, since you are *sixteen*.—Mamma sent you the photographs and films. The pictures are fine—particularly that one where three faces are grouped and taken at short range. I wish you'd catch Mildred in an unconscious attitude, and take a picture of her face and shoulders only. Let the picture be a *portrait* on a *dark* background.—Well, this is all, especially as you'll read Mildred's letter.

> Your loving
> Daddy

ALS

3 pp.

Envelope: Return to Box 111, / The Constitution, / Atlanta, Ga. / Miss Lillian Harris, / St. Joseph's Academy, / Washington, Ga., / *Wilkes county* / Ga. RR.

PM: 14 March 1898

1. The surprise was that JCH dedicated *Tales of the Home Folks in Peace and War* (1898) to Lillian.

[To Mildred]

> Sunday Evening, 13th March, [1898]

Sweetest Tommie: The rain falls *drizzle-drizzle*, when it doesn't come *mizzle-mizzle*—and it is very welcome, too, for the garden, and the roses, and the sweet peas all need it. Violets by the basketful! We had 'em all picked clean yesterday, and now they look as though not one had been pulled. I believe two come when one is taken away. The tulip-beds at the front door are green, and the first thing we know we'll have 'em all blooming.—The babies are getting on famously. Stewart can say a good many words. He didn't come see us all last week. His mama says it was on account of his teeth but he seems to be just as well as if he had all his teeth or none. Chubby says very little, and seems to be doing a great deal of thinking. Sometimes he laughs to himself, and when I ask him what the joke is, he merely blinks his eyes and pretends not to know what I am talking about. Oh, he's a shrewd one, Chubby is. And he's

so fat he looks like a bologna sausage painted white (*or* pale pink.) [.]
Nelly, the donkey, has been ailing, but she's better now; in fact, she's
able to holler back at Rosser's donkey[.] Rosser's yells out, "*A-h-h-h-e-r!*
What-er-are er-you er-doin', er-over-over er-there, er-anyhow, er-ow, er-
ow?" And Nelly replies in language that I fear is not always polite.—
You see I am writing another "private letter" to you. I'll tell you why.
The fact that Lillian is sixteen reminds me that someday *you'll* be sixteen, and then I'll have to be on my P's and Q's with you. So I may as
well begin practicing now. Lillian used to receive private letters from
me before you went to Washington, and I think you deserve to receive
some.—Your report has not made its appearance yet. Don't be afraid to
send it because it is imperfect. We are all imperfect. Besides, it will be
time enough for you to get to your books in earnest when you are a little
older. I'm glad to hear you are moving along in music. Some day when
you are grown you'll be very glad you went to St. Joseph's Academy, and
you'll remember the patient and gentle sisters as long as you live—you'll
remember them with love and wonder how they could manage so many
girls young and old so quietly.—I think you write very clever letters. I'll
be glad to have them a little longer occasionally. There are lots of things
about yourself you could tell me, or your mother. When you take up your
pen just say to yourself, ["]now I'm not going to *write;* I'm just going to
talk to papa and mama just as though they were sitting here listening
to every word I put down." That's the way I do when I write to you
and Lillian. You know, of course, that I do most of my talking with my
pen.—J.C. saw Mr. Bryan at Mr. Clark Howell's. Says J.C.: "Mr. Howell
looks like a baby by the side of Mr. Bryan. I saw Mr. Bryan take off his
hat and there's a bald place on top of his head." J.C. is now (I mean in
the week days) playing marbles part of the time, and base ball the other
part. He wants to get a standing collar for Sundays "with flaps on the
corners."—Mama has the headache, and Essie has been ailing for a week
or more. I don't think it is love, for I have been ailing myself[.] If you
or Lillian should chance to feel bad, don't forget that Celery Compound
is a good tonic. If Lillian needs any money, I can send it to her.—I'd be
glad if she'd save for me the pictures of you and her which were among
those we sent the other day.

My kindest regards to the sisters.

    Your loving

      Daddy

ALS

3 pp.

Envelope: The Constitution / Atlanta, Ga. / Return to Box 111 / Miss Mildred Harris, / St. Joseph's Academy, / Washington, Ga. / *Wilkes County.*

PM: 14 March 1898

[To Lillian and Mildred]

                Sunday Evening. [13? March 1898]

Dear Girls: I have a trade for you—first go. Someone wrote me a letter t'other day, and closed with these few remarks: "Your dear daughters are well, and are the dear, sweet, good children they always are." Now that's a great deal better than the praise I get in the newspapers, and it comes from a source that doesn't give praise lightly.—Now, as to news—well, you'll have to excuse me and Rufus this time. With respect to news, we have just simply run to seed, the seed thrashed and sent to mill, the meal ground and made into bread, and the bread cooked and eaten. Mama came home from church with the neuralgia to-day, and she has been grunting ever since. I'm sorry for her, but I have to laugh. It's all that can be done. It acts as a counter-irritant, she gets angry, and then her face doesn't hurt for quite awhile. She now has her head tied up in a red fascinator that is not at all fascinating. The trouble about neuralgia is that it is a horrible pain the doctors can't cure. There is no remedy for it. What helps some people doesn't help others. I sincerely hope mama will not be afflicted with it long. There's not much happiness or fun in the house when Mama is suffering.—The weather has been growing colder all the afternoon. The wind is doing business at the same old stand in the northwest. It seems funny that there should be so much wind in the northwest. You would think the supply would blow itself away, or get tired of blowing—but not a bit of it! It has been blowing thousands of years, and it is blowing now. And it is always cold. I suspect that the reason they can't find the north pole is because they are hunting in the wrong place. It is not in the north, but in the northwest. But, thank goodness! the violets are still blooming in profusion.—Rufus's "Mr. Banks" has returned to work.[1] He does right well when he's propped up.—Julian sent out some tickets and the folks went to the matinee yesterday—Shore Acres. You'll get even this summer.—Charles came over this afternoon and remained some time. The rest of the young men are not worrying us to any extent. Maybe they think I'm not good looking enough. Well, I'm going to have my hair cut and use magnesia for face powder.—Brader has now arrived, and I feel better. It is always a good thing to feel better; in fact, it is better to feel better.—I saw old Colonel Matthews on the car the other day—(maybe I wrote you about it)—and I never was so shocked in my life. Not so very long ago, he was hale and hearty, 'though nearly eighty years old. Now he is all bent, and his face could not look paler or more cadaverous if he were dead. I doubt if he lives a month longer. (Brader is now eating his third apple, and I fear *he* won't live long at this rate)—Grandma has improved considerably since she came. She seems to be livelier. She was really delighted with Sister Mary Bernard's souvenir. The truth is hardly a day passes that some reference is not made by someone to Sister Bernard. She is constantly talked of in this house. And, (believe me dear girls) this is better than fame—to make your influence felt on those who, hardly knowing you, yet constantly mention your name with emotions lively enough to bring moisture to the eye,—to be constantly talked of and remembered by those who have no claim on you. It is a great gift to make yourself at home in a house you have never seen. And this is the gift that Sister Bernard possesses. It is something new to me.

Positively there's nothing here to write about. The new book will be out in March,—about the 20th—and I'll send you a copy.[2] I've finished four short stories for Scribner's Magazine, making five in all.[3] They will hardly appear in the magazine till next year. I don't know what I'll be at next. The Thimblefinger business has about run out.[4] Maybe I'll take up and complete my revolutionary romance.[5]

My regards to the sisters.

> Your loving
> Daddy

ALS

3 pp.

1. Banks was the gardener.

2. *Tales of the Home Folks* (1898).

3. Aunt Minervy Ann is a realistic and forthright black female character and storyteller created by JCH. In all, seven Aunt Minervy Ann stories appeared in *Scribner's Magazine*, beginning in 1899 with the February issue; they were published in October as the book *The Chronicles of Aunt Minervy Ann* (1899). See Strickland, 91–92, 170. JCH's letter to Mr. Burlingame, 3 December 1897, says he's finished one of these Minervy Ann stories. See *Life and Letters*, 400.

4. Four of the six books in this series had appeared by 1898: *Little Mr. Thimblefinger* (1894), *Mr. Rabbit at Home* (1895), *The Story of Aaron* (1896), and *Aaron in the Wildwoods* (1897). *Plantation Pageants* (1899) and *Wally Wanderoon* (1903) concluded the children's series.

5. *Qua*, left incomplete, manuscript fragment edited by Thomas H. English and published posthumously (1946).

[To Lillian]

Sunday evening, 20. [March 1898]

Dear Billy-Ann:

The weather is really too fine for letter-writing. It is warm, and yet not too warm. The tulip beds—where we used to have pansies—are beginning to make a brave show, and in the poplars the mocking-birds are singing. The violets have been a real show. One day during the week, in fact, three or four days, they have been a mass of bloom. All the neighbors have been picking at them, and still thousands are left. People going along the street have stopped to gaze at the extraordinary display. Everything looks so fresh and green and promising that I am beginning to feel gay and skittish like a colt in a barley-patch.—At this point, Julian and Julia have just walked in.

After Supper.—I don't mean of course that they walked in after, or for, supper. Like all country folks, I instinctively say "*evening*" when I mean afternoon. I began this letter about four o'clock. It is now half-past seven, g.m. [*sic*] Julian and Julia stayed till sundown, and while they were here, Lucien and Alleen came in. Ellinor came, too, and she and J.C. had a boisterous time running around the house. Julian and Julia are looking well, and seem to be very happy. Julian's dignity is gradually wearing off. Like all married men, he has discovered that his wife walks on the ground as other folks do. Consequently he feels more chummy than he did. Of course this is a discovery that all lovers make for themselves after they marry. It is not disillusion; it is simply that they feel more "at home" with each other—and you know a human being of either sex could not possibly feel at home with a *real* angel.—Well, we had a very pleasant time. The mocking-bird gave a concert, the roosters crowed, and the cows lowed.—As usual, I have nothing of startling importance to relate in regard to that branch of society belonging to maidens of sixteen. These maidens seem to be skipping along the same as ever, putting on great dignity when a young man comes in view, and unbending again as soon as he is out of sight.—Grandma and Essie are going to the Mayor's before long to spend the day.—I think it is "in the cards," as the saying is, for J. & J. to visit the Collier boys at Sharon pretty soon. They will visit you and Mildred at the same time. I know you'll be glad to see 'em. You needn't feel shy of Julia. She's as simple and as sweet, and as unaffected as can be. A great deal more so than some other people I'm acquainted with—more so, I believe, than any other young woman of social prominence in the Town. "Social prominence" doesn't mean she's *in* society; it means that she could be if she wanted to.—There's a new boarder at Mrs. Abernathy's, a young man, and Essie has been introduced to him; in fact, she was there when he came. She says her presence just at that time was quite accidental. Maybe so; anyhow, it was providential. Essie imagines she is getting very old. She is having headaches, and the first thing we know she'll be an old maid in her own right. She has already fallen away from 112 pounds to 101½. Old maids are always—that is, 'most always—thin. I have seen a fat old maid, but she had the asthma, and seemed to be always on the point of having a mustache.—I have asked the publishers to send you an advance copy of the new book[.] [1] I suppose you'll receive it this week.—If J. & J. go to Washington soon, I'll send you some violets.

    Your loving

      Daddy

Mama and Grandma are well.

ALS
3 pp.
Envelope: Return to Box 111, / The Constitution, / Atlanta, Ga. / Miss Lillian Harris, / St. Joseph's Academy, / Washington, Ga. / *Wilkes county*
PM: 21 March 1898
1. *Tales of the Home Folks in Peace and War* (1898).

[To Mildred]

Sunday Evening, 20. [20 March 1898]

Dear Tommy:—Whatever you mean by *underwear*, I don't know, because I'm a nice old person; but no matter what it is, Mama says you are to take it off. She talks about it as if it were a rag on a cut finger, or a flax-seed poultice. Shucks! you women folks are too much for me. You—I mean the women folks—keep me puzzled all the time. When I ask Mama if I can have more gravy on my hominy at the table and she says "*Rats!*" I don't know whether she's talking about the ones that live under the barn or those you curl your hair on. The more I live the longer I learn. It's mighty sad when you think how smart men folks would be if they knew as much as the lady folks. I try to look wise sometimes, but, goodness knows, I'm ashamed of my ignorance.—All the ladies in the neighborhood have sauntered in to see Grandma, and soon she'll be sauntering out to see them.—Mama is well; she had to go out of the front gate sideways. Essie is not well; she could go out between the palings. And so it goes. Everybody is different from everybody else, except women and they are more than different.—J.C. has five more bantam biddies, making eleven in all. He says they are cute, and I'll not dispute his word in your private letter. You do very well with your letters. You manage to put yourself in them, and that's not easy for some of the best writers to do. What I mean is, you always say something that sounds like Mildred, and unlike anybody else. When a writer does this in a book, he (or she) is said to have an original style. (Essie is now playing the peanner and Brader is sitting around fixing his cuffs.) The donkey is getting well. Stewart has a very bad cold, and continues to cut teeth. It beats anything I ever heard of. The child has cut eleven hundred teeth during the past eight months, and still the cutting goes on. What he does with them after they are cut, goodness knows. I expect they fall out. If they staid [sic] in his mouth, his head and jowl would be as big as the clothes-basket. I'm sorry for him. He's puny and fretful, and has a bad cough. If he continues to cut teeth for seven or eight years, he'll be exhausted. Dr. Clarence Rosser says a baby couldn't cut eleven hundred teeth. But what does he know about babies? I simply make this remark, and I'll stand to it: If Stewart has cut as many teeth as they say he has, Essie's trunk wouldn't hold 'em. And if he hasn't cut 'em, why should they say he has?—Chubby is getting along finely. I haven't seen him in a week, but I hear from him. I hope he won't cut as many teeth as Stewart. Maybe he couldn't stand it.

Well, everything is the same here, except when the old woman comes by to sell lye hominy.—J.C. has set the old buff cochin on a couple of bricks, and we expect her to come off soon with a brood of brick-bats.

> Your loving
> Daddy

ALS
3 pp.
Envelope: The Constitution / Atlanta, Ga. / Return to Box 111 / Miss Mildred Harris, / St. Joseph's Academy, / Washington, Ga. / *Wilkes County.*
PM: 21 March 1898

[To Lillian]

Sunday, 27. [March 1898]

Dear Billy-Ann: The films and plates arrived yesterday too late to place them in the hands of the executioner. They will be so placed to-morrow. I think it would be impossible to give you any clear idea of my views on public affairs. Events follow each other so swiftly, and circumstances follow so hard on one another's heels, that mere "views" go for nothing. There may be no war with Spain after all. On the other hand, war may be declared before you get this letter. Whatever is done must be done quickly. A war means the ruin of Spain, though, for the matter of that it is ruined now. The Cuban revolution was brought about by the oppressive taxes levied by the Spanish government. The Cubans were taxed on every thing. This was unjust, and yet Spain was obliged to raise money to pay the interest on its bonds and to carry on its government. The Spaniards are out of date with the times. Once they laid claim to this whole continent, and actually held a large part of it. They held Mexico and all South America. And all has been lost to them by reason of their pride and folly—In old times, Catholics believed that a monarchy was of divine origin: This belief was held because all the Catholic countries were governed by kings or queens. It was a very natural belief. But times have changed. American Catholics do not hold any such belief. The Pope himself not very long ago wrote a letter to the bishops of France and warned them that they owed their political allegiance to whatever form of government the people found satisfactory. He did this because the bishops were opposed to the republic—and a very poor republic it is, being entirely different from ours. I gather from the Holy Father's letters (or encyclicals) to American Bishops that he admires the American republic. He is a very great statesman (aside from his holy office) and ranks—in my mind—even above Gladstone.—I can't tell you how long the war will last if it comes. War is one of the demons that are hard to pacify when once they break loose. We cannot wipe out the Spanish navy in a day—or we couldn't if their ships were manned by real men instead of pompous mannikins. I never have liked any of the Spaniards except Don Quixote and Sancho Panza—and the first was crazy, the second a clown. But I'm sorry for the poor little king. He is a small boy. I've a great mind to send him a Thimblefinger book.[1] It is so silly for a child to be "a-kingin' it," as Drusilla says. He should be playing marbles with other small boys.—You see I have written you quite a dull editorial essay, as becomes one who is addressing a mature lady of sixteen. It shall be "Sweet" sixteen no longer, but "old" sixteen!—The "surprise," so-called, is connected with the book, and that's all I shall tell you. You are getting me in a corner, and I refuse to be driven. I shan't tell you anything more about it—so there!—Such small gossip as I have I'll reserve for Mildred's "private" letter.—I hope Burdeene will be able to come out to dinner with you; two hours will give her time.—My regards to Sister Bernard, Sister Sacred Heart and Sister Mary Louis.

Your loving
Daddy

ALS
3 pp.
Envelope: Return to Box 111, / The Constitution, / Atlanta, Ga. / Miss Lillian Harris, /
St. Joseph's Academy, / Washington, *Ga.* / Wilkes county
PM: 28 March 1898
1. Reference to Harris's children's books and Drusilla, the teenaged black nurse in
them. See *Mr. Rabbit at Home: A Sequel to Little Mr. Thimblefinger and his Queer Country*
(Boston: Houghton Mifflin Co., 1895), 55, for Drusilla's observation about a young king.

[To Mildred]

Sunday evening, 27
[27 March 1898]

Dear Tom ildred:

It is with large symptoms of pleasure that I take up my fountain pen
to write you a private letter. And now, after taking it up, I find that I
have nothing much to say. The trouble is that I don't know what kind
of letter you like. Lillian, who is now sixteen, says she prefers editorial
essays—and long-winded ones at that—on foreign affairs. Until I hear
from you, therefore, I'll just go ahead and write as I do when I have
nothing to write about.—We had Charles to supper. He has been ailing
some and now he's trying to get well by coming over here occasionally. I suppose he comes to see the violets. Speaking of violets you'll see
a little article in the society column of the Constitution of Sunday by
Miss Sizzma Dooly on our violets.[1] She didn't see 'em when they were
in *full* bloom. The poppies—ah, no! I mean the tulips—are beginning
to bloom and they are ever so pretty—all sorts of colors, white, purple,
yellow, red, dark crimson, lemon, orange, pink, and some are varigated,
being streak*éd* and strik*éd*. And then there's the wisteria. You remember the old arbor. Well, the purple blossoms are banked up on top of it,
and spilling over the sides and ends, while there's a perfect cascade of
them on the side porch next to Bunker's.—Ellinor Collier had a birthday reunion last Saturday, and J.C. went. It was a very exclusive affair—
two McRae boys and J.C., and one Rawson girl and the Collier girls.
And they had ice-cream, too. At J.C.'s plate, he found a "favor"—a rabbit
putting eggs in an umbrella—a sort of easter device. Oh, why do I go

and use such big words? I mean easter trick.—Now, you see, a whole month has slipped away before you knew it. You have only two more months to stay in Washington. Awhile ago—only yesterday, it seems— you had *three* months to stay.—Your two nephews are fat and tolerably well. They would be quite well but for bad colds.—I am going over to Mr. Collier's to-morrow night to play whist. Think of that! A big fat sheep led to the mutton-maker! I can't get out of it; Mama says I must go, and Julia says she will be ever so happy (and so forth) if I will. So what is an old man to do? I'll be sure to cast a damper on the assembled multitude. And, then, to go out at night and see the big black shadows cast by the electric light; and to see your own black shadow following after you, or jumping suddenly ahead and stretching out like it was cast by some one a mile and a half high! Ugh! it makes my flesh crawl. I feel like squealing!—I don't know of any happenings in this neighborhood. It's not because we are too good, for Mama and Essie went to the mati- nee yesterday; but Mama made up for it by going to church to-day and paying her pew rent.—J.C. has had two teeth pulled recently to make way for new ones, and to-night he is complaining that the new teeth are aching. Well, we can't have fun all the time, especially when we are cut- ting teeth.—Grandma is getting on very well. She takes things easy, and doesn't allow anything to trouble her. I think she has improved some, but old people are naturally feeble.—Essie was making a waist Friday and so couldn't write. She said she'd write to-day but, she didn't. She could write to-morrow, but something will happen. Oh, she's very busy, you may depend on it. The only time she can call her own is when she's asleep, and I dislike to wake her and remind her to write.—I don't know when Julia and Julian will come down. They don't know themselves I'm afraid. Well, here I am at the end of the 3rd page. Love to Burdeene, and regards to the sisters.

> Your loving
> Daddy

ALS

3 pp.

Envelope: The Constitution, / Atlanta, Ga. / Return to Box 111 / Miss Mildred Harris, / St. Joseph's Academy, / Washington, Ga. / *Wilkes County*

PM: [ ]M 98

1. Miss Isma Dooly "conducted" a social column for women, written in florid prose, in the Atlanta *Constitution*. See for example her column in the *Constitution*, 12 November 1899, 6.

[3 April 1898]

Sunday Evening 3.

Dear Lillian: I am glad you were pleased with at least one page of the new book. I certainly wrote the few lines thereon with greater pleasure than all the rest gave me. It was just a whim of mine to make a little secret of the matter. I thought you would like it best if you came upon it unawares. At first I had only one line "To My Daughter Lillian," but when I made the title "Tales of the *Home* Folks," the publishers wanted to know [if] I could include the Canadian story under such a title. Then I added the rest of the dedication—"Who will know why," etc.[1] You know—because your mother is a French Canadienne and all your home folks on that side. The book you received was the first bound. It will not be *published* till the 9th of April—next Saturday.—I don't know how I failed to include Sunday's Constitution in you[r] last package. You see how careless old people can be. That's the reason I rarely reprove anybody for carelessness.—Doubtless you think from the newspapers that war is to break out the next minute. It seems so; there may be a declaration to that effect the day you get this; but somehow I have my doubts. The big bankers of Europe and New York have too much interest in Spanish bonds to permit Spain to go to war. This is what has been holding Mr. McKinley back. I don't mean by that that he is bribed, not at all. He is a good man; but the men who managed his election and raised the republican campaign fund, and who have his confidence are interested in the bank syndicates. These are the men who have been trying to bring about a peaceful settlement. And they are still trying. As I write, all the diplomacy of Europe is moving to compel Spain to submit to such demands as Mr. McKinley may make or has made. But the Spaniards are very vain, and if any concession is made by the Spanish rulers, the people may rise up and smash the government. They say the poor little King and his mother have a yacht ready to convey them out of the country at a moment's notice. All these things are going on behind the scenes. In front of the curtain (to continue the figure) the people are shouting their loyalty to the boy King and his dynasty.—It is all a depressing mixture in which I take interest only because it concerns our country. I'm very much of an American in my feelings (as you are) and so, if war comes, I shall be glad to see the Spaniards whipped out. I see the Holy Father is moving for peace. He does this for two reasons: first, because Christ's mission on earth was one of peace, and second, because the Spaniards are loyal Catholics. But this last fact, humanly speaking, has done a great deal to hinder the progress of the Church. The Span- iards are brutal and cruel; and a great many vicious people declare that these characteristics are due to the fact that they are Catholics. We know how false this is, but the charge has weight with a good many unthink- ing people. The native Cubans are also Catholics, but they are in every way superior to the Spaniards,—so observers say.—And, now what will you think? Here I am writing another editorial essay. But, being sixteen, you are now old enough to stand it. My regards to the sisters I know, and love to Burdeene. Mildred's letter will contain such gossip as I can pick up.

> Your loving
> Daddy

ALS

3 pp.

Envelope: Return to Box 111, / The Constitution, / Atlanta, Ga. / Miss Lillian Harris, / St. Joseph's Academy, / Washington, *Ga.* / Wilkes county. / *GaRR.*

PM: 4 April 1898

1. Complete dedication reads: "To My Daughter Lillian/who will know why I have included in Tales/of the Home Folks the little skit about/our friends in St. Valerien."

[To Mildred]

Sunday evening, 3d April [1898]

Dear Tommy: Your letter full of busses was received, and you must imag- ine that mine has twice as many, through I do not mark the places. Toodlum Boo and Chubby were here to-day. Stewart is smart and bois- terous, while Chandler is sweet, and quiet and fat. Alleen and Lucien took dinner and supper here to-day, and are still here as I write. The babies are at home and asleep. J.C. had seven more little bantams to hatch yesterday, and they are behaving very well for such young children. They have already learned to wipe their mouths, using blades of grass as napkins, and young as they are, they return thanks every time they take a drink of water. I wish that little hen would show people how to train their children as well as she has trained hers. Of course, I don't mean *my* children—especially my *girls*—but other folk's children. J.C. went out beyond the Stewart farm in Fritz's pony cart yesterday and brought back a load of sweet shrubs. To-day he rode with Fritz and Roy to Grant Park and made arrangements to swap some of his guinea pigs for black ones. He has four *tee-nine-chy* ones, and they are very prettily marked.—Julian and Julia were here this afternoon, and they seemed to enjoy themselves. Louise came with them. We tried to get Julian to fix a date for going to Sharon[1] and Washington, but he said he couldn't tell when; he didn't know; he hadn't made up his mind.—I was to go to Mayor Collier's last Monday night (with Mama) to play whist, but the wind blew and the rain fell, and we couldn't go. So we are to go to-morrow evening if nothing happens to prevent it. I haven't been feeling very jolly the last day or two. Indigestion.—The strawberries are blooming at a great rate. You'll be home in time to get some. We've had strawberry short cake three times, but the berries came from Florida.—The new Baptist Church is going up rapidly. They are building it in front of the old one, which is to be used as a Sunday school. Lucien and Alleen went to our church to-day.—We are having the house painted, and I can taste the paint. The color is lighter than before.—The wisteria is still a show for the passers-by. People stop and look at it. The violets are still blooming, but not so freely as before. During the past three months we have picked bushels of 'em. If I were to send some plants to the sisters when we divide them, is there a place to plant them around the academy? They make beautiful borders in summers, and are a delight in fall and spring. I could have the plants packed so they would keep. Mamma continues to have general spring house-cleaning twice a week, and I have heard her say to-day that she was only waiting for good weather to have a *genuine* spring-cleaning. I don't know where I'll go nor what I'll do. If I were a housekeeper I wouldn't live in a house that had to be turned upside down every day to get the dirt out of it. A *genuine* spring cleaning means that Chloë, and Johnson, and John, and Lizzie, and Rufus, and Banks and Calvin are to come in to the tune of Sousa's marches, played on the piano by Essie, tear up the carpets, knock down the plastering, break the clocks, and drop a stove in the back porch. Mama has made no attempt, as yet, to sun the bath-tub, but I'm expecting it every day. When it happens, I'm going to have the chimneys taken down and dusted. When this is done, I'll have the wood-pile cleaned and polished with that perfumed stuff they use on the stoves. And then I'm going to have all the dirt swept out of the garden. I think a *clean* garden—a garden with no dirt at all in it— is one of the loveliest sights on earth.

Well, this is all for this time.

Your loving

Daddy.

ALS

3 pp.

Envelope: The Constitution, / Atlanta, Ga. / Return to Box 111 / Miss Mildred Harris, / St. Joseph's Academy, / Washington, Ga. / *Wilkes County* / *Ga. R.R.*

PM: 4 April 1898

1. Sharon, a post office in Taliaferro County, Georgia. Incorporated in 1884, it had a population of 216 in 1900 according to Candler, s.v. "Sharon."

[To Lillian]

[9 April 1898]

Saturday, 9th.

My Dear Daughter:

I am the old Procrastinator—surnamed Mud! I ought to have sent you the money days ago. I enclose a cheque now.

Burdeene's plates were all ruined before they got here. They had been exposed to the light. Shall I have them re-sensitized for her? I use this word [re-sensitized] at random. Love to Mildred.

Your loving

Daddy

ALS

1 p.

Envelope: Return to Box 111, / *Atlanta, Ga.* / Miss Lillian Harris, / St. Joseph's Academy, / Washington, *Ga.* / *Wilkes County*
PM: 9 April 1898

[To Lillian]

[10 April 1898]
Easter Sunday.

Dear Bill-Ann: I sent your $10 yesterday. It is too bad that I should go on neglecting what I ought to do day by day, until at the last moment, I rush around, and make haste, and get in a hurry, and feel like I ought to be punished for my failure to do promptly what I intend to do at all. I assure you, I feel humiliated because you had to nag me about the money. I am sure you needed it for Saturday, or for Friday, so as to enable you to buy something you needed. Well, you were not more "put out" about it than I am at this moment. I am not at all satisfied with myself, and shall not be until you assure me that you forgive me for fretting you, if fret you I did.—You know as much about the war as I do; but you see that my prediction last Sunday was fulfiled [sic].[1] I suggested that there would be postponement. Now, everything is set for to-morrow; but I think you will see that, just in the nick of time, something will turn up to make the situation easier for the bondholders. These men have been carrying on a great work of education in Congress; and they have no idea of permitting the Cubans to be free unless there is something in it for the money-lending class. A friend of mine, a Catholic, suggested the other day, that the reason the Americans were so hot after the Spaniards was because they are Catholics. I suggested that the Cubans, whom the Americans desire to see politically free, are also Catholics. I also suggested to him that the Spaniards had done the Church untold harm by their Inquisition, which was a political, and not a religious machine, and which the Pope tried hard to suppress. There are millions of well-educated protestants who firmly believe the Spanish Inquisition was set up and operated by the Church, and the belief has deepened prejudice against Catholics. I believed it myself until a few years ago, but attributed it to the *age*—the *era*—the *epoch*—which was peculiarly bloody and cruel.—When I fail to say anything about matters that are mentioned in your letters, you may be sure it is because I have forgotten to do so. As to the adventure which you propose for yourself when you have graduated from St. Joseph's, why that is an affair which cannot be fairly settled now.[2] It is impossible to discuss measures for an event so far ahead. Let the day decide; I mean the day when the project can be discussed with an eye to the immediate (and not the remote) future. As likely as not you will have forgotten all about it by the time you are graduated; or you may have other views; or you may prefer to remain at home. In short, a thousand contingencies may arise, not one of which can now be anticipated. (Oh, just listen at that stilted language! *Don't* you wish you were not *quite* sixteen, so you might continue to receive free and easy letters from your Daddy?) I crave your pardon, fair maid, for getting on my high horse. One must be on one's guard when writing to a young lady who has had the remarkable good fortune to achieve sixteen long years.—Mama sent a box for you and Mildred. The pictures were enclosed with the substantials. And they were all good. Those of Mildred and Burdeene especially so. We want all those of Mildred and yourself (including Burdeene); so don't fail to save them.—Your report was good enough for me—or did I tell you that before? Your letters are also improving. The long one to Essie was especially good. The reason for that was that you were writing to a girl, and felt more at ease—you were more yourself. When one puts one's self on paper—*that* is what is called *good writing*; in fact it is the best.—Do tell Mildred to send back the slippers she don't want. The man has already come out for them. "What was the occasion of the detention?" as Jonah remarked to the Whale. Tommy is almost as bad about such things as I am. She should have selected the pair she prefers and sent back the others—but, alas the thought! Maybe it was because you two unfortunates had no money! Well!—this is enough. In Mildred's letter you'll find such poor news as I hear or can invent.—My kindest regards to the sisters, and my love to Burdeene.

Your loving Daddy

ALS

4 pp.

1. See letter to Lillian, 3 April 1898, re the Spanish-American War.

2. Perhaps a reference to Lillian's desire to become a nurse. JCH and family prevented that, according to Mrs. Elizabeth Chapman, daughter of Lillian's sister, Mildred. (Editor's interview with Mrs. Chapman, Atlanta, Georgia, 22 August 1990.) Until her marriage (15 January 1908), Lillian seems to have spent much of her time traveling and away from home. And JCH was frequently irritated by her absences.

Sunday, April 17 [1898].

Dear Mildred: I'm very sorry you failed to get the letter. I wrote you three pages, as usual, and put into it all the news I could find, a little praise for your nice letters, and some very sage advice. You know how old people are. They are always ready to put in advice if they can get it in edgewise, and sometimes they will cram it in where it has no business. I cant understand how the letter got lost. I directed it as usual, and put "Return to Box 111, Atlanta."—By the time you get this, you will have seen Julian and Julia. They wanted to give you a surprise. I didn't know they were going until Friday, when Julian came out and told us. Julian's wife is just as sweet and good as she can be.—In the letter you didn't receive, I told you that J.C. had a dude collar and cravat for Easter, and I drew a portrait of him the best I could—It was better than this one. He has only [portrait sketch] one collar and so he can only wear it once [sketch continued] every two weeks, which is quite often enough.—I also told you that he had swapped two of his guinea pigs for two black-and-tan ones from Grant Park. One of them killed a young one, and now the murderer, or assassin, is shut up in the adjoining pen by himself. I don't know whether he's in the penitentiary for life, or whether Governor Harris will pardon him. The two white bantam hens have weaned their chickens and are now laying again.— In the lost letter, I told you to thank Sister Mary Louis for allowing you to write your letters in pretty much your own way, and—oh, I don't know what all I said. I wish I did, 'cause then I could copy it all off, and wouldn't have to think up things that I don't know.—J.C. went to the great package party to-day at the Tabernacle, where 6,000 school children assembled with packages.[1] What I don't understand is how these packages are to be sent to the Cubans, when all the pac[ket] boats have stopped going there. Anyhow, J.C. did very well; he carried four potted-ham sandwiches, two cold potatoes, and three biscuits that were baked before Easter. And in spite of this the cry is for war!—Evelyn has not been well lately, and he's now off for a vacation. He went with Charles to Norcross last Tuesday. We haven't heard from him, but suppose he is having a good time. Charles was also ailing and had to take a rest. We are all well here, except one of the old black hens in the chicken-yard. She is not well at all, being unable to walk. I gave her to Rufus, who proposes to make her some crutches.—The weather was so cold Thursday that I had the strawberries covered. Yesterday and to-day were (and are) warm and pleasant; but the northwest wind and the cold snap at Easter have hurt the roses a little. The first blooms will not be as nice as they would have been.

Now, I'm not going to write a long letter, and you'll be glad I didn't—when you get Lillian's letter, which will be even briefer than this.

My regards to the sisters and love to Burdeene, whose nice letter Mama appreciates so much.

Your loving

Daddy

ALS

3 pp.

1. See Atlanta *Constitution*, 17 April 1898, 10, col. 2, "Children's Package Party." The Tabernacle Baptist Church, a massive brick building at the corner of Luckie and Harris streets, served as the city auditorium before such a facility was built. See picture and description in Martin 2:545–46. *Cf.* JCH's observations about the Spanish-American War in the letters dated 27 March and 3 April 1898.

[To Mildred]

Sunday afternoon.

1 of May [1898]

Dear M [ink blot shaped like a duck]: I made a blot on this page, and started to throw it away, but, before doing so, pressed the bottom ~~of it~~—no, I mean the lower end of the page on it, and the result is so curiously funny that I send it along anyhow. I don't know whether it's a duck, or a goose, or an ostrich. Anyhow it seems to have one leg in the air;

it is probably jumping for joy because the first of May has come. Sister Mary Louis can exercise the wits of the class in natural history on it, and report results in *Gleanings*.—Your report is superb, splendid. Perhaps that accounts for the fact that you are somewhat thinner than you were. Your poor little wrists look like the hind leg of a hedge sparrow.— Stewart was here to-day by a large majority. You couldn't tell what room he was in until he was somewhere else. Lucien, who has been at Lithia Spring[,] returned to-day. Evelyn is still there. Julia is there too. Julian goes up at night and returns early in the morning. Evelyn pretends to be enjoying himself, but you know what a home-loving boy he is. I hope, however, that he is really having a good time, and that [reverse of blot] [1] he is improving from the strain of the hard work he has been doing. He can write a better letter than his Daddy when he feels like it. The rye has grown a beard; perhaps I ought to have it shaved; but really, the soap and lather would cost too much.—Did I write you about the new cats? Well, we did have eight, but now we have only two, a white one for Bijou and a yellow spotted one for Trilby. The others have fallen victims to the chloroform habit.—J.C. went to town yesterday morning and had his hair cut and shampood [sic]. Then he went to the office and stayed with Julian until dinner time. In the afternoon he went all about the neighborhood with bat and ball.—Clark Frazier has the whooping cough, and Nora Belle the measles—no, the chickenpox. I think the Fraziers have more sickness than any family I ever heard of. They call in two or three doctors one day, and then the next day the whole family is up and about and in good health. I don't understand how anybody can be so suddenly sick and then so suddenly well again. "Old Kittens," who removed her trunk and valise over to Roy's Grandma's, has two new children. They have cut their teeth and are walking all about.—J.C. says he will write soon. But it is a great task for him. He handles a pen as if it weighed thirty pounds and was as big as a fence rail. His fingers are all thumbs and the thumbs are as big as a calf's leg. He wants to be a "catcher," on a base-ball team, as Julian was, and he goes about all day with his mask on. He is perfectly serious about it, and thinks it is better to know how to "catch" than it is to be rich. Maybe it is; I've never tried either one.—We've had another spring cleaning yesterday. Mama wanted to climb up and wipe off the ball on the lightning rod. She said she knew it was dusty. I suggested that the neighbors may say all sorts of things if they saw her riding the topmost pinnacle of the roof without bridle or saddle. She contended for some time that the neighbors wouldn't see her, but finally gave it up when I told her that the street cars would be passing every fifteen minutes.—There's nothing new here at all except the roses, and they are very beautiful.—When you get this you'll have only four more Sundays to be away from home. Time flies and so does the house—fly. One is buzzing around me now—not a house, but a fly. My regards to Sister Mary Louis.

> Your loving
> Daddy

ALS
3 pp.
Envelope: The Constitution / Atlanta, Ga. / Return to Box 111 / Miss Mildred Harris, / St. Joseph's Academy, / Washington, Ga. / *Wilkes County* / *Ga RR*
PM: Ma[y] 1898
1. Written around second ink blot: "This is the Twin."

> [1 May 1898]
> May-Day, Sunday.

Dear Lillian: The Gleanings came to hand, and I read your account of the pottery tour with great pleasure. It is particularly well done, and the reason is very plain. You had something to write about, you knew what you wanted to say, and you said it, briefly and clearly. There are two secrets of good writing that I will whisper in your ear. One is to write about something that interests you because you know it; the other is to be familiar with and believe in the ideas you propose to write about. One secret refers to descriptions, the other to views, feelings, opinions. Combined, or separate, they relate to everything that has been or can be written in the shape of literature. So far as merely correct diction is concerned, that can easily be acquired, especially by those who have a knack or a gift of expression. In nearly all the books and magazines that I read, diction is called *style*. Why, I don't know, for the two come together and combine only in the works of the very greatest writers, as for instance, Hawthorne—or, to name a greater still, Cardinal Newman. I have just been reading some of the Cardinal's works, and I am simply amazed at the beauty, power, fluency, vividness with which he uses the English tongue. In discussing the dryest [sic] subjects, he frequently thrills the mind with passages of such singular beauty as almost to take one's breath away. In these passages you cannot separate the style from the diction, for they are fused. Nevertheless, style is one thing and diction is another. If someone should compel me by force to explain the difference between the two, my answer would be something like this: Diction is the body—the flesh and bone—and style is the spirit. But some years ago, that able Heathen, Mr. Herbert Spencer had something he wanted to say about Diction, and so he wrote it out and called it an essay on Style, and ever since then the Heathens, the Pagans, and not a few who call themselves Christians, have persisted in referring to diction as style—just as our northern scholars refer to the "*provincialism of the South,*" when they mean the *provinciality* of the South,—Dear me! [1] I hope I am not wearying you with all this; more than all, I hope I have made myself understood. It is so easy to be vague and hazy when talking about writing as a gift and as an art. A person who has the gift must acquire the art, and that is to be done only by long practice. You will never learn English Grammar from the books. All you can learn is the parts of speech, and the dozen or more pages that deal with inflections. English grammar proper cannot be written. The worst English is written by those who call themselves grammarians. An article or a book may be grammatically perfect and at the same time be written in vile English. You will learn more from Latin grammar than you will from English grammar. And you will learn most of all by reading the best English books.—But really you will think some one else has taken your popsy's place in writing to you; but it's the same old fellow, subdued and sobered by the fact that you are now more than sixteen, and still looking puny. It's a good thing I've filled up the letter with all that talk about—By the by, permit me to congratulate [you] on that "bumpety feeling." *That* was quite a stroke. It tells the whole story, and gives the necessary touch of humor to light up the description. Don't be afraid of such passages.—Well, as I was going on to say, if I hadn't filled the letter up with all this highfalutin talk about style and diction, it would have been a very poor letter indeed, for there's nothing to write about; no news; no nothing. The cow begins to holler for Chloe at the same time every afternoon, and Rufus in the matter of shoes, has graduated from No. 8's to No. 9's, and feels that he has won a victory. Regards to the sisters, and love to Burdeene.

> Your loving
>
> Daddy

ALS

3 pp.

Envelope: Return to Box 111, / The Constitution, / Atlanta, Ga. / Miss Lillian Harris, / St. Joseph's Academy, / Washington, Ga. / *Wilkes county*

PM: [1] May 1898

1. Herbert Spencer (1820–1903), *Philosophy of Style: An Essay* (New York: D. Appleton and Co., 1871). Provincialism and provinciality is a subject that JCH takes up in essays elsewhere, particularly in *Uncle Remus's Magazine*.

[8 May 1898]

Sunday Evening, 8th.

Dear Lillian: If Mildred gets her letter before you receive this, it's because somebody accidentally mailed it this morning.—While I was writing it, I thought of several things to write to you, but the fact that it was mailed before I intended it should be has knocked them all out of my head.—But since the letter was written, we have heard from Mama, and she's been having a gay and glorious time. She went to the Boston Symphony concert in Chattanooga; she went to Chicamauga [*sic*], and saw the troops *looking* one another's heads; she was given a reception, which the fat and shy little dear persists in calling a *party*—did you ever?— she's in full view of Lookout Mountain, and can see the Inn, and behold the incline railway climbing up and climbing down; and she has seen the moonrise over Kennesaw ridge. In short, she's so elated with her trip that she begins her letter in a patronizing way, thus: "My dear Boy," etc., and says she'll come home, "*if possible*" to-night. If she comes, she'll arrive at home about half-past 8—it is now seven minutes past 7—and Charles is to meet her. She declares—in her letter—that Grandma had a lovely time, enjoying every minute of her stay.—Well, I'm glad they had a good time. We missed them a great deal—or, to be more grammatical—very much.—We had all the kids to dinner to-day, and they spent the afternoon. The Kidlets are in fine health, and Stewart continues to be as terrifying as a torpedo boat. In two more years we shall have to put armor plate on the house to prevent him from tearing it down.—You will see all about the war in the newspapers. There's little else in them. Dewey's victory is the most remarkable in naval annals, all things considered, and reads like a fairy tale. But it's true. I'm beginning to be sorry for the poor Spaniards. The Spanish people are to blame only for allowing themselves to be governed by a set of political rascals and corruptionists. Instead of building up their government and making the people prosperous, they have been engaged in stealing everything in sight in the name of Spanish "honor." Bad government is alone responsible for the fact that the Spanish navy is no better than a flotilla of doll's houses.—I see that the high price of wheat is causing bread riots in Italy. Well, the Italian government is as hopelessly corrupt as that of Spain. Even Crispi, the famous statesman, has been mixed up in bank embezzlements and failures, and the paper money in circulation isn't worth more than 20 cents on the dollar.[1] The King's party are claiming that the bread riots are stirred up by the clerical party—the Catholics. But it is folly to say so. The people are rioting because they are on the point of starvation, and this is the result of bad management of the finances by the King's party. If republicanism in Europe didn't mean infidelity and anarchy, I could wish to see the corrupt governments over there become republican: I'm looking for our little war with Spain, which will doubtless soon be over, to bring about some very queer changes and complications in European politics. For one thing, I look for an alliance between this country and Great Britain, with Japan as a party to it. Such an alliance would change the whole course of events, and doubtless result in an effort on the part of the rest of Europe to sweep the English speaking people off the Earth. Out of that contest the only European power to emerge sound and whole would be the Church of Rome and its spiritual followers, and congregations.—But, honestly now, does this editorial writing really interest you? If it doesn't, I'm presenting myself to you as the Parental Bore, and I'll be glad to return to my famous *role* of Popsy, the Clown, which I have successfully filled on many occasions.—Mama couldn't write to you and Essie has had company. She's to write to-morrow.—The cold weather has shriveled my mind and body (or so it seems) and I am unable to recall the various things I wanted to tell you, which is a sure sign that they are (or were) of small importance.—You asked me about your report. Well, I am so accustomed to receiving good reports from you, that I regard them now as a matter of course, something to be expected in the nature of things. You may be sure they please me; you may be sure I take note of them; but I take it for granted that you know all this. I should still be pleased with them if they were not quite so good as they are; for I can see from your letters and your compositions that you are steadily improving in the line that is the best of all the rest, namely, a knowledge of the correct and graceful use of English.—As gratifying as your report is the news that Burdeene is coming home with you. This will add to our pleasure, as you know, and I hope she knows it, too, by this time. I said something like this in Mildred's letter, but it is no harm to say it over again.—There now! I have written you a page too much, and I fear the extra page only adds to the dullness of a very tiresome letter—though it hasn't been tiresome to me. But if you don't like the editorial part of it, let me know. My love to Burdeene, and my best regards to the dear sisters, who have been so kind to you and, indeed, to us all.

     Your loving
        Daddy

ALS
4 pp.
Envelope: Return to Box 111, / The Constitution, / Atlanta, Ga. / Miss Lillian Harris, / St. Joseph's Academy, / Washington, *Ga.* / *Wilkes county* / *Ga. R. R.*
PM: 9 May 1898
1. Francesco Crispi (1818–1901), Italian political leader, resigned from public office in 1896.

[To Mildred]

                              Sunday, 15.
                              [15 May 1898]
Dear Tommy: You will please take notice that, as I write, the month of May is half gone, and by the time you get this, you'll have only 13

days to serve in St. Joseph's army before you get a furlough. (As I write, Mrs. Bunker is swinging her voice out of the window as you've seen auctioneers shake a bill.) I suppose you think the 1st of June is just as far off as it was several weeks ago. Maybe it is, but it doesn't seem so. It will be with you before you know it, and then when you get home, you'll do as Lillian did,—pine about the sisters and wonder why Sister Mary Louis doesn't write to you, and be anxious to get back. Anyhow, you'll soon get tired of playing, and likewise, you'll soon leave Stewart to paddle his own canoe, for he's coming to the age when children are hard to nurse. Right now he doesn't know what he wants, and he's so full of life that he's never still until he's sound asleep. Chubb, the baby, is entirely different. He's quiet and lazy. He's no sooner awake than he wants to eat and go to sleep again; and when he *is* awake, he's laughing all the time except when he's whining, he doesn't cry unless something is really the matter with him.—Saturday, J.C. went to a picnic with Roy. There were eight herdics[1] and all of them full. J.C. says he had a delightful time. They killed a snake in the road, and slipped up (or down) on the slick rocks, and ate dinner, and got dirty and tired, and, altogether, they had a roaring time—more fun than you could shake a stick at.— And then, on top of all that, we had home-made strawberry ice-cream to-day, and fried chicken, and ever so many things. And J.C. went into the woods with Fritz as far as McDaniels's pond, where they charge a nickel for bathing (in muddy water); and J.C. had no nickel, and, therefore, came home comparatively clean, still wearing his standing-collar, and still allowing his ring-streakéd and strikéd cravat to crawl over the back of his collar.—Nora Goodman is as big as a "hoss," and the Rosser children can holla louder than ever. And not only that, but the mildew is getting on my rose bushes and I'm fighting it with sulphur, and there is no telling which is going to come out ahead, me, or the sulphur, or the mildew. I felt right sorry for myself when I first found the mildew, but I'm feeling better now, especially since Mrs. Bunker has hauled her voice back in the house. Chloë had all her young ones here some this morning picking strawberries. They picked the milk bucket full and two boxes. So you can see we are having very gay times in Wes' Een', Atlanta, Georgy. The donkey's voice improves with age. It is no sweeter, but it is stronger.—I grew tired of seeing my chickens in the pen, and so con-

Grandchildren Chandler and Stewart Harris, 1898 (Joel Chandler Harris Collection, Special Collections Department, Robert W. Woodruff Library, Emory University).

cluded to kill and eat them; but Fritz wanted some Leghorns, and so I sold him five hens and the rooster for $3. I then gave the $3 to Mama, so you can see how much I made by the trade. The chickens cost me 75 cents a piece to start with, and then I sold them for 50 cents, and gave the money away. I don't think I'd make a good business man.— I've written all I can think of and more besides, and so I think this letter should be brought to a close.—Bring your music home so you can play your pieces for me. Regards to the good sisters.

       Your loving
       Daddy

ALS
3 pp.
Envelope: The Constitution, / Atlanta, Ga. / Return to Box 111 / Miss Mildred Harris, / St. Joseph's Academy, / Washington, Ga. / *Wilkes County* / *Ga RR*
PM: 16 May 1898
1. Herdic, "A two- or four-wheeled carriage named, after the inventor, Peter Herdic, of Pennsylvania. . . . It was much used from 1870 to 1890 for public hire. . . ." *Funk and Wagnalls New Standard Dictionary of the English Language* (1959), s.v. "herdic."

[15 May 1898]

Sunday, 15.

Dear Lillian: I thought I would show you how easy it is to write a dull letter. You asked for editorials, and you got them. I'm glad you know when you have enough. This thing of giving Information, and Advice, and making believe that everything in life is very, very serious, not to say melancholy, is tiresome to me. I remember when I was young some gentleman who thought he took an interest in me used to write me long and dull letters, and then, to cap the climax, he sent me William Cobbett's Letters to Young Men.[1] It was all very dreary, and I know now that it turned me against the man. But if he had sent me cheerful letters, I should have regarded him as a benefactor indeed.—Mama sent you a very mysterious box the other day. It seemed to be full of ruffles and riffles, and frills and furbelows. I suppose you received it.—Julian has gone to Tampa.[2] How he managed to make up his mind to separate from Dovey I can't imagine, nor can I understand how Dovey could allow Ducky to go.[3] I have been to Salt Springs (Lithia) to play whist twice, and I think that Ducky and Dovey are spoonier than Lucien and Alleen were.[4] But this is a great secret, and not even to be whispered save in the bosom of our family. Julian didn't want to go much; but he'll only stay two weeks; and if he doesn't get sick the trip will do him good.— Evelyn has been at home since Friday, but he left again this afternoon to remain until Wednesday. He has improved very much, or, at least, a good deal.—Grandma is well, and enjoyed her trip to Chattanooga very much. She talks about it constantly.—Essie has gone to Norcross with Mrs. Kelly. I hope she'll have a good time, but I'm afraid she'll find the country dull. I never have found it dull myself, but I have known people who thought it monotonous. Now I find something new and interesting every time I go out of doors. It is not so much what we see as the way we look at it. I can't get rid of the impression that my trees know me—and perhaps better than I know them.—Did it ever occur to you that by the time this reaches you—Tuesday, most likely, you'll have but <u>13</u> [triple underlined in MS.] days to stay at the Academy. This is enough to make Mildred have a fit. Only <u>13</u> [double underlined in MS.] days![5] Well, 9 times 13 are 117; add these last figures together and you have 9 again; which means that from next Sunday morning you'll have only 9 days to stay away from home.—I was going to say some time ago, but forgot it, that if you want to go to Canada you may; only in that case Essie will have to get some of her friends to stay with her. Moreover, I think home will be as new to you as Canada, and I have an idea you'll have a nicer time here than you would have in Canada. But you know how old people are; they think one way, and the young ones think another, and so there's always a conflict of opinions and a clash of ideas. Only, in this case, I don't propose to allow my opinion to overpower yours. I'd rather have you here, not only for my own pleasure, but for yours. Nevertheless, you will decide for yourself if your mind isn't already made up.— I'd like to have Burdeene stay just as long as she can—or will—if it's all summer. This is one place where we never get tired of the young ones. We like to have them around.—Well, it stands to reason there's no news here.—I see by the papers that Miss Eliza Bowen is dead.[6] She was a lady of fine mind and a good writer.—My regards to the sisters, and love to Burdeene. Tell her to come prepared to tire herself out with staying at this house. I hope to get James Whitcomb Riley to spend a week here during the summer.—This is all for the present.

    Your loving

      Daddy

ALS

4 pp.

Envelope: Return to Box 111, / The Constitution, / Atlanta, Ga. / Miss Lillian Harris, / St. Joseph's Academy, / Washington, *Ga.* / *Wilkes county* / *Ga. R. R.*

PM: 16 May 1898

1. William Cobbett (1763–1835), English journalist and radical reformer. *Advice to Young Men* (1829).

2. Julian was to cover the Spanish-American war from there. See Garrett 2:357.

3. JCH's names for Julia and Julian.

4. Lithia Springs, formerly known as Salt Springs, a well-known southeastern resort. See full note to the letter to Evelyn, Friday *afternoon*—late [c. 1896], p. 58.

5. First 13 in large figures, second one in even larger figures.

6. Eliza Andrew Bowen, Georgia writer, born 22 April 1828, died 10 May 1898. Wrote astronomy text for high school, essays, and reviews. See *Dictionary of Georgia Biography*.

[To Lillian and Mildred]

Sunday, 22d. [22 May 1898]

Dear Billy and Tommy: You'll have to put up with a letter between you this week. It was too hot to write this afternoon, and it's almost too hot now. We have had a good rain, and it is pleasant to sit on the porch, but I am under my lamp, and the flame seems to shed considerable heat.—I enclose with this a cheque for $10. If you choose, and the sisters can spare two such charming young ladies, you may come home this week—say Saturday. But that is for the sisters to decide. If you are engaged in doing anything special or particular, then, of course, you'll not come, but if you are just hanging around, waiting for the 1st of June to come, why you—but wait! I'm forgetting that Burdeene is to come with you on the 1st. Perhaps her aunt won't be willing for her to come with you before that date; consequently I'm sorry I said anything about it. But if our other daughter CAN get off on Saturday, then all three may come, and we'll have her with us just that much longer. But Sister Sacred Heart is not to change any part of her programme just because of a thoughtless whim of mine. Please remember that.—Brader took dinner here to-day, Charles came immediately after, and then, later Mr. Hartman and Mr. Harry Lewis came. But everything is quiet now, and we have no company except the old cow a-lowing in the pasture.—The rain will be the life of the strawberries, and I *think* I can promise you several short-cakes.—Again, to-day, we had strawberry cream, home-friz, and again I denied myself the privilege of making myself uncomfortable by eating of it. Self-denial is a great thing, especially when it prevents me from sitting down in a yellow jacket's nest, or from handling a red-hot poker.—Rufus continues to persist in going to the door with his breeches rolled up. [Small sketch of Rufus]—Miss Louise McIntosh has arrived at Lula's—and there seems to be great commotion in that neigh-borhood. Miss Laura wrote me a note to get her arrival in the paper—"thinking you was going to town"—but unfortunately "you" was done come back, and so the precious advertisement didn't come out to-day.—

A stray rooster wandered into the lot to-day, and at once I had him put in the pen. Nobody would ever think, just to look at me, would ever believe I was so serious-minded as to seize and appropriate a neighbor's rooster in this off-hand way. If I'm found out, I'll say it is a joke. If not, I'll—but wait! I started to say I'd put him in the dinner-pot. But I'll not go as far as that. *He's too old.* I'll be neighborly this once, that is if Mama doesn't want to make some chicken salad. In that case, I know how it will be. She'll say "Seef"—which is short for Josephus, though that never was and never can be my name—she'll say, "Seef, I want to make some chicken salad. Mrs. So-and-so had some the other day; and I'm *sure* if *she* can have chicken salad, *we* can have it too. I'll send her some just to show her she's not the *only* one who can have chicken salad." Then I'll reflect that maybe this stray fowl belongs to Mrs. So-and so, and as *she* is to have a share in the spoils, I'll look wise and say, "Well, *if you choose* you may kill the rooster." So the deed will be done, and Mama will remember how obliging I was, and she'll remark—*probably to the real owner of the rooster*—"My husband's the nicest man in the world; he let me kill his rooster the other day to make some chicken salad." And the real owner will say: "Well, I'm sorry I didn't know about it; I'd have given him a good price for a rooster. We lost ours the other day; *somebody stole him;* and I don't want to buy just *any* kind of a rooster." Then Mama will remember for the first time about the rooster, and she'll come home crestfallen and say: "Jowl!"—(no Seef now!) "Jowl! I think you played me a mean trick about that rooster.—I never did see such a man!" Then I'll lift up my voice and howl, and she'll add: "You don't appreciate how a woman feels about such things. Of course you think it's funny. But I'll tell you now, there's no fun in it."

And so you see how we poor men are treated! Even our innocent jokes are misunderstood. (Goodness know! I hope that old rooster isn't too tough for anything!)—Now when I began this letter I forgot that Mildred is to make her first communion next Sunday. This will make it impossible for you to come home this week. I know the sisters will think it's awful because I forgot this most important; but I hope they won't believe that I take no interest in it; for I do—a very great interest indeed: more than they can imagine.—Evelyn is still at Lithia. He will return Tuesday, whether for good or not, I don't know; though I think he'll stay another week.—Essie was writing to Lillian this afternoon, and no doubt she told her all the news. I can think of no more. Love to Burdeene, and my best and kindest regards to the sisters.

Your loving

Daddy

ALS

5 pp.

Envelope: Return to [. . .] / The Constitution / Atlanta, Ga. / Miss Lillian Harris, / St. Joseph's Academy, / Washington, *Ga.* / *Wilkes county*

PM: 23 May 1898

[May? 1898?] [1]

Sunday Evening.

Dear Mildred: Juvember will come before you know it. Pretend that you are not looking for it, and the first thing you know you'll wake up and find that the first of June has come and that your trunk is all packed for a long vacation in which to romp and play.—Your answer to the guinea pig problem was eminently correct. Please go head [sic].—Sister Julia says that their guinea pigs burrow so that it's hard to keep them in the pen. They got out the other night and the cat caught one. The funny part of it is that our guinea pigs never try to burrow. I think maybe it's because they have so much room in their pen.—Toodlum Boo visited us this morning, and this afternoon he and Chubby Chin-dler went to ride in the buggy. They also went to sleep in the buggy. Toodlum Boo is both tough and rough, and wants to have his own way. He succeeds in this without much trouble. We also have a little moo-calf two or three weeks old. And one of J.C.'s bantams has gone to setting. The little blue hen is setting on thirteen bantam eggs. If they all hatch we'll have most a hatful.—J.C. has a kite—or did have one until it unkited itself by falling in a tree. Before that he used to send it up, using two balls of cord. Lucien made it, and he says he'll make another. Meantime, J.C. is hunting for sparrows with an air-gun.—The donkey has not lost her voice nor Rufus his graceful figure.—We have cake sometimes for dinner, and keep it in the same old tin bandbox, and have to hide it where J.C. and Rufus can't find it.—Roy comes as usual, and continues to work his countenance as if one side of his face were about to drop off.—We planted English peas last Friday, and to-morrow we'll plant some sweet peas.—We don't have any chocolate here, and J.C. says it isn't fair for "you-all" to drink chocolate. I tell him that if he wants that kind of medicine he'll have to go to a girl's school.—We don't have any news here this time of year. The season is not good for news.—When you get homesick ask the sisters to give you more hash. That's what we have here. You must get used to it if you want to enjoy yourself at home—but I forgot: you are going to Canada, where they have nothing but stewed taters.

My love to Burdeene, and regards to the Sisters.

> Your loving
>> Daddy

ALS

2 pp.

1. See note to next letter for dating of it and of this letter.

July 7,—5 p.m. [1898?]¹

Dear Mildred: I received your nice letter. I have written to mama nearly every day, and now I'll write to you. It is raining now, and we have had a real good shower, which is something new in this climate. The ground must feel funny to be wet after being dry so long. But the grass and vegetables like the bath. They have also taken a big drink. I hope the grass in the pasture will get green again, but I'm very much afraid it's dead.—Lillian and Essie are at the matinee, and I think Evelyn carried a girl. Lillian will be sorry about the rain, for she was to go on a bicycle ride with Myra Cole and a few others, including Mitchy King. Lillian had a bicycle skirt made, and she also has some bicycle boots. She says the skirt is as long as mama wanted it, but it seems to me to be pretty short.

Anyhow it will show about half of the lower part of her hindlegs, but as this part will be covered by her boots, I suppose it is all right. I wonder how Essie would look in that kind of a rig! Maybe mama will have to get a skirt and some boots when she comes home[.] And (speaking of home) how is Mama feeling now? Home is a great place, when you look at it from a distance. I think it is a great place, no matter how close I am to it, and I never expect to be as far away from it as you are now. Isn't it about time for mama to be thinking about coming back? It seems like all of you have been gone a long time.—I'm afraid you are not having quite as much fun as you thought you would have.—As J.C. doesn't right (see how I spelled it!) write, I suppose he must be having a royal time. Give my regards to the smokestack of the factory, the puffing of which is so pleasant to mama; and you might say howdy to the river as it rolls by.—The yellow kitten has disappeared. I expect the sparrows caught him.—We had some canteleupes [sic] for breakfast this morning (3 for a quarter) and they were monstrous good (This will make mama's mouth water) [.] And I had a dish of figs besides. Yes siree! home's a fine place and don't you forget it. Lula Z. stayed all night last night. Charles came about 9, and after the whist game was over, he and Essie and Lula and Evy went on the porch and chattered until ½ past eleven, and came in the house and woke me from a sound sleep, and I got up and banged my door, and declared then and there that the price of a game of whist was too high for me to play anymore.—Chloë had the neuralgia to-day, and Rufus is no more bow-legged than he was when you left.—Stewart is lively as ever. He says "Millid gone way." I had my hair singed yesterday to get the cockroaches out of it.—I hope grandma is well again, and I hope Grandpa enjoys the war news.

This is about all the news I have to write. Give my love to all.

From your ever-loving

Daddy

ALS

3 pp.

1. Dated by references to Stewart's talking and to Rufus's working. Stewart was born 27 October 1896; Rufus quit as butler 15 January 1899. See letter to Lillian and Mildred of that date.

[To Lillian]

5 August. [1898]

You'll have to forgive me, my dear Bill; I wrote two pages to Evelyn last week, and then thought my duty was done. The act gave me the idea that I had written to you, and I went blissfully about my business dreaming that my letter would be on time, and that I'd soon have one from you. Not until I read your letter to Mama did I realize that I had neglected my gal; and even then I had to get the whole family to help me remember that I hadn't written, so sure was I that I couldn't possibly have omitted the duty, which is also a very great pleasure.—We gather from your letters that, through the kindness and thoughtfulness of Mr. and Mrs. Biechele and our dear Burdeene you are having the most glorious time of your life so far. I am glad of it, but at the same time, it makes me shiver when I think that we can never adequately repay those lovely people for their kindness. Well! we can only be thankful that there are such people in the world and that our daughter is fortunate enough to have fallen into their hands.—Mildred is gaining in weight and mischief right along. She's been threatening for some time to write to President McKinley and ask him how much it will cost to be his neice [sic]. To-day she was teasing Mama, who called for me to put an end to it. Before I could reply, Mildred called out in shrill tones, "Joel, I wish you'd speak to Mama; she's behaving scandalous!" What are you going to do with a gal like that?—We went down to Zachry's t'other night. Buss was there with a phonograph, and the horn on it was big as a hoss. The music and the recitations sounded as if nine brass bands were playing in your very ears. One or two pieces were good—especially a banjo solo. The trouble seems to be that the horn is on when the pieces are played or spoken into the machine, and this gives them a metallic twang that is very disagreeable. Mildred wanted a graph-o-phone for her birthday gift, and so, after much writing and selecting we've sent the order on. Speaking of brass horns and things, Mr. Buss doesn't seem to be a slam-bangy as I've heard gossips say. He's a very clever man, and has a remarkably good face. I wonder why human beings will persist in talking about one another, or why, if they will talk, they can't find something pleasant to say of those they meet.—Essie weighs ninety-

four, having lost two pounds since her engagement was announced.—
I was really grieved at the death of Bishop Becker. He seemed to be an
old and a very dear friend of mine, though I never met him but once.
He was so wise that he knew how to adapt himself to every one; and he
was very kind to me.—You are having so much pleasure that I hardly
know what you'll do when you return to this dull place. We can cut a five
cent watermelon the week after you return, or we can have batter cakes
for breakfast one Sunday in the month, or we can buy you a bottle of
soda. I'm afraid, though, that this programme (which would have been
deep dissipation for you before you went to Canton) will be no longer
interesting to you. Don't you remember how proud you were when you
could holler over the fence to Mary Richardson, "Oh, Mary! we're going
to have a whole watermelon week after next!" Well—this is all.

Your loving

Daddy

Love to Burdeene and regards to the family.

ALS

2 pp.

Envelope: Miss Lillian Harris, / 207 West Lake street, / Canton, *Ohio* / *care Edward A.
Biechele, Esq.*

PM: 4 August 1898

PART FOUR ❧ 1898–1899
MORE STORIES FOR THE GIRLS

Chewing heavily and earnestly on a dried fig, I seat myself to write to my dear gals, to ax' 'em howdy, and to tell them about such scraps of news as come fluttering my way.

—*Letter to Lillian and Mildred, 12 March 1899*

[To Lillian and Mildred]

Sunday, 18 Sept. [1898]

Dear Billy and Tommy:

It seems like old times to be writing to you again with nothing to write about. I intended to write a letter to each of you to-day, but the weather is too hot. Though the mercury is only 84° it seems to me to be as hot as any day we have had. Everything is quiet, too, except the jay-birds and the brown grasshoppers. The jays are making a big fuss, and the grasshoppers are making a noise like fat meat a-frying. Yes, and Miss Emma Bunker gives a yell once in awhile which serves to remind us that all is not gold that titters.—Nothing new has come to light in guinea pig society, except that one of them bit J.C. to-day. Mama didn't know about it till it was all over, consequently no harm is done. Miss Lena McGeehaughey is to be married to a Texas man next month. This shows that all a girl has to do is to be patient. My own experience shows that ugliness doesn't prevent a man from marrying a pretty woman, and Miss Lena's announcement shows that a girl can't be too ugly to marry. I hope they'll both be happy.

I hope also that Sister Sacred Heart will see to it that Miss Billy Harris takes plenty of exercise. My compliments to Miss Tommy Harris, and I hope she'll allow Miss Billy to make her own bed; and it wouldn't hurt Miss Billy to take up a broom every day and pretend to be sweeping the floor. And so Miss Tommy has now graduated into Sister Bernard's department? I hope both will be pleased; and it would please me to know that Miss Tommy does her best to please that gentle sister; and not to please me only but all.—I think Mama is fatter to-day than ever. She is not worrying much about the other house, or the other house's servants.[1] You know how we old people are. We have spells of that kind, and, for the time, we are not happy unless we are worrying about something.— I'd like to see Father O'Brien occasionally when he comes to town.— If I can remember it, I'll have the Journal sent to you and perhaps The Constitution.—You will say this is a dull letter and so it is. You haven't been gone long enough for news to accumulate, and the donkey is gone, and Rufus is more sedate than usual, so that there is nothing but dull-ness surrounding and enveloping us.—The babies are well, and Lucien was still playing whist at last accounts.—J.C. says he can ride the wheel [bicycle] with one hand. From the way he talks about it, that must be a great feat. Anyhow, I'll add nothing to it. You may expect longer letters hereafter.

Give my regards to the sisters, and to Lumpkin, who write such nice letters.

      Always your loving

         Daddy

ALS

2 pp.

Envelope: Miss Lillian Harris, / St. Joseph's Academy, / Washington, Ga. / *Wilkes county.* / *GaRR.*

PM: [torn off]

1. Home of Lucien and Aileen Harris, next door.

[To Lillian and Mildred]

                                [26 September 1898]

Dear Billy and Tommy: We are having great times here. Lizzie has gone to a Sunday picnic to-day, and Mama is in the kitchen. She calls it "watching" the dinner, but other people not so choice in their language would call it cooking. I don't suppose a man who was hanged would feel any better because the newspapers said he had been "suspended."— Joe Swartz is here. He came last night. He's a right nice looking boy, but seems to be somewhat dull. That may be in appearance only. I suppose he is somewhat shy. I hope we will find out how to make him enjoy himself during the time he stays.—And then, on top of that (as the negroes say) there is a sculptor, a Mr. Okaberg, making a bust of me. You may say that I am on a bust. He comes out every afternoon except Sunday, and I pose for him while he makes a clay model of my face and head. Julia came out yesterday afternoon to watch him, and she seemed to be very much interested. She discovered that the clay model favored Julian, and that seemed to make her happy. I think I rose in her esteem several degrees. Anything that looks like Julian is necessarily good: therefore the clay model is good, and therefore, also, I am much nicer than anybody would have supposed. The sculptor is a swede, and is not at home in the pronunciation of our language, consequently he will be able to catch on my face that "pleasant expression" which photographers demand and never get.—Tommy has two more guinea pigs— very pretty—and J.C. has three more.—Mama has had some new paper put on the walls of the vestibule and sitting-room, and she is feeling very happy. She seems really to enjoy that sort of thing, and if I were able I'd have some paper and new carpets every week. The vestibule is red, so it may now be said that not only the head of the house, but the house itself, is red-headed.—The young Caldwell who married Estelle Irby, has lost his position and has gone to St. Louis. It is said he was gambling and drinking. This is a pity; but it shows that a fond parent may be too fond. I was just fond enough of your brothers to larrup 'em, and now they are fond enough of me to be decent.—I am not writing any editorials to-day. I wrote some yesterday that were crowded out, and they'll either have to put 'em in to-morrow or leave 'em out, I don't care which.—Oh, yes! Mama has new portieres in the hall—if I spell 'em right, and she's had various new fixin's put in. We'll begin to look like we live on Peachtree after awhile, and this seems to be Mama's dearest wish—not to live on Peachtree, but to look like you could live there if you wanted to. We expect Mrs. Young and Mrs. Abernethy to be duly impressed when they plunge head foremost into our splendid mansion, and I'm only sorry that we are not on visiting terms with Mrs. Lovett, so that all our neighbors might see and feel our store-made magnificence. It's a very good thing I'm your pa, otherwise you wouldn't have a red-headed house to come to when you knock off for Christmas.—Essie tried to ride the wheel last night: in fact, she did ride it; and she now feels as if she wished there were no wheels. There's some piece of news I had stored up in my mind to write you, but I can't dig it out, and the fact that I can't worries me no little. It seems to be important, and yet if it were important I'd remember it,—and so the thought of it gallops up and down in my head and makes a bigger fuss than the news would—but it is something; something about your charming sex; something you'd smile to hear; something you'd gloat over; but it hides from me, and I can't get hold of it.—I often think of Father O'Brien and Spot, and I think I'll come down to see them in October.—Of course you'll bring

Burdeene home Christmas, but what about Lumpkin? Wouldn't she like to spend Christmas in Atlanta, or would she rather go home? I think she might come up, just for fun.—I'm writing with my old pen, which was sent to New York to be repointed. She writes from fifteen to twenty words to the line, and by the time you get through this letter you'll say it is a long one. I'm afraid the sisters will have to put on their specs to read it.[1] I can imagine Sister Bernard putting on her glasses, and asking with some curiosity, "What does the man mean?" Well, he only means to make himself pleasant to two little girls, and to give them some news of home that doesn't amount to much. The truth is, everything is going on here just as it would if both of you were on the spot. Perhaps the roses are suffering some from neglect, but they make no complaint, and the blue jays cry out as loudly as ever.—We have had so much house cleaning recently that it is too nice to be lived in, but we can't help ourselves. We are obliged to live in it or camp out next door to the street; but this would be an invitation to burglars, and so mama prefers to sleep in the mansion—though, really, the dust and dirt are horrible. Nobody knows where they come from. Chloë carries out seven barrelsful every Friday, and mama sweeps out seven barrelsful every Saturday. I suppose this is the way to enjoy life, but as for me, I'd prefer to live in a house that didn't have to be swept out but once every fourteen years.

My regards to the sisters, and love to all the girls you know.

    Your affectionate

      Daddy

ALS

2 pp.

Envelope: Miss Lillian Harris, / St. Joseph's Academy, / Washington, *Ga*. / *Wilkes county*. PM: 26 September 1898

1. Because JCH's script is unusually small in this letter.

[To Lillian]

                                        2 Oct. [1898]

"Is the bust to be of marble?" Oh, dear! What a funny question! No! it's to be of chalk, or, rather of the best grade of plaster of Paris. Marble would be too heavy for me to carry around in my valise and set up in the hotels when I travel. What I want, in the way of a bust, is something light and *durable* and *not* too heavy. I think from the way the Thing looks now, that it will be quite ornamental. At present its name is MUD. It is growing to be horribly real. I believe it would sneeze if you tickled it on the nose. I think I'll try it to-night when everybody has gone to bed. And if it *should* sneeze—well, my address will be Cavity, Isle of Goose-on, Philippine Archipellygo. On the base of it, in front, close to the Thing's manly Bosom, there is to be some small figures in relief— figures to show my trade, or stock in trade, namely: rabbits and other innocent reptiles. The man's name is Okerberg. He's a Swede and he talks English about as well as Mr. Vaigner. He is quite conscientious in his use of mud, and seems to be interested in his work. He's doing this work on his own responsibility. I suppose he wants to advertise himself. I told him he had come to a cold country for art; but that had no effect on him. If he zoomed when he was laying on the clay, he'd put me in mind of a huge dirt-dauber, or, as Sister Bernard would call it, a mud wasp.

Speaking of Mr. Vaigner, he went to town with me this morning. He snuggled up close to me on the seat, and began to talk. Says he, "Meester Airs, von't you tink Paw's failin' soom?" "Who?" says I[.] "Pa," says he, "Mein fader-in-law. He mighty good man. He tink more of me as he done ov his own child. One time dey come an' say, 'Paw, you mus' git out dat whoolsale leequor beeznis.' He say, 'Go shut your mout'.' Den, little while, I go too'm, an' I say 'Paw, you mus' take your name from doze sign in Anniston on dat whoolsale leequor house.' He say, 'you tink so, Frade?' I nod my haid. For two days he von't eat nuttings. Den he coom where I been, an' I say, 'Paw, dicken in de Bap's church mus' have no name on wholesale leequor house.' Den he git on train, an' go down dere an' have hees name struck out. Ah, he mighty good man, I tink he growin' more feeble, for why he aint got nuttings to do. He all right fer utter side!" Mr. Vaigner made this last remark with the air of one who knew that the old man had a through ticket in his pocket.

I know of no new transactions in society circles. The other family is well. Mrs. Bunker has returned. I suppose she has a Boston cold, or we should have heard her melodious voice ere this. J.C. rides the wheel every day, and seems to enjoy it. West Swartz will probably stay at the post here a year. He has nothing to do, and he knows how to do it to the queen's taste. I was just about to name him Mary R. Swartz when he retired. He's a very clever boy, but he is troubled with a revolving tongue, which moves like an electric fan—only it makes more fuss. Mama cleaned the house again yesterday, and to-day she's not feeling so well. If I worked as hard as she does, I'd be in the hospital. She doesn't have it to do; she just does it for the fun of the thing.—Rufus is getting more limber in the shanks and lazier. We'll have to send him home for good before long.—Essie and Charles are still spooning about in the corners. They love each other with the kind of love which makes you grit your teeth and bite nails in two. I'm thinking about my coal and gas bills this winter.—They say John Matthews no longer goes to Ray's. The old folks filed objections. Minette Lee is again with Mrs. Humphries. She says it's lovely in West End.—Essie and Lula went to Angela Otis's wedding, and also to Piedmont Park to see the soldiers drill.

If there is any more news, Mama and Essie will write it. I am now worried by the idea that the bust will be so much like me that it will chew tobacco. If that is the case we can't keep it in the parlor.

I enclose a cheque for $200. The bill is $194, and the $6 extra is for you both to use as pocket money[.]

My regards to the Sisters.

Your loving

Daddy

ALS

2 pp.

Envelope: Return to Box 111, / *Atlanta, Ga.* / Miss Lillian Harris, / St. Joseph's Academy, / Washington, *Ga.* / *Wilkes county*

PM: 3 October 1898

[To Lillian]

9 *October.* [1898]

Dear Billy: As usual, the dearth of news enables me to say that we are all well and thankful that matters are no worse. What matters? you will ask. Why, just anything and everything: For instance, Mrs. Z. borrowed Mama's cloak or cape Saturday night; maybe Mama is thankful that she didn't borrow a dress. I don't know. She never said so. I think she feels a kind of secret pride that she is able to lend something to Lucien's wife's mother. No doubt you'll have the same feeling some day when you are a mother-in-law.—There was a great uproar in Chloë's family last week. Her neice [sic] died and the remains had to be carried to Fayetteville. We had never heard of the neice before she died, and if Chloë had cared anything for her she would have said something about her. But now that she was dead and had to be carried to Fayetteville, and there was an opportunity for a picnic, it was very important that she should let us know how dear the neice had been in life. So she, and Lizzie and Johnson packed up their umbrellas and went off to Fayetteville, leaving Mama to do the cooking. Fortunately Mama is a pretty good cook, and we got along very well, but it was a great strain on her to be in that hot kitchen a day.—The other house is well. The babies are in good health. Alleen seems to be well. Lucien is about as usual. You never know whether he is well or not. Stewart spent the day with us recently, and seemed to enjoy the change.—I don't know who's sick at Frazier's; but it's somebody; nobody has told me, but I've never yet known the time when they were all well at the same time. Did you read Julian's article in last Sunday's paper about Mr. Bine?[1] I had the The Constitution sent to you for three months. If you want the Journal too, I'll have the time extended. I have just told Evelyn to have the Kodak fixed to-morrow. If it's ready in time, we'll send it by Burdeene. But don't pin any hopes on Evelyn's memory. Sometimes when he goes to bed he forgets to go to sleep. I think he is in love. He and Essie have what they call "hot and cold flushes."— Charles has now taken the place of Henderson, artist, and is on permanently. If he succeeds in filling it satisfactorily, he'll soon be drawing a comfortable salary, and then—"Oh, I wish you'd hush!" exclaims Essie and consequently I'll hush.

Speaking of Guinea pigs, another Lovett kid has come to town. Mr. Garnsey also has a son. He wrote me a letter about it the other day. Think of that man walking the floor in his pajamas,—trying for to get a squalling baby to sleep.—What are you homesick about? There isn't anything very enticing up here. If you were here you'd sit around doing nothing, and you'd have to take medicine every other day. I hope the sisters will make you take plenty of exercise. You should make up a dozen beds before breakfast and sweep all the rooms downstairs, including the porch, and then you might split up a cord of kindling wood before supper. Don't be homesick. Essie's homesick and she's at home. Sometimes she looks like she's sea sick.—The man is making considerable headway on my bust. He wants to make one of Colonel Johnston also—which reminds me to thank Father O'Brien for sending me the Catholic Mirror with the account of the funeral. I was also much interested in James R. Randall's letter.—Julia came out yesterday afternoon. She is very much pleased with the bust and continues to discover in it a great resemblance to Julian[.] Dovey and Lovey are off to Washington, D.C. to-day to escort Henrietta that far on her way to school. I don't know where she is going, but I know that Pop Collier is wasting his money. John is getting on finely in the high school. Roy says he is very smart. Myra Cole came over yesterday afternoon and said that Harry is trying for first honor. He is also president of the boys' debating society.

Well, I have followed my nose thus far, and have brought myself to the end of a very dull letter. My regards to the Sisters.

    Your loving

    Daddy

ALS

2 pp.

Envelope: Miss Lillian Harris, / St. Joseph's Academy, / Washington, Ga. / *Wilkes county / Ga. R.R.*

PM: [9] October [1898]

1. A comic family invented by Julian Harris to discuss current issues. The married couple, Cardigan and Constance Bine, first appears in "Factious Fractions and Fractious Factions Amuse the Bine family," Atlanta *Constitution*, Sunday, 2 October 1898, 15.

[To Mildred]

                        10 October. [1898]

Dear Tommy: I take my pen in hand for to send you a private letter, although there is nothing to write about[.] J.C. now considers himself the Prisoner of West Zend-ah! because I won't let him gad about this afternoon. He is now at Alleen's. Stewart came down just now with a note tied around his neck—a note to Lucien who had gone to sleep on the sofa. The note was from Alleen and read—"Lucien: Come home a minute." I suppose Alleen was by herself, but it seems to me that one of the two negroes might stay every Sunday.—One of J.C.'s young Guinea pigs was found dead to-day. His pigeons—he paid for them himself— are very pretty, but I don't think he'll have any success with them. He's too lazy, or, rather, he likes to gad about too much, to attend to them. We now have 53 guinea pigs in all, not counting the ones he sold, or disposed of, to Roy and Fritz.—To-day, Mr. Wagner's blind horse fell in the ditch that had been dug to put sewer pipes in. The ditch was so deep it took several people quite a long time to get the horse out.—I keep on forgetting to tell Lillian that our violets are not blooming. The foliage is so thick that they won't bloom till colder weather; or, it may be that they exhausted themselves last year. Anyhow there are thousands of bloom buds on the vines.—Miss Emma Bunker is well. Mrs. Bunker exercised her voice last night. She made it gallop through the air at a lively rate.— J.C.'s feet are growing very rapidly. We have tried four pairs of shoes on him, each pair larger than the other, and they are all too small. His instep is not on the bottom of his feet like Rufus's, but his feet are nearly as large as Rufus's. Chloe brought her baby to the house the other day. It is a very slick looking Senegambian. I believe this is all the important news I have, except that I forgot to tell Lillian that I may come down for a day after the man finishes my bust. Regards to the sisters and love to the girls.

>Your loving
>Daddy

ALS
1 p.
Envelope: Miss Mildred Harris / St. Joseph's Academy, / Washington, Ga. / *Wilkes County / Ga RR*
PM: 10 October [1898]

[To Lillian and Mildred]

>*Sunday, 16 October* [1898]

Dear Billy and Tommy: I, too, have been troubled with a headache, which is now nearly well. I'm sure you didn't enjoy my visit as much as I did. I had a splendid time all the time I was there, and enjoyed every moment. But when I got to Barnett Thursday afternoon, and found that the Augusta train was forty minutes late, I began to have that tired feeling.[1] And then, when I found that it was *one hour* and forty minutes late, I began to realize that I was in a strange country and a long, long way from home. It was eleven o'clock when I arrived at home, and Mama and Essie were in a terrible state for fear I wouldn't come. They had poor Brader to protect them, but even that frail prop was about to be removed, for Brader has his own folks to look after. Well—everything turned out all right, but I don't want the trains to be late the next time I go to Washington. I hope Burdeene didn't grow weary of trotting about with me. She had an air of fatigue, and a kind of pained expression on her face, which seemed to say, "Oh, when *will* the man go home and give us a rest?"

I don't think Lillian had entirely recovered when she wrote last. In addressing her letter she suppressed my surname, but I don't care; if she's going to suppress the Harris end of it, she'll have to be called Miss Lily Chandler. I enclose the envelope. It will give the sisters and Mildred something to laugh over. Friday I had symptoms of a headache and Saturday it came upon the scene with flying colors. I didn't go to bed, but I came very near it.—The weather has been very cold here, too. When I got home Thursday night the nor'west wind was blowing cold, but they had a fire at home[.] We have had three frosts: a big one Saturday morning.—On looking closer at the address Lillian wrote I find that it is "Joel C Handler" or "Joel C Dandler." This shows how notorious I am in the midst of my charming family. I was afraid I'd be sore from walking and riding so much, but I am not, and so I have only pleasant memories of Washington-Wilkes. Mr. Benson's crop of mint juleps is a very large one, but one is not compelled to eat too much of that sort of fruit. My face was sore from sun-burn, but a little violet vaseline cured it and caused the redness to vanish.—I neglected to go to the Academy and bid the Sisters good-bye. This shows that I'm not very polite; but I hope they won't think I'm ungracious. I need somebody to tell me what to do in matters of this kind, for my mind is constantly in the clouds.— In leaving I told you I'd be back yesterday week, which would be next Saturday. But don't expect me then. I may come on Saturday the 30th (or is it 31?)* and stay till the next Tuesday; but even this is not quite sure. I'll write you timely notice.—As for news, there's none to relate. Essie is not fattening any, but she seems to be feeling pretty well. Mr. and Mrs. Bine seem to be well.[2] The scalper, or sculptor, is making progress. Mr. Mud seems to "favor" me. I do hope he won't take to tobacco chewing. Mama is well, and apparently growing stouter. We have all the stoves up, but the weather has moderated this afternoon, and I'm perspiring in the dining-room. Evelyn is well and happy. The other household, including babies, is all serene; and the Martins have not yet "busted" their "melodion"—what a name for discord!—My regards to Sister Bernard and Sister Mary Louis. And to Sister Sacred Heart, to whom my gratitude is due for her kindness in "hauling" me from the depot, and for her courtesies of various kinds[.] My love to Burdeene.

> From your loving
> Daddy

*. So 'elf me gracious! it's the 29th!

ALS

2 pp.

Envelope: Miss Lillian Harris, / St. Joseph's Academy, / Washington, *Ga* / *Wilkes county* / GaRR.

PM: 17 October [. . .]

1. Barnett, Georgia, in Warren County.

2. The Bine family were invented by Julian Harris for his column in the Atlanta *Constitution*. The reference here may be to this fictional family or to Julian and Julia Harris (see letter to Lillian, 9 October 1898). Julia later used the pen name "Constance Bine" for some of her newspaper work.

[To Lillian and Mildred]

Wednesday, 26. [26 October 1898]

Dear Billy and Tommy:

Mama intended to write to-day, but her head is hurting her and she thinks that writing would make it hurt more. She is up and about; but she is not well yet. She has very little appetite, but she seems to be improving. The weather is very cold here to-day, the thermometer being down to 40°. Yesterday was warm and delightful, but last night a heavy rain fell, and, this morning the northwest wind was booming along at the rate of steen or stetty miles an hour. Such is the glorious climate of Atlanty, Ga.—Today is the anniversary of the marriage of dovey and lovey.[1] Someone suggested that I make them a present, but I frowned and said "No, I'll make no presents to those who are not willing to make me a present of a grandson or a granddaughter."—Mary T. Conley called on Essie this morning. Alleen has been here sewing on the machine to-day, the first time she has called since mama's been sick. Mama says she has already attended to the matter about Mildred's dress, and will send the slippers to-morrow. She's not too sick to look after things, but she's too sick to feel very good. She's languid—and no wonder! for she's taken enough pills of one sort and another to make anybody languid. Essie says she'll write to-morrow. I'll try and send the kodak to-morrow, but you know how forgetful I am. Evelyn has attended to the films, but has not yet got them from the photographer. He forgot to tell Julian that Mama is ailing, consequently Julian hasn't been out.—I'll have to get in my flannels to-night. This wind is what Shakespeare calls "a nipping and a nigger air."—As I am writing for Mama, I'll write only a page. The truth is there's nothing to write about. The Stanton lots in front of the house are to be auctioned off to-morrow. I hope the man will get good prices, but I doubt it. West was here Monday night.

Which is all I can think of at present.

Your loving Mama—

per

Daddy

ALS

1 p.

Envelope: Miss Lillian Harris, / St. Joseph's Academy, / Washington, Ga. / Wilkes county

PM: 27 October 1898

1. Reference to Julian and Julia Harris's marriage, 26 October 1897.

[To Lillian and Mildred]

Sunday 26. [26 October 1898]

Dear Billy and Tommy:

Mama has been sick all the week, not confined to the bed all the time, for she would get up and walk around, and still too ill to do anything but sit around and grunt. Last Sunday night she had a pain in her head, and, thinking to ease it, she poured some camphor on her handkerchief and held it to her temple. She must have gone to sleep with the camphorated handkerchief pressed against her face, for the next morning there was a big black scar near her right eye, the result of a blister, and her eye had a "blubber" under it. A stranger would have thought that she had been engaged in a prize fight, or that she had fallen out of bed and bruised herself. I have teased her a good deal about it, as you may imagine, but I was afraid all the time that she would have a serious illness[.] The whole cause of it is over-exertion at house-cleaning, of which there is no end in this mansion. Saturday, ill as she was, I saw her going around the house with a cup of tea in her hand, and enveloped in a cloud of dust, showing Chloë and Rufus what to wipe, and where to sweep, or scrub. It seems to be a mania that illness does not modify. The doctor called twice, and gave her a lot of medicine, but I am convinced that the partial rest she has been compelled to take has done her more good than all the medicine she has taken. It's no use to tell Mama that she's getting old. She seems [to] think the older she grows the more she should work. She climbs up the walls, perches herself on the very top of the step-ladder, and performs other startling acrobatic feats. But she is very much better now; in fact is up and about, and has a fairly good appetite; and I think she'll do fairly well if she doesn't try to walk the clothes line or climb on top of the house to see if the shingles have nails in them.—The man is through with the bust at last. The worst job of all was making a mould. First, he put a string over the head of the clay model; then he put on plaster of paris, flinging it on with his hands, as you would flirt water over flowers. In this way he built the mould up to be about four inches thick. Then, while the plaster was still soft, he seized the string by one end and pulled it through the soft stuff, thus dividing the mould into halves. Then when the stuff had hardened, he pulled off one half—the back of the head and shoulders. Then, with a trowel, he dug the soft clay from the face, and when that was all out, all he had to do was to put the two halves of the mould together, pour in plaster, and then, when it had hardened, knock the mould to pieces, and there was his first "cast," which he calls his "waste cast," since it is only to be used to make a "piece mould"—that is to say, a mould composed of pieces that can be put together and taken apart again without breaking. This "piece mould" will be used to make the casts that are to be preserved. All this as you can see, involves an immense amount of work, and really hard work at that. I'm glad the job over, for the sittings were getting to be somewhat monotonous, even to a patient man.—At church to-day, the Bishop said to the organist during the service, "Don't play such long preludes; we are not getting much music anyhow, and the shorter it is the better."—I'm sorry I didn't see Sisters Bernard and Mary Louis, except to shake hands with them; but it was all their fault. Goodness knows, I was hanging around the academy a great deal. I felt, indeed, as if I were interfering in some way with the exercises.—Essie had a fainting spell the other day while Mama was trying a waist on her. The episode upset Mama worse than it did Essie. She fainted, came to, and that was the end of it with her; but Mama went around all day heaving deep sighs and trying to recover from the shock. Essie is very thin and delicate; but she won't take outdoor exercise, and she won't do anything except take such medicine as the baffled doctor can prescribe.—I don't know where W. Higgins heard the astonishing news: not from here. I daresay there will be a match between Essie and Charles some day; I hope so for both their sakes; but it is impossible to say *when*. You shall be advised of it just as soon as I know anything about it.[1]—Rufus went to a "Singin'" to-day, and Milleage, his brer, took an' took his place. I hope Rufus sang with his feet. If he used his mouth, I'm sure the congregation fled:— There's no news here to speak of. The weather has been cold, but to-day fairly warm, and the roses are blooming. J.C. has gone 'simmon-hunting with Roy and Grace. The babies are well, and, in addition to being well, Stewart is mean and bad tempered. He and I will never be friendly till his doting parents use a shingle on him thirty or forty times a day. The various animals and creeturs on the place seem to be flourishing.

My regards to the sisters I know, and love to Burdeene.

Your loving

Daddy

ALS

3 pp.

Envelope: Miss Mildred Harris, / St. Joseph's Academy, / Washington, / Wilkes county / *Ga.*

PM: 27 September 1897[2]

1. Essie LaRose, Mrs. JCH's niece, did marry Charles Kelly. JCH often makes humorous comments about their protracted romance and engagement.

2. Dating of this letter is difficult. Supplied Emory date of 26 September 1897 and that of envelope postmark 27 September 1897 do not fit internal evidence. The sculpture referred to is the bust made of JCH in the Fall of 1898. Also Aileen's babies (mentioned) were Stewart (born 27 October 1896) and Joel Chandler Harris III (born 17 December 1897). Though both letters dated "Wednesday, 26." and "Sunday, 26." have salutations to both girls, the envelope of first is addressed to Lillian Harris and the second to Mildred. Also the first letter is by JCH on behalf of his wife. Perhaps the latter envelope was switched with an earlier one addressed to Mildred. Probably 26 October 1898 is the correct date of the second letter as the letter to Lillian and Mildred, 30 October [1898] mentions Mrs. JCH's camphor blister. Note also reference to hunting persimmons; they ripen only after a frost, an unlikely event in Georgia in September.

[late October 1898]

Dear Julian:

This will introduce to you Mr. K. Okerberg,[1] the gentleman who made a bust of me[.] The finished cast is on exhibition at the young men's library. It might help him to have the affair noticed in the paper.[2] You might have a photograph of it made and reproduce it in the paper for Sunday. The folks here say it is fine.

You will find Mr. Okerberg a very refined and agreeable gentleman, and I recommend him to your courteous attention.

> Your
>
> Father

ALS

1 p.

Envelope: Julian Harris, Esq. / City Editor / The Constitution / Present / Introducing Mr. K. Okerberg.

1. Knut Okerberg, sculptor. Harris first refers to bust and sculptor in his letter to Lillian and Mildred dated 26 September 1898.

2. An article headed "Clever Sculptor's Work," about exhibit of the bust of JCH by Knut Okerberg at the Young Men's Library Association, appeared in the Atlanta *Constitution*, Friday, 28 October 1898, 9. The bust had taken a month's work. Drawing of JCH's bust appeared in Atlanta *Constitution*, 6 November 1898, 4.

[To Lillian and Mildred]

Sunday, Oct. 30 [1898]

Dear Girls: Mama is better to-day than she has been. She was afraid to venture to church, but she rigged herself up in her Sunday-go-to-meetin' toggery, and is looking "Pretty-well-I-thank you;-how-do-you-do-yourself-?" The worst part of the camphor blister stills presents an inflamed appearance. I think when the scab comes off, there will be a scar there, such as a burn would leave. The camphor seems to have eaten into the flesh a little way. I never knew before that camphor was such a dangerous fluid to handle[.] Ordinarily, it evaporates so quickly that no harm comes from rubbing the skin with it; but Mama must have saturated her handkerchief with it and then placed it between her face and the pillow. I'm glad it's no worse, and I'm glad she's getting better. There isn't any fun in this house when Mama is ill.[1] Things get tangled. The system (or order) runs down and there's no one to wind it up.—I suppose you read of the murder on the street car.[2] Queer things are getting common. We seem to be coming to the verge of those days foretold in the Apocalypse, when there shall be strange happenings, and people shall run to and fro filled with delusions. It is very sad—or, rather, it would be very sad if we didn't know that in the Lord's good time every-thing will be straightened out.—I couldn't come down owing to Mama's ailing. To-day was to be her "bad" day, and though she was willing for me to go, I should have felt somewhat uneasy. This would have taken the edge off my enjoyment. But I'll come down before long.—Evelyn has been made night city editor in place of Royal Daniel, who went to the Journal. Evelyn got the place on his merits. Julian refused to appoint him, and Clark Howell took the matter out of his hands and made the appointment himself. Evelyn will have a better chance now to sleep. He gets home at 3 a.m. and sleeps till 1 p.m., about 9 hours. He will also have every Sunday off unless in case of an emergency.—Essie says that the firm of L. & E. now has 108 pennies in the box, which is pretty good for a beginning. Did Lillian say in her letter the other day that it was only a month to Christmas? If so she is somewhat mixed in *dates,* or stewed prunes. Anyhow, Christmas will be here before you realize it.—Mildred's report was the pleasantest kind of surprise. I got behind the door and hugged myself. I said to myself, "My Tommy is the nicest kind of a girl. She has found out that she can have fun and learn her lessons! too; and now she'll show everybody just how smart she can be." And I thanked my stars that both of you were in the hands of teachers who have the gift of teaching. I am certainly proud of that report. Mama says she's going to have it framed. I have know [sic] all along that when my Tommy began to take a real interest in her books she'd show folks that a girl may be healthy and rollicking and studious too.—Alleen and the babies are well.—I suppose the violets are blooming. I haven't been paying much attention to them owing to the weather. When the east wind blows, or when the nor'west begins to blow its breath in my face I always feel like going to bed and putting my head under the cover. There's nothing of any importance to write about. Brader continues to wear good clothes and deny a future existence (which he seems to be on the brink of) while his Aunt, (poor lady!) who supports him finds it difficult to make both ends meet. Mama says she feels sometimes like taking Brader and shaking him; but he'll be shaken soon enough.—The guinea pigs are all serene, but it is a hard matter to compel J.C. to feed them regularly. On two or three occasions, he's been closer to the back of the hair brush than he has any idea of. I don't suppose h[. . .] learning anything. Little Myra is clever enough, but I dare say she knows as little about the art of teaching as any person on the globe.—All the stoves are up now, and, while we don't want to see old Boreas, we are ready for him.—Mama will be well enough to write to you this week.—You see, I forgot the Kodak. As I have to go to the express office in the morning I'll try and think of it *And the films!* I declare! We are the pokiest set up here you ever saw. We never do anything right.

Right here is a good place to saw this rambling letter off. Regards to the sisters, and love to Burdeene.

Your loving

Daddy

ALS

2 pp.

1. *Cf.* reference to this accident in joint letter of "Sunday, 26." [26 October 1898].

2. Front-page story and sketch appeared in the Atlanta *Constitution*, 29 October 1898, entitled "Maniac Murders One Man and Injures Two Others"; he cut a passenger's jugular vein with a pocket knife on an Atlanta trolley car.

[To Lillian and Mildred]

The 6 of Nov. [1898]

Here comes the old Man, a-writing to his dear gals with nothing whatsomever for to write about. And it's a mighty bad fix for to be in, a-writing to somebody and with nothing whatsomever to write, but— . . . . As I was coming home from town yesterday, two negroes got on the car at High's corner[1]—two negro men. One had a valise and was from the country. The other had met him at the train. They were probably related. The town negro asked about many people whom he had formerly known in the town or settlement where the country negro came from. Finally, after a pause, he asked: "An' how is—ol' Tom Benson?" The country negro: "Humph! he dead; dat's how he is." Town negro: "Well, suh! Tooby sho, tooby sho. Why when did ol' Tom die?" Country Negro: "Day 'fo' yistiddy; dat's when." Town N. "Well, suh!—I thought he couldn't 'a' been dead so mighty long. What de matter wid him?" Country N.: "Trouble wid his Mu-ky-ous Membrine. It sho tuck an' tuck him off." Town N.: "De Mu-ky-ouse Membrine! Well, suh!" Country N.: Dat's what! An' I tell you right now, ef I has any trouble wid de Mu-ky-ous Membrine, I'm gwine ter sen' fer all de doctors in de town. I aint sayin' dee'l come, an' dee may not come; *but dee aint gwine ter sleep none dat night!*" Town n.: "I believe you!" In spite of myself, I had to drop a laugh to the memory of poor Tom Benson (whoever he was) and his Mu-ky-ous Membrine—which, I suppose, is another name for the Mucous Membrine.—Well! well! here comes the old man, a-writing to his dear gals and with nothing whatsomever for to write about. Mama went to church today, and it seemed to do her good. She has been very cheerful and chipper all day, and I hope she has weathered her bad spell. Things are very bad about the house when mama is ailing. It does no good for me to put on one of Chloë's frocks and try to keep things straight. They will go wrong. And I can't sit down and gossip with Mrs. Young, and Mrs. Abernethy, and the rest. I can listen but that doesn't satisfy them. When they tell something sweet about a neighbor or an acquaintance, they want to hear something sweet in return about somebody else. But how do I know that Mrs. So-and-so has taken off her mourning too soon, or that Mr. So-and-so is cutting his eye at Miss Prissy, and he old enough to be her father. No; everything goes wrong when Mama is ailing, and even the gossip gets stale. But, as I told you, she is getting better now, and everything will brighten up—nothing more so than poor me. Owing to the fact that Mildred's report was so good, and to the further fact that she is too large to be homesick, she has four new guinea pigs. Mama says that Lillian may buy Mildred a plain prayer book for every day service, and save the one at home for special occasions, or until she is old enough to appreciate and take care of it. Lillian asked me something about the Philippine question. There are two Philippine questions; one is agitated by our politicians and may be stated thus—"Is it good policy for the United States to take charge of these islands, considering their distance from us and the character of the population." On this point neither party knows where it is "at." There are inward divisions in both political parties on this question. But Mr. McKinley, thinking that the people will endorse annexation, has instructed our commissioners in Paris to demand the surrender of the islands from Spain. The Spanish commissioners have refused the demand, and negotiations have come to a standstill. As to the result, the papers this week will be able to [tell] you more about it than I can at this moment.[2]—Well, as I said before, here comes the old man a-writing to his dear gals, and with nothing whatsomever for to write about. Nevertheless, I think Lillian's letters are improving, not only as to handwriting, but as to expression. Mildred's would be better if they were longer. When she was a little girl, short and sweet letters were all that could be expected, but now that she is a big girl, and is beginning to see the necessity of studying, longer letters are in order. However, I'm not complaining. I know how hard it is for that restless young lady to compose her mind long enough to compose a letter.—Lillian's report was very good—extremely good in fact, so far as the studies are concerned; but there was one flaw in observance of the rules[.] I should think it would be easier to observe the rules than to learn all those hard lessons. Still, I am not complaining, merely making random comments.—Everything is the same here, now that Mama's well. The other family is well and happy. Mrs. Abernethy has been ill and is well again. Minette Lee has been to call on Essie. Charles followed suit and is here to-night. Brader has just gone. Mrs. Z. was here yesterday, as full of life as ever.[3] Evelyn seems to be improving since he has had regular hours. He sleeps now from 4 a.m. to 1 p.m. Julian has been slightly ill, but is well now. Nora Belle Rosser has had a slight relapse, not serious so far. Lillian's mistake about Christmas will not be a mistake very long. Thanksgiving will soon be here, and it's not a long jump from then to Christmas. [sketches of foot/paw and bent knee] Bill was here also, and J.C. went with Lucien and Stewart. Stewart said, "Man shoot, shoot, shoot." No more, dear gals, till next time, when I hope that the old man who comes a-writin' with nothing for to write about will have something more interesting to say.

Your loving

Daddy

(1,215 words, worth $35)

ALS

2 pp.

1. Atlanta department store of J.M. High, then at Whitehall and Hunter streets. A bequest from the family established the High Museum of Art.

2. One of the issues in the peace negotiations (1898) that concluded the Spanish-American War (1895–98). The treaty granted the Philippine Islands to the U.S.A. in December 1898 for $20 million.

3. Probably Mrs. Zachry, Aileen's mother.

[To Lillian and Mildred]

Saturday night: November 12. [1898]

If you'll believe me, dear gals, there were some queer goings on in this house yesterday and the day before. All is quiet now, but memory will linger around those queer doings. In the first place, there was mystery in the air. There was a bag of seedless raisins here, a bowl of scalded almonds there, and a jug of black 'lasses yonder: and then there was Mama running about between kitchen and dining-room, a business-like frown on her forehead and a streak of smut on her chin, as if she had been peeping in the recesses of the range. I pretended not to notice anything, but I was thinking hard, and trying to solve the mystery. After awhile a whiff came stealing from the kitchen and giving odor, as Uncle Shakespeare says, and then I knew, 'cause nothing else smells like a great, big, fat brown fruit cake. And then Mama said it was thirsty, very thirsty, and she gave it a wineglass full of raw red whisky. This made it drunk, of course, but she says that by Christmas it will be perfectly sober and ripe. At which time, dear gals I hope to sit back in my big arm-chair and watch you and Burdeene nibble at this famous cake: a cake, by the way, that is already causing trouble, for Mama, who has been watching over it like a hawk, has just discovered that someone has already been pinching pieces from it. A Rat did it, and Rufus is the Rat[.] And Mama! Well, *she* isn't angry; no, she's horrified, shocked, convulsed. How could anybody be so vicious and abandoned—so lost to all sense of patriotism and national honor, to say nothing of local and state pride—as to deliberately and with deep calculation nibble at that wonderful dark brown fruit cake; and so long before Nibbling-time at that?

Ahem! I am now—well:

Lucky Frank Stanton! Lucky not only in having the gift of writing the beautiful lyrics that are gathered together in his new book of poems called, "Comes One With A Song," but in having Joel Chandler Harris for critic! Mr. Harris, in the Atlanta Constitution says:

"This is the supreme test of lyric poetry, to give new energy and life to emotions and sentiments familiar to the heart and mind, to stir again the hopes of youth, and to rap with unfaltering hand upon the door of love and romance."

And of Stanton's book: "it is wholesome and mellow. It is more; it is hearty and honest and simple, it is homely and hopeful and helpful; above all, it is cheerful."

Lucky Atlanta! To have two such poets as Stanton
and Harris: one who writes in liquid verse, and
one whose prose is poetry.[1]

The Saturday Review—Atlanta—a woman's
club and society paper [Harris's comment written on
slip]

Oh, hush, dear gals! I feel too good! My *prose* is *er*-poetry! I always
thought I ought to wear a standing-collar!—There was great excitement in this neighborhood Thursday. Alleen's cook came running with a
scared face, calling for Mama to go up there, that Miss Alleen had cut her
hand and had fainted. "Gimme the turpentine bottle and some whisky!"
says Mama; but before anybody could get the turpentine or the whisky,
she was sailing across the field, waving her arms. She found Alleen on
the floor in the kitchen, soused her with water, had her put on the sofa,
and sent for the doctor. By that time J.C. had been to the Zachry's and
Mrs. Z. came running in wild-eyed and with her hair down. Alleen is
all right now, and so is Mama; they both went to Pinafore to-day. Mama
will describe the Alleen episode better than I can.—J.C. went to the
pony show to-day. After coming back he said he was sorry he didn't go
to Pinafore. "I've swallowed my cake, and, oh, how I wish it had been
candy!" Fiddlesticks! it's the way of the world, dear gals. No sooner does
one pleasure begin to weary us, than we wish it had been something
else; and the most of us never find out that a *cheerful, contented* mind
is the source of all pleasure and happiness (Oho! says Mildred—look at
papa trying to preach!—I declare, papa's too funny! says Lillian) What
was I saying when you interrupted me? Well, never mind—oh, yes! it
was about a cheerful and contented mind. We can't have that, you know,
unless we try hard to be good: we can't be *absolutely* good, try as hard
as we may, but the harder we try, the more contented we'll be. (Pull him
down from that platform! says Mildred. What about the violets? says
Lillian.) Oh, dear! I'll never be able to lecture if I'm to be thus flurried
and flustered by my dear gals. The violets are doing nicely, and so are the
roses; but there's no one to pluck them. Rufus? Well, you know Rufus's
legs are so arranged that he has to lie down when he squats, and he can't

pick violets long at a time. If I tell him to pick some Mama sends him to mail a letter, and when he comes back Essie sends him on an errand; and then the fires must be fixed, and more coal brought up; or the guinea pigs must be fed; or the back yard must be swept; or the cows must be attended to; or dinner must be put on the table; or Evelyn's bed must be made up, or he must be sent to West End for something we forgot to order; and so forth and so on the whole day long.—However, as I was saying, if we only try to be good (*Pa-Pa!* cries Mildred. Papa, *please* tell us something interesting, sighs Lillian) Let's see—um—um—um—oh, yes! the baby can shut his eyes and shake his head and play patty-cake when politely requested to do so: and Stewart is as mild as a buck.[2] Essie has had her purtygraph struck, and it is a splendid picture. Charles is to have one in a frame with a cloth-mat on which Essie is embroidering some sweet little forget-me-nots[.] I declare! it makes me feel ticklish all over when I think of the little thrills and throbs that will be embroidered into that mat. And the man (alas that it should be so!) will look at the picture and at the embroidered border, and never imagine all that has gone into the stitches. Heigho! it's the way with my lovely sex. I should have been a woman: I think I'm too tender hearted for a man; it frets me.[3] Shucks! here I am moralizing again!—

Sunday evening

—You see I had to break off yesterday at just the right point. I was getting sentimental, and that, in a middle-aged person, will never do. It becomes humorous. Sentiment is a thin crust over which the light feet of the young man tread safely, but we older ones would be sure to break through, and then what shouts of laughter from the giddy spectators on the bank!—The weather is heavy and cloudy, enough to make anybody but me a trifle gloomy. But the birds seem to take it sensibly, and why not I?—Harry L. called this afternoon and buzzed, and buzzed. Mama was not feeling so well this morning, but she has brightened up this evening. All the rest are well, including the dogs and the guinea pigs. The dogs have each a dry goods box to sleep in, and they are like the boy in the poem—Longfellow's, I believe. As the boy was toiling up the mountain, the maiden fair invited him to rest his head on her bosom, but he, far up the height, declared that he preferred "Excelsior!" Well, the dogs also have the privilege of sleeping on "Excelsior," and they seem to enjoy it.—Lula says that when she wrote her 17-page letter, she never thought about the sisters—that they would read it; and she's afraid they'll think her a very giddy and thoughtless creature; but I told her that the sisters would undoubtedly make allowances for letters written to give their pupils pleasure, and I asked her to write again. Moreover, I told her that the sisters had managed to survive *my* letters, and I knew hers were very much gayer and therefore much more interesting. The truth is, educated or uneducated, no one can write letters as well as women. They forget themselves entirely and that is the chief charm of a letter. During the talk with Lula, Alleen said she knew you thought it strange that she didn't answer your letters promptly; that she was afraid you'd think she cared nothing for you, whereas, she loves you as well as she does one of her own sisters. And she made the remark with some show of feeling. The truth is, her two children are now at an age when, nurse or no nurse, they demand her constant attention and she has little time to write.—Father O'Brien called and spent a very pleasant hour with us, and brought me a book. He is a charming man, wise and sympathetic. That was a beautiful letter Sister Bernard sent to Mama. I have had occasion recently to have the sisters in mind a good deal, and the thoughts of their patience, cheerfulness and devoted lives, have been a great help to me.—Essie says the penny fund amounts to 140 cents.[4]—Fritz and J.C. went rabbit-hunting Friday with Ovid and Muldoon.[5] In the field behind Lovett's they jumped a rabbit and Fritz fired away and accidently killed him. It was "a great victory for our side." They jumped two more, and Muldoon would have caught one if he hadn't taken refuge in a sewer. Fritz gave the shot rabbit to J.C. and he and I ate it Saturday. We could have eaten two or three others.

—Well, dear gals, don't you think I've written you a long letter this time? I'm afraid the sisters will groan over the length of it. They have to read it as a duty, and if I keep on writing such long letters they'll regard the reading of them as a penance.[6] Give my regards to them, and mama's love, and give my love to Burdeene.

As for yourselves, dear gals, you know you have it.

    Your loving
      Daddy

ALS

4 pp.

Envelope: Return to Box 111, / Atlanta, Ga. / Miss Lillian Harri[.] / St. Joseph's Aca[. . .] / Washington / *Wilkes county* / *Ga.R.R.*

PM: 14 November [1898]

1. Text of clipping pasted to letter.

2. The baby is Joel Chandler Harris III, born 17 December 1897; Stewart is his brother.

3. Interesting acknowledgment by JCH of his feminine nature. *Cf.* his use of female personae in his writings, such as Aunt Minervy Ann in his fiction and Anne Macfarland, his pen name as a book reviewer for *URM.*

4. According to tradition, any person who was out of sorts and grumbled at the dining room table had to pay a penny fine. See earlier reference to this fund, p. 123.

5. Fritz Wagener, a neighbor who later married Lillian; J.C. is Joel Chandler Harris, Jr., JCH's last child. Ovid and Muldoon were family dogs.

6. The Sisters of St. Joseph read all correspondence to and from their pupils as was the practice at that time. JCH refers often to this second audience of his letters to the girls.

[To Lillian and Mildred]

Saturday Evening, 19 November, 1898

I don't know, dear gals, how in the world I'm to finish this letter. Finish it! I don't know how I'm to begin it. I've made an *awful* discovery just simply AWFUL. You couldn't guess it—no, not if—not if each of you was eight inches taller and twenty pounds heavier; not if you were to guess until your tongues were tired and your heads aching with the same ache. It's just simply too terrible to think of; but I *must* tell it; I never could keep a secret, especially from my dear gals. Then listen that fruit-cake I wrote you of—it's old and wrinkled already, and no wonder!—That fruit cake is a confessed toper, a wretched inebriate, a habitual sot. I never would have found out if I were any less cunning than I am—if I were less shrewd than old man *Tallow Rand used to be.[1] Mama says to me, says she, "Cephas, have you any whisky?" At once I began to suspect something, but not a muscle betrayed my agitation. "Well," says I, "as likely as not there may be a thimbleful or two in the bottle. But who's ill?" "Nobody; I just wanted some for cooking purposes," says she. Aha! says I to myself, I smell a rag burning somewhere; but not a quiver of an eyelid betrayed me. "Then, we are to have mince-pie for dinner, or the stuff you call Trifle?" says I. "If you have no whisky, Cephas, say so, and I'll order a bottle through the grocer," says she. "I'll bet you a quarter you want it for that fruit cake," says I, not dreaming that my suspicions were correct. "I do," says she. "It must be kept moist and soft, till Christmas and whisky is the thing to keep it so." So the secret was out! Every week or two the fruit cake must have its dram, and it drinks so heartily you can almost hear it hiccough. It may happen that we'll have to send the cake to the Keeley Institute, the place where they reform poets and other geniuses.[2] I says to Mama, says I, "You needn't accuse anybody of nibbling at that cake if you find it broken. A tipsy cake can't walk any straighter than a drunk man, and if it gets up from that box it is sure to fall back and break." And Mama, says, says she, "Cephas, if you had married any other woman" ("Heaven forbid!" says I) "you wouldn't go on with that kind of nonsense."

> The Fruit Cake frowned at the young Mince Pie;
> "My friend, I fear you're 'fresher' than I."
> Then he up'd and laughed, did Young Mince P.;
> "With that, dear sir, I quite agree:
> I'm young and warm, but, then, you see,
> I'd rather be 'fresh' than 'full,' " says he.
> And then he bowed to the old F.C.
> And "the table groaned,"* and the crockeree
> Cracked itself with laughter free
> And the dishes joined in the Fruit Cake's spree.[3]

My Goodness! if Sam Jones knew the habits of our fruit cake he'd make a prohibition speech on it.[4] I knew the sisters won't expose us; and I hope the girls won't tell. Sh—! I hear somebody coming now! Keep right still—(no, "still" might remind 'em of the dram)—Keep quiet, and pretend you're reading—don't laugh!— ————Thank goodness! it was nobody but J.C. coming to tell us good-night. I feel right ticklish when I have a big secret like this. Essie's gone to bed, too; she doesn't know a word about the condition of that cake.

- - - - - - - - - - - - - - - - - Sunday night.—Evelyn stayed up all night last night in order to go to early church this morning. Lucien and Alleen went this morning, and the Bishop remarked that other churches than the Catholic were based on opinions. I'm afraid the good Bishop is wrong about this. I doubt if even opinions flourish[;] largely I think it is *prejudice*. I know it has been so in my own case; and a prejudice doesn't need even an opinion for its basis. It exists in the face of all other conditions of the mind, and is independent of them; it needs nothing but itself to feed on, and fattens on the diet.—Julian, Julia and the Collier Kidlets came out to-day, invited by the fine weather. I heard a mocking-bird singing this morning. It would have been quite a different thing if the bird had heard *me* singing. Imagine his consternation and dismay! Alleen and Stewart also came. Stewart is much the same. No foot-ballplayer can hold him a candle for roughness and toughness.— Charles has also been here to-day; in fact took supper here. He deposited a present with me for Essie's birthday, but she knows nothing of it and will not know till to-morrow. Thus I have two secrets to keep—about the sotty fruit cake and about the present. I can hardly sit still. I'll be sending my dear gals, presently, a book called "Shadows on the Wall."[5] I want them to see the pictures of the plantation negroes as I used to know them. They were painted first in Water-colors, but they are printed in the book in plain black and white. They are by an old maid of Huntsville, Ala. You may keep the book till you come home, or you can return it by mail. The sisters will be interested in these vivid pictures of the old-time negroes.—Up here the leaves are beginning to fall from the trees very rapidly, and before we know it we'll be in the midst of winter; and what will the poor guinea pigs do then? They are getting to be what the boys used to call a warm proposition. We have a whole drove of them and they seem to be hungry all day and all night, and Sunday too. If you find us sitting on the sidewalk when you come home and the guinea pigs in charge of the lot you needn't be surprised. I'll try to keep a warm place for you on the curbstone.—Lula Z. has a new blue "tailor-made" and a blue hat. She looks fine in it, and seems to enjoy looking fine. Alleen has a new marten fur—or is it a set of furs? I have nothing new but some views of things, for which I exchanged an old set I had had all my life.—Grace Abernathey is funny to see. She's as tall as this seems to be—[sketch of her across width of sheet] I hope she *will* begin to grow stout after awhile. Roy's cow came over this afternoon to see our cows. She concluded to stay to tea, and ate a panel of fence before the bell rang. Her appetite is almost as good as that of the guinea pigs.

You will see from all this that I really have nothing to write about

Manuscript page from Joel Chandler Harris's 19 November 1898 letter to daughters Lillian and Mildred. Harris frequently included caricatures, such as this drawing of Grace Abernathy, in his correspondence (Joel Chandler Harris Collection, Special Collections Department, Robert W. Woodruff Library, Emory University).

except this: that you may expect a barrel of apples[.] I'll start it on Tuesday afternoon, and address it to Lillian so that it won't disappear in the basement of the community house. The box will also start Tuesday, and I hope that my dear gals will enjoy everything and be as happy as possible[.] Love to Burdeene and regards to the sisters.

    Your loving

      Daddy

ALS

3 pp.

Envelope: Miss Lillian Harris, / St. Joseph's Academy, / Washington, *Ga.* / *Wilkes county.* / *Ga.R.R.*

PM: [illegible]

1. Note at bottom of Harris's page 1 after "that kind of nonsense": "*Mama says I have the name spelled wrong; that it should be Talleyrand—one word; but I don't see why we can't spell French names in English."

2. The Keeley Institute of Georgia, a sanitarium at 591 Whitehall, Atlanta, regularly advertised in the *Constitution* its promises to cure alcohol, tobacco, and drug addiction.

3. JCH's note to asterisk: "Don't you remember about the table groaning? It's an old trick they have, so the newspapers say."

4. Samuel Porter Jones (16 October 1847–15 October 1906), popular Georgia evangelist, known as the "Apostle of Prohibition." See entry in *Dictionary of Georgia Biography.* For additional information about Jones as a New South booster and fervent moral crusader and prohibitionist, see Kathleen Minnix, "The Atlanta Revivals of Sam Jones: Evangelist of the New South," *Atlanta History* 33 (Spring 1989): 5–34.

5. By Miss Maria Howard Weeden (1847–1905), an author/illustrator of books about Negro characters and life. Her first book was *Shadows on the Wall* (1898). JCH wrote the introduction to the second expanded edition called *Bandana Ballads* (1899). JCH admired her work very much. See Frances C. Roberts and Sarah Huff Fisher, *Shadows on the Wall: The Life and Works of Howard Weeden* (Northport, Alabama: Colonial Press, 1962).

[To Lillian and Mildred]

[24 November 1898]

Thanksgiving, 1898 [1]

We are just through with our Thanksgiving dinner, and I thought I would write to my dear gals, telling them just a word about it. Well, we had turkey, and cranberry, and celery, and cake, and nuts, and Miss Charlotte Russe, and lots of fixin's, and West, and Lucien, and Alleen, and Stewart, and Evelyn, *and* I don't know what all. And Mama and Alleen have gone to the White Flag matinee, and West and Lucien have gone to football, and Essie is playing the piano for the children, an' Lena has her [hair] twisted in front [small sketch of her head] till it looks like two crooked horns. J.C. had an invitation from the Collier Kids, but he preferred to go hunting with Fritz, returning with two field larks.

I hope you all had a nice time. I sent apples, Mama sent a box, and something tells me that you had a turkey too.—Did you see in the papers that Kenan Caldwell had married Ruby Morris? That's all the news I know up to date, and that isn't much. And—Oh yes! the sculptor brought the bust home, and I gave it an old hat to wear to keep it from catching cold. And, funny to say, the guinea pigs are not squealing to-day. They are in their boxes and keeping quiet. I guess they had a thanksgiving dinner to-day.

Well, this is not a letter, but just to remind you that we are thinking of our dear gals on big days as well as little ones, and to say that

It's Only A Month Till Christmas!

Love to Burdeene and regards to the Sisters.

  Your loving

   Daddy

ALS

1 p.

Envelope: Miss Mildred Harris, / St. Joseph's Academy, / Washington, Ga. / *Wilkes county.* / *GaRR.*

PM: 25 November 1898

1. Original letter and envelope held by the Uncle Remus Museum, Eatonton. Photocopy in Joel Chandler Harris Collection, SC, EU.

[To Lillian and Mildred]

       Saturday Evening, 26 November, 1898

If my dear pals will collect their thoughts, and put 'em in a box, and shake 'em up, they'll see that next Thursday is the First of December, with Christmas only TWENTY-FOUR days off. Thus does time fly when we're not looking; but the moment we begin to watch it, that moment it ceases to gallop and seems to be almost too tired to walk.—I wrote you a little note about our Thanksgiving, all of which you might have guessed since it's pretty much the same every year.[1] We should have been very

happy to have had you with us, but that fact will cause us to enjoy and
relish Christmas the more. And as for that Fruit Cake! Well, I wouldn't
advise a prohibitionist to take too big a bite if she doesn't want to walk
wobbly when she goes to bed. Mama says it needs more stimulants right
now, and if Christmas should happen to be put off this year by so much
as an hour we'll have to send it to the Keely University for a post graduate course.—I'm glad Mrs. Glenn was on time with the turkey. I didn't
order it because I thought you really needed it, for I knew better, but
because I wanted to give you a little surprise, and make you both feel a
little bit happier if that could be. But perhaps the whole truth about it
can be best expressed when I say that 'twas merely a little whim of mine,
a sort of a frolic for myself. I hope I'll never be too old to have some kind
of a frolic.—You know how neglectful I am. I intended to send the book
every day during the week, but here it is Saturday night, as cold as Flugens,[2] and the book not mailed yet. I have none of the original pictures,
which were done in Water-Color, but the reproductions in the book will
give you an idea of their beauty.[3] I'll send it first thing next week———
If I don't forget it.—I have received from some children in Virginia some
copies of a little paper they are publishing. I read them all through, and
I'll send 'em to you[.] I judge, from the many items about WeeWee's
baby that Jean, the junior editor, is another Mildred. If she had a paper,
half of the articles would be about Toody and Bumpers.[4] These Virginia
chaps seems to be very smart. I'm going to write to them and tell them
the incident of the negro and his Mucky ous Membrine.—[5]

Sunday night.—

No, on second thoughts, I'll send them a riddle that I wrote for my dear
gals. Viz:

> My Riddle lives in every zone,
> In every land when the Sun has shone
> (And where it has not, if the truth were known);
> It has wings without feathers, and I freely own
> I'd rather not meet it when I'm alone.
> You may put it in closets, but when it is grown,
> It fills half the earth, and, when shaped like a cone,

Flies as far as the moon: and when it has flown,
May be put in a thimble and will lie there prone.
   The wind may have blown on it,
   But the sun never shone on it,
And I hope that, in guessing, you won't have to groan on it.[6]
    From the pen of the Immortal Uncle Dremus, and
      respectfully dedicated to those who are not En it.

The answer to this remarkable riddle will be printed in our next. At present it is only necessary to say that the Fruit Cake has had another glass of grog.—Brader was to have had his knee operated on yesterday, but something interfered with the programme. The poor fellow continues to hope on, but the truth is the knee is getting worse all the time, and there is hardly any remedy for it now.—Mr. Bell called this afternoon, and spent an hour. Charles retired from the fray.—The Philps's and two bull-dogs have moved into the Cobb house. The first thing they did was to borrow three scuttles of coal. Well, we have to be neighborly. If I get errytated I'll borrow something from them—a sack of salt or a pint of coffee.—The northwest wind came out yesterday without any overcoat on, and the result is, we have to sit on the stove to keep warm. Mama is too heavy for the stove in her room, so she has to sit on the hall-stove. She biled a right smart while to-day.—You'll see by the way I'm writing that there's nothing to write about, and hardly that.—Clarence Caldwell's wife's pa is putting up a two-story house for them on the vacant lot opposite Mr. Daniel's.—West End beef is not affected by the weather. It's as hard to chew when it's hot as it is when it's cold.—Mr. Will Wilson is very low. He is too ill to go to Florida.—Charles went to church with Essie to-day.

But why go on at this rate? There's nothing to write about, and why not admit it?

    Your loving
    Daddy

ALS
2 pp.

Envelope: Miss Lillian Harris, / St. Joseph's Academy, / Washington, Ga. / *Wilkes county.*

PM: [torn off; none on back]

1. Letter to Lillian and Mildred, "Thanksgiving, 1898" [24 November 1898].

2. Flugens, colloquial word meaning "the extreme" or "the dickens"; first citation, 1830; used as degree of temperature, "cold as the flugens," or "colder 'n flugens" cited from Harris, *Tales*, 129. See entry in Mitford Mathews, *A Dictionary of Americanisms* (Chicago: University of Chicago Press, 1951); also Sir William A. Craigie and James B. Hulbert, *A Dictionary of American English* (Chicago: University of Chicago Press, 1940).

3. Reference to Howard Weeden's *Shadows on the Wall*, promised to the girls in the letter of 19 November 1898.

4. I.e., her nephews Stewart and Chandler Harris.

5. *Cf.* joint letter to girls, 6 November 1898.

6. On back of sheet two appears also the first two lines of the riddle poem: "My Riddle lives in every zone, / In every land where the sun has shone."

[To Lillian and Mildred]

Saturday evening, Dec. 3, 1898

Dear Billy and Tommy:

We enjoyed Sister Sacred Heart's funny and clever little drawings very much, but when I wrote my last letter, Mama had taken possession of them—they were not on my table—and though I had not forgotten them, I forgot to thank Sister for the pleasure she gave us. Sometimes in writing an editorial, I have a clinching argument in my mind. I begin the article, get interested in other arguments, and clean forget the clincher. That was the way with the drawings; I intended to say something about them, and then other things carried my mind away from them.—I saw in a magazine the other day that the author of "Alice in Wonderland,"[1] in writing to a little girl friend gave her a puzzle to work out, namely, to draw three overlapping squares without taking pen from paper or going over the same line twice thus: " ⌐⊡⌐ " It's very easy. As for that riddle—

> The simple riddle! so you couldn't guess it?
> Dear gals, I never would confess it!
> With all the wise heads St. Joseph's hazin
> Its walls. Why, first, there's Father Bazīn,

Then Mother Clemence, and that bright Sister
Sacred Heart, so keen, I wist, her
Mind must have solved it; and Sister Bernard
Who's so shy and gentle 'cause she's learn-ard;
And then there's Sister Mary Louis—
I own to you that it's mighty cu-is—
(These rhymes are worse than any hammer
To know the stuffin' out'n grammar,
And, while I'm in the way of tellin',
They knocked it, also, out'n spellin')—
   Now, where are you at night,
   When someone "outs" the light?
   In bed? Oh, yes! but mark, too—
   In bed and in the DARK, too.
      Yours respectfully, *Rinktum Riddler*

Dear gals, you ask so may questions in your letters that it quite takes my breath away, and by the time you get through asking them you are through with your letters. Now I don't think that's quite fair to a poor old man who expects to get letters every week and who goes solemnly to the post office to get them. Suppose *he* were to do that way? Suppose he were to write seven lines on a page, saying, "How's Mildred? I hope she is well. How is Lillian? I hope she is better than she was week before last. And how is Mrs. Glenn, and Mrs. Hen, and Mrs. Men, Men and Mrs. Wenn?"[2] Well, you'd say I was cheating; and you'd be correct— ahem!—in your surmizes. (I tell you, I'm right in the game when it comes to flinging big words at my esteemed correspondents!) But, by the way, *has* surmise a z in it, or an s—I mean two s's?— ———Things are beginning to smell like Christmas again, but the fruit cake will have to keep sober until the 15th, so mama says. Fine weather or foul, Mama will be seen slipping off to town next week, and the only way I'll know she's not at Aleen's will be when the door-bell rings four or five times a day, and men and boys come delivering all sorts of mysterious packages and bundles, the messengers remarking, "De lady say pintedly dat de bundle aint to be open tell she git back—if den." There's a good deal of

whispering going on in the house, and various half-remarks and references that nobody is supposed to understand but those who are in the
secret. As for me I sit and nod and write, and rouse up and write and
nod just the same as ever.—Brader has had his leg done up in plaster as
a sort of Christmas gift, and he seems to be very happy over it, tapping
it with a pencil and smiling placidly.

Sunday, Dec. 4.—George Obear came out to see Lucien yesterday,
and stopped here a few moments, interfering with the deep and sweet
silence that was taking place between Essie and Charles. He didn't stay
long, just long enough to warm his hands. The weather is very cold to-
day, thanks to a gale from the southwest. This morning we had blowing
snow, but the supply was shut off about ten and we haven't had any
since. I hope we'll have no more. Snow is beautiful to think about, to
remember, but it's not pleasant to deal with. I suppose you girls would
enjoy it, but if you had to go back and forth to town and the cars weren't
running, you'd soon say you had enough. I am willing you should have
as much as you want in Wilkes if you'll keep it there.—I'm sorry for the
poor little guinea pigs to-night; they have good quarters, but there are so
many of them, it's a problem to feed them when there's no grass.—I'm
afraid Stewart has a bad time Sundays when Lucien is home all day. He
is allowed to do as he pleases all the week, and then on Sunday Lucien
establishes laws, and rules, and regulations, and the result is a larruping
for the youngster every quarter of an hour—no, it's not that bad, but
anyhow Sunday is not a happy day for the kid. Brother can stand alone
and take a step or two. He's a very quiet baby—altogether different from
Stewart in his ways. But Stewart is really smart. His memory is as long
as a wire fence. He saw me shave a fortnight ago, and yesterday he got
a tooth-brush and said: "Alleen, Stewart goin chave,"—Last week's Life
never came. I ordered it, but it hasn't come yet. The news-man doesn't
know what the trouble is.—Ooh! the wind is howling up the chimney
as if it had got caught in the flue and couldn't get out; and I'm thinking
now, of the hundreds of poor little chilluns who have no fire to warm
by and who are shivering with cold. There are many thousands of them
in this broad land. Oh, what a pity that this should be so!—I started
out without having any news to write, and that's the way I'll have to

end—no news, nothing; even Rufus has gone home, and Charles has just retired. He went to church with Essie again to-day.

My kindest regards to the sisters, and ask them to excuse the friovle-iovle-ousness of an old man. Love to Burdeene.

> Your loving
>   Daddy

ALS

3 pp.

Envelope: Return to Box 111, / *Atlanta, Ga.* / Miss Lillian Harris, / St. Joseph's Academy, / Washington, *Ga.*, / *Wilkes county.* / GaRR

PM: 5 December 1898

1. Lewis Carroll. Interesting because JCH denied having read the Alice books before writing his own six fantasy novels for children.

2. Julia Harris alters this garbled sentence to "And how is Mrs. Glenn, and Mrs. Kerr, and Mrs. and Mr. Wenn?" in *Life and Letters*, 415. But JCH is simply extending a list of rhyming names by changing initial consonants, a usual practice for him in such doggerel.

[To Lillian and Mildred]

10 December, 1898.

No doubt my dear gals will be surprised to hear that I passed my fiftieth birthday yesterday—and it was not a pleasant day either. On the contrary, it was cloudy, and last night the sleet fell in such quantities that it seemed to be snow. To-night it is pretty much all melted, but the weather is cold—so cold, indeed, that I'm afraid to go out and shut the gate of the chicken pen. And the dogs are quarreling over their boxes. Each has a box to sleep in, but each wants to sleep in the box with the other. This doesn't suit the dog who is already in the box and has a warm place. It usually happens that Ovid is the outside dog, and so, about every five minutes he manages to discover a nest of thieves in Richardson's lot, and he runs after them barking as loud as ever he can. The noise attracts the attention of Muldoon, who comes charging out of his warm place. Thereupon Ovid rushes to the box and gets in, and then Muldoon begins to see thieves by the hundreds. This sort of thing is kept up until late at night—in fact, until it gets too cold for either of the dogs to dispute about a warm place.—Owing to the sleet on the ground, we thought we wouldn't have an early breakfast yesterday morning, but Lizzie managed to get here at half-past six.—Lula Zachry has been here for two days, and has made herself very agreeable.—I'm very glad Mildred wants a pony. A "pony" is a small glass of beer, and I haven't the slightest objection to her taking that. Some of her friends and acquaintances had selected other things as presents for her, but they are happy to know that a pony—which costs 5 cents—is all she wants. Maybe she would like to have a pill with the pony. The little puzzle she sent in her letter is very cute—too cute for me, though Mama says *she* can do it; in fact, she did it right before my eyes, but, try as I will, I can't do as she did. This makes me feel giddy.

Sunday and Monday.—Cuddled up in bed with a rag around my marbled brow.

Tuesday.—Able to be up and about—though the headache has dropped into the right eye-tooth. I discovered this morning that the tooth is a cold tooth. I opened my mouth getting on the street car, and could hardly shut it again owing to the terrible paroxysm of pain in tooth and jaw. It was quite an experience, being new to me, and made me feel like I resemble the man's bust of me. He has made some small ones, and they all look as if they had had some sort of strange experience with their teeth. They are the queerest little weazened affairs you ever saw. Julia has purchased one, and I think Julian will grow more jealous as he grows older.—Alleen and Lucien ate their anniversary dinner,[1] but, as for me, I was in bed and had nothing to eat but some nice medicine until this morning. Of course, under those circumstances, I had to hurry up and get well.—The shopping is still going. The streets to-day were a perfect jam, cold as it was. If everybody bought something, the stores did a rushing trade.—Tonight the weather is still colder and the weather-man has promised us some more as soon as ever he can unpack it—and I have just returned from turning the water off, though I found the stand-pipe in the front yard already friz. I hope it will thaw out in the morning without bursting. The exertion I had to undergo in turning off the water in the dark showed me that I am still suprisingly weak, and I am sure my dear gals will forgive me if this letter is neither as long nor as interesting as they might have reason to hope.—I enclose an autograph letter from Mr. Riley.[2] The part I cut out was simply some inquiries about our poor friend Mr. Stanton—such inquiries as need not be preserved, though they come from the heart of one of the best of men.

I shall have to close this dull letter. A man who has been in bed with a rag around his marble brow has no news of interest to relate. Regards to the sisters and love to Burdeene.

Your loving

Daddy

ALS

2 pp.

Envelope: Miss Lillian Harris, / St. Joseph's Academy, / Washington, *Ga.* / *Wilkes county.* / *Ga. RR.*

PM: 14 December 1898

1. They were married 11 December 1895.

2. James Whitcomb Riley.

[To Lillian and Mildred]

Saturday, 17 December, 1898.

Dear Billy and Milly: Here I am again, with not a scrap of news and hardly anything to remind you of home except the print of Rufus's thumb, which he made on the paper while moving my table from one room to another. I have been feeling very well since I wrote to you until to-day when I have another small supply of indigestion to remind me that I cannot hope to succeed in life if I continue to eat too much. The *menu* of your festival is very attractive. I should have been glad to be there. But [print of thumb] [1] if you didn't charge an entrance fee you had nothing with which to buy Father O'Brien a Jubilee souvenir.[2] It was a very happy thought to celebrate the anniversary. I am sure that no worthier, or better or kinder priest ever served his Lord and his church than Father O'Brien[.] Though I am not intimately acquainted with him I have always regarded him as my friend in a very special sense, and hardly a day passes that thoughts of him do not come into my mind.—Someone has been shooting the Lovett's pigeons and to-day Policeman Luck came over and told Mama that Mrs. L. and her cook said the pigeons were shot by J.C. When? Why, yistiddy. But yesterday J.C. was at a party at Hefner's. Well, may [sic] it was this morning. But he didn't take is [*sic*] gun out this morning. Well, anyhow, there are the pigeons—they were in the hands of Little Jim. Then Mamma: "Take those pigeons away from here, you little scamp you! And the next time I see you pulling the palings off my fence, I'll come out and spank you—that's what I'll do!" Luck: "Well, Mrs. Harris, I done what the lady said. *She* said J.C. killt the birds, and you know yourself how boys are." Mama: "Yes, and I know how those half-witted Lovett children are, too."[3]

And so on and so forth. It was quite a sensation—J.C. whimpering with anger, Luck grinning a sickly grin, Rufus cracking his knees together, and Mama with her dander up. I hope it won't get in the newspapers.—I am sending you in this letter a cheque for $31.50 as follows: For the sisters, $18.50; for railroad fare $10; for Mrs. Glenn, who has sent her bill, $3.00.[4] And please ask Sister Sacred Heart to do me the kindness to have the Glenn bill paid at once. It seems like putting her to unnecessary trouble; but when people are as kind as she is they always make more or less trouble for themselves.—Sunday night.—Mama says the Bishop roasted his congregation this morning, declaring that he wouldn't spend his Christmas with such a sordid crowd. There was some trouble about raising $300 of insurance money. An effort that was made failed, and the good Bishop was wrathy. Well, I don't blame him. I think it's a shame that a well-to-do congregation should be so stingy in church affairs. The Bishop then said that he wouldn't be here; he didn't want to preach to such a crowd. The whole trouble is that we need here for the pastor of this church a man who is a business man, and who knows how to address himself to the management of affairs that have become complicated by the lack of someone to manage them.—There is still a dearth of news. Harry spent the afternoon here. It was Charles's time, and he came, saw, and retired; consequently there is some trouble in our camp. But such is the course of true love.[5] It is a rocky passage, and needs a keen-eyed pilot.—J.C. is beginning to dispose of his guinea pigs. Mildred's are getting along all right; but, in time, they, too, will have to go—all except a few.—I don't think it's fair for me to write a letter and have no answer—oh, I forgot; you are going to answer it in person. I suppose Mama will meet you at the cyar-shed.[6] So will I if I can get my day's work far enough advanced—and I'll try mighty hard.

Well, this is all until next time. Regards to the sisters and love to Burdeene.

Your loving

Daddy

ALS

2 pp.

Envelope: Return to Box 111, / *Atlanta, Ga.* / Miss Lillian Harris, / St. Joseph's Academy, / Washington, Ga. / *Wilkes county.* / *Ga. R. R.*

PM: 19 December 1898

1. JCH's note around mark: "Behold the mark of Rufus's thumb!"

2. Father James M. O'Brien was chaplain to the boy's orphanage and probably also to the girl's school of Saint Joseph's. See full note elsewhere. A Jubilee signals fifty years in the profession.

3. JCH found the antics of his neighbors, the Lovetts, to be amusing.

4. Bill for the turkey sent to the girls. See letter of 26 November 1898.

5. Competing beaux of niece Essie LaRose.

6. Mrs. JCH's Savannah pronunciation of car?

[To Lillian and Mildred]

Sunday, 8 January, 1899.

I come limping, dear gals (including Burdeene), but still I come. I have a cough which is more tremendous than Lillian's (which I hope is better by this time), and every time I call on it to do its duty, it sounds like someone was pounding on an empty barrel. Consequently, you can imagine that I am not feeling well. This is worse than indigestion. It seems to be grippe, and if it is I'm afraid I'll have to go to bed and stay there two or three days. We hope to have a good report from poor Lillian the next time we hear from the academy, which ought to be soon. We received Burdeene's letter and were very proud of it. When I feel clear-headed I'll write her one all by herself. Meantime, she must remember that she gave us far more pleasure than we gave her. Our Christmas would not have been the same; a very lovely element would have have [*sic*] been lacking if she had been absent; and we hope she will be with us whenever she can and as long as she can.—Lillian wanted to know all the news. Goodness! What is the paper for! Charles took dinner here, and remained all the afternoon. Evelyn dined at Zachry's. Mr. Z.

has purchased the Haskell place, and Mr. Frazier still has more or less sickness in his family, though they all seem to be well. Mr. Bunker still continues to have his bad spells, and refuses to go to bed. He has an idea that if he goes to bed in a formal manner, as the result of sickness, and so he refuses [sic]. Nor will he have anybody to nurse him. Now, he's not like me; when I feel really ill, the first thing I think of is the bed, and I go to it cheerfully, grunting so everybody in the house can hear me and extend their sympathies. J.C. seems to be very well pleased at the convent. Naturally he thinks the discipline is strict, but when he hears me say that I hope the sisters will tan his hide, he seems to think matters might be worse than they are. He carried my copy to town yesterday for the first time, and seemed to be very proud of the feat.

Now, it seems that I have come to the end of my letter. Mama is at Alleen's—I am writing in the afternoon, so as to have nothing between me and bed—and the house is pretty quiet. In fact, it has been awfully quiet since my dear gals (including Burdeene) took their flight. You could hear a pin or a gum drop. What is there to write about? The weather has been very cold for two days, but when the sun shines out the violets are blooming. But there is no one to pick them. They are just as lonely as the house. J.C. has gone for a walk, and I hope he'll find it. I have one of my own, but I rarely ever use it. Bronchitis says "Shut up!" and I suppose I'll have to close now. I hope to be well enough to send you a longer letter next time, and I hope this will find my dear Lillian able to be up and about and to eat her "usual 'lowance." My regards to the sisters, and love to Burdeene.

Your affectionate

Daddy

ALS
2 pp.
Envelope: Miss Lillian Harris, / St. Joseph's Academy, / Washington, Ga. / *Wilkes county.*
PM: 10 January 1899.

[To Lillian]

[9 January 1899]
Monday

Dear Daughter,

I forgot to enclose stamps in my regular letter. I also forgot the cheque. In this you will find both.

All well. All send love.

Your'n

Daddy

When you want some pin-money, let me know [.]

ALS
1 p.
Envelope: Miss Lillian Harris, / St. Joseph's Academy, / Washington, Ga. / *Wilkes county*
PM: 10 January [. . .] [1]
1. Envelope is marked "After Xmas" and also contained two sketches of two little girls in dresses; the one with a skip rope has two handwritten notes: "Drawn by Bess." and "*B.S. so sweet.*"

[To Lillian and Mildred]

Sunday night, [January] 15, 1899.

I am now taking up my pen to write to my dear gals, and it has a very queer feeling in my hands, for it is the first time I have taken it up since writing to you last week. I was feeling ill when I wrote, and Monday I was coughing so I had to go back to bed. The week seems like a nightmare to me, for, on top of the illness was the miserable weather, the worst I have ever seen. Tuesday somebody sent for the doctor, and he came with his pills, his plasters and his boluses. Consequently I have been taking pink pills for pale people, vermifuge, Mrs. Pinkham's pellets for pettifoggers, sirup, sorup and serup, assafœdita, sassafras, and Wampules[?] wimples for warped men—to say nothing of nine kinds of cough medicine. I am gradually recovering from the medicine. To-day was warm and sunshiny, and so I went to town as usual, but did no work. I am feeling pretty well to-night, except a slight hoarseness, the effect of an abscess just behind my nose. That abscess, or congestion, was the main trouble after all, and when it broke I felt better at once. It was a horrible affair, and very painful until relief came.—Well, I hope you are both well. I could sympathize with Lillian's condition, for I was feeling that way myself, especially the cough. I hope she'll take care of herself and not have a relapse. Dr. Crow says a relapse in grippe is worse than the original disease.—Yes, Rufus has vanished from the places that once knew him. He left—or rather failed to return—after I had finished your letter, and I was feeling too ill to add it in. Lucien threatened to break his neck for disputing with Mama—poor Rufus was only trying to explain—and so he came in and told me he couldn't work any more. "Can't do what?" I inquired. "Can't work here no mo!" "Nonsense! you mean you can't play here any more. When did you ever work?" He scorned to make any reply to a remark so frivolous, and I haven't seen poor Rufus since.[1] Oliver's brother Wiley comes night and morning to attend to the fires and coal, and does it without making any fuss. I'm not at all sorry to get rid of Rufus. He wasn't worth the salt he ate in his food.—Lovey and Dovey were out to-day, with the two little girls. Dovey is complaining of muscular rheumatism, and if she has it, it won't be long before Lovey will be down with the same complaint. It is a case of two hearts that beat, two heads that ache, four arms that hurt as one.—We wanted to send Father O'Brien something for his jubilee, but we didn't know just what.—Mr. Bunker is still very ill, but seems to be gradually getting better. Beyond this, I know nothing of the neighborhood news. If I had heard any, my mind would have been too confused with quinine and things of that sort to retain it.—The violets have continued to bloom in spite of the cold gloomy weather, but there is nobody to pick them. Mama goes out occasionally and picks about a dozen, grunting all the time. Then she comes in with the back ache. Essie picks three or four (while hunting for caterpillars) and comes in with the toe-ache.—Stewart and the baby were here to-day for awhile. Brother is beginning to talk. He walks everywhere, and is about as busy as Stewart is.—Charles and Essie were hid about the house somewhere all the afternoon. Charles is having his eyes treated, and also his lips. The doctor is treating his eyes.—I must write a letter to Burdeene before long in answer to hers. Give her my love. My regards to the sisters. As I have nothing else to write, and as

I am not strong enough to write an extra long letter, I'll bring this dull thing to a close. All send love.

  From your affectionate

    Daddy

ALS

2 pp.

Envelope: Return to Box 111, / Atlanta, Ga. / Miss Lillian Harris, / St. Joseph's Academy, / Washington, *Ga.* / Ga.R.R.

PM: 16 January 1899

1. Rufus had been the long-time butler and general manservant in JCH's home. He was a member of Chloe Henderson's family, perhaps her son or husband. See *Life and Letters*, 179, and also letter to "My Dear Daughter [Lillian]," 25 April [1897].

[To Lillian and Mildred]

         Sunday [January] 22, 1899.

 Thank you, dear gals, I am feeling some better to-day—a trifle weak, but a great deal stronger than I have been. I hope that you are doing as well. There is nothing here to write about. The same thing happens every day; up in the morning, a one-hoss breakfast, house-cleaning, dusting, gossip about the neighbors, maybe a spot of a quarrel betwixt the feminine population; then dinner, and dawdling; then—supper, some writing, then to bed. They say in the house that as soon as I drop off to sleep a Thing called the Snorer comes and sits on my head and tries to strangle me. That's the tale they tell. I've never seen the Snorer, therefore I don't know what he looks like. He's never around when I'm awake; and if I ever catch him I promise you I'll strangle *him*.—Mr. Bunker is said to be better, but he's been very ill. Something is the matter with his heart. Every once in awhile it stops, and then, of course, there's a collapse. Brader seems to be gradually failing. He hasn't been over here for a week or more. He is very restless and nervous, and never stays in one place long. He seems to have a horror of staying at home. In a few weeks now he'll be confined to his bed, and when he's once there, he'll never get up any more. He will be 21 next Thursday, and he is then supposed to receive $2,500 left him by his Uncle. If he was well and in good health, you know what he would do with the money. He would throw it away. As it is, he'll not be able to throw it away, and his Mother and Aunt will get some of the benefit of it. I ought not to judge, but it does seem like the hand of Providence is in it, for the Mother and Aunt certainly need the money.—Mama is at Alleen's this afternoon, and Lucien is here. Essie is expecting Charles. Evelyn, who went to church to-day, has gone for a walk in the woods, the day being pretty.—J.C. went with Mama to see "Jack and the Beanstalk" yesterday. He liked it very much. J.C. is on the point of falling out with Charles Collier, Jr., who seems to be of an overbearing disposition. Well, he will push matters until finally your little brother will jump on him and hurt his feelings, and then we shall have a visit from Dovey, to know why J.C. has knocked Charles's nose out of joint.[1]—J.C. seems to like his teachers very much, and he takes a new interest in his studies. Thus far he has only one demerit mark. He had others, but he earned their withdrawal. These were not on account of poor lessons, but on account of his habit of talking. He forgets himself.—Mrs. Kelly has just come in. She's not Charles, but the next thing to him, and Essie seemed to be *very,* VERY glad to see her.[2] I heard the fuss in the dining room where I am writing. There have been thousands of violets, but nobody to pick them. Essie has been ailing, you know, and was not able to go out during the bad weather. It seems to me that the sisters' violets should be blooming profusely. Maybe they are not fertilized enough.—Mama wrote you several days ago. I wonder you didn't get the letter. Lizzie has been sick, and Chloë a-grunting, so that Mama has been a little busier than usual. Still she wrote. I am writing, too, but with nothing to write about, except that I have a new Thimble-finger book in the stocks, with two chapters done[.][3] The Aunt Minervy Ann stories will begin in the February Scribner now almost due.[4] This *is* all. Regard to the Sisters and love to that dear gal, Burdeene.

    Your loving

    Daddy

ALS

2 pp.

Envelope: Miss Lillian Harris, / St. Joseph's Academy, / Washington, *Ga.* / *Wilkes county.* / *GaR.R.*

PM: 23 January [1899]

1. J.C. is Joel Chandler Harris, Jr., and Charles Collier, Jr., is the younger brother of

Julia Collier Harris, whom JCH calls Dovey. Julia and Julian Harris lived in a new house next door and reared Julia's younger siblings, her mother having died in 1896. See *Life and Letters*, 373. They all lived together first in the Collier house, but it proved too large and was rented out.

2. As the mother of niece Essie's beau and later husband, Charles Kelly.

3. *Plantation Pageants* (Boston: Houghton Mifflin, 1899).

4. See note 3 to letter to Lillian and Mildred, "*Sunday Evening*" [13 March 1898].

[To Lillian and Mildred]

Sunday, 29 January, 1899.

I have two enclosures for my dear gals. One for Lillian, which is a harmless little letter from her cousin Arthur.[1] I send it, not to break any of the rules of the dear sisters, but because he is supposed to be one of the family. As to whether Lillian answers it or not, that is for the sisters to decide; and their decision will be correct, as it always is. The enclosure for Mildred is a letter I wrote to the children who sent me the little paper from Virginia[.] It is very funny, especially about Weewee's babies.[2]— Though I'm writing I'm not feeling very well. The weather has not been the pleasantest. We had snow yesterday though it is nearly all gone now, thank gracious! Evelyn has been in bed all day. He did some snow-balling on the roof of The Constitution at three o'clock in the morning in his shirt-sleeves. He will now do some of his no-bawling over Dr. Crowe's medicine. He has orders to remain in-doors for two or three days. He is very hoarse, but if he can be induced to be quiet, he will recover very rapidly.—From all I can gather, Mr. Bunker's illness was occasioned by the fact that we persisted in keeping Rufus. Mrs. B. told mama a day or two ago that Mr. B., even when he was very low, had wondered "Why the Harrises kept that negro boy"; and when she was able to tell him that Rufus was no longer a member of the family, Mr. B. began to get better directly, and the probability is that he will now get well.[3] This shows how influential a family may be without appreciating the fact. I feel pretty small myself, but when you count me in with the house and lot, and the cows and J.C.'s bantams it amounts to something. In other words, we never know how frequent we are until we see ourselves in a cracked mirror.—Harry Lloyd is to call to-night and Essie has been banging on the piano to ease her mind.[4] She has knocked "Yale" crank-sided, and the last notes sounded like somebody was beating a feather bed with a poker. But we cannot all be happy all the time, and we must all have our Harry Lloyds sometime or other. My Harry Lloyd is an old man who meets me at The Constitution every payday and says he is in a starving condition.—Mama diked out the other night and went to a sort of reception given to Mrs. Cole, who is going away for six months or more. Mama looked very nice, and received various compliments, as usual. Essie went too.—There has not been so much theatre-going as you might suppose. The weather has been bad, and the tickets have not been so numerous.—J.C. has been playing marble "for winance," and, as Julian did, he wins right along. This seems to be a sort of family knack. I watched him yesterday play with Charley Goodman and he won so constantly that it seemed like some trick of the fancy. But it was simply *good judgment* matched against *thoughtlessness.*

You will have to excuse this letter. It is not half a one. The film and other things will be sent to you to-morrow by express. You will probably get them when you get this. We are very remiss here when there's anything to be done, and I'm remiss now because I am going to bring this letter to a close. I'm feeling bad all over, and I'm going to bed. Goodnight, dear gals, and give my love to Burdeene, and my kindest regards to the sisters.

    Your loving

    Daddy

ALS

2 pp.

Envelope: Miss Lillian Harris, / St. Joseph's Academy, / Washington, *Ga.* / *Wilkes county*
PM: 30 January 1899

1. According to Lillian's daughter Mrs. LaRose Wagener Grant, Arthur was also Lillian's first beau. He was French-Canadian kin of Mrs. JCH. (Personal interview with Mrs. Grant, Charlotte, North Carolina, 27 October 1990.)

2. *Cf.* letter to Lillian and Mildred, 26 November [1898].

3. *Cf.* letter to Lillian and Mildred, 16 January 1898.

4. A beau of niece Essie LaRose. He is mentioned in next letter as a poor runner-up to Charles Kelly.

[To Lillian and Mildred]

Sunday aft. February 5, 1899.

I have been feeling so *droopy* all the week, dear gals, and ever since I had the grip, that I've about decided to spend a week in Florida. Clark Howell, Sr., and Henry Tanner are going down to St. Petersburg, near Tampa, to-morrow or Tuesday night. Young Clark wants me to go and has sent for railway passes, so that it will really be about as cheap to go as to stay at home. I don't like to go, but, really, I feel that it will do me good. I'm not ill, but Saturday I felt so weak and *faintified*, and nervous that I could hardly talk. It's all from the effects of the grippe. To-day, I am feeling about as well as ever, my greatest weakness being that I have no news of any importance to write. Nothing happens here but the weather, and that changes its complexion so often and so freely that you hardly know weather [*sic*] to write about it or not.—Evelyn has been home all the week, a part of the time in bed. He now seems to be fully recovered. For his amusement last night, I wrote this:

She—What is your favorite perfume?

He—Musk.

She—I never smell musk with but I feel like crying.

He—That's natural. You've heard of the three musky tears.

When Evelyn read it aloud, the whole family fainted except Trilby, the cat, and she rose and left the room, giving me a scornful look as she passed out. I don't blame the cat, but I do blame the people, especially when they belong to my own family.—It is said that Brader has received his money. The prospects are that he won't live long to enjoy it. He hasn't been here for a month. He goes to town and stays in the doctor's office all day, being afraid of heart failure. I hear that he is very despondent, and that he doesn't like for people to ask him how he is getting on. It is dreadful to think that this young man doesn't believe in God or a hereafter; at least he says he doesn't.—Harry L. is said to be very anxious to renew his addresses to Essie. He told the Zachry girls that he was sure to get her. Mrs. Walton called yesterday, and chatted awhile with me, Mama and Essie being at the matinee. She took occasion to intimate that Harry is very fond of Essie. But such is the perversity of human natur' that Essie and Charles are in the parlor right now, sitting close together on the sofa, and talking in very low tones. While Evelyn was sick, Charles called every morning to see how he was. Charles's solicitude about Evelyn was very touching.—Since this letter was begun, the Lannan's and Ryder have come in, and I have been showing Mr. L. around the place. He was amazed to see so many violets. Well, we walked around, and I was as silent as a country gal, not knowing what to say next. Finally I brought him in the house and excused myself on the plea that I must finish my editorial work: the said editorial work being this letter to my dear gals.—The babies have bad colds, and Stewart is cutting some more teeth—so they say. These will make 220 in all. Brother is also cutting them at the rate of seventeen a week. I've raised six children (or helped to do it) and all of 'em put together never cut one-half as many teeth as they say Stewart and Brother have cut.— Speaking of violets, Chloe is to bring in her brood of young ones tomorrow morning and pick all in sight. This means, of course, that the most of them will be sent to you. If they are withered when they arrive, put them in a cool place, and give them plenty of water with some salt in it. This will revive them in the course of an hour.—Mr. Bunker is about the same,—still in bed, and still having those spells with his heart. I'll write you from St. Petersburg, Fla., and let you know what it looks like—that is, if I go. Mama wants to write Mr. and Mrs. Lannan to spend a week with us, and she thinks the coming week as good as any. I guess that will give me a good reason for going. They are fine people, but I don't *know* them, and that makes all the difference in the world. Regards to the Sisters, and love to Burdeene.

> Your loving
> Daddy

ALS

2 pp.

Envelope: Return to P.O. Box 111, / *Atlanta, Ga.* / Miss Lillian Harris, / St. Joseph's Academy, / Washington, Ga. / *Wilkes county.*

PM: 6 February 1899

[To Lillian and Mildred]

> St. Petersburg, Fla.,
> (Near Atlanta, Ga.)
> Saturday evening,
> Feb. 9 (or 10) [1899]

Well, here I am, dear gals, in Florida—I mean as much in Florida as I ever expect to be.[1] Mr. Howell secured me passes all the way through, also sleeping car tickets. Armed with these I made up my mind to go. Clenching my hands, and pressing my lips firmly together, I went down to the Kimball,[2] and secured a berth[.] There I learned that I would have to change sleepers at Waycross. This deepened and hardened my resolution. I was now determined to go. So I went back home, packed my valise, and waited impatiently for the time to arrive when I would kiss the family on its various noses and flee from the northwestern gales. The train was to leave at 7:50. I was eager for the moment to arrive; I sat rocking to and fro and watching the clock, wondering if it registered the correct time. At a quarter past 7, I ceased rocking. The moment had now come. I was firm in my resolution. But something was needed besides firmness. I leaned back in the chair, and began the journey in my mind. I seized my satchel, flew down the terraces, boarded the car, and was soon in town—in my mind. Finally, I heard the clock strike the hour. It was half-past ten. I arose, shook myself, kissed 'em all good - - - - - - - - - - - - - night, and went to bed, where my journey was continued like a serial story in a French newspaper. I arrived safely the next day, and am still here. I have made special arrangements with the postal authorities, so that a letter addressed to Box 111 will reach me quicker than if it was sent to St. Petersburg, Fla. This is owing to the changes made by the recent war—and is also due to other things. The climate here seems to be as bad as that in West End, but still my trip has helped me. I am as well as ever I was if you leave Anna Domini out of the count.

I am very glad of the experience. You don't know how funny it feels to be in Florida and at home at the same time. It reminds me of a negro's description of an electric shock—"Boss, it feel des like sody-water tas'e." And yet there are people who say that I am no traveller. Mama laughs and says that I am a regular baby when it comes to travelling; but she little knows of the long and dangerous journeys I make while sitting in my room. I have fought in the American revolution; I was in the thick of the French revolution. On one occasion I saved a young lady's life in the Alps by allowing her to hold to my coat-tails as she hung over a crevasse in the ice. The coat I wore on that occasion was made by a tailor in Bordeaux who had formerly been King of Germany. He told me his name but I have forgotten it. So you see, I live in no pent-up Utica, (N.Y.) but in the wide, wide world.[3] But, honestly, don't you think it is better to have these adventures at home, in front of a warm fire, or on the veranda when the weather is warm, than to go traipsing over the earth after them? As it is, I need neither coat, nor staff, nor purse. If the tails of my coat had ripped when the young lady was holding on to them for dear life, no one would have been hurt. I can take a dozen trips to Florida a week, and still have all the comforts of home. Lucien was in bed with the grippe this morning, but is better this afternoon. The children have all been sick with colds, and look right puny, but they are getting better.—The weather has been very cold here. One of the water-pipes burst; nevertheless, that which gives trouble to the man of the house, gives bread to the plumbers; and the plumbers, knowing this, are careful to arrange their work so they will be called in again.—I've received no bill from the sisters. Did I pay up till June? I don't think I did.—J.C. started a letter to you last Wednesday. He is trying to finish it to-night, but it's a hard job. It's like ploughing with the trunk of a tree. He's a great talker. He gets up talking and talks all day, and then talks in his sleep. But writing is not his forte at present. On the coldest day perspiration reeks from him if he has to write.—Julian came out and spent the night, the day after Dovey left, but he hasn't been here since. His mission in life is to nurse the Collier kids, and he seems to be a success.[4] I hear, in a roundabout way, that Pop Collier has discharged the girl who used to look after the kids. Her services were unnecessary after Julian took hold. I suppose he acts as nurse as a sort of set-off for his board and it's just as well. I used to be a pretty good nurse myself.—I have been penned up in the house by the weather, and can tell you no news, except that Brader, having received his dowry has invested in $500 worth of Sanitarium. He is now there for treatment. I have not heard how he is getting on.—J.C. killed four robbins to-day, which reminds me that the cat caught one of his fan-tails the other night.—Regards to the Sisters, and love to Burdeene.

Your loving

Daddy

ALS

3 pp.

Envelope: Return to Box 111, / Atlanta, Ga. / Miss Lillian Harris, / St. Joseph's Academy, / Washington, Ga. / *Wilkes county.* / *GaRR.*

PM: 14 February 1899[5]

1. Letter describing JCH's imaginary trip to Florida and other places.

2. Kimball House, famous nineteenth-century Atlanta hotel.

3. Humorous allusion to the lachrymose novel *The Wide, Wide World* (1861), by Susan Bogert Warner, concerning the trials and tribulations of an orphan heroine.

4. "Dovey" is Julia Chandler Harris. The two Collier kids were her younger siblings for whom Julia was responsible after her mother's death.

5. Washington, Georgia, postmark; Atlanta postmark cut off.

[To Lillian and Mildred]

Sunday night—19 February 1899.

I am glad that my dear gals weathered the storm, but I'm sorry indeed to hear that Sister Bernard is still ill. The grippe is a most disturbing malady, as I know to my cost. I never have fully recovered my strength. My whole system seems to have been torn and shattered by it. I am not ill, but I have a sort of tired feeling occasionally. I hope Sister Bernard will soon recover. It pleases me to hear that our Tommy is fat and healthy. She says she doesn't feel any fatter; but if she *looks* fatter, that is something.—Lillian will be seventeen next Wednesday week, the 1st of March. Next year she will be eighteen on the 29th of February. Isn't that funny? A different birthday every four years—rather, every leap year—is something that everybody can't have for the asking.—What is the difference between a duck with two wings and a duck with one wing? It is the difference between a fly and no fly. If there's any other, I can't make it out now.—The children are well again. Stewart came down to-day, but would eat no dinner. Whether he was sulky or not hungry it is impossible to say. Brother is beginning to talk very plainly, and he's very cute—so Mama says.—There's still a little patch of snow by the chicken pen. We've had three burst pipes, and the water has been cut off for some time. We can use none in the dining room or in the bath-room. Before we had the pipes laid, we didn't feel the lack of water, but it is very inconvenient now. Dr. Rosser says all his rose bushes are killed to the ground. I don't think mine were hurt. Anyhow I found some violets to-day, and there's a little comfort in that.—We sowed some blue grass seed on the sow—no, we snowed—oh, shucks!—we sowed some grass seed on the snow. I wonder where the birds found food while the snow was on the ground. They certainly are well taken care of by the All-seeing, for they were as lively and as cheerful all that dreary time as if there were sno no—there I go again!—as if there were no snow at all. I think of the beautiful snow as the rejected fellow did of his beautiful's *No.*—J.C. has now arrived at that period in his career when he can carry my "copy" to the office, and it is a great relief to me, especially in bad weather. He is also becoming a great reader. He read a book called "Beautiful Joe," and then bought another book by the same author. Some of his young guinea pigs froze to death during the cold spell, and the old mammy pig—one of the first two he ever had—is dead. Oh, we had all sorts of a time!—Mr. Bunker is about the same except that he has his mother-in-law with him.—{Skip this when reading aloud[:] Mrs. Young's friends are going to give her a farewell reception—she's going to Washington to live,—and Mama has been invited. As the affair is to be at Mrs. Wiley Pope's, I thought Mama would refuse, but Mrs. Pope has insisted that she should come (*this is private and confidential*) and so she'll go.}[1]

There's no news here. As the poet says: "There's nowhere to get but on, nowhere to go but out." Consequently dulness [*sic*] broods over the scene like a mantle of snow and mud. I'll bet that not even Mr. Frazier is feeling real well.—Julian says he'll never allow Julia to go away without him again. Evelyn dined there to-day, and Pop Collier says he has some choice tales to tell Julia of Julian's antics while she was gone—the late hours he kept. "Julian," says he, "has had her room fixed up as a peace offering. This may save his life, but it won't prevent the clash of arms."— Mama has taken time to read several books lately. I think she is preparing to plunge head foremost into the Manning society, composed of ladies who never read anything the Cardinal wrote, and probably never heard his name till they joined the society. I think the lady who origi- nated it, intended it to be the Newman society, but the names got mixed. (This is simply a joke.) You see what the dearth of news leads me to.

Well, dear girls, this must do for to-night. Regards to the sisters and to Father O'Brien if you see him, and love to Burdeene.

Your loving

Daddy

ALS

2 pp.

Envelope: Miss Lillian Harris, / St. Joseph's Academy, / Washington, *Ga.* / *Wilkes County* / *Ga. R.R.*

PM: [?] February 1899

1. Passage put in braces by JCH.

[To Lillian and Mildred]

Sunday afternoon, Feb 26, 1899

If my dear gals were here to-day, they'd have to stay indoors. All natur' is soaked. Water is piled on top o' water on the face of the earth. But for Atlanta's excellent system of sewers (ahem!) I'd be afraid of another deluge on a small scale; and, even as it is, I have a great mind to haul out my boat—one of Rufus's old shoes which I have had rebuilt and carefully weather-boarded. In that I can place the whole family and row to a place of safety. Kennesaw would have to be my Arrasat.[1] It has now (3:15) ceased to rain, but the slosh of the waves against the side of the house can be distinctly heard*[2], and I'm afraid to go out after my boat. The rain started at half-past 12 and came down in sluices as big as a smoke stack, there being 27 sluices to the square yard. Lucien, who was here, was compelled to stay to dinner, but Mama, who was at his house came wading across the pasture with all three of the cows and both the dogs swimming after her.—J.C. has sold all the guinea pigs, and Mildred has $4.60 to her credit in his bank. The little things had come to be a nuisance. I had to raise a row every day to get them fed, and they were a constant burden on my mind. They had ceased to be pets, but became a charge. I feel as much relief as if I had had a carbuncle lanced or an aching tooth pulled. I am in constant misery for fear the dumb animals around me will be neglected. It must be due to nervousness. Other people have sympathy for them and look after them; but the bare idea that any dumb thing dependent on me has suffered or is suffering on account of neglect is enough to give me the all-overs.—The rain has begun again, and awhile ago there was a peal of thunder which spoke out from the solitude of the black clouds like a signal gun at sea.—I notice that Mama has been arranging to pack a box for Lillian's birthday, and though she and I go cahoots in the contents, I don't know what's in it, except a quarter of a pound of ring-streaked and strikëd peppermint candy, like you buy at the circus. I would have bought the circus itself, but there was no fresh one in town—all shop-worn.—Lucien says he would write to you, but he has no pens, ink or paper in his house; he's afraid to keep 'em. Stewart would eat the paper, drink the ink and jab Brother's eyes out with the pen.[3] Stewart was down there one day during the week, and he was so vicious I had to send him home. If he were mine I'd take a week off to smoothe his rough edges.—4:30. Again the rain, and this time worse than ever. What were sluices before are now solid sheets of water, reaching from the earth to the clouds—sheets that only come apart when the wind tears holes through them or the thunder and lightning jar them to pieces. Mama has gone to bed and covered up her head. My rye patch next to the street is a beautiful lake of yellow water. If the prow of my Venetian gondola were not stove in, I'd fetch it out for a promenade.—It is rumored around among the old ladies of the neighborhood that Mr. Bunker is losing his mind. This, if true, is hardly due to the fact that his mother-in-law is with him. *She* says he walks all night, so nobody else can sleep. J.C. saw him in the kitchen the other day, and waved his hand at him, but received no response. J.C. says Mr. B. stared at him and frowned as if trying to recall who he was. Well, I don't know whether it is true or not, but, if true, it is pitiable. He walks in his back yard occasionally, but seems to be very weak.—Mama went to see Brader yesterday, and he seemed very glad to see her. He has improved considerably, being now able to get the kind of food an invalid should have.—Now that Lillian is seventeen it will be easier for her to bear the burdens of eighteen, and when she's eighteen, it will be but a hop and a skip to twenty. I hope she will continue to give her Daddy as much pleasure in the future as she has in the past. And Mildred mustn't be jealous of these birthday remarks, for she has given me a great deal of pleasure too, and will give me more as she grows older. All I ask of my girls is that they shall be, first, *good*; if they are that they will be generous, sweet and charitable; second, that they shall be willing to take up cheerfully all the burdens that life brings. These burdens are its duties. I can truly say that neither one of my dear gals has ever given me cause for the slightest anxiety, except as to her health. They have been more than dutiful to me. They have been, and will continue to be, while we all live, my dearest chums and partners.

Now, then, after wiping your eyes, you will see that the page is full. I have written a long letter if a dull one. Regards to the Sisters and love to my dear Burdeene.

Your loving
Daddy

ALS

2 pp.

Envelope: Miss Lillian Harris, / St. Joseph's Academy, / Washington, *Ga.* / Wilkes County / *Ga. R.R.*

PM: 27 February 1899

1. Arrasat, JCH's comic spelling of Mt. Ararat. Kennesaw Mountain, outside Atlanta, would have to substitute.

2. Harris's note to * is " * At Tybee light-house."

3. Horizontal line here at bottom of page in Harris's manuscript; note 2 is below it.

[To Lillian and Mildred]

Sunday, March 5, 1899

Cold again, dear gals, in spite of the yeddytole I writ on spring in yistiddy's—no, in to-day's paper.[1] I had no sooner finished the yeddytole was no sooner finished [*sic*] and dispatched downtown than the mercury began to fall—there had been a hailstorm in the meantime—and last night the wind blow'd and then the thunder ro'd, and the lightning smacked and cracked, and the rain fell in some more torrents. Mrs. Lannan said "Oo," Mr. Lannan said "My!" and Mama dodged every time a flash came.—Mr. and Mrs. Lannan have been with us since Tuesday afternoon. Also Ryder; yes, more especially Ryder, aged 5, and red-headed. Since I was five, I have never known what it was to live in a house with a red-headed kid of that age. I know now; I know it all through and through, and up and down, and around and around. I can understand now why elderly people used to walk a block to avoid meeting me in the road when I was a kid; I know now why serious-minded ladies predicted some awful end for me. For the first time I can sympathize with them, and if I could meet them now, I'd shake hands with them and sob large sobs in their bosoms. But (as the girls say in their compositions) let us turn for a moment away from these gloomy reflections, these sad recollections, these—er—er—these dismal whats-his names. Every cloud (except a red-headed kid) has a silver lining[.] I know, as he goes running down the hall, that into each life some rain must fall, some days be dark and dreary; But [sic] when I hear him cry and bawl, I want his head tied in a shawl, for I am awful weary. Were I his daddy he'd sing small; I'd get a stick and him I'd maul. But I shall have to stand it all, or hunt the pole with Peary.[2]—Ahem! Anyhow I feel better [But see how shaky my writing is! I have been trying to shut the door of my stove in order to get my room warm—straining and tugging, and thinking awful things that I didn't dare to say out loud. And, then, bless Katie, Mama came along and shut the door with two fingers. She said she could shut forty doors like that with both hands tied behind her; and I believe it; but why, oh, why can women do so many things so much better than men?] Well, anyhow, I feel better after my tirade against red-headed kids, or lambs, if you choose. I feel as if I had got my revenge.—The Lannans are very nice people indeed. They have adapted themselves to their surroundings without any fuss or friction, and I feel quite at home with them—or, rather, quite at my ease. They know how to play whist, and, after I get through my literary work at night (I write three pages like this, about 1,200 words) we take a turn. Essie and Mr. L. play together, and Mrs. L. is my partner. Somebody asked Mr. L. if he played cards on Sunday. His answer was, "Well, I'm not a Methodist."—We've been having some very fine weather—that is, three days were fine—but now it is cold again. Friday we sat on the porch, and the mocking-birds were singing. The warm sun brought the violets out again, and several bunches were picked yesterday morning.—One of Chloë's children, Eugenius, is about to die with pleurisy.—We have nothing new here to write about.—Mr. Bunker seems to be improving. Mr. Ellis (Leonara Beck's husband) told me yesterday that Mr. B. would have been well by this time but for Mrs. Crosby, the mother-in-law. He said she compelled her daughter to neglect him, and misrepresented his case to the doctor, and has also circulated the report that he is losing his mind. I believe I wrote you about that rumor. Well, Mr. Ellis says there's nothing in it, and he says some very harsh things about Mrs. C. You know how quiet and gentlemanly he is. Well, his black eyes fairly blazed when he was telling me about Mrs. C's treatment of Mr. B.—There! you see what a gossip I am—just like a tea-drinking woman! This comes of keeping house for Mama while she goes shopping and visiting.—Miss Josie came out yesterday, and she says her sister is the finest elocutionist ever seen, and people rave over her, and she's had a grand offer to go on the stage, and she didn't accept it because the stage is not what it ought to be or might be, and certainly it might be bettered, and, as for Miss Josie herself, she didn't do a thing in the world but go out last Sunday and spoil a magnificent gown on the street car, and she's mad enough to sue the company for damages, and—and—Goodness! I wonder why I have to stop to catch my breath, while Miss Josie talked right along without breathing or batting her eyes? I find out more and more every day that women are really men's superiors. For me I'm willing to give them the privilege of voting and going into bar-rooms—if they want to.—The babies are well, and Alleen has a new cook and a new nurse.— This is all, and a great deal more than, I know. So you'll have to give the sisters my regards, and my love to Burdeene.—I enclose cheque for $199 which means

    For the Sisters $187.00
    "   "   Dentist   2.00
    "   "   Gals   10.00
                 - - - - - -
          $199.00

Oh, shucks! my calculation was all wrong![3]

>From your loving

Daddy

ALS

3 pp.

Envelope: Return to Box 111, / Atlanta, Ga. / Miss Lillian Harris, / St. Joseph's Academy, / Washington, *Ga. / Wilkes County / Ga. R.R.*

PM: 6 March 1899

1. JCH's comic spelling for editorial.

2. JCH's comic verse written as prose.

3. Initial figure of $200 was later scratched out and $199 written above.

[To Lillian and Mildred]

12 *March*, 1899.

Chewing heavily and earnestly on a dried fig, I seat myself to write to my dear gals, to ax 'em howdy, and to tell them about such scraps of news as come fluttering my way. The sensation of the hour in our small circle is the secession of Mrs. Bunker and her mother. They have packed up their belongings, even the lace curtains that used to hang in the windows, and have hied them back to their northern homes, leaving Mr. Bunker, as it were, to the mercy of the world and his creditors. There are two sides to the story. One is (I think I wrote you about it) that the mother-in-law wielded such a strong influence over her daughter as to cause her to neglect Mr. B. and to treat him shamefully. This is one side, and the side that I firmly believed until Mama, at the request of Mrs. Young, called on Mrs. B. to bid her goodbye. When Mama returned I heard the other side, and it is much the more plausible side, to-wit: That Mr. B. had not been physically ill a moment, but was only *mentally worried over a shortage* that had been discovered in his accounts—he was secretary and treasurer of Mr. Cofield's insurance company. It was discovered that this shortage had been going on from the time he took charge of the books—four years—and was at the rate of a thousand dollars a year, as far as the investigation had gone. He confessed this to Mrs. B. and she informed him that she despised a dishonest man. It was then he began the antics that led the two women to suspect that he was mentally unbalanced. He raved, tore his hair, threatened to throw himself over the bannisters of the stairway, asked for his pistol and made himself generally unpleasant. You can imagine the feelings of the two women left alone at night in the house with a man who acted like he was crazy. He wouldn't see the doctor, nor would he see friends who went to call on him. He cursed Mrs. Crosby and ordered her from the house many times, and then, with his hands to his head, he would cry out, "What did I say? What did I say? Oh, I didn't mean that!" Well, the officials of the insurance company came out and Mrs. B. and Kate signed away all their interest in his property of whatever kind, and he deeded his house and lot to the company. He had no money and no credit. Mrs. Crosby paid as many of the recent bills as she could, and she concluded that it would be better to take the daughter home, the daughter thought so too, and so they are gone, and that is the end of the whole miserable and unfortunate affair. Yesterday afternoon Mr. Bunker went to Mr. Ellis's, who knows nothing of all that I have been writing you, and still believes that Mr. B. has been badly treated. For four years, Mr. B.'s house has been mortgaged for three thousand dollars. Lucien discovered that some time ago. All that was unknown to Mrs. B.—Well, I'm truly sorry for all of them, and it may be that Mr. B., who is well on in years, and who has nothing to fall back on, deserves to be pitied more than the rest—for they have some one to care for them. The reason Mr. B. don't go to Kate's, as I have heard, is that the son-in-law will have nothing to do with him—repudiates him entirely. Where, then, is he going, and what will he do? See where sin and folly will land a man!— And then there's our old friend Ed. Wilson, who becomes a major. Four thousand dollars passed through his hands, and at last he took $122. He has been court-martialed and sentenced to forfeit his back pay and allowances, and to serve a term of three months in prison. The court rec- ommended that the imprisonment be commuted by the president. What possessed him, after $4,000 had passed safely through his hands, to take the paltry $122? Talk about mysteries! Here are two that will never be solved: An old man, after an honorable life, embezzles the money he has charge of—a young man with a wife and an infant child steals $122. Two families ruined! How easy it seems for ruin to fall on the innocent! It does seem to me that a man should think about the innocent people his folly is sure to hurt. But that is the real mystery after all.—Well, we are having tolerably jolly times at our house, whist at night, and occasionally the theatre for our good Catholic ladies. Mrs. L., Mama and the boys went to the minstrels Saturday, and seemed to enjoy it. J.C. has been telling me the old jokes ever since. One was "I want my wife to be like an almanac." "Why?" "Because I could have a new one every year."—Evelyn has bought a set of John L. Stoddard's lectures—very beautiful books.— I was sure I mentioned something about the puzzle in a former letter. I worried with it considerably, and intended to tell you that while it is admirable to whet the curiosity of students, it is too erudite for an old man. It is a very happy conception in all respects.—Oh! We had *turkey* for dinner to-day—We now have double tracks from the beginning of Park street to the corner by the drugstore.—The other family is well.[1]

This is all I know, and more than I like to know.—I mean about Mr. B. and Ed Wilson. Regards to the sisters and love to Burdeene.

> Your loving
> Daddy

ALS
3 pp.
Envelope: Miss Lillian Harris, / St. Joseph's Academy, / Washington, Ga. / *Wilkes county. / Ga. R.R.*
PM: 13 March 1899
1. Lucien and Aileen Harris and their children.

[To Lillian and Mildred]

> Sunday night, 19 March 1899.

Here I come a-runnin' for to say howdye to my dear gals and pass the time of day. And I want to say here, right at the very beginning that Lillian's composition is fine—not because she wrote it in half an hour, but in spite of that fact. The idea is good, and it is happily carried out. Indeed, I was surprised, for the piece has humor in it, and it is very rare for young girls of seventeen to display humor. But Lillian must remember that the very best things are the result of much thought and very hard work—though some people don't have to think as much or work as hard as others. As for myself—though you could hardly call me a real, sure-enough author—I never have anything but the vaguest ideas of what I am going to write; but when I take my pen in my hand, the mist clears away and "the other fellow" takes charge. You know all of us have two entitities [sic], or personalities. That is the reason you see and hear persons "talking to themselves." They are talking to "the other fellow." I have often asked my "other fellow" where he gets all his information, and how he can remember, in the nick of time, things that I have forgotten long ago; but he never satisfies my curiosity. He is simply a spectator of my folly until I seize a pen, and then he comes forward and takes charge. Sometimes I laugh heartily at what he writes. If you could see me at such times, and they are very frequent, you would no doubt say, "It is very conceited in that old man to laugh at his own writing." But that is the very point; it is not my writing at all; it is my "other fellow" doing the work, and I am getting all the credit for it. Now I'll admit that I write the editorials for the paper. The "other fellow" has nothing to do with them, and, so far as I am able to get his views on the subject, he regards them with scorn and contempt; though there are rare occasions when he helps me out on a Sunday editorial. He is a creature hard to understand, but, so far as I can understand him, he's a very sour, surly fellow until I give him an opportunity to guide my pen in subjects congenial to him; whereas, I am, as you know, jolly, good-natured, and entirely harmless. Now, my "other fellow," I am convinced, would do some damage if I didn't give him an opportunity to work off his energy in the way he delights. I say to him, "Now, here's an editor who says he will pay well for a short story. He wants it at once." Then I forget all about the matter, and go on writing editorials and taking Celery Compound[1]—which, by the by, would be a good thing for my dear gals to take occasionally in the spring weather—I go on writing editorials, and presently my "other fellow" says sourly: "What about that story?" Then, when night comes, I take up my pen, surrender unconditionally to my "other fellow," and out comes the story, and if it is a good story I am as much surprised as the people who read it.—Now, my dear gals will think I am writing nonsense; but I am telling them the truth as near as I can get at the facts—for the "other fellow" is secretive.—Well! so

much for that.[2] You can take a long breath now, and rest yourselves.—
Mr. Bunker has gone to Mr. Ellis's. Kate and Mrs. Ellis were supervising
a sale of his furniture the other day, and it struck me as a much sadder
sight than a funeral—this breaking up of a home, as it were, in broad
daylight. Don't think that I sympathize with a woman who deserts her
husband because he has taken a false step. He may have deceived her in
the first place, but it was her business to look out for that.[3] After she *has*
taken the marriage vow, that should settle the matter, unless his cruelty
or brutality takes a shape that she can not endure. I am sorry for both of
them; but I think I am sorrier for the man in his loneliness and weakness. I hope Heaven and the saints will guide my dear gals in marriage
as in everything else, and give them judgment enough to select only
good men, if they select any.—As you may well suppose, there's no news
here. Nothing out of the ordinary except our guests, who will go away
before easter. Outside news is to the effect that Mr. E. A. Howell can not
live many hours longer, and that young George Adair is at St. Joseph's
Infirmary in a very critical condition: Mr. Howell has hardening of the
liver (cirrhosis); I have not heard what George's trouble is.[4] We are going
to have a new sidewalk on Lawton street. Lucien wanted it, and I had
no objection. Julian and Julia were out to-day[.] Julian is busy writing
a play, and he told me the plots of several he had in mind.[5]—We are
very much pleased with the Lannans. Ryder is either less disagreeable
or I have become more accustomed to him. Chlöe's kid is getting well.[6]
The violets have come out again, and are beginning to bloom again; but,
after a tremendous rain-storm yesterday and last night, the weather has
turned cold again, and we don't know what is going to happen. O that
the mercury was 98° in the shade and I was sitting in the sun with my
overcoat and all my winter clothes on! I'd be happy then.

Well, there is nothing else. My best regards to the dear sisters, and
love to Burdeene.

Your loving

Daddy

ALS

3 pp.

1. Paine's Celery Compound, a patent medicine advertised in the Atlanta *Constitution.*

2. Famous acknowledgment by JCH of his creative side. *Cf.* JCH's use of numerous personae.

3. *Cf.* earlier letter in which JCH makes observations about Mr. Bunker's domestic and financial problems.

4. There is no E. A. Howell in the *Atlanta City Directory* for 1899 or the immediate years. Perhaps JCH meant to write E. P. Howell, his friend, neighbor, and the principal owner of the Atlanta *Constitution*. E. P. Howell died in 1905.

5. Julian made several attempts at being a playwright, including writing scripts for a musical play based on his father's Uncle Remus stories. None of these was successful. See mention of this material and various documents referring to the projected musical in the papers of Julian LaRose Harris, SC, EU.

6. Unidentified child of the milker Chloe Henderson, probably Eugenius, who earlier had pleurisy (letter to Lillian and Mildred, Sunday, 5 March 1899).

[To Lillian and Mildred]

Sunday, March 26, 1899.

This is one of the times, dear gals, when I have nothing to write about. Nothing has happened except weather, and as that is happening all the time, you wouldn't be interested in it.—Lillian asks me to suggest subjects for her graduation essay. That is out of my line somewhat. There is a certain set of conventional subjects that have become threadbare. You know what is coming as soon as you see a girl step out on the platform with her Manuscript held together by a blue ribbon[.] You know the whole thing by heart, from the launching of this petticoated thing on "the ocean of life" to the "farewell, dear classmates." Now, I hope Lillian will put a little ginger in her essay, and the only way she can do this is to select some theme she knows something about, and treat it as she did the composition on her seventeenth birthday. Make the stuff appear like it is written off-hand whether it is or not. She is supposed, when she graduates, to be at the beginning of a new career; but is that true? The idea is entirely a fanciful one, pretty enough when it was first used in the dim past, but not substantial enough to justify a thousand generations in using it. It is not easy, indeed, to hit off something entirely new; but I should think that Lillian would be able to get hold of a subject which she could drive over the same old road and yet give us a glimpse of fresh scenery. She has read enough to be able to take a somewhat comprehensive view of our age and time. She might contrast the aspiring new woman, bold, confident, and somewhat "sassy" with the woman who loves her home, and whose highest ambition is to make everybody about her happy. I mean, of course, the *good* woman. A woman who is not *good* in every sense of the word, can make nobody happy but herself, and her happiness is but momentary, being based on idle pleasures. I am not opposed to idle pleasures, but they should be the recreation, and not the pursuit, of women (and men too.) This sort of a subject might be too ambitious for Lillian—too hard for her. But it need not be treated ambitiously. Whatever subject she selects, she should treat it simply. Let it be written with the same care and freedom as she writes a letter home, avoiding those conventional and commonplace phrases that have rung in the same ears of thousands of people at graduation exercises. Many girls write, or have written for them, essays that leave the impression on those who hear them that the young lady believes the world is to receive a shock of surprise and pleasure when she leaves school and begins to circulate freely up and in it. This is because these essays are in to [sic] high a key.—Lillian could make her essay very much better than it would be otherwise by making it the subject of her letters to me.[1] Then I can return the letters to her with such criticism and comment as might be beneficial to her. The exercise of discussing the subject before writing it out formally would give her a mastery of it that she could obtain in no other way.—As I said at the outset, there is no news but the weather, and that is warm and cloudy.—Mrs. L. goes to-morrow. She seems to have had a very pleasant time. But for the fact that her discipline over Ryder is only intermittent, I should have enjoyed her visit more.—8:10 p.m.— Alleen has just come down to tell Mrs. L. goodbye.—Charles has just left after telling Essie goodbye all the afternoon.—Mr. & Mrs. L., Mama and Essie went to see "The Little Minister"[2] last night. Mr. L. furnished the flowers and I the tickets. They enjoyed the play very much.—I have nothing to interest Mildred, except that the babies are well and very cute. Brother looks like all the Zachrys rolled in one, and wants to smoke Lucien's pipe. Stewart knows all the Mother Goose poetry by heart, and also "The House that Jack Built." The two boys together make a roaring team.—The peach trees are just beginning to bloom. The poplars have no leaves as yet, but there are some tiny leaves on the apple trees. The roses are beginning to come up from the roots.—This is a dull letter, first on account of the essay, and, second, on account of the movement and agitation in the house on account of Mrs. L.'s preparations to leave.

Regards to the sisters, and love to Burdeene.

Your loving

Daddy

ALS

2 pp.

Envelope: Miss Lillian Harris, / St. Joseph's Academy, / Washington, Ga. / Wilkes county. / Ga. R.R.

PM: 28 March 1899

1. According to the commencement program of Saint Joseph's Academy in the Joel Chandler Harris Collection, her speech was entitled "School Girls." A handwritten draft entitled "Our Schoolgirl World" is in box 7, folder 9, Joel Chandler Harris Collection, SC, EU. Despite JCH's coaching in the previous letters, the speech is not remarkable in its contents.

2. *The Little Minister*, by James M. Barrie, dramatized (1897) from the novel (1891). Barrie is best known for *Peter Pan* (1904).

[To Mildred]

Sunday, 8th April. [c. 1899] [1]

B-u-r-r-r-r! but it's cold, dear Tommie. Yesterday the nor'wester came down from the mountains and swept over the plains, and we had to have fires in the hall and sitting-room, and in my room. I see from the papers that they had snow in Cincinnati Friday night. I'm afraid it will be snowing in Florida by to-night. I don't know what Mama and grandma will do up there on Kennesaw ridge. They are supposed to be coming home to-night, but we haven't heard a word from them. They left last Wednesday morning, but they carried neither pen or paper with them, consequently they couldn't write. And Essie, who is keeping house by eating, sleeping and playing the poor old piano—especially up in the bass notes where they growl loudest—Essie has not been able to write to Lillian.—The way we keep house here is to holler and tell J.C. to feed the guinea pigs, and to yell at Rufus to bring some fresh water in the house, or to put up his cattle—the cattle being three dry cows, a weak-kneed pony and a flabby looking donkey. And then when we don't want to keep house, we send for Chloë and get her to slam things around in the rooms, and bring in enough dry clay to raise soulful and satisfactory amount of dust. If Mama comes to-night she'll be ready to have another spring cleaning as soon as the weather begins to thaw and melt.—The poor roses have been whipped about by the wind until I'm really sorry for them. And they hadn't done a thing to derserve [sic] the thrashing. They were blooming their prettiest and looking their prettiest when down comes Uncle Wind from the northwest and lays about him with his thousand and one whips until the Roses are exhausted. They will not look saucy any more this summer—no, I mean this winter. But Uncle Wind has done one good thing. He has thrashed down hundreds of young apples, the ones that have the worms in them and the—well, the cramps.—J.C. now has thirty-two bantams and more a-settin'. It seems to be the easiest thing in the world to have more bantams; and, the first thing you know, they will begin to get in my rose beds, and then J.C. will have fewer bantams. It is just as easy to have fewer bantams as it is to have more.—The babes and their parents spent the day with us last—really one day is so much like another to me (except when it's cold) that I don't remember the date, but it was during the week just closed. Stewart is said to be cutting more teeth, though I don't see how it's possible, for he has cut two and three a week ever since he was two months old. By the time he is three years old he will have more teeth than a Florida alligator—if he keeps on cutting them. They say, too, that the baby is beginning to cut his teeth. I hope he won't have as many as a handsaw.—Everybody is well except me, and I'm well, too, except for this attack of weather.—Did it ever occur to you that when you get this letter you will have only twenty days in which to tell your friends goodbye at the academy?—I forgot to say anything in my last letter to Lillian about Burdeene, except to send her my love. I'll say now that we shall be delighted to have her come with Lillian. She seems like one of ours anyway.—Lula has been (and is now) staying with Essie.—Charles will meet Mama at the train to-night.—Friday night Mr. Hartman and Mr.—oh, I've forgotten the fellow's name—came out and played whist, or played at it. Brader, for a wonder, didn't come over. The serenaders caught him over here the night before, and he insisted on giving them a nickel.—Well, all the news has gone to war.

Your loving

Daddy

ALS

3 pp.

1. Lillian was still at Saint Joseph's Academy in 1899; note reference to her at school. Note also reference to cold weather in other letters about this time.

[To Lillian and Mildred]

[10 April 1899]

Monday night, Aprile the—the—

Oh, I've forgotten!—1899

I take my pen in hand to tell my dear gals the sad story of a piece of cheese, white and soft and thick, and covered severely with an overcoat of prepared mustard. Well, here was the cheese and close by was an elderly old man who should have known better than to get on speaking terms with this piece of cheese in its overcoat of French mustard. But he was reckless; age doesn't give some elderly old people judgment and discretion. The head of this elderly old man is hard and flat there bumps of judgment and discretion [sic]. He must have fallen up stairs once upon a time and broke the bumps off. He introduced himself to the piece of cheese with a large smile of affection. This was on Friday night. The next day the cheese reminded him that it was his guest. Sunday it told him so in still plainer language; so that it was not until Monday night that the elderly old man was able to seat himself at his Georgia mahogany desk, and write of his desperate conflict with the cheese in its mustard overcoat. Owing to this conflict some gals I know will wonder why they didn't get a letter from the seat of war by the usual mail, and they will imagine that the occasion of the detention is a whole cheese large enough to cause the electric car in Washington, Ga. to jump the track.—Anyhow the event has temporarily cut the elderly old man off from his base of supplies, so far as news is concerned. He can tell you all

the tidings he knows on three fingers: 1. There are two dime circuses in
town; 2. West Swarz [sic], the gay, the debenair [sic], is here; and, 3. J.C.
has a new ball mit [sic]. These things are important enough to afford
food for thought, as well as gossip, but no sooner do I make up my mind
to elaborate on them than a small camphorated voice calls out "Cheese
it!" West seems to be in fine health and spirits. He is making calls two
or three times a day, and finds time during the intervals to worry the
life out of Essie.—Evelyn won the big pound cake at the bazar. It was
a very fine one. Julia came out Sunday, and she and Mama discussed
it—well, a part of it—with some port wine. Julian was here also. His
head is full of an afternoon paper which he and some of his friends are
talking about starting at some future day. This, however, is, as we say in
French, under the frost-bitten rose-bush.[1]—The weather has been very
bad here. Some of my asparagus has been cut down—not by the cook,
but by the frost—and at last accounts the wind was still blowing from
the northwest. It was warmer this afternoon, but that means more rain
and another blizzard.—The children are well and happy.—We received
Burdeene's letter and appreciate it. I hope her cold is better now, and
that warm weather (if we ever have any) will drive it away.—We are
going to plant some corn to-morrow and trust to luck. Many of our small
vegetables are up, but they look very blue and lonely. The apple-trees are
beginning to bloom freely. The violets are blooming a little, but they are
waiting for better times. A lonely tulip in the front yard has been trying
to open out its blossom for three weeks. The roses are just now putting
up new sprouts. The hedges on the front walk have been cut close to the
ground. As a result the walk looks as big as a public road.—Johnson's
old mule, Beck, looks as if she'd have to be cut back on account of the
weather. And yet, there are open cars on our line—two at least.—Mr.
Bunker is still at Mr. Ellis's. They are certainly very kind to him.—Our
new neighbors are very exclusive. They don't lean over the back fence
and ask what we are doing in our yard. I don't see why people want to
be so stuck up!—J.C. says he'll write soon. Meanwhile he says "Tell the
girls the fan tail pigeons think that where there's a will there's a way,
and they're laying again"; and that "Mildred's Langshan hen is sitting or

setting on 12 eggs, which will hatch next Sunday if they hatch at all."—
There now! That's everything I know and more too.

Regards to the sisters and love to Burdeene.

> Your loving
>
> Daddy

ALS

2 pp.

Envelope: Miss Lillian Harris, / St. Joseph's Academy, / Washington, / *Wilkes county*, / *Ga.* / *Ga. R.R.*

PM: 11 April 1899

1. I.e., *sub rosa.*

[To Lillian and Mildred]

Sunday, 16 April 1899

Spring has again "jumped" her contract, dear gals and we are left to fight it out the best we can with a cold and dreary nor'west wind. It's about the same as winter, perhaps even more disagreeable, for in winter we expect these things.—We have an addition to the family that will interest Mildred. Bijou has three grand-children, one marked like old Kitty banks, one yellow, and one white. They cannot see to read without spectacles; in fact they refuse to open their eyes at all. This shows how obstinate young children can be.—Charles is in the parlor, eating the bread and honey of love, t-r-r-ew love.—A fine-looking young soldier, Sergeant L. E. Barnett, 202nd N.Y. Vols., from Buffalo, called on me today. He wanted me to write my name in "Sister Jane."[1] I did so, giving him a national salute, after which Mama whistled "The Stars and Stripes Forever," and then I had to go and feed the chickens. This shows that we are very busily engaged in literary work up here. If all the soldiers were to buy a copy of one of my books—however, that brings up the question of embalmed beef, and so I'll say no more about it.—Stewart is down here this afternoon. He says the boy stood on the burning deck eating goobers by the peck, and makes other remarks showing that he has inherited a memory that I never had.—West will be going home shortly. If Lillian were to see him and expect to find out anything about Cuba, she'd be badly disappointed. He knows he's been there and that's

all. What he saw, or heard, or found out seems to have passed as completely from his mind as if there were no such place as Cuba. I suppose
if he were placed on the witness stand, a clever lawyer could get some
facts out of him.[2] I have learned two important things from him, however. Fanny is going to San Francisco to spend a couple of days, and his
father has shaved off his beard because it was gray. This afternoon West
has gone to see Brader. I have no news of Brader; perhaps West will tell
me something.—What about Lillian's "A Valiant Woman?" [sic] Who
is she? Joan of Arc? Can't the dear gal give me an outline of her ideas
on the subject? In order to collect your thoughts, you have only to put
your mind on a subject about which you know, or can learn, something,
and the thoughts will come flocking of their own accord. But Lillian
can only put herself into the essay—I mean her individuality by writing
it out freely and almost at random, and then rewriting it half a dozen
times and painfully correcting it. Writing is an easy matter, but fairly
good writing is a matter of hard work, and the very best, like Cardinal Newman's, is simply the outcome of the most abject painstaking.
Still, nobody expects a school-girl's essay to be the best; it will be good
enough if it only stands for the very best she *can* do.—I'm glad to hear
that my dear Tommy is getting along so well in Music. I think she has
some talent for it; if she has her good and patient teacher will bring it
out.—I'm glad to hear, too, that Sister Mary Bernard has recovered from
her illness. My last encounter with grip has left me in a worse state than
any, and I find that I have to be prudent in every thing; I have to watch
myself when I eat. If I don't—well, it's off to bed I go.—Our new neighbors are Mr. and Mrs. Merinus—the Cable Piano Company's agent—
and their little boy.[3] They seem to be well-to-do, and are very quiet.—
Mrs. Young has been in West End, and has had a gay time with her
friends.—Lula spent Friday night here, and Mr. Lannan came out and
we played whist. Lula and I were beaten 8 *points* in 12 hands, a regular
Waterloo. Essie has developed into a very fine player.—J.C. went after
sweet shrubs this afternoon, but the bushes had been stripped. He found
only a few.—Julian and Mr. Woodruff came near having a collision in
the Journal office the other day—would have had one indeed if Mr. W.
had not swallowed some very salty talk.[4] I don't know where Julian gets

his combativeness from—certainly not from me.[5] 'Twas an old matter. Woodruff had misrepresented Julian to the Constitution's board of directors.—J.C. started to Sunday School to-day, and was delighted to find that Sister Ignatius is to be his teacher there, too. "Ain't that just *fine?*" says he. Sister Ignatius and Sister De Sailles (do I spell the name right?) came out Friday afternoon; rather they called on their way back to town. They had been visiting Miss Marion—at Stokes's. The good old soul has since died. She was 94, and kept her mind to the last. She saw Napoleon in 1812, and again in 1814 after Waterloo.

This is all. Regards to the sisters and love to Burdeene.

Your loving
Daddy

ALS

3 pp.

Envelope: Miss Mildred Harris, / St. Joseph's Academy, / Washington, *Ga.* / *Wilkes county.* / *Ga. R.R.*

PM: 17 April 1899

1. JCH's novel *Sister Jane* (1896).

2. I.e., regarding the Spanish-American War.

3. Actually H. B. Morenus. See Atlanta *Constitution*, 23 April 1899, 22, where he is listed as manager of Cable Piano Co.

4. Atlanta businessman Ernest Woodruff, father of Robert W. Woodruff, longtime president and chairman of the board of the Coca-Cola Co.

5. Julian kept his aggressive nature throughout his notable newspaper career. It may be that his investigative articles in the URM after the death of JCH were partially responsible for the loss of readers. Certainly his articles on the KKK and other controversial issues which brought him a Pulitzer Prize (1926) so offended many conservative Georgia readers that circulation dropped and he lost his ownership of the Columbus, Georgia, *Enquirer-Sun* in 1929. See William F. Mugleston, "Julian Harris, the Georgia Press, and the Ku Klux Klan," *Georgia Historical Quarterly* 59 (Fall 1975): 284–85, 286; also "The Perils of Southern Publishing: A History of *Uncle Remus's Magazine,*" *Journalism Quarterly* 52 (Autumn 1975): 515–21, 608; John M. Matthews, "Julian L. Harris: The Evolution of a Southern Liberal," *South Atlantic Quarterly* 75 (Autumn 1976): 484–85, 486–87.

[To Lillian and Mildred]

April 20, 1899.

We are all very proud of the Easter remembrances sent us by our dear gals (including Burdeene, of course) and think the various things,

cards and flower-pot, very beautiful. I say flower-pot simply through ignorance. Whatever the piece of chinaware is intended for, it is very beautiful. Some say it is for photographs; others, that it is for other uses. You'll see by that that we are stumped. The painting on it is nicely done.—I intended to go to church to-day, but I was not well enough, having a fit of indigestion. Mama says the services [were] very imposing, the church crowded, and the Bishop in high feather to preach a fine sermon. Essie aided in the decoration of the altar of the Blessed Virgin yesterday, and the Bishop was pleased to say that it was very beautiful, which pleased the young ladies immensely.—Stewart and Chandler send thanks for their Easter cards, and say they would write if they could. They are with us this afternoon, and I know what I'm talking about. Alleen sends love, and says she'll write just as soon as she can steal a half hour from town or from the babies.—Mr. Forbes and Cannon called awhile ago, but I had to deny myself the pleasure of seeing them.—It's funny that I have nothing to write about these days. Do you suppose it's because I'm getting old, or because we no longer have Rufus? Or is it because I have been thinking so hard about two or three books I want to write. I have just finished a new Thimblefinger book called Plantation Pageants, and it has been copied by a type-writer.[1] I came near sending the ms. to you so that it might be read and criticized before it goes into book form. It appears first in the newspapers, and in the fall will be put into a book. You'll see it in The Constitution, anyway.[2]—Mama and Essie have been making slippers and things for the bazar.—I hope my dear gals enjoyed their Easter trifles which were sent from here Friday. The box was heavy, and I know it must have contained something sweet and nice. I hope it did, anyhow.—Mildred's report was very good indeed, and I was very glad to see such a fine musical record. In short, I have nothing to complain about, but much to be proud of in the record my dear gals have made and are making.—Mama has suddenly developed a great fear of the cows, and she seems to gloat over it as a new sensation. The reason is that the cows are not used to very small children, and when they see Stewart and Chandler going across the pasture, they are curious to know what the little tots are, and so they run to investigate, shaking their heads and kicking up their heels. Of course Mama thinks

that this means war, whereas it is nothing but playful curiosity. Our new neighbors have arrived, and their first act, much to my gratification was to nail up their back gate—the one which the ladies of the neighborhood used when they called on Mrs. Abernethy or Mrs. Kelly.—It is a little warmer this afternoon, but still chilly. To-morrow or the day after it will be raining, and then there'll be one of Mildred's dear storms, followed by a freeze. I think the fig bushes will have to be cut down. The hedge along the walk will have to be cleared away. The lilac bush will not bloom any this year. The bloom buds were smashed by the freeze following the zero weather. The violets have grown out again and are trying to bloom,—succeeding very well, too.—So Lillian will spend only a week at home before going to see Jimmy McKinley? Well thank goodness! A week is seven days long anyhow. I hope she's going to bring Burdeene to spend that week with her.—I think Mildred will like Chandler better than Stewart. Brother is very cute, and is talking right along. Stewart can recite "Mary had a Little Lamb."—I suppose you saw about Mr. Haupt. He has been sentenced to ten years, but has moved for a new trial, and is now trying to get out on bond. I'm sorry for them all, and if I were rich I'd get him out of his trouble. And yet if I were rich I suppose I'd be like all the rest[.] Riches and benevolence refuse to sleep under the same roof together, and it's a pity, too.—Well, give my regards to the sisters, and my love to Burdeene.

> Your loving
> Daddy

[sketch of plate]³

Dinner-plate, barring the blot on the inner ring. The dark places are pale olive green and gold, and the edge is chased in gold. The four promontories are roughly fashioned like leaves.

ALS

3 pp.

1. Published under that title as a book in 1899. *Cf.* first reference in letter to Lillian and Mildred, 22 January 1899, of the completion of two chapters. "Type-writer" originally referred to the typist and only later came to mean the machine itself.

2. Usual marketing practice for his books.

3. Only this sketch and legend by JCH are on page 3.

[To Lillian and Mildred]

Sunday night, 23 April, 1899.

I awoke this morning with the headache, and I was afraid I wouldn't be able to write to my dear gals to-day. But it passed off this afternoon and I am feeling about as well as usual, only a little nervous.—For Mildred's information, I will state that we have four more new cats—two white and two dark gray. This makes seven new ones, three white ones, two gray, one splashed with yaller, and one yaller—making a very choice and beautiful collection; and now, ladies and gentlemen, what will you give for the lot? How much do I hear you bid? It will be some time before you have such another opportunity to secure bric-a-brac that is really alive. You have seen woolen cats, and china cats, and terra-cotta cats; but they were all imitation cats. These are the real thing, warranted to amuse you during the day and keep you awake all night. Speak up now; be brisk; we can't stand here all day. Am I to hear a bid, or shall I put these truly original and genuine cats back on the shelf? The first bid takes them. Fifteen cents! from the old lady with the steel spectacles. Fifteen cents, fifteen cents! going, gone! Here they are madam; take 'em and be happy. It is the same here as Mildred says it is in Washington— no news except that which you find in the papers. The neighborhood is dull. Mrs. Young has flitted and Mrs. Abernathy rarely comes over, so that I have no gossip to write you. Brader is still at the Sanitarium, and bids fair to remain there until his little dab of money is exhausted. Julian is a candidate for membership in the Board of Trustees for the Library. The library elects six and council elects six. Julian is a candidate before council for the four-year term. The terms of six will expire in four years, and the terms of the others in two years. In this way, the board will be in existence all the time. Julian's chances appear to be good. His friends say he has a sufficient number of votes pledged to him to insure his election. I hope so; I should be sorry to see him defeated in this first effort to run for office. He became a candidate at Clark Howell's suggestion.— I don't know what has become of Mr. Cramer. His wife is here keeping house for her mother, but Mr. C. has disappeared.[1] My impression is, though I may be wrong, is that he has gone for good. Mama and Essie went to Mr. Tommy's concert, and heard the little fiddles and flutes and the big bassoon. They are very quiet and secluded in their comments, and I judge by that that, while they may be willing to wash their hands in classic music, they don't like a shower bath of it. They say they liked it, but they don't insist on it. They don't go about the house hitting the walls and tables with their fists and daring anybody to say that classic music is not the only music.—In one of her former letters (to Essie), Lillian remarked that "No prayer was never known to fail." Did she mean that all fail sometimes, or that no prayer was ever known to fail? And why does Lillian pretend that she can't collect her thoughts? Can't she write ten lines of her essay at a time, or twenty? Can't she write a dozen pages and then rewrite them until she has her mind full of her subject? She thinks she can't, but doesn't even try. She should write, or try to write, a part of her essay every day. Then, when it is finished, rewrite it two or three times, making it simpler and simpler every time.—J.C. wrote to-day. It is a great trial to that child to write. It is like taking bitter medicine—his face is awry every time he thinks of writing a letter.

This is all I know and more—except that Evelyn went to the cremation of Sam Holt, and I expect to see a badly shocked young man to-morrow. He had to go for the paper. The whole miserable business is most awful—and we seem to be at the beginning of such things in Georgia.[2] My regards to the Sisters, and love to Burdeene.—Father O'Brien says he is going to bring Father Gunn out to see me.

Your loving

Daddy

ALS

2 pp.

Envelope: Miss Lillian Harris, / St. Joseph's Academy, / Washington, Ga. / *Wilkes county. Ga. R.R.*[3]

PM: 25 April 1899

1. Mr. Cramer, Clark Howell's brother-in-law, was editor of the *Evening Constitution* while it lasted a few months, and later a journalist on the Atlanta *Constitution*. *Cf.* earlier letter on this topic.

2. Sam Hose, alias Sam Holt, was a black man who confessed to the murder of Alfred Cranford and to the rape of his wife at their home near Palmetto, Georgia, 13 April 1899. He was sought by the authorities for several days. A front-page story in the Atlanta *Constitution*, 24 April 1899, reads "Sam Holt, Murderer and Assailant, Burned at Stake at Newnan." A crowd of two thousand witnessed Holt's torture, mutilation, and immola-

tion, afterwards choosing souvenirs of the body. JCH reflects on this sorry spectacle as a symptom of the deteriorating racial relations at the end of the nineteenth century in America, especially the South.

3. On back of envelope: list of rhyme words in JCH's hand:

"Bell, Cell,
Dell, Fell, Gell, Hell, Jell,
Kell, Lell, Mell, Nell, Pell,
Quell, Rell, Sell, Tell, Vell,
Well, Xell, Yell, Zell."

[To Lillian and Mildred]

Sunday, 30 April, 1899.

Though the weather is warming up, it is not too warm to put my head under the lamp shade to write to my dear gals. There is my dear Tommy: what is the matter with the school rules that she should find them so hard to observe? Maybe the summer-like weather is making her feel skittish and frisky. That's something of an excuse, but I notice that this friskiness has been going on for four weeks and I'm sure the weather wasn't warm the first two weeks of April. Well, I hope she'll clench her teeth together—(after cleaning them)—and resolve to stand by the rules.—And then there's my dear Billy's short and sweet letters: when she sits down to write she's in a hurry, when she writes, she's in a hurry, and her hurry is so great that she is compelled to finish pretty nearly as soon as she begins. Her last letter made me feel as if some one had run into the room and said "Howdye?" and then ran out again, slamming the door. If she would think the matter over, she'd find that she had a lot of interesting things to say about herself, her hopes, her aspirations and her desires, and if she started in on that line, she'd find a long and very interesting series of letters growing under her hands. I'm not complaining; I'm merely suggesting. I'm glad enough to get the letters as they are; but my dear Lillian is now seventeen, and occasionally serious thoughts must naturally come into her mind—I mean thoughts that may be called serious when compared with the ideas of very small girls. I'm sure I'm not making myself plain; but when I was seventeen every book I read, everything I saw started my thoughts in a new chan-

nel. What I call a serious thought is one that is new to the mind—
though it may have occurred to millions of people before.—Well, I'm
sure my dear gals will look at each other and say, "What a nice letter
papa could write if he didn't lecture!" But it isn't a lecture; it is simply
some of the good advice which old folks give and never take.—Ahem!
now then! Father O'Brien called to see me Friday, bringing Father Gunn,
of the Other-Side Church.[1] Says Father O'Brien, says he: "This is Gunn;
mind that he doesn't 'go off'!" Says Father Gunn, says he: "He'll be glad
enough for me to 'go off' ere I've been here long." Says Father O'Brien:
"This is Mr. Joel *Cand*ler Harris." Says I, "When did *C-h-a-n* spell *Can?*"
Says Father Gunn: "A good shot! a remarkably good shot!" I had a very
pleasant hour with the two. Father Gunn is young and has a beautiful
way with him. Indeed, he is almost as nice as Father O'Brien. He has
the gentlest voice and the merriest laugh you ever heard, and when he
was going away he wanted to see photographs of the girls. He says he's
coming out to see me again. Father O'Brien wouldn't accept any money
for the orphans, saying that he was paying a social call. I remember that
in my last letter I spelt the name of Sister de Sales *Sailles*. This was because I had been reading the *Reds of the Midi* by Felix Gras. These Reds
made up the Marseilles battalion which marched into Paris and started
the Revolution to the tune of a song that has since become known as
the *Marseillaise*—getting its name from the battalion.—Well, here I go
again! running along like a cricket a-fiddling under the hearth. There's
no home news except that Mama thinks of going to Chattanooga Tuesday for the May festival. Lula will stay with Essie.—Julian has been ill for
three or four days. This morning he went to Tate Spring[2] with Pop Collier to spend a week; meanwhile Evelyn is acting as City Editor. Julian,
as you will see by the paper, has been, or will be elected on the board
of library trustees.—The babies were down to see us to-day. Stewart is
just simply a terror.—J.C.'s fan-tail squabs are growing finely. They have
hair on them instead of feathers, and are as fat as butter.—The roses
have come up from the roots and presently they'll be blooming. But the
wind is from the east, and I must close. Regards to the Sisters and love
to Burdeene.

    Your loving
    Daddy

ALS

2 pp.

Envelope: Miss Lillian Harris, / St. Joseph's Academy, / Washington, Ga. / *Wilkes county. / Ga. R.R.*

PM: 1 May 1899

1. Father James O'Brien, formerly pastor (1878–80) of Atlanta's Shrine of the Immaculate Conception and then head of Saint Joseph's Home for Boys, Washington, Georgia; Father J. E. Gunn, rector of the Church of the Sacred Heart, then a new church organized for Catholics on the North Side. It remains at the intersection of Ivy Street (recently changed to Peachtree Center Avenue) and Peachtree Street. (Martin 2:570–72.)

2. Tate Spring, probably a resort in Tate, Georgia.

[To Lillian]

7 May, 1899: Sunday evening.

While Essie is thumping things on the piano, I thought I would take my fountain pen in hand to say that—

Mama returned in grand style from Chattynoogy, slipping upon us last night quite unexpected and also quite fat[.] She never lost a pound in Chattynoogy, and she says she had a good time. She said that when she first came in and before she had taken off her "things." But after she had taken a dose of tea, and began to feel confidential she talked a little different. Little by little the awful fact came out that Ryder was quite the same, if not worse. What made Mama mad (after she got home and was rested) was that she had to get down on the floor and play with that awful kidlet—not because she wanted to; goodness gracious, no! but because she "wanted to be polite to Cousin Ida!" Did you ever hear the like in all your born days? And imagine Mama at her age, and of her shape and size, down on her all-fours, galloping around a room, overturning furniture and shaking the very foundations of things just because Ryder wanted her to be a sure-enough hoss. I have asked her in vain to repeat the performance at home for J.C.'s benefit and mine. And when I even so much as refer to the subject, you should see the look of scorn she gives me. I'll say this, that when a woman four feet and a half high and five feet broad, the mother of a large and impoverished family plays hoss for a strange kid and stubbornly refuses to play hoss for her husband—the idol, as it were, of her gizzard—all I've got to say is that there's something wrong somewhere. Mama says she's very tired

from climbing hills—that's what she calls it now.—I saw Brader to-day
at the post office in the city. He is thin, but looks better. He says he is
coming home "next week." He seems to be a great deal healthier than his
mother just now.—Did I tell you that Miss Laura and Lula were keeping
boarding-house? Moddy is chaperoning them. Miss L. wanted me to buy
her diamond ring for you, only $70, and dirt cheap at that. I told her
that diamonds of that size and water were too rich for us. As a matter of
fact, I'd much rather give $70 to Father O'Brien's orphans than to buy
a diamond ring with it. My dear gals may have different ideas now, but
some of these days they'll feel as I do about such things; anyhow I hope
so. I never see a diamond flashing on a lady's fingers but I think of the
suffering that is going on in the world for the lack of money. (N.B.—
Mama's three little diamonds are family relics, and they don't flash like
some others I've seen.) Chandler has been very, very sick all the afternoon. He was taken with symptoms of *cholera infantum*, and came very
near collapsing. Dr. Crowe was called in and he succeeded in quieting
the youngster.—We have had a few strawberries out of the garden, but
they are not as fine as they should be. The weather has been too dry.
The garden is doing very well. We could have had some green peas for
dinner to-day if the cook had taken the trouble to gather them.—We
are to have a side walk on Lawton street; the curbing is already in place.
This will be more interesting when the city calls for money.—J.C. went
to the Baptist picnic near Hapeville. When it comes to free lunches, we
know no creed. Julian is pretty near well again. He has gained a pound
or two at Tate spring and will likely be home to-morrow.—Charles and
Mr. Bunker were here this afternoon. Mr. Bunker wants it understood
that the rumors of his cruel treatment of his wife are false. I tell you so
you'll know. But he is gradually getting gay again. He had an abscess
at the first or second base—goodness! J.C.'s base-ball fever has affected
me;—well, Mr. Bunker says he had an abscess at the base of the brain,
and that in the paroxysms of pain he might have made remarks that
would not have sounded polite in a Methodist church—but otherwise
he was very, very good. Regards to the Sisters and love to Burdeene.

    Your loving
      Daddy

P.S.—Miss Laura has a boarder by the name of BUSS. This completes the combination.

ALS

2 pp.

Envelope: Miss Lillian Harris, / St. Joseph's Academy, / Washington, *Ga.* / *Wilkes county.* / *Ga R.R.*

PM: 8 May 1899

[To Lillian and Mildred]

Sunday [May] 14, 1899.

Dear Billy and Milly: As you have discovered ere now—(doesn't that sound nice and romantic—*ere now!*—I hadn't thought of the beautiful expression in years and years, but I used to read it in the lovesick stories of Mrs. Sigourney[1])—you have discovered ere this (oh, it is such a lovely phrase) that time flies, tempus fergits us, as Aunt Minervy Ann would say.[2] Here it is all but the 15th, and before you know it vacation will lead you home, whereupon I hope that my dear Billy will cease to lose flesh at such a tremendous rate. What is the matter with her? Has she lost her appetite, or is she studying too hard? Why not try a bottle or two of Paine's Celery Compound?—anything so that she won't become a shadow.—We have the same news here that we have all the time, only more so. Our neighbors are so quiet that there's nothing to write about. None of them have the nerve to beat their wives or to kill their cooks, consequently there's nothing to write about. I believe things would be livelier if the chickens weren't penned up.—One of the little gray cats was found dead to-day, just after the cats were fed. Either it choked to death, or Muldoon got in the window of the wood cellar and killed it.—Our strawberries are not good this year. First the cold and then the drouth injured them, and while they are better than the berries that grow on the fruit stands, they are not as good as they should be. Still, they are good enough. Indeed, as reminders of what we might have had they are fine—poor in quality, but rich in suggestion.—For two weeks I have tried to get the Catholic News, but I find that they no longer keep it at the church on this side.[3] They didn't dispose of a sufficient number of copies to justify ordering it. Such is the supposition.

And it is very funny to me. No wonder the Bishop rails at the slovenly and penurious congregation; no wonder Father Schadewell is failing in health. Such a parish as this is enough to drive sensitive pastors wild. I hope my dear gals when they grow up will not weep over every penny they give to the church.—Speaking of surprises I think Billy will have one about graduation time if she is able to make a shadow. I'll not say what it is. Mama doesn't know it, nor Essie, nor anybody except me and one other, and I just heard about it accidentally.—I'm glad to hear that my dear Tommy is holding her own, and growing stouter and taller. That sort of news is good news. Bill's lost flesh is to be found in her reports. They are fine; but a little more weight on the bones and fewer marks of perfection on the reports would suit me just as well if not better. Health, health, is more important than anything save religion; and I believe a healthy person can serve the Lord just as acceptably as one who is ill. So I say once more: Dear Billy, don't study too hard; take exercise; take a tonic, Celery compound or something of that kind.—What is the name of the proprietor of the Johnson House? I want to write to him before Mama comes down.—Walter Forbes took dinner with Lucien to-day and called to see us this afternoon. He's a very fine fellow. Mr. Stanton—well, Mr. Stanton has made another escape from poetry; and Chloë and her tribe went to another funeral to-day. The peculiar thing about it is that the person whose funeral was preached has been dead for some time.— Both the children have been ill, but they are up and about now.—I don't know how the boarding house is getting on, but I shouldn't think it was flourishing.—Mr. Lannan took Mama and Essie to the Pearson Concert t'other night. He was in the chorus, and had on a claw-hammer coat, the tails of which nearly struck his heels. It was so funny that I came within one of calling Mama back and going with him myself. Regards to the sisters and love to Burdeene.

> Your loving
> Daddy

ALS

2 pp.

Envelope: Miss Lillian Harris, / St. Joseph's Academy, / Washington, Ga. / *Wilkes county. / Ga. R.R.*

PM: 18 May 1899 [4]

1. Lydia Huntley Sigourney (1791–1865), popular American author and poet, known as "the American Hermans."

2. Aunt Minervy Ann, a black character and storyteller created by JCH, appears in several of his books.

3. Saint Anthony's Catholic Church, West End.

4. Note discrepancy of date of letter and postmark.

[To Lillian and Mildred]

Sunday Evening, 21 May. [1899]

I'm sorry my dear gals missed my last letter—not because there was anything in it, but because it has become a sort of habit with them to receive a letter from me every Tuesday or Wednesday. Anyhow, my conscience is clear. I wrote the usual amount of nonsense, and Mama gave it to Chloë to post. Chloë says she sho did put dat ar letter in de mailbox up dar by Miss Frazier's: though for all we know she may have put it in the slop-barrel in the hope of educating her pigs.—Mamie Culberson has the measles, not one measle, but a whole swarm of them, Stewart has a stye on his eye, and Bessie Ray and May Smith are to graduate this year.—Of course, I am proud of the fact that Lillian received the first honor, very proud indeed, but somehow I can't help feeling sorry for the one that didn't get it. And yet if Lillian had been the disappointed one, I should have been sorrier still. So there it is! When a fellow gets old and his mind becomes wrinkled, he can't have any unmixed pleasures.—I judge from Lillian's chaney bill that she is becoming quite a successful painter of crockery.—And this reminds me that Mama had Ed. White washing the chicken-pen with an old broom. It was a beautiful sight to see the artist at work with a gunny bag sack for an apron, and the fork of the quince tree for a palette. J.C.'s squab-tail pangeons—oh, my goodness! I mean fantailed squabgeons—no!—fantail squabs are all feathered now, and the mother is setting, or sitting, again.—The puppies are doing as well as could be expected. We shall keep two—a white one for ourselves, and a mouse-colored one for Roy.—The weather has been trying to give us a rain to-day, with only partial success. It has been and still is very dry in these parts, and unless we have a good rain soon, our vegetables will dry up. The roses are doing only passably well. The trouble is that the new sprouts get top-heavy and break off. I think all except a very few will have to be replanted, after which I hope we'll have no more zero weather until the year 2999—not for *my* sake of course, but for the sake of other feeble-minded old men who may be alive at that time. But by 2999, folks will be able to distribute artificial heat over wide areas, so that a man—or a woman either—will be able to sit in West End and warm themselves (observe the truly English grammar) at a fire (say) in Cincinnati—or Canton. And then, instead of fan-tail squabs they'll have fan-tail buggies that will rise and fly or roll and run at the pleasure of the occupants; and Jim McKinley's descendants will be dukes and dukesses; and railway trains will be exhibited at county fairs as relics of the dark ages, to show how ignorant the people of this day were.—For Mildred's benefit, I'll say we had some tremendous thunder-claps about seven o'clock. Ovid, who was scratching off fleas on the front porch concluded to retire under our beautiful suburban villa. Mama brought out the holy candle, but didn't light it, for the supposed storm turned out to be no storm at all.—Brader is in a bad way again. He was riding out the other day, and had one of his spells. He had to be carried into a drugstore. His mother and aunt are very gloomy about him.—In the letter you failed to get I mentioned the fact that you'd probably be surprised about the time of your graduation. This is all I can tell you, since the secret is not mine. I simply heard that there was a surprise in store for you. Neither Mama nor Essie knows any more about it than I do, if as much.—Does Lillian intend to go barefooted in the afternoons when she returns home? I'm certain Mildred will. Both of you can play in the tub at the well.—The evergreen hedge has disappeared root and branch, and its place is taken by violets reaching from the second terrace to the front gate. I think the substitution of violet beds for the scraggly hedge is a great improvement. Anyhow, as Mama says, its [*sic*] something new.— Walter Howard, who was to marry Miss Newman, is critically ill in New York, and is not expected to recover.—This is all the news I know, and so I'll have to say ta-ta. Regards to the sisters and love to Burdeene.

Your loving
Daddy

ALS
2 pp.

Envelope: Return to Box 111, / Atlanta, Ga. / Miss Lillian Harris, / St. Joseph's Academy, / Washington, *Ga.* / *Wilkes county.* / *Ga. R.R.*
PM: 22 May 1899

[To Lillian and Mildred]

> Sunday Evening
> 28 May. [1899] (The last
> letter was dated April.
> typographical error.
> Please correct.) [1]

Dear Billy and Milly: I haven't the least idea what I'm going to write about. The only news I have is that my sensibilities are gradually recovering from the shock of the cold spell. Like the trailing mimosa, I feel like shutting up when the wind blows chill. The dry drouth continues. The cows have only the remnants of a pasture, and the ground sends up a cloud of dust if a chicken runs across the pen.—Johnnie-May Davis has the scarlet fever, and likewise Mattie Wagner. They must have contracted it at school.—The babes were with us to-day by a large majority, consequently the house and yard look as if a patent reversible steam plow had been turned loose on the premises to do its wild work.[2]—I see that Susie Lee Ray and John are determined to get married. They have had their pictures in the paper, and if the resemblance is correct, marriage is a horrible thing to anticipate. Yet they are both brave. They have allowed the affair to be announced. Oscar, John and Harry took dinner with Lucien to-day. Lucien went to see Brader yesterday. The doctor has put him to bed, and I suppose that is the beginning of the end.—Father Gunn's superiors gave him the option of going to the Philippines recently; but he preferred to remain in Atlanta, where he has a great many friends and admirers. He is a charming man, as far as I can judge from a brief talk with him.—I appreciate Father O'Brien's gift very much. The orphanage is a sort of hobby with me, and I am never tired of admiring the way in which Father O'Brien has made the fire turn out to be a blessing in disguise[.] The old orphanage was in no way comparable to the present one.—I hear the Wottons are going on the other side, a fact which doesn't displease Lucien.—The Zachrys don't know whether they are satisfied at Adrian or not. A letter comes one day to say that they are all coming home on the next train, and that train brings a letter saying they are perfectly charmed with the place. This is the report Lula gives of the correspondence. She may color it a little, but I suspect the exaggeration covers a fact Alas! Why are we never happy until we have chased our various bubbles out of sight? There is no more miserable sight in this world than the spectacle of a restless woman who can't accommodate herself to the ways of Providence. Poverty is a bad thing, but there is as much happiness and content in poverty as there is in riches if we know where to look for it.[3] We find them within us, or we find the lack of them. (*Uckychow!* egh! it's enough to make a body sneeze to find your *Daddy* putting on such wise airs. After this you needn't be surprised if he hits you between the eyes with a cold proverb or a chilled maxim. Keep your eyes on him, dear gals, and be ready to dodge.)—Evelyn has been ailing owing to eating late suppers, and was laid up for a day and night.—I'd be glad if you'd have the Catholic News sent to Box 111. Tell me what it costs and I'll enclose it in the lev'mty— lev'm cheque for the crockery ware. Fact is, I'm glad they don't sell it in the church any more. The temple is not a salesroom, and should never be made such.—Mama is going to have the chimneys cleaned out by chimney sweeps. As she is sure to superintend the job by sticking her head in the empty fireplace, trying to see what is going on up the flue, I hope nobody will call that day until she has been soused in the bath- tub. Mama was very much mortified because I chloroformed the puppies myself. She has put so many kittens to sleep that she feels herself to be an expert. House cleaning is still going on. Mama's room suffered Satur- day. The next thing is to have the ground ploughed up under the house and then leveled again by a steam roller with a big whistle. You miss a great deal by being away from home. However, girls are misses anyway. As Chloë says, "aint it de trufe!"

Well, regards to the sisters and love to Burdeene.

> Your loving
> Daddy

ALS
2 pp.

Envelope: Miss Lillian Harris, / St. Joseph's Academy, / Washington, *Ga.* / *Wilkes county.* / *Ga. R.R.*

PM: 29 May 1899

1. JCH's note in parentheses. Probably a reference to a missing customary individual letter either to Lillian or Mildred.

2. Stewart Harris and Joel Chandler Harris III, sons of Lucien and Aileen Harris.

3. Arrows drawn by JCH connect second "is" to "much" and third "is" to "much."

[To Lillian and Mildred]

Sunday afternoon, (hot and) June 4, 1899.

It may now be said, my dear gals, that summer is now in our midst. Speaking for myself, I can say I like it; but Mama and Essie are in a state of collapse until "dressing-time" comes, and then they proceed to wrap themselves around and about with vestments calculated to keep them hot at the north pole. Though the mercury is as high as the ceiling Essie now has her neck encased in two folds of blue ribbon. This is supposed to be the latest style at Cascade and other fashionable resorts.[1] The ribbon is five inches long and goes around Essie's neck twice, with an inch and three-quarters to spare. You can imagine what her condition will be in September.—Mildred's report is fine. Lillian's seem to overdo the thing as usual. I'm proud of it, of course, but it must be an unnecessary strain on the nerves to get 100 in everything. I want the Catholic News for a year; I could have published one myself by this time. I guess I'll enclose a cheque for $47 with this if I don't forget it— $46 for crockery ware and $1 for the News. Do I have to pay anything extra for Lillian's report?—Speaking of calves, one wandered into our barn early this morning and Daisy took charge of it.—Mrs. Zachry and all the children have returned. This is a new move, and I haven't inquired what it means. People who have been poor and then rich seem to be very unhappy when they become poor again. It seems to me that the best thing to do is to put a good face on everything and try to be contented with whatever happens. The happiest people are those who never try to be rich, and I thank heaven that I never had any real desire for riches. Yet I should like to have a surplus so as to help the unfortunate. Mrs. Z. didn't like the style of things at Adrian, and so she went and returned[.] Will she be any happier for returning? They say she is constantly weeping for fear she hasn't done the right thing. Dear gals, when you grow up be contented; don't be carried away by vain things; be good-humored and good-tempered, and knock disappointment in the head with a smile. Oh, it is *so* easy to be contented, and yet there is so little of it in this world. This is quite a homily. Well, it worries me to see grown women fretting their lives away about "style" and "good society"—when they know that these things are measured by money.— I send Lillian's stamps in a different envelope. If they get stuck on one another, a little warm water will cause them to separate.—I think Evelyn is making his arrangements to come down (not up) to Washington. If he lived in Augusta he would come "up" to Washington. I think we'll come down on the late train the day before commencement. We'd come in the morning, but Mama always has a headache after travelling, and so she'd better get there in time to go to bed rather than have to go to bed in the afternoon. I tell you, honies, we're getting old.—Could the two of you spend the night with us at the hotel? If so, you can meet us at the depot when the evening train gets in. Otherwise, we'll see you shortly after breakfast commencement morning.[2] If there's a concert on the night of examination day, I'll leave Mama at the hotel and bring J.C. Send me a programme in advance, and then I can tell you more about it.—Lillian says I should write long letters. So I would if there were anything to write about. The weather seems to have scorched the news, and the pasture, too—but we had a good rain three or four days ago. Regards to the Sisters, and love to Burdeene.

Your loving

Daddy

ALS

2 pp.

Envelope: Return to Box 111, / Atlanta, Ga. / Miss Lillian Harris, / St. Joseph's Academy, / Washington, Ga. / *Wilkes county.* / *Ga. R.R.*

PM: 5 June 1899

1. Cascade Springs, then six miles southwest of the city limits of Atlanta, was a popular resort and source of water for the community and of bottled water for Atlanta. See Russell A. Zaring, "Cascade Springs: An Atlanta Urban Spa," *Atlanta History* 31 (Fall 1987): 42–56, for a full account of its origins, development, and demise.

2. Lillian graduated in June 1899.

[To Lillian and Mildred]

Sunday Evening, 11 June 1899.

Here I come, dear gals, with my last letter during your school term; and I'm afraid it won't be much of a letter after all, for I'm starting out with nothing on hand except a couple of questions which Mama wants Billy to answer at once: 1. How many straps does Billy want on her slippers—one, two, or three? 2. How much ribbon does Billy want for Milly's bonny brown hair? These questions are to be answered post haste, on the spot, without delay, immediately, instanter, in a jiffy, in less than no time, in a twinkling, slap-dash, like a shot, forthwith, in a trice, and so forth and so on, because the box must be sent this week.

Now! I feel much better, in spite of the weather, which is cloudy and cold—too cold for me, though Mama and Essie are on the piazza, and seem to be enjoying the breeze.—Well, *of course,* we'll come Monday if it will please Mildred. I had an idea—you know how I am about such things, dear gals—that maybe Milly would feel embarrassed if she saw me in the audience ready to grin at her. But if *she* wants us to come in time for the examination, you can just bet—excuse me, young ladies; I am forgetting myself—Well, you may be sure we'll be there and glad of an excuse to come. The truth is, we can come just as well Monday afternoon as any other time.—I have a trade for Lillian—however, that is something I should say nothing about. The little calf is no more. Mrs. Chloë Henderson says she speck it got too much rich milk, and I specks so too. Anyhow, it will get no more.—The two surviving puppies are very fierce, if we are to judge from their barking and growling. Their mother is as wild as a weasel, and only comes to them at night. They are getting so they eat bread and milk, and in a few days they'll be ready to shift for themselves.—The rain to-day, which, so far, is a mere sprinkle, comes just in time to prevent the garden vegetables from crumbling up and blowing away. Cousin Dust has been having a regular picnic following the street cars from one end of the line to the other and back again, but Uncle Rain has put an end to this.[1]—Bessie Ledbetter came out to see Mildred the other day. She has become a Catholic, and is a very sweet girl. Her Uncle has brought her and her sister home. What possessed him to take the children from the Sisters, where she was so happy and contented, is more than I can tell. Bessie is only fifteen, and is just at the age when she needs good advice and a sustaining hand[.] Well, let us hope that it will all turn out all right in the end. She says she will seek the advice of the sisters here, and Mama will ask them to take a special interest in the child and her little sister. We hope, too, that Mildred will take an interest in her.—There is positively nothing to write about in this neck of the woods. The only new thing is the rain, which has just begun again, and which bids fair (I mean cloudy) to last all night.—Oh, Yes! we have a picture of Garnsey's baby—a very pretty child: which reminds me that I haven't heard of Mildred's Kodak. Has she swapped it for chewing-gum? She sends no films to be developed, and asks for none; nor does Billy. Something's the matter.—You should see the lovely dresses Miss Fanny has sent—and you shall! They are just simply altogether and especially too utterly fine for children to wear. I wanted Mama to wear one, while I wore the other, but she says we're too old for such furbelowed frivolity. But it's the honest truth,—these are the finest frocks I ever really admired. They are exquisitely made, and I hope my dear gals will be pleased with them. Regards to the Sisters and love to Burdeene.

> Your loving
> Daddy

ALS
2 pp.
Envelope: Miss Lillian Harris, / St. Joseph's Academy, / Washington, *Ga.* / *Wilkes county.* / *Ga. R.R.*[2]
PM: 12 June 1899
   1. *Cf.* JCH's story of "Uncle Rain and Brother Drouth" in *Mr. Rabbit at Home* (Boston: Houghton Mifflin, 1895), 252–65.
   2. Note in different hand on envelope: "Last letter from Papa while at school Tuesday June 13, 1899."

PART FIVE ❧ 1899–1900
ADVICE FOR THE ABSENT

I fear I am pretty nearly the only one now living who is willing to put his thoughts freely on paper even when writing to his own children. This is the result, as you may say, of pure accident.

—*Letter to Evelyn, 5 April 1900*

At Home:
June 21, 1899.

Dear Julian:

Mama and I are sending with this a little something to remind you that we are not too old to remember the day.[1]

I don't know how the anniversary affects you, but it is very queer to imagine (for it seems to be pure imagination) that the red and wrinkled affair, with the pained expression on its puckered countenance, which was placed in my arms on a Sunday in June, 1874, should have grown into a man big enough not only to be married, but to go about bulldozing ex-cabinet officers and library boards and things of that kind.

And mama and I are very happy to know that you have been successful enough to win for your wife one of the loveliest young women in the world; to whom and to you we send our love—send it and at the same time have more to send in our thoughts of and hopes for both of you.

To the which, as an evidence and a guarantee of good faith, we have hereunto set our hands:

to wit: Your loving
           Daddy
      and your loving,
           Mother

ALS
1 p.
Envelope: Julian Harris, Esq. / Aetat Twenty-Five
1. Julian's birthday in 1899; he was born 21 June 1874.

[To Lillian]

July the 3 eye, 1899.

Dear Billy: Your kind and courteous letter received, and I hasten to reply. In the first place, you sent no address, and I shall put on the envelope the first number and the first name of a street that pops in my head.

To-morrow is the glorious fourth, and by way of preparation for its celebration, Stewart and Chandler ate a cucumber apiece to-day. We shall await the explosions with some interest. The doctors of the neighborhood have been notified and no doubt the hospital ambulance will wait round the corner. As for ourselves, we are not having any quiet time at all. To-night Mildred tried to kick my hat off while I was standing in the hall reading the paper. Then she pretended to discover a bug on the floor. With a shriek she jumped on the sofa, and walked all over Essie who was fixing some of her lace "fixin's." I laughed until I had to hold my sides. Just before that, Shadrack had come for some buttermilk. When Mildred saw him coming up the walk, she began to call Charlie Goodman, who was not here. This startled the dogs, and they made a break for Shadrack. Naturally, this worried Mama, who saw in the attack on Shadrack an attack on Mrs. Kelly. She rebuked Mildred and wounded the child's feelings so that she wouldn't eat any meat for supper. In fact Mildred was so sensitive that she ate only five biscuits and a half pound of butter.

Everything here is pretty much as you left it except the terrapins. One of them has laid an egg. J.C. claims it for his terrapin, but Mildred is so sure her terrapin laid it that she says she can prove it. I have only one remedy left, and that is to call in the police.

How is my dear Burdeene? She should be happy now. She forgot to leave her diary for me to read, but Mildred quotes one sentence from it thus: "It is just horrid to pretend you are satisfied when you are not. Heigh! here I am at the Harrises again. As we understand each other dear Diary, I'll say no more." And how is that charming child. Gretchen? I hope that both are well and happy.—Mama is fairly well, though not so vigorous as she'd like to be. Essie had been enjoying herself for the past few days. Charles is taking his vacation, and comes over every evening. Essie took supper with Mom and Pop Kelly yesterday.

I hope you are enjoying yourself. There's no reason why you shouldn't. It's impossible to know Burdeene without knowing that her mother and father are lovely people. I judge from a photograph Burdeene showed me of her mother that Mrs. B. is full of fun. You must take care to give her and Mr. B. as little trouble as possible. If you'll conduct yourself there as Burdeene does here I'll be satisfied. She not only gives us no trouble, but adds to our enjoyment all the time she stays.

Well, there's nothing to write about. News doesn't develop here very rapidly. Give my love to Burdeene and Gretchen, and my kindest regards to Mr. and Mrs. Biechele.

    Your loving

      Daddy

ALS

2 pp.

Envelope: Miss Lillian Harris, / 207 Lake Street, / Canton, *Ohio* / Care Edward A. Biechele, Esq.

PM: 4 July 1899

[To Evelyn]

        Box 111

      6 *July,* 1899: After supper.

My dear Son: I am writing in reply to your letter rather more promptly than usual for the reason that I know you will be glad to hear from home at once—though I believe Mama has already written you a page or two. Thus, you see, I have in one sentence given you a reason for writing and have also strangled the reason at its birth. Well, anyhow, I am writing, and that is excuse enough.—We had a little over two inches of rain about noon to-day, and it has helped matters a great deal. Six or seven hundred such rains would go far toward building up the cow pasture to the butter point.—It is said that Tedford's play went off more successfully than Julian's and three reasons are given: 1. Hatch had the leading part; 2. The actors all knew their parts perfectly; and 3. The points made were perfectly obvious to the weakest intellect. This last is the most important reason of all. You will notice that Julian, even in writing, is disposed to be affected. Many of his references, suggestions, and illustrations are remarkable for their *aloofness.* They are good, once you have studied them out and mastered them; but the mind resents the demand made on it. It asks itself, unconsciously perhaps, why a writer who is seeking public approbation strives so hard to place difficulties in the reader's way. Please remember that you can't possibly spend too much time and labor in making your meaning perfectly clear. The best diction, as well as the most successful style, is that which is perfectly clear and transparent. Do you know how hard it is to be clear? The reason is that clearness is simplicity, and simplicity is the chief note of everything that is permanent in imaginative literature. You wouldn't read "The Sentimental Journey"; but old man Sterne has a very great style, whether we apply the word to his individuality or his diction. Suppose, then, you take a whack at Meredith. Don't read him for pleasure, but *study* him—the pleasure will come of itself by the bushel. I take great joy in that man's wonderful style. I mean his individuality;—and speaking of using one word for another in confusing sense, find out for me while you're in Maine why my yankee brethren speak of the "provincialism of the south!" when they mean "provinciality."—Don't allow any of your prejudices as a southerner (if you have any) prevent you from appreciating the people you meet. Next to genius, appreciation is the greatest boon a man can have; and it can be acquired. Don't ask everybody and everything to conform to your ideas and expectations before giving them a slice of your appreciation. The best man (apart from the truly pious) is he who is a critic without being critical.—But, gracious to goodness and back again! What am I doing? I started this letter merely to say howdy, and to tell you we are all well, and here I am "gwine on" as Chloë says. Why if this letter is ever resurrected after I have chased the worm to his den in the earth, folks will say it was written for print, be dinged if they don't. Yes, we are all well, and Mildred is more than well. She fills the house with her "devilment" from morning 'till night. She makes me laugh even when stern duty bids me be severe.—Mama has been telling me what she wrote, and I find, when it is too late that this particular letter is unnecessary. But no matter. Reply to it when you have time, and write as if you were writing to an old chum; and what better chum could you have than your loving   Daddy.[1]

ALS
2 pp.
1. Note on Emory typed copy: "This letter sent to Poland Springs, Maine."

[To Lillian]

Sunday, 9 July [1899]

Dear Billy: I'm glad to know from your letter that you are enjoying yourself so thoroughly. It is natural that you should. You are visiting those who know how to entertain and make themselves agreeable. I should be very glad to know that Burdeene enjoyed her visit here as much as you will enjoy yours; but that is impossible for two reasons. In the first place, she remains with us only a few days at a time, and we have no opportunity to make such arrangements as would enable her to get into the swim here. In the second place, Mama and I are two old slow coaches who can do nothing but eat and sleep and gossip. But Burdeene must have an opportunity to see what we can do when we try. The reason you are worrying Mr. and Mrs. Biechele to-day is because we want to have an excuse for having Burdeene with us not only next Christmas, but for a good part of the summer vacation, if not all.—Evelyn's address is Poland Spring House, Poland Spring, Maine. He was not seasick and therefore enjoyed every moment of his trip: You might write to him. I have neglected to send him your address, and if he doesn't write first you'll know why.—There's nothing new in this wilderness except the fact that Lucien has a new puppy. He is a very small puppy, about the size of forty-seven fleas stuck together, but he has a voice as big as a hogshead and as long as eleven fishing-poles. He yells all night and sleeps all day. Chandler will probably teach him how to bite, for both Stewart and Mildred are suffering from wounds made by Chandler's "tushes."—Mildred is as good as a show; she has kept me laughing nearly the whole time since you left. J.C. stares at her antics in astonishment, and seems to be grieved because I do not seize a chair or some other weapon and crush her. But she's a natural comedian and can no more be serious for long at a time than—than—well, than I can. She reminds me very much of the way I used to do when a boy; and I can see now, though I couldn't see then, why people laughed at everything I did and said. Now, I'm not praising her, for I don't think that such a nature as hers is likely to be appreciated. She's as full of tears as she is of laughter, and her extreme sensitiveness is likely to give her many a bad quarter of an hour.

Well, you see how I am running on—all because there is nothing to write about. The only change is that we have had some good showers of rain, and the young corn in the garden is just right, and canteleupes are coming in, and so forth and so on. But otherwise the place is as you left it. The house stands where it did, and the trees—and the birds flit around as usual. The only missing ones are you and Evelyn.

My love to Burdeene and Gretchen, and my kindest regards to Sister Sacred Heart.

Your loving
Daddy

ALS
2 pp.
Envelope: Miss Lillian Harris, / 207 West Lake Street, / Canton, *Ohio* / Care Edward A. Biechele, Esq.
PM: 10 July 1899

[To Evelyn]

12 July, 1899.
Lillian's address is 207 West Lake St.,
Canton, Ohio
Care E. A. Biechele

My Dear Son:

I enclose the bill of exchange, which I hope will reach you in time.— The report of the Dr. is no surprise to me; if it had been otherwise I should have known that he was engaged in flim-flamming in behalf of the hotel. It is part of the game for them to do so, as I have long known. What surprises me is that he should have made a correct report. Your urine is and has long been normal—the notion that albumen deposits in the urine are a sign of kidney trouble is exploded long ago, and is only kept alive in insurance offices to-day because their regulations—made when the notion was in full blast—prescribe it. The doctor here knew you were insurable, but he knew that insurance regulations would not permit him so to report. The urine of the healthiest men in the world will show traces of albumen at times, and occasionally much more than traces. This is so well known to modern doctors that they never bother their heads about the matter.—The Shakers will make a fine story. Howells, in his "Undiscovered Country[,]" deals with them; You'll find it in the hotel library perhaps. The way to write a good article on any subject is to deal with it sympathetically, or with the side of it that is purely human. I mean by that, let your sympathies play about the matter even though you have to condemn or criticise. Sympathy— especially literary sympathy—is not endorsement. We may sympathize (to put it roughly) with poor Folsom's weakness, but we don't endorse its manifestation.—I hope you'll cultivate Mr. Inman as much as possible—though he is as shy as I am. For myself, I have never been able to get close to him, owing to my own diffidence, but he is one of the best men in the world, and in the truest sense.—I'm sorry about that claw hammer coat and wes'cut. You might have known you'd need 'em sometime. I wouldn't like to appear disguised as a hotel waiter myself, but social customs have decreed the dress suit, and when a fellow needs one, he needs it mighty bad. In your case, however, you'll not be handicapped without it. You'll not think about it five minutes after you get in a crowd, nor will other people.—I hear in a quiet way that Tedford is making himself unbearable to the boys, and Julian intimates that he'll be compelled to put Ormand in his place.—Clark Howell said he answered your letter, and he appreciated the fact that you wrote to him. He paid you several fine compliments, and advised me to urge you to stay away from work till the 1st of September. He is more sympathetic about you than he is about anybody he has ever talked of to me. Forrest Adair was also very complimentary; in fact everybody that knows you seems to be "stuck on you."—Mama would write today, but she's up to her chin in dirt and dust, putting the winter clothes away and cleaning out trunks and closets.—Be sure and let me know if you get short of money.—I'm writing this in a hurry so as to get out for Ed to clean your closet.

All send love.

Your loving Daddy.

ALS
2 pp.

[To Lillian]

16 July, 1899

Dear Bill: Your request for stamps is too ridiculous—for anything. Do you intend it as a joke? Or do you really stand in need of money. Or do you dislike to get it from Sister Sacred Heart? I thought that by putting it in her charge, the responsibility of it would be taken off your mind, and that you would be freer to enjoy yourself. You are to use all except enough to pay your way back to Cincinnati—and you may use it all if necessary, and I'll send you more. I have a sort of sneaking idea that you feel somewhat "put out" because you were not given the money in charge. If so I am sorry. I consented to the present arrangement to relieve you of responsibility, and not to prevent you from spending it. I hope, therefore, that you will get what you want from Sister Sacred Heart, and if you want more, all you have to do is to sesso.—Oh, dear! it makes my head ache to talk about money. It is so tiresome. There's nothing new here except that Lucien has procured a puppy for the kids to abuse. They are not living up to their reputation in this matter, for they are treating the puppy well by letting it alone, and it is thriving. The Catholics of this-side church are to have a lawn party at our house next Wednesday from 4 p.m. to 10 p.m. Mildred wrote to the Bishop and extended him an invitation. She wrote a very nice letter, too—very cute and humorous. She is certainly a funny gal. She wears her hair pompadour when she "fixes up," and looks very well[.]—Evelyn has been examined by the physician at Poland Spring and has discovered that there's nothing the matter with him except the nervousness induced by overwork. Tedford was put in Evelyn's place on the paper, but he was so overbearing he had to be reduced to ranks. Sidney Ormand is now temporary night city editor.—Some complain of the warm weather, but the watermelons are good: some say the sun shines hot, but the canteleups [sic] are fine: some say they can't sleep at night for the heat, but, as for me, I'd rather be hot than cold.—It is now trying to rain, and we certainly need "something of the kind."—Evelyn writes some very funny descriptions of the people he meets at Poland Spring. He seems to have a knack at that sort of thing.—Mama's health has been better lately than for sometime. She now weighs more than ~~250 po~~ (*excuse ME!*) 150 pounds, and is still gaining.—Everybody is pretty well in this neighborhood, owing to the fine weather, and the "dog-wagon" hasn't come round yet. Your "long letters" consist of about 100 words—hardly that many.—You seem to be enjoying yourself thoroughly, and I'm glad of it. We are under many obligations to Mr. and Mrs. Biechele and Burdeene for their kindness to you, and hope to pay it back next summer in some way. Love to B. B. and regards to Mr. and Mrs. Biechele.

      Your loving

        Daddy

ALS

2 pp.

Envelope: Miss Lillian Harris, / 207 West Lake Street, / Canton, *Ohio*. / Care E. A. Biechele, Esq.

PM: 17 July 1899

[To Evelyn]

                    20 July, 1899.

My Dear Son:

Your letters have been received, and were inwardly digested and enjoyed. I'm writing, but not because I'm in the humor. Nothing but stem—in fact, the butt-end of—duty would make me do so. I've just passed through a lawn party for the benefit of the church, and I feel like a Chinese lantern looks when its bottom has dropped out. 'Twas 12 p.m. before I got to bed, and, having passed over my hour for wooing Morpheus, couldn't find him in the room. He had evidently gone off on a jag—would I had been with him!—Well, anyhow, I tried to make myself agreeable for Mama's sake, and I made myself quite conspicuous—for me. Two of the Marist Fathers were here, a visiting priest from Mobile, and Frs. Bazin and Schadewell. Father Schadewell took supper with us, so did Mrs. Corley, Mrs. Falvey and others. The lawn looked very pretty with lanterns hung in the trees, and the crowd seemed to enjoy themselves—at least to the amount of $37.90. We had some good music, too—vocal solo by a Mr. Majoribanks—or Marshbanks—violin by Hansel Crenshaw, and piano solo by a German lady, who gave us a very wonderful performance. I rather enjoyed the affair until today, when I find that enjoyment of that kind costs too much. All the women have headaches and are now asleep. They worked harder than cornfield niggers all day and half the night.—The status of Mrs. Croker at the hotel shows how strongly politics influence social life at the north. The Crokers are good people. The old man is especially attractive. He's well read, and is really a good talker. I suppose his family is equally refined if not more so. These things make me more of a Democrat than ever.—I knew you would like Mr. Inman. He is one of the few men really worth knowing.—I hear that Brooks has so far resented Ormand's appointment as to resign. That, however, is necessary weeding out. The idea that length of service is more important than natural capacity is one of those vicious ideas that wither wherever they are planted. The man who feels that simple length of service is worth any consideration whatever in a matter of this kind ought not to be tolerated in any situation where brains count.—However, you are hearing all the news and it is unnecessary to try to write you any.—Everything is on skids with Essie and Charles and the skids are greased. C. was here every day during his vacation, and one night when Mildred ran unexpectedly on the front porch, I heard this colloquy: Mildred—"Did you think I had a ball, Charles?"—C.—"No; why?"—M.—"Why you flung up your hand like you was trying to catch one!" Evidently Charles had his arm around Essie and was trying to get it away. Mildred had a lot of fun to herself about it, but she never teased Essie. M. will write you shortly. She wrote to the Bishop and he wrote a very nice letter in reply. However, it is time to repeat that I remain

> Your loving,
> Daddy.

ALS
2 pp.
Envelope: Evelyn Harris, Esq. / Poland Spring House, / South Poland, *Maine*
PM: 21 July 1899

[To Lillian]

Sunday, July 23 [1899]

Dear Bill: As I didn't receive a letter from you yesterday, I thought you had gone gypsying, but it came to-day, and you seemed to be all right, having apparently recovered from the desire to collect stamps in Atlanta. You are having such a fine time in Canton and the neighboring states that I wonder what you'll do when you return home. You'll find life insupportable; you'll sigh for variety; you'll miss your picnics, hobby horses, street fairs, moonlit lakes, music and dancing and the thousand and one things you are whirling through now.—Mildred says she always knew a president's neice [sic] must be sweeter and nicer than anybody else's neice; and it is as much as I can do to keep her from writing to Mr. McKinley to ask if she can't be his neice, and how much it will cost, etc. Well!! she's a whole show with the elephant thrown in. She keeps me laughing all day when she takes a notion.

Mama came near running herself to death at the lawn party, preparing for it, and then cleaning things up: so now she's "invalided" with a stiff and an aching neck and shoulder, and is this moment reading the paper and wearing a Red Cross mustard plaster instead of a linen collar. Everybody else is well. Essie's engagement will be announced next Sunday or the Sunday after. Mildred says she'll be glad of it, for then she'll know it for certain because it'll be in print.

I don't know any news whatsoever—except that the appointment of Ormond (instead of Tedford) temporarily in Evelyn's place, has caused some dissatisfaction. The idea seems to be that the man who has been working the longest is the one that expects to succeed, no matter whether he is capable or not. Julian tried Tedford, and the boys wouldn't work under him. I think Brooks has quit. He was next after Tedford. Evelyn doesn't know all this, or he would be for coming home; whereas, the paper isn't suffering at all. Evelyn is going to Canada about the 1st of August: he feels that he's as well as he wants to be. Fact is, he only needed a little rest and relaxation; but I don't want him to get back to work till the 1st of September.—Sister Bernard is in Lowell. She writes as if she would return in time for school. I hear Father O'Brien is getting along very well.—We have had one or two jolly good rains, and everything is looking better. The clouds continue, however,—and the mud on Whitehall, at the bridge where the paving is torn up is something terrific.

We are all very glad you are enjoying yourself at such a rate. It places us more and more under obligations to Mr. and Mrs. Biechele, and I fear these will grow so large we'll never be able to repay them. But we'll try. We'll have Burdeene here if we have to go to Canton after her.

Regards to the family and love to Burdeene.

Your loving

Daddy

ALS

2 pp.

Envelope: *S.A.P.* [1] / Miss Lillian Harris, / 207 W. Lake Street, / Canton, *Ohio.* / Care *Edward A. Biechele, Esq*

PM: 24 July 1899

1. *S.A.P.*=S.A.P. (As Soon as Possible?), JCH's joking way of continuing to urge Lillian to return soon.

[To Evelyn]

30 July, 1899

My Dear Son: I intended to write so a letter would reach you before you left Poland Springs, but I kept putting it off until now it is too late. So I send this to Upton—in spite of the fact that you may change your mind. Anyhow you won't miss much if this doesn't reach you.—We are all well here, and have been having a fine time with canteleupes. I'm afraid the season closed yesterday. Country water melons are now beginning to come in, and though they are small they're good. Alleen and Lucien spent the day here yesterday, and seemed to enjoy themselves fairly well. Alleen is not looking well, and I'm rather afraid she'll have some trouble when her time comes—though I hope not.—The latest news is that Buss has bought Lula a $50 graphophone, and they're having a lot of fun with it at Zachry's. What do you suppose the old cuss—I mean Buss—is up to? According to all I hear—though the rough estimate is mine—he is spending about half his salary on matinee tickets, street car checks, melons, marmalade, candy, flowers, silk parasols, and other articles that have escaped my mind.—Everything seems to be moving smoothly at the office. Little Clark is smiling and Julian seems happy, though they say Tedford is sour because he fell down. Dan Cary, I heard the other day, is going to Greenville, S.C. to take charge of a paper. I want to see it after Dan has hit it a few swipes with his powerful pen.—Charles and Essie's engagement is or was to be announced today.—I haven't seen the paper; but all during the week Essie has been looking very subdued, as though somebody had hit her for nothing.[1] Mamma's in a flutter because Essie, after binding her to secrecy, has told everybody in the neighborhood about. By that I mean she has told "Daught" and Lula. You'll wonder why I write you such nonsense. My dear boy, it's what we feed on; it's what we live for; it's what we're made for. I've breathed the atmosphere so much that when I see two women whispering together I'm dying to know who they're talking about and what they're saying. It's a disease as infectious as the measles and just about as irritating. I'm going to take a bath some day and see if that won't make me feel better.—Luther Rosser has begun to build in front of us. He's to have an 8-room two-story house.—Bunker is very spry and looks as if he wouldn't mind marrying again.—As to the crowd you run with, I know nothing about them and can give you no information on the subject[.] Your failure to receive a letter from your charmer every other day is not queer. No doubt she is testing you. Everything will come out all right in due time. You might do some testing yourself, but it takes nerve for a chap in love to pretend he doesn't care for his dearest. Still, it's the one way to settle all doubts. Well, that's all. My love to the folks.

> Your loving
> Daddy

ALS

2 pp.

1. Announcement of engagement of Essie LaRose to Charles J. Kelly of the *Constitution* staff appears in the *Constitution*, 30 July 1889, 13.

[continuation of letter to Evelyn, dated 30 July 1899]

Dear Evelyn: It is now Monday. After writing the letter I received your epistle, and held this over to enclose the draft.[1] It is payable to the Captain, and is for $5 more than you said, which will enable you and him to spend a day in St. Hyacinthe to get it cashed. I went to Zachry's concert and enjoyed it—partly. I rather like Buss, but the attitude of the family toward him is abominably free and familiar. Clark seemed to be much pleased with your last letter—and indeed, it is written in fine temper and style. *That* is what I mean by the *light touch:* I'm proud of that letter. It seems to fill the whole bill.

Well—everything's the same here as it was Saturday. Julian put the announcement in Sunday; but still Essie is not happy; there's something lacking—what I know not.

However I remain as ever

> Your loving
>
> Daddy.

ALS

1 p.

1. Note on typed copy at Emory: "Continuation of letter of July 30, 1899."

[ca. 1899/1900] [1]

Dear Julian:

Please take my bank book and have the McClure note, (due in August) discounted and put to my credit. Be good to yourself.

> Your
>
> Papa

See last page of bank book

ALS

1 p.

Envelope: Julian Harris, Esq. / Present

1. "Between 1899 & 1900" written on envelope in later hand. August 1899 is probable date.

[n.d.]

Dear Julian:

If you can spare the time run out and see Mamma a few minutes to-day. She would call if the elevator were running.

> Affectionately:
>
> Joel Chandler Harris

ALS
1 p.
Envelope: The Constitution, / Atlanta, Ga. / Julian Harris, Esq.

[To Evelyn]

7 August. [1899]

My Dear Son:

I hope the cheque will be sufficiently large for comfort. If it fits too tightly to your necessities, don't hesitate to let me know, and I'll send another. I saw Julian Saturday. He said he had $30 of yours, and also that he was coming out yesterday. If one statement is no truer than the other, he lacks 2.50 [sic] of having a cent for you: for he didn't come out. I'll see Clark about that pass—or, rather, I'll write him a note, as I am taking the balance of vacation due me.—I'm making a rearrangement of the Minervy Ann business. Frost could illustrate only four, and, as there are four unillustrated ones, I'm trying to make an octuple (or is it sextuple) sandwich. I find it a hard job: yet it's interesting, and it has enabled me to find a score of anachronisms; for instance, in one paragraph, I give the country printing office "a wooden imposing stone" and "a sheet iron imposing stone." It really seems that I'm the most careless writer the world ever saw.—I presume you'll find it dull where you are, but do you know it is a great field for a literary man? The engaging simplicity, the shrewd crudeness and the foreign atmosphere would all fit charmingly into a series of simple tales or sketches. You should take notes while you are there.[1] What you call loneliness is a part of the "atmosphere" and it attracts a man when he can read about it in the whirr of a city. Here, again, your observation can take you far. Note the characteristics. The question arises, what are these people existing for? The answer to it is a very pretty one, properly spun out. The good are living to be good, and the bad in order to be bad; but how few bad ones are there! And how quaint is the fact that here is a whole population which has preserved to this day the simplicity of the French peasants of three hundred years ago! Don't get into your mind the idea that the faith of these people in everything connected with their religion is "superstition." You know the Saviour, pointing to children, told his disciples "Unless ye become as one of these, ye cannot enter into the Kingdom of Heaven." Well, the faith of children is something wonderful, and no superstition is too gross for them to swallow. Superstition is so closely allied to the supernatural, that the wise men of the church have never discovered how to cut away one without wounding the other. They forbid the credulity that lends an ear to fortune-tellers, and the like, but that is as far as they can go. When it comes to the power of faith and the procession of Miracles nobody but a fool and an ignoramus will cry out "superstition!"—As I was saying, you are right in the midst of the most inviting literary field on the continent, and you must take notes. The ancestors of these grown children ripped up the bowels of royalty and made Napoleon great. They are worth any man's study. The Captain you have at your elbow, and he can introduce you to others. You'll not think much of this now, but in the time to come its importance will be borne in upon you.

All are well and all send love.

> Your loving
> Daddy.

ALS

2 pp.

1. Note on Emory typed copy: "refers to Upton, Canada."

Friday [25 August 1899?]

Dear Lillian: There's no date to this letter, because it is written on the last Friday in August, and the last Friday in August is not in the dative case. See?—I hope you are not having too much of a good time, because if you were you'd take a notion that you could always have a better time away from home and your poor old dad. I hope you sometimes think of me, sitting here on the porch with head bent down, and thinking of his dear daughter and all the rest. Yet you mustn't think too much about it, because when a man gets as old and as no account as I am, he isn't worth thinking about long at a time.—Everything is just about as you left it. One of your stockings is hanging on the water-shelf, and I have tried to get Ed to drop it in the well so as to flavor the water, but he hesitates over it. He thinks I am joking, when I am in dead earnest. Ed. says he never saw any ghosts himself, but his brother has seen 'em, 'cause his brother has fits, and cuts up all kinds of queer pranks. I didn't ask him his brother's name, but I suppose it must be the one who is bowlegged the wrong way.—No girls ever go by now. Their lovers must live on the other side of town.—Trilby's little kitten is dead, and I expect it died happy, because it had its mouth open as if it were laughing. Maybe it laughed itself to death—who knows? Ed. buried it in a hole in the ground, and I think he cried a little to think that such a small cat should have lived so long for nothing.

> "Oh, why was the kitten a kitten?
> In summer it seemed to be frost bitten.
> It was never old enough to put on a mitten—
> Skitten—skattin—skitten!"

You see that although Mr. Stanton is drunker than a biled owl that all the poets are not dead yet. Give my love to all inquiring friends, and write soon to your lonely

    Dad

[author's profile sketch of self as old man]

    ALS

    2 pp.

[To Mildred]

                      Sunday, 24 Sept. [1899]

Goodness gracious me! What is all this I hear about my dear Tommy? First they say she is not gay and festive, then that she is gloomy and pouty, and finally, to cap the climax, that she is homesick! A great big fourteen year old girl acting like a teenchy bit of a baby. And they say, too, that my dear Burdeene keeps up pretty well with Tommy. Just think of six feet of homesickness! Moreover, I hear that the two get up doll parties, and hide out together, and throw themselves into each other's arms and boohoo, and shed large weeps and drop countless sobs and sighs, and pretend to be very unhappy. From the various letters received at this house, one would imagine that St. Joseph's was a vale of tears, a penitentiary, a place of exile. Now, if I didn't know better than that, I'd take a fresh chew of tobacco, and sit on the porch and look glum, but, you see, I do know better. I know that Tommy can have lots more fun at St. Joseph's than at home. If I were there and felt lonely (which I never do) I'd immediately think about the good time I'd have when Christmas comes. I hope my dear gal, and also dear Burdeene, will brace up. A good dose of calomel would help you both. I'm told that my dear Tommy, though she's a famous elocuter, doesn't want to elocute until next year. Well, if she'll promise to be very smart in her music, and mend her ways by ceasing to be a cry-baby, she needn't Elocute this year. Therefore, dear Tommy, tell Sister Sacred Heart to please have you excused from Elocuting until next year. But when next year comes, just remember that whole barrels of tears won't prevent you from elocuting [.]—It's mighty funny that in all these many accounts of homesickness, I never hear of but one cure for it. It's "Oh, Lillian, hurry up and come," and "When are you coming, Bill?" and "We want to see you right now, sis[.]" Nobody says that she wants to see poor ME. I don't think that's fair; it's no way to play; and yet you'll be expecting me to send you boxes of things, and packages of goodies. Well, I'll know better next time.—Maggie (the beautiful and gifted) came down a while ago to say that the children were lost, and the news caused some excitement; but they have just been found in the backyard of Mrs. Walton's late mansion. And Mama is sitting on the porch telling herself in a loud voice what Maggie ought to do, and what ought to be done with her.—Mrs. Alleen Caldwell died Friday—Hugh Caldwell's wife.—I don't know of any more real news. J.C. went hunting with Fritz yesterday and Lillian cried to go with them. I guess that she too was homesick. You see how easy it is for a girl to cry. I hope you'll keep it up for sometime yet, for you always look beautiful after you have shed large gobs of sobs. Burdeene looks fine, too, after a spell of weeps.—I believe Lillian will be lovelier than any of you. There's nothing for her to do but sit down when she's not standing up. As the poet beautifully says, She has nowhere to come but in, nowhere to go but out. Give my kindest regards to the sisters, my love to Burdeene and Bessie, and don't forget about the elocution; you are not to take it until next year. I'll be writing again in a day or two.

   Your loving
   Daddy

ALS
2 pp.
Envelope: Miss Mildred Harris, / St. Joseph's Academy, / Washington, Ga. / *Wilkes County / Ga. R.R.*
PM: 24 September 1899

[To Mildred]

Saturday, 30 Sept. [1899]

Dear Jim-Tom: I'll bet you 85-cents that you get more letters than any other girl in school. I'll bet you 90 cents that you received this week more letters than any two girls in school. I mean, of course, with the exception of Burdeene.—Father O'Brien came out to see us, and I gave him a taste of the gram-o-phone. As he was looking very serious when he went away, I think the machine put his teeth on edge.—All the kittens are dead. They just died dry so [?], for the want of breath. Another one came to-day from somewhere, a stray kitten, with its hair combed the wrong way. Chloey was trying awhile ago to make the old cat take it, but I don't know whether she succeeded.—Essie and Charles seem to be getting along very sweetly. Essie comes over, sometimes every day, and sometimes every other day. She don't know whether she lives there or here. She thinks home is here, and feels that home is there. No doubt it is a very queer feeling, but she'll get used to living away from home after awhile.—We are having fires morning and night now. This is because Charles John Frost is beginning to leave his card in the yards and flower-gardens. The elephant ears are becoming deaf, and before many days they'll be all *swiveled* up; but the roses are finer now than they have been at any time during the year. Bill says she isn't cold, but I feel chilly, and I notice that Ovid, who is also an old fellow, is beginning to shiver, and the cats sleep close together. Late this afternoon, I heard the pigeons grumbling and growling as if they were afraid they wouldn't have enough cover to-night; and when a house-fly lights on my hand his feet feel as cold as mine.—Bill has the sniffles. She has found out that hot lemonade with whisky in it is good for a bad cold, and the prospect now is that she'll have a bad cold all winter. She went to the matinee with Mama this afternoon and was laced so tight she was afraid to cough.— The new baby has got out of the habit of resembling me, and is now said to look like somebody else. Babies have a very hard time, anyhow. They never look like themselves, but always have to "favor" some one. This new baby has a bass voice, and grunts when it wants to cry. Sister Alleen is now sitting up. Mama sent her some egg-nogg to-day by Bill, and I'm told it was the smallest egg-nogg ever seen by the time it got to Alleen. It seems that when Bill was close to the barn, she remembered that nogg is good for a bad cold—*well!*—

I don't know any girly-girly news, nor any girly-boy news. Jacque went to a foot-ballgame with Fritz this afternoon, and—Oh, yes! I forgot; he belongs to a military company, the Mohawk Braves, and Bill has sewed some red streakedy and strikedy stripes on his pantaloons; and he has a red cross band on his left arm. This band doesn't make him look much like a soldier. It is about the size and shape of a poultice, and a stranger would think the arm had a warm boil on it.—Yes, I owe Burdeene a letter, and if I don't write it soon, the dear child will imagine something or other, as girls insist on doing. But, really, I always include her in my thoughts when I write to you, so that in fact this letter is, as others will be, intended for both of you. I must write to Bessie, too.—I'm very glad that my dear little girl will try to make others happy. It is easy to tease and have fun without saying or doing anything spiteful. And if my dear girl sees any girl who is lonely or unhappy, she can do a great deal of good by paying the lonely one some attention.—But come now, Mr. Joel C'andler Harris, you must not begin any of your cold potato lectures. You did very well until you began to preach. Mildred is a warm-hearted child anyway, and *she*'ll know how to treat those who are unhappy. So, just shut off your grammyphone and go to bed. (You see how they treat me. I can't help myself. I have to obey orders. Regards to the Sisters and love to Burdeene; also to Bessie.)

Your loving

Daddy

[JCH's sketch of baby in bonnet]

Do Dransie's itty Toody lant 'im bottle? Yas' im doos!

ALS

2 pp.

Dear Mildred:

[18 October 1899] [1]

Dewey is to come on the 24th,[2] so you and Burdeene will have to leave Friday afternoon or Saturday morning[.] Send a telegram to 312 Gordon[.]

I see that your bill includes $13.50 for Elocution, which you are not taking[.] Tell Sister Sacred Heart to apply the amount to the matter about which I wrote her some time ago. She will understand. I enclose cheque for $112.50, which includes $4 for you to come on. If you have to pay full fare, use $1 of the money I gave you to spend.

> Your loving
> Daddy

Love to Burdeene and Bessie.

ALS

1 p.

Envelope: Miss Mildred Harris, / St. Joseph's Academy, / Washington, Ga. / *Wilkes County* / Return to Box 111 / Atlanta, Ga.

PM: 18 October

1. Washington, Georgia, postmark on back of envelope: October 18, 1899.

2. The city of Atlanta had made elaborate plans for several days of festivities, climaxing with Admiral George Dewey's presenting a ceremonial sword to local hero and Flag Lt. Tom Brumby for his role in the Spanish-American War, especially the battle of Manilla, 1 May 1890. Dewey accepted the invitation but canceled later because of health. The Atlanta *Constitution* fully covered the event (see Sunday, 8 October; Sunday, 15 October; Wednesday, 18 October; Thursday, 19 October; and cancellation notice in 23 October 1899 issue). Publicity for this patriotic event was synchronized with the opening of the state fair (18 October) and sales by local department stores. Gov. Allen D. Candler replaced Dewey in presenting the sword to Lieutenant Brumby at the capitol on 26 October. Harris wanted his daughter to avoid expected crowds on the train.

[To Mildred]

Saturday night, Nov. 4, 1899

Dear Little Chickadee:

We have received from you and Burdeene one or two scraps of paper. We call them letters because they came in envelopes and the envelopes had stamps on them. Anyhow, we are missing you very much, and we'd be glad if we had a Dewey day every week.[1] To-day was Schley day, and he sat up in his carriage, and smiled, and bowed, and grinned, and howdied, and took off his hat to the ladies and wiggled his fingers at the children, and seemed to be as happy as a sailor boy could be.[2] That's what they say. I didn't see him myself. He didn't ask for me, and so I didn't trouble myself about the matter. The engine collision the other day was a bloomin' fraud, so J.C. says.[3] According to his account the locomotives were not going as fast as he could run when they came together. They simply broke off their cow-catchers, and then stood still and looked at each other as much as to say, "Hello! Keep on your side of the road!" J.C. and Fritz went out again to-day, and J.C. brought home a hatful of stuff, pocket scissors, brass bracelets, memorandum books, copper pens, shoe strings, door hinges, nails, shavings, splinters, door knobs, pencil points, and various other things too numerous to mention, including a bad cold.—We haven't seen much of the kidlets during the last few days. The weather has been too cold for them to come down. Mama has gone up to night [sic] to stay while Alleen and Lucien are at the play. Mamma and Lillian went this afternoon, and came back saying it was fine.—Nora Goodman called this afternoon and wanted to see Mamma. She had on a long dress and a lady's hat and I didn't know her. She looks fine in a long dress.—Lillian is not gay since you and Burdeene left. I think she has had a number of gloomy moments. Burdeene is happy, of course. There is no silly old man down there to tease her.—Dewey couldn't come to Atlanta because he was busy courting a widow. Burdeene or Lillian can tell you what "courting" is. I used to know myself, but I've forgotten all about it long ago.—The weather has been so cold that the elephant ears are deaf. They are all swiveled and will have to be cut off. Mr. Morenus's cow continues to sing a bass accompaniment to the tenor of her calf. The latter I have named Mr. George J. Gaskin.—Our telephone rings every time one of Mr. Frazier's dogs begins to bark, which convinces me that electricity is one of the most mysterious things in the world.—I see Grace sometimes. She continues to look like a shoestring.—Lillian now has three beaus, Fritz, Roy and Alex. Sometimes they come over and they all sit and eat sugar-cane, and talk about cocoanut candy.—Speaking of sweet things, Roy killed a polecat in his barn the other day. This caused all the neighbors for two blocks around to sun their beds and bedclothes. They didn't know what the matter was.—Lillian has now become used to long dresses. I think she feels the responsibility of them. She is more dignified and doesn't talk in her sleep any more. As she gets older she will cease to snore.—Lucien went to the fair to-day, and, with Evelyn, proceeded to gamble on the hoss-races. They both won some money. When you grow up I hope you won't bet unless you are certain of winning. You can then make the bad money good by spending it in charity. When I have money to lose I'm going to bet with myself that I can do more good with it by giving it to those who need it than by spending it with a lot of gamblers. I tried to get in a lecture here, but you are not a young man, and so it would have been wasted.—Tell Bessie to take more exercise and then she won't be tired when she runs. My regards to the Sisters, and my love to Burdeene and Bessie.

> Your loving
> Daddy

ALS

2 pp.

Envelope: Miss Mildred Harris, / St. Joseph's Academy, / Washington, *Ga.* / *Wilkes County*

PM: 5 November 1899

1. *Cf.* note on abortive Dewey day in 18 October 1899 letter.

2. Rear Adm. Winfield Scott Schley, another hero of the Spanish-American War and known as the "Hero of Santiago," was honored in Atlanta, 4 November 1899. See Garrett 2:383–84.

3. Probably an exhibition-demonstration at the state fair. See advertisement in the *Constitution*, 15 October 1899, 19, for head-on collision of two trains to be held 24 October, 3 p.m. Tickets were sold for the event. Like our demolition derbies, such staged train crashes were familiar attractions at state fairs. See Robert Stanley, "Riding the Rails with Head-on Joe," *The Old Farmer's 1990 Almanac* (Dublin, N.H.: Yankee Publishing Inc., 1989), 118–21, for the career of Joseph Connolly, who staged seventy-three such shows (1896–1932).

[To Mildred]

Saturday night, Nov. 11, 1899

I have glorious news for you, dear child. Alex., or Ellick, was riding his bicycle on the sidewalk at the point where there is no paving on Whitehall—there where the car turns into the {tunnel/culvert}—when a policeman nabbed him. He tried to explain, but it was no go. He tried to beg off, but it wouldn't work. The policeman wanted to take him down in the Black Maria—

> Hello, Black Maria, hello!
> Oh, what's that a comin'? Please tell me if you know;
> Oh, What's that a rattlin' an'a gwine on so?—
> It's the old black Maria backin up to yo' do':—
> Hello, Black Maria, hello!—

The policeman wanted to take Ellick (or Alex.) down in the B.M., but he was finally persuaded to give the boy a copy of the charge, on the promise that he would appear in the police court the next day. So Alex. (or Ellick) went down and the judge, after hearing the policeman's tale of woe, asked Mr. Conley to please, sir, fork over $1.75, which he did. Result: when Ellick (or Alex) rides his wheel now, he takes the middle of the road; in fact, he's afraid to walk on the sidewalk. Such is justice in the neighborhood of Wes' Een'. The folks went to an Episcopalian cake walk at Mrs. Kelly's last night—shucks! What am I saying?—I mean they went to an Episcopalian social, where the only refreshments in sight were the man and his hat, into which (not the man but the hat) a dime had to be dropped. I was in bed and asleep when the folks came back, but I hear to-day that Lillian was awful angry because Harry Cole dared to be present. She never heard of such presumption and impertinence; and I think myself that it shows a considerable amount of cheek for any young man to go to an entertainment where there are young ladies. But now that Lillian has put on long dresses, and is wiping up the sidewalks with her skyirt [sic], or train, she is now in a position to deal some heavy blows at these impertinent boys. I am told she gave Harry only one heavenly smile, and then, after that, refused to recognize him even as a passing acquaintance. That's what he gets by being bold enough to attend an Episcopalian cake-walk, especially when there was no ice-cream on hand to induce him to do the handsome and manly thing.—Mama is feeling so much better to-night that she is going to Mrs. Abernathy's; and no wonder she feels better. She had one of her house-cleaning spells to-day, and has walked 932 miles. A part of the time she was walking on the ceiling like a fly. Once when I went to see what she was doing, she was clinging to the top of the door frame with one hand and wiping off the top of the wall with the other. Her last act before going to Mrs. A's (she has just gone) was to make a petticoat for a sofa pillow.—Lillian, if she can tear herself away from possible or probable Episcopalian cake-walks, will come down to Washington Friday or Saturday[.] As she will probably walk, you might go up the road and meet her, with a bottle of cold tea and a cracker. Essie doesn't come over as often as she did [.] In the words of Mr. Stringfellow, she has found that life is earnest, life is real, as tough as a steak as fresh as veal, and so she'll be a shero [sic] in the strife, a red-headed man's domesticated wife.—J.C. has been to the dog, pony, and monkey show, and now thinks he'll get up a show of his own with Stewart, Chandler, and the two dogs as the chief characters. Lucien's dog had the distemper and a few fits. And though there was no extra charge for the performance it was thought best to send the chief actor away, which was duly done; the Hon. Jeems Banks, taking charge of the affair.—Mama has been to the theatre once or twice, but she was not happy there. She missed the duster and the wet-rag, and they had no ladder there on which she could perch herself and fumble with the lamp chimneys. Old folks do not like to be deprived of their playthings anymore than children.—Everybody is well. The weather has been de-lightful—giving us a genuine Indian summer. It was sprinkling awhile ago, and as the weather man says it will be fair to-morrow, I expect it to rain all day. As for news,—well you know there's no more of that here than there is in Washington, perhaps not as much. We continue to eat three times a day, and Lillian sleeps late so as to weave romances in her dreams. She has an idea that some hero, name unknown will call her to the telephone and pour a hatfull of tender words into her ear. I hear it is against the rules of the company for impudent young men like Harry Cole to use the telephone, and I'm glad of it. It would be the height of impertinence for such young men even to speak above a whisper in a room where there's a telephone.—I intended to send "Plantation Pag-eants" down, but then I remembered that Burdeene has a copy.—Well, this is all I can think of and more too. My regards to the sisters, and love to the two B's.

Your loving

Daddy

ALS

2 pp.

Envelope: Miss Mildred Harris / St. Joseph's Academy, / Washington, *Ga.* / *Wilkes County*

PM: 12 November 1899

[To Mildred]

25 *November,* 1899.

Dear little chickadee: We receive your letters right along, but we find it impossible to carry out all your requests in person. To-day, for instance, it was raining so hard that we found it impossible to give your love and kisses to the kidlets, and so we wrapped them (not the kidlets, but the love and the kisses) in a piece of paper the sausages had come in, and placed them in the refrigerator where they will keep fresh until the weather gets so we can deliver them.—Did you see the notice of Julian's baby? It was under the head of "Births," and said that an "infant son" had been born to Mr. and Mrs. Julian LaRose Harris. A great many people have since asked Julian if he thought the public would believe that the newly-born son wasn't an infant. The result is that Bubba Juju has been badly rattled. He seems to be very proud of the event, though he pretends he wanted a girl. Well, we can't have everything we want in this world. If we could I'd have a big black beard and a hoss-pistol and play like I was a pirate. I'd hide behind the bushes, and when the little girls came along going home from school, I'd jump out at 'em, fire the hoss-pistol in the air and cry "Be-lud!" And then I'd form myself into an ambuscade, and when the Battle Hill dairyman came jogging along I'd stop him in the road and make him surrender nine quarts of blue milk; and then I'd make this milk into egg-nog for Bill and myself[.] Mama wouldn't want any. She's a temperance lady and doesn't want any sugar or raw eggs, or water in her toddy[.] She says that only drunkards and weak-minded people adulterate their whiskey. I think she'll want some

Julia Collier Harris, wife of Julian Harris, with their son
Pierre LaRose Harris, circa 1902 (Joel Chandler Harris
Collection, Special Collections Department, Robert W.
Woodruff Library, Emory University).

toddy to-night before she goes to bed, for she has been changing the furniture around again to-day. Also, she has been "straightening out" my book case, and says she feels like a misguided literary person. She'll soon recover, I hope, and be her own fat self again.—Bill has been very busy to-day hemstiching [sic] some hankchers [.] She has pulled one thread out of four hankchers, and she's pretty nearly fagged out. I tell her not to work so hard, but she says it's a duty she owes to society. I don't know what society she's talking about, and when I asked for information, she said I was too ridiculous for any thing. I hope she hasn't gone and joined the Free Masons or the Improved Order of Red Men.[1]—I don't see much of Essie these days. She's beginning to act as if marriage is a ticklish thing. She's more subdued. She wears solemnity as you would wear your cloak. She smiles, of course, but it is not the girly-girly smile; it is the deep and thoughtful grin of the married woman who is trying to find out what X represents on the blackboard of life:—we are all sorry to hear that Uncle Dick is very seriously ill—Aunt Sophia's husband. He has typhoid fever, and Uncle Frank writes that he is in a dangerous condition.—Lucille found a new calf in the barn this afternoon and she won't let any of the other cows pet it or claim it. I don't know what it's [sic] name is yet, but it, too, may turn out to be a Charles Collier Harris.[2] We can't have too many in the family.—J.C. and the Rossers have moved into the new house across the street and things are beginning to look cheerful in our neighborhood. If it hadn't 'a' been for J.C. the Rossers would never have been able to move in the world. He went to their rescue and toted a looking-glass, a hammer, a spittoon, a rug and a box of matches to the new house, and after that they had no difficulty.— Roy has a boil on his jaw, and has been unable to chew anything but soup for a day or two.—My news is exhausted, and I'll have to wait for another time to tell you howdy.—My love to Burdeene and Bessie, and to Gretchen and Brownie; and (what I should have put first) my best regards to those dear sisters each and everyone.

Your loving
Daddy

ALS
2 pp.

1. Improved Order of Red Men: The Atlanta fraternal organization had 2000 members in 1901, according to Martin 2:59; list of tribes and officers, 599.

2. The name of Julian's baby.

[To Mildred]

December-the-two-eye—and-getting-right
close-to-Christmas, Ga.

[2 December 1899]

Sweet chick: Of course Sister Bernard wouldn't "doctor" your report, consequently mama and I are very proud of it. But I don't want you to study *too* hard; I want you to scrap and play, and get to studying hard gradually. In that way, you'll always have health. I don't mean by that that you are to neglect your books; I mean that I want you to keep up your exercise in the fresh air as much as possible.—Please ask Mother Clemence if you and Burdeene can't come on the 20th, the 21st at latest. Mother Clemence is such a good mother that I bet you she'll say, "Yes, my little ones! go and have a joyful time; and when you return be better than you have been."—As for news, I don't know a bit except that the little bitsy baby was very sick last night and this morning; it is better to-night. Dr. Crow says its illness was caused by cold.[1] It is a fine baby, and just as good as can be. It cries only when it is hungry, and it will stop crying to laugh if anybody talks baby talk to it. Stewart was down here to-day, playing with one of your dolls. He got it to sleep and then went to sleep himself.—Essie is feeling—well, I don't know how Essie is feeling. She looks as if she had been sent for and couldn't come. She wanders over here and then wanders away again, and presently wanders back. This is the result of true love. It seems to be worse than the black measles, the kind they have in Canada. Better warn Burdeene about it. I don't know what would happen if she had a serious attack of it; she's restless now, but what would she be then.—J.C. has a yard full of boys (big and little) every afternoon playing hare and hounds. If boys are having fun when they holla and scream J.C. and his friends are having more than their fair share.—Lillian continues to go to matinees and pines when she can't—though she hasn't *can't*ed but once. She is so fond of the stage that I think she'll finally de[cide?] to become a tight-rope-walker. This will enable her to wear a spangled dress with no sleeves and very few skirt [sic]. She wants to see Miss Agler Leathersole play— I believe that's the name of the famous actress. (They are all famous.) I hear that Julian's kidlet is a very cute little duffer; I haven't seen it yet. They say it's about the size of a September fig, and has red hair— one red hair if not more.—Well, you see how I'm situated, a grandfather with four bald-headed responsibilities.[2] The two baldheadedest seem to be behind the age in a good many respects. Old as I am I have more teeth than both of them put together.—I don't know why J.C. *doesn't* write, unless it's because he's a boy, and boys are utterly worthless and selfish until they are old enough to think of something and somebody besides themselves. J.C. is good-hearted and he'll be all right after awhile. He has improved under the care of the sisters; they are splendid teachers; but there are no teachers anywhere equal to Sister Bernard, Sister Sacred Heart, and those other lovely sisters who make St. Joseph's Academy the finest school of its kind in the country. Of course the sisters will say I'm saying this in order to be pleasant, but, really, I can be pleasant without going out of my way to say what I don't mean. Not a day passes that I don't thank my stars that Lillian was educated there, and that you are now going through the same mill. Say to Sister Sacred Heart that on or about the 22nd or 23rd she'll hear from me on the subject we talked about when she was here—the little problem we were trying to settle or solve.—And now, my dear gal, I think I have reached the end of this dull letter. My best regards to all the sisters I know, and my love to Burdeene and Bessie.

 Your loving
  Daddy

ALS
2 pp.
Envelope: Miss Mildred Harris, / St. Joseph's Academy, / Washington, *Ga.* / *Wilkes County*
PM: 3 December 1899
 1. Probably Dr. W. A. Crowe. Baby referred to is probably Lucien, Jr., born 9 September 1899.
 2. I.e., Stewart; Joel Chandler III; Lucien, Jr.; and Charles Collier Harris.

[To Mildred]

December the X-and only 'lev'm more
days till (or to) the whatyoumaycallum.
[10 December 1899]

Dearest Tomas:

I couldn't write last night. I *had* just finished a story that must go off at once, and I wanted Bill to read it to me, which she did with great success, weeping heartily over the humorous passages and laughing sadly over the touches of pathos. So I'll write to-night though I haven't a thing in the world to write about. Nothing happens out here but the ringing of the *big* brass bell to call four people to their meals and the lighting of the lamps at night. Bill has now established herself in the office of lamplighter, and every evening when dusk falls she seizes the "toodly-too"—that's what Mama calls the thing you light with—and proceeds to set fire to all the gas in sight. She performs this duty with great dignity and modesty, and, also, I suppose, with a good deal of grace. If she has any pride, she doesn't show it when she's lighting the gas.—Bill is not having a very good time any way. Her appetite is bigger than her digestion, and this gives her trouble. Another trouble is that while she has been heretofore wearing shoes with soles about as thick as paper, she now has to wear shoes with fairly thick soles. She is greatly distressed about it. She doesn't want to go barefooted in hot weather; it's only when the cold weather sets in that she wants to get her feet wet. But the family fiat has gone forth in this shape: If she *will* wear long dresses she *must* wear thick soles. So there!—I see Augusta has had a big fire. Well, it will do the old town good in the end. Father McMahon has been in town, but he hurried back when he heard of the fire. He says that after the fire some time ago, a clairvoyant—a Mrs. Smith—predicted that in the fall a fire would destroy the block that was burned last night. One of the papers remarked at the time that if the fire occurred the clairvoyant ought to be arrested and put in jail. So Father McMahon said, and he has red hair—at least he used to have red hair.

As I said before, nothing happens here worth relating. The cows low; the dogs bark; Chloë tries to jar the house down when she walks through the hall; J.C. thinks there are a great many other places better than home, sweet home; Lucien still discharges nurses and pounds the children; Essie continues to look as if she had been sent for and couldn't come; Lillian continues to eat everything in sight and look out to see if Roy, or Fritz, or Ellick, is in the yard; Lucien Jr. is getting better, while Stewart is getting worse; Charles Collier Harris continues to be the only baby in Atlanta; Mama still insists on pulling up the house by the roots every Saturday, and sometimes on other days; and so on and so forth. You can just shut your eyes and imagine what is happening here every hour in the day, and every day in the week, especially if we are all well. You can also tell what we have for each meal, for there are no changes in our bill of fare. We have even gone back to chicken-pie on Sunday, so that now, we are right where we were when we started, except in the matter of age. A missionary to the negroes spoke in the church to-day. I'm sorry for him. He'll have a hard time converting that happy-go-lucky, thoughtless race. But if he ever gets them started, he'll have more converts than he knows what to do with.—Well, you see what a letter I have written. There's nothing in it but ink and good humor, and you'll have to put up with that for this time.—My love to the two B's, my highest regards to the dear sisters.

Your loving
Daddy

ALS
2 pp.
Envelope: Miss Mildred Harris, / St. Joseph's Academy, / Washington, Ga. / *Wilkes County*
PM: 11 December 1899

[To Mildred]

December the—oh, I've forgotten—anyhow, its [sic] Saturday night. [16 December 1899] "Ha—ha!" says I, with accent of pride and a gesture of-of-oh, well, I haven't time to look in a book and find a good word. Anyhow, "ha-ha!" says I laughing gleefully, "I won't have to write a letter to Mildred, since she's coming home Wednesday." My gloat must have been a loud one, for Bill, she ups and says, "Young man!"—she calls me young man when she's angry; it's a taunt she likes to fling in my teeth, or would like to, if I had any teeth—"Young man," says she, "you must *not* forget to send Mildred some money to come home on."—"But," says I, "she's not coming home on money; she's coming on the train."—"How perfectly ridiculous you are!" cries Bill; "it will be a *very* fine come-off, indeed, if in the midst of your poor jokes and your antics that are not at all becoming to the grandfather of four, you should forget that child's money."—"Child, indeed!" says I; "isn't she deep in a correspondence with a fiery young man?"—However, I was crestfallen. My ha-ha ceased to be a merry one. I was obliged to send the money, and if I sent the money, I must write a letter to go with it as its twin. Hence, I began to rub my chin, then I placed my forefinger on my marble brow. What was there to write about? "Ha! I have it!" cried I, in smothered tones.— "I think you have more than one," remarked Bill; "I've heard of the jimmies, but I never heard of a man having only one of them."—"Children," I said by way of rebuke, "should be seen and not heard." So I continued my train of thought—"Ha! I have it!" I repeated in a subdued whisper, "I'll pretend that I'm writing a letter, but I'll not write one; I'll not say a word about the presents, no, or the fruit cake, neither; and I'll not say that Burdeene is going to get a—however, we'll let that pass; and I'll not say a word about your four or five bundles marked M., and four or five marked B.; no, not a word. And in order to make sure about this, I'll cut this off right here, remarking that there's a $5 cheque on the inside (Lillian says the fare has been *reducted*) and that I also send $105 worth of love to Burdeene and Bessie; and $210 worth of regards to the dear sisters; remaining, in the meantime, Tommy's

      Loving
      Daddy

ALS
2 pp.
Envelope: Return to Box 111, / Atlanta, *Ga.* / Miss Mildred Harris, / St. Joseph's Academy, / Washington, *Ga.* / *Wilkes County*
PM: 18 December 1899

[To Mildred]

Janâwary the 27, 1900

And how is my dear gal?[1] The reason I ask is because I'm pretty well myself, and, have nothing on earth to write about. The only real fresh news I have is that Bill is about to take a bath, and she really deserves it; she has honestly earned it.—We have had some airish weather—mercury down to 20-odd, and the dogs and cats a-shivering just like they were paid to shiver.—Burdeene says to Lillian, says she, "Your father's letter is very clever." I know by that she's angry: not angry enough to be errytated (as Chloë says), but just angry enough to think to herself that her feelings are hurted. 'Cause why: she never before used that word "clever" as a club to hit me with. But just as long as she remains as sweet and nice as she is, I'm going to tease her. So there!—A new street car line is going down (on the ground) in West End. It comes up between Park street church and Dr. Longino's, turns down Park street, runs to Ashby, then turns into Ashby, and will run across Gordon. Where it will run to after that I don't know.—A new boy has come to West End—or was he here Christmas?—Phil Wade, and he has a sweet little Shetland pony, and a great many lovely chickens, and Lillian says he's her beau. He's a very clever chap. He works; yes'm—he milks the cow and 'tends to the horse, and takes care of the chickens, and is a very manly boy. He's quite a problem to J.C., who can't understand how a boy can work and make himself useful without whining and whimpering about it.— The babies are all well: Stewart and Chandler are very nice and polite. To everybody they say, "You old Priss, you!" or "I'm gwan ter cut you open wid a knife!" It's all so cute and charming that if they were mine I'd bump their heads together eleven times a day and fourteen times on Sundays for good measure.—Lillian will meet Aunt Kitty and they will both hunt for a rat. Charles Dusenbury—no, no! I mean Charles Collier was here to-day, together with a lot of the neighbor boys. These last brought their lunches and they all ate dinner in the yard. They are supposed to be hardening themselves for some war that will take place twenty or thirty years from now[.]—Lillian has just come in from her bath and looks like a different girl. Water and Ivory soap seem to clear her complexion. Her face is not muddy anymore. I hope she'll keep it up.—Well, there isn't anything else to say. Everybody is the same. The house is where it was, and we continue to have batter cakes for breakfast, and dried figs for dinner. Lillian eats like a hoss and then says she doesn't feel well. Mama has little snatches of headache occasionally, especially after she'd walked 250 miles with a wet rag in one hand and the duster in the other.—Lillian went to Mrs. Kelly's Episcōple Schentzenfest[2] the other night and saw Harry Cole, and she's feeling better now. And they had an auction of old clothes, and the affair passed off with a great *eclair*.

My regards to the sisters, and love to Burdeene and Bessie.

Your loving

Daddy

"Isn't Dad a sight?" I will write tomorrow,

Bill

ALS

2 pp.

Envelope: Miss Mildred Harris, / St. Joseph's Academy, / Washington, *Ga.* / *Wilkes County*

PM: 28 January 1900

1. Note reference to Lillian being at home; therefore, letter is to Mildred.

2. Harris's fractured German for dance; viz., *Schenkel* "shank or leg" plus *fest* "feast." Note also his deliberate comic spelling of Episcopal and *eclat*.

[To Mildred]

[4 February 1900]

February the-well, anyhow

it's the first Sunday, 1900

Dear Titmouse: I couldn't write last night because I had to go to the theatre to see Robson play Dr. Oliver Goldsmith.[1] I just had to go. The agent, a young man whom I had not met before, said that if I didn't go and see the play everybody in the company would go about heart-broken, especially the pretty ladies who took some of the parts. He said it wouldn't do to have these ladies sobbing through their lines, espe-cially in a comedy. And so, after much persuasion, I consented to go with Mr. Stanton and his mother-in-law. As mama and Lillian had been in the afternoon, I went with Essie. We had a box, and I sat crouched in the back end like a mouse in a chest. The play was fine all the way through. I think it's too fine to be a success. How many theatre-going people in Atlanta ever heard of Oliver Goldsmith except in a vague way? And how many know anything about Dr. Johnson, and Boswell, and Garrick and Burke? Not enough to fill a theatre, I can assure you. And it makes me sad to know that—this is so; and to know many women and men have missed all the finer things in life by snatching at shadows. Mama said that the character of Goldsmith reminded her of me. This didn't impress me until I heard one lady remark to another, as we came out of the theatre, "Was Goldsmith really such an idiot as Robson makes him out to be?" I wish I could be an idiot like Goldsmith. I enjoyed the evening very much.—Dr. and Mrs Durrance called a few evenings ago. Mama had gone to see the kidlets, and so Lillian and I were left to do the entertaining. Well, you know how I am: I was as embarrassed as a rabbit with a hawk after him. Then I happened to think of the gramophone and that showed me a way out. I made that old gramophone hum until it groaned and creaked in its very midst. The visitors thought—it was elegant, and it was, for it tided me over a very lively and hopeless quarter of an hour—no, over two hours and a half. The Dr. is a clever man, I think, but I didn't know him—consequently I didn't know what to say to him, and the strain of it gave me nervous prostration.—There's just as much news here as there was when I wrote last, and more; for I hear from J.C. that "the" is an adjective, and that "mood" is "mode." That's real news to me. If I were teaching school I wouldn't allow an English grammar inside its walls. I'd have Latin grammar, and I'd teach the children English grammar and English diction at the same time by dictating the best English prose to them. This I'd do one day, and the next day I'd make them rewrite the dictation in language of their own.— But what am I doing? Really, I am getting beyond my depths, and I'll wade back to shore with the remark that the stand-pipe in the front yard friz and burst the other day, and I've had a new one put in.—You have a pet rabbit, but Bill is ahead of you. She has a pet tapeworm, and feeds it every hour in the day. She made a lot of candy to send you girls the other day, and ate more than half of it. Her *menu* since this morning has been fried chicken, chicken pie, 2 oranges, 6 bananas, a half a gallon of black walnuts, a paper of peanuts, 3 cups of cocoa, 1 pound of steak, and 1 hatful of popcorn. I make no mention of tea cakes, raisins, dried figs and jam.—You must be getting fat. Well, keep up your exercise when you can, and stop catching cold. The way to keep from catching cold is not to get warm too quick when you're cold.—I feel sure that Bessie will get the medal. I have some fine trades for her from somebody who knows her well and sees her every day.—I hope Burdeene is well and happy. Give her my love, and Bessie also; and my regards to the sisters.

Your loving

Daddy

ALS

2 pp.

1. Stuart Robson played the lead role in Augustus Thomas's *Oliver Goldsmith* at the Grand theater, 2–3 February 1900. See the Atlanta *Constitution*, 1 February 1900, 11, for the announcement.

[To Mildred]

Febiwary the 10, 1900.

Dear Tommus:

There was once an old man who had a little daughter off at school—away off; yes, it was 'most 200 miles; and he was so mean that he forgot to give the poor child any pin money when she started. Yes, he was meaner than that. After she got there he forgot to send her any money, and the poor child didn't have so much as a copper with which to buy peanuts, and store candy, and chewing gum. This little girl was so fat and patient that she never asked for any money, and so the mean old man who was her father pretended to himself that this was a good excuse for not sending any. But his conscience had teeth like a mouse and it kept gnawing away in his bosom, until at last he thought of the money; and then he fixed up a cheque and sent it in a letter like this. It seems funny, too, but the cheque was just like the one I am sending to-day, and I think the same name was signed to it. Still I think the little girl was partly to blame. Why couldn't she ax her pa to send her some money? When a man is old and mean, he needs to be reminded of a good many things.— The Zachrys have retired, all except the three oldest girls. Laura and

Lula are stopping with some of their kinnery, and Mamie is with Lillian until Monday—only to-night she is at Alleen's.—She and Bill went to the Three Musketeers to-day, and I—I am almost ashamed to tell you—went last night. It was a full dose, too. I didn't want to go, but Julia wanted Mama to go, and then nothing must do but I must take Mama. Well, Mr. Jeems O'Neil doesn't cut a heroic figure at all. He is old and fat, and he doesn't play the character of D'Artagnan as it should be played. And then the play spoils the story. It jumbles the whole thing up in an awful manner. It's as long as a Chinese play. 'Twas after 12 o'clock when we arrived at the site of our domestic bliss, and plunged, as it were, into the bosom of our palatial cottage. Whereupon I made myself a long and fiery promise that it would be some time before I saw Grandma De Give sleeping soundly in her box while a play was going on.[1] I envied her. She was having a more comfortable time than I was. Her snoring between the acts, mingled with the hammering of the stage carpenters, and the shuffling of feet behind the scenes, made the evening one to be long remembered. In the midst of that giddy throng she had slipped away into a pleasant dream and sat there smiling in her sleep.—Bill has been invited to Mrs. Wiley Pope's reception, and Mama has been invited to Mrs. Luther Rosser's Valentine party. You see we are drifting right into the middle of the whirlpool of fashion, and I hope we'll only have all our clothes on when the mælstrom subsides.—The only news I know is some that is whispered around in regard to Mr. Bunker[.] The whisper says that Mr. Bunker's employees took advantage of his illness to make him sign papers that he should never have signed; and it says, further, that he will get his house back together with a good sum of money.— The weather is tolerably damp in this town, especially at our house. I believe that if a bedquilt had been left out on the clothes line last night and to-day, it would be too damp to sleep in to-night. But Bill is web-footed and doesn't mind wading.

Well, this is all and more too. My kindest regards to the dear sisters, and love to Burdeene and Bessie; also to those charming kids, Gretchen and Brownie.

> Your loving
> Daddy

ALS
2 pp.
Envelope: Return to Box 111, / Atlanta, Ga. / Miss Mildred Harris, / St. Joseph's
Academy, / Washington, *Ga.* / *Wilkes County*
PM: 11 February 1900
1. DeGive family built (1893) and owned the Grand Theater; the actor James O'Neill,
father of the playwright Eugene O'Neill, toured constantly in romantic dramas such as
The Three Musketeers.

[To Mildred]

Sunday, February 19, 1900

Dear Tommy,

On the other side of this sheet you'll see where I started to write an editorial, but I stopped short in the middle of a sentence because the weather is so cold and uncomfortable.[1] I didn't feel like spending my time grinding out editorials on Sunday, especially such a cold Sunday as this. I wanted Evelyn to telephone to Clarky [i.e., Clark Howell] that my editorial water-pipe has busted, but Clarky was gone, and so some poor chap will have to do extra work to-night just because your Daddy didn't feel like writing. It's cold as Flugens up here in this climate[.] The thermometer and the mercury caught hold of each other's hands and went down nearly to zero. I hope they like it; I'm sure I didn't. If I had the Tropic Zone here I'd sleep with it to-night and to-morrow night, much as I dislike to sleep with strangers. The water-back[2] in the stove burst this morning, and we've had to turn off the water. The outside pipe of the hall stove blew down yesterday, and if it rains the paper on the hall ceiling will be worse ruined than it is. So you see we are having a good deal of fun, one way and another.—J.C. is about to set his old Langshan[3] hen on a door knob, in hopes that she will hatch out a lock and key. I'm afraid he'll be disappointed. There seems to be nothing but disappointment in this world for those who have short hair and a romantic temperament. J.C. has four Wyandotte hens.[4] He thinks they are very fine. He also has a Sanshan [Langshan?] rooster and some hens; moreover, a few bantams. I don't know what he'll have next.—Mama and Bill went to Mrs. Wylie Pope's reception and "stood around" about three-quarters of an hour. They say it was very *swell*. Well, so is a gumboil. Anyhow, Mama has been stepping a little higher ever since. I guess I'll have to make the fence a few rails higher if I want to keep her in the pasture. Julian is improving. I went with Bill to see him Friday evening, and he appeared to be very bright and cheerful. He says he's going to have an operation performed as soon as he gets well. I'm so old-fashioned that I don't believe in operations of that kind unless it's a case of absolute necessity. Still, Julian is his own boss even if he has no beard. His baby is very ugly, just as Julian was at that same age. Lucien's youngest is now old enough to be good-looking and the cutest and sweetest chap you ever saw. He never cries, but laughs instead, and that's the kind of baby I like. Stewart and Chandler grow tougher every day. They mind nobody but Lucien, and they wouldn't mind him if they didn't have a dim idea that he is wanting a good excuse to break their necks. But when they are good—which happensinbetween [*sic*] times, like a streak of lean in a side of meat—they are very nice children.—Bill is so lazy that she rarely gets up to breakfast in the morning. At meals, she leans her head on the table while chewing her food. She'll wake up some of these days and begin to walk on the ceiling like your mama. Fritz comes and peeps through the palings at her, and so does the Byington boy, the boy with the cork leg. She didn't like the reception—says it's too tame. There was no skirt dancing—no ballet—nothing but talk and vittles.—I'm not feeling lively to-day. Cold weather always knocks me out. Therefore I'll have to walk backward to the door and make my best bow and bid you good evening, with a sort of feeling that I haven't made you have a good time. My regards to the sisters and love to Burdeene and Bessie.

> Your loving
> Daddy

ALS

2 pp.

Envelope: Miss Mildred Harris / St. Joseph's Academy, / Washington, Ga. / *Wilkes County.*

PM: 19 February 1900

1. On back of first sheet: "It is reported that Professor William G. Sumner recently stated that 90 per cent of marriages are unhappy alliances. If the report is correct, we are of the opinion that the sooner the professor is removed from the position where he can disturb. . . ."

2. Water-back: "A coil or chamber back of the fire-pot in a range or other stove, for heating water and usually a part of a circulating system." *Funk and Wagnalls New Standard Dictionary of the English Language* (1959), s. v. "water-back."

3. Langshan: a breed of hens from China.

4. Wyandotte: a breed of domestic fowls.

[To Mildred]

Saturday Evening, somewhere about the
24 of Febiwary, year 1900

My Dear Dr. Delim: Your esteemed favor of open date and current month has been received at the Langer now occupied by those notorious Boers the Harrises. The Kopje on which the langer is situated is the same as ever. People who reach it by the nearest route still have to trek across three veldts, and climb three terraced Kopjes.[1] The various and sundry kleiner boobies of the Harris tribe were alive and kicking, and also squalling, at last accounts. The Collier kidg [sic] drifted out yes'tiddy, and filled the whole house full of a warm and glaring ugliness that must be seen to be appreciated. His pa is doing very well. Evelyn tried to work to-day, but was compelled to return home. He is better than he was, but is still too weak to work. Lillian and Mama went to the matinee this afternoon, and as usual, (according to Bill) the play was the grandest thing ever acted, and the leading persons the most beautiful man and woman ever seen on any stage in any part of the world. The play is called "Glorious Duck" and the leading lady is named Vee-oh-la Partridge. They made a church out of a music hall, and because there is no dancing there any more, the hero Jack Thunderstorm runs off and joins an Episcopal monastery. As he had no reserved seat, he is compelled to stand while eating. He comes out after awhile, and at the end of the play everybody gets married to one another, including the stage-carpenter who is wedded to the lady who patches up the wardrobes of the company with a polished darning needle. You can imagine how exciting the play is.[2] It is from the glowing brain of Mr. Hall, who wrote it with his cane, and warmed it up with a red-hot poker. Lillian says everything was "just darling." She didn't know at the time that the hero was calling the heroine "names" behind the scenes because she forgot to emphasize a sentence so as to cause him to show why he was heart-broken for love of her. Oh, the stage! it is so lovely, and real, and handsome, and true, and romantic that I wish I had one at the barn for the cows to act on! If it is built when you come home, you, and Burdeene, and Bessie, and Gretchen and Brownie will have to pay fifteen pins at the door to see Rufus play Romeo to Lucille's Juliet. There'll be no hugging, for old Lucille might get her horn under Rufus's waistcoat and hurt him—and I don't want anybody to get hurt on my stage.—It is cold to-night, and I knew it would be, for Chloë came in this morning wearing Johnson's hat, overcoat and boots; and if I'm not mighty much mistaken she was smoking a cigar. J.C. has some Wyandotte chickens that look as if they had been tarred and feathered. He has an old Langshan rooster that crows 3,431 times every day, and his voice can be heard a mile or more. I think he was intended to be a donkey, but got some feathers on him and now they call him a Langshan.—Chloë says "When you see the rake er de hoe-handle pintin' to the norf whar it's accidentally been flung down, you may know it's gwine to be cold." We had a snow storm this morning but the weather was warm then and it melted. If we were to have one to-night, it wouldn't melt in a long time.

There, now! I have written you a heap of news that is real late, and I hope you'll turn around and hit me with a big wad from your end of the line. Regards to Father O'Brien, the sisters, and love to Burdeene and Bessie.

> Your loving
> Daddy

Evelyn doesn't believe he has a sister away at school. He hasn't heard from her in three months and he's been sick too.[3]

ALS

2 pp.

Envelope: Miss Mildred Harris / St. Joseph's Academy, / Washington, Ga. / *Wilkes County*

PM: 25 February 1900

1. The Boer War (1899–1902) is the occasion for Afrikaan words used humorously in this letter; i.e., Kopje, "head"; klein, "small"; veld, "field"; langer-lamderye, "farm-land"; trek, "journey/travel." The front yard of the Wren's Nest had three terraces.

2. Explanatory note in a later hand identifies the play as *Glory Quayle* and the actors as Viola Allen and Jim Storm.

3. Postscript in different hand, probably Evelyn's.

[To Mildred]

24th day of a backward
March, 1900

Dear Toodleum: Is anything serious the matter with you? We expected
a letter all day to-day and in between times. For a long time this afternoon Lillian sat out on the terrace (with Fritz) waiting for the mail man
to come along. It was quite late when she (and Fritz) concluded that
the mail man wasn't coming. Fritz had to go to supper, but he left his
picture as a guarantee of good faith.—Mama has a very bad cold. She
has the backache, the headache, a troublesome cough, and the sniffles.
In spite of all these drawbacks she worked hard all day, sweeping and
cleaning. It is enough to kill a horse, and how anybody who is really ill
can go through it all is more than I can tell.—Lillian is making herself
a ribbon and lace waist; I mean, Essie is making the waist while Lillian
looks on and superintends. I believe she did do some of the stitching—
or, rather, she believes it, for I heard her say so. She also picked some
violets and sat on the steps with Fritz.—Mrs. Wade sent over a package
of doughnuts. I don't know whether they are loaded or not. I was afraid
Mama was going to insist on my eating one, but she was not feeling
well. J.C. didn't insist because he wanted them all himself. As for Lillian,
she would have insisted, but she was engaged in sitting on the steps
with Fritz and smiling sweetly at his dear little picture.—Mrs. Hubert
Culberson came over this morning about the time Chloë arrived, and
informed us that she would help us pick the violets. If she had postponed her visit till the afternoon she'd have seen Lillian sitting on the
steps with Fritz, accepting—his picture. Lillian carried Stewart to town
yesterday, and the youngster seemed to enjoy [it]. When he returned
he was full of candy and curiosity. It is perhaps unnecessary to remark
that Lillian arrived at home yesterday in time to sit on the steps with
Fritz to-day. All of which goes to show that a person with energy can do
a great many things in two days, especially when he or she (especially
she) goes about it with the proper spirit of determination.—I ride to
town on the new Ashby street line sometimes. The cars run very rapidly,
and get to the Post Office in 20 minutes, in spite of the fact that they
turn every corner in town.—One of the Whitehall conductors said to-
day that I had a mighty pretty place. I judge from that that he saw Lillian

sitting on the steps with Fritz.—Julian was well enough to come out to see us Tuesday. He brought Julia and and [sic] the baby. He looks better than he did before his illness, but he says he still has a stitch in his side. I was sorry he couldn't come out to-day so as to see Lillian sitting on the steps with Fritz.—Charles took dinner here to-day (and carried it away with him, too) because Essie was fixing Lillian's waist. This brilliant garment is cut bias and forms a point d'applique in front and rear. The ribbon stripes are of the color of a full blown rose. It is a waist that will attract general attention, especially when she's sitting on the steps with Fritz.—I'm going to make mama a strong hot toddy directly and see if she'll talk in her sleep. Speaking of talking while asleep, I went out in the backyard the other night and heard J.C.'s pigeons snoring. Did you know that pigeons snore? It's news to me. I believe I'll write an essay on "The Snore of Pigeons." I'll also write a beautiful waltz song entitled "She sat on the steps with Fritz."—It is now getting on towards April, and I haven't received your school bill yet.—I hope you are not ill, and I hope the sisters are well. Lillian is not as lively as she was this morning. I'm afraid she'll take cold on account of sitting on the steps with Fritz.

Regards to the sisters, and love to Burdeene and Bessie, and the sweet little Miller gals.

> Your loving
> Daddy

ALS
2 pp.
Envelope: Miss Mildred Harris, / St. Joseph's Academy, / Washington, Ga. / *Wilkes County*
PM: 25 March 1900

[To Mildred]

> Next door to April the One-Eye, 1900
> [sketch of man's head in fool's cap all in a circle]

Dear Milsy: Time is rushing right along. It's only a matter of two months and a harf [sic], before you'll be home again, and Burdeene with you. You'll wonder why I'm telling you what you already know. It's because there's no news here that hasn't been written to you two times and a half. I think it's duller now than it has been for some time.—The little Collier gals were out to-day and took dinner. Julia and Lillian went to the matinee together, and I suppose the little gals were sent out to keep them from worrying Julian, who is not quite so well as he has been.—Of course I received Bessie's composition, and enjoyed it too. She has a talent for writing, and if she will cultivate it she can make something out of it. I thought the composition was wonderfully well done. As Bessie is a good girl, and a smart girl, and a sweet girl, she is sure to succeed in life.—I have nothing new to report in regard to Bill. The truth is, Bill is out of sorts. The season of the year has come when she wants to put a little salt on a ten-penny nail and bite it in two. She wanders around singing in a low key and feeling romantic. She made a waist for herself the other day—or, rather, she watched Essie make it, which comes to the same thing.—Julian and Julian [Julia] and the baby spent the day here—oh, I don't know when it was, but one day not long ago. The baby is as cute and as clean as a bowl of rice with milk in it.—Lucien is performing at the Athletic Club in order to take exercise. He seems to be improving on account of it.—I'm afraid Mother Clemence is awful mad about something or other, and I'm sorry she couldn't permit you and Burdeene to come at Easter time. However, she has some good reason, and instead of complaining we'll just knuckle down to our books and be good.—I know where Billy Bill is, but what has become of School Bill? I wish you'd ask Sister Sacred Heart about it again. I haven't the least idea what the amount is, or I would send it with this. Still, I'm not worrying about it. Sister S.H. knows what she's about. I'm only afraid that she thinks I should send the money anyway without waiting for it.—The weather feels to-night like we are going to have another Blizzard. B-r-r-r! I can feel the cold chills chasing one another up and down my back like lizards on a fence, or rats in the barn loft, or puppies playing in the grass. I had to buy another ton of coal, making 17 this winter. Such is life in the sweet sunny southland where the orange and myrtle are in bloom. We have three months of winter, and then three more of cold weather. I wish somebody would give me change for these two quarters.—And so Burdeene and Eva have bumped heads and made up. No doubt they have found out that there was no reason why they should have fallen out in the first place. What I want to know is, why girls are jealous of one another. I have asked doctors and preachers, and ice-cream peddlers, but none can give me any information on the subject. I can't find out even in the dictionary.—Well, Bill, after whistling to see if there are any boys hiding out in the front yard, has come in demanding to read this letter, and I suppose I'll have to bring it to a conclusion just to please. I don't want to have a case or Burdeene-and-Eva between Bill and me.—She went to ["]the children off they get, oh!" [*Children of the Ghetto*?] to-day and found another bright and beautiful and perfectly splendid and highly talented man on the stage.[1] She wanted to bring him home, but she knew the dogbox was full of fleas. Love to Burdeene, Bessie, and to the sweet little Miller Gals—but, first, my regards to the sisters.

    Your loving

      Daddy

ALS

2 pp.

Envelope: Miss Mildred Harris, / St. Joseph's Academy, / Washington, Ga. / *Wilkes County, Ga.* /

PM: 1 April 1900

    1. Perhaps a play based on the popular Victorian novel *Children of the Ghetto* (1892), by Israel Zangwill (1864–1924), about Jewish life in London.

                              Thursday Evening, 5th April [1900]

Dear Evelyn: Your letter was waiting for me when I came home, but was not the less interesting because I had seen you in the meantime. We usually say more in a letter than we do in conversation, the reason being that, in a letter, we feel that we are shielded from the indifference or enthusiasm which our remarks may meet with or arouse. We commit our thoughts, as it were, to the winds. Whereas, in conversation, we are constantly watching or noting the effect of what we are saying, and, when the relations are intimate, we shrink from being taken too seriously on one hand, and, on the other, not seriously enough.—But people no longer write letters. Lacking the leisure, and, for the most part, the ability, they dictate dispatches, and scribble messages. When you are in the humor, you should take a peep at some of the letters written by people who lived long ago, especially the letters of women. There is a charm about them impossible to describe, the charm of unconsciousness and the sweetness of real sincerity. But, in these days, we have not the artlessness nor the freedom of our forbears. We know too much about ourselves. Constraint covers us like a curtain. Not being very sure of our own feelings, we are in a fog about the feelings of others. And it is really too bad that it should be so. I fear I am pretty nearly the only one now living who is willing to put his thoughts freely on paper even when writing to his own children. This is the result, as you may say, of pure accident. I am really as remote from the activities of the world, and from the commotions that take place on the stage of events as any of the ancients were. It is the accident of temperament, for I am very sure that the temperament has been moulded by circumstances and surroundings. All that goes on has a profound significance for me, but I seem to be out of the way, a sort of dreamy spectator, who must sometimes close his eyes on the perpetual struggle that is going on.—But what is all this? *Bang!* Let us fire the sunset gun at such prosing, and forcibly bring on the twilight that belongs to modern and contemporary affairs. And the firing was timely, for the report had hardly died away before the doorbell rang and in walked Youth, Beauty, Love and Fashion, all combined in the person of sweet Lula Z., who has arrived to stay with Essie "for the looks of the thing," whatever that may mean. The phrase is a quotation from Mama's guide-book of Etiquette and Propriety. I hope the "thing," whatever it is, will look better now that this charming little filly has appeared in the pasture. It was a great thought to have her here, but it seems to me that I should have preferred, humanly speaking, the girl who has been taking you out among the ruins. But perhaps Age has no right even to hint at the propensities of Youth—especially after it has arrived at that period when it may go about with its trousers unbuttoned without bringing so much as a blush to the pink and sensitive cheeks of Propriety.—But perhaps you have your ears cocked for news. It is useless. We never get out an extra in West End until "Aunt Lol" pays us a visit and it has been a year and a day since she was here. We had

Lucien and Alleen to dinner to-day, "for the looks of the thing." Lucien said he liked to go to Lithia on account of the good eating. No doubt this is so, for, of a big hen, only the neck was left when he gave his mouth a final wipe. Mama and Grandma left on time, though she sat up all night for fear the man wouldn't come for the trunk. I haven't heard from her. When she writes I'll send you the letter unless there's some pestiferous piece of confidence in its vitals. You said nothing about money the other day—the fact is we didn't have time to say much of anything—but don't forget that I am to pay your expenses.[1]

> Your loving
> Daddy.

ALS
3 pp.

1. According to a later note, this letter was sent to Lithia Springs, Georgia, a popular spa. See the full identification of this resort in the letter to Evelyn, "Friday *afternoon—late*" [c. 1896].

[To Mildred]

April 7, 1900

I'm what do you reckon? and what do you think? says I, with a nod, says I, with a wink. It's nothing to eat, it's nothing to drink, as sure as I'm writing with Stafford's black ink. Oh, no, indeedy! it's far better than that; for Billy has bought her a brand new hat! And now she's obliged for to wear her Rat. It's partly a hat and partly a bonnet, with fluffy white chiffon and roses upon it. *Chiffon?* Well, I'm not at all certain (dog on it!) that I'm spelling it right, but Burdeene or Bessie can spell it for me; if not, there's Essie. "Now Popsy," says Bill, "don't you think it's quite dressy?" (If she reads about this she'll be giving me Jessy!) She's asking us all if we think it's becoming, and the tone of her voice shows she wants no humming (or hawing). Say "yes" if you want any chumming. The bonnet flares out like a grocer's scoop, and pink and black bows are caught in a loop, a sort of a beau-catcher that'll make the boys troop. "Room there, for the RAT!" it seems to announce; and the Chiffon is draped in a delicate flounce. *Oh, you just hush!* it'll make the boys bounce. It goes very well with her ring-streaked waist; it's choicy, and choosy, and it's *chicey,* and chaste, and 'twas surely selected with a good deal of taste.

Phew! that's the way with me. When I get started on the rhyme rails, it's hard to stop. I had to call Mama and ask her to put sand on the track and ring the gong. This she did, and so here I am—warm, but feeling better. Evelyn has been home for two days. His stomach is too much for him, and he persists in working too hard. He'll know more when he has a few serious set-backs, and then he'll settle down into a steady gait. Everybody else is well, especially Fritz. He and Lillian tried hard to-day to wear out the old red bench in the yard. They sat, and sat, and sat, and sat, and the breeze blewd and the birds flewd and the chickens shood, and the cows chewd, and the pigeons cooed, and the road rewd and Stewart stewd. And that aint all neither, but I've forgotten the rest. That's always the way; when I get hold of something interesting I sit right flat down and forget it.—Stewart spent the morning with Richard Morenus, and had a good time eating dirt and falling off the fence. He now has some "pants"; but that's nothing. Fritz also has "pants," and he and Lillian can sit longer in one place and flatter than Stewart can. Chandler tries to spend the day here sometimes, but his voice begins to drag on the ground and thrash about in the air and he has to be carried home. And all the time this is going on Mrs. Moseley's part is yelling "*All right! All right! All right!*" when she knows perfectly well that it's not all right. This parrot doesn't seem to disturb Fritz. Pauline came down to pick violets to-day. She is so fat that when she sits down she spreads out all around as if you had dropped 170 pounds of biscuit dough. Fritz isn't that fat, and, anyhow, if he was, it would be all right, because he's nothing but a boy. He hasn't seen our new bonnet yet, and he shan't look at it, so there!—My best regards to the sisters, and say to Sister Sacred Heart that we are always perfectly sure up here of the wisdom and justice of any decision that is made in regard to our dear kids.—Your report is very good, fine in fact. I see you are beginning to take to music.—We've had oodles of violets, so many, indeed, that we've been giving them away to the neighbors.—We have a new calf which is claimed by Daisy, and this is all the news. Love to Burdeene and Bessie.

Your loving
Daddy

ALS
2 pp.
Envelope: Miss Mildred Harris, / St. Joseph's Academy, / Washington, *Ga.* / *Wilkes County*
     PM: 8 April 1900

[To Mildred]

15 *Aprile, 1900*

Dear Tom: I didn't write to you last night because I didn't want to interrupt your conversation with Mama. I hope she arrived without any headache in her baggage. She always has the headache when she travels. If she starts from home without it she manages to pick it up somewhere on the road. I know you enjoyed her visit. She's a mighty nice lady when she's not dusting and tearing up the house.—I had an Easter present myself in addition to the pretty cards you kids sent me. James Whitcomb Riley sent me a complete edition of his works in ten volumes, with something original on the fly leaf of each one. This was in the first volume:

> To Uncle Remus.
> The Lord who made the day and night.
> He made the Blackman and the White;
>   So, in like view,
>   I hold it true
> That he hain't got no favor*ite*—
>   Onless, it's you.
>   - - - - - - /// - - - - -

Now, I am mighty proud of that—mighty proud. The first thing you know I'll be awfully conceited. Mr. Riley will be in Atlanta to-morrow (Monday), and I'm to meet him at the train. I don't know what he's going to do.—Now Mama, without intending to do so, has caused me lots of trouble. She has gone and went and told you all the news, and I haven't a-thing to write about except that Sidney Ormond has shaved off his pink water-color mustache, and I wouldn't have known that if

Evelyn hadn't told me. I reckon Mr. Ormond looks funny without that glowing little mustache. It sat on his face like a rose on a lady's hat and gave a charming touch of color to his make-up. I'm sure the girls will miss and mourn its fate—now that's all I know, and the truth is a gal who has her mama with her doesn't deserve and doesn't need to have a long letter from her Daddy.—Charles and Essie were over to dinner to-day. Essie was feeling too bad to go to church, and so she crawled through the crack of the fence and came over here.—Bill wore her new hat or bonnet to church this morning. Julian said she looked like a comic valentine, but I thought she looked fine—only her petticoats were too long. She wore one of her last summer's dresses, but it looked new. As for me, I went so far as to wear a white-and-purple striped cravat. This, I think, set off my peculiar style of beauty. Anyhow, the conductors and motormen looked at me and smiled more than once, and I was sorry I didn't have a lace fan so that I might temporarily conceal my blushes. As it was I could only snicker and say *"Oh, you stop!"* Stewart and Chandler are well enough to be up and about, and you know what that means. Stewart looks very well in "pants," and he's beginning to behave very well except at home. The small baby is the best of the lot. He laughs all the time, and consequently has no opportunity to cry.—Brader Warner has returned to his suburban home for the season, after spending all his legacy ($2,5000) [*sic*] on doctors and new cravats, and in cab hire. He's no better in health than he was, and so his money has been worse than thrown away.—We had fried hen to-day, the first I ever saw.—Bill's kid friends haven't been around to-day. I guess they are jealous because they saw her playing with Richard Morenus the other day.

Regards to the sisters, and love to Burdeene, Bess and the sweet little Miller kids.

>   Your loving
>   Daddy

ALS

2 pp.

Envelope: Miss Mildred Harris, / St. Joseph's Academy, / Washington, Ga. / Wilkes County

PM: 16 April 1900

[To Mildred]

Saturday, May 5, 1900

Dear Bridget: Your Unc. Jeems[1] has done gone and went, and the house feels as if all the furniture had been taken out (You see how my hand is trembling—I watered the violets for the first time this afternoon, and my arm is shaking so I can hardly write.) Your Unc. Jeems was very gay while he was here.—Mr. and Mrs. Stanton took dinner with us to-day.—Altogether, I have had a very enjoyable vacation. Bill has nearly laughed herself to death. Mr. Riley is a very fine actor and mimic. One minute he'd be taking the part of a six year old boy, declaring he was "the goodest boy in the world," and the next he'd be a very old man talking about another old man, and saying, "He's a-a'gin'—he's a-breakin'!" This sounds very silly on paper, but to hear your Unc. Jim say it, and see his actions and the movements of his face, was a spectacle as good as a show. He would have given you and the girls a good deal of enjoyment. However, he is gone, and the household will soon drop back to corn-bread and dumplings, and return to its old mutton and its warmed-over hash.—Julia took us to ride in the country, and we enjoyed it very much. We went to Westview,[2] and then out the country road two or three miles. The azaleas and rhododendrons were blooming in great style.— Did you ever see the cyclorama[3] here? I've been twice, and I'm ready to go again; but I believe I'll wait till you get home, and then we'll go out and shake hands (or snouts) with Clio.[4] Mr. Riley said he dearly loved Clio, but thought a great deal more of her at *a distanc*[5] (see how my hand shakes!)—at a distance of a hundred yards than he did at closer range.—We all regret very much to hear of the critical condition of Father O'Brien. I am very fond of him, so fond, indeed, that I have a very strong hope that he will be spared. One reason why I feel that way is because it will be impossible to fill his place. No other man c[an] take up his work and carry it out as successfully as he could. My hope may be doomed to disappointment; nevertheless, I entertain and nurse it.—I'm glad the bill came. I'll send a cheque under separate cover to Sister Sacred Heart.—What arrangements has Burdeene made after she graduates? Is she *obliged* to go home with her dear pa and ma? Isn't it possible to keep her here awhile? Something must be done.—What's all this about sending my letter to Mr. Riley? Don't you think he'll suspect a trick? It seems that Mama found the letter lying open on my table and permitted Jamesy to read it—or she told him I was saying some nice things about him, and he asked to read the letter. All this time I was out of the house. The letter wasn't intended for his eyes at all. I'm afraid he'll think we're a lot of gushers, and that would be bad.—Bill is just as anxious to go to Washington as you girls are to have her come. She'd go this minute if I said the word; and she is extremely anxious to go down with Mr. and Mrs. B., but I think that would be an imposition on those dear sisters who have been so generous in dealing with my gals. I know the sisters would be glad to be imposed on in this way. (They are ever thinking of others and not of themselves.) But, really, it seems to me best that Bill should go down sometime in June. That, of course, is subject to change. I am only telling you how I feel about it. We have come to no decision in the matter. We are hoping to have Mr. and Mrs. B. come out to see us on their way to Washington.[6] Give my kindest regards to the sisters, and my love to Burdeene, Bessie, and the Miller gals.

>Your loving
>Daddy

ALS

2 pp.

1. James Whitcomb Riley, who visited that year.
2. Westview cemetery.
3. Circular painting of the Battle of Atlanta housed at Grant Park, near the zoo.
4. Elephant at Atlanta zoo.
5. Italic text struck through in original.
6. Washington, Georgia, where Saint Joseph's Academy was located.

[To Mildred]

>Two Days fo' de 'Clipse,
>State of Georgy.
>[28 May 1900]

Before you get this, dear gal, you will have seen the Eclipse. Folks say it puts a mighty funny feeling in the atmosphere; the air gets chilly, and you have to put on your thick socks, and tie a hankercher round your neck and look at the front side of the moon through smoked glass. Evelyn says he's going to smoke some glass and a cigar too. One man says he was in the midst of an eclipse about forty year ago, and things got so dark that the chickens went to roost, and the cows came up and put their hindlegs through the bars to be milked, and the stars came out and winked, and the birds put their heads under their wings and took another nap. The man said it was truly a terrible time[.] A little boy who heard the man talking remembered enough of it to tell a tale to his mama. "I saw the 'clipse, mys'f," he said. "It was a drate big 'clipse, bigger'n the pennanner—bigger'n a house. An' it was hidin' in the bushes, 'n I dot my dun an' shooted it—right in de haid, 'n it falled down, 'n nen they want no 'clipse there; it flew'd 'way, '*way*, 'WAY, 'WAY off nonder."

One day fo' de 'clipse, state of Georgy.—You see I started this letter last night, and that is "all the far" I got. Nelly Forbes was on hand, and she and Bill kicked up such a racket that I couldn't write; and then other troubles jumped up like a lot of rabbits in the bushes, and I had to lay down my fountain pen in self-defence. And speaking of defence I'm mighty 'fraid I'll have to have a new one built on the side where we join on to Mr. Richardson's bald spot.—J.C. has a little fan-tail squab which lost its ma, and he is bringing it up by hand. The squab has no fan to its tail yet, but it is said by some very able prophets that it will have one some day if it lives and the cat doesn't catch it and use the fan during hot weather.—Bill went down to College Park to-day, and will return to-morrow evening in time to meet Mrs. B. the day after the 'clipse. Yesterday Bill went to the base-ball game, an' just 'cause she put on the Tech's colors, the Techs went and got beat. It was very, very sad, but somehow I couldn't weep.—Bill declares she can't come down with Mrs. B.'cause she's not fixed—she hasn't any clothes to wear until she gets a new dress, and anyhow she had her mind set on the first of June. So she says. She may come with Burdeene's ma, but I doubt it.—J.C. says please answer his two letters as soon as you can take time from your sewing.—Just think of it! I had to send your gramophone and all the records back to the factory, and so you can never play on the old machine anymore. Isn't that dreadful? However, I expect you'll be glad when—however, that's another story, as Mr. Bloodgood Whiffling would remark.—Mama and J.C. have gone up to Lucien's, and I'm here all alone with the squab and the canary bird. I tell you, I'm afraid of 'em both. The squab whistles when it wants food and after it gets full it snores; and the canary bird gets up in its swing and swings half the night; and the swing makes a squeaky creepy sound like a burglar burgling his way through the door. *Cluch!* What's that? I believe it's a man under my bed. No, it's Muldoon hitting the floor howdy with his tail.— Essie comes over occasionally. She is looking better than she has looked for a long time. Every hair in Charles's head is red, and he seems to be happy. Evelyn is off to-morrow night for Louisville, where he will try to find Uncle Sammy Roberts.—My best regards to the sisters, and love to Burdeene, Bessie, and the sweet little Miller gals.

 Your loving
  Daddy

ALS
2 pp.
Envelope: Miss Mildred Harris, / St. Joseph's Academy, / Washington, *Ga.* / Wilkes County
PM: 28 May 1900

[To Mildred]

3 of June, 1900

I resume my serial story, dear gals, but I have forgotten where I left off.[1] What was my heroine doing in my last letter? And what became of the hero? I have forgotten, too, whether the hero was named Fritz or Roy. The heroine, as well as I can remember was a bilious gal in more senses than one and never had anything to wear. Well, we will permit the serial story to take a much-needed vacation. One of the heroine's dresses has arrived and the others are expected on a special train to-morrow. The dressmakers say their hired help can't work as well after an eclipse as they worked before.—I presume Mildred and Burdeene are happy now. One has her sis and the other her ma. We liked Mrs. B. very much, and could like her still better if she would stop over a week on her way back home. Mama gave Mrs. B. her choice between my overcoat and the flannel sacque.—The news around here is about as plentiful as the feathers are on a Mexican canine. Julian's baby and the Collier kids all have the whooping cough, and I expect to hear every day that Julian has the rash, or that he has gone to teething again. Our kin on the corner lot are very quiet and conservative. The boys come down occasionally and do violence to a bushel or so of green apples. This seems to worry the apples more than it does the boys. Essie and Charles came over to supper and ate everything in sight; as a result Essie is feeling better.—Lizzie, the cook, went to Fayette yesterday, wearing a pair of number ten shoes. Chloe has taken her place and makes as much fuss among the pots and pans as a blindfolded cow. Two or three times to-day I have gone out to see if the range had caved in or the hot water tank had exploded. Ask Chloe about it, and her reply is, "Dey wan't no fuss out here. Maybe I mought er set the kittle down." I have concluded that what I heard was the dishrag dropping on the floor. Some day when Mama is feeling well enough to go to town, I'll ask her to buy a new dishrag and then I'll have the old one to split up for stove wood. I don't say that Lizzie's dishrag isn't *clean*; I simply say that it's *too hard*. Under the circumstances, it's no wonder that we have to put a new coat of paint on the crockery ware twice a year.—Bessie's complimentary verses would be very nice if I deserved all the nice things she says about me. Anyhow, I'm proud of her good opinion, and hope I'll be able to maintain with a straight face the deception I have been practising. If Bessie will take Bill off to one side and get her to tell the real facts of the situation there'll be a great opening of eyes in the neighborhood of St. Joseph's academy.—Fritz and Roy are both as well as they could be expected to be. Both look a little pale about the gills, but that is no doubt due to malaria. They both claim that I can't play the gramophone as sweetly as our Willie-lillie does.—Bill's blue dress has a white inlaid panel as a vest, and a white vine climbing around the skirt. The pallor of the vine is due to the fact that it was left out overnight in the early spring.—Well, I suppose that I must close, yet if I chose, I'd drop the prose, and rhyme you rows of verse's, so's to match my woes with Ah's and o's; but, goodness knows, it's time to hush. Regards to the Sisters and to Mrs. B., love to Burdeene and Bessie, and to the dear little Miller gals,

> Your loving
> Daddy

ALS

2 pp.

1. Letter to Mildred and school friend(s). Note reference to Lillian at home.

[To Lillian]

Send all replies to Box 111.

———————————

Saturday night, October 6, [1900]

Dear Bill: Evelyn received the telegram from Montreal, or Upton, Friday night but as he had to sit up all night with election figures, and didn't get up till 1 p.m. to-day, I never heard about it until just a while ago—well, a few hours ago. I wasn't worried, however. I have made up my mind, since the Taunton spree, not to worry about such matters. Mamma has always been so thoughtful and careful about such things, that I quite made up my mind you were both lost. In another hour Evelyn would have sent a telegram to Troy, and then there would have been nothing to do but send him to New York by the next day's train, and institute a search. Such was the programme we had mapped out—and it would have been vigorously carried through.—If there's any news here I don't know it's [sic] name. I did have several things to write about, but they seem to have slipped my mind. I told mamma that we were to have a new cook Monday morning. I don't know how she'll pan out, but I have great confidence in Dack Ezzard's (office man) judgment in such matters. I don't believe he would recommend a woman unless she had a good record, and was well known to him. Anyhow, it will be a welcome change at least for awhile, and if she's a fraud, why between Dack and Charley, there'll be no trouble in getting another. I'll let Chloë go on with the cows, and washing if she will. If she doesn't want to, Charley can milk Lucille, and I'll sell the other to the lowest bidder.—Chloë will go to a "Baptizing" to-morrow morning, leaving at 10 o'clock, and as Evelyn has asked Brooks out, I guess he'll find the dinner in exquisite shape, with no one to wait on the table. But it's all right. We'll manage in some way. Such things do not worry me. It's the failure of Taunton telegrams that worries me.[1]—Collier's Weekly wants a story for Christmas. More than that, I broke off one of my teeth to-night, and am feeling just as contented (probably more so) as if I had sprouted a new one.—Ray Stannard Baker has gone to Eatonton to find out things about me. He's going to write the stuff for McClure's Magazine. He saw Julian, and was very much struck by his gift of gab. He also admires Evelyn very much. In short, Mr. Baker appears to be a very nice man indeed. If Mamma had been at home, we could have entertained him, for he is a very quiet and unassuming [man?].—Roy is here to-night. He says he came to read the papers of the day. Just at present he and Essie are engaged in a very lively conversation in the sitting-room.—J.C. went to the D. & P. show,² and is now at Chaffee's, holding Marguerite's hand.—Essie appears to be feeling better to-night. She went to confession this afternoon.—Mrs. Wilson called to see her, but just at that time she was unbosoming herself to Father Bazoon.—Mamma remembers old Aunt Nancy Lamar, who used to cook for the Wilson's. She's with Potts now, and the other day she attempted to climb up in a wardrobe after something. The wardrobe toppled over, and buried her beneath its massive ruins, breaking one of her hind-legs.—I enclose some cards sent by Julia. I heard by telephone that she was not feeling so well to-day, but the baby's all right.—The last time I heard from Mrs. Kelly she had the backache, and knee-ache, the toothache, and her whole system was impregnated with malaria, vanilla, neuralgia, and cochineal.—Everything is the same around here except the violets. They are beginning to bloom. We have had several cloudy days, and one day it rained, but the weather and the mosquitoes are as warm as ever. I'll write alternate letters to you and Mamma, and you and she can alternate in writing, which will even matters up.—Give my love to the folks.—Paxon has his Harris window in full blast.³ It's a right good display.—The old cow's improving.

  Your loving
  Daddy

ALS
2 pp.
Envelope: *Return to Box 111,* / *Atlanta, Ga.* / Miss Lillian Harris, / Upton, / Province of Quebec, / Canada East.
PM: 11 October 1900
1. Changed erroneously to "worry" by JCH or other hand.
2. I.e., dog and pony show.

3. Probably the bookstore of the American Baptist Publication Society, located on Whitehall Street in the Chamberlin Building at the southeast corner of Hunter (now Martin Luther King, Jr., Drive) and Whitehall (now Peachtree Street SW). It was managed by Frederic J. Paxon (who became a partner of Davison-Paxon-Stokes Company, a department store, in 1901). See picture of bookstore and annotations in *Atlanta in 1890: "The Gate City"* (1890; reprint, Macon, Ga.: Mercer University Press, 1988), 27, 94. This edition has a new introduction by Timothy J. Crimmins. *Cf.* reference to Paxon's store in letter to Mildred, 2 April 1901.

[To Lillian]

Sunday, 14 October: 1900

Dear Bill: I am writing this on Sunday, but it will not be posted until tomorrow afternoon, because I want to send poor mamma some money. I'll send it in the shape of a bill of exchange, and the Captain can get it cashed at St. Hyacinthe.[1] He should get gold for it, or American money. I don't know when Mamma proposes to start back, but if she should chance to be in Troy about the 24th or 25th, I could run up there and see her. I've just received a letter from the McClure Co., in which they say in the person of Mr. Phillips: "I am sending for transportation for you to New York and return, and also from New York to Troy and return; also transportation for Mrs. Harris back to Atlanta. We will send it along in a few days." I suppose Mamma told you about the proposition they made.[2] I haven't quite made up my mind about it, and won't be able to until I can have a heart to heart talk with the poor worried lady who imagines that I am still grieving because she didn't send a telegram.— Julia, Julian and Rawson were out to-day for an hour, with the baby, who has a worried look on account of teething. Julia has a worn and weary appearance, but Rawson appears to be very chipper.—I've been able to do very little work, owing to various interruptions, propositions, and what-not; but before I come north I want to finish a short story, and write another Billy Sanders piece for "The World's Work," the first number of which will contain my purtygraph. I'm sorry I haven't got a patent medicine to offer to the public, for it is a pity to waste so much good advertising.—There isn't a spark, no, not a cinder, of news here. If anything happens it gets away from me.—You'll see in the paper about the fight between the Ryans and the Murphy's. It was started because Gus Ryan had made some remark about John's sister. Mrs. Murphy came to see me this morning to ask me to prevail on Evelyn to do John justice in any subsequent publication, and she told me the cause of the row. The fight was renewed at the police-station, and, as there were three to one, John got pretty well done up. Old Antony was there, but somebody held him.—There are thousands of violets, with no one to pick 'em, and they'll all be gone by the time you get back.—I thought Mamma had pruned her chrysanthemums, but the bushes are loaded down with buds, and the blooms will be about the size of dog fennel blossoms.— Mrs. Kelly brought her fatigue over the other day and took us down to Florida as usual.—I'll not write a long letter this time, for I am tired. Did you ever try to separate a young calf from its mother in a two-acre lot? No, you never did, and therefore you'll never fully appreciate my heroic qualities when I tell you that I have just succeeded in doing that very thing; and my whole nature is stirred and shaken, and the perspiration is gradually filling my shoes. I'll make this promise without compulsion— namely: that if there's forty calves with a cow I'll never try to separate them again unless I have a pack of hounds and a shot-gun. J.C. was with me, and it was as much as he could do to keep out of the calf's way. Phew! I'm tired! My love to all.

> Your loving
> Daddy

ALS

2 pp.

Envelope: Miss Lillian Harris, / Upton, / Providence of Quebec, / Canada East.

PM: 18 October 1900

1. Captain Pierre LaRose, Mrs. J. C. Harris's father.

2. The publishing company of McClure Phillips had offered him an annual salary in return for the rights to all of JCH's writings during the year. Doubleday, Page and Company had made a similar proposal. *Life and Letters*, 433–34, says that Harris accepted McClure's contract of $3,000 yearly and retired from the *Constitution*. Actually JCH retired from *Constitution* (5 September 1900) before signing the contract with McClure. See Cousins, 177. See also Atlanta *Constitution*, 7 September 1900, 4, for announcement of JCH's retirement for literary work. For various reasons, JCH did not renew the McClure contract in 1903.

PART SIX ❧ JANUARY– JUNE 1901
A TURNING POINT

As usual the news takes wing as soon as I get astraddle
of my type-writing machine.

—*Letter to Mildred, 1 June 1901*

Dear Mildred: Since you suggested it, I will write you a letter on the type-writer. I hope your cold is very much better by this time. I see by the newspapers that evrybody [sic] is having the influenza; but I hope it won't come your way nor mine. I've had it once or twice in spots, and I don't want to thvae [sic] it any more; I certainly hope you'll escape it. I have been so busy trying to write my long story that I can hardln [sic] get my mind in shape for writing you a letter, and you'll have to put up with a rather dull one this time.—If there's any news round here it hasn't drifted my way, it's the same old bill of fare every day: taters and steak during the week, and chicken pie for dinner every Sunday. Coran, our French cook still has trouble with her feet, and I'm afraid I'll have to buy her a horse and buggy so she can drive around the table and wait on it without disarranging her gout.[1]—Bill will leave for Canton to-morrow at 4 p.m. She doesn't make as much fuss about it as I thought she would; in fact she's very quiet and subdued since she purchased a pair of No. T dancing slippers[.] These slippers appear to fill a lon-felt [sic] want. They have tin buckles on top, and Bill holds them in her hand and looks at them by the hour. She says she thinks they were made for her, and I don't doubt it. Speaking of Bill, reminds me of the way you and she write letters. Do you recognize this? "How is evry [sic] body? I hope they are well. Tell Blanky I'll write as soon as my sore finger gets well. Well, I hope every body is well. I must stop now as it is nearly time for school hours. Give my love to everybody; I hope they are well."— The only news is that Mr. Morenus is going to move to Chicago, and we'll no longer hare [sic] his cow to play with. Fritz and Roy come no oftener than they did. The boys have inaugurated the kite-flying season, and J.C. is taking up all his time making kites that won't fly after they are made. It seems that kites are very contrary things; you may put just as much paste and paper on them as you please, and still they won't fly unless they want to. It's very exasperating, and it makes your poor little brother perspire a good deal[.]—No doubt Sister Sacred Heart is of the opinion that I have forgotten my promises, but it was the other fellow who did the forgetting; but it's all right now, and I'm enclosing in this letter a cheque that will tide me over till the next time.—Evelyn is going to Canton with Lillian. He will remain only a day or two, he says, but that depends on circumstances. Tell Bessie that we all enjoyed her presents very much. The handkerchief she sent me is the kind that when you wipe your mouth on it at Christmas, it'll stay clean all the year. The monogram in the corner is very prettily done, and altogether, Bessie is a fine girl. Sister Mary Louise and Sister Regius—I suppose that's the way to spell it—came out yesterday, and brought a cake for Mamma. It must have been a very good one, for it has been hid out evr [sic] since, and I haven't so much as smelt it. You see what [it] is to be a kind and forgiving old man. He receives flowers, but no cakes.— Marguerite is the same happy-go-lucky girl thaf [sic] she was when you were here. She doesn't come down now; I suppose she thinks it wouldn't be quite the proper thing for a young lady to call at a young gentleman's house unless the young gentleman's sister is at home. Maybe that's so, but she could call on the young gentleman's pa and ma, and get on the good side of them. As for the resf [sic], everything is pretty much as you left it. The old freezlin' hen is still moping about the place, and Eophia, the furnace, continues to make the house too hot when she is fired up. She was fired up yesterday for the first time in a week. The weather has been so warm up to then that we simply had a small fire in the sitting-room grate. If you were here, I daresay you go out [sic] in the yard and gather a few violets.—I have finished about fifty manuscript pages of a new story.[2] The pages are written in pencil, about three hundred words to the page. All this has been done since Aunt Sophia left. At that rate, I ought to have the book done by the first of March.—Lucien is in the back-room right now, making a kite for J.C., and Luther is looking on with watery eyes.—We are not feeling good about permitting you to go back with such a bad cold, and we are hoping that it will get no worse. But we know the dear Sisters will give you just as good attention as you could get at home. You must take care of yourself, so as to be strong and well.—I didn't say anything about your music while you were here, but I want to tell you now that I think you have made great improvement, and if you keep on improving in the same proportion, you'll do fine when you come home in June—and when you come to think about it right hard, June isn't so far off. Why, I don't believe I'll be able to write more than two books by that time. Your nephews are all well. The weather has

been so rainy that the boys haven't been able to get out much, but the[y]
were down this morning. My regards to the Sisters, and love to Bessie,
Gretchen and Brownie. Your loving

DADDY.

TL

2 pp.

1. The new cook was actually named Cora Smith Gann. (See letter to Mildred, 28 September 1901.) She replaced Chloe, who had served as temporary cook. (See letters to
Mildred, 3 June 1900, and to Lillian, 6 October 1900.)

2. Probably *Gabriel Tolliver*, finished June 1901 and published in 1902, first as a serial
in *The Era* and then as a book by McClure, Phillips, and Co. (*Life and Letters*, 454, and
Cousins, 184).

Sunday, 20 January, 1901

Dear Lillian: You are always so thoughtful and prompt about writing
that we are somewhat puzzled and disturbed because we have received
no letter from you. We feel that if you were ill, Mrs. Biechele or Burdeene
would surely let us know; and still we have an idea that if you were well
you would have written by this time. If we fail to get a letter from you
to-morrow morning, I propose to telegraph Mrs. B. and inquire what the
trouble is. Just a line, written on Wednesday or Thursday would have
been so reassuring and so pleasant. How true it is that those who go
away have all the fun, while those who stay have none! We have not
even heard from Evelyn, who has hertofore been so free with his fountain pen. He was to return to-day, but thus far he has not shown up.
So you see, we are all in the dark, and feeling as old people will, somewhat uneasy. We received a telegram in which you said you had arrived
safely and well, but there was no word about Evelyn, and since then all
is silence.

There is nothing to write about. Mamma was ill in bed one day last
week—sick headache. We could do nothing for it. She just had to sleep
it off. Mr. Bunker has sold his place to Mr. O'Donnelly of the Keely Co.,
and I'm told he wants to join me in buying the Richardson lot and divide
it between us to keep undesirable neighbors away.—Lucien has gone to
Florida for a week, leaving Alleen to the tender care of her sisters.—I'm
told that Agnes Ladson and Pauline Wagner are not on speaking terms.

It seems that Pauline invited Aggie to help her receive her guests at the party. Aggie went on time but before the guests began to arrive, she put on her things and said she had to go to a reception across town. It seems, also that the Heffner girl—not Lillian, but the next one, expected to be asked to receive with Pauline, and now *she's* warm under the chin. It is quite a tempest in a teapot.—Perhaps you remember Mr. Gerald Culberson. He died to-day at Hubert's of paralysis.—All the children are well. Yesterday and to-day the boys took dinner with us and seemed to enjoy it very much. This is all I know. Love to Burdeene, Mrs. B., and those lovely children, and kindest regards to Mr. B. Perhaps I shall be able to write more when I hear from you.

    Your loving
      Daddy

ALS
1 p.

[To Mildred]

                        Sunday, Jan. 20, 1901
Dear Tommus: Surely it's your fault that the literary man didn't send the literary book to the academy library. He told you (if you remember) that you were to take it back with you; and you said you would, and you didn't—so there!—We haven't had a line from Lillian. Tuesday we received a telegram that she had arrived safely—but the rest is silence. We have nothing from Evelyn either. Altogether it's a queer come-off. It's just the same as if Canton was a hole in the ground. L. and E. stand at the entrance, wave their hands and disappear in the cavern. There seems to be an epidemic of that sort of thing. For instance, you yourself, dear Tommus, haven't wasted more than a quart of ink on us since your return to school. But for a timely note from Sister Sacred Heart, in which she says you are well of your cold, we wouldn't know anything about it. You must learn to love your dear parents.—I had an invitation from Father Bazin to drive with Monseigneur Martinelli, but at 12 m. by the watch, Mama was compelled to go to bed with the sick headache, and therefore I couldn't go. Mama was very sick for awhile, and had to stay

in bed all day. She got the headache as the result of hiring a negro and paying him to watch her do the work. Mama can run up a step-ladder as nimbly as the kittens climb the apple-trees.—Mr. Morenus is going to move away, and Mr. Bunker has sold the place to Mr. O'Donnelly of the Keely Co.—Lucien has gone to Florida for a week. He left last Sat'day night.—I see Marguerite occasionally, and met her mother the day Mama was sick. She came in the rain. All Mama's friends call when it rains. They know they'll find her at home then.—You can just shut your eyes and guess that it's pretty lonesome here with only three at the table, and the house is bigger than four houses ought to be. When a drawer is pulled out it sounds like the chimney falling down, and when I go to bed I pull the cover over my head for fear the furnace, using the pipes for legs, will crawl in under the door and sit on me. Take warning by me, and don't never get to be an old man with children that won't write to you. If you do, you'll have some very pale hours peeping over your shoulders when you look in the glass.—I'm trying to write a story, and I'm stuck in the mud on page 75. Therefore, remember me, when this you see, for life is earnest, life is real, and corn-bread is not pound-cake by a good deal.—Your homesickness is like the measles. It breaks out when you have hot drinks. As a remedy, I'd advise you to bathe your feet occasionally and clean your teeth when you can steal a moment away from your studies.—Everybody here is well at this time, though Sister Alleen is complaining some.—We are expecting Evelyn home to-day, but he has no time set, and to judge by his silence, he'd just as lief not come as to come, and perhaps a little liefer.—Well, I don't know of anything to write, and if I did it wouldn't be interesting.

My kindest regards to the dear sisters, and love to Bess and the Miller gals.

> Your loving
> Daddy

ALS
2 pp.
Envelope: Miss Mildred Harris, / St. Joseph's Academy, / Washington, Wilkes County / *Georgia*
PM: 21 January 1901

[To Mildred]

Sunday, 27 January. [1901]

Dear Tommus: If you live up to all the nice things we hear about you—
we have various ways of hearing—you'll do well.—We have had only
five letters from Lillian thus far, if you can call them letters. They are very
short and flighty, and appear to be written between gasps. She writes
apparently because she thinks it is her duty, and not because she has
anything to write about. I can't make up my mind whether she's dazed,
or tired or ill. She speaks of gadding about, but we can get no satisfactory
account of what she is doing, or what she proposes to do.—Mr. Lowry
called this afternoon. When he went away, Messrs. Brooks, Fleming and
Cary came out to tea. As I write they are in the sitting-room, but I think
Mr. Brooks is preparing for to sing a few stanzas from a song adapted to
the bass fiddle.—We have had all sorts of weather, cold, warm and mid-
dlin', and Evelyn has taken charge of the furnace, having learned a few
points from Mr. Biechele.—Mr. Brooks has just sung "The Two Grenadiers,"—and now, Evelyn is giving a concert on the Zonophone.[1]—Since
I started this letter, the weather has grown three or four degrees colder,
and I think things will be friz up in the morning.—The cook continues
to have wounded and decrepid feet except when she wants to catch the
car, and then her feet are as good as anybody's. We have great times
with the servants, especially when Charley comes in the afternoon with
a thimbleful too much dram under his vest. You see we are progressing
slowly and with difficulty. I hope the time may come when we can get
a good, energetic cook and a pious butler. Anyhow, I shall look forward
to it as something to be hoped for.—Please find out from Gretchen how
she addresses letters to her mother. I want to write and thank her for
a very nice present she sent me by Evelyn. I should have written several days ago, but when I started the letter, I discovered that we didn't
remember her initials. Get the full address from Gretchen, name and
all, and send it by return mail, and I will be yours truly, Esquire. I see
Marguerite and Charlotte occasionally, and both are looking pretty and
sweet. M. always asks about you.—Evelyn had a fine time in Canton
and also in Lexington. We thought Mr. Harrison was a mighty nice man,
and we hope he'll come this way again. Gretchen seemed to me not to

enjoy her last visit here very well. I'm afraid the dear child didn't like the idea of going back to school. Nor poor little Brownie. Well, well—school is like a bitter tonic; it tastes bitter in the mouth, but it does good after awhile.—Essie and Charles are talking about boarding in town, the reason being that Charles has to walk home early in the morning.—I've had a little headache for a day or two, just enough to cause me to remember that I have a head. I'm thinking it's the dry air from the furnace.—Ooh! I hear the wind squealing outside like somebody had hurt its feelings. I don't know who did it but it wasn't me.—Lucien returned Saturday. Stewart and Chandler were already here; they didn't have to return. The reason I know they are here in West End is because I hear all sorts of funny noises all times of day.—Mamma is well, and Evelyn seems to be feeling good. The Friesland chicken is about the same if not more so. She never gets her feathers straight until it rains.

Well, this is all I know. Regards to the sisters, and love to Bessie, Gretchen and Brownie.

> Your loving
> Daddy[2]

ALS

2 pp.

Envelope: Miss Mildred Harris, / St. Joseph's Academy / Washington, / Wilkes County, Ga.

PM: 28 January 1901

1. The Zonophone, a disc phonograph player modeled after the earlier Gramophone, had better voice reproduction and was heavier with a more ornate case. It was known for its recordings by celebrity artists. Established by Frank Seaman c. 1899 and later incorporated as the International Zonophone Company in Berlin in 1901, the company was sold to the English-based Gramophone Company in 1903, and the American portion was sold to Victor and later discontinued. The label survived until the 1930s in Europe. See Roland Gelatt, *The Fabulous Phonograph* (Philadelphia: J. B. Lippincott Co., 1955), 95, 122–25. James Whitcomb Riley also had a Zonophone, and JCH sent him duplicate recordings to play on it according to Riley's letters to JCH of 8 May 1900 and 8 June 1900, in box 5, folders 2 and 3 (Joel Chandler Harris Collection, SC, EU).

2. Original letter and envelope are in Uncle Remus Museum, Eatonton. Photocopy in Joel Chandler Harris Collection, SC, EU.

February 22, 1901

Dear Lillian: I wrote to Mildred yesterday, thinking I would also write to you, but the effort was too much for me. I am up and about, but so weak, I can hardly see myself in the glass,—and I don't seem to gain in strength as I should. Grippe is a great thing; it is the most weakening disease that ever took hold of me. I was practically in bed for nearly three weeks. Mamma was also in bed, and but for Evelyn and Essie, I don't know what we would have done.—Essie is here to-day, arranging for her club meeting, and Mamma is flying around as if she had never been ill. This means that she will have to go to bed to-morrow, and she'll lie there and wonder what is the matter with her.—I hear this morning that the J. J. & J. E. Maddox block (on the site of the old Markham House, near the car-shed) is burned.—Everybody is well except the sick ones, and everybody is sick except those who are well[.]—There is no news here—at any rate, I know of none, and I'm just writing this because I think it is about time for you to hear from me. I am using a pencil because I am too weak to tote a pen across the paper.

Love to all. Your loving

Daddy

ALS

3 pp.

Envelope: Miss Lillian Harris, / 207 West Lake Street, / Canton, *Ohio*

PM: 21 February 1901 [1]

1. Note discrepancy in dates.

[To Lillian]

4 March—afternoon. [1901]

Dear Bill: To-day I began for to commence for to start work again, and as I am feeling pretty well, I thank you, only a little shaky in the hands, the result of cough-drops and whisky sours, I thought I would dash off a page to you if only to say howdye.—Dr. Clarence Rosser was buried to-day. Lucien, who saw him, said that his beard was iron grey. It is very sad, the way he must have suffered.—I presume Mamma keeps you informed in regard to the neighborhood news. I have been feeling too wobbly in the hind-legs to keep up with it. I went to town last Sunday, the second time since the 28th of January. Evelyn has been very good; he has attended to all of my correspondence, and has put all my papers in shape. In various other ways he has demonstrated his tenderness. He is a son and a brother worth having—if I do say it myself.—Do you know that the last letter you wrote to me was the first genuine letter you ever sent me? There was something in it besides questions not intended to be answered. You are beginning to have thoughts of your own, and although one of the Rogers Brothers says it make the eyebrows tired to think, I hope you will get in the habit of it. As you say, you are nineteen, with nothing to show for it but a beautiful disposition. Though this is not to be sneezed at, yet a good disposition doesn't carry one very far. It is possible to have serious views and intentions without being sad; it is possible to be serious and yet have plenty of fun. If you could see your way clear to taking up some sort of a vocation, even if it is only a fad, you would be happier. Don't think I'm preaching. I am perfectly sure that you will presently find a way of being all that I desire you should be, and therefore I'm giving myself no special concern about it.—Our friends are [cer]tainly exerting themselves to make your visit one long to be remembered. I wish we could give dear Burdeene one-half the pleasure that she and her family are giving you. We are going to do our best, but we'll fall short. But I'm tired now and will close. Love from all to all.

    Your loving *Daddy*

ALS
1 p.
Envelope: Miss Lillian Harris, / 207 West Lake Street, / Canton, Ohio
PM: 4 March 1901

[To Mildred]

                           March 5—night—1901

My deal little gal: You don't know how glad I am to be able to write to you in the old way—with the same old pen, and on the same old paper. I hope you missed my letters. I certainly wanted to write. Every Saturday and Sunday while I was held in bed by weakness that was stronger than

I was, I said to myself—"What a pity I can't write to both of my dear gals! I wonder what they'll think?"—Well, I'm feeling pretty well now. I'm a little weak, and somewhat shaky, as my handwriting will show, but I'm getting stronger every day.—I received your report, and think it is very good indeed. I notice you are surpassing yourself in music, and that is very gratifying. It will be a great consolation to you some day to be able to play the piano well. It will enable you to entertain yourself as well as your friends.—I had a book for the library before I was taken ill, but I can't find it, and so I'll have to get another. I'm afraid Sister Sacred Heart thinks I'm a tough citizen; but it's all due to my talent for procrastination. I have practiced it until it has become a fine art with me. While I was ill, Evelyn went through the hundreds of letters I had placed aside, intending to answer them "to-morow," and he found some very important ones. He worked over them, assorting and answering for nearly two weeks, and now, for the first time in my life, I find the decks cleared (as it were) and everything brought up to date.—There is no news, as usual. Sister Alleen has a very bad sore throat, and seems to be seriously ill. I hope she will be well soon. Julian's baby has had the crup. In fact, every thing seems to look toward sickness.—Mamma forgot to send you the papers last week, but you'll have a double dose of them by Friday. Yet we are sorry if you were disappointed[.] You see we are getting old and wobbly, and our thinking machines are getting rusty.—I have enjoyed your letters to Evelyn very much. The last one was very cute. Evelyn also enjoys them. Some young lady had the item put in the paper, and then telephoned to Evelyn asking if Mrs. Evelyn Harris was in. His reply was "No, she's just gone to a card party." "Oh," says the young lady, "I'm talking to the wrong person." Then Evelyn had to laugh.—The boys are fat and sassy. They have taken breakfast here for two mornings, and they were here all day to-day.—The violets have been outdoing themselves. I never saw so many in my life.—Well, this is a long letter, don't you think? I know I'm fagged out. Love to Bessie, Gretchen and Brownie. I enclose cheque. When you want money let me know. Regards to the sisters.

Your loving
Daddy

ALS

1 p.

Envelope: Miss Mildred Harris, / St. Joseph's Academy, / Washington, *Ga.* / *Wilkes County*

PM: 6 March 1901

March 12, Evening. [1901]

Dear Mildred: I thought I'd just drap in and say howdye. It seems as if I can never get my old habits on me since my illness. They say that a habit becomes second nature. Well, some habits, but not all. Formerly, I never forgot to write to you Saturday or Sunday; but now the time goes by (especially if I am feeling badly) and I never think about writing at all. I feel as if Evelyn had written, and so I make myself contented. Roy and his mother—and Grace are here to-night and I've been playing the Zoonophone [*sic*] for them.—Sister Alleen has been very ill, and is still in bed. The boys are as lively as crickets.—Your letter broke Evelyn all up— he blushed. He isn't angry. The reason he hasn't written is because he is writing what is called "subsidiary editorials" for The Sunny South— you saw it as a supplement to Sunday's Constitution.[1] Evelyn's contributions are in the nature of comments on the events of the week—I forget what the heading is: but there's something about Admiral Sampson and Govnr.[?] Morgan: you can find it. Well, that is the reason Evelyn isn't so prompt in writing this time. He has an arrangement by which he is to work four days in the week—but you know how he is: he will come nearer working ten days in a week than four. He enjoys your letters very much, even if they do make his ears burn occasionally.—I wish you'd ask Sister Sacred Heart if the committee will permit me to contribute $10 to Father O'Brien's monument.—Were some flowers received from Mrs. Lynch, of Canton, for Sister De Sales funeral? Lillian telegraphed here for $10 worth to be sent, and Evelyn gave the order to a florist.—I hope the flowers arrived all right.—Mr. Rosser is having a new 2-story house built on the corner of Culberson and Gordon, opposite our big gate.—Charles is sick in bed at his home. It seems that all our relations are in the way of getting ill. Indeed, some of us (you and I) are ill when we are well.—J.C. has joined the Y.M.C.A. gymnasium, and he thinks he is IT.—The O'Donnelly's have moved in, and they are as quiet as a dead chicken in a trash-pile.—I believe that's all.—I'm getting stronger by fits and starts. I'd be all right if I could control my appetite. Love to Bessie, Gretchen and Brownie, and regards to the sisters.

Your loving

Daddy [sketch profile of his head]

ALS

1 p.

Envelope: Miss Mildred Harris, / St. Joseph's Academy, / Washington, / Wilkes County, Ga. / Ga. R.R.

PM: 13 March 1901

1. The *Sunny South* became the nucleus of *Uncle Remus's Magazine*.

[To Lillian]

March 13, Evening. [1901]

Dear Bill: Mamma received a letter from Burdeene to-day. The poor child thinks she's going to put us to some trouble, and she takes advantage of our recent illness to try to get out of coming. I didn't know she'd treat sick folks that way. We were very ill, but we are both all right now— especially mamma—who goes to town shopping just as usual. She feels a little tired afterwards, but she soon recovers. My illness was severer than hers, and at one time I was too weak to think. I don't go to town every day, but the reason I am not going this week is because I was sum- moned on Judge Calhoun's jury, and had to get Dr. Crowe to give me a certificate. Consequently, I have to live up to the certificate. I could go to town very well, and will begin next week. All of which is the same as saying that, while it was very thoughtful of Burdeene and very kind of her to write, nevertheless, she will put Mama and myself to bed if she begins to entertain an idea that she will be in the way in this house. We need her and you to make us perfectly well. There is to be no change in her programme and yours. I'll be strong and hearty by the time you both reach home.—Alleen is better. She is able to sit up a little.—Charles is in bed at his home, but he also is better. Alleen has been without a cook for some weeks, and "Muddy" has had to do the cooking. The poor girl has had a hard time.—Mr. Rosser is building a two-story house oppo-

site our big gate, and you and Burdeene can run over there and play.—
By the by, when are you coming home? It is time for you to be thinking about it. You will need some money—how much? Let me know in
time.—I stay about the house so much that I have no news. Evelyn has
gone to work on the Sunday supplement of The Constitution. It is called
The Sunny South. He writes the subsidiary editorials, which are in the
nature of comments on passing events. All send love to all.

    Your loving

      Daddy

ALS
1 p.
Envelope: Miss Lillian Harris, / 207 West Lake Street, / Canton, *Ohio*
PM: 14 March 1901

[To Lillian]

Saturday Evening, 23rd
March. [1901]

Dear Willy:

    I am well now, and feeling gay, but somehow when I begin to write
a letter my mind becomes a perfect blank. I'd like to know why it is.
Perhaps the grip has destroyed my letter-writing faculty, if I had any.—
I am enclosing a cheque for $35 payable to Mr. Biechele. Evelyn says
that it will be enough to buy your ticket, berth, and leave some over. If
it isn't enough, send me a telegram and I'll increase the amount.—I hear
in a roundabout way that Burdeene threatens to return to Canton from
Lexington. I presume it is a joke—anyhow, you'd better not come without her.—The only news I know is that Alleen is still puny, and Charles
ailing, and Mrs. Warner has returned a book she borrowed. Also we
still have the Friesland hen with us. She makes so much fuss when she
lays that a casual observer would think she did it with her little cackle.
Evelyn is now working on the Sunny South, writing the subsidiary editorials—be jigged if I don't believe I told you that before.—The cook
still walks about on her ankles, and Sophia keeps the house warm.[1]—
The weather is like a wooden-legged man. It walks softly with one foot,

and comes down—*plunk!*—with the other[.] One day is nice and the next is ice.—I'm trying to write on my story, which, I fear, is going to be a failure. It hasn't got the go to it that it should have. I tell you what, gal, the grip business is enough to give literature a black eye. It's a good thing Shakespeare didn't have the grippe.—There isn't any home news; there never is, nowadays, when I start to write a letter. Every interesting thing escapes out of my mind like a rat out of a trap, and runs under the bed, or in the closet, or hides under the rug.—Chloë has never been to see Mamma: she even stopped sending for the slops. Such is life on a Southern plantation.—I suppose Julian and Julia are all right; I haven't heard from them in a day or two. It's the same thing all the time; they are both overworked, and both are tired. Julia doesn't look well at all. The baby is still delicate, and every zephyr gives him a fresh cold.— J.C. is not well. He is ready to cry if you look at him; he has a bad cold, and every day there is a pain over his right eye. I tell you we have been having hot times[.] Mamma sends love to all, and so do I[.]

> Your loving
> Daddy

ALS
3 pp.
Envelope: Miss Lillian Harris, / 207 West Lake Street, / Canton, *Ohio*
PM: 24 March 1901
1. Sophia, JCH's name for the furnace. See earlier letter.

[To Lillian]

[25 March 1901]

Dear Bill: I sealed up the letter and had it mailed, and then I suddenly remembered that I had forgotten to enclose the aforesaid cheque. So here it is.

> Your loving
> Daddy

ALS
1 p.
Envelope: Miss Lillian Harris, / Care E. A. Biechele, Esq., / 207 West Lake Street, / Canton, *Ohio*
PM: 25 March 1901

[To Mildred]

> Atlanta, Sunday,
> Sometime in March.
> [25 March 1901]

Hello, My Baby, How 'do!

Which means that I'm pretty well I thank you, though not quite as strong as I used to be. I feel that if I were to live fifty years longer, I'd be quite an old man—and there's nothing about the feeling to cause exultation. Evelyn says he wrote you a regular love-letter to-day. He's getting to be very sassy, which is a sign that his health is better. He seems to enjoy his work on The Sunny South Supplement. He has time to call on the gals and to go to the theatre. Nothing spoils him. He's a great guyer, but he's the best boy I ever saw. He has the tenderest heart and the highest principles of any boy I ever knew.—That reminds me of a tale that Mark Twain told me, a long time ago, about a railroad agent, who "had a harelip and a pure heart." I have forgotten the story itself, but the "harelip and pure heart" has stuck in my memory. As usual, all the news has broke its string and escaped, and I don't know where to find it.—J.C. is rather puny. He has had a bad cold in the head, a bad cough, and now he has a pain over his eye every day at certain hours. I haven't seen Marguerite for sometime, but she's alive and well.—Mamma doesn't know whether she's well or not. Sometimes she is, and then again, she aint, and that's about the way I feel. The fact is we're both getting old and wobbly. When we sit down we don't want to get up, and when we get up we want to flop right down again.—The frieslin' hen has been sent to Georgia's, where there's another frieslin chicken. We had a hen for dinner to-day, and the cook fried her. I tried to eat of this feast, but I had to fall back on J.C.'s rubber ball. I sliced it up, put a little butter and mustard on it, and made a very hearty meal. Compared to the old hen it was as tender as a fried egg.—Alleen is not very well, but she's better 'n she has been. Essie is well and Charles is on the lift.—The weather has been cutting up queer capers. One day it is hot and another day it is cold, and Sophia, the furnace, groans under this inconsistency.—Dan C. and Ed L. [Latham?] came out this afternoon and carried Evelyn off with them. Providence was with us in this, for we didn't have anything for supper but fragments of the fried hen, all as hard as a cow's horn.—It's been drizzling all day so that Mama couldn't go to church. We've been warned so often of a danger of a relapse, and Evelyn is so nervous about it that we hardly dare put our noses out of the door. I haven't been to town but four times since the 29th of January. Don't you think that's worse than going to school? I know of a gal who, if she continues to make high marks in music, is going to have a big surprise before long. I mention no names—nuff ced till Easter. Regards to the Sisters and love to Bessie, Gretchen and Brownie.

Your loving

Daddy

ALS

4 pp./ 1 folded sheet, front and back

Envelope: Miss Mildred Harris, / St. Joseph's Academy, / Washington, Ga. / *Wilkes County.*

PM: 25 March 1901

[To Lillian]

[1 April 1901]

Aprile the 1-eye—

Evening: 7:40

Feeling that you would be able to spare a few moments from Maurice, and Fred, and William Henry, I seat and reseat myself, dear Bill, to drop you a few lines in regard to Matters and things about which I know nothing. Evelyn had E. Lowry and Fred Lewis to tea. I used to know Fred long ago, when he was a boy—he's about 22 now—and it turns out that he's Harry Lewis's brother. Fred is on the Constitution now, and he's all sorts of a clever chap except the wrong sort. Julian also came out to-day with Julia.—Mamma was just now showing the Uncle Remus crockery to the boys.[1] True to his advance notices and the declarations on his handbills, the distinguished author modestly retired to his own room, fell into a chair, and began to compose a letter to his travelled daughter. The audience, understanding the joke, applauded wildly and tried hard to recall him before the curtain. Feeling that to respond to the Encore would Ruin everything and Expose the Hollow Mockery in Which his

Modesty is Kept Sizzling Hot, he remained in his room, although he was strongly tempted to go in the sitting-room and boldly claim that he was the author of the crockery as well as the books. But his strong will prevailed, and he refrained from showing himself again. (However, Fred and Ed came in a moment ago, and I read them the foregoing. Strange to say, they regarded it as a Good Joke and Laughed Heartily.)—But, honestly, there is no news here—except this: that Mr. Clasidy [?] died suddenly last night.—The violets have been and still are simply gorgeous. We have never had so many and such large ones. I hope there will be some left when you two gals get home.—I think I'll send this letter to Lexington. It wont [sic] leave here till to-morrow afternoon, and would reach Canton after you had gone. If I send it to Lexington, it will be there when you arrive. Nuff ced.—And, by-the-by, that expresses it exactly. I can't think of anything that would interest you. We have been having some tremendous storms and rains, and the three cats are still with us. It rained yesterday, but to-day has been fine, chilly enough to have a smouldering fire in the furnace.—I'm about half through my story, having written forty-odd thousand words in spite of my illness. But it's no good; I can't write a long story. I put all my strength in the episodes and leave the thread of the main story hanging at loose ends.—I've been reading "My New Curate," "Gosta Berling," and a French Catholic romance—the first being one of the best books I ever read.[2]

Regards to all, and love to B.B.

Your loving

Daddy

ALS

1 p.

Envelope: Miss Lillian Harris,[3] / St. Joseph's Academy, / Washington, *Ga.* / *Wilkes county* / Ga. R. R.

PM: 3 April 1899

1. Reference to a set of brown pottery ice cream dishes with scalloped edges and rubbed gold decoration made by Rookwood Pottery Co. (est. 1884); individual Uncle Remus scenes are painted on each. Six of these were given to Joel Chandler Harris Collection, SC, EU, in 1986 by Mrs. Mildred Wright, daughter of Mildred Harris Camp.

2. Patrick Augustine Sheehan (1852–1913), *My New Curate* (1900), a popular novel and play; Selma Lagerlöf, *The Story of Gösta Berling* (1898).

3. Contents suggest that this is not the original envelope and that the letter is later than 1899; *cf.* copyright date (1900) of *My New Curate* in note 2.

[To Mildred]

April 2-eye, 1901-eye.

Dear Tommus: I didn't write Sunday night because I had to write some letters that had been put off and put off until they could be postponed no longer, and certainly not shorter; one was to Uncle Jamesy.[1]—Since I've come to think it over, you'll have three surprises, two in one, and one by itself. Riddle me the riddle.—Say to the Sister who was astonished by the Bap. Pub. Co. that it was mamma who did the wrapping. Paxon had given me some of his office paper to use in my type writer when it was new and before I had bought any paper of my own.[2] I don't know where Mamma found it; but she's always piroutin' [sic] around in strange corners and cuddies. She has cleaned house four times since she got well, and is now able to walk forty miles a day, carrying a rag and a dusting brush.—I know of no news, except that Mrs. Rosser is having a hard time with neuralgia.—All the family are well. I'm a little short-winded, but aside from that my health is as good as ever it was. I need more exercise, but haven't been able to take much, owing to the bad weather. Up here it rains half the time, and when the sun is shining, the wind is blowing hard: But every thing will be all right some day, especially toward the last of June. We have been (and are still) having oodles upon oodles of violets. To-day it is raining and an east wind is blowing, but when the weather is fine, the people going along the street have to stop and look at the violets, the display is so fine. The girls around and about have tried hard to pick all of them, but Sunday, when the sun was shining, the walks and border were literally blue with blooms.— Evelyn enjoys your letters so much that he—however, that's another story.—The little boys come down every day, especially if they think there are apples in the pantry. T'other little boy comes out to see us occasionally.—Mamma is fixing up a box of Easter goodies. I suppose it is intended for some one; but she simply sorts over the things and looks wise. It will be funny if she sends it to Bill, for Bill has been having such a good time that she doesn't want an easter box. Well—my regards to the sisters and my love to Bessie, Gretchen, and Brownie.

Your loving

Daddy

ALS

1 p.

Envelope: Miss Mildred Harris, / St. Joseph's Academy, / Washington, Ga. / *Wilkes County*

PM: 3 April 1901

1. James Whitcomb Riley.

2. *Cf.* reference to Paxon's store in letter to Lillian, 6 October [1900].

[To Mildred]

Big Rain Day:

April 13, 1901

I didn't write to you last week, sweet girl, because I sent Evelyn, and he was ever so much better than any letter: he was, as you may say, the real thing, including that sweet little mustache. We are all proud of that mustache; it's the only one we have in the family except mine, which is beginning to fade, as all beautiful things must. But Evelyn's is young and fresh and tender, so much so that a breath of frost would wither it.— Would you believe it? Lillian will not be home till Tuesday! In some way she has coaxed Mrs. Roberts to write, and Mr. Roberts to telegraph, begging that she be allowed to remain until Tuesday, so as to see Jefferson— and all the rest of the boys. Of course, I said yes—I always do on such occasions. I am looking for another letter or telegram Monday asking me to let her go back to Canton; and I'll say yes, of course: what else is there for an old man to do?—If there's any news here I haven't heard of it; it has performed the usual feat of getting under the bedl [sic] The Rossers have a new telephone, and now Luther and Julia can converse with the rest of the world to their hearts' content.—Judging from her letters, Bill has been having royal times on her triumphal march through the west; she is particular to mention the names of all the young men she meets, and the list is quite a formidabke [sic] one. Both she and Burdeene will doubtless sigh for the good times, but they know what to expect here, and they'll have to settle down to crochet or embroidery, or something of that kind.—Evelyn seemed to enjoy his trip very much; But [sic] on the train coming back, he relieved a weary lady of the care of her baby, a very lively kid, and he was somewhat fagged out when he reached home.—

He told us—Oh, shucks! I don't like this kind of type at all. [Change
in typewriter face.] There! that is better—he told us that you certainly
needed some new skirts; and Mamma has been bestirring herself to get
them. By all means you should let your mother know when you need
anything, even if it's a scolding!—Charles has been on the jury all the
week, and last night he had to be locked up because the other fellows
wouldn't agree with him. Essie stayed over here, and is here now.—The
kids in both ends of town are well and happy. Brother Lucien has improved greatly, both in health and in conduct; I mean by that that he is
no longer afraid of evrybody [sic] he meets. He is trying hard to talk,
and can say a few words. So his grandmother says; to me his talk sounds
more like the grunting of a satisfied pig, and in fact that is the way all
baby talk sounds to me when they are first beginning.—Charles has just
returned, and Essie has been chewing his ear; it is thought here that she
is really fond of him—at least that is the report. His experience on the
jury is much the same as mine, except that he is younger, and can stand
it better. Essie is going to have her Club here next Thursday, and Alleen
is to have a reception in honor of Burdeene; she has already made out
her list of invitations.—It has been raining hard all day, and the weather
is gloomy enough to suit the sickest kind of a man. As for me, I am well,
and refuse to feel gloomy in spite of the invitation the weather is extending me.—It is rumored here that J.C. and Marguerite are at outs, but I
think the report is exaggerated, for he was carrying violets to her by the
armful last week. The violets are nearly all gone now, but we have had
them in sufficient quantities to satisfy the most greedy—we've had 'em
by the bushel.—The new Rosser house on the corner opposite our big
gate is to be occupied by the Spratlings, who used to live in one of the
Daniel houses on Lee street. Confidentially, they say that the Spratling
boy is a very handsome young fellow. Should this prove to be the case,
we'll have him over when you return.—I can't help feeling sorry for Bill
and Burdeene. When they get here and find every thing so dull and old
fogy, they'll feel like two pieces of banana peeling. Well, they'll have to
get used to it. When they get too gloomy, we'll enliven them up by giving
them permission to go to the cemetary for a walk.—Our new neighbors
are very quiet, the O'Donnellys, I mean. You'd never know that anybody

lived in the house. That suits me to a T. They say that Miss nell [sic] is a very nice, sweet girl. She's the only one of the family I have seen stirring about.—I see some mistakes in this, but you'll have to correct them yourself, for it's too much trouble to go over the whole thing. If you'll count the words, you'll see that this letter is nearly twice as long as those I write with a pen.—Well, give my regards to the Sisters, and my love to Bessie, Gretchen and Brownie.

Your loving
DADDY

TL
1 p.
Envelope: Miss Mildred Harris, / St. Joseph's Academy, / Washington, Ga. / *Wilkes County.*
PM: 13 April 1901

[To Mildred]

Wes' Een, Ga.:

Aprile Twenty-eight, 1901

Dear Tommus: If you'll skuzen pen and ink, I'll try to drop you a line for to let you know that we are all pretty well at this time and hope that your base-ball bruises are healed by this time. My advice to all who play base-ball is that they should never get in front of a ball unless they are going to catch it. It seems that you had your hands in your pockets— but you caught it nevertheless; did you catch it hard enough to make you cry? You know the old saying: A woman cries twice after she's forty for every tear she sheds between fourteen and twenty.—The girls seem to be enjoying themselves to a certain extent. The boys are calling right along, and yerking 'em out to the theatre. They had a box party at the Columbia the other night, and Evelyn was with Miss Newman. The girls said they enjoyed it immensely. The plays there are of the melodramatic variety, taken from dime novels. You can imagine what fun it was to the girls. My private opinion is that they really enjoyed the blood and thunder stuff—I know I used to enjoy it when a boy. Burdeene spent one night at Cary's and had to borrow a nickel to get back home: she went off and forgot her purse. Several of the girls have called, including Miss Leila Culberson.—Did I tell you I was sitting for my portrait, which is to be placed in the boy's [sic] high school?[1] Mr. Field, the artist, is painting it. He comes out in the afternoons, and then I have to brace up and look purty for an hour and a half[.] It's mighty hard work, but he won't be painting all the year.—I thought I had my story nearly finished, but I am afraid that I'll have to work it all over again. It doesn't sound right; I haven't hit the right key somehow. That comes of writing a story at somebody else's suggestion.—The weather is beautiful to-day, just the kind you'd like to have all the time. It is neither too hot nor too cold. You can be perfectly comfortable in the house, or on the porch, or out of doors. When I was out in the yard just now, I heard a catbird singing softly, and peculiarly. I watched her a moment, and soon found that she was building her nest in the Chinese quince tree, for she flew down, still singing, and picked up some feathers, and went into the tree again, singing all the time. This cat-bird is the only lady I know who can sing with her mouthful of building material. I suppose all the birds are nesting by this time. As for the Plague-taked English sparrows, they've been laying and hatching ever since Christmas. I wish there was a hawk big enough to get them in a corner and catch them all at once. I saw a thush [sic] to-day. I mean thrush, of course.—The tennis-court is rigged up and the girls rose at six Friday, (no, Saturday) morning to play. When they came in to breakfast, you could have put them in a cigar-boxx [sic], they were so limp and tired. Yet, they felt better all day as the result of the morning exercise.—But I hardly think they will try it again.—Burdeene and Evelyn are on the front porch now making believe to quarrel. The young bachelor is a famous tease, and he keeps the girls in hot water, though I don't see why they take him so seriously.—We had spring lamb with mint sauce to-day, and it was very fine; also the inevitable chicken dumpling, or pie, or whatever you choose to call it.—The strawberry vines are covered with blossoms, and if there is a berry wherever there is a bloom, we'll certainly have oodles of strawberries; but I'm afraid they'll all be gone when you get home. That is the trouble about these summer schools—but never mind: you have only six or seven more years to go, and then you'll be home when strawberries are in season. However, you'll be here in time for the green apples, and I've already ordered a supply of paregoric and vermifuge. The trees are simply one mass of blooms.—The children are all well, and the weather is so fine that it takes two or three people to keep up with the two boys.—The city is going to put down a new sidewalk for me, and it's going to cost money. Mamma is already looking gloomy for fear her pin money will be cut off. But I tell her to brace up, for I don't have to pay for the sidewalk all at once. It is consoling to know that all the property owners out in West End have to put down new walks, or widen the new ones, so that we have company in our supposed troubles. The truth is I am glad it is to be done, for my sidewalk has long been a disgrace to the family.—All are well and all send love. My regards to the Sisters, and love to B., G. and B.

> Your loving
> DADDY.

More boys were out to-night: Mr. Brooks came and brought his bass voice tied up in a handkerchief. When he turned it loose there was trouble in the air. I enclose check for music.[2]

TL
1 p.
1. Atlanta Boys High School.
2. Handwritten postscript.

[To Mildred]

Five of May, 1901

Deear Tommus:

You will notice the two e's in "Dear"; well, I didn't go to do it. It just happened so. It seems that this machine has its own way of spelling, and I can't help myself. In fact, I don't try; I just let her go ahead and do her own spelling.—As usual, there is no news, except that we found a stray horse in the lot this morning, and Charles turned him into the pasture. He is there now, taking a nap. He is a tall, long-legged horse, and looks as if he had seen service.—The kittens are coming on finely, and Lucien's Marechal Neil roses are gorgeous.—J.C. is trying hard to play baseball, but he isn't making much headway. You will have to give him some points when you come home; you'll have to learn him how to Pitch, and how to catch a ball. His team got licked ten to five yesterday.—Fritz has been down to play tennis two mornings, but I haven't seen him to give him your messages.—The girls are having a good deal of company, such as it is. Walter Ormond called to see them yesterday afternoon. He is Sidney's brother, and is a very lively chap. Miss Nora Belle Stark and Miss Emily Harrison called yesterday.—Sister Sacred Heart sent her notes too late for Burdeene; for that restless kid couldn't be happy until she finished her essay. She went at it like a whirlwind, dashed it off, and had it mailed before you could say Jack Robinson with your mouth open.—Bessie's verses were good, and I hope she will continue to prac-tise such exercises. She seems to have a talent that way, and it may develop into something worth while. She's a mighty smart girl, and it's pleasant to know that she remembers me once in awhile.—I picked two ripe strawberries out of the garden yesterday, but if we don't have some rain soon, the thousands of green ones will not amount to much. But the roses are beginning to bloom for all they are worth, and they are a great deal better than the strawberries. You can taste one strawberry only once, but a rose will last you two hours or more; and if you will pet it up a little, it will last you two whole days.—Rawson Collier came out last evening, and the girls had a game of whist. Bill is getting so she plays pretty well, but she and Rawson were defeated last night by Evelyn and Burdeene.—The weather has been fine here for several days, and the leaves on the trees have come out wonderfully. Everything is beautiful, or, as the girls say, just grand, and it is worth while to be out of doors and become a part of the procession, as it were.—Julian's baby came out to see us the other day, and spent the afternoon. he' [sic] weasly, but awful cute, and is beginning to talk. It's funny that he never forgets me. He'll come to me when he wont [sic] go to any one else but his nurse; and he smiles at me every time he sees me, as much as to say, "You think I don't know you, but I'll show you!" The t'other kids are all well, and as rude as ever. They can make more fuss than a circus train.—This morning, the girls, in order to be entirely fashionable, went to church on the other side, where they have good music, and a congregation that is willing to contribute something to the support of the Church. On this side, the congregation is too stingy for anything. The priests are compelled to lecture them every Sunday; but lecturing does no good; they give no more after the lecture than they did before.—Mama has been on the grunt again. She had a bad headache yesterday, and was frowning all day; and you'll not wonder at it when you once have the sick headache. Otherwise everybody is well. The warm weather just suits me, and I am feeling fine.—I don't see much of Marguerite these days, but she's just as sweet as ever.—Mamma bought some spring chickens the other day, and one of them is already beginning to lay; which shows that Mamma is a fine judge of fancy poultry.—Bill has already begun to complain about the heat, and as she always complains to me I suppose I'll have to move away before the summer is over. She is warm only in her mind.— Well, I've about come to the end of my rope. My regards to the Sisters, and my love to B., G., and B.[1]

      Your loving

      Daddy

TLS

1 p.

1. Initials refer to Brownie, Gretchen, and Bessie, Mildred's school chums at Saint Joseph's Academy. See earlier letters where they are named.

[To Mildred]

          May the Twelve 1901.

No matter how hard I might try, dear Tommus, it would be impossible for me to send you a letter as large and interesting as Mamma, and you now have her with you. I know you are pleased, and I hope you were surprised: it is so nice to have a pleasant surprise; it makes you feel ticklish all over, because you don't know what is coming next.— As for news, why Mamma will tell you more than I could think of in a wek [sic]. She seems to keep it in her mind, and all she has to do is to lift the lid, and out it pops. The truth is, there is really no reason for me to write you a letter this week. I venture to say that, with Mamma to whisper in your ear, you know more about what has happened here the past week than I do, for I can't keep up with the little things—except the kittens; and I couldn't hardly keep up with them the other day. They disappeared and couldn't be found; but after everybody had tried to find them I tilted my hat on the side of my head, and went down into the cellar, and found them at once. They were hiding behind some old junk.—Miss Newman came out last night with a Mr. Jones. I thought from his name that he was a foreigner, but he speaks better English than I do; so I judge he has been in this country some time. Miss N. is a very bright young woman, and in some ways reminds me of you.—I sometimes think Burdeene is a little homesick, but she says not. Anyhow, she has spells of seriousness. Otherwise, she seems to be having a fairly good time. The neighborhood girls have been very kind. Several have called, and Miss Newman has done her best.—We have had greenpeas [sic] from the garden three times, and the strawberries are coming in nicely. Some of them are very large; but I'm afraid they'll all be gone when you get home. However, you'll have plenty of green apples and salt, and maybe I'll buy you a nickel's worth of candy, and give you a piece of chewing gum.—It has been trying to rain this afternoon, but it hasn't succeeded very well; it—I wonder what that "it" stands for?—will have to try again. But there was one big clap of thunder; it sent Burdeene to bed, and took all the starch out of Bill. The telephone was ringing just now, and she wouldn't go near it. She insisted that the lightning was playing with it.—You will have to teach J.C. how to play base ball [sic] when you come home. He belongs to a little team which gets beat every time it plays. Charley Goodman is the manager.—I see Marguerite occasionally, and she's always smiling. There's nothing more becoming to a girl than a genuine smile. I hope you'll bring home a supply with you, enough to last till you go back to your dear lessons—This typewriter is like a woman; it runs right along in its conversation, and doesn't give me time to put in a period.—We have had the usual supply of cat-birds, and also a couple—doesn't it look funny to divide that word [In ms., "coup-" ends a line and "le" begins another.]?—of thrushes. The cat-birds have discovered that the strawberries are good to eat, and they have left their autograph on some of the largest.—Speaking of autographs, I think you asked me to send you one for one of your friends. Well, I'll enclose it

with this if I don't forget it by the time this letter is finished. I hope
it is some young person that wants it, for I never will believe that any
grown person can [care] for the autograph of a cornfield author.—Well,
I have written more than I know, and I reckon it is about time to close
the blinds and feed the canary bird. Mamma left him in my charge, and
I have turned him over to Bill.—Everybody is well; in other words all
are able to eat their allowance. The kids are doing as well as could be
expected. My regards to the sisters, and love to B., B., and G.

Your loving
DADDY.

TL
1 p.
Envelope: Miss Mildred Harris, / St. Joseph's Academy, / Washington, *Ga.* / Wilkes
County.
PM: 13 May 1901

[To Mildred]

Atlanta, Ga.:
May 19, 1901

Dear Tommus:

I hear in a roundabout way that you have decided to sweat it out in
Washinton-Wilkes [sic] until afer [sic] the Jubilee. Well, you can do as
you please about that; you have the option of coming home the first of
June, or staying until the affair is over. But if you come home you can't
go back with the girls when they go; you will have to stay at home with
your poor old Daddy. I am giving Mamma the right of way this time.
She enjoys such things very much—and, anyhow, the girls will have to
be accompanied by a chaperone if they are to stay at the hotel. I may
come down one day; but I dislike very much to go away and leave the
house in other hands. Invariably it happens that some dispute arises,
or something goes wrong.—Stewart fell out of a swing this morning,
and split a gash just atove [sic] his right eyebrow. It happened while
Lucien and Alleen were at the Methodist church, and there was nobody to do anything until Mamma went up quite by accident. He and
Chandler were playing at the negro houses behind our place, having

been carried there by their nurse, who is not much bigger than Stewart. I am not surprised that he was hurt, but I am surprised that he hasn't broken his neck long ago. But you know the old saying—Providence looks after drunk men and children.—I presume the girls are having a pretty good time; at any rate, they look as if they had both been on a spree. Lillian is to have some kind of a party next Wednesday, and she and Burdeene are looking forward to it with many anticipations. Bill has invited about twenty-six, and thus far all she has heard from have accepted.—We have strawberries every day, some of them very fine. If we could get a little rain, we'd have thousands, and the flowers would be finer, and evrybody'd [sic] feel better, though I don't know of anybody around here who is feeling badly. In fact, we are all well, though Mamma had another spell the first of the week. She's all right now. The reason the girls look so puny is because they have been gadding about a good deal and sitting up late.—J.C. still thinks he can play baseball, and he seems to be considerably stuck on the game; he wants to go to all the college games that are played here. The Tech. has a very fine team this year; the pitcher gets down to his work like a professional.[1] He struck out eleven men in the game yesterday.—Oh, I forgot to tell you! Julian is thinking about building on his lot. In fact, he is having plans maxe [sic] for a nice house. Rawson is going to marry a nice little yankee gal, and he is going to housekeepimg [sic] on his own hook.[2] I think the plan is to vacate the Collier house, and rent it out.—John and the little girls will live with Julian, and henrietta [sic] and Charlie with Rawson. At least that is the plan now; but I don't know whether it will be carried out. Marguerite says that she and you are going to give a party when you get back—a party that will be a stunner.—Mma [sic] enjoyed her little trip very much; and I know she'll relish coming down again commencement week. She is very fond of such outings, while I much prefer to stay where I can see the lawn and the flowers, and hear the birds, and run the chickens out, and chunk old Ovid out of the violet beds.— Those dogs are a perfect sight. They have been fighting with other dogs ever since the beginning of Spring—if we have had any Spring—and they have a very disreputable appearance.—The girls had a new caller the other night—young Mr. Sprat Hooklin, and also a Dr. Adair, whose

head is about the size of a chinquepin. Oh, pshaw! I've got the first fellow's name wrong; it is Hook Spratlin, and his pa lives just across the
streetin [sic] Mr. Rosser's new house.—It has begun to rain a little since
I set down to write this letter, and it is to be hoped that it will keep up
the lick until far into the night.—Well, I am coming to the limits of my
letter, and I have written nothing that will either amuse or instruct you;
nor have I given you any news. In fact, I grow duller and duller every
week. Regards to the Sisters, and love to B., G. and B.—Dr. Crowe came
and took two stitches in the gash over Stewart's eye.[3]

> Your loving
> Daddy

TLS

1 p.

Envelope: Miss Mildred Harris, / St. Joseph's Academy, / Washington, *Ga.,* / Wilkes
County. / Ga. R.R.

PM: 20 May 1901

1. Georgia Tech, or more correctly Georgia Institute of Technology.

2. Rawson Collier was the brother of Julia Collier Harris.

3. Last sentence—handwritten.

[To Mildred]

> Next Door to Atlanta, Ga.,
> 26 May, 1901

Dear Tommus:

Your imaginary ball of electricity probably frightened you as badly as
if it had been real. I'm glad that Mamma wasn't there, for she grows in
fear of lightning. I tell her that a woman of her age should set an example to those who are younger; but she says she doesn't want to make
her hair any grayer than it is by trying to set an example that nobody
would follow.—Well, Bill had her party, and everybody says it was quite
a success. They would say that in any event, but we all believe 'em, and
snuggle up to oneanother [sic], and feel proud. Bill was frightened the
whole time, and looked like the kitten in the picture that sees a rat for
the first time, and doesn't know whether to grab it, or tuck tail and run.
The affair was supposed to be in pink, and I have been seeing red ever

since. They had red ice-cream moulded in the shape of roses, and red cakes of s [sic] size to suit the delicate appetites of the dear young ladies. You—or I—could put four in your or my mouth at a time, and never know they were there. I have no idea what they painted the ice-cream with. It must have been some sort of an innocent stain, for I have not heard of any cholera morbus as the result of eating it. All the young ladies remained long enough to say that they had a very enjoyable time. Now that Bill has had a party, I suppose you must have one; and then J.C. will cry if he doesn't have one. Heigh-ho! you'll never know the cares of a father until you become one.—Marguerite has been over to look at the pictures, and she says her mouth will water till you come home.—We have a new Mildred—Mildred Spratlin, who is about as large as Marguerite. She seems to be a very nice girl.—J.C. is having a hard time with Sister Alphonsus. She doesn't seem to understand the boys, and the boys don't understand her, and so there's a perfect mixture of misunderstandings. He thinks he's imposed upon, and I have no doubt that the good Sister is of the opinion that she's imposed upon. I wouldn't be a teacher for a million dollars a year. It is the most trying position that can be imagined. You should remember that, and try not to worry your teachers. If you'll just sit down a moment and think of all they have to go through, and all they have to endure from so any divferent [sic] persons, I am sure you will have more consideration for their nerves. The reason I mention this is because I sometimes see you have low marks for behavior in the school-room. You have done pretty well, but when you come to think about the matter, you will agree with me that there is not much excuse for not conforming to the rules.—J.C. belongs to a new baseball club called the Diamond Hustlers. His club was defeated yesterday 20 to 2, and when he came home, with "D.H." sewed on his manly bosom in letters of white, we all wanted to know if they stood for Dead Heads. Sister Julia wants him to go with John and Charles to Porter Spring, and I supposed we'll have to let him go.[1]—The boys continue to come out and smoke my cigars, and the girls continue to go to the matinee. Burdeene says she is having a fine time, but there is a kind of tired look about her which xeems [sic] to say that she'd like very much to be at home or at Lexington. She nearly fainted the other day, when her Aunt Jean wrote to say that she could probably stay until some time in July. Poor child! she's in for it, and don't know how to get out of it. However, her Oxford trip and her visit to Washinton [sic], which she is looking forward to with great impatience, will be a sort of relief for her. But for these events, she would actually pine away, and we'd have to call in the doctor.—You can't tell about Bill. She saws wood and says nothing. She doesn't talk much; in fact, she doesn't talk as much as she use used [sic] to. I am beginning to believe she is in love, and I don't know whether it is Dan Cary, or one of the street car conductors. I am giving her Swamp Root as an antidote, and though she has been taking it for some days, it doesn't seem to have much effect. She still has that far-away look in her eyes, as if she were trying to find a rhyme for dove. Did you ever try to find a rhyme for dove? They say all the girls try when they get old enough to spell words of ten syllables. Burdeene has found the rhyme. She says it came to her in Lexington. She wasn't thinking about it at the time, and it came to her so suddenly that she thought some one had hit her with a rock, and she had to go in a drug store and order something cool. Bill has had her head washed. She seems to think that this will help her to find the rhyme. Do you think it will?—Our neighbor in the Bunker house is adding two stories to the rear. And since there is so much building going on, I have been thinking of getting Cora a wooden leg. I don't know what architect I'll engage, but if she is to have a wooden leg, I think it should be in the old Colonial style—something elegant and yet simple.—Ah, well! if I run on this way, the good Sisters will think that I am frivolous, and I wouldn't have them to think that for the world. Distribute my regards and my love, as usual, or as the merchants say, as per invoice.

Your loving
DADDY.

TL
2 pp.
Envelope: Return to Box 111 / Atlanta, Ga. / Miss Mildred Harris, / St. Joseph's Academy, / Washington, Ga. / *Wilkes County.*
PM: 27 May 1901

1. "Porter Springs, a post-hamlet and noted summer resort of Lumpkin county, is about eight miles north of Dahlonega. Lula is the most convenient railroad station" (Candler 3:116).

[To Mildred]

Atlanta, Ga.: June the One-Eye. [1901]

Dear Tommus:

Though goodness knows that I want to see you, yet I am glad you concluded to stay over for the Commencement and Jubilee exercises. The option I gave you was a sort of test. I wanted to see if you were really taking an interest in the affairs of the school; and it is really very gratifying to me to know that you are willing to forego your own natural desire to come home, in order that you may be able to help out in the programme. You say that you want to stay because you are curious to see what the affair is to be like. Well, curiosity is one form of interest. You wouldn't be curious about it if you were not interested in it.—As usual the news takes wing as soon as I get astraddle of my type-writing machine. Evelyn has been to Memphis and has returned. He says he had a good time, but that I doubt very capitally, for I don't see how any-body can have a good time in the midst of such a crowd as that which gathers at these reunions. I never have been able to have a good time in a large crowd. I always want to get away and run home to my own house.—Cannon Forbes has come to take dinner, and Mamma says she don't know what he will think when he sees what we have to live on.— Cora's rheumatism flew from her feet to her hands, and she had to give up and go home. (Be switched if I haven't dated this letter wrong. It should be June the Two-eye. Anyhow, today is Sunday.) Well, Cora had to quit cooking several days ago, and Mamma had to go in the kitchen, where shae [sic] has been every day until to-day. This morning bright and early, a woman came to hire, and Charlie put her to work in the kitchen. She had already promised to come. She is said to be colored, but she is nearly white. She looks exactly like a Georgia cracker. Her name is Octavia, and I judge from the sound of the name that we are about to get into high society, so as far as cooks are concerned. Mamma seemed to enjoy he [sic] experience in the kitchen. She rose at six, G.M., [sic] and went out, and such a rattling of pots and pans you never heard in all your born days. Then, when the rattling was over, she'd begin to sing. I thought I was the only person in the country who had an appetite for singing before breakfast; but Mamma showed that she could not only sing louder, but better. My private opinion is that she made the racket because she wanted to wake up evrybody [sic] in the house, but it would be injudicious to make such a suggestion where Mamma could hear it. When I make public reference to the subject at home, I say that the singing was due to the fact that she had been trained bt [sic] a good-natured husband; but even this modest suggestion causes Mamma to turn up her nose and make a mouth at me. I think she learned that trick from you. J.C. is still in trouble with his teacher, and is not at all happy. It is a pity, but it can't be helped at this time. He also continues to get awful drubbings when he plays baseball. Yesterday, the score was 15 to 3 against his side.—Lucille, the old cow lay down and died the other day, but her last calf, which has been named B.B., after Burdeene, is as pretty as a picture, and I think she will make a fine cow. Meanwhile, I suppose I'll have to buy a new cow. To do this while Father Bazin is complaining that his congregation won't contribute to the church half as much as they should, will be a piece of extravagance, but it can't be helped. I suppose there is not to be found in all the world a congregation as stingy and ax [sic] close-fisted as that of the church over which Father Bazin presides. It is a fact that I have heard Protestants talking about it on the street-cars, and I am ashamed when I hear it. The church on the other side, however, is booming along, and seems to be on the high road to prosperity. But why should I be writing all this to you? I don't know, I am sure, unless it is because I don't like to see Mamma fret over what she can't help—and she worries all the time because the prosperous members of the congregation refuse to come dowm [sic] with the dust.— Everybody in all the families are well, except, perhaps, Julian's baby, which seems to be condemned to all the ills that flesh is heir to. The girls seem to be enjoying themselves in first one way and then another. Alma Pope brought ot [out] a feller last night—I don't know what his name is. And then there's the matinees—I don't suppose you'll have an opprtunity [sic] to go when you come home, for by that time Bill will have the habit so bad that we'll have to send her to some kind of an institute for the cure of matinee girls. Burdeene is looking forward to her Oxford trip with a good deal of pleasure, and we hope she will have a nice large time. I think Alma Pope is going, and she seems to think a good deal of Burdeene.—You'll have to excuse mistakes in this letter, and correct them yourself, for I can't afford to go back over this stuff with a pen, and amke [sic] it right where it is wrong. It seems that I'll never get so I can hit the right letter at the right time.—Marguerites [sic] mother has been very ill, and if you haven't heard from the child, you mustn't blame her——and at this juncture, in walks Mamma, and wants to know if you have been so kind and obliging as to write to Miss Fannie and tell her how your dress fits. (And I'm mighty glad you've got a dress at last!) She's now engaged in reading what I hare [sic] written, and so I suppose I'll have to close in order to give her an apportunity [sic] to read the whole letter. Scatter my regards and love in the usual directions.

Your loving

DADDY.

TL

2 pp.

Envelope: Return to Box 111 / Atlanta, Ga. / Miss Mildred Harris, / St. Joseph's Academy, / Washington, Ga. / Wilkes County.

PM: 3 June 1901

[To Mildred]

June 9, 1901.

Dear Tommus:

I take up my pen with the same old complaint. I have nothing to write about. The only New thing we have here is a cook, who is as white as white folks, although she says she is a negro. Her name is Octavia, and she is shaped like a shoestring. She looks like some of the thin, scrawny women that come into town from the country with butter and eggs to swap for snuff ans [sic] red calico. She's a pretty good cook, but Mamma doesn't like her, and is pining for Cora to return. We haven't heard from

Cora since she left, and the probability is that a change of climate has driven the rheumatism from her feet into her head—though I haven't heard of any explosion in that direction.—I went to the ball game yesterday in order to see Henley pitch. He is a good one and no mistake. The truth is, he is better than some of the professionals. The game was very pretty, and I was very sorry you weren't here to see it. At one time, in the first inning, it looked like (I mean as if) mercer [sic] [1] were going to walk away with the Techs.[2]—Lillian is not feeling well since Burdeene left. This morning, she had a spell of dizziness, and has been feeling dizzy all day. That means a compound pill to-night. I have a headache myself, and that means another pill for Bill. I never take medicine myself when I have some one to take it for me. I think it is the duty of children to take medicine for their parents. When you come home you can assist Bill in taking medicine when your Mamma and I are not feeling well.— Burdeene left on schedule time, and we miss her very much. I suppose, however, she was glad to go, for, ordinarily, we are a dull crowd here. If Bill is well enough, she will leave here on the 12th, meet B.B. in Covington, and reach Washington sometime afterwards. She is very glad of an excuse to get away from home—and so is J.C., who is billed to go with the Collier boys to Porter Sprong [sic]—of course I mean Spring. You must correct the errors for yourself; I don't believe I ever will learn how to write correctly on the nasty old machine. I can write fast enough, but it is almost impossible to strike the right letter every time.—As I said before, there's nothing doing here in the way of news. Even the weather is beginning to settle down to something commonplace and dull. Even the roses are dull-looking. This all owing to the absence of news.—J.C. is worrying about going in bathing at Mc's pond. He acts just like he was the same age as Chandler; he whines, and tears come in his eyes, and he wheedles his mother, and worries everybody with his own selfish wants and desires. If he ever thinks of anybody besides himself I have never heard of it. Sometimes at night, he tells his mother that he loves her, but the next day you soon find out why he told her that. He always has some request to make. No doubt he thinks I am one of the hardest hearted men in the world, simply because I don't agree with everything he says. And yet, he is thirteen years old. Maybe he'll do better after awhile. His selfishness keeps him thin, so that if you met him in the road you would think he had had a spell of sickness. I am writing you this to say that I hope you are going to be unselfish, and think about others rather than yourself. After piety, it is the rarest and more beautiful trait, or quality that the human mind can cultivate, because it covers and includes several other virtues, such as charity, and patience, and humility. I suppose the other boys were like J.C. when they were several years younger than he is, but when they were thirteen, they were manly young fellows, and if they were not unselfish, at any rate they didn't think of themselves alone. They sometimes thought of others.—Julian's baby spent the day here recently. He is a cute baby, but very frail, and the last I heard from him he was having another spell of teething.[3] It seems that they never do get over teething. Lucien's youngsters, according to my count, have cut over seven hundred teeth apiece, and I bnever [sic] have found out what they do with them after they cut'em.—Well, this is all. Regards and love same as usual.

    Your loving DADDY.

You must take what I say about J.C. with a grain of salt. He's no more selfish than other boys of his age.[4]

 TLS
 1 p.
 Envelope: Miss Mildred Harris, / St. Joseph's Academy, / Washington, Wilkes Co. / Ga. PM: 10 June 1901
 1. Mercer University.
 2. Georgia Tech.
 3. Charles Collier Harris, Julian's first son, who died very young on 29 December 1903.
 4. Handwritten postscript.

[To Lillian and Mildred]

            16 June, 1901

Dear Bill and Tommus:

 Things are beginning to look squally with respect to Mama's visit. In spite of his last Sunday's illness, J.C. went to Phil's Friday and gorged himself on cherries, and now he's in bed. We have had to have the doctor twice, once for the original illness, and once for the certain weak spells which attacked the voracious youngster. The doctor thinks he will be all right in a day or two, but he seems to me to be very weak. I'm just telling you these things now, so that if it should turn out that Mama can't come, you'll have the edge taken off your disapointment. We think she can come, and certainly I hope so, but if she doesn't, why you will know the reason, and it is a great deal better to know the reason than to belong to the crowd of guessers.—Evelyn is at Lithia today. The water there seems to do him a great deal of good, and we hope he will continue to "patronize" it.[1] There are also some young ladies up there who seem to be very attractive. Well, as Evelyn is to be an old bachelor any way, there is no reason why he shouldn't enjoy the days of his youth in pretending that the girls interest him.[2] He tries hard to be interested in them, and sometimes he almost makes himself believe that he has succeeded, but amounts to the same thing in the end. The effort exhausts him; and I think that is one of the secrets of his illness.—Mama is not feeling well herself; she gets up in the morning feeling dizzy, and she comes to the breakfast table looking like she is witch-ridden. She has a bad taste in her mouth and red eyes; and she is beginning to have suspicions in regards to her inwards, as Mr. Sanders would say, that are quite distressing.[3] She imagines that her gizzard is in conflict with her kidneys; and swamp root does her no good. Well, such are the symptoms of age, and you two may as well prepare for it now, while you are young. Take your swamp root now, and you won't have to take so much when you are old. In fact, now is the golden hour when you should take all the patent medicine that you see advertised int he [sic] newspapers. As I write, I have the headache, and I know the reason without asking the doctor: it is because I wasn't raised on Mellen's Food.[4] Babes who have been fed on the syrup of Squills always show it in their old age. Their teeth wear off, their hair turns from a beautiful auburn to a dingy brown, and they stammer when they try to say anything serious even if they are writing a letter.—Old Darling is on the Constitution, and they say he is burning the air so rapid are his movements, and so voluminous his conversation. I'd be happy if I could swap talking-machines with him.—They say Burdeene never slept a wink while she was in Oxford. Her record is ten boxes of candy, which entitles her to the degree of E.C.E. in the Ipsalon

Upsalon Alpha Fly Beater Society. I hope she feels better now. The dear child never knew what life in Georgia was until she joined the Methodists in Oxford.—Well, it is experience that makes us experienced. I found that out once when I fell in a well. Important movements do not go backwards, otherwise I should have fallen upwards.—We received B.B.'s letter, and appreciated it. She was not in a hurry when she wrote it—fourteen strokes of the pen and five shrugs of the shoulders. The fact is there's [sic] no busier girls in the world than those who visit St. Joseph's Academy on the occasion of the silver-lined jubilees.—We have to buy butter now; we buy it from Mr. Baker. We bought two pounds yesterday, and it was so strong that it walked through the pasture and tried to get in his wagon again. The dogs caught it, however, and we'll have to get a barber out to shave it. Like Samson, its strength is in its hair. Julian and Julia took supper with us Friday but to-day at dinner, there were only two at the table, your Mama and me. Such a thing has not happened before in many years. It was quite a lonely affair.—Well, as I have the headache, I'll close this remarkable epistle. My regards to the sisters, and my love to the girly-girlies.

> Your loving
> DADDY.

TL

1 p.

Envelope: Misses Lillian and / Mildred Harris, / St. Joseph's Academy, / Washington, / Wilkes County, / Ga.

PM: 17 June 1901

1. Lithia Springs, a popular Georgia resort. See note in letter to Evelyn, Friday *afternoon*-late [c. 1896].

2. Evelyn Harris. He married Annie Louise Hawkins, 27 October 1903.

3. Mr. Sanders, a middle Georgia cracker created by JCH as literary character and occasional persona, appears in several books and essays.

4. Mellen's Food for infants, a popular patent food advertised in the Atlanta *Constitution*. Also Squills, a competing brand.

PART SEVEN ᴈ⸰ 1901–1908
RENEWED SPIRITS & NEW PROJECTS

Julian is still in wild pursuit of the magazine idea, and I think it will pan out all right before long. The announcements are to be sent out next week, and, meanwhile, I have written letters to every author in creation, including some dead ones. I wrote to the dead ones because it wasn't their fault.

—*Letter to JCH, Jr., 20 October [1906]*

Saturday, June 29. [1901]

Dear Son:

Your little bit of a letter was duly received, and of course we were very glad to hear from you. Your letter was so short that you didn't have room to say how you like the place, or to give any description of your surroundings. I'll bet you a quarter that when John writes home he uses more paper, and tells more of what he sees than you did.—We are all well here, except Evelyn, who is still ailing. He's off for Lithia again. Mildred is in fine health and spirits, and is funnier than ever. Mamma returned with her usual headache, and consequently she has been somewhat disgruntled during the last few days; but she is feeling better to-day. The girls have all gone to the matinee and there is no one here but your mamma and me—two old has-beens. Marguerite comes down every night, and last night she brought two young fellows who were paying a brief visit to the Chaffees. One of them could imitate a cat to perfection, and consequently he is Mildred's beau-ideal of what a hero in real life should be. He could also talk like a frog, and the girls were charmed with him.—The puppy is all skue-vee, and so are the kittens.—I bought two new tennis balls for the girls, but somehow or other they don't take to the game. However, the boys can use the balls.—West End was defeated in the tennis contest, but Roy and his parner [sic] put up a very warm game, and I really believe they are better players than the others—but you know how Roy is: he gets rattled, and that puts an end to his playing. I didn't see the game yesterday, but I hope to see a part of the one this afternoon, before I finish this letter, and I'll let you know about it.—It is funny, but when I start to write a letter, all the news crawls under the bed, and I can't pull it out to save my life. I thought I had a number of things to tell you, but they have escaped, and I don't believe the bloodhounds could catch them—Essie is getting along finely, and her baby is a very pretty one, being as red as a beet and as fat as butter. It is in fine condition, and has an appetite that lasts all day and all night.[1]—I have just come back from the tennis game. The contest was between those who deafeated [sic] the West End Lobsters, and consisted of a team from the St. Charles and one from the Highland Avenue Clab [sic]. I didn't remain to the finish. The small boys were too

407

noisy for me; but the St. Charles Club team seems to be the best so far as artistic playing is concerned—and the girls have just come from the grounds (they had hardly got there before the game was over) and they say that the St. Charles won. This team will now hold the silver cup for which the tournament was played.—Roys [sic] two puppies seem to be thriving; at any rate, I can hear then [sic] fighting all day, and they make more fuss at it than a colony of johnthomas cats—I am glad to hear that you have so much spending money. Two dollars and a half is almost a fortune in the mountains. I don't know what you mean by "incidentals." That seems to be a piece of commercial slang. When a party of young men are going fishing, and you hear them talk of "incidentals," you may know they are referring to beer and whiskey. You already have five or six tablespoonsful of "incidentals," and that is enough to last you several days. Don't be worried about money; in fact stop wrrying [sic] about anything. You were sent to the mountains to cure your worries. Every-thing will be all right. You have about as much need for money at Porter Spring as a hen has for teeth. If things are as they used to be when I went into the mountains, you can buy a house and lot for seventy-five cents, and the man you buy it from will make his wife cook for you a whole year for nothing. Don't fail to drink freely of the water. We want you to be thoroughly well when you return home, and I hope you will stop eating trash. Don't bother with Gainesville bananas. By the time they get to that town, they are not fit for an Italian to eat. Be good; don't attempt to do anything that you think we wouldn't approve. It is so easy to be good that I sometimes wonder why all of us are not as good as we should be.—Give my regards to John and Charles, and be sure and consult John in regard to matters about which you are doubtful. He will be sure to give you the right kind of advice. I also send my regards to Colonel Farrow.[2]

> Your loving
> Daddy

TLS
1 p.
Envelope: Master J.C. Harris, / Porter Springs, Ga. / Care Colonel H. P. Farrow
1. Niece Essie La Rose, who married Charles Kelly.
2. End of letter—"send . . . Daddy"—handwritten.

[To JCH, Jr.]

At home, July 6. [1901]

My dear Son:

I hear dreadful tales of your adventures with the terrible bugs that are to be found at all summer resorts. John writes home that you would have had a sanguinary conflict with a cockroach if you had stood your ground. But you saw the roach shake his wings in a threatening manner, and at once fled. And then there are the beetles. Now that I think of it, there is a great scarcity of beetles and roaches in our house, and I suppose that is the reason you find them so terrible. Well, you must brace up. The bugs and beetles will not hurt if you are good.—Mamma is thinking about sending the things you wrote for, and I suppose will start them off Monday, and you will likely receive them Tuesday night.— The letters you write are very good ones, surprisingly good when I remember what a task it is for you to make up your mind to write one. I notice that the one you sent to Marguerite was beautifully written, while those you sent us looked like the writing had been scrambled. I mean the writing looked as if it had been scrambled. Otherwise the letters were all right.—The girls had a box party yesterday, with Marguerite as their guest, and all say they had a fine time. Bill and Tom rose early this morning for the purpose of playing tennis. They played until half-past six, and then Bill said she was too hungry to lift a racquette, and so they came in the house at the very time when they should have been playing. Julian says you must play tennis all the time—that is, when you have the opportunity to play. The match game that I saw was very fine. The team that was defeated was much the best-looking, and made a better appearance than the others in every way; in fact, the St. Charles boys had the appearance of country scrubs. They were thin and scrawny-looking, but they had a way of being where the ball was, and their style of serving was entirely superior to the Highlanders.—Evelyn has been at Lithia Spring all the week, and will go back to-night. He is not well at all. Brother Lucien—I mean the baby—is still ailing, and the doctor has been to see him several times.—Julian's baby is in fine condition, and his Pa says that he is the smartest baby in the universal world—and he certainly is cute. He has never forgotten me, and is always ready to come

Joel Chandler Harris with his grandsons Chandler, Lucien Jr., Charles, and Stewart, 1900 (Joel Chandler Harris Collection, Special Collections Department, Robert W. Woodruff Library, Emory University).

to me whenever he sees me.—Essie is getting along finely, and her baby is very fat and very red. It is also very sleepy. Charles Kelly says it snores, which shows that it takes after its Aunt Essie Harris.—I hear that you and Charles have to grab for the food as it comes in. Is this because there is a lack of it, or is it ona ccount [sic] of your appetite? I hope you won't eat anthing [sic] that doesn't agree with you. That is the trouble with Evelyn. When he feels well, he will eat stuff that his stomach can't manage, and the result is acute indigestion.—The puppy is growing finely, and everything about the place is the same as usual—even Cora has the same old trouble in her hind-legs. One of her friends—Emma—is cooking in her place, while she is lying up in bed.—I haven't watched the rain-crow's nest very closely, and therefore don't know whether the eggs have hatched. Sometimes they build a nest and then desert it.— The small boys sometimes play tennis, but they haven't been over since the Fourth.—Mildred seems to be having a good time. Sometimes she reads, and then again she is flying about causing the other girls to squeal and laugh. She's just as full of mischief as ever.—Well, this is all I can think of. I don't know why I write such dull letters; it has come to be a regular habit with me. Maybe it's because I'm getting old and wobbly, or maybe it's because the hendersons [sic] are not here any more. I saw Rufus going by the other day, and he was looking at his mule's tail as intently as if he were reading a book.[1]—My regards to John and Charles, and likewise to Colonel Farrow. Tell the Colonel to send me the amount of your bill—or you can find out from him—three or four days before you leave, and I'll send him a cheque for the amount.

Your loving DADDY.

TL

1 p.

Envelope: Master J.C. Harris / Porter Spring, Ga. / Care Col. Henry P. Farrow

PM: 8 July 1901

1. Rufus had resigned as butler in January 1899. See letter to Lillian and Mildred, 15 January 1899.

[To Evelyn]

[13 September 1901]

Atlanta

Friday night, 13.

My Dear Son:

Your letter came to hand this morning. Mamma is packing your things now, and they will leave to-morrow. I sent you a cheque this morning which I hope will reach you in safety.—I see that Dr. Janeway has gone to Buffalo, but he will probably return before you are ready to leave Washington.—You must suit yourself about the hotel. The Fifth Avenue is the most convenient. You reach it by way of the Courtlandt Street Ferry. The street cars run from the Ferry door on the other side straight to the hotel, which is on Broadway. The Dewey Arch is right in front of it.

We are glad to know you are feeling well. I enjoyed your dispatch, which was in your best style. It shows me that that is the sort of newspaper work you are best fitted to do. We are all well here—and as this is Friday night, the house is full of children.—I tried to see Clark this morning, but he wasn't in. Ed White is jubilant over the change, and I think everybody about the office is pleased. There is no news.

Your affectionate
Daddy.

ALS

2 pp.

1 folded sheet of logo paper

Envelope: Mr. Evelyn Harris / Sturdevant Hotel / N.Y. City [forwarded from] Metropolitan Hotel / Washington, D.C. / 9/15/01

PM: 14 September 1901

At Home.
18 Sept. 1901.

Dear Evelyn: Your letter was highly welcome. I didn't write last week because your Mother had written and had included in her letter practically all the answers to your inquiries. I see you have fallen in with some of the gay companions of your days of health, and that you are having a good time. New York is certainly a town where a fellow, old or young, can see sights. It is a place where money will buy anything in sight besides things that for some reason or other are kept under cover. I am sure you will commit no indiscretion calculated to give you a set-back. On the score of your health your friends will excuse you from joining in the festivities that represent wear and tear.—We think you would enjoy a week at Troy if you are so minded, and certainly your Aunt Sophia will be glad to have you. She says so in a letter received to-day. But you will know best what to do. Don't go if you feel that the trip will prove to be in the least irksome.—I was afraid you would miss the cheque, as your change of base was very sudden. You seem to have caught the malady of Geigerism[1] to perfection. May you soon cure it!—Mildred left for school Monday, yesterday it rained all day, and to-day we have had our first real touch of fall, which we have met by a counter blast from the furnace.

With that exception there have been no changes here.—Cora writes that she will be home Saturday or Sunday, meanwhile Georgia is cooking and doing very well.—Lillian and Mildred went over to see the new baby recently. They say it "is the perfect image of Julian," from which I imagine it is in the habit of drinking milk toddies with Sidney O. Charles and Essie are safely bestowed in their new home, and seem to be contented.[2]

Otherwise I know of nothing to write.

> Your affectionate
> Daddy.

ALS

1 p.

1. Note not in ALS but in typed Emory copy: "Geigerism" refers to Mr. Geiger, a friend of James Whitcomb Riley who traveled extensively.

2. Essie LaRose and Charles Kelly, the newly married couple.

[To Mildred]

> Monday, 25 Sept. [1901]

Hello, Baby! How' do!

Glad to hear you're feeling better. And how is Baby Burdeene! Keep dry eyes, both of you, and be happy. But we just had the biggest old time Sunday morning. Mr. Herbert Culberson's roof cotch on fire, the 'larm was turned in, and in about 1 Minute, here come No. 7, hosses just a-pantin', gong a-ringin', and wagon a-rattlin'—and then, after so long a time, here come some more hosses and wagons, and gongs, and firemen, and dogs, and folks, and "Gee-whizz!" says Bill, "I'm going to the fire. Jake, oh, Jake! less go see where the fire is!" and off they put, Bill a-runnin' and Jake a-flyin'. And then, by that time, the fire was out, but the folks kept on a-runnin' to the place, and Mr. Culberson had more company than he has had since the last fire.

Say to Burdeene that she must certainly try for first place. It won't hurt her to fail to get it, but it would certainly hùrt her if she gave it up without trying for it. She's bright enough to get it if she tries. And as for you, dear girl, I want you to buckle down to music, and you must begin to think of something else besides your own personal pleasure. Try to make others happy, and never repeat anything you know or hear when it is calculated to make any one else feel uncomfortable. By making others happy uou [sic] will be happy and contented yourself, and this sort of happiness will last much longer than the enjoyment of eating candy, or than temporary "fun."

I couldn't tell you why, not even if I was to try, the reason I thought last night was Friday. But the idee got in my head and I didn't get it out until to-day. That's why you won't get this letter Monday. But you have Sweet William instead and so you won't need a letter until you get this. Bill is now a great traveller. She has made a journey all by herself with no chaperone but a carpet-sack and a box or two of candy. I've no doubt she feels proud because she was so bold and self-possessed. As for me, I always feel frightened when I go away from home. One time I was on a train and it ran off a bridge; I mean it ran on the bridge and then off again. If this hadn't happened the train would have been on the bridge to this day. We had seven puppies at our house the other day, and now we have only two, and nobody knows what has become of the rest. Maybe the mammy dog carried them off for fear we would chloroform them. Charles and Essie came over awhile ago, and they both seem to be very much subdued. They have found out what a solemn thing marriage is, and they have been eating onions. Charles bears up very well for a young man. Otherwise he would have begun to eat onions several weeks ago. Nothing happens when you are not here, and now that Bill is gone everything will be still nothinger. I guess Mrs. Rosser is about to move, 'cause Ruth fell off the back steps yistiddy and broke one of her golden curls. Fortunately the blacksmith can mend it.

Bill's beaus don't materialize. Alex (or Ellick) drops in occasionally (to see J.C.), and Roy comes over because he has something to say to J.C., but the rest of them are hiding in the bushes. But Bill doesn't care for boys so long as she can have a dress with a small train attached to it. She loves those dear trains with all her heart, so much so that she won't let me tickle her under the chin. Isn't that what you call *cooglin'*? It certainly is absurd for a young lady in long frocks to be ticklish under the chin. Alleen brought the baby down yesterday. He is the best of the lot. He laughs and coos and sleeps and rarely cries; that's the baby for my money. Stewart and Chandler rise shrieking in the morning, shriek all day, and go to bed shrieking at night. All this is very cute, of course, but I'd rather have less cuteness and more silence. I'm going to adopt the baby. J.C. went hunting with Roy and Fritz yesterday. He was armed with a single-barrel shot-gun as big and as heavy as a musket. You would think that one load fired promiscuously in the woods would fetch down all the game for miles around, including the turkey buzzards; but all he brought home was one golden winged woodpecker, which he had no business to kill. Roy killed a jay and Fritz a red-bird. And yet to hear them talk you'd think they had exterminated a tribe of wild Indians, slaughtered a herd of buffaloes, and killed seventeen grizzlies. Mr. and Mrs. Lannon are coming out Tuesday. The reason I know this is because Mama has been talking to her Cousin Ida at the top of her voice in the telephone. This is a dull letter, I know, but you'll have to charge it up to Old Uncle Indigestion who comes to see me occasionally, and sits up with me chatting of old times. He tells me of the days when I could eat everything in sight and call for more, and then he shakes his head, and points to the medicine bottle. The first thing you know I'll be on a diet of mush and milk, or Mellin's food.

My kindest regards to the sisters, and love to Lillian, Burdeene and Bessie.

> Your loving
> Daddy.

TL
3 pp.

[To Mildred]

Saturday night, 28 Sept. [1901]

Dearest Tommus: Your letters are all to hand, and we are very much pleased at your threats to do a little studying—I sent you some cards in the box, but you had better turn them over to Sister Sacred Heart during study hours. If she finds you solitairing when you should be studying, I hope she'll confiscate the cards for the term.—Mamma and Sis went to the Burgomaster mat. [matinee] this afternoon, and had a grand time with their tickets, which had been sent by mistake to the Lyceum. Mamma returned home with her feathers up, and I don't blame her much. We have the hardest time with deadhead tickets of any dead-head family in the country.—Evelyn has returned, and is very much better. Dr. Janeway assured him that there was nothing serious the matter with him, and he's been improving ever since. He and Dan are going to the theatre to-night.—Jerd called on Lillian last evening, and the fat rascal stayed until it was nearly time for him to go. He's almost as high around as he is up and down; he's a sort of oblong spheroid. Mildred and Marguerite have both called on Bill once or twice, and the youngsters are to play over here to-night—Marguerite has just arrived, and I showed her a song I wrote. She says it's fine; indeed, she enjoyed it so much that I shall enclose it in this letter, and if you want to have it set to music you can do so.—There isn't a mite of news. Ovid is getting better, and Cora Smith Gann is getting.[1] She walks around as if her feet were caught in cigar boxes. It would be better for her if she had wooden [legs? rest torn off]. [Mr.] Riley sends his regards to you every time he writes.—J.C. and one or two of the boys have a fad of making battleships and cruisers out of paste-board. They are ferocious looking vessels, but they have to keep them hid from the puppy, who is pretty well.—Lillian began teaching Stew and Chan last Monday. They came the next morning, but I haven't seen them since except at long range. In the matter of studying they seem to have the complexion of their Aunt Mildred.—I went over to see the new baby the other day, and it's as fine as a fiddle. It is very much like Julian, and Julia, strange to say, seems to be proud of the fact. Well, some people have strange tastes.—Mamma has stained the dining-room floor with a mixture of fish-oil and red paste, a mixture that is not much more agreeable than "awdy colone," as we French say.—As Clarke F. was going out just now, he slipped up and broke the seat of his trousers in two. He was going after Mildred S. with J.C.—As I was saying when he interrupted me, there is no news here, and you'll have to make the most of a letter that is like Cora's feet—too heavy for anything.—My regards to the sisters and love to Bess and the sweet little Miller kids.

Your loving
Daddy

Way Over Jordan!
As I was out walking I heard a bird sing—
    Bird—oh, Bird—ee!—
He warbled and trilled and made the woods ring—
    Bird—i, Bird—ee!—
I thought I could translate one of his notes—
    Bird—oh, Bird—ee!—
For Birds can talk away down in their throats—
    Bird—i, Bird—ee!
And these were the words as they sounded to me—
    Bird-i, Bird—ee!—
The singer was not very high in his tree:—
    Jerdy, Jerd! Jerd-ee
    Jerd!—Jerd!—Jerdee
    Jerdee! Jerdee! Jerdee.[2]

ALS
3 pp.
Envelope: Miss Mildred Harris, / St. Joseph's Academy, / Washington, / Wilkes county, Ga.
PM: 29 September [rest illegible]
Washington PM on back: 30 September 1901
1. The only time the full name of this cook is given.
2. Later note on envelope: " 'Jerd' was one of the girls' beaux[.]"

The championship Marist baseball team, 1904; Joel Chandler Harris, Jr., is in the first row, second from right (courtesy Marist School Archives).

[To Mildred]

5 October, 1901

Times flies, Dear Tommus: Here we are in October, and presently we shall be in November, and then will come December and Christmas. Several of the children are over here to-night, and they are chattering like a treeful of English sparrows. The colony is composed of Marguerite and the Rosser gals, Luther, Wallace and J.C. Luther came home with a bad cold, and he has been here for a week.—J.C. appears to like affairs at the Marist college. He is taking both Latin and French, and seems to have no trouble in getting his lessons. He doesn't like Latin, but I tell him he'll get used to it before he's a hundred and twenty years old. Consoling thought! I wish some one had suggested it to me when I was stuttering and stammering through my lessons years ago.—As usual, there is no news. I have it in hand some times, but when I come to use it, it has flewd away, and I can find it no more.—The gals here have been trying to induce Mildred to come over, but she says she can't. She spent a large part of the afternoon over here yesterday and I played the zonophone for her.[1]—Jerdy has been here twice. He was here Thursday night, and stayed till half-past ten.—The reason I write with a pencil is because my pen is out of order, and refuses to give forth ink.—The weather has been right coolish, and we have had fire in the furnace in the mornings. There was a big frost Thursday morning, so the car-conductors say. And it's about time. We are getting along towards the middle of Fall, the time when possums and muscadines are ripe.—I am glad Sister Sacred Heart enjoyed the book.—"My New Curate!" It is a piece of real literature, and it is the finest book I have read in many a day.—Oh, I heard the children say that Myra Cole is engaged to a Mr. Roberts. Myra is staying at Chaffee's. Marguerite stayed at Julia's last night—wouldn't that jar you? J.C. and Marguerite are sitting side by side, live, right now, and they seem to be as happy as Christmas. All the youngsters are eating hoss-apples, and I can hear their mouths smacking away in here—I mean when Luther isn't talking. Bill is the queen of the May. She's sitting in there with a paper napkin bundled and bowed and pinned in her hair.—Mamma went to the mat. to-day with Mrs. Stella G. Humphries, the young lady who lives on the corner with a lot of red-haired children.—We have been thing [thinning] out the violets, and still we have oodles and oodles of 'em.—The Journal has bought a part of the material of the News and that paper will suspend. It's pretty hard on some of the boys.—Evelyn is looking fine and feeling prime.—Julian will soon begin to build. I notice that some lumber has been thrown over the fence at the corner.—We are going to have chicken pot-pie to-morrow. Don't you wish you were here?—The very thought of it has so overcome me that I'll have to quit right here. All send love, and all are well. Regards to the Sisters and love to B., G., and B.

> Your loving
> Daddy

ALS
2 pp.
Envelope: Miss Mildred Harris, / St. Joseph's Academy, / Washington, Ga. / *Ga. R. R.*
PM: 6 October 1901

1. See note on Zonophone in letter to Mildred, 27 January 1901.

October 19, 1901.

Dear Mildred:

J.C. is now very angry with me because I wouldn't let him go to the fair to-night—he has a bad cold—and so I will console myself by writing to you who are not angry with your Daddy; though, really, I don't think there is much consolation in writing when you have not much of anything in particular to write about. That seems to be my luck these days, and I account for it by the fact that my mind is so much taken up with the fluttering phantoms that I put in my books. I have noticed ever since I quit the paper that my letters to you are not as lively as they were before. The reason is that when I was writing for the paper, my mind was not seriously on my literary work until after nightfall; but now I am thinking about it all day, and the result is that I forget most of the things that would interest you.—I went to the fair this morning with Lillian, and while it was the same old thing to me, I was sorry you were not there to enjoy it, for it would have been new to you, especially the Angora cats, the pretty pigeons, and the beautiful pheasants. Some of the pheasants have more color on them than the rainbow, or rather, more combinations of colors. And then there was a little railway train there about as high as—I mean the locomotive was about as high as Muldoon. The man that ran it had to sit on top of the tender. Small small [sic] as it was, the children had great fun with it. It had small cars attached to it, and the youngsters rode on them. The little engine was almost as snorty as a big one, and ran along on its toy trip at a pretty good clip. And then there was the baloon [sic] which kept on carrying the Reubens[1] up in the air two at a time. I didnjt [sic] see many things, for I began to get tired before I had been there very long, and Bill said she had a headache in the top of her head. J.C. was out there somewhere, but I didn't see him. I concluded that home is a better place than a fair, and so we got on the car and retired to West End in good order, and with no vain regrets.—Mary Lou and Ruth Leonard, and Agnes Leverette took dinner here the other day, and seemed to enjoy themselves. Ruth is pretty as a picture, and I think she has found it out in some way—it's funny how pretty girls find out such things—and yet she doesn't seem to be vain.—The kindergarten club continues ti [sic] hang around on Sundays. Some of the members were here the other day and took some pictures of one another, including Bill. She said she intended to send the pictures for you to look at, but I think her courage forsook her when she happened to think that the whole school would see them, and make them the subject matter of considerable merriment.—Jerd insists on looking fat in the face, and comes occasionally. Marguerite received your letter, and says she was mighty thankful to get it. She says I must send you her love every time I write, even if I write every day. She went to the fair to-day, but I didn't see her—in fact I felt so much out of my element that I didn't see much of anything.—Evelyn continues in good health, and is looking well. I think he will gradually get back to night work. If he does, I'm not going to worry about him any more. I think he will be an old bachelor. He goes to see the girls, but he doesn't seem to care very much for them.—J.C. is getting along well at school, so his teachers say, and if he can keep his health he will come out all right. He studies hard every night, and I presume gets his lessons well, for he hasn't been kept in yet.—By the by, he says he wasn't mad awhile ago, and I hasten to give him the benefit of the statement. If he wasn't pouting, he looked very much like a boy that I saw pouting once upon a time.—Bill was to go to the fair agin [sic] to-night with Tootsie, Alleen and Walter Ormond, but I suppose the trip has been called off, for it is now 8:10, and I've heard nothing about it.—Anyhow, I bet you I don't go to the fair to-night, nor to-morrow, nor the next day, nor the day after. I believe Mamma and Mrs. Rosser, and Bill have arranged for Evelyn to take them to the horse-show. They didn't arrange with me to take them—don't you think that's funny?——Wait! Listen! Yes, it's "them!" They have just come for Lillian, and now they are chasing a car. And "Why don't you wear your furs, Lillian?" cries Mamma; but Lillian is nearly to the gate, and Mamma comes into the house remarking that she wished Lillian would fix up to look like something. Alas! it's always the way! these fond mothers are so anxious for gheir [sic] girls to look well that they want to load them down with clothes. Well, I hope the girls appreciate it; but do they? I'm afraid not. I know I didn't appreciate the things that were given to me when I was a slip of a lad.—We'll say no more about it. Regards to the Sisters, and love to my gals.

> Your loving
>
> Daddy.

TL

2 pp.

Envelope: Miss Mildred Harris, / St. Joseph's Academy, / Washington, Ga. / *Wilkes County.*

PM: 20 October 1901 [2]

1. I.e., rubes.

2. Original of the letter and envelope were in the Uncle Remus Museum, Eatonton. Only a photocopy was found there, 9 December 1991. Photocopy of the letter and envelope are also in the Joel Chandler Harris Collection, SC, EU.

[To Mildred]

Sunday night, October 25, 1901.

Dear Tommus:

You will observe that the very second lick I hit the machine I made a mistake. I left "u" out of Sunday.[1] Well, any how, such mistakes come natural to old men. Everything is new, the spelling and the grammar, and the manners. They won't even allow me to eat with a knife at the table; they say I'll cut my mouth. But there's no more danger of that than there is that the rest of them will jab a fork prong in their tongues. Bill is getting very particular since Jerd and the other kids have begun to hang around the house and whistle at the gate. She wants me to comb my hair even for breakfast, and she says it is low to chew tobacco, and suggests that I would do well to smoke cigarrettes like Jerd and the other birds. I put too many r's in cigarette, but I was thinking how they smell.—Bill went over to Abernathy's last night to play with Grace and another little girl that had come to spend the night there. Of course Jerd and the other birds were on hand. About hal-past [sic] ten, Jerd and the birds came out of the house and began to howl like a parcel of demons. I took it for granted that these hideous noises were the signal for their retirement to their own homes, and I thought that some of them were on their way home with Bill, but she didn't come, and at a quarter after eleven I sent Evelyn for her. Well—I've had more fun over thaf [sic] caper than a box of monkeys. She's been going around all day with a peculiar expression on her face, as if she don't know whether to laugh or cry—and as for me, I have been stepping pretty thin. The kids came again this afternoon, and Bill played with them in the swing. They must have had a nice time, for I heard marguerite [sic] laugh once. The kids all looked like they had been sitting up all night eating pickles. It is a sad, sad sight to see them when they think they are having fun, and to hear one cry out "Oh-ho!" in a deep base [sic] voice. The Lyceum aint in it with these unconscious performers. If every day was Sunday, I never would hare [sic] to go to the Lyceum to be amused.—Julian's house is coming along. He came out to look at it this afternoon, so J.C. says, and, seeing the little boys playing around it, begrudged them their enjoyment, for he told them that he wasn't building a playground. Some of my children are so nice and kind that I am tempted to go out in the backyard and have a couple of duck fits. In fact nothing prevents me but the fact that Mamma might be frightened.—Evelyn is still in good health, and seems to enjoy his work. He went with Mamma and Mrs. Rosser to the horse-show. Bill was along too, and although the night was warm, they made her wear her new coat with a heavy fur collar. I don't think they enjoyed the affair very much; in fact there was nothing to enjoy, as there was nothing interesting to be seen but a few one-hoss hosses. Oh, yes—the Peachtree swells were out with their fine duds, and the rest of the folk went to see the clothes and be envious. I am not speaking of Bill, for she isn't envious of anything or any body. I mean the great majority of the women who were at the show. Peachtree was in Bloom too, and it promenaded in front of the poor white trash that sat in the galleries, and shook out rustling skirts, and shook its plumes, and in this the way the hoss-show was a great success.—J.C. is getting along firstclass [sic]. He won a medal in Latin, a study that he doesn't like. If such things happen in the green leaf what will happen in the dry? But he has to study at night, and the fact that he has already got a medal will help him along considerably. Like all the brood, he is ambitious. I went to the Lyceum with Bill Thursday afternoon, and enjoyed the show very much, so much, indeed, that I prevailed on Mamma to go Saturday. But she came back and tossed her head a time or two, and said she didn't like it much. 'Twas ever thus from childhood's hour; I never made a pan of dough, but what 'twas sure to up and sour; I never went to see a show, but some one said 'twas dumpy-dour.—We see by the papers that a Captain J. B. Richardson, of Macon, who died in Lagrange [sic], was carried home for burial. If it is our Mr. Richardson—the one who was once our neighbor, it will be a very sad event for his wife, for it is only a short time ago that Buck died, and a year or two ago, Johnny. I don't know what the poor lady will do.—I have no other news that's worth relating, except that you'll not know Whitehall street, or rather Trinity Hill, when you come back. The low part at Formwalt street has been filled in five and a half feet.— My regards to the Sisters, and my love to all my gals.

> Your loving
> Daddy.

TL

2 pp.

Envelope: Miss Mildred Harris, / St. Joseph's Academy, / Washington, Ga. / Wilkes County.

PM: 28 October 1901

1. Missing "u" inserted by hand.

[To Mildred]

> Nov. the Two-Eye, 1901.

Dear Tommus:

We have been in a perfect whirl of adventure and excitement during the week. First there was the flowere [sic] show. Mamma is a member of the club, and she succeeded in raising several very large and sassy-lookingchrysanthemums [sic]. You know how she is on such occasions; the famous hen who scratched her eyes out to feed one chicken isn't a circumstance to mamma when she is cleaning out the range or looking after her handful of flowers in the aforesaid show. You would think to hear her talk that she had charge of the whole thing; and yet there are times when she sits down and begins to think right good and hard that she has a suspicion that her flowers have been somewhat snowed under by the others. I head [heard] her say awhile ago that the Culbersons thought they had a patent on the show and likewise on all the flowers— the show is held at Miss Kate's. I went up this morning and saw the show. I remember that the old maid who chased you from the tree where you had no business to be was one of the first chrysanthemums I saw; but otherwise the show was quite a success. Mrs. Burnett has the finest ones, I think, and yet all the club have some fine ones. They are as large as those grown under glass and a great deal fresher looking. They have one variety that they call the Paderewski, because it doesn't comb its hair at all; and they have some that look as though they had been caught in a whirlwind. I enjoyed the show very much, but I didn't think they would have the heart to put your old maid on exhibition. Mamma has been up there twice a day for three days, and she's going again to-night.—Charlie was arrested for gambling Thursday night, and stayed in the calaboose until after his trial. I didn't pay his fine, and I didn't in-quire about him, and so this afternoon he telephoned to know whether his place had been filled; if not could he come back? I told Mamma to tell him to come back to-morrow morning if he would behave himself. He hasn't got more than half sense anyway, but he's a good servant, and so we thought we'd try him again.—I have told you two exciting adventures, and now I'll relate a most awful and harrowing tale, to-wit, viz. Marguerite and J.C. have fallen out; Mildred and J.C. have fallen out; and nobody remains true to anybody else in this neighborhood ex-cept *Ducas, J.C. and Julia. Charlootte [sic] spent the day with Julia to-day, and to-night wouldn't speak to her. Oh, it's just simply terrific and awfully heartrending. Mrs. Chaffee saw J.C. on the car to-night— she had gone to borrow some coffee from the grocery store—and asked him what the trouble was between him and Marguerite, and he said that so far as he was concerned there was no trouble at all. She said he would do well to come back to Marguerite, and he said Marguerite would do well to come back to him. And then Mrs. C. asked him if he stole the pumpkin she had at her house on hallow eve. Indeed and indeed it is a pretty state of things, and coming just after the visit of Mr. and Mrs. C. to Mamma and me, it is enough to make the heart of an elephant ache. I see the fun in it, but J.C. takes it all as seriously as if the course of the sun, moon and stars depended on it. I have never been able to discover what the trouble is all about, and I don't believe anybody knows. Over on Oak street there is the same trouble among the boys and girls; it seems to be an epidemic. Julia is of course perfectly happy, and has a right to be, for the larger girls have not always treated her just right.—The Chaffees had a Halloween party, to which the admission was ten cents, and I presume some of the boys carried off the pumpkin to get even. J.C. went as a Brownie—you remember his suit—Clake was blacked up, Phil was an Indian, and Lafayette was a policeman. Bill painted in the colors.— Yesterday was Mamma's reception day at the flowers show, and she was in a perfect whirl and flutter of excitement. She had a good crowd, too, among them the Spaldings. She has gone back to-night, with Bill and Alleen.—Jerd hasn't been around but once this week.—Mrs. Rosser is going to give a reception before many days, and Bill volunteered to write her invitations, and address the envelopes. I tell you, it has turned out to be a job. She has been writing on cards and addressing envelopes every day for a week past. Bill says she likes that kind of thing and if she does she has had the kind of thing she likes—which is no joke so far as I can see.—In the way of really interesting news there is nothing doing— nothing whatever.—We are having a most beautiful fall. There has been but one frost, and that not a killing one, and all we need is a little bit of fire in the grate in the morning.—Well, this is all. My regards to the Sisters, and love to my various gals.

      Your loving   DADDY.

*Alas! Ducas has revolted, and is now trying to kidnap Marguerite. [handwritten at the bottom of page one]

    TL

    2 pp.

    Envelope: Miss Mildred Harris, / St. Joseph's Academy, / Washington, / *Wilkes County*, Ga.

    PM: 3 November 1901

[To Mildred]

Sunday, November 10. [1901].

Dear Tommus:[1]

Once more I take up my pen for to write you a few lines in regard to matters and things in general. First, as to the justly celebrated fuss, or feud, which threatened the lives and happiness of Marguerite and J.C.: It was all a mistake, a myth. The two parties to the misunderstanding are now chummier than ever.—Julian took dinner here to-day; he had come out to look at his new house. It is getting along quite rapidly, and he seems to be of the opinion that it is the only hiuse [sic] in town worth talking—so true is it that we always like our own dolls and playhouse the best.—Essie had to dismiss her nurse to-day, and, consequently, she is in Pecks of trouble. Her baby is as pretty as a picture, and very smart.—J.C. and the boys went hickory nut hunting yesterday and to-day, and have managed to pick up quite a number. J.C. is getting along very well in his studies, though he is sometimes kept in for misbehaving. Your last report was fine. I hope you'll keep it up. I want to be proud of you for something else besides your love of fun. Evelyn is holding up very well, though he doesn't go to bed as early as he should perhaps. At any rate, he slept until one o'clock to-day, and missed church, something that he doesn't do often. He'll make up for it, for I am thankful to say that he sticks to his religious principles and attends to his duties as regularly as if he were a pious woman.—Bill went to Mrs. Connally's reception, and enjoyed it better than she thought she would.—She was quite ill with fright beforehand, but she had Mamie Culberson to go with her, and this took some of the sting away. Before she went, she said she would never go to another one, but I haven't heard her make the threat since she came back. She is also going to Mrs. Rosser's reception this week, and by the time she goes to a few more, she will be broken in.—Mamma and Alleen also went to Connally's. They must have had a goof [sic] time, for they came back licking their chaps—we used to call 'em chops where I lived when a boy—Jerd comes occasionally; he is here now, and J.C. is leaning on his shoulder in the friendliest manner, thus interfering with any possible courtship. You needn't get jealous. Bill treats him just as she does one of the small boys—Friday night, the youngsters played out over here; but somehow they don't seem to have the fun they did when you were here. I don't think a higher compliment could be paid to your mischievousness.—Everything is just the same here, except Julian's house, which rather changes the aspect of affairs. The old cow is well, and the calf is getting along all right. Ovid has entirely recovered from his recent crippled condition, and Muldoon does very well with one tooth. Joe Lively passes the time by trying to catch the flies on the back porch. This is a task calculated to keep him busy. The cats all know when it is time for Charlie to milk, and they meet him half way between the house and the lot. The weather is fine as split silk, and I say this in spite of the fact that I have a bad cold in the head, as well as a bad cough. But such is life in the merry autumn, when you don't know whether to have a fire in the furnace, or whether to order a hundred pounds of ice to sit on. The truth is, we are living in a great country and should be proud of our privileges.—J.C. has an invitation to Mrs. Rosser's reception, and he is the only boy who has received one. Francis will be there, and Julia, and so he will probably have a nice time, for Francis [sic] is as pretty as a pink, and as sassy as a barley fed colt.— Jerd is just going, and so I suppose we shall not see him till next time.— Alleen is not well. Mamma, who has just come from there, says she looks badly.—Well, we've had supper, and I don't know whether I feel better or not. Yes, I feel better; we had nut salad, and I refused to eat any, and so, if I don't feel better now, I will after awhile. If I had eaten the stuff— and I'm sure I wanted to—I would have felt worser, and, consequently, as I don't feel worser, I must feel better.—Julia and Mildred are all right. All of them seem to be getting along peacably, and I hope they will continue to do so.—Lucien's kids come down every day, and seem to be improving. Brother ran away from home and came down twice last week. He came through the crack of the fence, and seemed to be very proud of the fact that he was able to run away.—Well, this is positively all that I know, and perhaps a little more than I thought I knew when I started out. Regards to the Sisters, and love to my gals.

> Your loving
> DADDY.

TL

2 pp.

Envelope: Return to Box 111, / Atlanta, Ga. / Miss Mildred Harris, / St. Joseph's Academy, / Washington, / Wilkes, Georgia

PM: 11 November 1901

1. Handwritten note: "I enclose a cheque for the sisters."

[To Mildred]

Saturday, 16 November, 1901.

Dear Tommus:

As you know, the celebrated feud between the infant lovers has been adjusted. There are no more tears, no more heart-burnings; everything is peace and joy. The gals and boys were here last night, and Bill made them some chocolate candy. You wil [sic] will know what kind of candy it was when I tell you that J.C. had to go to bed ill five minutes after he had eaten it. He recovered, however, in time to get up and talk with the children. They all went into the sitting-room, and there, in the presence of Roy, had one of those heart-to-heart talks that you read about. Margaret related some of the experiences of Myra Cole, who is shortly to be married to a Mr. Harry Roberts. The way Marguerite told it was funny enough to choke on. She mimicked Myra, and I could see her as plain as day. Then Charlotte related what she had seen, and that was funny, too. My advice is to all girls who are engaged—beware of the small person. Evidently Marguerite has teased Myra until the poor girl is nearly wild. Then Marguerite related some of her experiences with the girls at school, and that was as funny as the other. The child is a good talker, and she knows how to describe the peculiarities of people.—The weather has been really cold for the first time to-day. J.C. wanted to go hunting this morning but the boys didn't call by for him. He also tried to go to a foot-ball game this afternoon, but the other team failed to put in an appearance. So he has a bad day of it all around; but he's none the worse for it. He is at the head of his Latin class, and has more marks to his credit than any of the others. Which shows that he is doing fairly well.—You will observe that November is more than half gone. Pretty soon it will be all gone, and then December will fly by until you come to the 18th, when the little Miller gals are to start home, and I want you to come with them, just for company. I don't know what sort of a Christmas Mamma and Bill propose to get up, but they'll doubtles [sic] fix it so everybody will have a good time.—Mamma went to Mrs. Rosser's reception, and so did Bill, and they bith [sic] say they had a fine time. Thursday Bill went to a buffet luncheon given by Miss Lucy Newman. She says that Miss Lucy was very attentive to her. She sat by poor timid Bill the whole time and held her hand. Doesn't that look kinder quare? Why, the first thing you know she'll be holding my hand.—Evelyn continues to be in good health. As for myself, I have a bad cold in the head and a sort of hacking cough; but I'm better now than I was. I was to be a pall-bearer at Mr. Moran's funeral to-morrow, but I don't feel well enough, and they'll have to get somebody else. I didn't even know that Mr. Moran was sick. He had two editorials in the paper that announced his death. He had congestion congestion [sic] of the lungs and heart failure.—Julian's house is coming along very rapidly. The roof is all on, and looks very pretty. The ends of the shingles were dipped in green paint before they were put on, and you would think that the whole shingle was painted. The walls are to be shingled too, and the shingles are to be silver gray. But the four seasons are the greatest painters the world has ever seen, and they'll soon have the huse [sic] colored to suit themselves.—As I remarked on a previous occasion, the news has all run out at the window, and I can't get my hands on it.—Charles and Essie took dinner here the other day. The baby is very pretty and very smart, and they are both crazy about it. They are not well satisfied with their experiment at house-keeping. It is the old story of too many fingers in the pie, too many spoons a-stirring the soap-pot, too much Me, Me, Me, and not enough You, You, You! And the nurse they had had to be sent away, and all the time there is something or other happening, and Essie thinks that it never happened to anybody in the world before, when the fact is, it is happenning [sic] to all young people every hour in the day and will continue to happen until the end of the world, when we'll all go out of the business of house-keeping.—Bill sent off and got a quart of bump remover, and Mamma has bought a half pint of hair restorer. As for me

I prefer to keep my freckles and my lovely chinquepin—NO! chestnut hair.—We have so many cats the mice are about to take the place. We caught one in a trap this afternoon, and I gave it to one of the half-grown kittens. Well, he wouldn't even smell of it—he didn't know what it was, and probably thought I was trying to poison him.—If you hear a gun go off some night don't be alarmed; it will be me killing cats that don't know a rat when they see one.—Well, this is all I can write to-night. My kindest regards to the Sisters, and love to the girls.

      Your loving
      DADDY.

TL
2 pp.
Envelope: Miss Mildred Harris, / St. Joseph's Academy, / Washington, / Wilkes County, *Ga.* / Ga. R. R.
PM: 17 November 1901

[To Mildred]

      Saturday Evening, Nov. 23, 1901.
      Right after Supper.

Dear Tommus:

We are having all sorts of a time in this neighborhood. Charlie, the butler, has been sent to the stockade for conduct not becoming to a gentleman—otherwise drunk and disorderly—and now he wants me to get him out, promising to become a reformer if I will be so kind as to interfere in his behalf. More than that, Alleen has no cook. She had Hulda again for a few days, but Hulda failed to show up, and the last I heard of her was thaf [sic] she was trying to hire out to some one else. Then, on top of that, here comes the northwest wind blowing like fury, and causing the furnace to open wide its mouth for coal. . . . I paused here to fetch the little kittens and their mother into the house from the back porch. . . . Mamma and Mrs. Rosser went to the theatre to-day, and I suppose they enjoye [sic] it as it wzs [sic] one of these crying plays. . . . Julian's house is getting on rapidly. The roof is all on and the chimneys finished. It will be avery [sic] pretty house when finished, and will contain all the modern improvements, including the two babies. . . . Essie sent her baby over the other day, and it is as pretty as a picture, and very cute. . . . Gharley's [Charley's] wife came down to-day to beg us to get him out of the chain-gang. One of her reasons for wanting him out is, as she says, "her only lawful husband." The trouble with him is that if I get him out, it won't be a week before he will be cutting up again. He never cuts up here, but waits till he is through with his work. . . . J.C. got another medal for leading his Latin class, and he is naturally very proud of it. This is the second now, and I think he is to try for the third one. These medals are not very valuable intrinsically, but they are gold, and J.C. can save them and show them to his grandchildren. . . . The children tried to play out last night, but they made no great success of it. Julia and Earle had a dispute about something and she slapped his face— she is very quick with her hands. Marguerite says she is counting the minutes for you to come home. . . . You see what a dull letter I am writing? Well, it is because I have some stories in my head. One about Wally Wanderoon, who carries Buster John and Sweetest Susan into his own country. They have a very easy time going, but I don't know how they'll get back home. To go they only had to catch hold of a pine sapling, and suddenly the woods and the fields, and the fences began to fly by them, as they do when you are on the train. It was the longest time before the children could realize that they were travelling. They thought the other things were moving. Finally, when they got there they found that the new country was down hill all the way and in all directions. The only way they could do to keep from worming themselves off the earth, was to walk sidewise. This kept them on level ground. Wally Wanderoon has an old-fashioned story-teller shut up in a big box, and he makes him tell stories for the children.[1] I don't know how it is all going to turn out, but I will dig away at it until I make something of it. . . . I haven't seen the Chloe tribe in some time. Mrs. Richardson, who is now a widow, wants to collect some back rent from them. She might as well try to make them use soap. As soon as anything is said about money, Johnson takes down his crutches, and begins to limp, Chloe goes to bed with typhoid fever, and Rufus's legs lean in further than ever. If they hear that they have to pay back rent, three or four of them will permit themselves to be buried alive. . . . Cora still continues to cook for us and for the old black Cat. Joe Lively has disappeared entirely, and I don't suppose we will ever see him again.[2] The funny thing is that nobody seems to care very much. J.C. has made no sort of effort to find him in the neighboorhood. As soon as he gets back from school he has to go to Frazier's so as to be close to Marguerite, or to Wade's where he can stand around and look gloomy. I don't see much of Mildred Spratlin. I presume her mother is making her walk a chalk line as the saying is.—Jerd sometimes comes around with a smile on his face the size and shape of a ball of twine. Roy was here last night, and seemed to have a good time talking to Bill's bad cold. He talked and she sniffled, and thus they had a pretty nice time. . . . I heard something said about Thanksgiving—something, I don't remember exactly what; but Bill was in it, and a bottle of pickles, and a bottle of olives, and things like these, but nothing substantial. They were to be packed in a cigar box that Evelyn brought home, and were to be sent off to some winter resort. . . . I'm not sur [sic] that I know anything else, and maybe I don't know that. I've just been down to fix up the furnace, and the first news you know, it will be as warm in the house as it is in Florida. I am trying to make the place a summer resort on Bill's account. She won't wear flannels, and I am compelled to protect her by keeping the house warm, the heat being all the way from 72° to 80°. . . . My regards to the Sisters, and love to the gals. I enclose you a cheque for some money, which I suppose will last you till you start home.

> Your loving
> DADDY.

TL

2 pp.

Envelope: Return to / P.O. Box 111 / Atlanta, Ga. / Miss Mildred Harris, / St. Joseph's Academy, / Washington, Georgia / Wilkes County.

PM: 24 November 1901

1. Published as *Wally Wanderoon and His Story-telling Machine* (1903).

2. Joe Lively, JCH's comic name for the dog in the letter to Mildred, 10 November 1901.

[To Mildred]

Saturaday [sic] Evening, Nov. 30. [1901]

Dear Tommus:

You will see by the date line, not only that time is rocking along, but that I have not yet learned to write with accuracy on this bewitched machine. I don't know how it is down there, but time certainly flies up here. The sun goes down at half-past four, and it is dark before the chickens can get to roost, and some of them have to walk around in the dalk [sic] in their stocking-feet and hunt for their beds. A chicken is the most unprogressive person in the world. It is funny, but neither roosters or hens have come to the point where they use candles to light themselves to bed. If they don't find the place before dark they don't find it at all. . . . The boys and girl [sic] girls played out over here last night, and as it was a little too chilly to play out of doors they played out in the house; and they had a sensation, too, please don't forget that off of your mind. While they were in the full swing of playing some game or other, what should Wallace Thompson do but collapse! Yes, miss, he did. His eyes were sot, his face drawn, his hands clenched, and he fell back in his chair unconscious. It was a frightened crowd, and the frightenedest of all was poor J.C., who came near having a conniption fit on his own account. He called me, but you know how I am when something is to be done— I don't know what to do nor how to do it. Anyhow, Bill was there, and she rubbed him off with some cold water, and he recovered after awhile and went home. He has been ill in bed to-day, and last night, after his collapse, he had a high fever. Poor J.C. was so frightened that his hands shook loke [sic] like he had the palsy, and it was the longest time before he could go to sleep—I heard him talking to his mother after I had gone to bed. He was already in a nervous condition, having been ill the day before. . . . Bill had her celebrated bonfire yesterday, and she says it was very fine, but to tell the truth, I didn't see anything but smoke, and I'm sure I didn't breathe anything else. The youngsters were all on hand, and it seemed to please them very much. But there was something the matter with the leaves and trash they had piled up. It was the first pile of leaves I ever saw that wouldn't blaze up. They were like some of the cigarette fiends—they were great smokers. . . . Charley, the butler, came out of the stockade Wednesday. The judge reduced the fine and I paid it, and now Charley will pay me back in weekly installments, unless he gets drunk again, in which event, he will not be fined, but will be sent to the stockade for a good term. He is very meek-looking now, and has been working hard all the week. He declares he will go into bad com-

pany no more. . . . I have written you every thing of interest that I can think of, so you will see we are having the same old same old [sic] dull time. All the news seems to be a month old before I can get around to it. . . . Bill has subscribed to the Booklover's Library, and will get three books a week. The volumes are delivered at the house and are called for by a representative of the library. The headquarters of the concern are in Philadelphia, and it seems to be doing a good business. . . . In one, if not two of your letters, you refer to various so-called improvements that have been made in the front yard of St. Joseph's Academy. As I understand it, all the shrubbery has been taken away, and a grass yard will be attempted in its place. This is indeed bad news. The shrubbery was very beautiful and gave the grounds a character of their own, and I think it is a pity that it shoul [sic] be removed. I don't like changes of that kind; and you must say to the Sisters that I enter a respectful protest against such wholesale changes. Why it won't seem like the old place where I have had many pleasant moments, yes, hours. . . . However, I have about come to the end of my row. There is nothing more to write about. Julian's house is coming on so rapidly that he comes out every once in awhile to eat dinner, and to-day, Julia and the two little girls came out for a visit. I hear that Charles Collier's insteps are breaking down. He has no pain, but for some reason or other, the instep of each foot is falling away, and he has to wear braces on both ankles. It is a pity—and it is also very unusual, for the doctors say they have never known of a similar case. . . . Give my regards to the Sisters, and say to Sister Sacred Heart that I haven't forgotten that other matter—she'll understand. And give my love to Bessie, Gretchen and Brownie.   Your loving
                                   DADDY.

TL
2 pp.
Envelope: Return to P.O. Box 111, / Atlanta, Ga. / Miss Mildred Harris, / St. Joseph's Academy, / Washington, Georgia, / Wilkes County
PM: 1 December 1901

[To Mildred]

Monday morning, Dec. 9 [1901]

Dear Tommus:

I am feeling a good deal better, and as this is my 153d birthday, I thought I would drop you a few lines concerning matters and things in this neck of the woods. I had some kind of a sore throat that threw me into a fever, so that I was unable to write Saturday nigh [sic], and I was feeling kind of sneaky all day yesterday; but I sent for the doctor, and took his pills and capsules, and sprayed out my throat with a mixtur [sic] that tastes like a photograph gallery, and now I am feeling a good deal better. In fact, but for a little weakness, due to my age and general condition, I am feeling as well as I ever did. . . . Bill is thinking a good deal about Christmas. She thinks she has tremendous responsibilities resting on her shoulders, and she is going around with the air of a lady who has charge of the cash department of a dry goods store. She dont know what to buy, nor how much to pay for it after she buys it. It is her business this year to do the buying for you and herself, and she is making a great many calculations. . . . I don't know of a thing of interest, except that J.C. put his finger in a squirrel's mouth with the usual result. The wound is a perfect treasure to him. He can now sit in his mother's lap, and get Bill to blow his nose for him, and have everybody waiting on him except me. He wants to show the wound off to all the neighbors, and I think he made the rounds yesterday afternoon for that purpose. . . . Bill had some callers last night—Walter Ormond and Fred Lewis, but she was not feeling well, and didn't seem to enjoy herself. After they left, I had to give her a big drink of whiskey and put her to bed. She was glad to get there, but this morning she says she didn't sleep well. . . . I don't know any gal news at all. They come over to see Bill occasionally, but I don't hink [sic] J.C. takes the same interest in Marguerite that he used to, nor she in him. Children, you know, soon get over their puppy love, and they feel better forever after, or after. . . . Stewart and Cahndler [sic] have been eating dinner down here quite regularly lately. They are very well behaved except when their mother is around, and then they want to show off, just like you and I used to do when we were children. . . . Bill is making some handkechiefs [sic] for Christmas. They are all full

of lace, and are hardly big enough for a rabbit to blow its nose on. . . .
Friday night, the tennis club had a surprise party at Mizzers Vogner's.
Hook went with Bill, and they are said to have a good time. Jerd was
there, and he paid so much attention to Bill—and the other boys did
too—that Mizzers Vog said it was perfectly scandalous, and I speck it
was. Bill is always cutting-up when she is out of my sight. At home you
would think that the butter wouldn't melt in her mouth; but when she
gets out—well, she makes up for lost time. . . . I am putting this down
for Bill to read, and she will be properly shocked when she takes it in[.]
"Oh, papa. what do you mean? Don't you know that the Sisters read
Mildred's letters? What will they think of me?". . . Bill says if the Sisters
have a bazar, it will be a good opportunity for you to buy a number
of little presents such as might strike your eye. I am sending with this
another cheque for five dollars. Of this, save enough to fetch you home;
the rest you may spend there for presents for your friends. . . . Julian's
house is coming slowly along. It sometimes brings him out to take dinner with us, and occasionally Julia sends the kids out. Charles is very
cute and smart, and Pierre is the finest baby I ever saw. . . . The boys
say they are going to have a surprise party here before long. . . . I hope
they will postpone it until after your arrival. They get up such informal
affairs that I am sure you would enjoy them. . . . Well, this is all I know.
My regards to the Sisters, and love to Bessie, Gretchen and Brownie.

> Your loving DADDY.

TL
2 pp.
Envelope: Miss Mildred Harris, / St. Joseph's Academy, / Washington, Ga. / Wilkes
County
PM: 9 December 1901

[To Mildred]

> Most Christmas Time;
> Atlanta, Ga.: 13 Decem. [1901]

Dear Tommus:

Bill is expecting you every minute. Day after day and all day long, she
is declaring that you'll soon be here; and she has insisted on it so often

that I am beginning to feel that perhaps she may be right about it. But Marguerite came down this afternoon to say that you don't know when you are coming, and the poor child is quite put out about it. I suppose she is mistaken as to the meaning of your letter to her. We have all got our expectations fixed on the 19th, and I don't see how the performance can be postponed. There's a considerable smell of Christmas in the air, not only in the kitchen, but all about the house, and packages are piled in every room—all of them containing something mysterious, which is not to be talked about, much less seen until the very day of Christmas. J.C. hasn't bought his presents yet, and from the way he talks he intends to make quite a demand for money when the proper moment arrives. He is very quiet about it now, but he has given me to understand that he'll be heard from when he gets good and ready to go up town and storm the stores. Mamma and Alleen have been to town every day this week, rain or shine, and if to-morrow wasn't Sunday they'd go again. They have made all their arrangements to start bright and early Monday, and I think they are going to carry their dinners with them and eat it on the curbstone. Marguerite is afraid she'll be taking her music lesson the afternoon you come, and she has a good deal to say that is not complimentary to her teacher. The others are not as enthusiastic as Marguerite. They'll be glad to see you, but they are not bubbling with anticipation as Marguerite is. During the last two or three times that I have seen her she has talked of nothing else. . . . The boys have been eating dinner down here every day for a week, except to-day, and they would have been here to-day, but for the rain which has been pouring down pretty much all the time. The weather has changed now, and to-night, even as I write, the wind is blowing very cold, and we are promised weather for to-morrow that will make us close kin to Uncle Zero. . . . I haven't been well this week. My throat, which was better, got worse again, and I have been having it treated by Crichton. It is better now, but as I write, I have a dull headache, which makes me feel stupid and out of sorts, as the asying [sic] is. I am in that sort of a fix that if any one was to hit me right hard with a stick in a tender place, I'm afraid I would be angry, or something of that kind. . . . Bill, who is very fond of cold weather, is warming her feet over the register. I take notice that as soon as real cold weather begins to feel around for a place to light, Bill is the first to get under cover. But she is consistent; even when she is shivering, with the blankets piled high on her bed, she complains that it is fearfully warm. Now, if there's anything I like it is consistency, which is said by the poet, who didn't know, to be a jewel. The jewel is Bill's, and she wears it both night and day. She's hot when she's hot, and she's hotter when she is freezing. And if you don't believe it you can just ask Jerdy, who was here last night, and stayed as long as he dared to. . . . J.C. has taken no more medals. The two he got seem to have been too much for him. He studies, however, but I judge that he is not trying very hard for the medals. Two of 'em make a pretty good sized dose for a small boy. . . . We are going to have electricity in the house next year sometime. I am afraid that for awhile, it will make your mamma miserable, for she has an idea that electricity attracts lightning; and it's a fact that they are mighty close kin. We are going to put it in to help Julian to get it. The company won't fetch a wire out unless three persons, or families, will agree to take the current. . . . I began this letter at seven, and it is now nine. I have been talking with Mr. Walter Page, of the New York firm of Doubleday, Page & Co.[1] He came out in a cab, and while he was talking to me the weather got so cold that the cabman rung the door-bell, and told him time was up. . . . It is a positive fact that the weather had changed quicker than I ever knew it to change. The mercury has dropped at least 15° since I began this letter, and Bill is still hovering over the register like a sitting hen over her nest. It is cold in my room, and yet the hot air is sweeping through the register at a great rafe [sic]. If we freeze to-night, I will have the consolation of knowing that we would have friz a great deal quicker if we had had no furnace. . . . This is all I know. My regards to the Sisters, and love to Bessie, Gretchen and Brownie.

 Your loving
 DADDY.
Dear Tom,[2]
 You must come Thursday at noon without fail as I can't wait any longer. Let me know for sure as Jordan & I are going to meet you.

 Lovingly,
  Bill

Leave W. in the morning. I hope the girls can come then, but we will meet them when they do come.

Bill

TL

2 pp.

Envelope: Miss Mildred Harris, / St. Joseph's Academy, / Wasington [sic], / Wilkes County, / Georgia

PM: 15 December 1901

1. According to business correspondence from Doubleday, Page and Co. for 1900 and 1901, there were several proposals on the table. Doubleday had published in the fall of 1900 *On the Wing of Occasions*. JCH finessed the offer of a yearly contract from them in return for his output for the year. In addition, the publisher sought to make JCH the titular editor of *Everybody's Magazine*. All of the negotiations by Walter Hines Page were aimed at wooing JCH to Doubleday as his exclusive publisher. They included a discussion of taking over Appleton's rights in the first Uncle Remus book (1880), publishing Harris's historical novel and new short stories, and his doing Billy Sanders essays for *The World's Work*, a new magazine to be edited by Page. But instead, Harris signed a yearly contract in October 1900, with McClure Phillips, who became the publisher of his next books (letter to Lillian, 14 October 1900). See box 1, folders 8, 9, 10, and 11 of the Joel Chandler Harris Collection, SC, EU. Page's letter of 9 February 1901 (box 1, folder 11), which contains a royalty check for *On the Wing of Occasions*, promises a return visit to discuss these earlier matters as well as publishing a uniform edition of his entire works. Page had first met Harris on 28 September 1881. The collection at Emory contains thirty-two letters written by Page. See *Life and Letters*, 177–78; *Cousins*, 117.

2. Handwritten postscript by Lillian.

[To Mildred]

[c. 1900–03] [1]

At Home: 26 January.

Dear Tommibus: I was too lazy to write yesterday, and so I write this morning. You'll say I was ill—but it's pure laziness.—Burdeene has been having a hard time recently. She heard from her Aunt Ann that Wm Arnold was critically ill, and she nearly went crazy until Evelyn telegraphed and found that there was nothing much the matter with the child. I think Aunt Ann is a little nervous, and Burdeene is simply strung on wires. She is coming to Washington to-day, and I'll send this letter by her. She will stay only four days, so she says. I suggested to her to set her cap for Mr. Benson, and I've had a lot of fun planning what she will do when she is a widow with plenty of money. She has had callers galore since she has been here, and I hope she has had a good time. She certainly deserves it.—There were half a dozen yesterday—Hook, Duncan, Simmons, Crumley, and Steve Brown. Last night Dan and Fred Lewis were here and played cards with the girls until a late hour.—J.C. is still ailing, and feels too bad to go to school to-day. We hardly know what his trouble is. He complains of nausea and weakness. I think he plays too much, and I'm going to stop him for awhile.—Bill is still playing on her light catarrh, and seems to be having a good time with it. Pretty near all the children in the neighborhood have the measles—the Wikles, the Dobbins, the Chaffees, and so forth. We thought Esther had them, but Doc Crowe says not. Mamma has a breaking out on her face, and seems almost as proud of it as Bill is of her cold. I am very much better—in fact as well as ever, but the weather was so fine yesterday that I loafed and walked about in the sunshine instead of writing to you.—Brother has had a relapse, and is still ill. He seems to be having a pretty hard time, but is very patient and good.—We had Father Jackson to tea the other night. He seems to be as nice as possible, and I like him very much.— I had Mamma on pins just before he arrived. I said that I intended to tell him that she asked me if she should place a crucifix on the table. You would have smiled to see her consternation. Of course I didn't tell him any such thing; 'twould have been irreverent. He stayed until nine o'clock and we had a very pleasant time.—If there were any news I'd make this letter longer, but I can think of nothing at all. Besides I must get to work. Regards to the Sisters and love to Gretchen.

> Your loving
> Daddy

ALS

3 pp.

Envelope: Miss Mildred Harris. / Kindness of Miss Burdeene / Biechele.

1. Lillian graduated June 1899 and was at home; Mildred was at Saint Joseph's Academy until April 1903, according to surviving letters.

[To Mildred]

At Home, Ga.: May 6, 1902

Dear Tommus:

I received yuor yuor [sic] double-barreled letter to-day, and was charmed to hear from you. Matters are pretty much the same here, with this exception, or, rather, these exceptions: the roses are are [sic] in bloom, and strawberries have come in. Bill picked a big panful out of the garden this morning, and seemed to enjoy it. The truth is, Bill is coming out; she was up at half past five this morning, and cut the asparagus and lettuce, and picked the strawberries. She doesn't like to do it, but her pride sustains her; she just grits her teeth, and sticks to the work. But I think it is doing her a great deal of good; her appetite, which didn't need improving, is very much better, and I think that her color is better.— Moll and Coll have moved into their new house, and so have Jule and Julia. We had the whole shooting match over to supper last night, and I tell you they formed a tired and a hungry brigade. Molly is a dumpling-girl, just as jolly as she can be, and full of the energy that marks the yankee gal. Both houses look very neat with their furnishings. Julian has a little patch that he calls a garden, and he seems to think that it is the biggest thing this side of the celebrated truck-gardens of Florida. It is more than probable that he will get at least three messes of greens out of it, and maybe a couple of Irish potatoes. Our garden is in very good ahpe [sic] this year; we will soon have green peas.—I'm improving very slowly, but yet surely. I'm vey [sic] weak, and yet I get a little stronger every day. I get up soon in the morning, and during the day I take a good deal of exercise. In fact I take more exercise now than I did before I was sick, and in some respects I feel better than I did then. The doctor says that when I do get well, I'll feel a great deal better than I did before. I never knew what it is to be perfectly helpless until this spell. Why, I was so weak that your mamma could have secured a divorce on the ground of non-support. She had to lift me about and turn me over in bed. It is not a fine thing to be ill.—Cora is still limping. When she starts from her house to the kitchen, she has to stop half way, and rest herdelf [sic] on a clod of dirt. I can symlatise [sic] with that sort of thing for the first time in my life.—There is no news worth writing about. I have told you

Lillian Harris with her nephews (left to right) Lucien, Stewart, and Chandler, 1902 (Joel Chandler Harris Collection, Special Collections Department, Robert W. Woodruff Library, Emory University).

about the moving, and that is the only excitement we have had here. It will be very pleasant to have the children here, and I do hope that they will make themselves agreeable to one another.—Well, I am properly tired and my shoulders ache from writing. My regards to the Sisters, and love to the gals.

     Your loving   DADDY.

TL

1 p.

Envelope: Return to Box 111, / *Atlanta,* Ga. / Miss Mildred Y. Harris, / St. Joseph's Academy, / Washington, *Georgia* / Wilkes County.
   PM: 7 May 1902

[To JCH, Jr.]

> Box 111.
> Atlanta, Ga.:
> August 5, 1902.

My dear son:

   I received your letter yesterday, and enjoyed your collection of fish tales immensely, as well as your very cute pretended misunderstanding of Mildred's bad spelling.—It is all the same here as it was before you left—that is, except the fact that you and Mamma are not here. That makes a great difference of course. I mean the days go by just as they do when nothing is happening. I have caught myself more than once getting up from my chair in the porch and coming to the back part of the house to see what mamma was doing, and a half dozen times I have been on the point of calling you, especially when Julian's cow could get out. Which reminds me that she is the worst cow I ever saw, and the greediest.— Forrest Adair's bull terrier has five puppies, four dogs and one female, and he says I can have my choice of the litter. They are sired by Wood- cote Wonder, the fine dog that was on exhibition at the dog show. It seems to me that I heard you talk about him at the time you were going to the bench show. Well, anyhow, I told him I'd be glad to have one, and thanky too; and then I asked him why he was so generous, and, being generous, why he had been good enough to think of me. He said that his wife had heard that one of our dogs was poisoned, and she told him that not one of the puppies was to go away until I had had my choice. I am sure she couldn't have done anything that I would appreciate more.— Miss Pauline seems to be having a very pleasant time, and has made herself thoroughly at home. To-night the girls are going to Susie May's, to-morrow night to Evan Howell's, and on Wednesday night, Bill is to give some sort of a lay-out in honor of Polly.—Tell mamma that every- thing is getting along all right in every way. The new milker does his best, and gets as much milk as William. He milks the cows until their bags are no bigger than my two fists. No rain yet, and I am so tired of watering things that I don't know what to do.—I saw Georgia the other day—she was helping Alleen to get off—and I said to her that I hadn't seen her before in a long time. She said she had been superseded down here. I don't know what she meant by that, but it reminded me of something that Buck Adair told on old Ceily, who cooks for Mrs. G. A. Howell. She wanted old Mrs. Adair to hire one of her children named Lije. She said that Lije was one the hardes [sic] working and best exposed niggers that she could find.—Sunday School goes on all right, and the children appear to enjoy it. They were all ahead of time last Sunday.[1] We see very little of the crowd you used to go with. There is Luther, of course, but he is very dignified and reserved, and besides he goes to town with his pa every morning. He seems to have very deep thought—problems of some kind.—Alleen has been heard from. She says the place is right in the midst of the mountains, and she seems to be enjoying herself.—There has been no tennis playing since you left. Ping-pong is the onliest thing, and I continue to take most of my exercise that way.—I have putting down some things that are not interesting to you, and I will add others; as, for instance: The bell peppers have taken a new start, and the bushes are now fuller than they were at first. The tomatoes are still holding out, but they are beginning to get scarce.—We had Mr. Lewis and Hook to supper Sunday night; Dan and Evelyn went to Lithia.

Well, this about exhausts my budget of news—if you can call it news. Nothing happens, not even rain. I'd give a dollar and a half if I could look out and see Julian's old cow strangling at the wire fence. O'Donnelly's big dog got in the yard yesterday, and Muldoon rode him out. I never saw a worse frightened dog in my life. All here are well and have tremendous appetites. I am kinder one legged in the mouth now. The doctor pulled the tooth that I did most of my chewing on. And now I have to limp when I chew. But I'll soon have plenty of teeth to chew on. My health is as good as it ever was. I haven't taken a pill nor medicine of any kind in a long time, and I continue to get up early in the morning, and watch the birds catch worms.—You will have to correct the typographical errors in this letter.—All send love to all.   Your loving

DADDY.

TL
2 pp.
Envelope: Joel Chandler Harris, Jr., / Upton, Quebec, / Providence of Canada East.
PM: 5 August 1902

1. Mrs. JCH and a friend taught a Sunday school class at the Wren's Nest for neighborhood children.

[To JCH, Jr.]

August 11, 1902.

My Dear Son:

It seems that the more letters you and mamma get the more you want. I can't write every day, nor every two days, for when I get through with my work, I'm feeling somewhat worn out. That is the reason my letters are so dull. I write them in the afternoon, when I have finished my work for the day, and all my stupidity gets into the letters. The girls write regularly, for I mail their letters myself. I guess both of you must be getting homesick; if you are, letters won't cure it. For mamma's information, I'll say that I have written about fourteen thousand words, but the stuff didn't suit me, and so I began all over again.—Polly left for the Pope's today, and the house seems rather quiet. She appeared to be really sorry to go. The big tennis boys did their duty, and paid her considerable attention—and Mr. Cay and Mr. Lewis came out. So Polly had nothing to complain of in the way of attention.—Charles Kelly has been over only twice. There must be something the matter with his liver.— A few drops of rain are falling as I write, but there is not much danger of a good shower. Everything is parched up. The pasture is so dry that the grass breaks under foot with a crackling sound. It is impossible to keep everything watered as it should be. The girls, with the best will in the world, cannot water everything, and I—well, I am an old stick, you know, and the only thing I can do is to wish everything well done. The chrysanthemums are looking well, but they are not growing to suit mamma. They are growing some, but not as they would if they could get rain. Banks is working them to-day, and fertilizing them, and I hope they will do better, but river water can't take the place of rain.—Charley Goodman came over to see me the other day for the sake of old times. We talked about you and had quit [sic] a pleasant time together.—Julian's cow is not in a thriving condition. We have nailed up the fences so that she can't break through, and since then she seems to be grieving. She lies down all day, and doesn't give as much milk as BB.—Sister Alleen wrote a very pretty answer to my letter. She is having the time of her life, and so are the children. Lucien will go up next Saturday. He has been very genial and good natured sine [sic] he has been eating down here. He even goes so far as to play ping-pong with me every night after supper, and sometimes allows me to beat him a set. They all say that I have improved in my play, but somehow, I don't look at it that way.—Evvy has not been very well during the past few days. He eats too much one day, and for the next four starves himself.—Mr. Brown has returned, and took breakfast with us Sunday morning—at which meal I ate two whole waffles! It seems that Lizzie told him that Miss Harris expected him to breakfast, and he, being unused to the lingo of the niggers concluded that Miss Harris could be no other than Lillian, when, in fact it was Julia. He found it out for himself, however, and seemed to be much embarrassed, which was very foolish, for we are always ready to take in those who are willing to put up with our fare.—Really, there is no news to write about, and if there was I fancy I should forget it until after I had sealed up my letter.—By the by, the set with which you go have organized a crokinole [?] club. Luther elected himself president. They are to give parties every week. The boys are not thinking about giving a party for the girls, the boys are thinking about giving one to the boys. They gather together everynight [sic] and talk about what they are going to do; and it thus happens that so far nothing has been done. It would be far otherwise if you were here. Everybody sends love to all, and Mildred says you must answer her letter whenever you get good and ready. You must be cheerful and thus cheer Mamma up. She is in a bad fix; in a strange land, and far from home. Tell her to brace up and be good. Give her my love.

> Your loving
> DADDY.

TL
2 pp.
Envelope: Joel Chandler Harris, Jr. / Upton Station / Province of Quebec, / Canada East
PM: 12 August 1902

[To Lillian]

Saturday evening
October 11. [1902]

Dear Bill: It is too chilly to use the type-writer, which is in my room—
and so I fall back on the uncomfortable pen. There is nothing doing here,
of course, since you are gone. Everything and everybody has fallen into
Cora's gait, and we all go wobbling about, sometimes stopping to lean
against the door jamb, and sometimes sitting flat on the floor. The children rarely come over, which, in a way, leaves me to write in peace.—
Julia has finally hired Rosa, and seems to be very well satisfied; but she
had a time before she got her—tho not as hard a time as she would have
had but for the hospitable Hotel Harris.—John passed his examination
all right, so Julia says, and by this time, he has settled down to work.
He was so restless that I sometimes thought he had the itch, but I suppose that was just a fancy of mine—Yet, such things have happened.—
The puppy is growing very fast, but he is inclined to be a rover. He will
follow anybody that comes along, and I am afraid we will finally lose
him. The little boy who delivers The Constitution has already stolen him
once, but we recovered him. But nearly every morning since then the
little boy has lingered around the big gate waiting for an opportunity to
repeat his theft. Meanwhile, I have been lingering where I could keep
an eye on the little boy. He has found this out, and now he delivers the
paper and goes on about his business.—Evelyn, when last heard from,
was at Sophia's. Monday he will be in New York. He had a glorious time
at Mr. Riley's, and from there went on to Chicago. He reports a good
time everywhere.—Mamma had a birthday. She received an Austrian
Celery dish from Evelyn, and a hankcher from Mrs. Abernathy. I never
thought to give her any.—I am improving in ping-pong, and I think J.C.
resents the situation. Last night and to-night, I beat him a set. He went

out to the fair to-day, and says it is fine. It will be better next week, and I think I'll take a day off and see what it looks like.—Alleen entertained her club yesterday, and made quite a success of it. Your club, I hear, is reserving your place for you.—I have at last become convinced that the Tennis Club boys didn't come to see me, for I am still here, and they have failed to show up. Even Ray remains away. But such is life in a frontier town, where everybody stays at home for fear the Injuns or the Booger Man will get him.—We have had no frost yet, but the trees are putting on their fall clothes, and in a few weeks they will be undressed for the winter—Naughty trees!—Mamma has had some of the carpets cleaned, and, as the weather is damp, they smell like a couple of niggers in a barrel of soap suds.—There is a diptheria [sic] card on Wikles' house, next door to Alleen's, but I don't apprehend any danger. The doctors are getting so that they can control diptheria [sic] to a certain extent, and it is no longer the terror that it used to be.—Susie May asked after you the other day, but at that time you were engaged in making up your mind to write some other day. I should think that in a small town like Canton, you could find plenty of time to write. I suppose you will be coming home before long. I remember you said that you didn't want to stay till we missed you.—As the washerwoman said, I have about run out of soap, and will have to postpone this until next week. Give my regards to Mr. and Mrs. Biechele, and my love to Burdeene. I suppose she has grown taller and thinner, and this is what she gets by staying away from Georgia. Lee Duncan went to the train to see you off just because you were going to Canton.

    Your loving

      Daddy

ALS

4 pp.

Envelope: Miss Lillian Harris, / 207 West Lake Street, / Canton, *Ohio*

PM: 12 October 1902

[To Lillian]

Saturday Evening,
October 18, 1902

Dear Bill:

Evelyn will be home Monday, and since that is the case, I'll take up my pen to address you these few lines. We are all well and as comfortable as you can expect human beings to be. J.C. is at the fair to-day, and will remain to the fireworks. I went out the other day, but soon returned to my cosy cottage in West End, a wiser and, I hope, a better man. The whole business doesn't amount to a row of pins. The only thing they have had that was worth seeing, was Walthour's relay race with ten horses—distance ten miles, with a fresh horse for every mile. He beat 'em out and had time to spare. But wait—I forgot another thing, and that was the fancy drill of a picked company of the Seventh Cavalry. That was even better than the Walthour ride. They did everything that men can do on horseback, and laid the circus in the shade.—Cora has been on the lift since Monday, but Zack came Wednesday, and has been cooking ever since. He does pretty well, too. He will be very handy about the house. He neither smokes nor drinks, and he makes a good appearance in his white jacket.—Alleen and the kids went to the fair to-day and came back with a bushel or two of squealing balloons. Consequently they are all supremely happy—though I believe they've had a fight, the result of a dispute as to which could make the loudest noise.—Some of the chrysanthemums are very fine, but the majority show some kind of a flaw in the blossom. This is the case with nearly all the plants raised by the ladies of the Flower Club, and they met to-day, and seriously discussed the propriety of omitting the show for this year. They haven't decided as yet, but if they have a show, it will be a very poor one.—Really, I don't know any news. I have been so busy trying to think out a new story that I haven't had time to find out what is going on. Dan and Mr. Lewis took supper with us last Sunday night, and they threatened to come back to-morrow. But such is life (I changed my cambric pen for a stub one, but couldn't stand it) But such is life in a West End flat. You never know what to expect next.—Otherwise there is nothing out of the ordinary.— The puppy is growing both in appetite and in size.—Rosa is cooking for

Julia, and seems to be giving satisfaction. She looks more like a Cherokee squaw than other.—I haven't seen Mrs. Warner since she ate a pod of red pepper at Alleen's suggestion. I suppose she is trying to get the puckers out of her countenance. This is a funny world if you look at it right—and left.—I received Burdeene's nice letter, and appreciated it very much. She is lovely as ever, and very cute. I'll answer her to-night or to-morrow. Meanwhile, dear Bill, it is up to you to come when—or about the time—that we decided on before you left, and be sure and bring Burdeene with you. A couple of months here during the winter would greatly benefit her—and us, too.—All the kids are well, and Essie is able to eat a full meal occasionally—when she can get it.—I saw old lady Conley up town the other day. She is very spry, and her beard is getting longer. I hear she is courting Miss Mattie Burchell. It would be funny if the two were to get married—wouldn't it? Don't worry about Mildred[.] She gets her letters just the same, and the papers likewise.— Evelyn called on the McClures. He writes that the first edition of Gabriel Tolliver was exhausted, and another edition of 6,000 has been called for. Meanwhile, I haven't received my supply.—I went in Julia's back-yard to-day, and this is principally what I saw: [sketch of crying baby labeled "Pierry"]

     Your loving *Daddy*

[around rabbit logo at top of sheet on page 5 is written: "As Mildred would remark: This is the place to kiss."]

ALS
5 pp.

[To Lillian]

                                    Oct. 28. [1902]

Dear Bill:

I had so many letters to write yesterday, that I postponed yours till to-day—you know how easy it is for me to postpone anything. I can do it and not half try. I answered one of Burdeene's letters, and now she has written me another. That gal's a great wheedler. I believe she could wheedle her way into Heaven, if she wasn't going there on her own mer-

its, which of course she is. She wrote so fast, and said so many nice
things that I don't remember exactly what she said—my head was in
such a whirl. As well as I can remember, she wants you to wait until she
can get ready, which will be the last of December next year. Wasn't that
the idea? If I am wrong you must correct me. Anyhow, she wants you to
postpone your trip for a month or two, and then she'll return with you.
Well, that proposition is so fetching that I agree without firther [sic]
argument—for what is the use of arguing with a sweet girl who writes
like a whirlwind, and says all sorts of nice things with the speed of a
cyclone? So I say yes, if Burdeene is to return with you, you can wait
any reasonable time. We haven't seen her in such a long time, and she's
so nice when we do see her, that I am willing to do almost anything
in reason to get her with us again.—Mildred complains that you never
write to her now; she's exaggerating of course, but I suspect that you do
[not?] have as much time to write as you did when you were at home.
You have so much to do, so many functions to attend that you hardly
have time to sleep, much less write letters. And Mildred is getting along
all right. She must have had some trouble awhile ago, but when I began
to inquire about it, lo! it had all passed away.—There is no news here,
except what you know already. Essie is with us, and she is able to say
that she has the worst young one that was ever brd [bred] in West End.
She is spoiled in every way, and her chief amusement is to yell at the top
of her voice. Over at the Kellys they think this is cute, and I think the
child has been taught to do it. However, she is very sweet and cute with
it all.—The new butler lost his mother the other day, and has benn [sic]
somewhat put out about it, but he is all right now, and really does very
well.—Everybody is well so far as I know, and all the children are in
daily evidence.—Alleen has been thrown on her own resources again, as
Callie's mother is ill and the child had to go to her. I think that trouble
of this sort follows Alleen as the stream follows its bed.—Mamma is
having daily duck-fits over her chrysanthemums. She [sic] afraid they'll
shatter before the show, and then again she's afraid they won't. They are
really very fine ones, and they are no earlier than those of our neighbors,
so that if the show is too late for one it will be too late for all. Mamma
goes down into the dry well every morning, and when she comes her

head looks like some new kind of chrysanthemum. She was complaining just now that she never has time to do anything, and she has so many things to do. She and Mrs. Wilson are as thick as two in a bed, and I believe they both think secretly that they [sic] may be other women in the world, but thank goodness, they are not in West End. (Mamma will rip me up the back when she reads this letter.) I always am particular to write nothing but the sober truth to my dear children, for I don't want them to become frivolous when they grow up. (I think you are grown and a half.) However, I have about reached the limit of my paper, and as I have been writing to you when I should be at work, I'll bring this beautiful letter to a close. My love to all the folks.[1]

    Your loving
      Daddy

TLS
1 p.
1. "Folks" is handwritten.

[To Lillian]

               At Home, Ga., Nov. 2. [1902]

My Dear Bill:

You know perfectly well that I wrote to you last Monday, and that you received the letter. The trouble was that you didn't have time to open it; you were too sleepy, or too busy.—Mamma received your interesting note this morning, and was very glad to get the twenty-seven words that it contained. We read it and said that if everybody would be as brief as that, there would be less trouble in the world. But you should not have said that you received no letter from me. It is an easy matter to write when there is nothing to write about, and that is the reason I am always so willing to write.—Mrs. Wilson came down to Sunday school this morning with her singing apparatus, and it sounded pretty well when she got it going. She and mamma are always in such a hurry to get through with the Sunday school, in order to catch the ten o'clock car, that the children think there is a storm coming up, and they are constantly looking out of the window to see if they can get home before it rains. Mamma goes in to them putting on her skirt over her head, and trying to get her garter right, and Mrs Wilson looks out at the window to see if that is her car—though I don't know how she can tell her car from any of the rest—and then mamma has to fix her garter, so that it seems to be a race between "Who was the first man?" and the sitting room clock. But the children are growing very pious, for when Mrs Wilson asked "Is that clock right,["] one of them said, "You'll have to ask God." So you see we have a regular whirlwind of a Sunday school, with no one to bet on the outcome.—Essie has retired to the palatial home of the Kelly's. She didn't want to go, but she was obliged to pull Molly off of Zach, in order to get her to do anything. It seemed to be a case of true love at first sight, though I don't see, for the life of me, why true love should have kinky hair and a bad breath. But such seems to be the way of the world.—There is hardly anything doing in social circles. Mrs Forrest Adair is giving five o'clock teas to beat the band, and Miss Nell is following suit.—The Guild out here advertised a Hallowe'en party, but recalled the advertisement for fear no one would come.—According to all accounts, Mildred hasn't heard from you but once since you left; but she hears from me, thank gracious.—If Burdeene can hold out till she gets here, she will have a royal rest. She will come to a place where ther [sic] is nothing doing, and nothing to be done. The old hens have the upper hand, and they are having most of the fun. They insist on chaperoning everything that the young ones do, and the result is that there are always more chaperones than there are youngsters. The presence of the older ones gives to every affair the flavor of stale ale. They know they are out of it, and they should stay out altogether, and do their knitting at home. We young people would like them better if they did.—I see some of the girls going to school during the week, and swap bows with them, but conversation seems to be interdicted.—The Piskerpoleons[1] had a Hallowe'en party, and made thirty cents with a hole in it.—Everybody is well except me, and I'm in better health than any of 'em. I am now eating malta vita for breakfast. I know nothing else, and, having told you all that I don't know, I had better close. All send love. With my regards to Mr. and Mrs. B., and love to Burdeene and the children, I am

    Your loving
    DADDY.

TL
2 pp.
Envelope: Miss Lillian Harris, / 207 West Lake Street, / Canton, Ohio. / Care of Miss Burdeene Biechele
PM: 3 November 1902
1. I.e., Episcopalians.

                                    At Home:
                                    Saturday night, 15th. [15 November 1902]

Dear Lillian:

I didn't write to you last week. I thought you were having such a good time that a letter from me would probably strike a false note and turn your Joy into discord. I am well, and so are all. The teas and things that were arranged for you will probably get cold before the 29th, and you will arrive when the social season is on its last legs. You won't mind that, of course. You don't like to visit and attend social functions when you are at home, and so you will not be put out to any great extent, so far as I can see. But I am sorry for Burdeene. You have prolonged your visit, holding on to Canton by tooth and toenail that she will not have a very stirring time here. For her every passing day will have a funereal aspect, and she will seek to escape the dullness by retiring on her reserve force at Canton.—What is the difference between social functions in Canton and in Atlanta? If you were here you would turn up your nose at them, but in Canton you rush at them with open mouth and outstretched hands. You see, there are a great many things I don't know, and this is the chiefest.—We have been a considerable stew for several days about the puppy. He went away Sunday night, and we never saw him again until to-day. He had been taken in hand by a family which lives on the corner between Oglethorpe and nowhere. We had some difficulty recovering him, and now we propose to chain him at night until his love of home is developed as large as a tumor. We thought he had been stolen, but he merely wandered off, like so many young fellows, with a frolicsome companion. When you return some time toward the close of the year, I propose to send him to your Sunday school. He is equally intelligent as the majority of your pupils, and has a great deal more piety. He never consciously committed a sin in his life and would scorn to tell a fib. He didn't even know he had fallen into bad company, and so he went gaily off, and had to be toted back. Take warning—I toted the puppy back home, but I'll not tote you.—Evelyn said he forwarded you a pass. I hope you received it. I enclose a cheque that will probably take you to Cincinnati, where you will have to look out for yourself.— Essie and Charles stayed a week and that was long enough to establish the fact that they have the meanest kid, with the exception of Julian, that has ever been seen in a civilized community.—Mildred seems to be happy. As you are not here we shall send her nothing for Thanksgiving, and she'll enjoy herself every bit as well.—This letter is not three words to the line and six lines to the page, but I'll send it along anyway. All send love to all.

> Your loving
> Daddy

Just write your name across the cheque's back, and Mr. B. will cash it.

ALS
4 pp.
Envelope: Miss Lillian Harris, / 207 West Lake Street, / Canton, *Ohio*
PM: 16 November 1902

[To Lillian]

Home, Sweet Home: Nov. 22. [1902]

Dear Bill:

I am sorry your feelings were hurt, and Burdeene's heart broken all to pieces by my would-be funny letter. I expect it was your conscience gnawing away at you, and you were just dying for an opportunity to shed a few bitter tears. Well, you feel better now. Evelyn received a telegram last night signed "Papa Biechele," which he answered this morning to your satisfaction. He left the telegram on his desk, and by chance Forman, and Duncan, and Timmons were in his room and saw it. It is said that one turned green, one yellow, and another one white when they read the telegram. They had to aid each other out of the room, and I heard from Mr. Fleming that they wouldn't take the elevator, but went down the stairs and stopped on each landing to shed a few sobs.—Thus is Burdeene well paid for her abuse of a poor innocent old man: thus does fate come to my rescue when I am supposed to be in a hole: thus am I vindicated.—I can promise you one thing—you will have Burdeene with you until next April, at the very least, and then Mr. and Mrs. B. will be sorry, for they will discover that I am the most selfish old fellow they ever heard of. It is all right: you needn't say a word to them: just wait until Burdeene gets here, and then we'll see who is who and which is t'other,—All these little troubles that you seem to be having now won't look so large when you are as old as I am.—Mildred says you are not coming until December and so I thought it would be well for her to quit school until next year, so I could have some company. Mamma is gone all day evry [sic] day, and when she isn't gone she [sic] doing worse by stirring up the dust, and having the yard swept when the wind is blowing right into the house, and all the windows up up [sic] and the doors open.—She has some new piano polish which she thinks is very fine, and she has used some on the stove, and on the dining room table. I expect that that was it she put on the table, for when I tried to wipe my mouth on the table cloth to-day, it was sticking to the table so tight that it tore when I jerked at it. But you needn't be alarmed. Mamma is equal to all emergencies. She will have the torn place darned by the time you get home. She says she can easily get the table cloth loose by using warm water. It's the same one we had on the table when you went away. You would hardly know it now; its color has changed from a pure white to a dapple grey, with coffee ground markings near the tail, where I sit.— Mamma has gone to the matinee with Essie this afternoon. She threatens to change the table cloth before you get home; but I want you to see it.— Cora is still moving around, using the stove and the chairs for crutches, and she is having a pair of shoes made at the cabinet-makers—the man took her measure by means of a cheese-box.—Molly takes dinner over here every other day, and then goes back home and eats with Rawson. Her appetite grows more delicate day by day; I think she is pining for her native clime—which we are sure to have with us before very long. Just at present the violets and the roses are trying themselves, and the xenias; and the quinces are beginning to fall. I saw one the other day as big as a dog. Julia made three tumblers of jelly from it.—I have been saving the collards for Burdeene. I have enough to last her three months, and by that time some other vegetable will have come in.—Everybody is well here, in spite of the fact that you didn't answer my letter and have written to me only twice since you have been away[.] My love to all. There is more news I reckon, but I have forgotten it.

> Your loving
> DADDY.

TL

1 p.

Envelope: Miss Lillian Harris, / 207 West Lake Street, / Canton, *Ohio* / Care of Miss Burdeene Biechele

PM: 23 November 1902

[To Mildred]

> House of the Bazaar
> April 12, 1903.
> Also Easter Sunday.

Dear Tommy Prof.:

It is only two days till the Bazaar, and Mamma is in bed. She is fagged out, she is don [sic] done up, she is out of business, she has been struck out by Time, the well known pitcher, she has been put out at third. She has run until she can run no more, and is now curled up in bed and wondering why she isn't made of iron. During the past two weeks she has turned the place upside down several times, and has worked the tongue out of several niggers. She has climbed on the step-ladder 999 times, and has clung to the ceiling by her eyelids time and time again; even at night she has found something to do, and when we are all in bed, we can hear her when we wake plunking about the house in her stocking feet. Why does a woman who walks lightly in her shoes, shake the whole fabric of established things when she gets in her stocking feet? I have often asked that question, but have never received a satisfactory answer.—The things from St. Joseph's came all right, and as each one was unwrapped, there were cries of delight from the admiring spectators. If I were to tell you everything that was said, you and Gretchen would be quite vain;

and the Sisters, especially Sister Sacred Heartwould [sic] feel—however, the Sisters are not supposed to have any vanity. I'm glad they weren't here, for they would have had a terrible temptation, For myself I thought that everything in the package was beautiful. In fact, the articles are the nicest we shall have at the Bazaar.—Billy is somewhat under the weather to-day, and I am going to give her some medicine to-night. She looks worse than she has looked in a long time, in spite of the fact that Hook came over and played flinch the other night.—Mamma will write to you and to Sister Sacred Heart as soon as she is able—Cousin Mayme continues to go to town and come back dead. She and Bill walked all over town yesterday, and while Bill is under the weather, the chronic invalid seems to be none the worse for her tramp. Honest to goodness, I don't see how the women can stand it to tramp from store to store and from street. Such a trip as that would do me up for a month, if not for good.—I don't know of anything that would interest you. I am feeling pretty well, but not as funny as usual—I don't feel ticklish anymore. I am afraid I am getting too mellow.—We had a very pretty day for Easter services, but it is cloudy this afternoon. It is warm, however, and that much I thank the Lord for. Gi' me Summertime—the good old summertime!—There is absolutely nothing new in our domestic circles, nothing worth writing about except what I've already written; and you see how little that is.— Georgia has been helping mamma clean house, and the steam hs [sic] been rising from her so thick you could cut it with a knife. Such is the state of things in Africa, and I wish that all that state of things would stay there.—As I don't know what else to write, I might as well acknowledge my ignorance of the news, and retire from the arena. My regards to the Sisters, and love to Gretchen and the teenchy little Bickers gals.

          Your Loving   DADDY.

TL
1 p.
Envelope: Return to Box 111, / Atlanta, Ga. / Miss Mildred Harris, / St. Joseph's Academy, / Washington, Ga. / *Wilkes County*.
PM: 13 April 1903

[To Lillian]

[31 October 1903]
At home: August 31.

Dear Bill:

Your letter was like the flutter of a bird's wing—a whiff and a whirl and it was so far done for that I wondered what it was begun for. Nevertheless, it was enjoyed, especially as it came from the young lady, who, only the other day, was boasting that she never went anywhere that she didn't immediately announce her safe arrival by telegraph. She considered that to be her first duty, before which everything else had to give way. If I remember correctly your letter was not dated the day you arrived, nor the day after.—Mildred received Dan's letter, and asked me if I thought it was a love-letter; to which I responded that it most certainly was. She didn't think so, or pretended she didn't, and I had to tell her that the reason I knew it to be a love-letter was because it had tobacco stains on it just like the letters I wrote to Mamma before we married. She seemed to be entirely satisfied with this explanation, hove a sigh, and gazed vacantly into the fire.—The Hallowe'en party at Chaffee's seems to have been a howling success. I didn't go mself [sic], but the children did, and I know not at what hour they returned. Rosalind T. blacked herself, put on a short skirt, and tried to kick holes in the ceiling. The real pie of the occasion, however, was when she washed the black off her face, and with arms bare to the shoulders, and still wearing the abbreviated skirt, proceeded to dance every dance that was danced. From the way Mildred talks, she was not very pleased with the performance. Otherwise she had a good time, and was brought home safely about twelve o'clock by Monroe Norman.—They installed the Stations of the Cross last night, and J.C., who was to serve, preferred to go to the party—you know how boys are. I think mamma was somewhat put out about it, but she kept her displeasure to herself better than I have ever seen her—with the result that J.C. will serve better than ever, and with a better grace.—Everything is about the same here, except myself. I ate some rare steak the other day, and it has somewhat upset me. I think I will have to stop eating gradually, for I feel better when I have eaten nothing for twelv [sic] or fifteen hours.—Mildred got acquainted with some of Marguerite's girl friends from town and seems to like them very well—I mean the Goode and Talbot girls.—The weather is very fine now, neither too cold nor too hot. The same old cat is here, and also Cora and Helen.—We received a telegram from Evelyn when he arrived at Washington, which was on the Morning of the 29th. Both were doing as well as could be expected of two young creatures who, for fourteen long hours, had drawn upon them the audible grins of the travelling public.[1] Let us hope that they will get used to it by the time they reach home again. If their wedding affected them as it did me, they were not feeling so well the next day, for I shook off the cover with a tremendous headache—as usual when I sit up beyond my bed-hour.—Well, this will have to be a short letter, though not as short as yours. You said nothing about coming home, and I suppose you consider yourself a fixture there. Write when you can.

 From your loving
  DADDY.

TL
1 p.
1. Evelyn was married 27 October 1903 to Annie Louise Hawkins in Atlanta, Georgia. Therefore JCH got month wrong in dating his letter; correction to 31 October 1903 made by later hand on Emory ms. Note also reference to Halloween party at Chaffee's.

[prior to 1904]

Dear Julian:

If you can, save Lillian two matinee tickets for to-morrow. If you can't, send word by Evelyn.

Lillian received a letter from Mamie Richardson stating she would arrive Saturday (tomorrow)[.] I don't know whether this will be agreeable to Julia. We are helpless in the matter. Mama leaves Canada on the 29th. Will reach home the latter part of the first week in August.

  Yours affectionately
   Pop

ALS
1 p.

[6 June 1904][1]

Dear Evelyn:

I am not sure that I clearly understood your purpose in proposing to go to Macon if you could prevail on Clarkie to give you fifty dollars a week; but since thinking it over, I imagine that there must have been some sort of a wager between you and Annie Lou as to how the proposal would be received out here. If that isn't the solution of the matter then I am at a loss to know what it means. I never heard of any grown person, brought up in Atlanta, who would be willing to go to Macon for fifty dollars a week when he could get thirty or thirty-five here. It is true that there are many good people in Macon, fine people, the very top of the pot, as we say in Georgia; but you wouldn't like it—neither would Annie Lou—and I have not the slightest idea that either one of you has ever wasted a serious thought on the subject. For if Annie-Lou has no serious object to going to Macon, she certainly can have no serious objection to coming to West End as our guest, to remain with us just as long as she can put up with us.—It is very true that we have extended no pressing invitation; but is it necessary to extend such an invitation to you and to her? And there is another reason why we have not pressed the matter. I have felt all along that Annie-Lou has an idea that she will not like West End; all her friends are on the other side—all her kin people— and the feeling is a perfectly natural one. I should feel the same about the Northside. But I think that Annie Lou would like it out here for a month or two, or for three months, or for just as long as she could stand it; and I have been waiting for some hint or intimation that she and you are ready to come. She knows us pretty well by this time—I am sure she has seen me at my worst—and she knows just what to expect; so why not put an end to the Macon flirtation and come right out and make yourselves at home? I had intended to say something of the kind if you had come last Sunday night, but your barbecue intervened. That, I am inclined to think, was providential, for I can write what I want to say so much better than I can talk it. Don't you think that this will be ever so much better than going to Macon?—and don't you think you can convince Annie-Lou that this is the solution to your financial problem? You can tell her how pleased we shall be to have her, and how we shall

Editorial staff of the Atlanta *Constitution,* 30 March 1902: (seated) Frank L. Stanton, poet and writer; Clark Howell, editor-in-chief, at desk; (standing) Evelyn Harris, city editor; Sam W. Small, editorial writer; John Corrigan, state news department; Lucien Knight, library editor; Julian Harris, managing editor (Joel Chandler Harris Collection, Special Collections Department, Robert W. Woodruff Library, Emory University).

try our hardest to make it as comfortable for her as possible, and all that sort of thing; and you will know how to convince her that we mean it, though I am very far from saying that she needs to be convinced. With love for you and love to her.

> Your affectionate
> Father.

TLS
1 p.
1. Date added in Emory typed copy.

[To Lillian and Mildred]

[2 October 1904]

At home in Georgia, Sunday.

My dear Gals: I thought I would write you just a little one to-day, simply to tell you that the house is in the same old place. (You must correct mistakes as you come to them.) Everything is the same as when you left, except that you two are not here—and the hole that you pulled your-selves out of constantly grows bigger, and will continue to grow bigger until you come back and tumble into it again, and then there'll be no cavity at all. The pony is well, and the puppy is weller, which means a great deal. Momma is well and so is J.C. This last distinguished citizen seems to be very fond of his school, though this does not mean that he is fond of his books. Julia has a friend visiting her—a Miss Grace Nor-ton, who is the living image of what poor Winnie Bunker would have been if she had lived.[1] Her appearance gave me the all-overs, and for a brief moment I seemed to be somewhere else. All her gestures, every little movement of hands and head, every turn of her features are the same that Winnie used to have. It was quite a queer experience a queer experience [sic], to say the least. Well, Winnie was nice and clever, and attractive, and so is Miss Norton. Julia brought her over last evening, and we had quite a pleasant time together. Her resemblance to Winnie made me feel quite at home with her—and then she plays the piano beautifully, and was perfectly willing to play when asked.—We received a pretty letter from Burdeene the other day, and were very glad to get it. She seems to think that it is not as easy to get married as it is to fall off a log, but what I meant was that it is easy after you get used to it. The poor child isn't used to getting married yet, but after next Wednesday, she'll laugh to think that she was frightened, and she'll snap her fingers at Paul, and tell him that she wouldn't mind marrying him again.[2]— Aleen and the baby are getting along very nicely, both of them setting up.[3] Evelyn and Annie Lou continue to drop in occasionally, but, in a general way, it is very lonely, and Cora will tell you the same. Cora says "You tell 'em ter make the most of this trip, for they'll not go again in a hurry!" To-day I was at the dinner table before anyone else. Cora came in and sighed, saying, "Mr.Harris, aint it awful?" I'll not write again, for

I suppose you will be coming home pretty soon. I hope the wedding will go off all right, and that Burdeene will not be too badly scared to enjoy the sensation of standing up before her friends and giving herself away to a great big grown man. And I hope mildred [*sic*] won't have one of her nervous spells. The new house is to be painted white—in fact, it is already painted white, and I'm afraid I shall have to change my writing-place in the afternoons. I have been trying to finish a short story, but the call of Miss Norton knocked it in the head for the time being—I was to mail it to-day. There is nothing else to write about, and even if there were, I couldn't do it, for the white house is in my left eye as big as the agricultural building at the world's fair. Love to all.

Your loving

Daddy

TL

3 pp. / 2 folded sheets

1. Perhaps the Winnie in the early letters to Julian or perhaps Mr. Bunker's daughter. See letters about the Bunker neighbors.

2. Burdeene Biechele, school friend of Lillian and lifelong friend of JCH's family. Lillian and Mildred were attending her wedding to Paul Irwin.

3. Aileen Harris, born 25 September 1904, was the first daughter of Lucien and Aileen Zachry Harris.

At Home: 7 December, 1904.

Dear Evelyn:

I have a story on the stocks—a story, not a novel—dealing with certain imaginary episodes of the war in Tennessee. It is a narrative of the adventures of a soldier, a young fellow, who having lost a foot in Virginia, grows restless when he finds that he is as much of a man on horseback as he ever was. He finally concludes to offer his services to Forrest at a moment when that commander is glad to get any recruit who seems to be more than usually intelligent, and he details him on special duty. There are two or three women in it, the young fellow's sweetheart among the rest. This story is a little more than half done.[1]

Of course I don't know how the story will strike the public, but The Little Union Scout went off very well and is still selling.[2]

Tell my dear A.L.H. that I have had the distance to West End measured, and I find that we are two miles further from the town than the town is from us.[3]

Your Affectionate

Daddy

TLS

1 p.

1. Probably the manuscript of *The Shadow Between His Shoulder-Blades*, published 1909.

2. *A Little Union Scout*, published 1904.

3. Evelyn's wife, Annie Lou Harris.

[To Lillian and Mildred]

At Home, 5 July—8 A.M. [1905]

My Dear Gals—which includes Annie Lou:[1]

Evelyn rolled in this morning about six, with a very thoughtful look on his face. He had nothing extraordinary to report, from which I gather, that a few people at the beach are not getting their money's worth. The situation reminds me of that beautiful old song that I used to sing to Mildred when she had the ear-ache—

When Adam delved and Miss Eve span

They sang the song of the bald-headed man.

The truth is, Evelyn flung a large pitcher of cold water on my hopes; I had an idea that Bill and Mildred were having the time of their lives; whereas, they are moping around and hiding out for fear some awful man will speak to them in a hoarse tone of voice. However, they are the blushing products of West End, and they cannot at once shake off the mantle of their environment.

There is nothing doing here; everything runs to peace and there is a restful quiet brooding over the barn in which we live, that promises a great deal until Julian's old cow begins to bawl, and then there is small chance of sleep for those who are weary and heavy-laden. J.C. retired yesterday morning, and by this time he should be safe in or at Porter Spring. C. Collier, Dope Pope, Frank Baker, and Hagy Boynton went with him; there are enough of them to keep the boogers off one another. I hear that Mildred is not feeling so spry. I'm sorry, for old Ocean is always feeling well, and if she will wade out deep enough, he will help her to hide her shanks. Esther is still subsisting on what she finds in the trash barrel, and seems to be very well satisfied with the situation. Essie is getting along very well. Aileen's baby has the whooping-cough, and is not as lively as she might be, a fact that doesn't speak very well for the whooping-cough.[2] It is a pity that babies cannot walk around such things, instead of stumbling over them. The Hon. Charles Dennis is spending his vacation at Lithia Spring—that is, he intended to, but for all we know he is at this moment occupying an airy room at the police station.

Evelyn says that you are worried because you haven't received a letter from me. I intendede [sic] to write you as soon as I got a letter from you. Thus far two little notes have reached us, one with a striking likeness of Mildred's shanks, and the other a polite note from Bill. There is nothing like etiquette.—Our 4th of July seems to have been a big one up town. Bessie Ledbetter came through it all, and was quite in a persweat [sic] when she arrived at our well known mansion. She was very sorry to find you out, and wasn't afraid to say so. The Guild was in session at the same time, and between the voice of Bess, and the various languages of Mrs. Rosetti and Mrs. Burtsch, I had a very enjoyable hour or two hours and a half.—Julia is quite ill, but not dangerously so. She is suffering from a nervous collapse and has a trained nurse with her.[3]—This is all, and I positively refuse to write to any or all of you until I receive at least one decent letter.

> Your loving
> Daddy

TLS
1 p.
Envelope: Miss Lillian Harris, / The Continental Hotel, / Atlantic Beach, / *Fla.*
PM: 6 July 1905
1. Lillian and Mildred Harris and Annie Lou Hawkins, who married Evelyn Harris.
2. Aileen Harris, born 25 September 1904, daughter of Lucien and Aileen Harris.
3. Both of Julia and Julian's sons died young in 1903 and 1904. Subsequently, Julia suffered ill health for several years and took periodic rest cures in various sanitaria. *Cf.* following letters and the papers of Julia Harris in SC, EU. She recovered her health to be-

come an accomplished journalist, writer, and partner with her husband in the newspaper business.

[To Lillian and Mildred]

All-round-the-House, Ga.
9 July. [1905]

My Dear Gals:

Some of your letters came duly to hand; others went astray. Mildred's was such a little bit of one that I was afraid she had a fiddler-crab up her britches leg—which would have been just awful. I don't know whether Evelyn's trip helped him or not. He came home last night, after staying with Fred Lewis for a few days, and he didn't look well to me. I suppose he is all right. The first thing he said to me I couldn't understand. It sounded like this: "Popdon't cherthinkanniloo fines girlinth eworl'?" I asked him if he thought I could understand Japanese so soon after a hearty supper, whereupon, he drew a heavy breath, and went solemnly to bed, and tried to smother himself with two pillows and the lounge blanket.[1]—It has been raining here nearly every day, and our corn and grass is simply grand. the [sic] weeds also are doing well.—It is now half-past eleven a.m. and mamma hasn't returned from church. but [sic] Cora is here, and Charlie, and I suppose everything will be all right. Esther continues to haunt the house, and is quite as much of a nuisance as ever. The only good quality she has (except her appetite) is that she minds me perfectly.[2] Mollie Rawson has taken her kid out of the whooping-cough belt, and carried her into the typhoid zone near Tocoa [sic].—There is nothing here to write about, and if there was, I am not feeling equal to the occasion. Julian came over last night, and talked for some time, and when I started to bed, I found it was after eleven o'clock. The result is that I feel this morning like (or as if) I had been to Atlantic Beach.—Evelyn is somewhat nervous for fear all of you will fail to enjoy yourselves. I tell him that it doesn't make a bit of difference whether you do or not. All we can do is give you the opportunity, and if you fail to take advantage of it, the fault will not be ours.—I don't know where Esther is this morning. The place is deserted. Even Julian's old cow refuses to bawl, and I am going out directly for to see if there's anything the matter with her.—Julian proposes to take Julia to Highlands—wherever that may be.³ She is better, but greatly run down.—A letter from J.C. assures me that he is about to have the time of his life; that is to say, he thinks he is. Colonel Farrow, who used to roar like a lion cannot now speak above a whisper. The Colonel is the man who is supposed to own the spring.⁴—Essie is getting along very well, and Charles is the same old stick-in-the-mud.⁵ I don't believe he has shed a hair since you left.—The only thing of interest is the fact that the heifer in some way got a bran sack on one of her horns and couldn't get it off. She thought that the best way to do this would be to have a circus in the lot, and she had it all right. She waltzed and two-stepped, and then she walked about on her hind legs, and was very gay.—I am getting fat again, and I'm like Annie Lou—I'm afraid it will spoil my figure.—Mamma and Evelyn send some love; they want to keep some to send another time.—Love to all.

> Your loving
> DADDY.

TL
1 p.
Envelope: Misses Lillian & Mildred Harris, / The Continental Hotel, / Atlantic Beach, Fla.
PM: 9 July 1905
1. This may be a humorous exaggeration designed by JCH for Evelyn's wife Annie Lou, who was with Lillian and Mildred.
2. Perhaps Mary Esther Kelly, daughter of Mrs. JCH's niece Essie LaRose Kelly and Charles Kelly.
3. Highlands, North Carolina; perhaps to the sanitarium there.
4. Probably the owner of Porter Springs, a Georgia mineral spring and its resort. See envelope of letter to JCH, Jr., 29 June [1901].
5. Essie LaRose and Charles Kelly.

[To Julian]

> Somewhere Around Home,
> on or about the 8th of Aug. [1905]

My Dear Son:

I am not feeling like writing a very gay letter at this time. I went to the Howell funeral this morning, and the strain it put upon me was nerve-

racking, as such things always are to me.[1]—My remarks about finance
in my letter awhile ago were not intended seriously. But they might well
have been serious. Take the case—the hypothetical case—of a man who
has been working for the benefit of other people for forty-six years. He
never has had any need of money for his own uses, but always looked
forward to the time when he would have a family. Well, he did have
a family, a wife and a number of children. They were always supplied
not only with the necessities but the luxuries of life to the extent of
his means. Time went on, and he falls sick of an illness more serious
than they could imagine, a sickness that almost unfitted him for work.
Meanwhile, he has a home, and a few thousand dollars in bank; but he
is earning little or nothing.[2] Now, the question is should the children
and the wife economize—not to save money for the man, but to save
something for themselves in case of the man's death? Well, let us say
that the man suggested it in as many ways as he could without being
downright disagreeable abput [sic] it, and that the word went roun [sic]
round among the younger children, with the approval of the wife, "Papa
is getting mean and stingy!" And then let us suppose that the drain on
the man's resources continues just as if he were earning as much as ever,
the bank account gets lowere [sic] and lower, and finally the time comes
when the happy home, the only one that wife and children have ever
known, is put on the market, or sold to the highest bidder at auction. Do
you suppose the children will be glad of it? I think that in this case they
will, since they have been instrumental in bringing it about.—There is
no news here that I know of. It is the same old routine of events and
people, the same cows, the same dogs, the same street cars, the same old
things for breakfast, dinner and supper, with several of us needing new
digesting apparatuses—the same houses in the same place, the same
people passing by, the same bugs flying against the screens, the same
whicker of the same pony, the same old washerwoman after soap and
starch, or money to buy wood to bile the clothes, the same old clothes
in the wash, and the same old holes in the same old clothes, the same
old fence, the same claves[?], and the same old whooping-cough show
under the able management of the accomplished Mademoiselle Peacherina Kelley, the same folks in the house, and the same house for to house

'em. I enclose cheque for eight dollars to aid you in returning to the same old house, the same old meals, and the same old dad.

Your loving
DADDY

TL
1 p.
1. Evan Park Howell, half-owner of the *Constitution*, died 6 August 1905.
2. Harris had been seriously ill with septic fever in spring of 1902. He had retired from the *Constitution* in 1900 with no pension. Note that he snaps out of the doleful mood in last part of letter with a catalogue of "same things" and an offer of check for $8.

[To Lillian]

Right around Home,
12 October, in the Same Year [1905]

My Dear Daughter:

Life is so varied in its aspects that I now find time to write you a letter of the large gray variety. Everybody is gone—mamma, no one knows whither; Annie Lou, ditto; and Mildred Mildred [*sic*] has gone to Mrs. McClelland's in company with Miss Nell—please put on the soft pedal and keep it on during the rest of the concert. Essie has had another spell—sore throat, a creeping feeling along the backbone, and shivers up and down her hind legs. Mamma, Mildred, and Nona have been waiting on her, while Charles sits in the dim liht [*sic*] and light, and reads the popular news of the day. I went to see the County Chairman, and enjoyed it very much. It seems to be a cross between a country play and a melodrama—pretty good as far as it goes, but it stops a long way this side of perfection. Julia has had something of a relapse, and mamma has been going over with great regularity—which shows that a wild and woolly mother-in-law can do all sorts of stunts. (So much for the consolation of Hook.) You can't tell me anything about Macon. I once lived there, and liked it very much. The people are fine. You must see Rose Hill Cemetery—not professionally, nor as a matter of necessity, but casually, as an interested visitor. It used to be a beautiful place, and it must be beautiful now, if the landscape gardeners haven't destroyed its wonderful natural attractions. I haven't seen much of Aleen lately, though sometimes the children pass throug [sic] the lot. Molly is invisible. We play hearts at night just as before, and in that way manage to endure your atsence [sic]; but the place is not the same without you. Why you have got the gadding bee in your boonet [sic] is more than I can imagine. You didn't get it from me. Old man Gann carried a jug of whiskey home with him last night, and Cora reports that he made a rough house at home.[1] He fanned out both Bush and Alma, literally tearing their hides off. If the jug causes such a necessary reform, I shall send him another in about three weeks. Bush told him that she would stay with him till she died, a fact that shows how the battling-stick calls forth the affections of our children. J.C. is getting along about the same, with a strong desire to array himself like the son of a millionaire, with the intention no doubt of deceiving the public, which is made up of bothe [sic] male and female. His room isn't finished yet, owing to the numerous engagments which interfere with his work, though they do not interfere with his meals. He continues to be very Chi Phious. The fair is on, and there are a good many country people in town. They look at the big buildings and open their mouths like they are trying to swallow them, brick and all. I have never been able to find out why they open their mouths when they come to town. It is a trick that even the girls have; and these same girls also have a trick of wearing mighty funny shoed [sic]. I wish I could get you in the habit of wearing just such shoes.[2] This blamed type-writing machine is doing its best to make me stop, and I expect I'll have to obey the warning. Give my love to Polly and Hook, and tell them that I am wishing and hoping the very best for them that life hold [sic] for any one, and wishing and hoping it all the time.

    Your loving

    DADDY.

TL

1 p.

Envelope: Miss Lillian Harris, / 422 Spring Street, / Macon, Ga. / Care of Mrs. James Hook Spratling

    PM: 12 October 1905

    1. Cora Smith Gann's home. She was the cook.

    2. JCH changed typeface.

February 21, [1906]
Next door to Washington's Birthday.[1]

Dear Lillian:

I am writing this letter to you, but it must be in a measure accepted by all as intended for them. Yesterday was a most beautiful day; the mockingbirds sung [sic] in a dozen trees, and the warm wind made the waters of the bay sparkle and dance in the sun; but to-day is different— the east wind is blowing, and the wind sifting down. In spite of this, however, the day is not unpleasant. The windows of my room are up, and yet I feel no dampness such as is to be found in the atmosphere of Atlanta. I was coming from Julia's rooms Monday night when I met a Kentuckian named Tom Phillips, who was accompanied by Col. Ewing, of Missouri. "Come with us," says Captain Tom. I had no idea where they were going, but I went. We walked up the street to the Mayor's house, entered the gate, and walked boldly up the steps. I supposed, of course that Captain Tom would ring the bell or knockat [sic] the door, but he did neither. He opened the door and entered, your dad at his heels. We had hardly crossed the threshold before I heard a series of loud shrieks, the sound of running feet. Out went the light, but it was as promptly turnrd [sic] on again by T., and then I saw the cause of the dismay[.] Every unmarried girl in the place was there, clad only in kimonos; they were having a kimono party, and had no idea that the house would be invaded by a trio of males. They hid in closets, in corners, and behind sofas, but no matter where they hid, Phillips, who is an old bachelor and well acquainted with them all, seized them and pulled them into the glare of the electric light, which was for some reason about as brilliant as I ever saw. Among the girls present were those from Sea-Ora and the Sea-view that he has doubtless told you about. After they found out that no one would bit [sic] them, they quieted down, and we all had a mighty nice time, with ice-cream and cake, which I couldn't eat, and conundrums which I can't remember, I tried to strike a period here, but hit a comma instead. I received a letter from J.C., which I appreciate very much. He can shed more light on the situation in a sentence than all the rest of you can in a whole letter. He seems to be getting there sure enough. The raise in his salary, so soon after his beginning, shows what is in store for him if he doesn't get impatient. Tell him I understand and appreciate his comparison of two of our well known friends and acquaintances.—There is a tree here of a very strange character. Pluck two of its leaves and hang them close together, and from one leaf will spring a tiny tendril which will attach itself to the other. There is a sermon in this for all the families on earth, with which remark I will bring this dull letter to a close; only pausing to remark that I always thought Mildred would marry a jew or a dago—she is so romantic. With love to all, and kind remembrances to Cora and Charles, and a fond hope that the roses will be nourished with cow fertilizer, I am your loving

DADDY.

TL
1 p.
Envelope: Miss Lillian Harris, / 312 Gordon Avenue, / West End, / Atlanta, Ga.
PM: [. . .] 1906
1. This date in JCH's handwriting.

Friday, 9 Mrch. [1906]

Dear Julian:

Your note received. I presume I should be satisfied with the verdict of Dibble and Camp; both are capable men; but they are thinking about the style, while I am mostly concerned about the Statement. After R.R.[1] has passed upon it, wouldn't it be possible to have a copy made for me, so that I can brood over it, and take it to my bosom and go to bed with it? I sincerely hope that Julia will recover rapidly: but it is a pity she can't go out of doors. I didn't want to bother you about the matter, and so I telegraphed to Evelyn the other day to see J. B. Wallace, 3d floor Austell building, and settle up my insurance. Please ask E. if he has accomplished this. If so, send me a statement of the amount he paid out, and I'll send him a cheque. If he hasn't attended to it, please see Wallace yourself and settle the matter. I shall leave here about the 27th. I want to go to Tampa and then to Tarpon Springs.

Love to all.

J.C.H.

P.S.—The girls are not writing any letters these days.

ALS

1 p.

Envelope: H,/ Clearwater, Fla. / The Constitution / Atlanta, Ga. / Julian Harris, Esq. / The Constitution Office / Atlanta, Ga.

PM: 9 March 1906

1. Probably Roby Robinson. Letter may refer to the beginning of *Uncle Remus's Magazine* in which Roby Robinson was instrumental. Harris was in Clearwater, Florida, on vacation at this time. *Cf.* envelope's return address, "H,/ Clearwater, Fla.," and note "From Clearwater Fla."

[To Julian]

16 Mch, 1906

Dear Son-ier:

I'll be coming home shortly, but I write this to say that I endorse all you said to Wood. There were but two omissions in your statement to him? I. I am not going to put Uncle Remus's name to things about the Salmon, but only to what is characteristic of negro folk-lore. I don't care anything about the folk-lore, but do care most dementedly for the characteristics and things. II. The final disposition of the verse. I am not going to give away the book rights to it.[1] These things probably never occurred to you, because they are not essential in a contract not yet made. But I hope you'll land the fellow[.] Did it ever occur to you that R.R. is manifesting an interest in your plan simply to keep you on The Constitution?[2] That he will dilly-dally and make-believe until you have lost interest in it, and then finally declare that he has tried his best to raise the capital, but has failed? I may be too suspicious; mamma says I am; but people are so selfish and so in the habit of looking out for number one—and I have seen so much of it, and so often been the victim of it, that I am always looking behind promises to see if I can detect motives.

Miss Kamenski kodaked me the other day, and the result is one of the best pictures I have ever had taken. I am laughing because Riessa is holding my coat-tail, but nothing is shown of her but the scrawny arm. Miss K. has had the photographer to develop one on a postal card, and this she will send to Mamma. Mr. Ewing left this morning for N.O. via Tampa, and as I write the Inn is completely deserted save for

Crocker. Tom Phillips has gone fishing, and the Judge is interviewing old Mrs. Law, the crazy woman. Julia will be interested in the fact that Mrs. Aiken has been compelled to return to Clearwater. Her visit to the East coast did her no good. I have had several talks with her, and she impresses me more and more by her singular resemblance to Julia. She is a lovely woman in every way, and so patient with her beast of a daddy. Love to all. Affectionately your

Father

ALS

2 pp.

1. Probably verses printed in magazines such as *McClure's* and newspapers such as the Atlanta *Constitution*, which were reprinted in *Uncle Remus and Brer Rabbit* (1906). Some of the verse he published in magazines and newspapers in 1905–6 remains uncollected. See Strickland, 116–17, 179–81.

2. Probably Julian's organizational plans for *Uncle Remus's Magazine*. See William F. Mugleston, "The Perils of Southern Publishing: A History of *Uncle Remus's Magazine*," *Journalism Quarterly* 52 (Autumn 1975): 515–21, 608.

[To Lillian]

[16 May 1906][1]

At the Door of Spring, Sometime in May.

Dear Child:

Should you forget to receive this, it will be well to remember that it was written. We have been having great times here in our minds, where there is a large hole occasioned by the fact that you have pulled yourself out, as though you were a sliver, and betaken yourself to the Metropolis of Evil. I trust in heaven that you will be able to get some good out of it, though you will have to hunt for it a long, long time.—I am writing while all the family are asleep, especially Mildred and J.C. As to Mamma, I am not so certain. If she is asleep now, it will be the first time that I have ever caught her in that attitude—I suppose you can call it that. I am afraid to investigate, because she would raise her hoary head, with the question, "What is it?" or "Who is that?" or, "Why in the world don't you stay in bed like other people?" Whereas, the whole town is awake— men going to work, and women preparing to attack the bargain counter;

Photograph of Joel Chandler Harris in Clearwater, Florida, taken by Miss
Kamenski in March 1906 (Joel Chandler Harris Collection, Special Collections
Department, Robert W. Woodruff Library, Emory University).

and, as I have hinted, Mamma may be awake herself. So I'll not venture to see.—Mildred has been having some new experiences. Her case of Noteatess has given way to a huge appetite for Johnson and Camp. She says she is Knott going to Forsyth, but you know how her mind changes without changing! Mrs. Collar Cord came down to see me last evening, and read me a letter from a girl I used to know long before I was gray— something about trying to get Carnegie to subscribe something for the library of Monroe college. This was bad enough; cold sweat was dripping from my hat and shoes, and the whole world turned around as usual— it is curious how the world keeps right on in spite of everything we can do!—and then Mamma came out with a dose of some kind, mainly ammonia, and I lost control of my stomach for the space of—I mean the time—about five minutes. Then, of course I had more sympathy and attention than I knew what to do with, and if some nice-looking woman had come along I suppose I should have eloped with her without asking the color of her name or religion.—All this is the same as saying that everything is tripping along just the same as when you left. The roses bloom, the birds sing, and Julia comes over once in awhile—also Essie and Alleen.—Charley is doing business at the same old stand, the cow is sold, and Cora scrubbed the kitchen yistiddy.—Mildred and I had a great time yesterday afternoon with Willie West, Essie's cook. She gave us an inside view of the social aspirations of the new negro, and, while she was perfectly earnest, it was the most comical account of the ways and doings of the new, or educated negro, that I have ever heard. The Lord knows we ought to be sorry for the unfortunate creatures, who seem to grow more ignorant with the book knowledge they obtain.— The street is in a fix with the paving and the double track, but I suppose it will be all right in a few weeks. You are having a good time, of course, and we are all glad of it. Mildred is preparing to learn how to make passover bread in Eastman, and, as it is nearing breakfast-time, I'll just say at a venture that we are all sending our love just as soon as we can get the crumb [sic] crumbs out'n our mouths. Give my love to Burdeene and Paul, and write when you can.[2]

    Your loving
    DADDY.

TL

1 p.

1. Date added to Emory ms. by later hand; also address "L. Harris, Richmond Hill, L.I."

2. Burdeene had married Paul Irwin.

[To Lillian]

[June? 1906] [1]

My Dearest Bill:

I've been ill, but I love you still, think what you will. I've had my fill of soup and pill, and have the will to climb a small hill. I had indigestion till I thought I would die of a red-hot chill.

To Eastman [2] Mildred has gone; she went in the early morn, and left us all forlorn. She'll have a good time as sure's you're born—which reminds me of my corn.

Well, that's as much as you can stand of such silliness, any way it's as much as I can stand. Everything is all right here, and I am now as well as ever. I could write you a long, gossippy letter—note the spelling!— but I have n't the time to-day, as I have some contract work to do which must be done at once. I'll write again—to-morrow, perhaps—and send you some money thouh [sic] I haven't the slightest idea how much you want. Love to Burdeene and Paul.

Your loving DADDY.

TL

1 p.

1. Date written on front of sheet in another hand and also address on back: Miss Lillian Harris, 427 N. Beech, Richmond Hill, L.I.

2. Eastman, New York. *Cf.* letter to Lillian, 16 May 1906.

"At the Sign of the Wren's Nest:" [1]

June 8 [1906]

Dear Lillian:

Just a line by way of sending the Exchange. I have a piece of work in my type-machine that I can't take out. Mildred has had all sorts of a time. Checks were mixed at the station, and her trunk went with Mrs. William

Jenkins to Waverly Hall, and the Jenkins trunk went to Eastman—So you can imagine the situation. Mrs. J. went to a wedding, and of course all her finery was in the trunk. I presume Mildred has been weeping and moping. I am feeling all right now, and will write you a longer letter Sunday. Mamma is a little off to-day with the Summer Complaint, but, otherwise, we are all well and happy.

    Your loving

      Daddy

Love to Paul and Virginia.—no, I mean Burdeene. Evelyn's deal with Bobbs Merrill didn't pan out.

    ALS

    2 pp.

    Envelope: Return to Box 111, / Atlanta, Ga. / Miss Lillian Harris, / 427 N. Beech Street, / Richmond Hill, / Long Island, / N.Y.

    PM: 9 June [1906]

    1. This much of return address typed.

[To Lillian]

Most anywhere around,

sometime in June. [1906]

Dear Billian:

    You might hare [sic] guessed why I didn't write to you, if you had just taken a sober second thought. Haven't I always been a prompt correspondent, writing you letters so long that you couldn't take time to read them? You didn't say how much money you wanted, and so I sent you ten dollars. Evelyn's deal with the Bobbs Merrill company fell through, and so I am that much to the bad. Mildred has never received her trunk. She had Mrs. William Jenkins trunk, and we supposed, of course, that Mrs. Jenkins had hers. But no, the trunk she had belonged to Mrs. M. L. Lipscomb, of 25 Oglethorpe street, and this lady has gone to Orlando, N.C. It is a sad mess all around, and I haven't slept much for two nights, thinking of the worry that Mildred has had. I suppose that all the employes of the baggage company were drunk last Wednesday morning. I am not at all certain that we shall ever see the trunk again, and it contains all of Mildred[']s decent summer clothes. Her pleasure has been effectually spoilt. I am feeling a great deal better, but I am very nervous, and I can hardly write on my type machine, my touch is uncertain. For this reason I am going to write you a very short letter. The weather has been very warm here, the humidity ranging almost as high as it sometimes does in New York. Everyone is well here with one exception, and he doesn't count much. The families also are well. The sweet peas have been gorgeous; I never saw anything like the show they made on the vines day before yesterday—it was like one huge bank of flowers. Old man Walter died the other day, and other people in various parts of the country will die before long if they are not already dead; that is the way the world progresses and improves. Give my love to Burdeene and Paul, and tell 'em that when they get old their hand-writing will be like mine. When you write for money, nominate the sum you want.

> Your loving
> DADDY.

TL
1 p.

[To Lillian]

Close-at-Home:
June 21. [1906]

Dearest Bill:

I have been very busy on that syndicate work,[1] and at the same time have been somewhat under the weather because I eat too much. It seems utterly impossible for me to control my appetite. For Instance [sic], I ate yesterday some tomatoes with green pepper, and the result was that I was ill all day, and half the night. Cora has been ill, in fact, she was in bed two or three days; but when she was told she must go to the hospital for an operation, she got well immediately. Mamma and I browsed around with Essie and our daughters-in-law, and in that way got along very well. Mildred received her trunk, after a week had passed, and I suppose she was glad to get it. The boys paid her a great compliment last Sunday. Roy went down to seeNeila [sic], but Knott, Fritz and Joe went down to see Mildred. I am sending you exchange for forty dollars, which I suppose will be sufficient for your return trip. Love to Burdeene and Paul.

Your loving
DADDY.

TL
1 p.
Envelope: Return to Box 111, / Atlanta, Ga. / Miss Lillian Harris, / 487 N. Beech Street, / Richmond Hill, / Long Island, N.Y.
PM: 21 June 1906
1. JCH's syndicate consisted of several newspapers to which he sold his UR sketches.

At Home: Monday, 24 Sept. [1906]
Dear Julian:

As you have seen by the papers, we have been having stormy times in town; but it will be well for you to read between the lines, remembering who sends out the stuff from here. There has not been and will not be any trouble in the neigborhood [sic] of West End, and the town is safer now than it has been since the war, guarded as it is by the justly famous Georgia malishy. The occasion of the trouble was four assaults in various parts of the town on Saturday, combined with some sweet-scented extras of The News. This stirred up the Saturday night crowd, and the chance they had, they began to chase negroes, killing some and wounding others, and kicking up the devil generally. In West End we had no suspicion of what was going on until we read the Sunday papers.[1]—J.C. stayed at your house last night. I went up for awhile, and found Julia as serene as it is possible for a human being to be. One thing is certain: she is not afraid, and I think that is the most fortunate thing in the world for her. She was not feeling very well yesterday, but she is all right this morning. She rode out with Rawson and the girls for some golden-rod yesterday, and the ride in the carriage fatigued her as it always does.—I am enclosing the cheque for $29, and with it the so-called song that has bothered me so to write. I have added to it a little note to Mr. T., which will enable him to shuffle it about to suit himself.—Mamma has a bad cold in the head, and, with it some fever, so that she was very nervous last night. She had me awakened about 2 o'clock a.m., and the result is I feel as though I had been on a tear. I say nothing about the play, as that is out of my line.—Is there another song to be written for the first act? If so, I'll get about it.[2] Write whenever you can.

Your affectionate

FATHER[3]

TL

2 pp./1 sheet

1. Referring to the 1906 race riot in Atlanta, brought about largely by inflammatory newspaper articles about the rape of white women by black men. JCH gave protective shelter on his premises to a number of black men and women, both on the back porch and in the cook's house. See photostat copy of his letter to Mr. Francis Garrison, 22 October 1906, in box 6, folder 9, Joel Chandler Harris Collection, SC, EU. The original is in the collection of Alexander William Armour, Princeton University Library.

2. Probably in reference to Julian's persistent efforts to turn the Uncle Remus material into a musical.

3. Later note added to letter in another hand: "Written to Julian at New York at the time of the Atlanta race riots."

[To JCH, Jr.]

In and out, and Roundabout:

20 October [1906]

My Dear Son:

Mama has been taking it for granted that you were lost, Mildred was sure that something had happened to you (and you so far away from home!) while Bill and I have compromised our uneasiness by laughing at the others. You have been deluged by a perfect flood of new experiences. First, you were seven hours late, and when you did arrive in Montreal, you had to stiffen up as a pall-bearer. Now you have unbent, pretending to learn French because there is sugar in it. Ah, that little postal card that Miss Albumen sent tell [sic] its own sweet little story. But such is life among les habitan's [sic]—We are much the same here. Mamma is in fine health, while the girls have their ups and downs of indigestion. To-day, Mildred has gone to the matinee with Alma—not the house-girl, but Alma the neighbor. Cora limps a little occasionally, but she manages to keep braced up on that drug-store whiskey, of which I still have a small supply. Alleen, the elder, and Esther Kelly have both been ill with sore-throat and fever.[1] Both are up and about to-day. Lucien read your letter, with the remark, "That kid's a peach!" Julian is still in wild pursuit of the magazine idea, and I think it will pan out all right before long. The announcements are to be sent out next week, and, meanwhile, I have written letters to every author in creation, including some dead ones. I wrote to the dead ones because it wasn't their fault.[2] We have violets by the hundred, and I'm sorry I can't send some to Ma'mselle Albumen. Like everything else that's nice, they'd wither and fade before they got there. Please don't get into any controversies with the Captain: you know how we old men are, how sot in their ways, and how overbearing they are. I broke my shuttle, and I have to put on another. The first word in the line above—or, rather, the first two words that are written over are "with the." I hope you are feeling as well as you were when you left. I used to have to get a pencil or a pen before I could write a letter, but I never used such a large thing as a trunk. Did you think there was no stationery in Upton? Well, well—if you can write with a trunk, it is a great accomplishment.—By the way, there is a big thick letter here from Betsy. I may enclose it with this, or I may open it and send you a copy. She says on the front, "Please forward." but I had never heard that she was of a military disposition. It is the Captain of a company that says "forward!" and he doesn't put any "please" to it either. But I suppose Betsy is trying to be polite, and she deserves great credit for it, just as the Captain of the Banks County Guards deserved it. He used to say, "Gentlemen of the Banks County Guards: Attention   You'll have to put in the scare mark and the quotation marks after attention; I couldn't quite come it. I haven't a bit of news to write you, and therefore I have to pad out with nonsense—which I hope you'll not find disagreeable, especially when you are so far from home. All news takes to the bushes when I seize my type machine. The magazine's name is funny: Uncle Remus's Magazine! Love to the Captain, and write when you can.

Your loving DADDY.

TL

1 p.

Envelope: J.C. Harris Jr. / Upton Station, / Province of Quebec, / Canada East, / Care of Captain LaRose

PM: 20 October 1906

1. Esther Kelly, daughter of niece Essie La Rose and Charles Kelly.

2. *Uncle Remus's Magazine*; addresses of newspaper editors and drafts of letters by

Joel Chandler Harris (left), his wife, Esther (far right), their children Evelyn, Julian, and Lillian (in rear), and daughter-in-law Julia (left center), in the backyard of the Wren's Nest. The woman between Julia and Esther Harris is probably Esther's niece Essie LaRose Kelly; the young girl in front is Essie's daughter, Esther LaRose Kelly (Joel Chandler Harris Collection, Special Collections Department, Robert W. Woodruff Library, Emory University).

JCH to them and to authors promoting the magazine are in box 1, folder 13, Joel Chandler Harris Collection, SC, EU.

[To JCH, Jr.]

Considerably at Home: October 28. [1906]

Dear Son: Your last letter was quite the thing, and I liked it very much. It was interesting and well-written; in other words, there seemed to be no effort on your part to write well and yet the well-known-sign of style was there—the thing that everybody recognizes instantly, though nobody can say precisely what it is. I call it the flavor of individuality. But there is not one person in a million that can put himself on paper. The way I do, I just imagine that I can hear my thoughts, and that gives them a certain vitality that they could not have if I did otherwise.

There is no news here except that the long talked-of announcement of the new magazine appeared in the three Sunday papers this morning. Everybody seems to take some degree of interest in it. It is full of mush about me (I mean the announcement) and I can hardly realize, after reading it, that I am such a "dam genius."[1] Maybe that's what's the matter with my feet and legs when they feel wobbly. I hope to goodness that it won't strike in like the measles, and take me off in the prime of senility—which is another name for a sick old age.

Essie had a chill yesterday, and a high fever last night, but she is better to-day. Mr. Crowe thinks she has a touch of the grip. To-day, Mildred, with that access [sic] of benevolent kindness characteristic of her, brought the baby over home to take care of it, and went to ride. She is the kindest hearted child I ever knew, and some day she will have a crown so grand that it will be too heavy for her head, and someone else will have to wear it. She can always find some one to do that she ought to do herself. With the exception noted, everybody is well. Evem [sic] Cora is not complaining. Mrs. Eckford dragged us out to the carriage-makers' barbeque, and I had a specially good time. You see, since I have discovered what a distinguished man I am, I am taking advantage of the fact, or condition, to get a free meal occasionally. I am afraid it will develop into a habit.

The boys come down occasionally for to play set-back, and last night Mildred and Alton won over Bill and Roy. The winners were so hilarious over it that I am thinking there will be many games of set-back before the season is over. We've had a circus, and now Pawnee Bill is to be on hand with a wild west show. The boys with whom you associate have dropped out of my life, as the girl said when her stocking dropped. I don't know what else we are to have, but whatever it is, the girls will pant over it. Speaking of letters, you must remember that a letter from Upton consumes eight days of good time before it can be answered and the answer received. The girls have written, and they have sent you a package of papers, and another was shipped this morning. I suppose you are getting along well with Miss Albumen. I hope her feet are not fat. Give my love to grandpa, and keep him cheered up. Old people can stand a good deal cheerfulness if it be not too boisterous.

To-day has been very cold, calling for overcoats and jackets; yet if the wind should cease blowing, the weather would be unusually pleasant. The leaves are falling so fast when the wind blows that I have the impression a flock of sparrows is flying to the ground. Julian is still hard at work on the affair, and I have written hundreds of letters to editors whom I used to know. All the responses have been more than kind, even cordial, and there seems to be no doubt that the magazine will receive more free advertising than any other new publication ever received. This is due to the remembrance of [my] winning smile—you've seen it in action.

Well, there's nothing worth writing about except what I've already written, and you'll hardly think that that is worth while. Send me a letter when you are in the humor.

Your loving

DAD.

TL
1 p.
Envelope: Mr. Joel Chandler Harris, Jr. / Upton Station / P. of Q., Canada
PM: 29 October 1906
1. See picture of JCH and article by S. W. Dibble, Atlanta *Constitution*, Sunday, 28 October 1906, B-5; also, the Atlanta *Journal*, Sunday, 28 October 1906, 4.

[To Lillian]

[18 November 1906][1]
Saturday, 17, 1906

Dear Bill:

I have just placed a new ribbon on my type-machine, and I'm going to try it first on you if it kills every cook in Macon, Bibb county, Ga. I am going to write to you, and yet there is nothing to write about. The various kinnery are about as usual, especially the children. The Kelly kids continue their peculiar habit of swallowing bottle stoppers—glass ones—and chewing up eye-droppers, and eating pieces of coal. The diet seems to agree with them. The baby chewed one the other day and another yesterday; she seems to have a weakness for them, and is in better health now than she has been for a long time. Consequently, I have ordered twelve dozen of these eye-droppers, and I think these will last her during the winter. I hope Polly's baby won't get into the habit of using such a diet, for it is somewhat costly. Mildred and Essie have gone to the matinee to-day, and Cora is tending to the children for her; I don't know who is to pick the chickens for to-morrow, but I suppose the duty will fall on me. Well, such things are among the diversions of married life, and I am used to them. There is absolutely nothing in this neighborhood worth writing about. If there is, I go out so little that it never comes my way. You saw about Addison Snodgrass getting drunk at the thratre [sic]. Well, he was fined $25 and the man who sold him the whiskey was bound over to the State courts. Addison is certainly a grown man now. (You see that the new ribbon on my machine is a little too narrow.) Isn't it funny that none of our boys ever sought distinction in a bar-room! But, as I said, there is positively nothing to write about. I hear nothing but magazine from morning till night.[2] Julian is going to New York on the 30th, and Julia is coming over here while he is away. Love to Polly and the baby.

　　Your loving
　　　Dad.

TL
2 pp.

1. Date in brackets supplied by later anonymous hand. Date in letter appears to be overstrike, changing 14 to 17; i.e., "Saturday, 17, 1906."

2. Plans for the *Uncle Remus's Magazine.*

[To JCH, Jr.]

In the Neighborhood of
Home: 17 November, 1906.

Dear Son: The postals that you have alluded to so often are held in the Dead Letter office in Montreal. It seems that you wrote on them and then placed them in an envelope. This was fatal to the 1 cent idea, and so notices have come hither addressed to Neila, Lillian, and Mildred, informing them that if they would send another cent, the postals would be forthcoming. This they have done, and are expecting to receive them any day. We learn a great deal that we didn't know before as we grow older; sometimes the acquisition of new knowledge irritates us, and sometimes we merely laugh at it. But we must have our dose, based on experience, circumstance, and opportunity. I have no doubt that you now know something about postal cards that you didn't know before, no matter whether the knowledge is amusing or irritating.—There is absolutely nothing here to write about. Things are going on in the same old way. You don't want to hear that the Kelly kids are still in the push, swallowing bottle-stoppers, and chewing up eye-droppers. That would be no news at all, for you already know what is likely to happen in that well-conducted mansion. The bottle-stoppers, and the crushed glass seem to agree with the kids better than any medicine they ever took; they actually fatten on it. Well, it's a blessing! If my hopefuls had been similarly constituted, I should have fed them on broken tumblers and vases, and in this way, saved quite a number of dollars.—Along towards the middle of December, you will begin to press your nose against the window-pane, and cry, "Me for home!" It is a long, long journey, but you will be able to make the trip, by arriving on a late train.—Your friend Addison Snodgrass went to the Grand the other night in an intoxicated condition. As a result, he was arrested, and fined $25 by the Recorder.

Incidentally, he told who sold him the liquor, and the saloon man was bound over to the state courts. Addison got more good advertising than he'll ever get again.—Everybody is well here, and we hope you are the same. Love to the Captain and to yourself.

> Your loving
>
> DADDY.

TL
2 pp. / 1 sheet folded
Envelope: Joel Chandler Harris Jr., / Upton, Quebec / Canada East.
PM: 18 November 1906

[To JCH, Jr.]

2 December, 1906

Dear Son:

This is the note paper that Julian has had fixed for the great editor—don't you feel proud? Moreover, this is the first letter I have written on it, and that should make you prouder.[1] I notice that you are getting very coltish, since you arrived in Upton. That is a very good idea; be coltish, but not horsy, and all will beforgiven [*sic*]. Mamma and the gals have been away day and night since the fair began five days ago. Yesterday they stayed in bed until half-past eleven, and I am not certain they are up yet. According to all accounts, the fair was a great success; Lucien thinks that it made at least $1,800, but I suppose the amount will be something less than that. It has been a perfect orgie for Mamma, and partially so for the girls, for during the closing hours, both Alton and Fritz were largely in evidence, and everything seemed to be all serene. The latch-key was great puzzle, like the game of who's got the thimble? The sister that didn't have it, would hurry home with her escort, and, finding it missing, would endeavor to sit out in the cold for fear of waking Dad. I caught on to the game at last, and, Saturday night, when Not and Mildred put in an appearance without the key, I donned my raincoat, to hide my nakedness, and called them in. It was a great blow to young love, but they could do nothing bet [*sic*] respond gracefully to the voice of parental authority; yet it was a sad hour!

There isn't a bit of news. All the suicides and wife-beatings are on the other side of town. I tell them all that the epidemic will spread in this direction presently, and they seem to believe it, for they are very quiet and good-humored these days. In fact, you will hardly know your own home if this keeps up. I sent you some exchange in Mildred's letter, which I trust you have received by this time. I suppose you know what to do. Just get some one to identify you at a Montreal or St. Hyacinthe bank, and ask them to give you American money. Everybody is well and maintain exasperating appetites, in the face of the fact that people shouldn't eat too much. There is nothing else to say, and I shall proceed to say it by sending my love to the Captain.

Your loving
DADDY.

TL

2 pp. / 1 sheet folded

Envelope: Joel Chandler Harris, Jr., / Upton, Providence of Quebec / Canada East

PM: 4 December [1906]

1. Note JCH's first use of monogram in a rabbit shape on business stationery with the heading *Uncle Remus's Magazine.* Oliver Herford, illustrator of *Little Mr. Thimblefinger* (1894) and *Mr. Rabbit at Home* (1895), had devised the rabbit monogram for the first book. The monogram was first used in JCH's personal stationery and then in the magazine by permission of the publishers of the children's books. The monogram in this particular letter has been cut out.

[1907]

Dear Julian:

Hereafter, I hope you'll not accept stuff for the magazine until I have passed on it.[1] One expensive mistake you have made could have been so easily avoided by submitting it to me, that I am induced to write you about it. That is the Dr. Massey stuff about the dead towns in Georgia. It is copied almost literally from a book written by Colonel Charles C. Jones, and is not of the slightest interest to anybody in the world.[2] Another mistake you have made is the Octavia Walton Levert business by Mrs. Horton. Mrs. Levert has sounded the death-knell of every Southern magazine that ever was started, and I am not going to allow her to sound ours. She was the Mrs. Joseph Thompson of her time as I understand it, and nobody living now has the slightest interest in her career.[3] Please let me see the stuff about her before you put it to print. No matter how well it is done, it will have to be postponed indefinitely, or until the magazine reaches a point where it cannot be killed by it. These two mistakes are not caused by a lack of judgment or taste on your part, but by a lack of perspective. If you had fifty years behind you it would be impossible for you to make them.

You told me some time ago that you intended to submit to me the proposed contents of the first issue. I understand that you and Mr. Camp[4] have consulted over it, but, as yet, I have not seen the lay-out, so to speak. It is my business to see it, and I shall think it very peculiar if I do not. I am not trying to worry you or hamper you; but if you had your name as prominently connected with the magazine as mine is, I am afraid you would kick up a tremendous row over the situation as it stands, especially the impossible MS. of Dr. Massey, and the almost equally impossible stuff of Mrs. Horton. We cannot afford to be provincial in such matters; we have got to make a modern magazine, and a successful one, no matter whose feelings are hurt. I am prepared to take the responsibility in such things. But before we shelve Octavia Walton Levert, let me see the stuff.[5]

Affectionately yours:
Joel Chandler Harris

TLS

2 pp./1 sheet

1. Re contents of first issue (June 1907) of *Uncle Remus's Magazine*. Note Harris's firm hand as editor and concern for high quality of magazine.

2. Charles Colcock Jones, Jr. (28 October 1831–19 July 1893), lawyer and prolific writer, author of *The Dead Towns of Georgia* (1878), opponent of Grady's New South, supplier of Gullah tales to Harris (*Dictionary of Georgia Biography* 1:546–47). See his letters in Robert Manson Myers's *The Children of Pride* (1972).

3. Octavia Walton LeVert (18 August 1810 or 11 August 1811–12 March 1877), social notable and descendant of George Walton, Georgia signer of the Declaration of Independence (*Dictionary of Georgia Biography* 2:616–18). Mrs. Joseph Thompson, late nineteenth-century Atlanta social leader.

4. Future son-in-law, Edwin Camp.

5. Mrs. Horton's "Letters from Henry Clay to Mme. Levert" appears in *URM* 1, no. 1 (June 1907), 18–20; "Madame LeVert and Her Friends," in *URM* 1, no. 3 (August 1907), 19–21.

[To Lillian]

Purty Close to Home,

Sometime in Jinnawary, 1908.

Dear Bill: If you knew what a vacant spot you had left behind you—
what a tremendous vacuum you have created, you'd take another breath
before you began to spout about your happiness.[1] Of course you are
happy, not only because you deserve to be, but because Fritz is such a
fine fellow. I knew what you were getting; I have kept my eye on Fritz
ever since he was a kid, and he has always been one of the substabtial
[sic] and dependable sort. He has been my favorite among all the boys
that have been coming here. He didn't know it, of course, and there was
no need that he should, but I felt gratified when he justified my ideas of
him by picking you out as his mate. He certainly showed that he was a
wise one, for there never was a girl more deserving, or one better fitted
to meet all the responsibilities that fall to the lot of a wife. This is not
taffy. The only fault I have ever found with you is a tendency to be a little
extravagant—a sort of ignorance as to the value and power of money.
Both of you are young, and if I were you, and knew as much about such
things as I know now, I'd buckle down and save all the money I could.
That is the way to get along in this world, and I wouldn't be surprised
if it don't turn out to be a pretty good plan for the next.—Things are
just like they used to be, except for your absence. If you were here we
couldn't tell 'em apart, as the twin said to the stranger. Mamma has shed
a few natural tears, but she hasn't forgotten to buy lye hominy when the
man comes around; she'll keep on fooling with such stuff until we have
to call in the cow-doctor.—Cora seems to be in low spirits, and I don't
know whether she is troubled by prohibition, or by your absence.[2] She
says she has been cookin' here eight years, sick and well, and she never
felt lonesome before. She reckons it must be the weather, which has been
very cold during the last few days.—I see by the paper that Charles has
been made managing editor. I expect Essie to celebrate it with another
baby in March. Essie says I don't seem as cordial as I used to be, and
she wonders what the matter is. The trouble is that I never know when
I'm speaking to one person or two when she walks in the door—and
it's embarrassing. You will see that Fritz feels the same way about it.—I

Lillian Harris's bridal portrait, 1908 (Joel Chandler Harris Association, Atlanta, Georgia).

knew you would like Cordele. The people in the country towns are the salt of the earth. I would give anything if my lot had been cast in a country town. It is a very happy life, simply because it lacks the ambition of what is called the smart set. Just be yourself, and you'll never lack for warm friends.—News is might skace [sic]; it all runs away when I take my type-machine between my teeth. Mildred Spratling called Friday. Our Mildred was asleep on the sofa, but I just brought her in regardless, and I wish you could have seen the tableau. It was as good as the By Jo. One was astonished, and the other surprised, but M.S. had on brown pumps with gold buckles, and she dangled her hind legs at Mildred until I thought the child would have a fit, or fall in a faint.—As Frances is away, J.C. is staying at home at night, and trying to be very good.— Annie-Belle will go next week, and Mildred will be the maid. She is not capable, but we'll rty [sic] to get along the best we can. This is all I can think of now. I'll try to write once a week, but you must remember that you are married, and have no time to read so many letters. Give my love to Fritz, reserving a small slice for yourself.

    Your loving

      DAD.

TL

1 p.

1. Lillian married Frederick "Fritz" Wagener, Jr., 15 January 1908.

2. Georgia passed a statewide prohibition law on 2 August 1907 to take effect 1 January 1908.

[To Lillian and Mildred]

At the Same Old Place,

Especially on Sunday.

[16 March 1908]

Dear Bill and Mill:

We are having a very quiet and restful time, but I am still suffering from my cough and cold. I am doping on Chaney's expectorant, and I think I am getting better. Edwin is not getting any better, however; he looks as if he had a bile on his elbow. Everybody is well that ought to be, and a good many that don't deserve it. We have the same old cat, and the same old cook, and you would think, to look at us and hear us talk, that we are getting along just as well as ever. But appearances are deceitful, for I forgot to get me some tobacco Saturday, and I am afraid I will need it before Monday. Cora says she is beginning to feel signs of rheumatism in her hind-legs, and if her feet begin to swell, I am going to get her some hat-boxes for slippers; I think she will be able to get around with these. At any rate, I am going to try it; maybe she won't have the rheumatism if she knows she'll have to wear hat-boxes for shoes. I went to walk this afternoon, and came home very tired, which shows that I am getting older every day.—The weather is fine up here, but no one knows what a day or two may bring forth. All the fruit trees are in bloom, eacept [sic] the apple, and if we have a frost, we shant have any fruit. One consolation is that if we had it, nobody could eat it on account of its toughness, and its close kin to the stummy-ache [sic].—I thought I had some news to write, but since I sat down it has all gone under the bed and I can't coax it out, although I have put a nice piece of apple on the floor.—Essie got a bed bug in her washing and came running over here to ask if it was contagious.[1] I told here she had better have everybody vaccinated, and she smiled a sickly smile just as if she had on a wool hat that flopped down over her ears. At last, I told her to have the bug dropped on Camp's front porch, and this seemed to relieve her; she said she'd put it in a basket, and make brother take it. Thus you see there are just as many funny things happening as when Mildred was here. They happen and nobody sees them but me.—Tell Mildred I had a fine time at the vaudeville, and that Louise gets sweeter and sweeter every day; it seems as if she just can't help it. She slept over here last night in Mildred's bed in order to give Julian and sister an opportunity[2] to go to the theatre. Ask Mildred not to be too jealous. I don't know about the Langford girl; I haven't seen her, but it is said that she has been in this neighborhood for several nights—it's so hard to teach[3] some girls how to play the piano!—I don't know of a single scandal in the neighborhood; everybody seems to be trying to keep the lid on. I received a letter from the guests of the Verona Inn at Clearwater ordering me to come down or be tried by a court martial. Charlie's case is over; I had to pay a fine of twenty-five dollars, and he has already begun to pay it back; nevertheless, he was drunk on Saturday.[4] It was one of these giggling drunks; the kind that makes you love all your friends and their children. There is no prohibition in the alley back of Cora's because the express wagon visits the place sometimes twice a week. It is funny how an express wagon can change the whole appearance of an alley, bringing sunshine where there had been gloom. But such is life! Good-bye; be good, and give my love to Fritz and the housekeeper.[5]

Your loving DADDY.

TL

1 p.

Envelope: UNCLE REMUS'S / MAGAZINE [monogram] / EDITED BY JOEL / CHANDLER HARRIS / ATLANTA, GA. / Mrs. Fred. Wagener, Jr., / The Suwanee House, / Cordele, Ga.

PM: 16 March 1908

1. Niece and later neighbor Esther LaRose Kelly.
2. *t* typed over *y*.
3. *learn* struck through and *teach* written above.
4. Charlie was the butler. See mention of him in previous letters.
5. Letter used through permission of owner, Myrtle W. Wagener.

[To Lillian and Mildred]

27 March. [1908]

Dear Gals:

It wasn't altogether meanness that prevented me from writing to you last week; but it was pretty close to it. In other words, the last cold spell stirred up my bronchitis again and aroused my light catarrh, and I wasn't feeling any better than a sick man should. I haven't done any work in two weeks, except write a piece of nigger doggerel for the Children's Department.[1] Then I have had indigestion, which is always a bad companion for an old man. I noticed in one of Mildred's letters last week, she asked what had become of Camp. I thought it so funny that I asked Camp if he had written to her. To convince me that he had, he showed me copies of twelve letters that he had mailed to her, and she had only been in Cordele eight days. He also had nine from Mildred. May the Lord help the prevaricators! J.C. and I have come to the conclusion that it wouldn't be well for me to come down there until Fritz has been cured of his tumors and warts. I hope he is better now. The weather is fine

here—the lilac blooming, and the wisteria arranging to make a great show. They will all probably be killed by a freeze or a frost, for such is life in our hand-made city. Frank and J.C. are still at it, while old Lije is fumbling in his britches pocket for some tobacco crumbs. We have been having a nice quiet time here, with nobody to pester us. Mama has been constantly cleaning house for two weeks, and when night comes you can't tell whether she's been shuffling in the ash-pile, as the settin-hens do, or whether she's been taking a dust bath with the sparrows. It's all one to her. Your orange spoons came, and we divided them up: J.C. took three for Frank, and I gave two to Cora, and one to old Mary. The Bible says we must remember the poor you know. Dip up water with orange spoons and the microbes will float into you. I had to wash the stickiness off my hands after reading extracts from the Camp-Harris correspondence.[2] Mildred says she wants more money; it's curious how much she has spent for postage stamps and drug-store loblolly. Here's one little West End convulsion: Julian forgot to pay his telephone bill, and he's been cut off. Sister is in great distress, but she's mighty pretty when she gets a little angry.[3] The apple trees are beginning to bloom and the bumble-bees are as drunk as lords all day. If the Sons and Daughters of Human Temperance were to find that out, apple trees would be abolished and prohibited, and we'd have to send to Chattanooga for our cider. Well, I'm tired between my shoulder-blades, and, besides, I have nothing more to write. I am enclosing a cheque for Mildred. Love to Fritz.
Your loving DADDY.
I've made the cheque out to Fritz.[4]

TL
1 p.
Return: UNCLE REMUS'S MAGAZINE [rabbit monogram] / EDITED BY JOEL CHANDLER HARRIS / ATLANTA, GA.
Envelope: Mrs. Fred. Wagener, Jr., / The Suwanee House, / Cordele, Ga.
PM: 27 March 1908
1. In *Uncle Remus's Magazine*, a section that JCH began.
2. Mildred and Edwin Camp were married 27 October 1909.
3. "Sister," probably Julian's wife, Julia Harris.
4. Last sentence is JCH's handwritten addition; Fritz Wagener, Lillian's husband.

[To Lillian]

Roundabout Home, April 4. [1908]

My Dear Gal:

I take my type-machine between my two hands to inform you that I am fairly well—not too well, but just about well enough to remember my ailments. Speaking of Vaudeville, Camp went to Macon to meet Mildred, and had to run clear across town in order to catch the Central train. He pulled off the stunt all right, but I couldn't help thinking all the time that his family needed the money he had spent. They have to pay the Langford girl for Mary['s] music lessons;.—unless she is giving them just to keep in touch with Edwin. It is a sweet name, Edwin, and I am determined to name my next son Edwin. If it is a girl, she shall be called Edwina. It is a name that trembles on your lips, and makes you want to take another drink—which I invariably do, especially if my fat old prohibitionist is too busy to watch me. Tell Fritz that old man Spratlin has introduced a bill in council to increase taxation[.] It's a cured ham for him, since he pays no taxes. Mildred Spratlin hasn't borrowed anythin[g] from Mrs. Wagner this week, but she has evened things up by borrowing some clean underclothing from Julia Rosser. You see we live in a hospitable neighborhood, and the next news you hear I will be wearing a pair of Mr. Rosser's pants. Think of your dear old father becoming a sport to this extent. The Magazine seems to be booming. The May number will have more than eleven thousand lines of advertising, and this means about seven thousand dollars worth of business. Fortunately for the publication, I will handle none of this, and things will go on just as they have been going. And yet you can't always sometimes inginer'lly [sic] tell. By looking for the worst, you are agreeably surprised if it doesn't happen. I hope Fritz wasn't offended about my remarks about carcbucles [sic] and warts; I was just simply trying to tease you. I think, however, that you have become case-hardened since you married—nevertheless, there is a way to tease married women, and I give you fair warning. We'd like to have Fritz with you when you come up for Easter. There is no lack of room since you ran off with him. I don't know any neighborhood news, and I have no grievance against anybody—not even against Spratlin. I wish I could hear what the feeling is in regard to Joe Brown in your section; up here it is all against Hoke Smith; I never heard of such changes.[1] Get Fritz to tell you of the situation down there; he can easily find out from the traveling men. I know he doesn't take an interest in such things; neither do I, but there has been such a remarkable reaction in North Georgia, that I would like very much to know what the feeling is in South Georgia. Mildred says she had the time of her life in Cordele, and she says it in such a way that I am bound to believe it. She gone to town to have a pearl put in Stoy's Elk pin. Everybody* is well, and apparently doing well. Neila is going to have an operation for appendicitis performed to-day, and I'm rather dubious about the result, she is so big and fat. Her mother is with her, and that's a blessing. Mrs. Ab. is still in Florida, I think.[2] Lord 'a' mercy! I've written you too much; if I don't write next week, just take out this letter and read it over; it will do you good. Love to Fritz.

> Your loving
> DADDY.

*In our families, I mean. [handwritten addition][3]

TL

1 p.

Envelope: UNCLE REMUS'S MAGAZINE [monogram] / EDITED BY JOEL CHANDLER HARRIS / ATLANTA, GA. / Mrs. Fred Wagener, Jr., / The Suwanee House, / Cordele, Ga.

PM: 4 April 1908

1. Previous letters mention these candidates for the governor of Georgia.
2. Probably a neighbor, Mrs. Abernathy. See earlier letters.
3. Letter used through permission of owner, Myrtle W. Wagener.

[To Lillian]

> [6/7 May 1908]
> Along about May 6 or 7

Dear Bill:

The only news I know is that the police are about to arrest J.C. for going to Connally's so much, and when that happens I am going to have Camp put in the chain-gang. Mildred is not the same when you are not here; in fact, she is the most disagreeable character I eve [sic] met. The fact that she and Camp hold hands all day and nearly all night doesn't make her temper any better, and you will hear before long that I have knocked her from the front door to the sidewalk. Don't be surprised when you hear it, and don't judge me harshly[;] you know the provocations I have. I wish Camp could get her right away; in a year he would be better cured than a country ham. I want to see him suffer; I think it will make him strong. Annie Lou and Evelyn come over when they want anything; otherwise they are too busy to visit us. I paid them my first and last visit the other Sunday, and I haven't recovered yet; Peachtree cooking is too much for me.—Speaking of dreams, I had one the other night that made me sit up and take notice. I dreampt [sic] I was a rosebush, not a large one, but a small and shy one. I thought I had four blossoms, pink and very beautiful. This was all right, but in addition to the blossoms, I thought there were two caterpillars on me. I wanted the wind to blow and shake them off, but there was no wind, and I could feel them crawling up my branches slowly but surely. I was so glad when I woke up and found it was a dream that I didn't know what to do. I know now how a rosebush feels when it has worms on it; it wants to move and shake them off, and yet it doesn't know how.—All the families are well, as far as I know; only Julia and myself have been ailing during the bad weather—and it has been bad. I hope Fritz is well; some young men, you know, go through a great deal of suffering when they are first married. They have a kind of gallopy feeling. I think Peruna is good for it.—You seem to be having a good many changes down there; I expect to hear next that the hotel has been turned into a Hoke Smith bar-room.[1] or that it has been moved to Fitgerald [Fitzgerald]. In fact, I am expecting any kind of queer news from there, but, thank goodness, I am not compelled to believe all I hear. One question I asked you has not been answered: When is Fritz going to break up his headquarters down there, and come to Atlanta where it will cost you two nothing to live. I am asking in the interests of economy. His railroad fare back and forth would cost him a little more, but he would save his tremendous board bill. As a matter of course, it is none of my blooming business, but it is sad to see two young people, in the very heyday of their career, throwing away money that could be saved. But I am not lecturing this season; I am merely repeating some remarks that I delivered before the Young Men's Christian Association last year—or was it forty years ago?

All time looks alike to me, except winter time. Tell Fritz, if he has become absentminded, to wear his left shoe on his right foot, and turn his
coat wrongside outwards twice a day; that's what an old fellow told me
some time ago. I haven't tried it, and I believe I'd prefer for Fritz to try
it first.—Well, this is all. Love to Fritz.

> From your loving
>> DADDY.

TL

1 p.

Envelope: Box 111 UNCLE REMUS'S MAGAZINE [monogram] / EDITED BY JOEL CHANDLER HARRIS /
ATLANTA, GA. / Mrs. Fred Wagener, Jr. / The Suwanee House, / Cordele, Ga.

PM: 7 May 1908

1. Hoke Smith—progressive politician (2 September 1855–27 November 1931), lawyer, businessman, secretary of the interior under Grover Cleveland (1892–96), governor of Georgia (1906–8; 1910–11); U.S. senator (1911–20). A statewide prohibition law
adopted 2 August 1907 made the legislature less tractable in implementing Hoke Smith's
reform platform after his defeat of Clark Howell (*Dictionary of Georgia Biography* 2:898–
900). Hoke Smith was defeated in the 1908 election by Joseph Brown and his slogan
"Hoke and Hunger, Brown and Bread," referring to the panic of 1907. Smith was reelected
in 1910.

[To Lillian]

> At the Old Stand,
> Tuesday. [1908]

Dear Bill,

We took dinner at Annie-Lou's last Sunday, and I suffered from it all
Monday. But such is the fate of society people the world over; they eat
all sorts of cooking and die before they are a hundred years old. Roy
didn't come down as he said he would, and I reckon it is just as well.
Mildred and mamma would have put on long faces, and the whole business would have been brought back to him as vividly as ever. There was
no news at Annie-Lou's, so that you may know there is none here. The
weather has been something fierce—rainy, windy and cold. Cyclones
have looked in on us, and the lightning has come close to ripping up
our backs. I went to Dr. Troutman's silver anniversary, and found my-

self the observed of all observers; in fact, I had to stand in the same room with the aged bride and groom, and hold a reception of my own. Mrs. Candler, the Bishop's wife talked one ear off and the rest of them walked off with the remains of the other.[1] I never heard so much talk in my life. Some woman caught hold of the lower corner of my vest, and held on as though she was afraid she'd drown if she turned loose. You may be sure that I had surfeit of all this. Enough is enough, and too much is a plenty. It was all mighty funny to me. As I was going, Dr. T. whispered that he wished everybody would go but me. He and his wife must have been tired, for they stood up—as I did—all the time. When I got out, I panted right heartily, and felt as if I had done a day's ploughing. And yet, in spite of this, I rather enjoyed the affair, for it enabled me to see with my own eyes what durn fools nice women can be. There is no let-up in the Brown boom up here; in fact, it seems to be growing.[2] Nevertheless, you can't always sometimes inginerlly [sic] tell. Why don't you get a mosquito net? You'll come back here with malaria if you allow the skeeters to bit you. Alleen's Grandmother Zachry is dead; Lamar Collier married her daughter. Everything is just as usual with the various families, including mine. Nothing seems to pall on their appetites; nothing is too raw for them to eat. You seem to have symptoms of a person who is seasick; if so, I'd advise you to pull up your panties and wade to land. We have the same old cook and cat, and your room is waiting for you. When will Fritz make up his mind to break away from down there? He'll have to leave some day in self defence; moreover, I have cigars for him. We are sending you by express a bottle of champagne. We intrusted [sic] it to J.C., so there's no telling when you will receive it. Mildred has Nancy this week, and has been sticking by her work quite steadily. Charley lambasted Annie-Belle the other night, and now she has left him. He doesn't seem to be suffering. Everything else is just as you left it, so I will close this rambling letter, and let you go to sleep. Give my love to Fritz.

Your loving
DADDY.

TL
1 p.

1. Probably the wife of Bishop Warren Akin Candler, who became the first chancellor of Emory University.

2. Reference to Joseph M. Brown–Hoke Smith gubernatorial race. *Cf.* letter to Lillian "Tuesday, 12 [1908]."

[To Lillian]

[12 May/June 1908]
Purty Close to home.
Tuesday, 12. [1908]

Dear Bill:

The only new thing in this neighborhood is Corley's cow, and she wouldn't be new if she hadn't shed her winter coat of hair. As it is she looks pretty frisky. Pace has a new calf—or, rather, his cow has. We think this is a great victory for West End, though I don't know what has become of the calf. Everybody is well, especially mamma, who is healthy enough for to make a sick king bite his finger-nails. There has been a tremendous row over at Kelly's to find out what color to tint the rooms, and what kind of matting to lay down. I think a decision has finally been made, and now there is peace in the land. At times like this I can see where we need four more battleships and a number of submarine family destroyers. Randolph Rose has sent me some whisky that I didn't order, and now mamma is making a novena to prevent me from developing into a high-toned drunkard.[1] It is a little too much for me—I mean the whisky—and I wish Fritz were here to sample it; meanwhile, I'll save some of it for him. I had a bad day yesterday; I ate some stewed beef, and got stewed. So, don't you see, forsooth, forsooth! 'Twas ever thus in early youth? The Magazine seems to be getting along very well; we have six thousand dollars' worth of business for June—which seems to be shaking the bushes some.[2] Mrs. Fleming has had her house painted inside and out, Father Rosser has had his front porch made as broad as his mind, and Miss Nell has had a new room added to the back for the accommodation of her mother, and to prevent such a gittin' up stairs. More than that, my beloved fellow-countrymen, Brown is running just like he had a tincan tied to his tail.[3] So you see, we are having both progress and politics, together with long-winded discussions on the street cars, where you usually find one Hoke man to do all the discussin', while the others sit back and laugh at him. But such is the way of the cold and cruel world. Camp is still tied out in the front yard, just as though he were a calf belonging to the place. Not ambles down sometimes, followed by Cecil Myer, and then occasionally Henry Troutman comes to supper. He is a very fine boy. The Browns, including Frank, are going on a long trip, and I don't know what J.C. will do. They are trying to wean the girl away from him, and they may succeed; you can never tell about hearts and lungs, and livers and lights. This thing you call love is like breaking into a confectionary shop, where you don't know where the right kind of candy is kept. But such is life in this giddy old world, where the vaudeville show has a continuous performance, with no recess for dinner. We have had more fires, but they are nothing to the sight we'll see hereafter; so be good and kind and gentle, and forgive the Cordele cook his trespasses.

Your loving

DADDY

Love to Fritz.

TL

1 p.

1. Former owner of Atlanta's Four Roses Distillery. Statewide prohibition had begun 1 January 1908, according to a new law.

2. The first issue of *Uncle Remus's Magazine* appeared June 1907; the letter is probably a year later.

3. Reference to the 1908 gubernatorial race between Joseph M. Brown and Hoke Smith. News of Brown's election, *Atlanta Constitution*, 24 June 1908.

APPENDIX
REGISTER OF PREVIOUSLY PRINTED LETTERS

UNCLE REMUS'S MAGAZINE

Following JCH's death in 1908, the editors of *Uncle Remus's Magazine* published both portions and whole letters from those written either individually or jointly to Lillian and Mildred while they were students at Saint Joseph's Academy. Placed first in "The Children's Department," a feature that JCH had begun and personally edited, later such letters were set apart in the table of contents. The magazine changed its name to *Uncle Remus's The Home Magazine* in May 1908 after a merger and then to *Uncle Remus's Home Magazine* in August 1909. The abbreviation *URM* is used regardless of variations of title. As the editorial information supplied with these (recipient and date) is so unreliable in the early issues, each will be identified by the information in the originals. But the heading will be the title supplied in *URM*. This portion of my list is a corrected version based on the one found in William Strickland's invaluable bibliographic dissertation on JCH's works (pp. 201–5).

1. To: "My Dear Daughter [Lillian]"; date: "25 April [1897]." *URM* 24, no. 1 (September 1908): 28. No heading.
2. To: "My Dear Daughter [Lillian]"; date: "1 November [1896]." *URM* 24, no. 2 (October 1908): 29. Heading: "An 'Uncle Remus' Letter."
3. To: "Dear Lillian"; date: "7 February [1897]." *URM* 24, no. 3 (November 1908): 30. Heading: "An 'Uncle Remus' Letter."
4. To: "Dear Girls [Lillian and Mildred]"; date: "*Sunday evening* [December 1897]." *URM* 24, no. 4 (December 1908): 28. Heading: "An 'Uncle Remus' Christmas Letter." Incomplete in Emory collection; this printed version continues further.
5. To: [Lillian and Mildred]; date: "The 6 of Nov. [1898]." *URM* 24, no. 5 (January 1909): 24. Heading: "An 'Uncle Remus' Letter."
6. To: [Lillian and Mildred]; date: "Saturday Evening, 26 November [1898]." *URM* 24, no. 6 (February 1909): 28. Heading: "An 'Uncle Remus' Letter."

7. To: "Dear Billy-Ann [Lillian]"; date: "*31 Jan.* [1897]." *URM* 25, no. 1 (March 1909): 28. Heading: "An 'Uncle Remus' Letter."

8. To: "Dear Tommus [Mildred]"; date: "Aprile Twenty-eight, 1901." *URM* 25, no. 2 (April 1909): 28. Heading: "An 'Uncle Remus' Letter." This letter is heavily edited and combined with a second one; date: "May the Twelve 1901."

9. To: [Mildred]; date: "April 7, 1900." *URM* 25, no. 3 (May 1909): 28. Heading: "An 'Uncle Remus' Letter."

10. To: "My dear Daughter [Lillian]"; date: "*Sunday before Lent* [28 February 1897]." *URM* 25, no. 4 (June 1909): 28.

11. To: "My dear daughter [Lillian]"; date: "11 *October* [1896]." *URM* 25, no. 5 (July 1909): 26. Heading: "An 'Uncle Remus' Letter."

12. To: "Dear Billy ann [Lillian]"; date: "30 May [1897]." *URM* 25, no. 6 (August 1909): 22. Heading: "An 'Uncle Remus' Letter."

13. To: "My Dear Daughter [Lillian]"; date: "26 *September* [1896]." *URM* 26, no. 1 (September 1909): 30. Heading: "An 'Uncle Remus' Letter."

14. To: "Time flies, Dear Tommus [Mildred]"; date: "5 October, 1901." *URM* 26, no. 2 (October 1909): 29. Heading: "An 'Uncle Remus' Letter."

15. To: "Dear Billy and Tommy [Lillian and Mildred]"; date: [26 September 1898]. *URM* 26, no. 3 (November 1909): 41. Heading: "An 'Uncle Remus' Letter."

16. To: [Lillian and Mildred]; date: "Saturday night: November 12 [1898]." *URM* 26, no. 4 (December 1909): 5. Heading: "Christmas Flavor, Philosophy and Some Fooling."

17. To: "Dear Miss Pods [Lillian]"; date: "4 January.[1897]." *URM* 26, no. 5 (January 1910): 23. Heading: "An 'Uncle Remus' Letter."

18. To: "Dear Lillian"; date: "*Sunday Evening* [14 February 1898]." *URM* 26, no. 6 (February 1910): 4. Heading: "An 'Uncle Remus' Letter."

19. To: "Sweet little Tom [Mildred]"; date: "Sunday evening, 6th [6 March 1898]." *URM* 27, no. 1 (March 1910): 16. Heading: "An 'Uncle Remus' Letter."

20. To: "Dear Tommy [Mildred]"; date: "Sunday evening, 3 April [1898]." *URM* 27, no. 2 (April 1910): 4. Heading: "An 'Uncle Remus' Letter."

21. To: "Dear Miss Billy-Ann [Lillian]"; date: "2 of May [1897]." *URM* 27, no. 3 (May 1910): 14. Heading: "An Uncle Remus Letter."

22. To: "Dear Billy and Tommy [Lillian and Mildred]"; date: "Sunday, 22d [22 May 1898]." *URM* 27, no. 4 (June 1910): 4. Heading: "An Uncle Remus Letter."

23. To: "Dear Billy [Lillian]"; date: "July the 3 eye, 1899." *URM* 27, no. 5 (July 1910): 17. Heading: "An Uncle Remus Letter."

24. To: "Dear Lillian"; date: "May-Day, Sunday [1 May 1898]." *URM* 27, no. 6 (August 1910): 4. Heading: "An Uncle Remus Letter."

25. To: "My Dear Daughter [Lillian]"; date: "*Sunday Night.* [February/March? 1897]." *URM* 28, no. 1 (September 1910): 4. Heading: "An Uncle Remus Letter."

26. To: "My Dear Daughter [Lillian]"; date: "7 March [1897]. "*URM* 28, no. 2 (October 1910): 27. Heading: "An Uncle Remus Letter."

27. To: "Dear little chickadee [Mildred]"; date: "25 *November,* 1899." *URM* 28, no. 3 (November 1910): 6. Heading: "An Uncle Remus Letter."

28. To: [Mildred]; date: "December the—oh, I've forgotten—anyhow, its Saturday

night [16 December 1899]." *URM* 28, no. 4 (December 1910): 16. Heading: "An Uncle Remus Letter."

29. To: [Mildred]; date: "Janâwary the 27, 1900." *URM* 28, no. 5 (February 1911): 15. Heading: "An Uncle Remus Letter."

30. To: "Dear Tommus [Mildred]"; date: "Febiwary the 10, 1900." *URM* 28, no. 6 (March 1911): 25. Heading: "An Uncle Remus Letter."

31. To: "My Dear Dr. Delim [Mildred]"; date: "Saturday Evening, somewhere about the 24 of Febiwary, year 1900." *URM* 29, no. 1 (April 1911): 15. Heading: "An Uncle Remus Letter."

32. To: "Dear Toodleum [Mildred]"; date: "24th day of a backward March, 1900." *URM* 29, no. 2 (May 1911): 17. Heading: "An Uncle Remus Letter."

33. To: "My Dear Daughter [Lillian]"; date: "25 October [1896]." *URM* 29, no. 3 (June 1911): 4.

34. To: [Mildred]; date: "Two Days fo' de 'Clipse, State of Georgy. [28 May 1900]." *URM* 29, no. 4 (July 1911): 17. Heading: "An Uncle Remus Letter."

35. To: "My Dearest Tommy [Mildred]"; date: "*16 September* [1897]." *URM* 29, no. 5 (August 1911): 14. Heading: "An Uncle Remus Letter."

36. To: "My Dear Daughter [Lillian]"; date: "20 October [1896]." *URM* 29, no. 6 (September 1911): 42. Heading: "An Uncle Remus Letter."

37. To: "Dear Lillian"; date: "13 December [1896]." *URM* 30, no. 1 (October 1911): 15. Heading: "An Uncle Remus Letter."

38. To: "My Dear Pods [Lillian]"; date: "Sunday evening [December 1896]." *URM* 30, no. 2 (November 1911): 28. Heading: "An Uncle Remus Letter."

39. To: "Dear Billy and Tommy [Lillian and Mildred]"; date: "Saturday evening, Dec. 3 [1898]." *URM* 30, no. 3 (December 1911): 21.

40. To: "Hello Baby! How' do [Mildred]"; date: "Monday, 25 Sept. [1901]." *URM* 32, no. 1 (October 1912): 22. Heading: "An Uncle Remus Letter."

JULIA HARRIS'S BIOGRAPHY

Julia Collier Harris. *The Life and Letters of Joel Chandler Harris.* Boston: Houghton Mifflin Company, 1918. Julia Harris used many of the letters written by JCH to his children, quoting short excerpts in blocks in her chapters to provide a running narrative. Page numbers below are to her book; dates are those of the originals.

Dates in brackets are supplied dates or those given in *LL* if original is lost; i.e., not present in Special Collections, Woodruff Library, Emory University. Such lost letters are identified by an asterisk.

1. Seventeen letters to Julian:
pp. 260–61 (date: "Sunday [July 1890].")
pp. 263–64 (date: "6 July, 1890.")

pp. 265–67 (date: "July 20 [1890].")
pp. 267–68 (date: "July 27 [1890].")
pp. 269–70 (date: "3 August [1890].")
pp. 271–72 (date: "1st September, 1890.")
pp. 274–75 (date: "15 September [1890].")
pp. 276–77 (date: "22 September, 1890.")
pp. 280–81 (date: "6 October [1890].")
pp. 281–82 (date: "26 Octo. [1890].")
pp. 282–84 (date: "Sunday, [November] 16, [1890].")
pp. 284–86 (date: "7 December [1890].")
pp. 286–88 (date: "1 January, 1891.")
pp. 289–90 (date: "10 February [1891].")
pp. 293–94 (date: "7 December [1890].")
pp. 347–48 (date: "Wednesday, May 20 [1896].")
p. 523 (date: [February 1906])*
2. Four letters to Lucien:
p. 302 (date: [Fall 1892])*
pp. 303–4 (date: [4 September, 1892])*
pp. 305–6 (date: [n.d.])*
pp. 306–8 (date: [5 October, 1892])*
3. Nineteen letters to Lillian:
pp. 240–41 (date: "*9 May* [1897].")
p. 243 (date: "7 March [1897].")
pp. 244–45 (date: "At the Old Stand, Tuesday [1908].")
p. 273 (date: "Sunday 15 [15 May 1898].")
pp. 348–50 (date: "7 March [1897]"; not 1896 as in *LL*.)
pp. 351–52 (date: "*25 April* [1897]"; not 1896 as in *LL*.)
pp. 352–55 (date: "2 of May. [1897]"; not 1896 as in *LL*.)
pp. 356–57 (date: "25 October [1896]."
p. 358 (date: "1896—27 Oct. (night)/10:30 o'clock.")
pp. 358–60 (date: "Sunday evening. [November 1896].")
pp. 361–63 (date: "30 *May* [1897].")
pp. 370–72 (date: "4 January [1897]."
pp. 386–88 (date: "*Sunday evening, 20* [Mar. 1898].")
pp. 391–92 (date: "Sunday, 27 [27 March 1898].")
pp. 393–96 (date: "May-Day, Sunday [1 May 1898]."
p. 397 (date: "Sunday Evening 3 [3 April 1898].")
pp. 434–36 (date: "Sunday, 14 October: 1900.")
pp. 444–45 (date: "February 22, 1901.")
pp. 446–47 (date: "4 March—afternoon [1901].")
4. Thirteen letters to Mildred:
p. 240 (date: "Sunday, 15 [15 May 1898].")
p. 253 (date: "July 7,—5 p.m. [1898])."
p. 253 (date: "May 19, 1901.")

pp. 364–66 (date: "3 *September* [3 October 1897].")

pp. 366–67 (date: [22 September 1897].)

pp. 367–70 (date: "*16 September*. [1897]"; not September 26 as in *LL*.)

pp. 379–81 (date: "Sunday evening, 6th [6 March 1898].")

pp. 381–83 (date: "Sunday Evening, 13th March, [1898].")

pp. 388–90 (date: "Sunday evening, 3d April [1898]"; not April 30 as in *LL*.)

pp. 422–23 (date: "15 *Aprile, 1900*.")

pp. 425–26 (date: "Saturday, May 5, 1900.")

pp. 447–48 (date: "March 5—night—1901.")

p. 482 (date: "Saturday Evening, Nov. 23, 1901./Right after Supper.")

5. Ten joint letters to Lillian and Mildred:

p. 242 (date: "*Sunday Evening* [late November 1897].")

pp. 242, 253 (date: "Sunday afternoon, (hot and) June 4, 1899.")

p. 243 (date: [26 September 1896])

pp. 376–78 (date: "Saturday Evening, 19 November, 1898.")

pp. 384–86 (date: "Sunday night, 19 March 1899"; not 1898 as in *LL*.)

pp. 409–11 (date: "The 6 of Nov. [1898].")

pp. 411–14 (date: "Saturday Evening, 26 November [1898].")

pp. 414–16 (date: "Saturday evening, Dec. 3. 1898.")

pp. 416–17 (date: "Sunday, Dec. 4. [1898]"; continuation of December 3 [1898] letter.)

pp. 417–20 (date: "10 December, 1898.")

6. Three letters to Joel Chandler Harris, Jr.:

pp. 470–72 (date: "August 5, 1902.")

pp. 472–73 (date: [n.d.])*

pp. 529–30 (date: "Considerably at Home: October 28[1906].")

JULIA HARRIS'S ARTICLE IN *LADIES HOME JOURNAL*

Julia Collier Harris. "'Uncle Remus' to His 'Gals': How Joel Chandler Harris Kept His Place in His Daughters' Hearts While They Were Away at School," *Ladies Home Journal*, April 1919, 45, 126. As a promotion for her biography, Julia published excerpts from fourteen letters to the girls. This was the last use of the letters before they were given to Special Collections, Woodruff Library, Emory University.

The letters are identified below according to their original correspondent and date, retaining JCH's spelling and punctuation:

1. "Dear Lillian"; date: "7 February [1897]."
2. "My dear Daughter [Lillian]"; date: "11 *October* [1896]."
3. "My Dear Daughter [Lillian]"; date: "26 *September*[1896]."
4. "Dear Daughter [Lillian]"; date: "1 *November* [1896]."

5. "My dear Daughter [Lillian]"; date: "*Sunday before Lent* [28 February 1897]."

6. "Dear Billy and Tommy [Lillian and Mildred]"; date: "Sunday, 22d [22 May 1898]."

7. [Lillian and Mildred]; date: "Saturday night: November 12 [1898]."

8. [Lillian and Mildred]; date: "Sunday, March 5, 1899."

9. [Lillian and Mildred]: date: "Sunday night, 23 April, 1899."

10. "Dear Daughter [Lillian]"; date: "*Sunday night* [February/March? 1897]."

11. "Dear Tommus [Mildred]"; date: "Febiwary the 10, 1900."

12. "Dear Tommy [Mildred]"; date: "Sunday, February 19, 1900."

13. [Mildred]; date: "April 7, 1900."

14. [Mildred]; date: "December the—oh, I've forgotten—anyhow, its [sic] Saturday night [16 December 1899]."

RECOMMENDED READINGS

No effort has been made to compile an exhaustive bibliography. Nor does this one include all the sources used in the notes to the letters. Instead it gives a selection of important works on the life and writings of Joel Chandler Harris and directs the reader to more extensive bibliographies.

The two earliest biographies appeared in the same year. A revision of his doctoral dissertation at the University of Virginia, Robert Lemuel Wiggins's *Life of Joel Chandler Harris: From Obscurity in Boyhood to Fame in Early Manhood* (Nashville: Publishing House Methodist Episcopal Church, 1918) consists of a rather skimpy biography that does contain, however, important quotations from contemporary sources. Two-thirds of the book consists of reprints of the early literary work of Harris that had not been put in books: work in *The Countryman* (1862–66) and the Atlanta *Constitution* (1876–81) and the complete text of his first novel, *The Romance of Rockville*, published as a serial in the *Constitution*. Julia Collier Harris's *The Life and Letters of Joel Chandler Harris* (Boston: Houghton Mifflin Co., 1918), an affectionate portrait by his daughter-in-law, draws extensively on the letters to the children and letters from contemporary writers such as William Dean Howells, James Whitcomb Riley, and Mark Twain. But often the letters are edited and altered to preserve the benign grandfatherly image she knew best and wished to pass on to readers. Some dates and facts are erroneous. The good general coverage includes chapters on such bypaths as Harris's letters to Dorothy Loye and the book reviews Harris did under the name Anne Macfarland. Paul Cousins's *Joel Chandler Harris* (Baton Rouge: Louisiana State University Press, 1968), the standard biography, effectively places Harris in the social and literary climate of Middle Georgia, especially Putnam County, of the latter nineteenth century. Started many years before publication as a doctoral dissertation, it contains valuable interviews with contemporaries of Harris and goes into great detail about his journalistic experience prior to work on the *Constitution*. Chapters 7 through 11 shift to a chronological analysis of the writer's works and give much less about his life. The most recent biography is by R. Bruce Bickley, Jr., *Joel Chander Harris* (Athens: The University of Georgia

Press, 1987). It is a well-written interpretative study of the psychological relation between the complexity and contradictions of elements of Harris's life to
his various literary works. Chapters 1 and 2 give a detailed accounting of the
important facts of his life. The other five chapters group the works by genres
in exploring this relationship. The book contains a useful chronology and an
annotated bibliography.

Various reprints of Harris's works appear from time to time. But the most
accessible and useful are the paperback reprint *Uncle Remus: His Songs and
His Sayings*, edited by Robert Hemenway (New York: Viking Penguin, Inc.,
1982) and *The Complete Tales of Uncle Remus*, edited by Richard Chase (Boston:
Houghton Mifflin Co., 1955), a compilation of 184 tales from nine books containing tales in Black English dialect. Professor Hemenway's introduction gives
an analysis of the tales in the first book in relation to the author's character
and their didactic and propagandistic slant. Chase's collection contains most
but not all of the stories Harris told in Black dialect. The most generous published selection of Harris's journalism for the Savannah *Morning News*, the New
York *Sun*, the Atlanta *Constitution*, the *Saturday Evening Post*, the *World's Work*,
and *Uncle Remus's Magazine* appears in *Joel Chandler Harris: Editor and Essayist*,
edited by Julia Collier Harris (Chapel Hill: The University of North Carolina
Press, 1931). She drew upon JCH's scrapbook and the files of the *Constitution*
and *Uncle Remus's Magazine*.

Critical Essays on Joel Chandler Harris, edited by R. Bruce Bickley, Jr. (Boston: G. K. Hall & Co., 1981), gives an extensive selection of contemporary book
reviews and comments by Harris's fellow writers, plus twentieth-century re-
assessments. Among these, important ones are those on folklore by Kathleen
Light and Florence E. Baer, Louis Rubin's essay on the writer in relation to
his work, and Thomas H. English's assessment of Harris's achievements and
attitudes in relation to his time. The psychological readings by Jesse Bier and
Michael Flusche are countered by the more moderate views of Louis J. Budd.
This collection also contains an essay by Joseph M. Griska, Jr., that is based on
his detailed study of Harris's business correspondence (begun first in Griska's
1976 dissertation). A more recent collection of conference papers is *Joel Chandler
Harris: The Writer in His Time and Ours*, edited by Hugh T. Keenan, *Atlanta
Historical Journal* 30, nos. 3–4 [Fall–Winter 1986–87]). Especially important are
the initial survey essay by R. Bruce Bickley, Jr., on the contradiction and para-
doxes in the life and work of the author; the genealogical research of Kenneth H.
Thomas, Jr.; Lee Pederson's linguistic reassessment of the syntax of Harris's

black dialect; another essay by Joseph M. Griska, Jr., based on Harris's unpublished business correspondence; and Eric L. Montenyohl's tracing of the shifting alliances between Harris and folklore and folklorists. The book contains both a primary bibliography of Harris's works and a selected annotated bibliography of criticism. *Joel Chandler Harris: A Reference Guide* (Boston: G. K. Hall & Co., 1978), by R. Bruce Bickley, Jr., with the collaboration of Karen L. Bickley and Thomas H. English, is the standard comprehensive annotated bibliography, listing all commentaries in English from 1862 through 1976. It gives book reviews, dissertations, scholarly articles, and books and has a subject index. The introduction gives an overview of the various critical approaches taken to Harris's works.

A few more specialized works worth seeing are the pioneer study by Stella Brewer Brookes, *Joel Chandler Harris: Folklorist* (Athens: The University of Georgia Press, 1950), a basic study of the folklore elements in the Uncle Remus stories, proverbs, and songs; and Florence E. Baer's *Sources and Analogues of the Uncle Remus Tales* (Helsinki: Suomalainen Tiedeakatemia Academia Scientiarum Fennica, 1980), a more detailed and restricted study tracing two-thirds of the Uncle Remus tales in Chase's collection to African sources. Walter M. Brasch's *Black English and the Mass Media* (Boston: The University of Massachusetts Press, 1981) provides a context for dialectal writing in Black English by tracing the cyclical popularity of such works from 1650 to 1980. Brasch places Harris in the context of other such dialectal writers both black and white during Reconstruction, one of the high points of this cycle. Finally, James Stafford's "Patterns of Meaning in *Nights with Uncle Remus*" (*American Literature* 18 [May 1946]: 89–108) is an often-overlooked essay on the most artistically complex of the Uncle Remus books. It reminds the reader that Harris as a literary artist reshaped the materials that he chose and that he aimed to be more than a compiler of folktales or the author of materials designed simply for entertainment. He sought to teach as well.

INDEX

Adair, Bob and Jack, 31
Adair, Buck, 445
Adair, Forrest, 311, 444
Adair, George, 150; illness of, 275
Adair, Mrs. Forrest, 454
Adamson, Mr., 90, 95, 133
Ade, George, xxv, 144n
Adrian, 298, 299
Agnes Scott Institute, 61
"Alice in Wonderland," 245
Alphonsus (Alphonso?), Sister, 67, 396
American Baptist Publication Society, 363n, 384
American Catholics, 183
Apocalypse, 228
Apples, loss of barrel of, 159, 161–62
Appleton Publishing Company, 440n
Atlanta: 1906 race riots in, 482–83; sewer system of, 266
Atlanta *Constitution,* xxvii, 184, 213, 233, 258, 284, 285, 377, 475, 476; office gossip at, 52–53
Atlanta *Journal,* 90, 95, 117, 138, 142, 148, 161, 213, 219, 283, 419
Augusta, Ga., 300; fire, 335

Bacon, Augustus O., 35, 36n
Baker, Mr., 404
Baker, Ray Stannard, 362

Barnett, Sergeant L. E., 282
Barrett, E. W. (correspondent for the *Constitution*), 6
Bazin, Father, 77, 161, 164, 313, 370, 399
Beautiful Joe, 265
Becker, Bishop, 210
Benson, Tom, 230
Bernard, Sister, 67–156, 172–283 passim, 315, 333, 334
Bickley, R. Bruce, Jr., xviii
Biechele, Burdeene, 149, 216, 404, 451–52, 464–65, 379, 400
Biechele, Mr. and Mrs., 209, 307, 309, 313, 316, 357, 358, 359, 369, 370, 372, 379, 449, 454, 456, 457
Bier, Jesse, 518
Bijou (theater), 282
Bine, Mr. and Mrs., 223
Black Maria, 328
Black narrator, xxi
Blessed Virgin, 285
Bob, 167
Bobbs Merrill, 480
Boers, 345
Booger Man, 157, 449
Boston Symphony, 197
Boswell, James, 340
Bowen, Miss Eliza, 203, 204n
Boynton, Hagy, 466

Brooks, 314, 315

Brooks, Mr., 372, 389

Brown, Joseph M., 500, 505; "Hoke and Hunger, Brown and Bread," 502

Brownie, 173, 332, 342, 346, 369–87 passim, 426, 435, 437, 439

Brownies, 173

Brown-Smith gubernatorial race, 504

Brumby, Lt. Tom, xxvii

Bryan, William Jennings, xxvii, 176; lecture by, 86, 89n

Bunker, Mr., 71, 292, 317, 369; marriage of, 77; new wife of, 84

Bunker, Mrs., 90, 92, 126, 147, 217

Burchell, Mattie, 451

Burgomaster matinee, 416

Burke, William, 340

Butter, 404

Byington, Mattie, 107

Caldwell, Alleen, 322

Caldwell, Clarence, 164, 244

Caldwell, Hugh, 322

Caldwell, Kenan, 242

Calhoun, Judge, 378

Camp, Edwin, 492–505 passim; courtship of Mildred, 498, 500–501

Candler, Bishop Warren Akin, 504n; wife of, 503

Canton, Ga., 210, 296, 315, 316, 370, 383, 385, 449, 455

Carnegie, Andrew, 478

Carter, Mrs. Joshua, 31

Carter's Little Liver Pills, 76

Cary, Dan, 317, 397

Cascade Springs, 299

Catholic fiction, xxix

Catholic Mirror, 220

Catholic News, xxix

Catholics, 187, 190, 198, 312

Ceily (cook for G. A. Howell), 445

Century Magazine, xxii, 11

Charlotte Russe, 241

Chattanooga, Tenn., 130, 498

Chicago, Ill., 448

Chicago Times Herald, xxii

Children of the Ghetto, 350

Children's Department (section of URM edited by JCH), 497

Christmas, 242, 246, 322, 338, 358, 388, 436, 438

Church of Rome, 198

Cincinnati, Ohio, 278, 456

Clemence, Mother, 333, 349

Cleveland, Grover, 502

Clio (elephant), 356

Cobb, Jesse, 85, 127

Cobb, Lucy, 114

Cobbett, William: Letters to Young Men, 202

Cole, Myra, 220

Collier, Charles Augustus, 185, 188, 263, 265; and trip to Tate Spring, 290

Collier, Charles, Jr., 257, 263, 338, 435, 466

Collier, Ellinor, 184

Collier, George, 38

Collier, Lamar, 503

Collier, Rawson, 390, 457

Collier kids, 239, 242; and whooping cough, 360

Collier's Weekly: Christmas story, 361

Columbia (theater), 387

Corbett, "Gentleman Jim," 105, 106
Cord, Mrs. Collar, 478
Cordele, Ga., 495, 500, 505
County Chairman (play), 471
Courtlandt Street Ferry, 412
Cousin Dust, 301
Cousins, Paul M., xxviii
Covington, Ga., 401
Cox, Palmer, 173n
Cramer, Mr., 90, 133, 287
Crenshaw, Hansel, 313
Crispi, Francesco, 198, 199n
Critic, 233
Crowe, Dr. Walter A., 18n, 130, 153, 258, 292, 333, 378, 395, 441, 486
Cubans, 187, 190, 192
Culbertson, Gerald, 370
Culbertson, Mamie, 295
Cyclorama, 356, 357n

Dame Gossip, 97
Daniel, Charles, 95
D'Artagnan (*Three Musketeers*), 342
Davis, Johnnie-May, 297
Dead Letter Office, Montreal, 489
De Give, Grandma, 342
Dennis, Charles, 467
de Sailles (Sales), Sister, 284, 290, 377
Dewey, George, xxvii, 198, 325, 326
Dewey Arch, 412
Diamond Hustlers (baseball team), 396
Dixon, Mallory, 107
Domestic animals: Kitty Banks (cat), 58; Thompson (goat), 64, 65, 92, 100; Nelly Harris (donkey), 64, 65, 145–46, 159, 176; Lily Harris

(horse), 67, 159, 162; Lucille Harris (cow), 92, 159, 332, 346, 361; Daisy Harris (cow), 159, 353; George J. Gaskin (calf), 326. *See also* Pets
Don Quixote, 183
Dooly, Miss Sizzma, 184
Doubleday, Page & Co., 439, 440
Drusilla (character), xxvii, 183, 184n
Duncan, Lee, 449
Durand's (restaurant), 86
Durrance, Dr. and Mrs., 340

Easter, 172, 193, 349, 354, 459, 499
Eatonton, Ga., 35, 362
Eclipse, 357–58
Editorial mark: JCH's use of, 55
Electricity, 439
Ellis, Mr., 270, 275, 281
Ellman, Richard, xx
Embezzlement, 271–73
English grammar, 196, 340
Episcopalian cake-walk, 328–29
Episcopalians, 454, 455
Erysipelas, 156
Eusebius, 101
Evening Constitution, 90, 95, 97, 111, 112; first issue of, 96
Everybody's Magazine, 440
Ezzard, Dack, 361

Fair, 420
Farrow, Colonel, 408, 411, 469
Fitzgerald, Ga., 501
Flannagan, 138
Flower Club, 450
Flusche, Michael, 518
Forbes, Cannon, 398

Forbes, Nelly, 358
Forbes, Walter, 285, 294
Formwalt Street, 424
Forrest, Nathan Bedford, 465
Four Roses Distillery, 505
France, 10, 501
Frazier, Clark, 108
Free Masons, 332
Frost, A. B., 319
Frost, Charles John, 323
Fruit-cake, 237, 238, 243, 244, 246
Furnace, 368, 379, 381

Gainesville bananas, 408
Garnsey, John Henderson, 47, 49n,
    104, 219, 302
Garrick, David, 340
Geigerism, 413
Gilder, Miss (of *The Critic*), 29
Gleanings, 76, 194; and Lillian's
    account of pottery tour, 195
Glenn, Mrs., 251
"Glorious Duck," 345
Goldsmith, Dr. Oliver, 339–40
Goodman, Bob, 91, 94, 100, 102, 123
Goodman, Charley, 259, 447
Goodman, Harold, 68
Goodman, Louise, 169
"Gosta Berling," 383
Grant Park, 188
Gras, Felix: *Reds of the Midi*, 290
Great Piedmont Exposition, 21n
Gretchen, 332, 342, 346, 369, 372,
    373, 376, 378, 382, 384, 387, 435,
    437, 439, 441, 458, 459
Grigsby, Ida, 46
Gross, Archbishop, 128
"Grumble-box," 123, 228, 236, 237n

Guinea pigs, 137–38
Gunn, Father, 288, 290, 297

Hall, Mr., 345
Halloween party, 454, 460
Harper's Round Table, 63
Harris, Aileen, 39–47, 239, 445–83
    passim; birth of daughter, 464; first
    pregnancy of, 55; children of, 104,
    229, 323, 467
Harris, Annie Lou, 462, 471, 501, 502
Harris, Charles Collier, 332, 336, 437
Harris, Esther LaRose (Mrs. Joel
    Chandler Harris), xxi, 33, 46, 51,
    55; French Canadian Catholic, xxx;
    and clothing, 47, 147; illnesses of,
    70, 124, 145, 165, 177, 224–25,
    228, 369, 370–71, 391, 403; and
    housecleaning, 70, 188–89, 194–
    95, 218, 225, 298, 328–29, 371,
    384, 457, 498; and pony, 95; visits
    St. Joseph's Academy, 111, 300,
    402; and California violets, 112;
    and kitten killing, 118; and
    redecoration of Wren's Nest, 215;
    and neighborhood gossip, 231; and
    Christmas shopping, 246; visits
    Chattanooga, 290, 291; and
    preparation for lawn party, 315;
    drinking habits of, 330–32; and
    canary, 393; cooking of, 398–99;
    singing of, 399; and staining of
    dining-room floor, 416–17; and
    flower show, 424–26; birthday of,
    448; and preparations for church
    bazaar, 458–59
Harris, Evelyn, xxiii, 8–69, 90, 95,
    97, 114–26; marries Annie Louise

Hawkins, 461; letters to JCH, 35, 40, 44, 56–57; JCH's letters to, 35–37, 40–47, 56–58, 133–34, 307–8, 310–11, 313–14, 316–18, 319–20, 350–53, 411–13, 462–63, 465–66; JCH's advice to on newspaper work, 57; JCH's advice to on letter writing, 57, 350–51; at Lithia Springs, 194, 206, 296, 403, 407, 409, 445; as city editor, 290; kidney trouble of, 310; at Poland Spring, 312; JCH's literary advice to, 319–20; and trip to Louisville, 359; and trip to Canton, 368, 372; and trip to Lexington, 372; and *Sunny South* subsidiary editorials, 377, 379, 381; character of, 381; and trip to Memphis, 398; attitude toward women, 403, 421; in New York, 412; in Chicago, 448; at Mr. Riley's, 448; considers job in Macon, 462; and invitation to live at Wren's Nest, 462–63; visits J. B. Wallace, 474; and deal with Bobbs Merrill, 480

Harris, Joel Chandler, xiii, xx, xxii, xxxix, 70, 156, 165, 175, 182, 200, 206, 233, 290, 324; journalistic assignments for *Scribner's*, xviii; empathy of, ix–x; literary technique of, x; relationship with sons, xxi, xxiv; use of alcohol, xxvi; female personae of, xxvii; as "Queen of May," xxvii; as "The Parental Bore," xxviii, 198; as the "Other Fellow," xxviii, 274, 420; contributions to Boys' Orphanage at Saint Joseph's, xxix; relations with ministers, xxix; and the Roman Catholic Church, xxix–xxx, 120n; and Spanish-American War, xxx; birth record of, xxxix; literary advice of, 19, 22; syndicate venture of, 33, 481, 482; illnesses of, 34, 78, 124, 128–30, 148, 222, 249, 253, 254, 256, 280, 352, 374, 375, 415, 436, 442, 471, 495; dramatic sketches, 50, 110; sketch of play, 54; gardening news, 54–55; advice to Lillian, 89–90, 108; on photography, 113–14, 117; Catholic beliefs of, 119–20; remarks on Lillian's "street-car" story, 123; and outbreak of small-pox, 152; motive in writing letters, 166; content of letters to Lillian, 173–74; advice on letter-writing, 174–75, 176; letters of, as "editorial essay," 187, 202; as Popsy, the Clown, 198; in Salt Springs (Lithia), 202; and neighbor's rooster, 205; visits St. Joseph's, 221–22; bust of, 223, 225–26, 249; and riddles, 243–44, 245–46; criticism of letters from Lillian and Mildred, 246; as "Rinktum Riddler," 246; fiftieth birthday of, 248; as the "Snorer," 256; and imaginary vacation trip to Florida, 260–61, 262, 263; advice for Lillian's graduation essay, 276–77; interest in women's gossip, 317; observations on courtship of Lillian and Fritz, 347–48; as "Billy Sanders," 363, 403, 404; and typewriter, use of, 367, 384, 422, 433, 472, 479, 481, 488, 495, 499;

Harris, Joel Chandler (*continued*)
as literary man, 370; lonesomeness
of, 371; advice to Lillian, 375; on
character of Evelyn, 381; advice to
Mildred, 387, 414; portrait of, 388;
autographs of, 392–93; fifty-third
birthday, 436; *Everybody's
Magazine,* 440; Appleton
(publisher), 440; Doubleday
(publisher), 440; McClure Phillips
(publisher), 440; concern for
income, 470; Kimono party, visit
to, 473; concern for use of Uncle
Remus's name, 475; in Clearwater,
Florida, 475, 476; and *Uncle
Remus's Magazine,* 484, 486–87,
490, 491
—LETTERS, x, xiii, xvii; in *Uncle
Remus's Magazine,* xviii, 507–14; as
professional correspondence, xxi;
in *Uncle Remus's Home Magazine,*
xxx, 507–9; as newspaper copy,
xxxvii; monetary value of, 145,
232; as lectures, 234, 290
—WORKS: variety of, xviii; *Aaron in
the Wildwoods,* xxvi, 75, 77, 79, 87,
99, 102, 126, 179n; *Balaam and His
Master and Other Sketches and
Stories,* xxii, 13n, 29; *The
Chronicles of Aunt Minervy Ann,*
xxvii, 179n, 257, 293, 319; *Daddy
Jake the Runaway and Short Stories
Told After Dark,* xxi, 24n, 67;
*Gabriel Tolliver: A Story of
Reconstruction,* 368, 369n, 451;
*Little Mr. Thimblefinger and His
Queer Country,* xxviii, 52n, 179n,
491n; *A Little Union Scout,* 465,
466n; *Mr. Rabbit at Home,* xxiii,
44n, 52n, 179n, 184n, "An Ode on
Weeps," 141; "1 Mile to Shady
Dale," 96, 102; *On the Plantation,*
20, 24, 27n; *On the Wing of
Occasions,* 440n; *Plantation
Pageants,* 179n, 258, 285, 329; *Qua,*
179n, 257; *The Shadow Between His
Shoulder Blades,* 465, 466n; *Sister
Jane,* 49, 98, 282; *Stories of
Georgia,* 74; *The Story of Aaron,* 65,
67, 76; *Tales of the Home Folks in
Peace and War,* 162n, 175n, 178,
181n, 186; Thimblefinger books,
51, 178, 183, 257; *Uncle Remus and
Brer Rabbit,* 476; *Uncle Remus: His
Songs and His Sayings,* xviii, 52n;
Uncle Remus's Magazine, 475, 492;
*Wally Wanderoon and His Story-
Telling Machine,* 179n, 433n
Harris, Mrs. Joel Chandler. *See*
Harris, Esther LaRose
Harris, Joel Chandler, Jr. ("J. C.,"
"Jake"), xxiii–xxix, 8, 30, 49, 401–
2; illnesses of, 149, 156; and
clothing, 192, 221; accused of
shooting pigeons, 250; goes to see
"Jack and the Beanstalk," 257; and
baseball, 292, 394; and Rossers,
332, 428; comment on character
of, 334, 401–2; kite flying, 367;
joins Y.M.C.A., 377; and Sister
Alphonsus, 396; letters from, 407,
444; letters to, 407–11, 444–48,
483–87, 489–91; JCH's advice to,
408; and studies at Marist school,
418; and Latin studies, 423–24,
429, 432, 439; and feud with

Marguerite, 425–27, 429; at Porter Spring, 466; and missing post-cards, 489

Harris, Joel Chandler III ("Chubby"), 159, 162, 164, 187, 264, 267, 285–309, 329, 338, 344, 355, 373, 393, 401–2, 415, 416, 436

Harris, Julia Collier, xxi, xxxi, 54–55, 58, 138–52, 163, 169, 173, 179, 185, 188, 192, 214, 220, 239, 249, 255, 257, 263, 275, 281, 349; *The Life and Letters of Joel Chandler Harris,* ix, xxvii, xxx; use of letters in *Ladies Home Journal,* xxx, 511–12; "social prominence" of, 180; at Lithia Springs, 194; anniversary of marriage to Julian, 224; children of, 348, 349, 437; moves into new house, 442; illness of, 467, 471; death of sons, 467; trip to Highlands, N.C., 469; use of letters in biography, 509–11, 517

Harris, Julian, xxii, 30–45, 58; autobiography of, xxxii; and French studies, 3, 7, 12, 14, 21, 30, 33; letters to, 3–34, 37–38, 47–56, 227, 305, 318–19, 461, 469–71, 474–77, 482–83, 491–92; and clothing, 3, 13–14; *Washington Post* notice of disappearance, 4; letters from, 7, 10, 28, 29, 31, 45, 51, 56; study of shorthand, 7, 21; and law profession, 19; as black sheep of the family, 20; and newspaper business, 20, 21; keeps a journal, 21; advice to, 22, 26, 34, 52; and pipe smoking, 28; homesickness of, 30, 33; experience of, on Chicago

newspaper, 50; letter in *Constitution,* 52; letters to mother, 53; *Times-Herald* apprenticeship of, 55; publications in *Alkahest,* 56; and vacation in Nassau, 90; marriage of, 147, 224; at Lithia Springs, 194; in Tampa, 202; article in *Constitution,* 219; and Board of Trustees for the Library, 287, 290; in Tate Spring, 290, 292; birthday of, 305; writing skills of, 307; sons, 330, 334, 344, 349, 360, 376, 390, 399, 402, 409, 467; and new house, 419, 423, 427, 428, 430, 431, 435, 437, 442; in Highlands, N.C., 469; organizational plans for *URM,* 476; efforts to write an Uncle Remus musical, 484; in New York, 488; and *URM* article on dead towns in Georgia, 491–92

Harris, Lillian, x, xvii, xix, 35, 489, 493; dedication of books to, 174, 175n; marriage of, xxvii, 493; letters to, 61–134, 140–41, 142–44, 146–48, 168–71, 173–75, 179–81, 182–84, 186–87, 189–92, 195–99, 202–4, 209–10, 216–20, 291–93, 305–7, 309–10, 312–13, 315–16, 320–21, 361–64, 369–70, 374–75, 378–80, 382–83, 448–58, 460–61, 471–74, 477–82, 488–89, 493–95, 499–505; story criticized, 65; grades of, 73, 83, 85, 96, 97, 111, 113, 116, 127, 170, 199, 231–32, 252, 299; letters from, 77, 78, 108, 140, 222, 231, 375; and toothache, 75, 76, 77; and Miss Pods, 84, 86n, 97; story in *Gleanings,* 85–86;

Harris, Lillian (*continued*)
  advice to, 89–90, 108, 174–75, 375;
  letters to Charles, 89–91, 96; and
  photography, 97, 99, 104, 113, 114,
  117, 175, 219; dramatic sketch, 110;
  sixteenth birthday of, 164, 170,
  172, 176, 184; account of pottery
  tour in *Gleanings,* 195; letters and
  compositions of, 199, 273; and
  Christmas, 232; letters from
  Arthur, 258; and graduation essay,
  276–77, 283; as Joan of Arc, 283;
  commencement of, 300; behavior
  of, 335; diet of, 340–41; clothing,
  352, 367, 415; trip to Canton, 367,
  368; and party, 394, 395–96; and
  tennis, 409; and beaus, 414; at
  Mrs. Connally's reception, 427; and
  subscription to Booklover's
  Library, 435; comment on her
  letters, 460. *See also* Harris, Lillian
  and Mildred
Harris, Lillian and Mildred: letters to,
  148–57, 158–68, 177–79, 204–6,
  213–16, 221–27, 228–78, 280–91,
  293–302, 402–4, 464–65, 466–69,
  495–98; school friends, xix, 301–2,
  459. *See also* Brownie; Biechele,
  Burdeene; Gretchen; Ledbetter,
  Bessie
Harris, Linton, 8, 16, 18
Harris, Lucien ("Tootsie"), 352–93,
  421, 428, 447, 483, 490; starts
  school, 17; letters to, 38–40; letters
  from, 38; and new house, 98, 102;
  at Lithia Springs, 194; children of,
  247, 344, 402; and the Athletic
Club, 349; and trip to Florida, 369,
  371
Harris, Lucien, Jr., 336, 409
Harris, Mildred ("Tommy"), x, xix,
  xxvii, 370, 468; as elocutionist, 8,
  151, 322, 325; confirmation of,
  121; letters to, 137–38, 141–42,
  145–46, 157–58, 172–73, 175–77,
  181–82, 184–86, 187–89, 192–95,
  199–202, 206–8, 220–21, 278–80,
  321–50, 352–61, 367–69, 370–73,
  375–78, 381–82, 384–402, 413–
  44, 458–59; letters from, 149,
  153–54, 231, 288; and chocolate,
  168; and "private letter," 175; first
  communion of, 205; and graph-o-
  phone, 209; grades of, 229, 231,
  285, 299, 333, 376, 396; and
  "pony" pun, 249; and letter from
  JCH to Virginia children, 258; and
  Kodak camera, 302; comic nature
  of, 306, 309, 315; homesickness of,
  321–22, 371; allowance of, 341;
  and tennis, 409; love letter to, 460;
  puns about her beaus, 478; and
  loss of trunk, 479–80, 481; visits
  to Eastman, N.Y., 479; courtship
  of, 500–501
Harris, Percy, 151
Harris, Pierre LaRose, 437; birth of,
  416; sketch of, 451
Harris, Stewart ("Toodie"), xxv, 75,
  86; description of, 73, 83; illness
  of, 145; teething of, 181–82; and
  nursery rhymes, 277, 286; accident
  of, 393
Harrison, Emily, 390

Hartman, Mr., 204
Harvey, William H., 52, 53n
Hawkins, Annie Lou, 464, 466, 469
Hawthorne, Nathaniel, 196
Henry, John Thomas, and the Tabitha Ann Cats, 165–66
Herford, Oliver, 491n
Highland Avenue Club, 407, 409
High's Corner, 230
Hill, Gov. Dave, 32
Hobbs, Dr. Arthur G., 18n
Holliday, Jim, 115
Holt, Sam, 288
Hooklin, Sprat, 394–95
Hoppie, Miss Philadelphia Baltimore, 159
Howard, Walter, 296
Howell, Annie, 114
Howell, Clark, 49, 51, 54, 55, 176, 228, 287, 311, 318, 319, 343, 412, 462, 502
Howell, Clark, Sr., 260–61
Howell, E. A., 275
Howell, Evan Park, xxiv, 56, 444; drinking habits of, 49; candidacy of, 76; political defeat of, 76n; funeral of, 469–70; death of, 471
Howell, G. A., 445
Howells, William Dean, 311
Hurricane, 66

Improved Order of Red Men, 332
Influenza, 367
Inman, Mr., 311, 314
Ipsalon Upsalon Alpha Fly Beater Society, 403–4
Irby, Estelle, 215

Irwin, Paul, 478, 479, 480, 481; marriage of, 465

Jackson, Father, 441
Jackson cotton, 140
Janeway, Dr., 416; and trip to Buffalo, 411–12
Jerd (suitor of Lillian), 419, 421, 422, 426, 427, 428, 433; description of, 416; poem about, 417
Job, Book of, 152
Johnson, Samuel, 340
Johnson House, 294
Jonah and the Whale, 191
Jones, Bob, 133
Jones, Charles Colcock, Jr., 491, 492
Jones, Samuel Porter, 108, 109n, 238
Josephine, Aunt, 143, 153
Joyce, James, xx
Jubilee, 393, 398
Judge, 95

Kamenski, Miss, 475
Keeley Institute, 238
Keely Co., 67, 68n, 369, 371
Kelley, Mademoiselle Peacherina, 470
Kelly, Essie LaRose, 483, 484, 486, 496; baby of, 407, 410
Kelly, Mary Esther, 468
Kelly kids, 489
Kennedy, Father, 77
Kennesaw, Ga., 197, 266, 278
Kimball House (hotel), 262
King, Mitchy, 207
Kingdom of Heaven, 319
"King Philpo," xxi
Kipling, Rudyard, 29, 67

Kodak, 97, 99n, 104, 113–14, 219, 229, 302
Kohlsaat, H. H., 51

Ladson, Agnes, 369
LaGrange, Ga., 424
Lakewood Park, 132, 133n
Lamar, Aunt Nancy, 362
Lannan, Mr. and Mrs., 261, 268, 269, 275, 277–78, 283, 294, 415
Lannan, Ryder, 261, 269, 275, 277, 291
LaRose, Esther DuPont ("Essie"), xxiii, xxviii, 35–42, 373–86, 413, 414, 427, 430, 452, 454–93 passim; marriage of, xxviii; estrangement of, 41, 43; at St. Hyacinthe, 143; and trip to Norcross, 202; engagement of, 210, 317; courtship of, 218; birthday of, 239; and "The Little Minister," 277
LaRose, Josephine, 24n, 41–42
LaRose, Pierre, 14, 27, 41, 42, 208, 317, 320, 363, 484, 490, 491
LaRose, Mrs. Pierre, 42, 153, 161–65, 178–85 passim, 197, 202, 208, 278, 352
Leathersole, Miss Agler, 334
Ledbetter, Bessie, 301–2, 322–87, 349, 390, 415, 417, 435–39, 467. See also Harris, Lillian and Mildred: school friends
Leonard, Cephas, 20
Leonard, Pat, 43
Leonard, Ruth, 421
Leverette, Agnes, 421
Leverette, Nona, 20
Levert, Octavia Walton, 491, 492

Lewis, Fred, 382, 436, 468
Lewis, Harry, 204
Life, 247
Light, Kathleen, 518
Lilliputians, 159
Lithia Springs, Ga., 57, 404, 467
Lloyd, Harry, 163, 258
Longfellow, Henry Wadsworth, 235
Longino, Dr., 93, 167, 338
Lookout Mountain, Ga., 197
Louisville, 359
Lovett family, 102, 143, 215, 236, 250–51
Lowell, James Russell, 171
Lowry, E., 382
Lowry, Mr., 372
Loye, Dorothy, xxi, 517
Lumpkin, Ga., 214, 216
Lycett Studio, 117, 118n
Lyceum (theater), 159, 416, 423, 424

McClure Phillips (publisher), 440
McClure's, 29, 65, 318, 362, 363, 476
MacFarland, Anne, xxviii
McGeehaughey, Lena, 213
McIntosh, Louise, 119, 204
McKinley, James, 150, 186, 209, 231, 286, 296, 315
McMahon, Father, 335
Macon, Ga., 154
Maddox, J. J. & J. E., 374
Majoribanks (or Marshbanks), Mr., 313
Manning, Cardinal, 101, 103
Manning society, 103, 265
Markham House, 374
Marseillaise, 290
Martinelli, Monseigneur, 370

Mary Louis, Sister, 82–148, 122, 138–200 passim, 223, 226, 368
Matthews, Billy, 168
Matthews, Colonel, 178
Matthews, John, 218
May, Susie, 444, 449
Mellen's Food, 403, 404n, 415
Merinus, Mr. and Mrs., 283
Methodists, 269, 404
Mint julep, 222
Miracles, 320
Mobley house fire, 156
Mohawk Braves, 324
Montreal, Can., 153, 483, 491
Moody, Mrs. Sheehan, 101
Moran, Mr., 430
Morgan, Governor, 377
Morris, Ruby, 242
Mugleston, William F., 476
Muse and Co., 53
Myer, Cecil, 505
Myers, Robert Manson: *The Children of Pride,* 492
"My New Curate," 383, 419

Napoleon, 320
Neighbors in West End: Grace Abernathy, 239–40; Mrs. Abernathy, 72, 81, 92, 151, 180, 215, 232, 286, 287, 328; Alex (or Ellick), 327–28; Nora Belle, 194; Emma Bunker, 213, 221; Mr. Bunker, 253, 255, 256, 258, 261, 265, 267, 270, 271–72, 275, 281, 342, 371, 397; Mrs. Bunker, 200, 271; Winnie Bunker, 464; Marguerite Chaffee, 368–438 passim; Harry Cole, 328, 329, 339;

Myra Cole, 207, 419, 429; Mr. Conley, 328; Mrs. Connally, 427; Mrs. Crosby, 270; Herbert Culbertson, 413–14; Leila Culbertson, 388; Mamie Culbertson, 427; Mrs. Fulgin, 154; Clark Frazier, 194; Mr. Frazier, 326; Charley Goodman, 392; Nora Goodman, 200, 326; Stella G. Humphries, 419; Mrs. Kelly, 46, 328; Charles Kelly, xxiii, 46, 57, 69, 77, 127, 193, 218, 279, 314, 317, 323, 348, 355, 359, 360, 373, 377, 381, 386, 389, 410, 413, 414, 430, 446, 484; Mrs. Kelly, 69, 78, 202, 306, 362, 364; Molly Kelly, 454, 472; Richard Morenus, 326, 353, 355, 367, 371; O'Donnelly family, 369, 371, 378, 386, 445; Sidney Ormond, 312, 315, 354; Walter Ormond, 390, 421, 436; Alma Pope, 399; Wiley Pope, Mrs., 342–43; Captain J. B. Richardson, 424; Mrs. Richardson, 432; Mamie Richardson, 461; Mary Richardson, 210; Brader Warner, 40, 42n, 106, 244, 247, 256–57, 260, 263–64, 355; Lula Zachry, 239, 249, 351; Mamie Zachry, 130, 148; Zachry family, 86, 133, 147, 232, 297, 299, 341
Newman, Cardinal, xx, xxix, 103, 196, 283
Newman, Lucy, 430
Newman, Miss, 296
Newman, Mrs., 392
Newman society, 266
News, 419

Norman, Monroe, 460
Norton, Grace, 464
Nuns, 236. *See also* Alphonsus, Sister; Bernard, Sister; de Sailles, Sister; Mary Louis, Sister; Regius, Sister; Sacred Heart, Sister

Oak Street, 426
O'Brien, Father James M., 82, 121, 140, 141, 161, 164, 167, 168n, 169, 173, 213, 215, 220, 236, 250, 255, 266, 288, 290, 291n, 292, 297, 315, 323, 346, 356, 377
Okerberg, Knut: and bust of Harris, 214, 216–18, 220, 221, 227
Old Uncle Indigestion, 415
O'Neill, James, xxv, 342
Osborne, Dorothy, xvii, 174
Oxford, Ga., 397, 404

Paderewski, 426
Page, Walter Hines, xxvii, 439
Paine's Celery Compound, 140, 144, 176, 191, 274, 275n, 294
Park Street, 338
Park Street Methodist Church, xxx, 93, 338
Partridge, Vee-oh-la, 345
Pawnee Bill, 487
Paxon, Frederic J., 362, 363, 384
Peachtree swells, 423
Pearson Concert, 294
Peary, Admiral, 269
Penny fund, 236
Pets: Flip (dog), 39; Ovid (dog), 39, 42, 65, 79, 130, 236, 248, 296, 323, 394, 416, 428; Muldoon (dog), 124, 127–28, 130, 138, 140, 154–55, 236, 248, 293, 359, 420, 428, 445; Mingo (dog), 128; cats and chloroform, 194; "Old Kittens," 194; Trilby (cat), 260, 321; Aunt Kitty (cat), 338; Mrs. Moseley (parrot), 353; canary, 393; Joe Lively (dog), 428, 432. *See also* Domestic animals
Philadelphia, 435
Phillips, Tom, 473, 476
Piedmont Park, 218
Pinafore (play), 234
Poland Spring, Ga., 312
Pope, Dope, 466
Pope, Ella, 114
"Popsy the Clown," xxviii
Porter Springs, Ga., 45, 316, 396–408 passim, 466, 469
Prohibition, 495
Protestants, 399
Provincialism, 196, 308
Puck, 95

Rawson, Mollie, 468
Ray, Susie Lee, 297
Reed, Wallace P., 11, 14, 16, 22, 31, 53, 74, 75n
Regius, Sister, 368
Rich's (department store), 78
Riley, James Whitcomb, xxvii, 203, 249, 356, 357, 384, 416, 448; inscription to JCH, 354; visit of, 354; departure of, 356; letters of, 517
Roberts, Harry, 385, 419, 429
Roberts, Mrs., 385
Roberts, Uncle Sammy, 359
Robinson, Roby, 475

Robson, Stuart, 339–40, 341n
Rockwood Pottery Company, 383n
Rogers Brothers, 375
Rose, Randolph, 504
Rose Hill Cemetery, 471
Rosser, Dr. Clarence V., 131n, 182, 374, 377, 378, 395
Rosser, Mrs., 384, 414, 421, 423, 426, 427, 428, 430, 431
Rosser, Julia, 499
Rosser, Luther, 317
Rosser, Mrs. Luther, 342
Rosser, Nora Belle, 68, 232
Rosser family, 332, 385, 418
Round Table, 65

Sacred Heart, Sister, 67, 138–48, 151–68, 204–23, 245, 310, 312, 322–459 passim
St. Anthony's Church, xxix, 313–14
St. Charles (tennis club), 407–9
St. Hyacinthe, 318, 363, 491
St. Joseph's Academy, x, xvii, xix, 61, 92, 116, 131, 141, 144, 176, 321, 322, 334, 360, 398, 404, 435, 458
St. Joseph's Home for Boys, 167
St. Nicholas, xxii, 29, 31, 63, 65, 142
St. Petersburg, 260, 262
Sampson, Admiral, 377
Sancho Panza, 183
Santa Claus, 155
Saturday Review, 234
Savannah, Ga., 121
Sawyer, Belle, 104, 119
Sawyer-Goodman card club, 94
Scarlet fever, 108, 167
Schadewell, Father, 117, 294, 313
Schley, Rear Adm. Winfield Scott, xxvii, 325, 327n
Scribner's Magazine, 178. *See also* Harris, Joel Chandler
Sea-Ora, 473
Sea-view, 473
Servants at Wren's Nest: James Banks (gardener), 64, 92, 122, 140, 150, 158, 178, 189, 329, 446; Calvin, 150; Celia, 32; Charley, 372, 426, 428, 431, 432, 434–35, 468, 478, 496, 497; Ed, 63, 118, 152, 311, 320, 321; Cora Smith Gann (cook), 367, 397–417, 432–98 passim; Georgia (cook), 413; Chloe Henderson, xxv, 39, 40n, 47, 64, 90, 107–28, 140, 151, 172, 189–208, 216, 219, 221–30, 257, 261, 270, 275, 279, 294–308, 323, 335–46 passim, 360, 361, 380, 432; Mattie Henderson, 82, 84n, 85, 92, 107, 118; Johnson, 118, 189, 432; Lena, 242; Lizzie, 118, 120, 189, 214, 233, 249, 255, 257, 346, 360, 447; Octavia (cook), 398, 400; Rufus (butler), xxv, 57–85, 100, 109–20, 137–78, 189, 193, 197, 204–85 passim, 346, 411, 432; Zack (butler), 450
Seventh Cavalry, 450
Shadows on the Wall, 239
Shakers, 311
Sharon, Ga., 169, 180, 188
Shore Acres, 178
Shropshire, Uncle Bob, 39
Sigourney, Mrs., 293
Silver campaign, 52
"Slav Tales," 130
Small-pox, 155

Smith, Hoke, 500, 501, 502, 505
Smith, Mrs., 335
Snodgrass, Addison, 488, 489–90
"The Snore of Pigeons," 348
Sons and Daughters of Human
    Temperance, 498
Sophia, Aunt, 332, 368, 412
Sousa, John Philip, 189
Spanish-American War, 182–83,
    186–87, 190–91, 192–93, 198, 231
Spanish Inquisition, 190
Spencer, Herbert, 196–97
Spratlin, Hook, 395
Spratlin, Mildred, 396, 417, 433, 495,
    499
Spratlins, 386
Stanton, Frank, xxvi, 11, 14, 53, 90,
    107, 133, 233, 250, 321, 339
Stark, Nora Belle, 390
"The Stars and Stripes Forever," 282
Stations of the Cross, 460
Sterne, Laurence: *The Sentimental
    Journey,* 308
Stoddard, John L., 273
Strickland, William, 507
Stringfellow, Mr. (James Wadsworth
    Longfellow), 329
Style, 195, 196, 197
Sunny South, 105, 106n, 379. *See also*
    Harris, Evelyn
Swamp Root, 397
Swartz, Joe, 214
Swartz, West, 217, 281
Syrup of Squills, 403, 404

Tabernacle Baptist Church, 192–93
Tallow Rand (Talleyrand), 237
Tallulah, Ga., 45

Tampa, 474, 475
Tanner, Henry, 260–61
Tar Baby, 40
Tarpon Springs, 474
Taunton, 361
Tedford, Mr., 311
Temple, Sir William, xvii, 174
Tennis Club boys, 449
Thanksgiving, 242, 433
Thompson, Mrs. Joseph, 491
Thompson, Wallace, 434
The Three Musketeers (play), xxv, 342
Thunderstorm, Jack, 345
Toombs, General, 128
Trains, 326
Trinity Hill, 424
Tropic Zone, 343
Troutman, Dr., 502–3
Troutman, Henry, 505
Troy, N.Y., 412
Turner, Joseph Addison, xxiv, xxxix,
    56
Twain, Mark, 381, 517
"The Two Grenadiers," 372
"The Two Orphans," 169

Uncle Rain, 301
Uncle Remus crockery, 382–83
Uncle Remus's Magazine, x; Children's
    Department of, xxi; editor-in-chief
    and editor of, xxii; plans for, 489;
    success of, 499, 504; use of JCH's
    letters in, 507–9. *See also* Harris,
    Joel Chandler; Harris, Julian
Uncle Remus tales, xxi
Uncle Wind, 279
Uncle Zero, 438
Upton, 484, 487, 490

Vaigner, Mr., 217
Verona Inn, 496
Vogner, Mizzers, 437

Wade, Edna, 108
Wade, Mrs., 347
Wade, Phil, 338
Wagener, Frederick ("Fritz"), 156,
    236, 242, 322–60, 390, 415, 490,
    497–504 passim; marriage to
    Lillian Harris, 493
Wagner, Mattie, 297
Wagner, Mr., 221
Wagner, Pauline, 369
Wallace, J. B., 474
Walton, Mrs., 322
Warm Springs, Ga., 40
Washington, Ga., 62, 85, 87, 107, 111,
    116, 122, 131, 168, 171, 173, 185,
    188, 222, 280, 287, 300, 329, 357,
    397, 401, 412, 440, 461
Waycross, Ga., 262
Weeden, Maria Howard, 241n
Welsbach lamp, 132, 133n
West, Willie, 478
West End, 63, 64, 70, 92, 103, 105,
    114, 122, 162, 173, 200, 218, 296,
    338, 373, 421, 450, 466, 504

West End Lobsters (tennis club), 407
West End Society, 65
Whiffling, Bloodgood, 358
Whiskey, 504
Whist, 269, 279, 390
White, Ed, 412
White Flag, 241
Wiggins, Robert Lemuel, 517
Wilkinson, Mr., 81, 113
Wilson, Ed, 272, 273
Wilson, Mrs., 453–54
Wiseman, Cardinal, 103
Wiseman Society, 103
Woman's exchange, 159
Woodcote Wonder (stud dog), 444
Woodruff, Mr., 283, 284
Wooten, Kathrine, 91, 98, 119
World's Work, xviii
Wotten, Mrs., 94
Wottens, 297

"Yale," 259
Yellow Kid, 81, 82n
Y.M.C.A., 377, 501
Young Harris Institute, 85
Youth's Companion, 65

Zonophone, 372, 373n, 419